Lecture Notes in Computer Science

Commenced Publication in 1973
Founding and Former Series Editors:
Gerhard Goos, Juris Hartmanis, and Jan van Leeuwen

Dengguo Feng   Dongdai Lin
Moti Yung (Eds.)

Information Security and Cryptology

First SKLOIS Conference, CISC 2005
Beijing, China, December 15-17, 2005
Proceedings

 Springer

Volume Editors

Dengguo Feng
Dongdai Lin
Chinese Academy of Sciences, Institute of Software
State Key Laboratory of Information Security
Beijing, 100080, P. R. China
E-mail: {feng,ddlin}@is.iscas.ac.cn

Moti Yung
RSA Laboratories and Columbia University
Computer science Department
Room 464, S.W. Mudd Building, New York, NY 10027, USA
E-mail: moti@cs.columbia.edu

Library of Congress Control Number: 2005937143

CR Subject Classification (1998): E.3, D.4.6, F.2.1, C.2, J.1, C.3, K.4.4, K.6.5

ISSN   0302-9743
ISBN-10   3-540-30855-5 Springer Berlin Heidelberg New York
ISBN-13   978-3-540-30855-3 Springer Berlin Heidelberg New York

Springer is a part of Springer Science+Business Media

springeronline.com

© Springer-Verlag Berlin Heidelberg 2005
Printed in Germany

Typesetting: Camera-ready by author, data conversion by Scientific Publishing Services, Chennai, India
Printed on acid-free paper   SPIN: 11599548   06/3142   5 4 3 2 1 0

Preface

The first SKLOIS Conference on Information Security and Cryptography (CISC 2005) was organized by the State Key Laboratory of Information Security of the Chinese Academy of Sciences. It was held in Beijing, China, December 15-17, 2005 and was sponsored by the Institute of Software, the Chinese Academy of Sciences, the Graduate School of the Chinese Academy of Sciences and the National Science Foundation of China. The conference proceedings, representing invited and contributed papers, are published in this volume of Springer's Lecture Notes in Computer Science (LNCS) series.

The area of research covered by CISC has been gaining importance in recent years, and a lot of fundamental, experimental and applied work has been done, advancing the state of the art. The program of CISC 2005 covered numerous fields of research within the general scope of the conference.

The International Program Committee of the conference received a total of 196 submissions (from 21 countries). Thirty-three submissions were selected for presentation as regular papers and are part of this volume. In addition to this track, the conference also hosted a short-paper track of 32 presentations that were carefully selected as well. All submissions were reviewed by experts in the relevant areas and based on their ranking and strict selection criteria the papers were selected for the various tracks. We note that stricter criteria were applied to papers co-authored by program committee members. We further note that, obviously, no member took part in influencing the ranking of his or her own submissions. In addition to the contributed regular papers, this volume contains the two invited papers by Serge Vaudenay and Giovanni Di Crescenzo.

Many people and organizations helped in making the conference a reality. We would like to take this opportunity to thank the Program Committee members and the external experts for their invaluable help in producing the conference program. We would like to thank the Organizing Committee members, the Co-chairs Dongdai Lin and Chunkun Wu, and the members Jiwu Jing and Wenling Wu. Dongdai Lin also served as a "Super Program Chair", organizing the electronic program discussions and coordinating the decision making process. We thank the various sponsors and, last but not least, we wish to thank all the authors who submitted papers to the conference, the invited speakers, the session chairs and all the conference attendees.

December 2005   Dengguo Feng and Moti Yung

CISC 2005

First SKLOIS Conference
on Information Security and Cryptology

Beijing, China
December 15-17, 2005

Sponsored and organized by
State Key Laboratory of Information Security
(Chinese Academy of Sciences)

Program Chairs

Dengguo Feng	SKLOIS, Chinese Academy of Sciences, China
Moti Yung	RSA Labs and Columbia University, USA

Program Committee

Dan Bailey	RSA Laboratory, USA
Feng Bao	Institute for Infocomm Research, Singapore
Carlo Blundo	University of Salerno, Italy
Felix Brandt	Stanford University, USA
Ahto Buldas	Tallin Technical University, Estonia
YoungJu Choie	POSTECH, Korea
Zongduo Dai	GSCAS, Chinese Academy of Sciences, China
George Davida	UWM, USA
Ed Dawson	QUT, Australia
Cunsheng Ding	HKUST, Hong Kong, China
Keqin Feng	Tsinghua University, China
Keith Frikken	Purdue University, USA
Jun Furukawa	NEC, Japan
Guang Gong	University of Waterloo, Canada
Jiwu Huang	Zhongshan University, China
Kwangjo Kim	ICU, Korea
Xuejia Lai	Shanghai Jiaotong University, China
Dongdai Lin	SKLOIS, Chinese Academy of Sciences, China
Mulan Liu	AMSS, CAS, China
Wenbo Mao	Hewlett-Packard Labs, UK
Tsutomu Matsumoto	Yokohama National University, Japan
Sjouke Mauw	EUT, Netherlands
Bodo Moller	Calgary, Canada
Svetla Nikova	K.U. Leuven, Belgium
Thomas Pornin	Cryptolog, France

Michel Riguidel   ENST, France
Eiji Okamato   Tsukuba University, Japan
Duong Hieu Phan   ENS, France
Bimal Roy   Indian Statistical Institute, India
Ahmad-Reza Sadeghi   Bochum, Germany
Kouichi Sakurai   Kyushu University, Japan
Tom Shrimpton   Portland State University, USA
Willy Susilo   University of Wollongong, Australia
Vijay Varadharajan   Macquarie, Australia
Xiaoyun Wang   Shandong University, China
Chuan-kun Wu   SKLOIS, Chinese Academy of Science, China
Yixian Yang   BUPT, China
Huanguo Zhang   Wuhan University, China
Yuliang Zheng   UNCC, USA
Hong Zhu   Fudan University, China
Yuefei Zhu   Information Engineering University, China

Organizing Committee

Dongdai LIN (Co-chair)   SKLOIS, Chinese Academy of Sciences, China
Chuankun Wu (Co-chair)   SKLOIS, Chinese Academy of Sciences, China
Jiwu JING   SKLOIS, Chinese Academy of Sciences, China
Wenling WU   SKLOIS, Chinese Academy of Sciences, China

Table of Contents

Signature Schemes

Symmetric Key Mechanisms

Zero-Knowledge and Secure Computations

Threshold Cryptography

Intrusion Detection Systems

Protocol Cryptanalysis

ECC Algorithms

Applications

Secret Sharing

Denial of Service Attacks

On Bluetooth Repairing: Key Agreement Based on Symmetric-Key Cryptography

Serge Vaudenay

EPFL,
CH-1015 Lausanne, Switzerland
http://lasecwww.epfl.ch

Abstract. Despite many good (secure) key agreement protocols based on public-key cryptography exist, secure associations between two wireless devices are often established using symmetric-key cryptography for cost reasons. The consequence is that common daily used security protocols such as Bluetooth pairing are insecure in the sense that an adversary can easily extract the main private key from the protocol communications. Nevertheless, we show that a feature in the Bluetooth standard provides a pragmatic and costless protocol that can eventually repair privateless associations, thanks to mobility. This proves (in the random oracle model) the pragmatic security of the Bluetooth pairing protocol when repairing is used.

1 Setting Up Secure Communications

Digital communications are often secured by means of symmetric encryption and message authentication codes. This provided high throughput and security. However, setting up this channel requires agreeing on a private key with large entropy. Private key agreement between remote peers through insecure channel is a big challenge. A first (impractical) solution was proposed in 1975 by Merkle [19]. A solution was proposed by Diffie and Hellman in 1976 [12]. It works, provided that the two peers can communicate over an authenticated channel which protects the integrity of messages and that a standard computational problem (namely, the Diffie-Hellman problem) is hard.

To authenticate messages of the Diffie-Hellman protocol is still expensive since those messages are pretty long (typically, a thousand bits, each) and that authentication is often manually done by human beings. Folklore solutions consist of shrinking this amount of information by means of a collision-resistant hash function and of authenticating only the *digest* of the protocol transcript. The amount of information to authenticate typically reduces to 160 bits. However, collision-resistant hash functions are threatened species these days due to collapses of MD5, RIPEMD, SHA, SHA-1, etc. [9, 23, 24, 25, 26]. Furthermore, 160 bits is still pretty large for human beings to authenticate. Another solution using shorter messages have been proposed by Pasini and Vaudenay [20] using a hash function which resists second preimage attacks (like MD5 [21]; namely: collision resistance is no longer required) and a commitment scheme. Other solutions such as MANA protocols [13, 14] have been proposed. They can reduce the amount of information to be authenticated down to 20 bits, but they work assuming a stronger hypothesis on the authenticated channel, namely that the authentication occurs without any latency for the delivery. Some protocols based on the Diffie-Hellman one were

D. Feng, D. Lin, and M. Yung (Eds.): CISC 2005, LNCS 3822, pp. 1–9, 2005.

proposed [11, 15] with an incomplete security analysis. A provably secure solution was finally proposed by Vaudenay [22]. This protocol can work with only 20 bits to authenticate and is based on a commitment scheme. Those authentication protocols *can* be pretty cheap (namely: without public-key cryptography) and provably secure (at least in the random oracle model). So, the remaining overwhelming cost is still the Diffie-Hellman protocol. Since key agreement is the foundation to public-key cryptography, it seems that setting up secure communications with an authenticated channel only cannot be solved at a lower expense than regular public-key algorithms.

The Bluetooth standard starts from a slightly different assumption, namely that there is a private channel between the two devices involving the human user. Of course, this channel should be used to transmit as few bits as possible. This would, in principle, be possible by using password-based authenticated key agreement. A first protocol family was proposed (without security proof) in 1992 by Bellovin and Merritt [8]. SRP [27, 28] is another famous protocol, available as the RFC 2945, proposed in 1998 by Wu. The security analysis followed a long research program initiated by Bellare and Rogaway [5, 6]. Specific instances of the Bellovin-Merritt protocols with security based on the random oracle model were provided in [3, 4, 7, 10, 18] starting in 2000. Finally, another protocol without random oracles were proposed in 2001 by Katz, Ostrovsky, and Yung [16]. All those protocols are however at least as expensive as the Diffie-Hellman protocol.

Despite all this nice and extensive piece of theory, standards such as Bluetooth [1, 2] stick to symmetric-key techniques (for cost reasons) and continue to use insecure protocols.

In this paper, we review the Bluetooth pairing protocol and its insecurity. The Bluetooth version 1.2 [1] mentioned (in a single sentence) the possibility to refresh keys. More details (namely, how to do so) were provided in Bluetooth version 2.0 in 2004 [2]. We finally show that this feature (that we call *repairing*) substantially increases the security and may be considered as a pragmatic costless solution. Security is based on the assumption that the radio channel (considered to be insecure by default) *sometimes* provides privacy in an unpredictable way, i.e. that the adversary Eve can in principle easily listen to the channel from time to time, but it is unlikely that she can do it *all the time* throughout the history of the devices association. This assumption is quite reasonable due to the mobility context of Bluetooth applications.

2   Bluetooth-Like Pre-pairing and the Security Issue

We assume a set of N possible participants with identifier strings ID_i. (Note that the notion of identity is rather weak since authentication will be based on a human user manipulating physical devices: it can just be a mnemonic identifier like "laser printer", maybe extended by a MAC address.) We assume that they all manage a local database of (K_j, ID_j) pairs, meaning that the current private key to be used with participant ID_j is K_j. The goal of a pairing protocol between Alice of identity ID_A and Bob of identity ID_B is to create (or replace) an entry (K, ID_B) in the database of ID_A and an entry (K, ID_A) in the database of ID_B so that the key K is the same and private to both participants.

Alice   Bob
input: $\widehat{\mathsf{ID}}_B$ **input: $\widehat{\mathsf{ID}}_A$**
private input: π_A   **private input: π_B**

$\text{pick } R^i \in_U \{0,1\}^\rho \xrightarrow{\quad R^i \quad}$

$K_A^i \leftarrow G(\mathsf{ID}_A, \widehat{\mathsf{ID}}_B, R^i, \pi_A)$ $K_B^i \leftarrow G(\widehat{\mathsf{ID}}_A, \mathsf{ID}_B, \hat{R}^i, \pi_B)$

final key for $\widehat{\mathsf{ID}}_B$: K_A^i   **final key for $\widehat{\mathsf{ID}}_A$: K_B^i**

Fig. 1. A One-Move Preparing Protocol

For cost reasons, nowadays wireless devices (e.g. Bluetooth devices) only use symmetric-key cryptographic protocols for establishing secure communications over insecure channels. When they connect to each other for the first time, they establish some initial private key materials K^i. Both devices, Alice and Bob, start with their identities ID_A and ID_B, pick some random numbers R_A^i and R_B^i. Additionally, a user types some random one-time private code π on both devices and both devices run a π-based authenticated key agreement protocol. When they prompt the user to type π, they may display a piece of the identifier strings (a mnemonic) for user-friendliness reasons. Due to the state of the art on symmetric-key primitives, the protocol must leak R_A^i and R_B^i so that we have

$$K^i = G(\mathsf{ID}_A, \mathsf{ID}_B, R_A^i, R_B^i, \pi)$$

for some function G. In a one-move variant, R_B^i is void so that only R_A^i (which is rather denoted R^i) needs to be sent. (See Fig. 1.)[1]

Following our setting model, π has low entropy. Indeed, the private code is typed by a human user and is typically pretty small. Eventually, exhaustive search leads to guessing π. Hence, an adversary can typically compute K^i from R^i by guessing π. The adversary only needs some information about K^i to check whether π is correct or not to run an *offline* dictionary attack. Peer authentication protocols based on K^i are based on symmetric-key cryptography. They eventually leak such an information by releasing some S and $F(S, K^i)$ for some function F from the protocol. In the Bluetooth case, this attack was described by Jakobsson and Wetzel [17].

This attack can be completed by a man-in-the-middle attack. Namely, an adversary can claim to have identity ID_B to Alice of identity ID_A and to have identity ID_A to Bob of identity ID_B. Even though the adversary does not get π from the user who wants to pair the real Alice and Bob, the adversary can easily infer it from the previous attack. The consequence is that Alice and Bob would be independently paired with the adversary even though they think they are paired together.

Those protocols can nevertheless be secure *in principle* provided that

– either enumerating all possible values for the code π is infeasible
– or the transmission of R^i is confidential.

In Section 6 we prove it in the random oracle model.

---

[1] By convention, notations without a hat are sent values and notations with a hat are received values. If no attack occurs, the value should not be changed by putting a hat.

3   The Two-Round Bluetooth Pairing

The Bluetooth standard [1, 2] is quite interesting in the sense that it uses a 2-round pairing protocol that we call *preparing* and *repairing*. Fig. 1 and Fig. 2 illustrate the two rounds, respectively. In a first round, a 128-bit (ephemeral) initialization key K^i is established from some random numbers R^i and π. In a second round, the final key is established from new random numbers R_A and R_B, the identities of Alice and Bob, and K^i. More precisely, the second round works as follows.

1. Bob picks a random R_B and sends $C_B = R_B \oplus K^i$ to Alice.
2. Alice picks a random R_A and sends $C_A = R_A \oplus K^i$ to Bob[2].
3. Both compute $K = H(\mathsf{ID}_A, \mathsf{ID}_B, R_A, R_B) = H(\mathsf{ID}_A, \mathsf{ID}_B, C_A \oplus K^i, C_B \oplus K^i)$.

We assume that (K, ID_B) (resp. (K, ID_A)) replaces (K^i, ID_B) (resp. (K^i, ID_A)) in the database of ID_A (resp. ID_B) so that K^i is discarded.

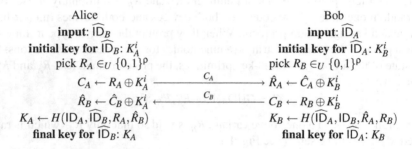

Fig. 2. The Bluetooth Repairing Protocol

Note that the internal structure of H in Bluetooth is of the form

$$H(\mathsf{ID}_A, \mathsf{ID}_B, R_A, R_B) = H'(\mathsf{ID}_A, R_A) \oplus H'(\mathsf{ID}_B, R_B).$$

Obviously, this does *not* instantiate a random oracle since we have unexpected relations such as

$$H(\mathsf{ID}_A, \mathsf{ID}_B, R_A, R_B) \oplus H(\mathsf{ID}_B, \mathsf{ID}_C, R_B, R_C) = H(\mathsf{ID}_A, \mathsf{ID}_C, R_A, R_C).$$

We further note that if Alice and Bob were already the victims of a man-in-the-middle attack, they can remain in the same attacked state if the adversary can continue an active attack. When the adversary becomes out of reach, the repairing protocol fails and Alice and Bob end in a state so that they can no longer communicate.

In Section 6 we prove that the repairing protocol alone is secure if either the initialization key is private or the communication of either C_A or C_B is private. We deduce that the preparing and repairing together achieve a secure pairing protocol provided that either π is large or the communication is private: repairing does not decrease the security. The incremental role of the repairing protocol will be made clear in the following section.

---

[2] It is worth noticing that Alice and Bob actually exchange R_A and R_B by using a (safe) two-time pad.

4 Repairing and Forward Secrecy

The Bluetooth standard [1, 2] already suggests that a key K could be refreshed. Indeed, new pairing protocols could just skip the first round and use the old K as the K^i initialization key. (Note that the user no longer needs to type a private code in this protocol.) If the old key was not known by the adversary, it could not be guessed like π. So the new link key would be safe as well. Now, if the old key K had leaked out, but the adversary did not listen to the new pairing protocol, then the new key would be safe: the secure communication would be repaired. This way, we claim that the new link key is at least as safe as the old one.

Similarly, mobility and repairing can detect man-in-the-middle attacks as previously discussed. This repairs the weak notion of authentication.

Furthermore, frequent repairs provides *forward secrecy* when we make sure that old link keys are destroyed. Indeed, if we let K_j denote the link key generated by the jth pairing protocol, assuming that this pairing was safe and that K_{j+t} is the first key which is leaked after the jth pairing, then none of the link keys $K_j, K_{j+1}, \ldots, K_{j+t-1}$ can be recovered by the adversary. In the mobility context of Bluetooth, it is reasonable that the adversary does not listen to *all* pairing protocols. Since security only increases here, communications are eventually secure between Alice and Bob. It is indeed the case where mobility can help security.

What can happen in the case of active attacks? The two devices will end up in an unpaired state. Due to the mobility and the inability for the adversary to follow both devices, the user will eventually realize that the two devices are not paired and launch a new pairing protocol. An adversary could use this behavior and try a denial of service attack combined with social engineering: indeed the adversary could make sure that the two devices are unable to communicate, making as if the two devices were not well paired. The consequence would be for the user to launch a new pairing protocol with a humanly selected π. This would clearly provide openings to the adversary. This problem can only be fixed by clear human-machine interfaces and education of users. A pairing should not be perceived a benign action.

Another helpful feature would be, if possible, to enlarge the database by adding a new field telling the length of π in the preparing protocol and the number of repairs. Keys with low length for π and low number of repairs would have a low security confidence, but would become more trustable as the number of repairs increase.

To conclude, we believe that the repairing protocols provide a truly pragmatic and costless security solution for lightweight wireless communications.

5 Adversarial Model

The launch *and* send *oracles.* We adapt the security model of [5, 6] and [22]. We assume that the powerful adversary can launch instances of the preparing/repairing protocol on chosen inputs by making a chosen participant to play the (chosen) role of Alice or Bob with a chosen input. For instance, the $\Pi \leftarrow$ launch$(n, \text{Alice}, \text{ID})$ query creates an instance π of Alice with input ID, played by node n. We assume that the adversary can play with all participants in a concurrent way and basically run the protocol step by step. The adversary is the central node of the communication channels, can send an arbitrary message to any instance and get the response message in return. For instance, $y \leftarrow \mathsf{send}(\Pi, x)$ sends the message x as being the current protocol message to instance Π, makes this instance step the protocol, and tells the protocol answer y of Π.

The test *oracle.* We assume that the adversary can make $\mathsf{test}(n, k, \mathsf{ID})$ oracle calls which tell whether (k, ID) is an entry of the database of node n. We say that an adversary wins if one test query positively answered. Note that contrarily to the traditional Bellare-Rogaway [5, 6] model, the adversary can make as many test queries as he wants. The reason is that, in practice, information leaks so that the adversary can simulate this oracle in an offline way.

Every key K in a database can be seen as a random variable. In that case, every (unsuccessful) test query reduced the entropy by telling the adversary that K is not equal to a given k.

The remove *oracle.* We also assume that the adversary can make $\mathsf{remove}(n, \mathsf{ID})$ oracle queries which make node n remove any entry with ID from its database. This simulates a user managing the database of paired devices.

The inputPIN *oracle.* The preparing protocol assumes a special channel which privately sends the same random value π to two instances. We model this by the ability for the adversary to make some $\sigma \leftarrow \mathsf{inputPIN}(n_1)$ and $\mathsf{inputPIN}(\sigma, n_2)$ oracle calls which make n_1 receive a new random input π attached to a fresh tag σ, then n_2 receive the same input π. We assume that π is discarded by $\mathsf{inputPIN}(\sigma, n_2)$ after that (namely, a single π cannot be input more than twice). The distribution of π (namely, the entropy) will play a role in the analysis.

The reveal *and* corrupt *oracles.* Participating nodes are assumed to be honest by default. In the traditional Bellare-Rogaway model [5, 6], the adversary can nevertheless make $\mathsf{reveal}(n)$ queries which simply dump the private database of a node n, and corrupt (n, code) queries which go beyond that by further installing a malicious code on the node so that this node can no longer be assumed to follow the protocols. For simplicity reasons we assume that adversaries have no access to these oracles here. Extensions of our results is left to further work. Note that excluding malicious participants de facto exclude the adversary from getting any π form inputPIN.

The secureLaunch *oracle.* The repairing protocol assumes that communication between two prepared participants can sometimes be private. Additionally, we sometimes consider instances of the preparing protocol that are also run in a private environment. In such a case, we assume that an oracle query $\mathsf{secureLaunch}(n_A, n_B, x_A, x_B)$ launches a complete run of the protocol on nodes n_A and n_B with input x_A and x_B respectively. The adversary has no access to the transcript of the protocol.

6   Security of the Preparing Protocol

Theorem 1. *Given an integer* ρ *and a random oracle G which outputs u-bit strings, we consider the preparing protocol of Fig. 1. We assume that* inputPIN *selects* π *uniformly* distributed in a set of S elements. For any adversary limited to t test queries, the wining probability is at most $t/S + \frac{1}{2}t^2 2^{-u}$.

A key that was set up by secureLaunch can only be successfully tested with probability at most $\min(2^{-\rho}, 2^{-u})$.

We can easily tune u so that $t^2 \ll 2^u$. This result thus tells us that the protocol is secure when S is large. Typically, for $S = 2^{80}$ and $u = 128$, an adversary requires at least nearly 2^{64} trials so succeed. The theorem also says that if ρ and u are large and R^i is privately sent, then the protocol is secure.

Proof. Let us consider the ith test query $\text{test}(n_i, k_i, \text{ID}'_i)$ and assume that all previous test queries were negative. We want to compute the probability that the answer is positive. Due to the protocol, it relates to some random variable $K_i = G(\text{ID}_i, \text{ID}'_i, R_i, \pi_i)$ where R_i is known but π_i is a priori not.

Let L be the number of pairwise different $(\text{ID}_i, \text{ID}'_i, R_i)$ triplets. Let s_ℓ be the number of occurrences for the ℓth triplet, for $\ell = 1, \ldots, L$. Since G is a random oracle, it produces no collision $G(\text{ID}_i, \text{ID}'_i, R_i, \alpha) = G(\text{ID}_i, \text{ID}'_i, R_i, \beta)$ with probability higher than $1 - \frac{1}{2}s_\ell^2 2^{-u}$ where ℓ is the number of the triplet for the ith test. Let us focus in this case.

Clearly, the protocol leaks no information about any π, so information only comes from previous test oracles. Since G is a random oracle, any previous test query (let say the jth one) leaks some useful information about K_i only if $(\text{ID}_j, \text{ID}'_j, R_j, \pi_j) = (\text{ID}_i, \text{ID}'_i, R_i, \pi_i)$. Hence, the maximal information is that K_i is one value out of $S - s_\ell + 1$. The wining probability for this query is thus at most $1/(S - s_\ell + 1)$. The loosing probability for all queries related to this triplet is thus $1 - s_\ell/S$.

The overall loosing probability is thus at least

$$\prod_\ell \frac{S - s_\ell}{S} - \frac{1}{2}\sum_\ell s_\ell^2 2^{-u}$$

with constraint $\sum_\ell s_\ell = t$. The probability is the lowest for $L = 1$ for which it is $1 - t/S - \frac{1}{2}t^2 2^{-u}$.

When a key was set up by secureLaunch, we can best assume that the adversary caught π but no other information leaked. The best strategy to guess K^i is either to guess K^i or to guess R^i. with probability at most $\min(2^{-\rho}, 2^{-u})$.   □

We similarly prove the following result.

Theorem 2. *Given an integer ρ and a random oracle H which outputs u-bit strings, we consider the preparing protocol of Fig. 2. We assume that initialization keys are randomly preset. For any adversary limited to t test queries, the wining probability is at most $t^2 2^{-u}$.*

A key that was repaired by secureLaunch can only be successfully tested with probability at most $\min(2^{-\rho}, 2^{-u})$.

7 Conclusion

We have shown that the pairing concept of Bluetooth can in principle lead to a secure protocol, provided that repairing is frequently done and is eventually privately run. This is proven provided that G and H behave like random oracles. This provides a pragmatic costless alternative to key agreement based on public-key cryptography.

We also proposed to store the length of the used PIN in the preparing protocol and the number of performed repairs in order to better assess the security of a given link key. This could help audit and increase the confidence in the Bluetooth security.

One open question would be to extend this result to the specific structure of the Bluetooth primitives. Another challenge would be to consider (namely to model and prove) security when the adversary has access to reveal or corrupt oracles.

References

1. Specification of the Bluetooth System. Vol. 2: Core System Package. Bluetooth Specification version 1.2, 2003.
2. Specification of the Bluetooth System. Bluetooth Specification version 2.0, 2004.
3. M. Abdalla, O. Chevassut, D. Pointcheval. One-Time Verifier-Based Encrypted Key Exchange. In *Public Key Cryptography'05*, Les Diablerets, Switzerland, Lecture Notes in Computer Science 3386, pp. 47–64, Springer-Verlag, 2005.
4. M. Bellare, D. Pointcheval, P. Rogaway. Authenticated Key Exchange Secure against Dictionary Attacks. In *Advances in Cryptology EUROCRYPT'00*, Brugge, Belgium, Lecture Notes in Computer Science 1807, pp. 139–155, Springer-Verlag, 2000.
5. M. Bellare, P. Rogaway. Entity Authentication and Key Distribution. In *Advances in Cryptology CRYPTO'93*, Santa Barbara, California, U.S.A., Lecture Notes in Computer Science 773, pp. 232–249, Springer-Verlag, 1994.
6. M. Bellare, P. Rogaway. Provably Secure Session Key Distribution: the Three Party Case. In *Proceedings of the 27th ACM Symposium on Theory of Computing*, Las Vegas, Nevada, U.S.A., pp. 57–66, ACM Press, 1995.
7. M. Bellare, P. Rogaway. The AuthA Protocol for Password-Based Authenticated Key Exchange. In *Contribution to the IEEE P1363 study group for Future PKC Standards*, 2002. (Available from http://grouper.ieee.org/groups/1363/)
8. S. M. Bellovin, M. Merritt. Encrypted Key Exchange: Password-Based Protocols Secure Against Dictionary Attacks. In *IEEE symposium on Research in Security and Privacy*, Oakland, California, USA, pp. IEEE Computer Society Press, 72–84, 1992.
9. E. Biham, R. Chen, A. Joux, P. Carribault, C. Lemuet, W. Jalby. Collisions of SHA-0 and Reduced SHA-1. In *Advances in Cryptology EUROCRYPT'05*, Aarhus, Denmark, Lecture Notes in Computer Science 3494, pp. 36–57, Springer-Verlag, 2005.
10. V. Boyko, P. MacKenzie, S. Patel. Provably Secure Password Authenticated Key Exchange Using Diffie-Hellman. In *Advances in Cryptology EUROCRYPT'00*, Brugge, Belgium, Lecture Notes in Computer Science 1807, pp. 156–171, Springer-Verlag, 2000.
11. M. Čagalj, S. Čapkun, J.-P. Hubaux. Key Agreement in Peer-to-Peer Wireless Networks. To appear in the Proceedings of the IEEE, late 2005.
12. W. Diffie, M. E. Hellman. New Directions in Cryptography. *IEEE Transactions on Information Theory*, vol. IT-22, pp. 644–654, 1976.
13. C. Gehrmann, C. Mitchell, K. Nyberg. Manual Authentication for Wireless Devices. *RSA Cryptobytes*, vol. 7, pp. 29–37, 2004.
14. C. Gehrmann, K. Nyberg. Security in Personal Area Networks. In *Security for Mobility*, C. Mitchell (Ed.), pp. 191–230, IEE, 2004.
15. J.-H. Hoepman. The Ephemeral Pairing Problem. In *Financial Cryptography, 8th International Conference (FC 2004)*, Key West, Florida, USA, Lecture Notes in Computer Science 3110, pp. 212–226, Springer-Verlag, 2004.

16. J. Katz, R. Ostrovsky, M. Yung. Efficient Password-Authenticated Key Exchange using Human-Memorable Passwords. In *Advances in Cryptology EUROCRYPT'01*, Innsbruck, Austria, Lecture Notes in Computer Science 2045, pp. 475–494, Springer-Verlag, 2001.
17. M. Jakobsson, S. Wetzel. Security Weaknesses in Bluetooth. In *Topics in Cryptology (CT–RSA'01)*, San Francisco, California, USA, Lecture Notes in Computer Science 2020, pp. 176–191, Springer-Verlag, 2001.
18. P. MacKenzie. The PAK Suite: Protocols for Password-Authenticated Key Exchange. Technical report No. 2002-46. DIMACS Center, Rutgers University, 2002. (Available from http://dimacs.rutgers.edu/TechnicalReports/abstracts/2002/2002-46.html)
19. R. C. Merkle. Secure Communications over Insecure Channels. *Communications of the ACM*, vol. 21, pp. 294–299, 1978.
20. S. Pasini, S. Vaudenay. An Optimal Non-Interactive Message Authentication Protocol. To appear in the proceedings of CT-RSA'06, Springer, LNCS, 2006.
21. R. L. Rivest. The MD5 Message Digest Algorithm. RFC 1321, 1992.
22. S. Vaudenay. Secure Communications over Insecure Channels Based on Short Authenticated Strings. In *Advances in Cryptology CRYPTO'05*, Santa Barbara, California, U.S.A., Lecture Notes in Computer Science 3621, pp. 309–326, Springer-Verlag, 2005.
23. X. Wang, X. Lai, D. Feng, H. Chen, X. Yu. Cryptanalysis for Hash Functions MD4 and RIPEMD. In *Advances in Cryptology EUROCRYPT'05*, Aarhus, Denmark, Lecture Notes in Computer Science 3494, pp. 1–18, Springer-Verlag, 2005.
24. X. Wang, H. Yu, L. Y. Yin. Efficient Collision Search Attacks on SHA-0. In *Advances in Cryptology CRYPTO'05*, Santa Barbara, California, U.S.A., Lecture Notes in Computer Science 3621, pp. 1–16, Springer-Verlag, 2005.
25. X. Wang, L. Y. Yin, H. Yu. Finding Collisions in the Full SHA-1. In *Advances in Cryptology CRYPTO'05*, Santa Barbara, California, U.S.A., Lecture Notes in Computer Science 3621, pp. 17–36, Springer-Verlag, 2005.
26. X. Wang, H. Yu. How to Break MD5 and Other Hash Functions. In *Advances in Cryptology EUROCRYPT'05*, Aarhus, Denmark, Lecture Notes in Computer Science 3494, pp. 19–35, Springer-Verlag, 2005.
27. T. Wu. The Secure Remote Password Protocol. In *Proceedings of the 1998 Internet Society Network and Distributed System Security Symposium*, San Diego, CA, pp. 97–111, The Internet Society, 1998.
28. T. Wu. The SRP Authentication and Key Exchange System. RFC 2945 standard track, The Internet Society, 2000.

You Can Prove So Many Things
in Zero-Knowledge

Giovanni Di Crescenzo

Telcordia Technologies Piscataway, NJ, 08854, USA
giovanni@research.telcordia.com

Abstract. We present a short survey of known notions of zero-knowledge proof systems in the interactive model and main results about these notions. We then introduce a new notion, an extension of proofs of knowledge, which we call *Proofs of Non-Zero Knowledge*, as they allow a prover to convince a verifier that he knows a secret satisfying some relation, without revealing any new information about the secret *or even the relation* that the secret satifies with the common input. We prove a number of basic results about proofs of non-zero knowledge, and, in the process, revisit previously studied protocols, described as 'proofs of partial knowledge', which are particular cases of proofs of non-zero knowledge.

1 Introduction

The seemingly paradoxical notion of Zero-Knowledge protocols, introduced in [24], has received a great amount of attention in both the Cryptography and Computational Complexity literature. Very informally, a zero-knowledge proof is a method allowing a prover to convince a verifier of a statement without revealing any additional information other than the fact that the theorem is true. In other words, all the verifier gains by interacting with the prover on input a true statement is something that the verifier could have generated without help by the prover. While the two requirements of 'convincing a verifier' and 'not revealing anything else' may seem hard to coexist, zero-knowledge proofs have found rigorous formulations and numerous theoretical and practical instantiations in various settings. Furthermore, the general zero-knowledge methodology of revealing only the necessary minimal information in communication in the presence of adversaries has become a fundamental tool having wide applicability throughout Cryptography. As a consequence, zero-knowledge protocols are studied along several dimensions, with respect to: adversary computational models (e.g., proof systems sound against infinitely powerful provers and zero-knowledge against polynomial-time verifiers, or argument systems with dual security guarantees); provability notions (e.g., zero-knowledge proofs of membership, knowledge, computational ability, decision power, decision); setup models (e.g, interactive, non-interactive, pre-processing, public-key models); and security notions (e.g, sequential, concurrent, resettable, non-malleable, universally-composable security).

D. Feng, D. Lin, and M. Yung (Eds.): CISC 2005, LNCS 3822, pp. 10–27, 2005.

In this paper we present a short survey of known provability notions for zero-knowledge proof systems (and argument systems)in the most basic setup model (the interactive model) and security notion (sequential zero-knowledge). We then introduce a new provability notion, (an extension of proofs of knowledge), which we call *Proofs of Non-Zero Knowledge*, as they allow a prover to convince a verifier that he knows some information about a secret satisfying some relation, without revealing anything new about the secret *or even the relation* that the secret and the common input satify. We prove a number of basic results about computational zero-knowledge, perfect zero-knowledge and relation-indistinguishable proofs of non-zero knowledge. In the process, we revisit certain previously studied protocols, also denoted as 'proofs of partial knowledge', which turn out to be particular instances of proofs of non-zero knowledge. We point out and fill some gaps in the claimed theorems and proofs for results on this type of proofs.

2   Known Notions of Proof Systems

We review known notions of interactive protocols, such as proofs of membership, proofs of knowledge, proofs of computational ability, proofs of decision power, and proofs of decision. For each notion, we recall informal definitions and discuss their main results.

2.1   Proofs of Membership

We start by recalling the formal definition for zero-knowledge proof systems of membership, introduced in [24].

A zero-knowledge proof system of membership is an interactive protocol in which a prover convinces a polynomial time verifier that a string x belongs to a language L. Informally, the requirements for zero-knowledge proof systems of membership are three: completeness, soundness and zero-knowledge. The completeness requirement states that for any input x in language L, the verifier accepts with overwhelming probability. The soundness requirement states that for any input x not in the language L, the verifier rejects with overwhelming probability. The zero-knowledge requirement can come in three main variants: computational, statistical and perfect zero-knowledge. The perfect zero-knowledge (resp., statistical zero-knowledge) (resp., computational zero-knowledge) requirement states that for all probabilistic polynomial time verifiers V', the view of V' on input $x \in L$ and the output of an efficient algorithm, called the 'simulator', on input the same x, are equal (resp., have exponentially small statistical distance) (resp., are indistinguishable by any polynomial-time algorithm).

Applications of zero-knowledge proofs of membership can be found in essentially all types of cryptographic protocols: encryption and signature schemes, financial cryptography schemes (electronic cash, digital elections and auctions, etc.), and, more generally, in private multi-party computation. A major application in the latter area, from [23], is that of compiling protocols secure in the presence of honest parties to protocols secure in the presence of malicious parties, where the latter are forced to prove their honesty by using zero-knowledge proof of correctness of their messages and computations.

A variant on the definition of interactive proof systems is *public-coin* proof systems, which can be defined from the definition of interactive proof systems by requiring the verifier to send only its random coins.

Another variant on the definition of zero-knowledge is *honest-verifier* zero-knowledge, which can be obtained from the definition of zero-knowledge by requiring the same property to hold only with respect to the honest verifier, rather than with respect to all probabilistic polynomial time verifiers.

A major result in this area is the existence of a computational zero-knowledge proof system of membership for any language in NP, assuming the existence of non-uniformly secure one-way function families [23]. This result has found many applications in theoretical cryptography and has also played an important role in enlarging as much as possible the class of languages having zero-knowledge proof systems of membership, as proved in [25, 5]. We note that the class IP of languages having an interactive proof system of membership has been proved equal to PSPACE in an important result in [27]. It follows then that any language in PSPACE has a computational zero-knowledge proof system of membership under the existence of non-uniformly secure one-way function families. On the other hand, as proved in [7, 19], it is very unlikely that all languages in NP have a statistical or perfect zero-knowledge proof system (as otherwise the polynomial hierarchy would collapse to its second level). An important consequence of these results is that a way to give evidence that a language is not NP-complete is to construct a perfect zero-knowledge proof system for it.

Protocol games. Most zero-knowledge proof system of membership can be abstrated as relatively simpler protocol games, perhaps the most important one being the so-called 'meet-the-challenge games', first formally defined in [16]. We start by considering a basic version of such games and later discuss some extensions of interest. Informally, in such games, the prover sends a single message to the verifier; the verifier sends a single random bit as a challenge; and the prover's goal is to answer properly for each value of the challenge and with a single message. At the end the verifier accepts if it received a proper answer, according to whether the received transcript satisfies a prespecified polynomial-time predicate.

Definition 1. *A meet-the-challenge game* (A, B) *for language L is a perfect zero-knowledge proof system of membership for L having the following form. On common input x, game* (A, B) *can be divided into three phases: in the first phase the prover A computes a string com, called the* first message, *and sends it to the verifier B; in the second phase B uniformly chooses a bit b, called the* challenge, *and sends it to A; then A replies by computing a string ans, called the* answer, *and sending it to B; finally B outputs ACCEPT or REJECT according to whether predicate $\rho(x; com, b, ans)$ is equal to 1 or 0.*

Note that the above definition implies that the prover can answer to one value of the challenge if the statement it is proving is false, and to both values otherwise.

By using results in [28, 24, 23], we directly obtain the existence of a meet-the-challenge game for every random self-reducible language (these include several languages related to the graph-isomorphism problem, residuosity problems modulo composite integers, and discrete logarithm problems modulo primes). By using results in [13], we directly obtain the existence of a meet-the-challenge game for various boolean formula compositions over random self-reducible languages membership statements, including monotone formulae.

Let S be the simulator associated with a meet-the-challenge game, and let $s(n)$ be the number of random bits used by S on input a string x of size n. For $b \in \{0, 1\}$, define distribution $S_{x,b} = \{r \leftarrow \{0, 1\}^{s(n)}; (com, c, ans) \leftarrow S(x, r) : r \mid c = b \land \rho(com, c, ans) = 1\}$. An element com returned according to $S_{x,b}$ will also denote the first message sent by the prover to the verifier. We observe that any meet-the-challenge game for L satisfies the following: for each $x \in L$, the two distributions $S_{x,0}$ and $S_{x,1}$ are equal; for each $x \notin L$, the distributions $S_{x,0}$ and $S_{x,1}$ have disjoint support sets.

2.2   Proofs of Knowledge

The concept of proof systems of knowledge has been alluded to in [24], developed by [17, 18, 28] and fully formalized in [2].

A proof system of knowledge is an interactive protocol in which, on input a string x, a prover convinces a poly-bounded verifier that he knows a string y such that a polynomial-time relation $R(x, y)$ holds. The requirements for proof systems of knowledge are two: verifiability and extraction. The verifiability requirement states that for any input x in the domain of relation R, the verifier accepts with overwhelming probability. The extraction requirement states that there exists an extractor that, for any input x in the relation domain dom$R$, and interacting with any prover that forces the verifier to accept with 'sufficiently high' probability, is able to compute a string y such that $R(x, y)$ holds, within a 'properly bounded' expected time. A proof system of knowledge is witness-indistinguishable if for any probabilistic polynomial-time V', any input $x \in$ dom$R$, and for all y_1, y_2 such that $(x, y_1) \in R$ and $(x, y_2) \in R$, the view of V' when P uses y_1 is identical to the view of V' when P uses y_2. A proof system of knowledge is zero-knowledge if it is zero-knowledge over language dom$R$, analogously as for proofs of membership.

Applications of proofs of knowledge include secure entity authentication, as originally suggested from [17], where parties prove their identity by witness-indistinguishable proofs of knowledge of a secret that was previously assigned to them by an appropriate authority. More generally, the concept of extraction has proved very useful in several other cryptographic protocols, such as bit commitment, non-malleable auction protocols, etc.

For all known languages having a meet-the-challenge game (using protocols in, e.g., [28, 24, 23, 13]), one can define a natural relation such that the meet-the-challenge game is also a proof of knowledge for this relation. Given a meet-the-challenge game (A, B), in the sequel we will also need a proof of knowledge for a relation $R_{x,(A,B)}$ with some special properties, where $R_{x,(A,B)} =$

$\{(com; (b, ans)) \,|\, (com, b, ans) \in S(x, \cdot) : \rho(x; com, b, ans) = 1\}$. For all languages that are known to have a meet-the-challenge game, i.e., random self-reducible languages and monotone formulae over them, a proof of knowledge for the associated relation $R_{x,(A,B)}$ has been given in [23, 13]. A protocol for all languages having such games can be obtained by combining the mentioned properties of meet-the-challenge games with techniques from [26, 5]. We have the following

Fact 1. *Let L be a language, x be an input string and k be a polynomial. Let (A, B) be a meet-the-challenge game for L and let S be the simulator associated with (A, B). Then there exists a proof of knowledge (C,D) for relation $R_{x,(A,B)}$, with the following properties:*

1. *(C,D) has soundness error $2^{-k(|x|)}$,*
2. *if $x \in L$ then (C,D) is witness-indistinguishable,*
3. *C's program can be performed in probabilistic polynomial time, when given an auxiliary input.*

2.3   Proofs of Computational Ability

The concept of proving the ability to perform a certain task has been introduced in [29]. A formalization of this concept, in the spirit of the formalization for proofs of knowledge given in [2], has been first given in [14]. (In fact, proofs of knowledge can be seen as a particular case of proofs of computational ability.)

An interactive proof system of computational ability is an interactive protocol in which, on input a string x, a prover convinces a poly-bounded verifier that for each string z in a certain domain, it can compute a string y such that relation $R_x(z, y)$ holds. Informally, the requirements for proofs of computational ability are two: verifiability and extraction. The verifiability requirement states that for any input x there exists a prover that convinces the verifier with probability 1. Extraction states that there exists an extractor that, for any input $z \in \text{dom}(R_x)$, and interacting on input x with any prover that forces the verifier to accept with 'sufficiently high' probability, is able to compute a string y such that $R_x(z, y)$ holds, within a 'properly bounded' expected time.

Applications of proofs of computational ability, as discussed in [29, 4, 14], include the following: 1) if an efficient factoring algorithm being discovered, the owner of such an algorithm would like to prove that he has the ability to factor, without revealing information about his algorithm [29]; 2) proving the ability to compute a trapdoor permutation [4]. In addition to the mentioned results in [29, 4], ideas in [14] can be extended to show the following result for many languages L that are known to have a meet-the-challenge game (A,B): for any input $x \notin L$, the proof system of knowledge for relation $R_{x,(A,B)}$ from Fact 1, is a proof of computational ability of the function that associates to each input com the bit b such that $(x, com, b, ans) \in S(x, \cdot)$, where S is the simulator for (A,B). Furthermore, [14] shows (informally speaking) that this proof is *not* a proof of knowledge for the naturally associated relation, unless the language considered is trivial, thus proving a separation between proofs of knowledge and proofs of computational ability.

2.4   Proofs of Decision Power

The idea of proving the knowledge of whether a string belongs to a language or not has been given in [17]; a related concept of proving computational power has been introduced in [29]; the formal definition of zero-knowledge proof systems of decision power has first appeared in [15].

A zero-knowledge proof system of decision power is an interactive protocol in which a prover convinces a poly-bounded verifier that he knows whether a string x belongs to a language L or not, without revealing which is the case, or any other information. Informally, the requirements for zero-knowledge proof systems of decision power are three: verifiability, extraction and zero-knowledge. Verifiability states that the verifier accepts with high probability for any input x, in the language L or not. Extraction states that there exists an extractor that, for any input x, and interacting with any prover that forces the verifier to accept with 'sufficiently high' probability, is able to decide whether $x \in L$ or not, within a 'properly bounded' expected time. This differs from proofs of knowledge in which the extractor exists only for input in the language and is required to output a string satisfying a polynomial relation with the input. In particular, note that this approach allows to consider even languages above NP. Finally, the zero-knowledge requirement states that for all probabilistic polynomial time verifiers V', the view of V' is efficiently simulatable, and the simulation is correct for all x (in L or not).

Applications of this type of protocols include an even larger class of entity authentication protocols than in the applications obtained using proofs of knowledge. In [16] it was shown that every language having a meet-the-challenge game has a perfect zero-knowledge proof of decision power, which we now describe. Informally, the main idea is that of replacing the challenge sent by the verifier by the outcome of a 'language-dependent coin flipping' subprotocol, whose distribution depends on whether $x \in L$ or not.

The Proof System of Decision Power (A,B)

- A uniformly chooses an $s(n)$-bit string r, runs algorithm S on input x, r, and lets (com, a, ans) be its output. If $\rho(x; com, a, ans) = 0$ then A sets $acc = 0$ and $mes_1 = (r, acc)$ else A sets $acc = 1$ and $mes_1 = (com, acc)$. A sends mes_1 to B.
- If $acc = 0$ then B runs algorithm S on input x, r and lets (com, a, ans) be its output; if $\rho(x; com, a, ans) \neq 1$ then B outputs: ACCEPT and halts else B outputs: REJECT and halts.
- If $acc = 1$ then A and B run the following coin flipping protocol:
  - B uniformly chooses an $s(n)$-bit string r_2, run algorithm S on input x, r_2 and lets (com_2, b, ans_2) be its output; if $\rho(x; com_2, b, ans_2) \neq 1$ then B sets $mes = r_2$ and $acc_2 = 0$ else he sets $mes = com_2$ and $acc_2 = 1$. B sends mes, acc_2 to A.
  - If $acc = 1$ then B and A run protocol (C,D) on input (x, com_2), where B runs algorithm C and A runs algorithm D. If D outputs: REJECT then A halts.

- If $x \in L$ then A uniformly chooses $c \in \{0,1\}$. If $x \notin L$ and $acc_2 = 1$ then A computes b such that there exists a string ans_2 for which $\rho(x; com_2, b, ans_2) = 1$ and sets $c = a \oplus b$. If $x \notin L$ and $acc_2 = 0$ then A runs algorithm S on input x, r and lets (com, b, ans) be its output; if $\rho(x; com, b, ans) = 1$ then A halts else she sets $c = a \oplus b$. A sends c to B.
- B sends b, ans_2 to A; if $\rho(x; com_2, b, ans_2) \neq acc_2$ then A halts.

- If $x \notin L$ then A sets $mes_2 = ans$. If $x \in L$ then A runs algorithm A on input $(x; com, b \oplus c)$, obtaining ans_d as output, and sends $mes_2 = ans_d$ to B.
- If $\rho(x; com, b \oplus c, mes_2) = 1$ then B outputs: ACCEPT else B outputs: REJECT.

The verifiability property of (A,B) can be easily verified to hold. The extraction property follows by showing an extractor that, by properly rewinding the prover, obtains, in correspondence of the same first messgae from the prover, multiple independent executions of the special flipping-coin protocol, for which the verifier later accepts. By correlating the values of these executions with the first message from the prover, the extractor has an advantage over the verifier in understanding the the prover's behavior and can therefore compute whether $x \in L$ or not.

These techniques were crucial in [16] towards proving that any language having a honest-verifier statistical zero-knowledge proof of membership has a honest-verifier statistical zero-knowledge proof of decision power.

2.5 Proofs of Decision

The model for zero-knowledge and result-indistinguishable proofs of decision has been introduced in [21]. A zero-knowledge and result indistinguishable proof of decision is an interactive protocol in which a prover convinces a poly-bounded verifier of whether a string x belongs to a language L or not, without revealing which is the case, or any other information to any eavesdropper, and without revealing any other additional information to the verifier.

Zero-knowledge and result-indistinguishable proofs of decision have three requirements. The completeness requirement states that for any input x, with overwhelming probability the verifier accepts and can compute the value $\chi_L(x)$. The correctness requirement states that for any input x and any (possibly dishonest) prover, the probability that the verifier accepts and receives the wrong value $1 - \chi_L(x)$ is negligible. The zero-knowledge requirement states that for all probabilistic polynomial time verifiers V', the view of V' is efficiently simulatable, by a simulator that queries an oracle returning $\chi_L(x)$. Moreover, the simulation is correct for all x (in L or not). The perfect result-indistinguishability requirement states that for all input x, the conversation between prover and verifier is efficiently simulatable.

An important application of this type of protocols are interactive encryption schemes that are secure with respect to stronger definitions, based on languages with such proofs. In [16] it was shown that every language having a meet-the-challenge game has a perfect zero-knowledge transfer of decision, which we now describe. Informally, the main idea is that of replacing the challenge sent by the verifier by the outcome of a 'result-revealing and language-dependent coin flipping' subprotocol, whose distribution depends on whether $x \in L$ or not. Additionally, the verifier's final output depends on whether an equality among messages in the coin flipping subprotocol is satisfied or not.

The Proof of Decision (A,B)

- A uniformly chooses an $s(n)$-bit string r, runs algorithm S on input x, r, and lets (com, a, ans) be its output. If $\rho(x; com, a, ans) = 0$ then A sets $acc = 0$ and $mes_1 = (r, acc)$ else A sets $acc = 1$ and $mes_1 = (com, acc)$. E sends mes_1 to B.
- If $acc = 0$ then B runs algorithm S on input x, r and lets (com, a, ans) be its output; if $\rho(x; com, a, ans) \neq 1$ then B outputs: ACCEPT and halts else B outputs: REJECT and halts.
- If $acc = 1$ then A and B run the following coin flipping protocol:
  - B uniformly chooses r_{21}, r_{22}, runs algorithm S on input x, r_{2j} and lets $(com_{2j}, b_j, ans_{2j})$ be its output, for $j = 1, 2$; if $\rho(x; com_{2j}, b_j, ans_{2j}) \neq 1$ for some $j = 1, 2$ then B sets $mes = (r_{21}, r_{22})$ and $acc_2 = 0$ else he sets $mes = (com_{21}, com_{22})$ and $acc_2 = 1$. B sends mes, acc_2 to A.
  - If $acc = 1$ then A and B run protocol (C,D) twice in parallel, first on input com_{21} and then on input com_{22}, where B runs algorithm C and A runs algorithm D. If D outputs: REJECT then A halts.
  - If $x \in L$ then A uniformly chooses $c_1, c_2 \in \{0, 1\}$. If $x \notin L$ and $acc_2 = 1$ then A computes b_1, b_2 such that there exist strings ans_{21}, ans_{22} for which $\rho(x; com_{21}, b_1, ans_{21}) = \rho(x; com_{22}, b_2, ans_{22}) = 1$ and sets $c_1 = a \oplus b_1$ and $c_2 = a \oplus b_2$. If $x \notin L$ and $acc_2 = 0$ then A halts. A sends c_1, c_2 to B.
  - If $b_1 \oplus c_1 = b_2 \oplus c_2$ then B sets $d = b_1 \oplus c_1$ and $e = 0$ else he sets $e = 1$ and uniformly chooses a bit d. B sends d to A.
  Let e be the bit computed by B denoting whether the equality $b_1 \oplus c_1 = b_2 \oplus c_2$ was satisfied or not during the execution of the coin flipping protocol.
- If $x \notin L$ then A sets $mes_2 = ans$. If $x \in L$ then A runs algorithm A on input $(x; com, d)$ obtaining ans_d as output and sets $mes_2 = ans_d$. A sends mes_2 to B.
- If $\rho(x; mes_1, d, mes_2) = 1$ then B outputs: (ACCEPT,e) and halts; else B outputs: REJECT and halt.

The completeness and correctness properties of (A,B) can be easily verified to hold. The perfect zero-knowledge property follows from the following two facts: 1) a simulator can rewind the verifier's proof of knowledge and extract bits b_1, b_2; 2) by having access to $\chi_L(x)$, a simulator can successfully simulate transcripts of the coin-flipping subprotocols for each value of $\chi_L(x)$. The result-indistinguishability property follows from the fact that a simulator is now given the verifier's random coins and can use the knowledge of b_1, b_2 to successfully simulate the observer's view.

We remark that these techniques were crucial in [16] towards proving that any language having a honest-verifier statistical zero-knowledge proof of membership has a honest-verifier statistical zero-knowledge proof of decision.

3   A New Notion: Proofs of Non-zero Knowledge

Our new notion can be seen as a generalization of the previously discussed proofs of knowledge. Specifically, according to the zero-knowledge variant of the previous notion, a prover can convince a verifier that he knows a "secret" related to the common input according to a known "relation", without revealing anything new about the value of the secret. More formally, a prover and a verifier share a common input x and a relation R of size polynomial in $|x|$, and the prover can convince the verifier that he knows a string y such that relation R is satisfied (i.e., $R(x, y) = 1$), without revealing any additional information about string y.

According to the zero-knowledge variant of proofs of non-zero knowledge, we would like the prover to be able to convince a verifier that he knows a "secret" related to a common input, according to "some relation", without revealing anything new about the value of the secret *or the relation*. More formally, a prover and a verifier share a common input x and the prover can convince the verifier that he knows a string y and a relation R of size polynomial in $|x|$, such that relation R is satisfied (i.e., $R(x, y) = 1$), without revealing any additional information about string y or relation R, not even its size. Here, the "knowledge" concept is formalized by extending the same formalization for the same concept in proofs of knowledge.

The formal definition for proofs of non-zero-knowledge requires that these are interactive protocols satisfying two requirements. First, the verifiability requirement states that for any input x, if the prover uses as input y, R such that $R(x, y) = 1$, then the verifier accepts x with overwhelming probability. Second, the extraction requirement states that there exists an extractor that, for any input x, and interacting with any prover that forces the verifier to accept with 'sufficiently high' probability, is able to compute y, R such that $R(x, y)$ holds, within a 'properly bounded' expected time.

Definition 2. *Let P be a probabilistic Turing machine and V a probabilistic polynomial-time Turing machine that share the same input and can communicate with each other. Let $err : \{0, 1\}^* \to [0, 1]$ be a function. We say that a pair (P, V) is a* PROOF SYSTEM OF NON-ZERO KNOWLEDGE *with knowledge error err and with respect to polynomial-size relations if*

1 (Verifiability). For all x, and all y, R such that $|y| + |R|$ is polynomial in $|x|$, with probability 1 the verifier outputs ACCEPT, when given as input the transcript of an execution $(P[y, R], V)(x)$, where y, R are P's private input and x is the input common to P and V.

2 (Extraction). There exists a probabilistic oracle machine E (called the extractor) such that for all x, and for any Turing machine P', and letting $acc_{P'}(x)$ the probability that V outputs ACCEPT, when given as input the transcript of an execution $(P', V)(x)$, the following holds: if $acc_{P'}(x) > err(x)$ then,

- *$\text{Prob}(E_{P'}(x)) = (y, R)) \geq 2/3$, where $R(x, y) = 1$ and $|y| + |R| = poly(|x|)$.*
- *E halts within expected time bounded by $\frac{poly(|x|)}{(acc_{P'}(x) - err(x))}$.*

Remark. It directly follows from the definitions that a proof of knowledge for a relation R does not satisfy the relation-indistinguishability requirement for proofs of non-zero-knowledge (as the proof of knowledge obviously reveals which relation R it works for). Furthermore, we note that a proof of knowledge for a relation R does not necessarily satisfy the verifiability or extraction requirements. In particular, the attempt of using the verifier or extractor for the proof of knowledge as a verifier or extractor for a proof of non-zero knowledge fails in general, as the latter algorithms have no access to any relation, but only to the common input x.

Parameters and Extensions. It may be useful to consider proofs of non-zero knowledge for a class of relations. In fact, the above definition of proofs of non-zero knowledge already refers to the class of polynomial-size relation, which seems to combine generality and applicability. Extensions along this line are possible. For instance, one could define proofs of non-zero knowledge with respect to relations bounded by size $t(n)$, for some function t (bounded by a specific polynomial or not), or even practical examples of relations obtained by boolean formula composition. We study both variants in Sections 4 and 5. A formal definition of *arguments of non-zero knowledge* is obtained by modifying the extraction requirement in the formal definition of proofs of non-zero knowledge so that it holds with respect to all polynomial time provers P'.

Security Against Verifiers. We now define relation-indistinguishable and zero-knowledge requirements for proofs of non-zero knowledge. The former requirement states that the verifier cannot distinguish which relation R and which string y satisfying R is used by the prover. The latter requirement states that the verifier does not obtain any information at all about y, R or anything else that he could not compute before. Formal definitions follow.

Definition 3. *Let (P,V) be a proof of non-zero knowledge with error function err and with respect to polynomial-size relations. We say that (P,V) is* COMPUTATIONALLY RELATION-INDISTINGUISHABLE *(resp.,* PERFECTLY RELATION-INDISTINGUISHABLE*) if for any probabilistic polynomial-time V', for any x, and any $(y_1, R_1), (y_2, R_2)$ such that $(x, y_1) \in R_1$, $(x, y_2) \in R_2$, and $|y_1| + |y_2| + |R_1| + |R_2|$ is polynomial in $|x|$, the following two probability distribution are computationally indistinguishable by V' (resp., equal): the view of V' in $(P[y_1, R_1], V')(x)$ when P uses y_1, R_1 as private input and the view of V' in $(P[y_2, R_2], V')(x)$ when P uses y_2, R_2 as private input.*

Definition 4. *Let (P,V) be a proof of non-zero knowledge with error function err and with respect to polynomial-size relations. We say that (P,V) is* COMPUTATIONAL ZERO-KNOWLEDGE *(resp.,* PERFECT ZERO-KNOWLEDGE*) if for any probabilistic polynomial time verifier V', there exists an efficient algorithm $S_{V'}$, called the simulator, such that for any x, and any (y, R) such that $(x, y) \in R$, and $|y| + |R|$ is polynomial in $|x|$, the probability spaces $S_{v'}(x)$ and $P(y, R)$-$View_V(x)$ are computationally indistinguishable (resp., equal).*

Applications of proofs of non-zero knowledge obviously expand the applications of proofs of knowledge. In particular, one could use proofs of non-zero knowledge in arbitrary knowledge-based transactions, where a party needs to convince another party about his state of knowledge on some public data, without revealing anything at all about the nature of this knowledge. Knowing this knowledge state of other parties may be relevant in incentive-based transactions.

4 Computational Zero-Knowledge PNZKs

We start the study of the new notion by investigating computational zero-knowledge proofs and arguments of non-zero knowledge with respect to classes of generic polynomial-size relations. We discuss two simple protocols that are obtained as applications of protocols from [23, 6] and [1], respectively.

Proofs of Non-zero Knowledge. The first protocol is a computational zero-knowledge proof of non-zero knowledge for all relations whose size is bounded by a fixed polynomial. Specifically, we obtain the following

Theorem 1. *Let p be a polynomial. If non-uniform one-way function families exist, then there exists a computational zero-knowledge proof system of non-zero knowledge (with negligible knowledge error) with respect to the class of relations having size at most $p(n)$, where n is the size of the common input.*

We sketch the proof system (P,V) that proves Theorem 1. The tools used by (P,V) are a computationally-hiding and statistically-binding commitment scheme (Com,Rec) and a computational zero-knowledge proof system of knowledge for any polynomial-time relation. Using well-known results, we can implement both primitives under the existence of non-uniform one-way functions.

Let x be the common input to P and V, and let y, R be P's input such that $R(x, y) = 1$, and $|R| \leq p(|x|)$. The prover P, on input R, y, uses algorithm Com to commit to the two strings $s_R = R|10^{p(|x|)-|R|}$ and $s_y = y|10^{p(|x|)-|y|}$, sends the resulting commitment keys com_R, com_y to the verifier, and keeps secret the decommitment keys dec_R, dec_y, respectively. This implicitly defines the relation $R' = \{((com_1, com_2, s_1, s_2); (y, R, r_1, dec_1, r_2, dec_2)) \mid R(x, y) = 1 \land (com_1, dec_1) = Com(s_1, r_1) \land (com_2, dec_2) = Com(s_2, r_2)\}$. Then the prover proves to the verifier the knowledge of a witness for input (com_r, com_y, s_R, s_y) with respect to relation R', using a computational zero-knowledge proof system of knowledge for R'. The verifier accepts if and only if this proof is convincing.

Arguments of Non-zero Knowledge. The second protocol is a computational zero-knowledge argument of non-zero knowledge for all polynomial-size relations (that is, relations whose size is bounded by *any* polynomial). We obtain the following

Theorem 2. *If collision-intractable hash function families exist then there exists a computational zero-knowledge argument system of non-zero knowledge (with negligible knowledge error) with respect to all polynomial-size relations.*

We sketch the argument system (P,V) that proves Theorem 2. (P,V) uses a collision-intractable hash function family $H = \{h_w\}$, a computationally-hiding and statistically-binding commitment scheme (Com,Rec), and a zero-knowledge universal argument of knowledge for any polynomial time relation (such as the one in [3]). We use here two properties of the universal argument in [3]: 1) the argument of knowledge is a *single protocol* that can be used to prove knowledge of any polynomial-time relation (that can be decided by the prover during the protocol); 2) when the common input is in the relation domain, there is a polynomial-time witness certifying this fact and the extractor returning this witness runs in polynomial time. (We remark that, contrarily to [1,3], in this paper we are not addressing any soundness property, and therefore we are not facing extractors running in super-polynomial time.)

Let x be the common input to P and V, and let y, R be P's input such that $R(x, y) = 1$, and $|R| \leq p(|x|)$, for some arbitrary polynomial p. (This also implies that $|y| \leq p(x)$.) The verifier sends a random index w for a hash function h_w in family H to the prover. The prover P, on input R, y, uses function h_w to hash pair (R, y) to a fixed length string s, and uses algorithm Com to commit to s. Then P sends the resulting commitment key com_s to the verifier, and keeps secret the associated decommitment keys dec_s. This implicitly defines the language $L' = \{com \mid \exists (y, R, r, dec)) \text{ s.t.} R(x, y) = 1 \land (com, dec) = Com(s, r) \land s = h_w(y|R)\}$. Then the prover proves to the verifier that $com_s \in L'$ using a computational zero-knowledge universal argument system (of knowledge), and using (y, R, r_s, dec_s) as a witness. The verifier accepts if and only if this proof is convincing.

5   Perfect ZK and Relation-Indistinguishable PNZKs

We continue the study of the new notion by investigating perfect zero-knowledge and relation-indistinguishable proofs of non-zero knowledge with respect to more specific classes of polynomial-size relations.

Specifically, given a language L having a meet-the-challenge game, as defined in Section 2.1, we consider the (sub)class of such relations whose domain contains m instances $x_1, \ldots, x_m$ and the boolean variables $\chi_L(x_1), \ldots, \chi_L(x_m)$ denoting their membership (or not) to L satisfy some given boolean functions $\phi_1, \ldots, \phi_q$. More formally, let ϕ a boolean function over m variables, and define relation $R_\phi = \{(\boldsymbol{x}, \boldsymbol{\chi}) \mid \boldsymbol{x} = (x_1, \ldots, x_m), \boldsymbol{\chi} = (\chi_L(x_1), \ldots, \chi_L(x_m)), \phi(\chi) = 1\}$. In general, we consider as an interesting problem that of presenting a proof system of non-zero knowledge for a class of relations of the type $\{R_\phi \mid \phi \in \{\phi_1, \ldots, \phi_q\}\}$, any such class varying over all possible choices or descriptions of $\phi_1, \ldots, \phi_q$.

In the sequel, we study two examples of such classes. In Subsection 5.1 we study 3-round perfect zero-knowledge proof systems of non-zero knowledge with constant knowledge error. (These can be transformed so that they have negligible knowledge error using well-known techniques increasing the number of rounds.) In Subsection 5.2 we study 3-round relation-indistinguishable proof systems of non-zero knowledge with negligible knowledge error.

5.1   Perfect Zero-Knowledge PNZKs

We study proofs of non-zero knowledge for classes containing relations only indexed by monotone formulae, and for classes containing relations indexed by monotone and negations of monotone formulae.

Proofs of Non-zero Knowledge for Classes of Monotone Formulae.
In our first example we consider the class $\text{MON}_{L,q,\phi}$ of relations R_ϕ, for $\phi \in \{\phi_1, \ldots, \phi_q\}$, where all boolean functions in $\phi = (\phi_1, \ldots, \phi_q)$ are monotone(that is, they contain OR, AND operators but no NOT operator), and, moreover, we assume that all quantities $m, q, |\phi_1|, \ldots, |\phi_q|$ are polynomial in the size n of instances $x_1, \ldots, x_m$. We obtain the following

Theorem 3. *Let L be a language having a meet-the-challenge game. Let q be a polynomial and let $\phi = (\phi_1, \ldots, \phi_q)$ be a q-tuple of boolean functions. Then there exists a 3-round perfect zero-knowledge proof system of non-zero knowledge (with constant knowledge error) with respect to the class $\text{MON}_{L,q,\phi}$ of relations.*

We sketch the proof system (P,V) that proves Theorem 3. Informally, (P,V) is obtained by proving the OR, for $i = 1, \ldots, q$, of the statement "formula ϕ_i over χ is true". Using for this protocol a 3-round proof of knowledge as the one in [13], we inherit a property implying that an extractor for our protocol obtains a witness certifying that one of the m formulae $\phi_1, \ldots, \phi_m$ is true.

Protocol (P,V) uses the fact, directly following from results in [13], that the language of monotone formula ϕ_i over χ has a meet-the-challenge game (A_i, B_i), for $i = 1, \ldots, q$. The prover P, on input i^* such that ϕ_{i^*} is true, does the following. For $i = i^*$, it generates the first message mes_{i^*} using algorithm A_{i^*}, and, for $i \neq i^*$, it generates the first message mes_i using the simulator S_i associated to (A_i, B_i). Also, P denotes as a_i, ans_i the values obtained in the output from S_i; that is, such that $(mes_i, a_i, ans_i) = S_i(x_i, r_i)$, where $a_i \in \{0, 1\}$ and r_i is a random string. P sends $mes_1, \ldots, mes_q$ to V, that replies with a single random bit b. Now, P computes ans_{i^*} by running algorithm A_i on input mes_{i^*}, c, where $c = b \oplus a_1 \oplus \cdots \oplus a_{i-1} \oplus a_{i+1} \oplus \cdots \oplus a_q$. Finally, P sends $ans_1, \ldots, ans_q$ to V, that uses algorithm B_i to verify that (mes_i, a_i, ans_i) is an accepting conversation of the meet-the-challenge game for ϕ_i. Finally, V accepts if and only if all these checks are satisfied and $a_1 \oplus \cdots \oplus a_m = b$.

Proofs of Non-zero Knowledge for Classes of Monotone and Negated Monotone Formulae. We now consider the class $\text{NEG-MON}_{L,q,\phi}$ of relations R_ϕ, for $\phi \in \{\phi_1, \ldots, \phi_q\}$, where all boolean functions in $\phi = (\phi_1, \ldots, \phi_q)$ are either monotone (that is, they contain OR, AND operators but no NOT operator), or negated monotone formulae (that is, they can be written as the NOT of a monotone formula). Moreover, as in our first example, we assume that all quantities $m, q, |\phi_1|, \ldots, |\phi_q|$ are polynomial in the size n of instances $x_1, \ldots, x_m$. We obtain the following

Theorem 4. *Let L be a language having a meet-the-challenge game. Let q be a polynomial and let $\phi = (\phi_1, \ldots, \phi_q)$ be a q-tuple of boolean functions. Then there exists a 3-round perfect zero-knowledge proof system of non-zero knowledge (with constant knowledge error) with respect to the class $NEG\text{-}MON_{L,q,\phi}$ of relations.*

We sketch the proof system (P,V) that proves Theorem 4. Interestingly, an approach for obtaining (P,V), similar to that in our first example, fails. Specifically, if we design (P,V) by proving the OR, for $i = 1, \ldots, q$, of the statement "formula ϕ_i over χ is true", for instance, using a proof of knowledge as the one in [13], it is unclear how to design an extractor that always obtains a witness certifying that one of the m formulae is true. Instead, we prove the OR differently, by extending the meet-the-challenge games for the monotone formulae so that the challenge bit is determined by a language-dependent flipping-coin protocol ([16]) based on the meet-the-challenge game for the negated formula. Then we can design an extractor that can compute which formula is known to be true by the prover, by obtaining several outcomes for the language-dependent flipping-coin protocol with respect to the same first message in the meet-the-challenge games for the monotone formula. We present protocol (P,V) for the simple case of $q = 2$, and assuming that formula ϕ_1 is monotone and formula ϕ_2 is negated monotone. Protocol (P,V) uses the fact, directly following from results in [13], that, for $\phi = \phi_1, \overline{\phi_2}$, the language of monotone formula ϕ over χ has a meet-the-challenge game (A_ϕ, B_ϕ); furthermore, protocol (P,V) uses protocol (C,D) from Fact 1.

The prover P, on input $i^* \in \{1, 2\}$ such that ϕ_{i^*} is true, does the following. First, it generates the first message mes_1 by using algorithm A_1 if $i^* = 1$ or the simulator S_1 otherwise; in the latter case, P denotes by a_1, ans_1 the values obtained in the output from S_1; that is, such that $(mes_1, a_1, ans_1) = S_1(x_1, r_1)$, where $a_1 \in \{0, 1\}$ and r_1 is a random string. Now, V sends the first message mes_2 by using the simulator S_2 for the meet-the-challenge game (A_2, B_2) for $\overline{\phi_2}$; here, V denotes as a_2, ans_2 the values obtained in the output from S_2; that is, such that $(mes_2, a_2, ans_2) = S_1(x_2, r_2)$, where $a_2 \in \{0, 1\}$ and r_2 is a random string. Now, P and V run subprotocol (C,D) on common input x_2, com_2, where V plays as C and P plays as D. If D rejects at the end of this subprotocol, then P stops. Otherwise, P computes a_2 from com_2 and sets $c = a_1 \oplus a_2$ if $i^* = 2$, or sets c equal to a random bit if $i^* = 1$. P sends c to V that replies by returning a_2, ans_2. If (com_2, a_2, ans_2) is not an accepting conversation of the meet-the-challenge game for $\overline{\phi_2}$, then P stops; otherwise, P uses algorithm A_1 on input $x_1, com_1, c \oplus a_2$ and sends ans_1 to V, that accepts if and only if $(com_1, c \oplus a_2, ans_1)$ is an accepting conversation of the meet-the-challenge game for ϕ_1.

The extractor works as follows. First, the extractor plays as V and obtains one accepting conversation $(com_1, com_2, tr_{(C,D)}, c, a_2, ans_2, ans_1)$ from P, and then rewinds P to the state just after sending com_1. Now, it keeps playing independent executions of the language-dependent flipping-coin protocol and rewinding the prover to the state just after sending com_1 until it obtains a new accepting conversation, with bits c', a_2'. At this point, if $c' \oplus a_2' = c \oplus a_2$, then the extractor returns: 2; otherwise, it returns: 1.

5.2   Relation-Indistinguishable Proofs of Partial Knowledge

We now study *relation-indistinguishable* proofs of non-zero knowledge with respect to more specific classes of polynomial-size relations. Although we target a weaker security guarantee against the verifier (relation-indistiguishability instead of perfect zero-knowledge), we obtain more efficient protocols in terms of both communication and rounds, when negligible soundness error is required. In particular, we are interested in proving results analogous to the previous two theorems, with the only difference that we start with languages having a large-challenge meet-the-challenge game, where we recall that these games are honest-verifier zero-knowledge, rather than any-verifier zero-knowledge, as for (standard) meet-the-challenge games.

It would appear that an analogue of Theorem 3 in this setting would directly follow from results in [10] (which are, in turn, very similar to techniques in [12, 13]). Unfortunately, a bug in Proposition 1 of [10] was pointed out by [30], which also invalidates all main subsequent results in [10]. As a further complication, the explanation suggested by [30] to fix Proposition 1 in [10] is incorrect as well, as we later show. We therefore revisit [10], prove a number of simple results that clarify the state of the art on this topics, and propose a simple fix that, when applies to all techniques in [10], makes those results valid by only a loss of a factor of 2 in the communication complexity of the resulting protocol. (Indeed, this may be relevant as some papers applying results from [10, 13] cite constant factors in the communication complexity to argue efficiency of their results.) Moreover, in certain cases, including our application of relation-indistinguishable proofs of non-zero knowledge, we can achieve our goals without increase in the communication complexity.

Revisiting the "Proofs of Partial Knowledge". Proposition 1 in [10] states that any 3-round public-coin honest-verifier zero-knowledge proof system for a language L in NP is also witness-indistinguishable (against any verifier) over L. Using this proposition as a starting point, several other results are proved in [10] on the witness-indistinguishability of threshold compositions of 3-round public-coin honest-verifier zero-knowledge proof systems.

In [30] it was observed that the proof of Proposition 1 in [10] is flawed; furthermore, a converse of this proposition is proved in [30]: specifically, that there exists a 3-round public-coin honest-verifier zero-knowledge proof system for a language L in NP that is *not* witness-indistinguishable (against any verifier) over L. In footnote 3 and beginning of Section 3 of [30], it is suggested that perhaps Proposition 1 holds if the 3-round public-coin proof system for language L in NP is actually "special-honest-verifier zero-knowledge". We remind that a 3-round public-coin proof system is defined to be *special-honest-verifier zero-knowledge* if there exists a simulator that, on input the challenge message b generated by a honest verifier, returns a conversation (com, b, ans) that is indistinguishable from the transcript of a real execution of the 3-round proof system.

In the following fact, we show that even this suggestion from [30] is false. We actually show a stronger statement, by showing that it is false even if the zero-knowledge type of the original 3-round proof system is of *statistical* type.

Fact 2. *Let L be a language having a 3-round public-coin and special-honest-verifier statistical zero-knowledge proof system of membership. Then there exists a 3-round public-coin and special-honest-verifier zero-knowledge proof system of membership for L that is not witness-indistinguishable over L.*

SKETCH OF PROOF. Let (P,V) be a 3-round public-coin and special-honest-verifier statistical zero-knowledge proof system for L. We construct a new proof system (P′,V′) as follows. First, we use simple padding techniques to modify P and V so that the length of the first message from P is equal to the length of the message from V. Then we define V′=V; and P′=P with the only difference that if the message from V′ is equal to the first message from P′ then P′ sends the witness as a third message. Note that (P′,V′) is a 3-round public-coin special-honest-verifier statistical zero-knowledge proof system; to see that, just note that the special-honest-verifier simulator uses the same simulator as for (P,V). The statistical difference is still exponentially small. Then note that (P′,V′) is not witness-indistinguishable as a malicious V′ just sends its message equal to the first message from P′ and therefore obtains the witness.   □

One consequence of Fact 2 is that many theorems in [10] do not hold any more. Furthermore, several other papers use Proposition 1 in [10] as a black-box (see, e.g., [22,9,11,20]) and therefore they inherit the same problem. The following simple observation suggests a way for fixing all these results.

Fact 3. *If there exists a 3-round public-coin honest-verifier zero-knowledge proof system of membership for language L then there exists a 3-round public-coin witness-indistinguishable proof system of membership for L.*

SKETCH OF PROOF. Let (P,V) be a 3-round public-coin honest-verifier perfect zero-knowledge proof system with simulator Sim. We use the OR technique from [12,13] (also used in [10]) to construct a perfect zero-knowledge proof system (P′,V′) for the statement "$(x \in L) \vee (x \in L)$", starting from protocol (P,V). (Also used in the proof of Theorem 3; recall that (P′,V′) is some particular composition of two executions of subprotocol (P,V).) Assume (P′,V′) is not witness-indistinguishable. Then there is an efficient algorithm distinguishing $P'(w_1, w_1)$-$View_{V'}(x)$ and $P'(w_2, w_2)$-$View_{V'}(x)$, where the notation $P'(w^1, w^2)$-$View_{V'}(x)$ denotes the view of V′ in an execution of (P′,V′) for proving statement "$(x \in L) \vee (x \in L)$", where P′ uses witness w^i in the i-th execution of subprotocol (P,V). Then the same algorithm can be used to distinguish either: $P'(w_1, w_1)$-$View_{V'}(x)$ and $P'(w_2, w_1)$-$View_{V'}(x)$; or: $P'(w_2, w_1)$-$View_{V'}(x)$ and $P'(w_2, w_2)$-$View_{V'}(x)$. Consider the first case (the second being similar). An algorithm distinguishing $P'(w_1, w_1)$-$View_{V'}(x)$ from $P'(w_2, w_1)$-$View_{V'}(x)$ can be used to distinguish either: $P'(w_1, w_1)$-$View_{V'}(x)$ from (Sim+$P'(w2)$)-$View_{V'}(x)$; or (Sim+$P'(w2)$)-$View_{V'}(x)$ from $P'(w_2, w_2)$-$View_{V'}(x)$; where the notation (Sim+$P'(w_2)$)-$View_{V'}(x)$ denotes the view of V′ in an execution of (P′,V′) for proving statement "$(x \in L) \vee (x \in L)$", where P′ uses witness w_2 in the second execution of subprotocol (P,V), and the first execution of subprotocol (P,V) is generated using simulator Sim. Using the fact that the challenge to the first execution of (P,V) in (P',V') can always be chosen before the protocol starts, this violates the honest-verifier zero-knowledge property of (P,V).   □

Fixing Other Results. We note that thanks to Fact 3, Theorem 8,9 and Corollary 12,13,14 in [10] can then continue to hold when their Proposition 1 is replaced by the above Fact 2 and each construction is preceeded with the transformation in Fact 3. We note that the construction in Fact 3 increases the communication complexity by a multiplicative factor of 2. Actually, the problem in Theorems 8,9 and Corollary 12,13,14 in [10], as written, only lies with monotone formulae of the form $\phi = \phi_1 \wedge \phi_2$. Instead, for monotone formulae of the form $\phi = \phi_1 \vee \phi_2$, the construction of Fact 3 is actually not necessary, although the proof needs to be modified to incorporate arguments similar to the proof of Fact 3, thus resulting in no loss in communication complexity.

Our Results on Relation-Indistinguishable PNZKs. Following the above observations, we can use essentially the same protocol from the proof of Theorem 3 and 4 (with the only modification that we use large challenges, and, consequently, a suitable large-challenge extension of meet-the-challenge games) to have no loss in communication complexity and obtain the following results.

Theorem 5. *Let L be a language having a large-challenge meet-the-challenge game. Let q be a polynomial and let $\phi = (\phi_1, \ldots, \phi_q)$ be a q-tuple of boolean functions. Then there exists a relation-indistinguishable proof system of non-zero knowledge (with negligible knowledge error) with respect to the class $MON_{L,q,\phi}$ of relations.*

Theorem 6. *Let L be a language having a large-challenge meet-the-challenge game. Let q be a polynomial and let $\phi = (\phi_1, \ldots, \phi_q)$ be a q-tuple of boolean functions. Then there exists a relation-indistinguishable proof system of non-zero knowledge (with negligible knowledge error) with respect to the class NEG-$MON_{L,q,\phi}$ of relations.*

References

1. B. Barak, *How to Go Beyond the Black-Box Simulation Barrier*, in Proc. of the 42nd IEEE Symposium on Foundations of Computer Science (FOCS 01).
2. M. Bellare and O. Goldreich, *On Defining Proofs of Knowledge*, in Proc. of CRYPTO '92, LNCS, Springer-Verlag.
3. B. Barak and O. Goldreich, *Universal Arguments and Their Applications*, in Proc. of IEEE Conference on Computational Complexity '02.
4. M. Bellare, and O. Goldreich, *Proving Computational Ability*, manuscript, 1992.
5. M. Ben-Or, O. Goldreich, S. Goldwasser, J. Håstad, J. Kilian, S. Micali, and P. Rogaway, *Everything Provable is Provable in Zero Knowledge*, in Proc. of CRYPTO 88, LNCS, Springer-Verlag.
6. M. Blum, *How to Prove a Theorem So No One Else Can Claim It*, Proc. of the International Congress of Mathematicians, Berkeley, California, 1986.
7. R. Boppana, J. Hastad, and S. Zachos, *Does co-NP has Short Interactive Proofs ?*, in Information Processing Letters, vol. 25, May 1987, pp. 127–132.

8. G. Brassard, C. Crépeau, and D. Chaum, *Minimum Disclosure Proofs of Knowledge*, Journal of Computer and System Sciences, vol. 37, no. 2, pp. 156–189.
9. R. Cramer, I. Damgard and P. MacKenzie, *Efficient Zero-Knowledge Proofs of Knowledge Without Intractability Assumptions*, in Proc. of Public Key Cryptography 2000, LNCS, Springer-Verlag.
10. R. Cramer, I. Damgard and B. Schoenmakers, *Proofs of Partial Knowledge and Simplified Design of Witness Hiding Protocols*, in Proc. of CRYPTO 94, LNCS, Springer-Verlag.
11. R. Cramer, M. Franklin, B. Schoenmakers, and M. Yung, *Multi-Authority Secret Ballot elections with Linear Work*, in Proc. of EUROCRYPT '96, Springer-Verlag.
12. A. De Santis, G. Di Crescenzo, and G. Persiano, *Secret Sharing and Perfect Zero-Knowledge,* in Proc. of CRYPTO 93, LNCS, Springer-Verlag.
13. A. De Santis, G. Di Crescenzo, G. Persiano and M. Yung, *On Monotone Formula Closure of SZK,* in Proc. of the 35th IEEE Symposium on Foundations of Computer Science (FOCS 94).
14. G. Di Crescenzo and R. Impagliazzo, *Security-Preserving Hardness Amplification for any Regular One-Way Function,* in Proc. of STOC 99.
15. G. Di Crescenzo, K. Sakurai and M. Yung, *Zero-Knowledge Proofs of Decision Power: New Protocols and Optimal Round-Complexity*, in Proc. of ICICS 98.
16. G. Di Crescenzo, K. Sakurai and M. Yung, *On Zero-Knowledge Proofs: 'From Membership to Decision'*, in Proc. of the 2000 ACM Symposium on Theory of Computing (STOC 00).
17. U. Feige, A. Fiat, and A. Shamir, *Zero-Knowledge Proofs of Identity*, in Journal of Cryptology, vol. 1, 1988, pp. 77–94.
18. A. Fiat and A. Shamir, *How to Prove yourself: Practical Solutions to Identifications and Signature Problems*, in Proc. of CRYPTO 86, LNCS, Springer-Verlag.
19. L. Fortnow, *The Complexity of Perfect Zero Knowledge*, in Proc. of the 1987 ACM Symposium on Theory of Computing (STOC 87).
20. M. Franklin and T. Sander, *Committal Deniable Proofs and Electronic Campaign Finance*, in Proc. of Asiacrypt 2000, LNCS, Springer-Verlag
21. Z. Galil, S. Haber, and M. Yung, *Minimum-Knowledge Interactive Proofs for Decision Problems*, in SIAM Journal on Computing, vol. 18, n.4.
22. J. Garay and P. MacKenzie, *Concurrent Oblivious Transfer*, in Proc. of the 41st IEEE Symposium on Foundations of Computer Science (FOCS 00).
23. O. Goldreich, S. Micali, and A. Wigderson, *Proofs that Yield Nothing but their Validity or All Languages in NP Have Zero-Knowledge Proof Systems*, Journal of the ACM, vol. 38, n. 1, 1991, pp. 691–729.
24. S. Goldwasser, S. Micali, and C. Rackoff, *The Knowledge Complexity of Interactive Proof-Systems*, SIAM Journal on Computing, vol. 18, n. 1, 1989.
25. R. Impagliazzo and M. Yung, *Direct Minimum Knowledge Computations*, in Proc. of CRYPTO 87, LNCS, Springer-Verlag.
26. T. Itoh, Y. Ohta, and H. Shizuya, *A Language-Dependent Cryptographic Primitive*, in Journal of Cryptology, vol. 10, n. 1, 1997, pp. 37–49.
27. A. Shamir, *IP=PSPACE*, in Proc. of the 31st IEEE Symposium on Foundations of Computer Science (FOCS 90).
28. M. Tompa and H. Woll, *Random Self-Reducibility and Zero-Knowledge Interactive Proofs of Possession of Information*, in Proc. of IEEE FOCS 87.
29. M. Yung, *Zero-Knowledge Proofs of Computational Power,* in Proc. of EUROCRYPT 89, LNCS, Springer Verlag.
30. Yu. Zhao, C. H. Lee, Yi. Zhao, and H. Zhu, *Some Observations on Zaps and Its Applications*, in Proc. of ACNS 2004, LNCS, Springer-Verlag.

Improvements on Security Proofs of Some Identity Based Encryption Schemes

Rui Zhang and Hideki Imai

Institute of Industrial Science, The University of Tokyo
zhang@imailab.iis.u-tokyo.ac.jp, imai@iis.u-tokyo.ac.jp

Abstract. Concrete security reduction plays an important role in practice, because it explicitly bounds an adversary's success probability as a function of their resources. In this paper, we study the security reductions of Boneh-Franklin identity based encryption (IBE) schemes and its variants, focusing on the efficiency of their security reductions:

Improvements on proofs of Boneh-Franklin IBE and variants. The proof of the Boneh-Franklin IBE (BF-IBE) scheme was long believed to be correct until recently, Galindo pointed out a flawed step in the proof and gave a new proof, however, the new reduction was even looser. We give a new proof of the BF-IBE scheme that essentially improves previously known results. Very interestingly, our result is even better than the original underestimated one. Similar analysis can also be applied to Galindo's BF-IBE variant, resulting in a tighter reduction.

A new BF-IBE variant with tighter security reductions. We propose another variant of the BF-IBE that admits better security reduction, however, the scheme relies on a stronger assumption, namely the Gap Bilinear Diffie-Hellman (GBDH) assumption.

Keywords: IBE, tight security reductions, BDH assumption.

1 Introduction

Identity Based Encryption. Identity Based Encryption (IBE) provides a public key encryption mechanism where an arbitrary string, such as recipient's identity, can be served as a public key. The ability to use identities as public keys avoids the need to distribute public key certificates. Such a scheme is largely motivated by many applications such as to encrypt emails using recipient's email address.

Although the concept of identity based encryption was proposed two decades ago [11], it is only recently that the first full-fledged IBE schemes were proposed. In 2001, Boneh and Franklin proposed the first secure IBE (BF-IBE) [3, 4], and defined a security model, namely *Indistinguishability under Chosen-Ciphertext Attack for ID-based encryption* (IND-ID-CCA) and gave the first efficient construction provably secure in the random oracle model based on the Computational Bilinear Diffie-Hellman (CBDH) assumption.

Justification on the BF-IBE. The Boneh-Fraklin scheme has attracted much focus since the very beginning and the correctness of its security proof was

D. Feng, D. Lin, and M. Yung (Eds.): CISC 2005, LNCS 3822, pp. 28–41, 2005.

never challenged until recently. Galindo [9] noticed that the proof regarding security reduction given in [4] contains a flawed step, he then gave a new proof. However, for the modified reduction result given in [9], as in the sense of IND-ID-CCA security, its security is reduced only *loosely* to its underlying intractability assumption.

Concrete Security Reductions. It is crucial to note that an inefficient security reduction would imply either the lower security level or the requirement of larger key size to obtain the same security level. In fact, if considering a practical adversary breaking the security of the BF-IBE, it is not sufficient to say that such an adversary can be used to solve the CBDH problem in a meaningful sense.

We remark that all the analyses above [3,9] are in the random oracle model [7,2]. A proof in the random oracle may not guarantee the security when this random oracle is instantiated with any particular hash function [5]. However, a proof in the random oracle model indicates there is no "inherent" weaknesses in the scheme thus is certainly better than no proof at all.

1.1   Our Contributions

Improvements on Proofs of the BF-IBE and Variants. We give a new security proof of BF-IBE scheme which significantly improves Galindo's result. More exactly, we show how to solve the problem of applying Coron's technique [6] in BF-IBE and variants. Very interestingly, this shows a better security reduction than that given by Boneh and Franklin in [4], though the original proof was in fact underestimated. We then apply similar analysis to improve the security reduction of Galindo's BF-IBE variant.

A New BF-IBE Variants with Tighter Security Reductions. We propose a variant of BF-IBE, called CIBE, whose security can be reduced to the difficulty

Table 1. Comparison of Schemes

Scheme	Assumption[†]	Security Notion	Reduction cost[*]	ciphertext size[‡]
BF-IBE ([4])	CBDH	IND-ID-CCA	$O(\frac{1}{(Q_E+Q_D)Q_H^2})$ ([4])	$|r| + 2|M|$
\\	\\	\\	$O(\frac{1}{Q_H^3})$ ([9])	\\
\\	\\	\\	$O(\frac{1}{Q_E Q_H})$ (this work)	\\
G05 ([9])	DBDH	\\	$O(\frac{1}{Q_H})$ ([9])	$\approx 2|r| + |M|$
\\	\\	\\	$O(\frac{1}{Q_E})$ (this work)	\\
Ours (ZIBE)	GBDH	\\	$O(\frac{1}{Q_E})$	$|r| + |l| + |M|$

[†] CBDH, DBDH and GBDH are referred as Computational, Decision and Gap Bilinear Diffie-Hellamn assumptions.

[*] Q_D and Q_H are the numbers of decryption queries and hash queries, respectively.

[‡] $|r|$ is the bit-length of an element of $\mathbb{G}_1$ (an optimistic parameter choice could be $|r| = 171$bits). $|M|$ is the length of plaintext, $|l|$ (typically 160bits) is the bit length of the output of a hash function.

of solving the Gap Bilinear Diffie-Hellman (GBDH) problem, which is a stronger assumption than the BF-IBE. A supplementary remark is that GBDH assumption is very helpful and many efficient schemes are based on it. A comparison of the results of security reduction is listed in Table 1.

2   Preliminaries

We review the model and the security notion of IBE scheme. The definitions are similar with [3, 4]. We also give a brief review of bilinear maps and related computational assumptions.

2.1   ID-Based Encryption: Algorithms

An IBE scheme $\mathcal{E}$ is constructed by four efficient algorithms (**Setup, Extract, Encrypt, Decrypt**).

Setup: takes a security parameter k and returns params (system parameters) and master-key. The system parameters include a description of a finite message space $\mathcal{M}$, and a description of a finite ciphertext space $\mathcal{C}$. Intuitively, the system parameters will be publicly known, while the master-key will be known only to the "Private Key Generator" (PKG).

Extract: takes as input params, master-key, and an arbitrary ID $\in \{0, 1\}^*$, and returns a private key sk. Here ID is an arbitrary string that will be used as a public key, and sk is the corresponding private decryption key. The Extract algorithm extracts a private key from the given public key.

Encrypt: takes as input params, ID, and $M \in \mathcal{M}$. It returns a ciphertext $C \in \mathcal{C}$.

Decrypt: takes as input params, $C \in \mathcal{C}$, and a private key sk. It returns $M \in \mathcal{M}$ or *"reject"*.

These algorithms must satisfy the standard consistency constraint, namely when sk is the private key generated by algorithm Extract when it is given ID as the public key, then $\forall M \in \mathcal{M} :$ Decrypt(params, C, sk) $= M$, where $C =$ Encrypt(params, ID, M).

2.2   Security Notion

In [3, 4], Boneh and Franklin defined chosen ciphertext security for IBE under a chosen identity attack. In their model the adversary is allowed to access both an Extract oracle and a Decryption oracle.

We say that an IBE scheme $\mathcal{E}$ is semantically secure against an adaptive chosen ciphertext attack and a chosen identity attack (IND-ID-CCA) if no polynomially bounded adversary $\mathcal{A}$ has a non-negligible advantage against the challenger in the following IND-ID-CCA game:

Setup: The challenger takes a security parameter k and runs the Setup algorithm. It gives the adversary the resulting system parameters params. It keeps the master-key to itself.

Phase 1: The adversary issues several queries $Q_1, \cdots, Q_m$ where query Q_i is one of:

- Extraction query $\langle \mathsf{ID}_i \rangle$: The challenger responds by running algorithm Extract to generate the private key sk_i corresponding to the public key $\langle \mathsf{ID}_i \rangle$. It sends sk_i to the adversary.
- Decryption query $\langle \mathsf{ID}_i, C_i \rangle$: The challenger responds by running algorithm Extract to generate the private key sk_i corresponding to ID_i. It then runs algorithm Decrypt to decrypt the ciphertext C_i using the private key sk_i. It sends the result to the adversary.

These queries may be asked adaptively, that is, each query Q_i may depend on the replies to $Q_1, \cdots, Q_{i-1}$.

Challenge: Once the adversary decides that Phase 1 is over it outputs two equal length plaintexts $M_0, M_1 \in \mathcal{M}$ and an identity ID^* on which it wishes to be challenged. The only constraint is that ID^* did not appear in any Extraction query in Phase 1. The challenger picks a random bit $\beta \in \{0, 1\}$ and sets $C^* = \mathrm{Encrypt}(\mathsf{Params}, \mathsf{ID}^*, M_\beta)$. It sends C^* as the challenge to the adversary.

Phase 2: The adversary issues more queries $Q_{m+1}, \cdots, Q_{max}$ where each query is one of:

- Extraction query $\langle \mathsf{ID}_i \rangle$ where $\mathsf{ID}_i \neq \mathsf{ID}^*$: Challenger responds as in Phase 1.
- Decryption query $\langle \mathsf{ID}_i, C_i \rangle \neq \langle \mathsf{ID}^*, C^* \rangle$: Challenger responds as in Phase 1.

These queries may be asked adaptively as in Phase 1.

Guess: Finally, the adversary outputs a guess $\beta' \in \{0, 1\}$ and wins the game if $\beta = \beta'$.

We refer to such an adversary $\mathcal{A}$ as an IND-ID-CCA adversary. We define adversary $\mathcal{A}$'s advantage in attacking the scheme $\mathcal{E}$ as:

$$Adv_{\mathcal{E}, \mathcal{A}} = \Pr[\beta = \beta'] - 1/2$$

The provability is over the random bits used by the challenger and the adversary.

Definition 1. We say that the IBE system $\mathcal{E}$ is $(t_{\mathsf{IBE}}, \epsilon_{\mathsf{IBE}})$-adaptive chosen ciphertext secure under a chosen identity attack if for any t_{IBE}-time IND-ID-CCA adversary $\mathcal{A}$, we have $Adv_{\mathcal{E}, \mathcal{A}} < \epsilon_{\mathsf{IBE}}$. As shorthand, we say that $\mathcal{E}$ is IND-ID-CCA secure.

2.3   Bilinear Maps

We briefly review several facts about bilinear maps. Throughout this paper, we let $\mathbb{G}_1$ and $\mathbb{G}_2$ be two multiplicative cyclic groups of prime order q and g be a generator of $\mathbb{G}_1$. A *bilinear map* $e : \mathbb{G}_1 \times \mathbb{G}_1 \to \mathbb{G}_2$ satisfies the following properties:

1. bilinearity: For all $u, v \in \mathbb{G}_1$ and $a, b \in \mathbb{Z}$, $e(u^a, v^b) = e(u, v)^{ab}$.
2. non-degeneracy: $e(g, g) \neq 1$.
3. computability: There is an efficient algorithm to compute $e(u, v)$ for any $u, v \in \mathbb{G}_1$.

Note that a bilinear map is symmetric since $e(g^a, g^b) = e(g^b, g^a) = e(g, g)^{ab}$.

2.4 Complexity Assumptions

We review three problems related to bilinear maps: the Computational Bilinear Diffie-Hellman (CBDH) problem, the Decision Bilinear Deffie-Hellman (DBDH) problem and the Gap Bilinear Diffie-Hellman (GBDH) problem. Let $\mathbb{G}_1$ and $\mathbb{G}_2$ be two groups of order q and g be a generator of $\mathbb{G}_1$.

CBDH Problem. The CBDH problem [3] in $\mathbb{G}_1$ is as follows: given a tuple $(g, g^a, g^b, g^c) \in (\mathbb{G}_1)^4$ as input, output $e(g, g)^{abc} \in \mathbb{G}_2$. An algorithm $\mathcal{A}_{cbdh}$ solves CBDH problem in $\mathbb{G}_1$ with the probability ϵ_{cbdh} if

$$\Pr[\mathcal{A}_{cbdh}(g, g^a, g^b, g^c) = e(g, g)^{abc}] \geq \epsilon_{cbdh},$$

where the probability is over the random choice of generator $g \in \mathbb{G}_1 \backslash \{1\}$, the random choice of $a, b, c \in \mathbb{Z}_q$, and random coins consumed by $\mathcal{A}_{cbdh}$.

Definition 2. We say that the $(t_{cbdh}, \epsilon_{cbdh})$-*CBDH assumption* holds in $\mathbb{G}_1$ if no t_{cbdh}-time algorithm has advantage at least ϵ_{cbdh} in solving the CBDH problem in $\mathbb{G}_1$.

DBDH Problem. The DBDH problem in $\mathbb{G}_1$ is defined as follows: given a tuple $(g, g^a, g^b, g^c, T) \in (\mathbb{G}_1)^4 \times \mathbb{G}_2$ as input, outputs a bit $b \in \{0, 1\}$. An algorithm $\mathcal{A}_{dbdh}$ solves DBDH problem in $\mathbb{G}_1$ with advantage ϵ_{dbdh} if

$$\left| \Pr[\mathcal{A}_{dbdh}(g, g^a, g^b, g^c, e(g, g)^{abc}) = 0] - \Pr[\mathcal{A}_{dbdh}(g, g^a, g^b, g^c, T) = 0] \right| \geq \epsilon_{dbdh},$$

where the probability is over the random choice of generator $g \in \mathbb{G}_1 \backslash \{1\}$, the random choice of $a, b, c \in \mathbb{Z}_q$, the random choice of T in $\mathbb{G}_2$, and the random coins consumed by $\mathcal{A}_{dbdh}$.

Definition 3. We say that the $(t_{dbdh}, \epsilon_{dbdh})$-*DBDH assumption* holds in $\mathbb{G}_1$ if no t_{dbdh}-time algorithm has advantage at least ϵ_{dbdh} in solving the DBDH problem in $\mathbb{G}_1$.

GBDH Problem. The GBDH problem in $\mathbb{G}_1$ is as follows: given a tuple $(g, g^a, g^b, g^c) \in (\mathbb{G}_1)^4$ as input, output $e(g, g)^{abc} \in \mathbb{G}_2$ with the help of a DBDH oracle $\mathcal{O}$ which for given $(g, g^a, g^b, g^c, T) \in (\mathbb{G}_1)^4 \times \mathbb{G}_2$, answers "*true*" if $T = e(g, g)^{abc}$ or "*false*" otherwise [10]. An algorithm $\mathcal{A}_{gbdh}$ solves GBDH problem in $\mathbb{G}_1$ with the probability ϵ_{gbdh} if

$$\Pr[\mathcal{A}_{gbdh}^{\mathcal{O}}(g, g^a, g^b, g^c) = e(g, g)^{abc}] \geq \epsilon_{gbdh},$$

where the probability is over the random choice of generator $g \in \mathbb{G}_1 \backslash \{1\}$, the random choice of $a, b, c \in \mathbb{Z}_q$, and random coins consumed by $\mathcal{A}_{gbdh}$.

Definition 4. We say that the $(t_{gbdh}, \epsilon_{gbdh})$-*GBDH assumption* holds in $\mathbb{G}_1$ if no t_{gbdh}-time algorithm has advantage at least ϵ_{gbdh} in solving the GBDH problem in $\mathbb{G}_1$.

3   The Missing Details

We briefly review the justification on BF-IBE by Galindo [9] in this section. Towards the proof, some intermediate schemes, BasicPub and BasicPub^{hy}, are devised to help complete the proof. FullIdent and BasicPub are reviewed in Figure 1 and Figure 2.

BF-IBE (FullIdent)	
Setup (1^k): $\quad s \leftarrow \mathbb{Z}_q^*; g_{pub} := g^s$ $\quad$ params $:= \langle q, \mathbb{G}_1, \mathbb{G}_2, e, n, g, g_{pub}, H_1, H_2, H_3, H_4 \rangle$ $\quad H_1 : \{0,1\}^* \to \mathbb{G}_1^*, H_2 : \mathbb{G}_2 \to \{0,1\}^n,$ $\quad H_3 : \{0,1\}^n \times \{0,1\}^n \to Z_q^*, H_4 : \{0,1\}^n \to \{0,1\}^n.$ $\quad$ master-key $:= s;$ $\quad return$ (params, master-key)	**Extract**† (ID, params, master-key): $\quad h_{ID} := H_1(ID);$ $\quad d_{ID} := (h_{ID})^s;$ $\quad return \ d_{ID}.$
Encrypt (ID, params, M): $\quad h_{ID} := H_1(ID);$ $\quad \sigma \leftarrow \{0,1\}^n;$ $\quad r := H_3(\sigma, M);$ $\quad c_1 := g^r;$ $\quad c_2 := \sigma \oplus H_2(e(g_{pub}, h_{ID})^r);$ $\quad c_3 = H_4(\sigma) \oplus M;$ $\quad C := \langle c_1, c_2, c_3 \rangle.$ $\quad return \ C$	**Decrypt** $(C, \text{params}, sk_{ID})$: $\quad$ parse $C = \langle c_1, c_2, c_3 \rangle.$ $\quad$ if $c_1 \notin \mathbb{G}_1$, $return$ "reject". $\quad \sigma := c_2 \oplus H_2(e(c_1, d_{ID}));$ $\quad M := c_3 \oplus H_4(\sigma).$ $\quad$ set $r := H_3(\sigma, M);$ $\quad$ if $c_1 \neq g^r$ $\quad\quad return$ "reject"; $\quad$ else $\quad\quad return \ M.$

† **Extract** first checks if d_{ID} has been generated before. If it has, the previously-generated d_{ID} is output.

Fig. 1. The algorithms of FullIdent

BasicPub is a semantically secure public key encryption scheme where $h_{ID} \leftarrow \mathbb{G}_1$ (once chosen then is fixed), r is generated random rather than $H_3(\sigma, M)$, and M is encrypted as $c_2' := M \oplus H_2(e(g_{pub}, h_{ID})^r)$. The resulting ciphertext is $C = \langle c_1, c_2' \rangle$. BasicPub^{hy} is the public key encryption scheme where the Fujisaki-Okamoto (FO) conversion is applied [8] to have chosen ciphertext attack (CCA) security for BasicPub. Refer [4] for details.

In order to establish the reduction from FullIdent to BasicPub^{hy}, Coron's technique was used in simulation the random oracle H_1 [4]. But as pointed out in [9], by the simulation given in [4], the random oracle H_3 is not controlled by the simulator then any decryption queries that implicitly with call to H_3 will in fact cause the simulator to abort with overwhelming probability.

BasicPub	
Setup (1^k): $\quad s \leftarrow \mathbb{Z}_q^*; \; g_{pub} := g^s$ $\quad$ params $:= \langle q, \mathbb{G}_1, \mathbb{G}_2, e, n, g, g_{pub}, H_1, H_2 \rangle$ $\quad H_1 : \{0,1\}^* \to \mathbb{G}_1^*,$ $\quad H_2 : \mathbb{G}_2 \to \{0,1\}^n.$ $\quad$ master-key $:= s;$ $\quad$ *return* (params, master-key)	**Extract**[†] (ID, params, master-key): $\quad h_{\mathsf{ID}} := H_1(\mathsf{ID});$ $\quad d_{\mathsf{ID}} := (h_{\mathsf{ID}})^s;$ $\quad$ *return* $d_{\mathsf{ID}}.$
Encrypt (ID, params, M): $\quad h_{\mathsf{ID}} := H_1(\mathsf{ID});$ $\quad r \leftarrow \{0,1\}^n;$ $\quad c_1 := g^r;$ $\quad c_2 := M \oplus H_2(e(g_{pub}, h_{\mathsf{ID}})^r);$ $\quad C := \langle c_1, c_2 \rangle.$ $\quad$ *return* C	**Decrypt** $(C, \text{params}, sk_{\mathsf{ID}})$: $\quad$ parse $C = \langle c_1, c_2 \rangle.$ $\quad$ if $c_1 \notin \mathbb{G}_1,$ *return* "reject". $\quad M := c_2 \oplus H_2(e(c_1, d_{\mathsf{ID}}));$ $\quad$ *return* $M.$

[†] **Extract** first checks if d_{ID} has been generated before. If it has, the previously-generated d_{ID} is output.

Fig. 2. The algorithms of BasicPub

4   An Improved Proof for the BF-IBE

The BF-IBE was proven via several intermediate steps, where each defines a scheme with small modifications. However, this happens to be the reason why the proof is flawed: some of those steps are not meaningfully linked for independent parameter choices in each scheme.

In this section, we give another proof of the BF-IBE. The main difference lies in that the simulator simulates itself all the oracles: the random oracles, Extract oracle, Encryption oracle and Decryption oracle. The intuition is that if all the oracles are simulated "properly", then an IBE adversary will not distinguish the simulated oracle from the real oracles. Interesting enough, this small modification is all that needed to have a better reduction cost. In the rest of this section, we prove the following theorem:

Theorem 1. *Assume* $(t_{cbdh}, \epsilon_{cbdh})$-*CBDH assumption holds in bilinear group pairs* $(\mathbb{G}_1, \mathbb{G}_2)$, *then the BF-IBE is* $(t_{\mathsf{BF-IBE}}, \epsilon_{\mathsf{BF-IBE}})$-*secure against* IND-ID-CCA, *where*

$$\epsilon_{cbdh} \geq \frac{(\epsilon_{\mathsf{BF-IBE}} - (Q_{H_3} + Q_{H_4})2^{-n})(1 - Q_D/q)}{e(Q_E + 1)(Q_{H_2} + Q_{H_3} + Q_{H_4})} \approx O(\frac{\epsilon_{\mathsf{BF-IBE}}}{Q_E Q_{H_2}})$$

$$t_{cbdh} \geq O((Q_D Q_{H_3} + Q_{H_2} + Q_{H_4} + Q_E)\tau) + t_{\mathsf{BF-IBE}}$$

Here τ *is the maxium time of one running step of* $\mathcal{B}$, *e is the base of natural logarithm,* Q_{H_1}, Q_{H_2}, Q_{H_3} *and* Q_{H_4} *are the number of random oracles queries to* H_1, H_2, H_3 *and* H_4, Q_D *and* Q_E *are the number of Decryption oracle queries and Extract oracle queries, respectively.* $q = |\mathbb{G}_1| = |\mathbb{G}_2|$, *is the order of* $\mathbb{G}_1$ *and* $\mathbb{G}_2$.

4.1   The New Proof

We want to show the reduction of the security of the BF-IBE to the hardness of CBDH problem. We start with the description of the CBDH adversary $\mathcal{B}$ who interacts with an IND-ID-CCA adversary $\mathcal{A}$. In Phase 1, $\mathcal{A}$ may access Extract oracle and Decryption oracle. At the end of Phase 1, $\mathcal{A}$ submits a pair of messages with equal length (M_0, M_1) to Encryption oracle. After Encryption oracle creates the challenge, in Phase 2, $\mathcal{A}$ may behave exactly as Phase 1 except that $\mathcal{A}$ may not query C^* to Decryption oracle.

Recall that $\mathcal{B}$'s input is a 4-tuple $(g, g^a, g^b, g^c) \in (\mathbb{G}_1)^4$ whose goal is to output $T \in \mathbb{G}_2$, such that $T = e(g,g)^{abc}$. For convenience, let $g_1 = g^a$, $g_2 = g^b$ and $g_3 = g^c$.

Setup: $\mathcal{B}$ gives $\mathcal{A}$ params $= \langle q, \mathbb{G}_1, \mathbb{G}_2, e, n, g, g_1, H_1, H_2, H_3, H_4 \rangle$ as the system parameter, where n is the length of the plaintext, and H_1, H_2, H_3, H_4 are random oracles controlled by $\mathcal{B}$, described as follows (Phase 1,2):

H_1-oracle: $\mathcal{B}$ maintains an H_1-list, initially empty. When a query ID_i comes, if there is already an entry $(\mathsf{ID}_i, s_i, h_{\mathsf{ID}_i})$, $\mathcal{B}$ replies h_{ID_i}; otherwise, $\mathcal{B}$ internally flips a biased coin $coin_i$ with $\Pr[coin = 0] = \delta$, and δ will be decided later. If $coin = 0$, $\mathcal{B}$ selects $s_i \leftarrow_R Z_q^*$, replies to $\mathcal{A}$ $h_i = g^{s_i} \in \mathbb{G}_1$; if $coin = 1$, $\mathcal{B}$ returns $h_i = g_2^{s_i}$. In both case, $\mathcal{B}$ adds $(\mathsf{ID}_i, s_i, h_i, coin_i)$ to H_1-list.

H_2-oracle: When a query $t_i \in \mathbb{G}_2$ comes, if there is an entry (t_i, v_i) in H_2-list, $\mathcal{B}$ returns v_i to $\mathcal{A}$; otherwise, $\mathcal{B}$ chooses $v_i \in \{0,1\}^n$, returns v_i to $\mathcal{A}$ and adds (t_i, v_i) to H_2-list.

H_3-oracle: When a query (σ_i, M_i) comes, if there is an entry (σ_i, M_i, r_i) on H_3-list, $\mathcal{B}$ returns r_i to $\mathcal{A}$; otherwise, $\mathcal{B}$ chooses $r_i \leftarrow_R Z_q^*$, returns r_i to $\mathcal{A}$ and adds (σ_i, M_i, r_i) to H_3-list.

H_4-oracle: When a query σ_i comes, if there is an entry (σ_i, w_i) on H_4-list, $\mathcal{B}$ returns w_i to $\mathcal{A}$; otherwise, $\mathcal{B}$ chooses $w_i \leftarrow_R \{0,1\}^n$, returns w_i to $\mathcal{A}$ and adds (σ_i, w_i) to H_4-list.

Extract oracle: When a query ID_i comes, $\mathcal{B}$ in the H_1-list for $coin_i$. WLOG, we can assume ID_i has already been asked before. If $coin_i = 1$, $\mathcal{B}$ reports "*abort*" and quits the simulation. If $coin_i = 0$, $\mathcal{B}$ sets $d_{\mathsf{ID}_i} = g_1^{s_i} = (g^a)^{s_i} = (g^{s_i})^a$ which is a valid secret key for ID_i, and returns d_{ID_i} to $\mathcal{A}$.

Decryption oracle: When a query (ID, C) comes, $\mathcal{B}$ searches in H_1 for $(\mathsf{ID}, h_{\mathsf{ID}}, coin_i)$, in H_2 for (t, v), in H_3 for (σ, M, r), in H_4-list for (σ, w), such that $(\mathsf{ID}, h_{\mathsf{ID}}, r, \sigma, t, v, w, M)$ satisfy below equations:

$$h_{\mathsf{ID}} = H_1(\mathsf{ID}) \qquad\qquad r = H_3(\sigma, M)$$
$$t = e(g_1, h_{\mathsf{ID}}) \qquad\qquad c_1 = g^r$$
$$c_2 = \sigma \oplus H_2(t^r) \qquad\qquad c_3 = M \oplus H_4(\sigma)$$

If there exists such an M and (σ, t, v, w, r) in those lists, $\mathcal{B}$ returns M to $\mathcal{A}$ as the answer. Otherwise, $\mathcal{B}$ returns "*reject*" to $\mathcal{B}$.

Encryption oracle: On $\mathcal{A}$'s input ID^* and (M_0, M_1), if $coin_{\mathsf{ID}^*} = 0$, $\mathcal{B}$ aborts the simulation; otherwise, $\mathcal{B}$ chooses random $v^* \leftarrow_R \{0,1\}^n$, $d \leftarrow_R \{0,1\}$

and sets $c_2^* = M_d \oplus v^*$ and $c_3 = \{0,1\}^n$. Especially, $\mathcal{B}$ sets $c_1^* = g_3^{-s_{ID^*}}$ and returns $C^* = \langle c_1^*, c_2^*, c_3^* \rangle$ to $\mathcal{A}$ as the challenge ciphertext. For convenience, we shall associate the variables that are related to the Challenge ciphertext with a "$*$" hereafter.

$\mathcal{B}$ keeps interacting with $\mathcal{A}$ until $\mathcal{A}$ halts or aborts. If $\mathcal{A}$ doesn't halt in polynomial time, $\mathcal{B}$ also terminates the simulation. Finally, when $\mathcal{A}$ terminates, $\mathcal{B}$ first searches H_1-list for the entry with $(ID, h_{D_i}, s_{ID_i}, coin_{ID_i})$. Then $\mathcal{B}$ chooses: an arbitrary t from H_2-list and computes $t^{-s_{ID_i}}$ as its answer to the CBDH problem. This completes the description of $\mathcal{B}$.

Then all that remains is to bound the success probability of $\mathcal{B}$.

Lemma 1. $\mathcal{B}$ doesn't abort in simulating Extract oracle and Encryption oracle with probability at least $\frac{1}{e(Q_E+1)}$, where Q_E is the number of Extract oracle queries made by $\mathcal{A}$.

Proof. Notice that $\mathcal{B}$ only abort on Extract and Encryption queries. It is sufficient to show that $\mathcal{B}$ succeeds in answering Q_E Extraction queries and one Challenge query, i.e., $\mathcal{B}$ succeeds with probability $p_0 = \delta^{Q_E}(1 - \delta)$. This probability gets maximized at the point $\delta = Q_E/(Q_E + 1)$, and $p_0 = 1/(e(q_E + 1))$, where $e \approx 2.72$ is the base of the natural logarithm. Furthermore, if $\mathcal{B}$ doesn't abort, Extract oracle and Challenge oracle are simulated perfectly.

Lemma 2. If $\mathcal{B}$ doesn't abort, Decryption oracle can be simulated with probability at least

$$(1 - 2^{-n})^{Q_{H_3}}(1 - 2^{-n})^{Q_{H_4}}(1 - 1/q)^{Q_D} \approx (1 - Q_D \cdot q)(1 - (Q_{H_3} + Q_{H_4}) \cdot 2^{-n}),$$

where Q_{H_3}, Q_{H_4} are the numbers of random oracle queries to H_3 and H_4, Decryption oracle queries made by $\mathcal{A}$.

Proof. To ensure the correct simulation of Decryption oracle, all valid ciphertexts should be answered correctly and all invalid ciphertexts are correctly answered (with probability 1), and all invalid ciphertexts will get rejected. However, all but a small proportion of ciphertexts may be rejected by the simulated Decryption oracle. We bound the probability of this misbehavior as follows.

From the description of $\mathcal{B}$, all random oracle queries are simulated identically to a real random oracle except $(\sigma^*, *)$ is asked to H_3 or σ^* is asked to H_4. Additionally, a random tuple $C = \langle c_1, c_2, c_3 \rangle$ outsides $\mathcal{B}$'s lists forms a valid ciphertext with probability at most 2^{-n} and this happens at most Q_D times. Combines all above, we achieve the claimed bound on $\mathcal{B}$'s success probability of simulating Decryption oracle.

Lemma 3. If $\mathcal{B}$ doesn't abort, $\mathcal{B}$ succeeds solving the CBDH problem and this happens with probability at least $\frac{1}{Q_{H_2}+Q_{H_3}+Q_{H_4}}$.

Proof. We have to show that when $\mathcal{B}$ terminates, the answer to the CBDH problem is already in H_2. Notice that if $\mathcal{A}$ doens't abort, since C^* contains no information of M_b, which contradicts that $\mathcal{A}$ should get non-negligible advantage in guessing C^*. Then $\mathcal{A}$ must have already abort (even internally). This can be achieved by asking $T = e(g, g)^{abc}$ to H_2 oracle, or by queries to H_3 or H_4 oracles, by the time $\mathcal{B}$ terminates. The probability of $\mathcal{B}$'s success is then given by:

$$\frac{1}{Q_{H_2}} \cdot \frac{Q_{H_2}}{Q_{H_2} + Q_{H_3} + Q_{H_4}} = \frac{1}{Q_{H_2} + Q_{H_3} + Q_{H_4}}.$$

Combine above lemmas, we conclude the bound given in the statement of Theorem 1. The bound on time complexity can be verified easily.

4.2 Generalizations

The above proof technique can be generalized to a variety of IBE schemes. For example, we can prove the following theorem. The proof of Theorem 2 is similar to that of Theorem 1 and will be omitted here.

Theorem 2. *Galindo's BF-IBE variant is (t', ϵ')-secure against* IND-ID-CCA, *if (t, ϵ_{dbdh})-DBDH assumptions holds in the bilinear group pairs $(\mathbb{G}_1, \mathbb{G}_2)$, where*

$$\epsilon \geq \frac{(\epsilon' - Q_{H_2} 2^{-l})(1 - Q_D/q)}{e(Q_E + 1)} \approx O(\frac{\epsilon}{Q_E})$$

$$t \geq O((Q_D Q_{H_3} + Q_E + Q_{H_1} + Q_{H_2} + Q_{H_4})\tau) + t'$$

Here τ is the maxium time of one running step of $\mathcal{B}$, e is the base of natural logarithm, Q_{H_1}, Q_{H_2} and Q_{H_3} are the number of random oracles queries to H_1, H_2 and H_3, Q_D and Q_E are the number of Decryption oracle queries and Extract oracle queries, respectively. $q = |\mathbb{G}_1| = |\mathbb{G}_2|$, is the order of $\mathbb{G}_1$ and $\mathbb{G}_2$.

5 A New BF-IBE Variant

In this section, we propose a new BF-IBE variant called ZIBE, which is compact in size and with better reduction cost. The scheme can be viewed as an adoption of the tag-based KEM-DEM framework [1] in the IBE setting.

5.1 Construction

The algorithms of ZIBE is described in Figure 3. A possible speedup can be achieved by computing $e(g_{pub}, H_1(\mathsf{ID})) \in \mathbb{G}_2$ offline and regarded as a public parameter for a particular ID.

5.2 Security

We prove that the security of our IBE scheme in the random oracle model via the following theorem:

ZIBE	
Setup (1^k): $s \leftarrow \mathbb{Z}_q^*;\ g_{pub} := g^s$ params $:= \langle q, \mathbb{G}_1, \mathbb{G}_2, e, n, l, g, g_{pub}, H_1, H_2 \rangle$ $H_1 : \{0,1\}^* \rightarrow \mathbb{G}_1^*,\ H_2 : \mathbb{G}_2 \rightarrow \{0,1\}^n,$ $H_3 : (\{0,1\}^n)^2 \times \mathbb{G}_1 \times \{0,1\}^n \times \mathbb{G}_2 \rightarrow \{0,1\}^l.$ master-key $:= s;$ *return* (params, master-key)	**Extract**[†] (ID, params, master-key): $h_{\mathsf{ID}} := H_1(\mathsf{ID});$ $d_{\mathsf{ID}} := (h_{\mathsf{ID}})^s;$ *return* $d_{\mathsf{ID}}.$

Encrypt (ID, params, M):
$h_{\mathsf{ID}} := H_1(\mathsf{ID});$
$r \leftarrow \{0,1\}^n;$
$c_1 := g^r;$
$c_2 := M \oplus H_2(\mathsf{ID}, e(g_{pub}, h_{\mathsf{ID}})^r);$
$c_3 = H_3(\mathsf{ID}, M_i, c_1, c_2, e(g_{pub}, h_{\mathsf{ID}})^r);$
$C := \langle c_1, c_2, c_3 \rangle.$
return C
	Decrypt $(C, \text{params}, sk_{\mathsf{ID}})$:
	parse $C = \langle c_1, c_2, c_3 \rangle.$
	if $c_1 \notin \mathbb{G}_1$, *return "reject"*.
	if $c_3 \neq H_3(\mathsf{ID}, c_1, c_2, e(c_1, d_{\mathsf{ID}}))$
	    return "reject";
	else
	    $M := c_2 \oplus H_2(\mathsf{ID}, e(c_1, d_{\mathsf{ID}}));$
	    return $M.$

[†] **Extract** first checks if d_{ID} has been generated before. If it has, the previously-generated d_{ID} is output.

Fig. 3. The algorithms of ZIBE

Theorem 3. ZIBE *is* $(t_{\mathsf{ZIBE}}, \epsilon_{\mathsf{ZIBE}})$-*secure against* IND-ID-CCA, *if* (t, ϵ_{gbdh}) -*GBDH assumptions holds in the bilinear group pairs* $(\mathbb{G}_1, \mathbb{G}_2)$, *where*

$$\epsilon_{gbdh} \geq \frac{1}{e(Q_E + 1)}(\epsilon_{\mathsf{ZIBE}} - (Q_D + 1)(2^{-n} + 2^{-l})) \approx O(\frac{\epsilon_{\mathsf{ZIBE}}}{Q_E})$$

$$t_{gbdh} \geq O((Q_D + Q_E + Q_{H_1} + Q_{H_2} + Q_{H_3})\tau) + t_{\mathsf{ZIBE}}$$

Here τ *is the maximum time of one running step of* $\mathcal{B}$, *e is the base of natural logarithm,* Q_{H_1}, Q_{H_2} *and* Q_{H_3} *are the number of random oracles queries to* H_1, H_2 *and* H_3, Q_D *and* Q_E *are the number of Decryption oracle queries and Extract oracle queries, respectively.* $q = |\mathbb{G}_1| = |\mathbb{G}_2|$, *is the order of* $\mathbb{G}_1$ *and* $\mathbb{G}_2$.

Proof. Our goal is to show that any IND-ID-CCA adversary $\mathcal{A}$ against ZIBE can be used as a subroutine to construct a GBDH adversary $\mathcal{B}$. Let $(g, g^a, g^b, g^c, \mathbb{G}_1, \mathbb{G}_2, e, q, \mathcal{O})$ be the input to $\mathcal{B}$, where g is the generator of $\mathbb{G}_1$ and $\mathcal{O}$ is the decision oracle on input (g, g^a, g^b, g^c, T) outputs *"true"* if $T = e(g, g)^{abc}$. Let $g_1 = g^a$, $g_2 = g^b$ and $g_3 = g^c$. $\mathcal{B}$ interacts with $\mathcal{A}$ as follows:

Setup: $\mathcal{B}$ gives $\mathcal{A}$ params $= \langle q, \mathbb{G}_1, \mathbb{G}_2, e, n, l, g, g_1, H_1, H_2, H_3 \rangle$ as the system parameter, where n is the length of the plaintext, l is the output length of H_3, and H_1, H_2, H_3 are random oracles controlled by $\mathcal{B}$, described below:

H_1-oracle: $\mathcal{B}$ maintains an H_1-list, initially empty. When a query ID_i comes, if there is already an entry $(\mathsf{ID}_i, s_i, g_2^{s_i})$, $\mathcal{B}$ replies $g_2^{s_i}$; otherwise, $\mathcal{B}$ internally flips a biased coin $coin_i$ with $\Pr[coin = 0] = \delta$, and δ will be decided later. If $coin = 0$, $\mathcal{B}$ selects $s_i \leftarrow_R \mathbb{Z}_q^*$, replies to $\mathcal{A}$ $h_i = g^{s_i} \in \mathbb{G}_1$; if $coin = 1$, $\mathcal{B}$ returns $h_i = g_2^{s_i}$. In both case, $\mathcal{B}$ adds $(\mathsf{ID}_i, s_i, h_i, coin_i)$ to H_1-list.

H_2-**oracle:** When a query $(\mathsf{ID}_i, t_i) \in \{0,1\}^n \times \mathbb{G}_2$ comes, $\mathcal{B}$ queries $\mathcal{O}$ on (g, g^a, g^b, g^c, t_i), if $\mathcal{O}$ outputs *"true"*, which indicates that this is a BDH tuple, $\mathcal{B}$ terminates the simulation and returns t_i as its answer to the GBDH problem. Otherwise, if there is an entry $(\mathsf{ID}_i, t_i, v_i)$ in H_2-list, $\mathcal{B}$ returns v_i to $\mathcal{A}$; otherwise, $\mathcal{B}$ chooses $v_i \in \{0,1\}^n$, returns v_i to $\mathcal{A}$ and adds $(\mathsf{ID}_i, t_i, v_i)$ to H_2-list.

H_3-**oracle:** When a query $(\mathsf{ID}_i, M_i, c_{1i}, c_{2i}, f_i)$ comes, $\mathcal{B}$ queries (g, g_1, g_2, g_3, f_i) to $\mathcal{O}$. If $\mathcal{O}$ outputs *"true"*, then $\mathcal{B}$ terminates and report f_i as its answer to the GBDH problem. Otherwise, if there is an entry $(\mathsf{Id}_i, M_i, c_{1i}, c_{2i}, f_i, w_i)$ on H_3-list, $\mathcal{B}$ returns w_i to $\mathcal{A}$; otherwise, $\mathcal{B}$ chooses $w_i \leftarrow_R \{0,1\}^l$, returns w_i to $\mathcal{A}$ and adds $(\mathsf{ID}_i, M_i, c_{1i}, c_{2i}, f_i, w_i)$ to H_3-list.

Extract oracle: When a query ID_i comes, $\mathcal{B}$ in the H_1-list for $coin_i$. WLOG, we can assume ID_i has already been asked before. If $coin_i = 1$, $\mathcal{B}$ abort the simulation. If $coin_i = 0$, $\mathcal{B}$ sets $d_{\mathsf{ID}_i} = g_1^{s_i} = (g^a)^{s_i} = (g^{s_i})^a$ which is a valid secret key for ID_i, and returns d_{ID_i} to $\mathcal{A}$.

Decryption oracle: When a query (ID, C) comes, $\mathcal{B}$ searches in H_1 for $(\mathsf{ID}, h_{\mathsf{ID}}, coin_i)$, in H_2 for (t, v), in H_3 for $(\sigma, M,)$, in H_4-list for (σ, w), such that $(\mathsf{ID}, h_{\mathsf{ID}}, r, \sigma, t, v, w, M)$ satisfy below equations:

$$h_{\mathsf{ID}} = H_1(\mathsf{ID}) \qquad\qquad f = H_2(e(g_1, h_{\mathsf{ID}})^r)$$
$$c_2 = M \oplus f \qquad\qquad c_3 = M \oplus H_3(\mathsf{ID}, M, c_1, c_2, f)$$

If there exists such an M and (σ, t, v, w, r) in those lists, $\mathcal{B}$ returns M to $\mathcal{A}$ as the answer. Otherwise, $\mathcal{B}$ returns *"reject"* to $\mathcal{B}$.

Encryption oracle: On $\mathcal{A}$'s input ID^* and (M_0, M_1), if $coin_{\mathsf{ID}^*} = 0$, $\mathcal{B}$ aborts the simulation; otherwise, $\mathcal{B}$ chooses random $c_1 \leftarrow g_3^{-s_{\mathsf{ID}^*}}$, $c_2 = M_d \oplus v$, where $d \leftarrow_R \{0,1\}$ and $v \leftarrow_R \{0,1\}^n$. $c_3 = \{0,1\}^l$, and returns $C^* = \langle c_1^*, c_2^*, c_3^* \rangle$ to $\mathcal{A}$ as the challenge ciphertext.

When $\mathcal{B}$ terminates, $\mathcal{B}$ search H_2 for t_i such that $\mathcal{O}(g, g_1, g_2, g_3, t_i) = 1$.

Lemma 4. *The probability that $\mathcal{B}$ doesn't abort in simulating Extract oracle and Encryption oracle is at least $1/(e(Q_E + 1))$.*

The proof is similar to that of lemma 1 and will be omitted here.

Lemma 5. *If $\mathcal{B}$ doesn't abort, it can simulate Decryption oracle with probability at least $(1 - 2^{-n} - 2^{-l})^{Q_D}$.*

Proof. It is noticed that the simulated Decryption oracle functions similar as a real Decryption oracle except that it may reject some valid ciphertexts, however, we can bound the probability below. All valid ciphertexts will be replied correctly. The simulation is successful except the case that for the challenge C^* if it has been queried via previous decryption queries. We have that this will not happen with probability at least $(1 - 2^{-n} - 2^{-l})^{Q_D}$. Combining the discussions, we have $\mathcal{B}$ succeeds in simulating Decryption oracle with probability at least $(1 - 2^{-n} - 2^{-l})^{Q_D}$ as claimed.

Lemma 6. *When $\mathcal{B}$ terminates, $T = e(g, g)^{abc}$ must have been in either H_2 or H_3 lists with probability at least $(1 - 2^{-l} - 2^{-n})$.*

Proof. Since H_2 is a random oracle, M_d is perfectly hiding by the one-time pad if either $T = e(g, g)^{abc}$ is not queried to H_2 or M_d is not queried to H_3. Moreover, once M_b and r^* are chosen, C^* is uniquely determined. Then for any IND-ID-CCA adversary $\mathcal{A}$ who distinguishes M_d with non-negligible advantage, T must have appeared somewhere in H_2 or H_3 lists except that $\mathcal{A}$ correctly guessed b without even looking at the challenge. But this happens with probability at most $(1 - 2^{-l})$. Then $\mathcal{B}$ can find T with the help of $\mathcal{O}$ with probability $(1 - 2^{-l} - 2^{-n})$ at least.

Combine above three lemmas, we get $\mathcal{B}$ succeeds with probability at least

$$\frac{(1 - 2^{-n} - 2^{-l})^{Q_D}(1 - 2^{-l} - 2^{-n})\epsilon_{\mathsf{ZIBE}}}{(e(Q_E + 1))} \geq \frac{1}{e(Q_E + 1)}(\epsilon_{\mathsf{ZIBE}} - (Q_D + 1) \cdot (2^{-n} + 2^{-l})).$$

It is easily to verify the correctness of the claimed time complexity t_{ZIBE}.

6   Conclusion

In this paper, we revisit the proof the Boneh-Franklin IBE scheme in the random oracle model. By simulating all the oracles at a time, we manage to acquire an improved security bound. We also apply a similar analysis to Galindo's BF-IBE variant. Finally we propose a new variant of BF-IBE that enjoys essentially better security reduction to the hardness of the GBDH problem.

Acknowledgement

Rui Zhang is supported by a JSPS fellowship.

References

1. M. Abe, R. Gennaro, K. Kurosawa, V. Shoup: "Tag-KEM/DEM: A New Framework for Hybrid Encryption and A New Analysis of Kurosawa-Desmedt KEM." In Eurocrypt'05, LNCS 3494, pages 128-146, 2005.
2. M. Bellare and P. Rogaway, "Random oracles are practical: A paradigm for designing efficient protocols." In Proc. First Annual Conference on Computer and Communications Security, pp62-73, ACM, 1993
3. D. Boneh and M. Franklin, "Identity Based Encryption from the Weil Pairing," In Advances in Cryptology–Crypto'01, LNCS 2139, pages 213-229, 2001.
4. D. Boneh and M. Franklin, "Identity Based Encryption from the Weil Pairing," SIAM Journal of Computing 32(3):586-615, 2003, full version of [3].
5. R. Canetti, O. Goldreich and S. Halevi. "The Random Oracle Methodology, Revisited. In Proc. of the 30th STOC, pages 209-218, 1998

6. J.S. Coron, "On the Exact Security of Full Domain Hash," In Crypto'00, LNCS 1880, pages 229-235, 2000.
7. A. Fiat and A. Shamir. "How to prove to yourself: practical solutions to identification and signature problems. In Crypto'86, pages 186-194, 1987.
8. E. Fujisaki and T. Okamoto, "Secure Integration of Asymmetric and Symmetric Encrytion Schemes," In Advances in Cryptology–Crypto'99, LNCS 1666, pages 537-554, 1999.
9. D. Galindo, "Boneh-Franklin Identity Based Encryption Revisited," to appear in Proc. of ICALP'05, available as IACR ePrint Report 2005/117.
10. T. Okamoto and D. Pointcheval, "The Gap-Problems: a New Class of Problems for the Security of Cryptographic Schemes," In Proc. of PKC'01, LNCS 1992, pages 104-118, 2001.
11. A. Shamir, "Identity-Based Cryptosystems and Signature Schemes," In CRYPTO'84, LNCS 293, pages 341-349, 1984.

An ID-Based Verifiable Encrypted Signature Scheme Based on Hess's Scheme[*]

Chunxiang Gu and Yuefei Zhu

Network Engineering Department, Information Engineering University,
P.O. Box 1001-770, Zhengzhou 450002, P.R. China
gcxiang5209@yahoo.com.cn

Abstract. This paper proposes an efficient ID-based verifiably encrypted signature scheme based on Hess's ID-based signature scheme [3]. We provide some theoretical discussions for the security model of ID-based verifiably encrypted signature schemes, and show that our new scheme can be proven to be secure in the random oracle model. Our new scheme can be used as primitives to build efficient ID-based optimistic fair exchange protocols, which can be widely used in signing digital contracts, e-payment and other electronic commerce.

Keywords: ID-based cryptography, verifiably encrypted signatures, bilinear pairings, fair exchange.

1 Introduction

In 1984, Shamir [1] first proposed the idea of ID-based public key cryptography (ID-PKC) to simplify key management procedure of traditional certificate-based PKI. In ID-PKC, an entity's public key is directly derived from certain aspects of its identity, such as an IP address belonging to a network host or an e-mail address associated with a user. Private keys are generated for entities by a trusted third party called a private key generator (PKG). The direct derivation of public keys in ID-PKC eliminates the need for certificates and some of the problems associated with them.

Recently, due to the contribution of Boneh and Franklin [2], a rapid development of ID-PKC has taken place. Using bilinear pairings, people proposed many new ID-based signature schemes, such as [3, 4, 5, 6]. With these ID-based signature schemes, a lot of new extensions, such as ID-based blind signature schemes, ID-based proxy signature schemes [7, 8], and so on, have also been proposed. ID-based public key cryptography has become a good alternative for certificate-based public key setting, especially when efficient key management and moderate security are required.

Verifiably encrypted signature scheme (VESS) is a special extension of general signature primitive. VESSs enable user Alice to give Bob a signature encrypted

---

[*] Research supported by Found 973 (No. G1999035804), NSFC (No. 90204015, 60473021) and Elitist Youth Foundation of Henan in China (No. 021201400).

D. Feng, D. Lin, and M. Yung (Eds.): CISC 2005, LNCS 3822, pp. 42–52, 2005.

using an adjudicator's public key, and enable Bob to verify that the encrypted signature is valid. The adjudicator is a trusted third party, who can reveal the signature when needed. VESSs provide an efficient way to enable fairness in many practical applications. Suppose Alice wants to show Bob that she has signed a message, but does not want Bob to possess her signature of that message. She can achieve this by sending Bob a verifiably encrypted signature. Bob can verify that Alice has signed the message and the encrypted signature indeed contains such a signature, but cannot deduce any information about her signature. Later in the protocol, when a certain event has occurred, e.g., Bob had given Alice his signature while Alice refused to reveal her signature, Bob can ask the adjudicator to reveal Alice's signature. The adjudicator (an off-line trusted third party) works in an *optimistic* way. That is, the adjudicator does not participate in the actual exchange protocol in normal cases, and is invoked only in case of disputes for fairness.

Verifiably encrypted signature schemes can be used as efficient primitives to build many practical optimistic fair exchange protocols, such as optimistic fair signature exchange protocols [9, 10], certified delivery of E-Goods [15], certified e-mail protocols [16]. In the last couple of years, researches on verifiably encrypted signature schemes and fair exchange protocols have been fruitful. Several new constructions of verifiably encrypted signature scheme and fair exchange protocols [9, 10, 11, 12, 13, 14, 15, 16] have been proposed. Very recently, new verifiably encrypted signature scheme [12] and corresponding protocol [13] for fair signature exchange from bilinear pairings have also been proposed. However, all these works are in traditional certificate-based PKI setting. How to construct new ID-based verifiably encrypted signature schemes and build fair exchange protocols in ID-based setting is an open problem.

In this paper, we propose an efficient and provably secure ID-based VESS based on Hess's ID-based signature scheme [3]. The rest of this paper is organized as follows: In Section 2, we introduce the bilinear pairings and the hard problems which our scheme relies on. In Section 3, we present a new ID-based VESS with an analysis about correctness and efficiency. In Section 4, we provide the exact security proofs for our new scheme in the random oracle model. Finally, we conclude in Section 5.

2   Bilinear Maps

Let $(G_1, +)$ and $(G_2, \cdot)$ be two cyclic groups of order q. Let $\hat{e} : G_1 \times G_1 \rightarrow G_2$ be a map which satisfies the following properties.

1. Bilinear: $\forall P, Q \in G_1, \forall \alpha, \beta \in Z_q, \hat{e}(\alpha P, \beta Q) = \hat{e}(P, Q)^{\alpha\beta}$;
2. Non-degenerate: If P is a generator of G_1, then $\hat{e}(P, P)$ is a generator of G_2;
3. Computable: There is an efficient algorithm to compute $\hat{e}(P, Q)$ for any $P, Q \in G_1$.

Such an bilinear map is called an *admissible bilinear pairing*. The Weil pairings and the Tate pairings of elliptic curves can be used to construct efficient admissible bilinear pairings.

Let P be a generator of G_1, and $a, b, c \in Z_q$. We are interested in the following mathematical problems:

1. Computational Diffie-Hellman problem (CDHP). Given $P, aP, bP \in G_1$, compute abP.
2. Bilinear Diffie-Hellman problem (BDHP). Given $P, aP, bP, cP \in G_1$, compute $\hat{e}(P, P)^{abc}$.

We assume through this paper that CDHP and BDHP are intractable, which means that there is no polynomial time algorithm to solve CDHP or BDHP with nonnegligible probability.

3   A New ID-Based VESS Based on Hess's Scheme

3.1   Description

Let $(G_1, +)$ and $(G_2, \cdot)$ be two cyclic groups of order q, P be a generator of G_1, $\hat{e} : G_1 \times G_1 \rightarrow G_2$ be an admissible bilinear pairing. We propose the following ID-based VESS, which consists of seven polynomial-time algorithms:

- **Setup:** Given $(G_1, G_2, q, \hat{e}, P)$, pick a random $s \in Z_q^*$ and set $P_{pub} = sP$. Choose three hash functions $H_1 : \{0, 1\}^* \rightarrow G_1^*$, $H_2 : \{0, 1\}^* \times G_2 \rightarrow Z_q$ and $H_3 : G_2 \rightarrow Z_q$. The system parameters $\Omega = (G_1, G_2, q, \hat{e}, P, P_{pub}, H_1, H_2, H_3)$. The master key (PKG's private key) is s.
- **Extract:** Given an identity $ID_X \in \{0, 1\}^*$, compute $Q_X = H_1(ID_X) \in G_1^*$, $D_X = sQ_X$. PKG uses this algorithm to extract the user secret key D_X, and gives D_X to the user by a secure channel.
- **Sign:** Given a private key D_X and a message m, pick $k \in Z_q^*$ at random, and output a signature (r, U), where $r = \hat{e}(P, P)^k$, $h = H_2(m, r)$, and $U = hD_X + kP$.
- **Verify:** Given a signature (r, U) of an identity ID_X for a message m, compute $h = H_2(m, r)$, and accept the signature if and only if $r = \hat{e}(U, P) \cdot \hat{e}(H_1(ID_X), P_{pub})^{-h}$.
- **VE_Sign:** Given a secret key D_X, a message $m \in \{0, 1\}^*$ and an adjudicator's identity ID_A,
  1. choose $k_1, k_2 \in Z_q^*$ at random,
  2. compute $r = \hat{e}(P, P)^{k_1}$, $h = H_2(m, r)$, $h' = H_3(\hat{e}(Q_A, P_{pub})^{k_2})$,
  3. compute $U_1 = h'P$, $U_2 = k_2P$, $V = hD_X + (k_1 + h'k_2)P + h'Q_A$,
  4. output the verifiably encrypted signature (r, V, U_1, U_2).
- **VE_Verify:** Given a verifiably encrypted signature (r, V, U_1, U_2) of a message m, compute $h = H_2(m, r)$, and accept the signature if and only if

$$\hat{e}(P, V) = r \cdot \hat{e}(hP_{pub}, Q_X) \cdot \hat{e}(U_1, Q_A + U_2).$$

- **Adjudication:** Given the adjudicator's secret key D_A, and a valid verifiably encrypted signature (r, V, U_1, U_2) of ID_X for message m, compute $U = V - H_3(\hat{e}(D_A, U_2))(Q_A + U_2)$, and output the original signature (r, U)

We call our new scheme ID-VESS. Readers can see that (**Setup, Extract, Sign, Verify**) constitute Hess's scheme-1 in [3].

3.2 Correctness

Validity requires that verifiably encrypted signatures verify, and that adjudicated verifiably encrypted signatures verify as ordinary signatures, i.e., for $\forall m \in \{0,1\}^*$, $ID_X, ID_A \in \{0,1\}^*$, $D_X = Extract(ID_X)$, $D_A = Extract(ID_A)$, satisfying:

1. $VE\_Verify(ID_X, m, ID_A, VE\_Sign(D_X, m, ID_A)) = 1$;
2. $Verify(ID_X, m, Adjudication(D_A, ID_X, m, VE\_Sign(D_X, m, ID_A))) = 1$

The correctness is easily proved as follows: For a verifiably encrypted signature (r, V, U_1, U_2) of an identity ID_X for a message m.

$$
\begin{aligned}
\hat{e}(P, V) &= \hat{e}(P, hD_X + (k_1 + h'k_2)P + h'Q_A) \\
&= \hat{e}(P, k_1 P + h \cdot D_X) \cdot \hat{e}(P, h'(Q_A + U_2)) \\
&= \hat{e}(P, k_1 P) \cdot \hat{e}(P, h \cdot D_X) \cdot \hat{e}(h' \cdot P, Q_A + U_2) \\
&= r \cdot \hat{e}(P_{pub}, Q_X)^h \cdot \hat{e}(h' \cdot P, Q_A + U_2) \\
&= r \cdot \hat{e}(h \cdot P_{pub}, Q_X) \cdot \hat{e}(U_1, Q_A + U_2)
\end{aligned}
$$

That is, $VE\_Verify(ID_X, m, ID_A, VE\_Sign(D_X, m, ID_A)) = 1$.
   On the other hand,

$$
\begin{aligned}
U &= V - H_3(\hat{e}(D_A, U_2))(Q_A + U_2) \\
&= hD_X + (k_1 + h'k_2)P + h'Q_A - H_3(\hat{e}(Q_A, k_2 P_{pub}))(Q_A + U_2) \\
&= k_1 P + hD_X + h'(Q_A + U_2) - h'(Q_A + U_2) \\
&= k_1 P + hD_X.
\end{aligned}
$$

So we have $\hat{e}(U, P) \cdot \hat{e}(H_1(ID_X), P_{pub})^{-h} = \hat{e}(U - hD_X, P) = \hat{e}(k_1 P, P) = r$. That is, $Verify(ID_X, m, Adjudication(D_A, ID_X, m, VE\_Sign(D_X, m, ID_A))) = 1$.

3.3 Efficiency

Some general performance enhancements can be applied to our scheme. Pairings are usually been constructed with the Weil pairings or the Tate pairings of (hyper)elliptic curves. For a pre-selected $R \in G_1$, there are efficient algorithms [17] to compute kR by pre-computing. We may assume that such a computation is at most $1/5$ an ordinary scalar multiplication in $(G_1, +)$. In our scheme, P, P_{pub} are fixed. An identity's private key if fixed for himself. For most instance, Q_A is also fixed. The signing operation can be further optimized by pre-computing $\hat{e}(P, P)$ and $\hat{e}(Q_A, P_{pub})$.

   VESSs constructed with interactive zero knowledge proofs generally need a number of message exchanges and Exp. operations. The ID-VESS needs no message exchanges, which will bring us convenience in applications. Recently, Boneh et.al. [12] and A.Nenadic et.al. [15] proposed new noninteractive VESSs. Denote by M a scalar multiplication in $(G_1, +)$, by E an Exp. operation in $(G_2, .)$, and by $\hat{e}$ a computation of the pairing. For RSA-based scheme [15], denote by Exp

an Exp. operation. We do not take other operations into account. We compare our ID-based VESS with the schemes in [12, 15] (not ID-based) in the following table.

	Sign	Verify	VE_Sign	VE_Verify	Adjudication	certificate
Nenadic [15]	$1Exp$	$1Exp$	$6Exp$	$2Exp$	$1Exp$	needed
Boneh [12]	$1M$	$2\hat{e}$	$1.4M$	$3\hat{e}$	$1M$	needed
Proposed	$1E + 0.4M$	$2\hat{e} + 1E$	$2E + 1M$	$3\hat{e} + 0.2M$	$1\hat{e} + 1M$	not needed

A.Nenadic's scheme is a RSA-based scheme which is less efficiency, because of the larger parameter's size (at least 1024 bits). Comparatively, our new scheme is a little less efficient than Boneh's scheme. But our new scheme is an ID-based scheme, which needs no certificates and has a simple key management.

4   Security Proof of the ID-VESS

Security proof is a sticking point for the construction of new cryptographic schemes. Besides the ordinary notion of signature security in the signature component, Boneh et.al. [12] proposed two security properties of verifiably encrypted signatures:

- **Unforgeability:** It is difficult to forge a valid verifiably encrypted signature.
- **Opacity:** It is difficult, given a verifiably encrypted signature, to extract an ordinary signature on the same message.

In this section, we extend this security notation to ID-based VESSs.

The ordinary signature algorithm of the ID-VESS is the same as that of Hess's scheme-1 [3]. The signature unforgeability has been shown in the random oracle model under the hardness assumption of CDHP in [3]. We do not repeat the proof here.

4.1   Unforgeability

Definition 1. *An ID-based VESS is said to be **existential unforgeable secure under adaptively chosen message, ID and verifiably encrypted signature attacks (EUF-ACMISA)**, if no polynomial time adversary $\mathcal{F}$, which we call ACMIA adversary, has a non-negligible success probability in the following game:*

1. *A challenger $\mathcal{C}$ runs **Setup**, and give the system parameters Ω to $\mathcal{F}$.*
2. *$\mathcal{F}$ can issue queries to the following oracles adaptively:*
   - *Extract oracle $E(.)$: For input an identity ID_X, this oracle computes $D_X = Extract(ID_X)$, and outputs the secret key D_X*
   - *VE_Sign oracle $VS(.)$: For input (ID_X, m, ID_A), this oracle computes and outputs a verifiably encrypted signature $\pi = VE\_Sign(D_X, m, ID_A)$, where $D_X = Extract(ID_X)$.*

 – *Adjudication oracle $A(.)$: For input (ID_X, m, ID_A, π), where π is a valid verifiable encrypted signature, this oracle computes and outputs the corresponding ordinary signature $\delta = Adjudication(D_A, ID_X, m, \pi)$, where $D_A = Extract(ID_A)$.*
3. *$\mathcal{F}$ outputs $(ID_X^*, m^*, ID_A^*, \pi^*)$, such that ID_X^* is not equal to the inputs of any query to $E(.)$ and (ID_X^*, m^*) is not equal to the inputs (or part of inputs) of any query to $VS(.)$ and $A(.)$.*

$\mathcal{F}$ succeeds in the game if π^* is a valid verifiably encrypted signature of ID_X^* for m^* with adjudicator's identity being ID_A^*.

Note: An ordinary signing oracle is not provided, because it can be simulated by a call to $VS(.)$ followed by a call to $A(.)$. In the random oracle model, the adversary also has the ability to issue queries to the hash function oracles $H_1(.), H_2(.), H_3(.)$ adaptively.

If the adversary has got an ordinary signature or a verifiably encrypted signature of ID_X^* for message m^*, he can easily to forge another verifiably encrypted signature. Because the encryption uses the adjudicator's public key, this is an inherent property of VESS. However, this kind of forgery is insignificant since it can't forge a verifiably encrypted signature for a new message.

Without any loss of generality, we may assume that the set of signers Σ do not intersect the set of adjudicators Γ, which means that a user can't acts as both an ordinary signer and an adjudicator.

Theorem 1. *In the random oracle model, if there is an ACMISA adversary $\mathcal{F}_0$ which performs, within a time bound T_0, an existential forgery against ID-VESS with probability ε_0, then there is an ACMIA adversary $\mathcal{F}_1$ which performs an existential forgery against Hess's scheme-1 with probability no less than ε_0, within a time bound $T_0 + (4M + 1\hat{e})n_{VS} + (1\hat{e} + 1M)(n_A + 1)$, where n_{VS} and n_A are the number of queries that $\mathcal{F}_0$ can ask to $VS(.)$ and $A(.)$, respectively.*

Proof. From $\mathcal{F}_0$, we can construct $\mathcal{F}_1$ of Hess's scheme as follows:

1. A challenger $\mathcal{C}$ runs **Setup** of Hess's scheme, and gives the system parameters $\Omega = (G_1, G_2, q, \hat{e}, P, P_{pub}, H_1, H_2)$ to $\mathcal{F}_1$.
2. $\mathcal{F}_1$ selects hash function $H_3 : G_2 \to Z_q$, and runs $\mathcal{F}_0$ with input $\Omega' = \Omega \cup \{H_3\}$. During the execution, $\mathcal{F}_1$ emulates $\mathcal{F}_0$'s oracles as follows:
   – $H_1(.), H_2(.), E(.)$: $\mathcal{F}_1$ replaces these oracles with his own $H_1(.), H_2(.), E(.)$ oracles respectively. That is , $\mathcal{F}_1$ asks his $H_1(.), H_2(.), E(.)$ oracles with the inputs of $\mathcal{F}_0$, and lets the outputs be the replies to $\mathcal{F}_0$, respectively.
   – $H_3(.)$: For input $x \in G_2$, $\mathcal{F}_1$ checks if $H_3(x)$ is defined. If not, pick a random $h \in Z_q$, and set $H_3(x) = h$. $\mathcal{F}_1$ returns $H_3(x)$ to $\mathcal{F}_0$ as the reply.
   – $VS(.)$: For input $ID_X \in \Sigma$, $ID_A \in \Gamma$ and a message m, $\mathcal{F}_1$ emulates this oracle as follows:
     1. Request to his own signing oracle $Sign(.)$ with input (ID_X, m) and get reply (r, U).
     2. Pick a random $k_2 \in Z_q^*$, and compute $h' = H_3(\hat{e}(H_1(ID_A), k_2 P_{pub}))$.
     3. Compute $U_1 = h'P$, $U_2 = k_2 P$, $V = U + h'(H_1(ID_A) + U_2)$.
     4. Let (r, V, U_1, U_2) be the reply.

- $A(.)$: For input $ID_X \in \Sigma$, $ID_A \in \Gamma$, a message m and corresponding verifiably encrypted signature (r, V, U_1, U_2), $\mathcal{F}_1$ emulates this oracle as follows:
  1. Request to his own $E(.)$ oracle with input ID_A and get reply D_A.
  2. Compute $h' = H_3(\hat{e}(D_A, U_2))$, $U = V - h'(H_1(ID_A) + U_2)$.
  3. Let the ordinary signature (r, U) be the reply.
3. If $\mathcal{F}_0$ outputs $(ID_X^*, m^*, ID_A^*, \pi^*)$, where $\pi^* = (r, V, U_1, U_2)$, $\mathcal{F}_1$ computes $U = V - H_3(\hat{e}(D_A, U_2)) \cdot (H_1(ID_A^*) + U_2)$ and outputs $(ID_X^*, m^*, (r, U))$, where D_A is the reply of the Extract oracle $E(.)$ with input ID_A^*.

If $\mathcal{F}_0$ win in his game, then $\mathcal{F}_1$ has not asked his **Extract** oracle and **Sign** oracle with input ID_X^* and (ID_X^*, m^*) respectively, and (r, U) is a valid ordinary signature of ID_X^* for m^*. So we can see, $\mathcal{F}_1$ succeed in existential forgery against Hess's scheme-1 with probability no less than ε_0,

$\mathcal{F}_1$'s running time is roughly the same as $\mathcal{F}_0$'s running time plus the time taken to respond to $\mathcal{F}_0$'s oracle queries and to transform π to ordinary signature in step3. Neglect operations other than pairing and scalar multiplication in $(G_1, +)$, the total running time is $T_0 + (4M + 1\hat{e})n_{VS} + (1\hat{e} + 1M)(n_A + 1)$.

4.2   Opacity

Definition 2. *An ID-based VESS is said to be **opaque under adaptively chosen message, ID and verifiably encrypted signature attacks (OPA-ACMISA)**, if no polynomial time adversary $\mathcal{F}$ has a non-negligible success probability in the following game:*

1. *A challenger $\mathcal{C}$ runs **Setup**, and gives the system parameters Ω to $\mathcal{F}$.*
2. *$\mathcal{F}$ can adaptively issue queries to the **Extract** oracle $E(.)$, the **VE_Sign** oracle $VS(.)$ and the **Adjudication** oracle $A(.)$ described the same as those in Definition 1. In the random oracle model, $\mathcal{F}$ can also issue queries to the **hash function** oracles $H_1(.), H_2(.), H_3(.)$ adaptively.*
3. *$\mathcal{F}$ outputs $(ID_X^*, m^*, ID_A^*, \pi^*, \delta^*)$ satisfying: ID_X^* and ID_A^* are not equal to the inputs of any query to $E(.)$, and (ID_X^*, m^*) is not equal to part of the inputs of any query to $A(.)$.*

$\mathcal{F}$ succeeds in the game if π^* is a valid verifiably encrypted signature of ID_X^* for message m^*, with adjudicator's identity being ID_A^* and $A(ID_X^*, m^*, ID_A^*, \pi^*) = \delta^*$.

Theorem 2. *In the random oracle mode, let $\mathcal{F}_0$ be an ACMISA adversary which has running time T and success probability ε in opaque attack. We denote by n_{h_1}, n_{h_3}, n_E, n_A and n_{VS} the number of queries that $\mathcal{F}_0$ can ask to the oracles $H_1(.)$, $H_3(.)$, $E(.)$, $A(.)$ and $VS(.)$ respectively. Then there is a polynomial-time Turing machine $\mathcal{F}_1$, which can output $\hat{e}(P, P)^{a(b-a)c}$ with probability $\varepsilon/(n_{h_1}^2 n_{h_3} n_{VS})$, or can output $\hat{e}(P, P)^{abc}$ with probability $\varepsilon/(n_{h_1}^2 n_{VS})$ on input of any given $P, aP, bP, cP \in G_1^*$ in expected time $T + (5M + 3\hat{e})n_{VS} + (2M + 1\hat{e})n_A + (n_{h_1} + n_E)M$.*

Proof. Without any loss of generality, we may assume that for any ID, $\mathcal{F}_0$ queries $H_1(.)$ with ID before ID is used as (part of) an input of any query to $E(.)$, $VS(.)$, and $A(.)$, by using a simple wrapper of $\mathcal{F}_0$.

From the adversary $\mathcal{F}_0$, we can construct a polynomial-time Turing machine $\mathcal{F}_1$ as follows:

1. A challenger $\mathcal{C}$ generates $(G_1, G_2, q, \hat{e})$ and selects randomly $P, aP, bP, cP \in G_1$. $\mathcal{C}$ gives $(G_1, G_2, q, \hat{e}, P, aP, bP, cP)$ to $\mathcal{F}_1$ as inputs.
2. $\mathcal{F}_1$ selects $H_1 : \{0,1\}^* \to G_1^*$, $H_2 : \{0,1\}^* \times G_2 \to Z_q$ and $H_3 : G_2 \to Z_q$ as hash functions and sets $P_{pub} = cP$.
3. $\mathcal{F}_1$ sets $v = 1, z = 1$, and picks randomly t, u and ι satisfying $1 \le t, u \le n_{h_1}$, $t \ne u$, and $1 \le \iota \le n_{VS}$.
4. $\mathcal{F}_1$ picks randomly $x_i \in Z_q, i = 1, 2, ...n_{h_1}$, and sets $VS_{list} = \Phi$, $H_{list} = \Phi$.
5. $\mathcal{F}_1$ runs $\mathcal{F}_0$ with input $\Omega = (G_1, G_2, q, \hat{e}, P, P_{pub}, H_1, H_2, H_3)$. During the execution, $\mathcal{F}_1$ emulates $\mathcal{F}_0$'s oracles as follows:
   - $H_1(.)$: For input ID, $\mathcal{F}_1$ checks if $H_1(ID)$ is defined. If not, he defines
   $$H_1(ID) = \begin{cases} aP & v = t \\ x_v P & v \ne t \end{cases}, \text{ and sets } ID_v \leftarrow ID, v \leftarrow v + 1. \mathcal{F}_1 \text{ returns}$$
   $H_1(ID)$ to $\mathcal{F}_0$.
   - $H_2(.)$: For input (m, r), $\mathcal{F}_1$ checks if $H_2(m, r)$ is defined. If not, it picks a random $h \in Z_q$, and sets $H_2(m, r) \leftarrow h$. $\mathcal{F}_1$ returns $H_2(m, r)$ to $\mathcal{F}_0$.
   - $H_3(.)$: For input $e \in G_2$, $\mathcal{F}_1$ checks if $H_3(e)$ is defined. If not, it picks a random $g \in Z_q$, sets $H_3(e) \leftarrow g$. $\mathcal{F}_1$ returns $H_3(e)$ to $\mathcal{F}_0$ and adds e to H_{list}.
   - $Extract(.)$: For input ID_i, if $i = t$ or $i = u$, $\mathcal{F}_1$ returns with $\bot$. Otherwise, $\mathcal{F}_1$ lets $d_i = x_i \cdot P_{pub}$ be the reply to $\mathcal{F}_0$.
   - $VS(.)$: For input a signer's identity ID_i, an adjudicator's identity ID_T and a message m, $\mathcal{F}_1$ emulates VE_Sign oracle as follows:
     - If $z = \iota$, $i = u$ and $T = t$,
       1. Pick randomly $\mu \in Z_q$. And let $U_1 = \mu aP, U_2 = bP - aP$.
       2. Pick randomly $V \in G_1, h \in Z_q$.
       3. Compute $r = \hat{e}(V, P) \cdot \hat{e}(H_1(ID_i), P_{pub})^{-h} \cdot \hat{e}(\mu aP, bP)^{-1}$.
       4. If $H_2(m, r)$ is defined, then abort (a collision appears). Otherwise, set $H_2(m, r) = h$.
       5. Add $(z, i, T, ., r, V, U_1, U_2)$ to VS_{list}.
     - Otherwise,
       1. Pick randomly $U' \in G_1, h \in Z_q$;
       2. Let $U = U', r = \hat{e}(U, P) \cdot (\hat{e}((-h)H_1(ID_i), P_{pub}))$.
       3. If $H_2(m, r)$ is defined, then abort (a collision appears). Otherwise, set $H_2(m, r) = h$.
       4. Pick randomly $k_2 \in Z_q^*$, and compute $h' = H_3(\hat{e}(H_1(ID_T), k_2 P_{pub}))$;
       5. $U_1 = h'P; U_2 = k_2 P; V = U + h'(H_1(ID_T) + U_2)$
       6. Add $(z, i, T, k_2, r, V, U_1, U_2)$ to VS_{list}

In the (unlikely) situation where $r = 1$, we discard the results and restart the simulation. Set $z = z + 1$ and let (r, V, U_1, U_2) be the reply to $\mathcal{F}_0$.

- $A(.)$: For input ID_i, m, ID_T and a valid verifiably encrypted signature (r, V, U_1, U_2) of ID_i for m with adjudicator's identity being ID_T, $\mathcal{F}_1$ obtains the corresponding item $(z, i, T, k_2, r, V, U_1, U_2)$ (or $(z, i, T, ., r, V, U_1, U_2)$) from the VS_{list}. (With Theorem 1, verifiably encrypted signature is unforgeable. Hence (r, V, U_1, U_2) is in the VS_{list}.) If $T = t$ and $j = \iota$, $\mathcal{F}_1$ returns with $\perp$. Otherwise, $\mathcal{F}_1$ computes $U = V - H_3(\hat{e}(Q_T, k_2 P_{pub}))(Q_T + U_2)$, and replies to $\mathcal{F}_0$ with (r, U)

6. If $\mathcal{F}_0$'s output is $(ID_i, m^*, ID_T, r^*, V^*, U_1^*, U_2^*, U^*)$, then $\mathcal{F}_1$ obtains the corresponding item $(z, i, T, k_2, r^*, V, U_1, U_2)$ (or $(z, i, T, ., r^*, V, U_1, U_2)$) from the VS_{list}. If $z = \iota$, $i = u$ and $T = t$, $\mathcal{F}_1$ computes $R = V^* - U^*$, $e_1 = \hat{e}(R, P_{pub})^{\mu^{-1}}$, picks a random item e_2 from H_{list}, and outputs e_1 and e_2. Otherwise $\mathcal{F}_1$ declares failure and aborts.

This completes the description of $\mathcal{F}_1$.

Because of the randomness of r, the probability of $\mathcal{F}_1$ aborts as a result of collision of $H_2(m, r)$ is negligible. On the other hand, if $\mathcal{F}_0$ has not asked to $H_3(.)$ with $e = \hat{e}(aP, (b-a)cP)$, then the simulation of $H_3(.)$ generate a random distribution.

If $\mathcal{F}_0$ succeeds in his attack, then ID_u and ID_t are not equal to the inputs of any query to $E(.)$, and (ID_u, m^*) are not equal to part of the inputs of any query to $A(.)$. Now, let discuss in two cases:

- $\mathcal{F}_0$ has not asked to $H_3(.)$ with $e = \hat{e}(aP, (b-a)cP)$. In this case, the responses of $\mathcal{F}_1$'s emulations are indistinguishable from $\mathcal{F}_0$'s real oracles. If $T = t$, $i = u$ and $z = \iota$, then $R = abP$, $e_1 = \hat{e}(R, P_{pub})^{\mu^{-1}} = \hat{e}(\mu abP, cP)^{\mu^{-1}} = \hat{e}(P, P)^{abc}$. Because t and u are chosen randomly in 1 and n_{h_1}, and ι is chosen randomly in 1 and n_{VS}, $\mathcal{F}_1$ can output $\hat{e}(P, P)^{abc}$ with probability $\varepsilon/(n_{h_1}^2 n_{VS})$.
- $\mathcal{F}_0$ has asked $H_3(.)$ with $\hat{e}(aP, (b-a)cP)$. In this case, $\hat{e}(aP, (b-a)cP)$ is in the H_{list}. So the probability of $\mathcal{F}_1$'s output e_2 satisfying $e_2 = \hat{e}(aP, (b-a)cP)$ is $1/n_{h_3}$. That is, $\mathcal{F}_1$ can output $\hat{e}(aP, (b-a)cP)$ with probability $(\varepsilon/n_{h_1}^2 n_{h_3} n_{VS})$.

$\mathcal{F}_1$'s running time is roughly the same as $\mathcal{F}_0$'s running time plus the time taken to respond to $\mathcal{F}_0$'s oracle queries. Neglect operations other than pairing and scalar multiplication in $(G_1, +)$, the total running time is bounded with $T + (5M + 3\hat{e})n_{VS} + (2M + 1\hat{e})n_A + (n_{h_1} + n_E)M$ as required.

Theorem 3. *For input $P, aP, bP, cP \in G_1$, suppose there is a Turing machine $\mathcal{M}_1$, which outputs $\hat{e}(P, P)^{a(b-a)c}$ with probability ε, in a time bound T. Then from $\mathcal{M}_1$, we can construct a Turing machine $\mathcal{M}_2$ which outputs $\hat{e}(P, P)^{abc}$ on input of any given $P, aP, bP, cP \in G_1^*$ with probability ε^2 in expected time $2T$.*

Proof. From $\mathcal{M}_1$, we can construct a Turing machine $\mathcal{M}_2$ as follows:

1. $\mathcal{M}_2$'s input is $P, aP, bP, cP \in G_1^*$.
2. $\mathcal{M}_2$ runs $\mathcal{M}_1$ with input P, aP, bP, cP. If $\mathcal{M}_1$ outputs $\xi_1 = \hat{e}(P, P)^{a(b-a)c}$, then goto the next step.

3. $\mathcal{M}_2$ runs $\mathcal{M}_1$ with input $P, -aP, bP, cP$. If $\mathcal{M}_1$ outputs $\xi_2 = \hat{e}(P,P)^{(-a)(b+a)c}$, then goto the next step.
4. $\mathcal{M}_2^*$ computes and outputs $\gamma = (\xi_1/\xi_2)^{(q-1)/2}$.

Obviously, $\gamma = (\hat{e}(P,P)^{2abc})^{(q-1)/2} = \hat{e}(P,P)^{abc}$. That is, in expected time $2T$, $\mathcal{M}_2^*$ can output $\hat{e}(P,P)^{bcd}$ with success probability ε_2^2.

With Theorem 2 and Theorem 3, we can get our conclusion. That is, the ID-VESS is OPA-ACMISA under the hardness assumption of BDHP in the random oracle model.

5   Conclusion

This paper proposes an efficient ID-based verifiably encrypted signature scheme, which we called ID-VESS, based on the ID-based signature scheme due to F.Hess [3]. Our new scheme can be proven to be secure with the hardness assumption of the bilinear Diffie-Hellman problem in the random oracle model. Our new scheme is an entirely ID-based scheme, which provides an efficient primitive for building fair exchange protocols in ID-based public key cryptosystem.

References

1. Shamir, A.: Identity-based cryptosystems and signature schemes. In: Advances in Cryptology - CRYPTO'84. Lecture Notes in Computer Science, Vol. 196. Springer-Verlag, Berlin Heidelberg New York (1984) 47-53.
2. Boneh, D., Franklin, M.: Identity-based encryption from the Weil pairing. In: Advances in Cryptology- CRYPTO 2001. Lecture Notes in Computer Science, Vol. 2139. Springer-Verlag, Berlin Heidelberg New York (2001) 213-229.
3. Hess, F.: Efficient identity based signature schemes based on pairings. In: Selected Areas in Cryptography 9th Annual International Workshop, SAC 2002. Lecture Notes in Computer Science, Vol. 2595. Springer-Verlag, Berlin Heidelberg New York (2003) 310-324.
4. Cha, J.C., Cheon, J.H.: An identity-based signature from gap Diffie-Hellman groups. In: Public Key Cryptography - PKC 2003. Lecture Notes in Computer Science, Vol. 2567. Springer-Verlag, Berlin Heidelberg New York (2003) 18-30.
5. Yi,X.: An identity-based signature scheme from the Weil pairing. In: IEEE Communications Letters 7(2)(2003), pp. 76–78.
6. Paterson, K.G.: ID-Based Signatures from Pairings on Elliptic Curves. In: Electron. Lett., Vol.38, No.18, 2002, pp.1025-1026.
7. Zhang, F., Kim, K.: Efficient ID-based blind signature and proxy signature from bilinear pairings. In: ACISP 03. Lecture Notes in Computer Science, Vol. 2727. Springer-Verlag, Berlin Heidelberg New York (2003) 312-323.
8. Gu, C.X., Zhu, Y.F.: Provable Security of ID-based Proxy Signature Schemes. In: Proc. 2005 International Conference on Computer Networks and Mobile Computing (ICCNMC'05). Lecture Notes in Computer Science, Vol. 3619. Springer-Verlag, Berlin Heidelberg New York (2005) 1277-1286.
9. Asokan, N., Shoup, V., Waidner, M.: Optimistic fair exchange of signatures. In: Advances in Cryptology - EUROCRYPT 1998. Lecture Notes in Computer Science vol. 1403. Springer-Verlag, Berlin Heidelberg New York (1998) 591-606.

10. Camenisch, J., Shoup, V.: Practical verifiable encryption and decryption of discrete logarithms. In: Advances in Cryptology - CRYPTO 2003, Lecture Notes in Computer Science vol. 2729. Springer-Verlag, Berlin Heidelberg New York (2003) 195-211.
11. Poupard, G., Stern, J.: Fair encryption of RSA keys. In: Proc. of Eurocrypt 2000, Lecture Notes in Computer Science vol. 1807. Springer-Verlag, Berlin Heidelberg New York (2000) 172-189.
12. Boneh, D., Gentry, C., Lynn, B., Shacham, H.: Aggregate and Verifiably Encrypted Signature from Bilinear Maps. In: Eurocrypt 2003. Lecture Notes in Computer Science, Vol. 2248. Springer-Verlag, Berlin Heidelberg New York (2003) 514-532.
13. Li, M.D., Yang, Y.X., Ma, C.G., Cai, M.C.: A scheme of fair exchange of signatures based on bilinear aggregate signatures. In: Journal of China Institute of Communications, 25(12):59-64. Dec. 2005.
14. Dodis, Y., Reyzin, L., Breaking and reparing optimistic fair exchange from PODC 2003. In: Proc. of the 2003 ACM Workshop on Digital Rights Management. ACM Press, New York (2003) 47-54.
15. Nenadic, A., Zhang, N., Cheetham, B., Goble, C.: An RSA-based Security Protocol for Certified E-goods Delivery. In: Proc. IEEE International Conference on Information Technology, ITCC 2004, Las Vegas, USA, IEEE Computer Society (2004), 22-28.
16. Ateniese, G.: Verifiable Encryption of Digital Signatures and Applications. In: ACM Transactions on Information and System Security, Vol. 7, No. 1, February 2004, Pages 1C20.
17. Sakai, Y., Sakurai, K.: Efficient Scalar Multiplications on Elliptic Curves without Repeated Doublings and Their Practical Performance. In: ACISP 2000. Lecture Notes in Computer Science, Vol. 1841. Springer-Verlag, Berlin Heidelberg New York (2000) 59-73.

ID-Based Signature Scheme Without Trusted PKG

Jian Liao, Junfang Xiao, Yinghao Qi, Peiwei Huang, and Mentian Rong

Department of Electronic Engineering, ShangHai JiaoTong University,
Shanghai 200030, P.R. China
{liaojian, running, qyhao, pwhuang, rongmt}@sjtu.edu.cn

Abstract. Key escrow is an inherent disadvantage for traditional ID-based cryptosystem, i.e., the dishonest PKG can forge the signature of any user. On the other hand, the user can deny the signature actually signed by him/herself. To avoid the key escrow problem, we present an ID-based signature scheme without trusted Private Key Generator (PKG). We also presented the exact proof of security to demonstrate that our scheme is secure against existential forgery on adaptively chosen messages and *ID* attacks assuming the complexity of Computational Diffie-Hellman (CDH) problem. Compared with other signature schemes, the proposed scheme is more efficient.

1 Introduction

In a traditional Public Key Cryptosystem (PKC), the association between a user's identity and his public key is obtained through a digital certificate issued by a Certification Authority (CA). The CA checks the credentials of a user before issuing a certificate to him. To simplify the certificate management process, Shamir [1] introduced the concept of ID-based cryptosystem in 1984, which allowed for a user's identity information such as his name, IP address, telephone number, email address, etc. to serve as his public key. Such a public key is clearly bound to the user, and doesn't need a certificate to indicate the legitimate owning relation between the key and the user. Compared with the traditional certificate-based cryptography, the main advantage of ID-based cryptography is to reduce largely the amount of computation and memory requirements for certificate management. Hence, after Shamir's initial work several practical identity based signature schemes [4,5,8,9,10] have been constructed. However, those schemes confronted with an open problem in constructing ID-based signature scheme from bilinear pairings, "key escrow".

Key escrow is a fatal disadvantage for ID-based cryptosystem, which leads its only to be applicable to small close environments. This problem results from the fact that the PKG generates private keys for users. Namely, the PKG inevitably has users' private keys. It is brought two problems to ID-based cryptosystem. Firstly, the PKG can impersonate any user to sign any message as their wish. Secondly, the user can deny the signature actually signed by him/her because s/he can indict that the PKG also forges the signature of any user. In recent years, researchers have been trying to solve the key escrow problem to allow for ID-based cryptography to be used in open

D. Feng, D. Lin, and M. Yung (Eds.): CISC 2005, LNCS 3822, pp. 53–62, 2005.

environments. Sattam et al. [2] introduced the concept of certificateless public key encryption (CL-PKE) scheme from bilinear pairing, which avoids the inherent escrow of ID-based cryptography and yet which does not require certificates to guarantee the authenticity of public keys. Similarly to [2], Gentry [3] proposed certificate-based encryption avoiding the inherent problems "key escrow" in ID-based Encryption (IBE). In [13], Dae Hyun Yum provided a generic secure construction of a certificate-less signature and presented an extended construction whose trust level is the same as that of a traditional public key signature scheme. Avoiding "key escrow" problem in encryption scheme is preventing the PKG from knowing the message encrypted by the user, but in signature scheme is impeding the PKG to forge the signature signed by any user. For this purpose, Chen, Zhang and Kin [5] presented ID-based signature scheme from parings to solve the key escrow problem and extended their scheme to apply in group signature. However, we think their scheme is less efficient and have no exact security proof. The discussion of [5] will be presented below.

In the paper we propose an ID-based signature scheme without trusted PKG. There still needs a PKG in our scheme to generate the private key of the user. However, the private key embeds some particular information chosen by the user. If the dishonest PKG impersonate an honest user to sign a message, the user can provide this particu-lar information to verify the dishonest of the PKG. Because the PKG is no longer treated as a trusted party, so we must present the exact secure proof in two cases: forgery with no participation of PKG and forgery with participation of PKG. The conclusion of our analysis on security is that our scheme is secure against existential forgery on adaptively chosen message and *ID* attacks assuming the complexity of Computational Diffie-Hellman (CDH) problem. Compared with Chen's signature schemes, we think proposed scheme is more efficient.

The rest of paper is organized as follows: The next section contains some prelimi-naries. Our scheme is proposed in Section 3. We present the secure proof in Section 4 and efficiency in Section 5. Finally, Section 6 concludes our paper.

2 Preliminaries

2.1 Bilinear Pairing and Gap Diffie-Hellman Groups

Let G_1 be a cyclic group generated by P, whose order is a prime p, and G_2 be a cyclic multiplicative group of the same order p. The discrete logarithm problems in both G_1 and G_2 is hard. Let $e : G_1 \times G_1 \to G_2$ be a pairing which satisfies the fol-lowing properties:

1. Bilinear: $e(P_1 + P_2, Q) = e(P_1, Q)e(P_2, Q)$ and $e(aP, bQ) = e(P, Q)^{ab}$;

2. Non-degenerate: there exists $P, Q \in G_1$, such that $e(P, Q) \neq 1$;

3. Computability: There is an efficient algorithm to compute $e(P, Q)$ for all $P, Q \in G_1$.

Definition 1. *Given a generator* P *of a group* G *and a 3-tuple* (aP, bP, cP), *the Decisional Diffie-Hellman problem (DDH problem) is to decide whether* $c = ab$.

Definition 2. *Given a generator* P *of a group* G, (P, aP, bP, cP) *is defined as a valid Diffie-Hellman tuple if* $c = ab$.

Definition 3. *Given a generator* P *of a group* G *and a random triple* (P, aP, bP), *the Computational Diffie-Hellman problem (CDH problem) is to compute* abP.

Definition 4. *If* G *is a group such that DDH problem can be solved in polynomial time but no probabilistic algorithm can solve CDH problem with non-negligible advantage within polynomial time, then we call* G *a Gap Diffie-Hellman (GDH) group.*

We assume the existence of a bilinear map $e : G_1 \times G_1 \to G_2$ that one can solve Decisional Diffie-Hellman Problem (DDH problem) in polynomial time.

2.2 Security Model of ID-Based Signature Schemes

We consider the following security model, which is acceptable as a standard model of security for ID-based signature schemes. An ID-based signature scheme consists of four algorithms: Setup, Extract, Sign, and Verify. An ID-based signature scheme is secure against existential forgery on adaptively chosen message and *ID* attacks if no polynomial time algorithm A has a non-negligible advantage against a challenger C in the following game [4]:

1. C runs *Setup* of the scheme. The resulting system parameters are given to A.
2. A issues the following queries as he wants:
Hash function query. C computes the value of the hash function for the requested input and sends the value to A.
Extract query. Given an identity *ID*, C returns the private key corresponding to *ID* that is obtained by running Extract.
Sign query. Given an identity *ID* and a message m, C returns a signature that is obtained by running Sign.
3. A outputs (ID', m', δ'), where ID' is an identity, m' is a message, and δ' is a signature, such that ID' and (ID', m') are not equal to the inputs of any query to *Extract* and *Sign*, respectively. A wins the game if δ' is a valid signature of m' for ID'.

3 Proposed ID-Based Signature Scheme Without Trusted PKG

In this section we present new ID-based signature scheme. Let G_1 be a Gap Diffie-Hellman group of prime order q, G_2 be a cyclic multiplicative group of the same order q. A bilinear pairings is a map $e : G_1 \times G_1 \rightarrow G_2$. Define two cryptographic hash functions $H_1 : \{0,1\}^* \times G_1 \rightarrow G_1$, $H_2 : \{0,1\}^* \times Z_q^* \times G_1 \rightarrow G_1$.

Setup:

PKG chooses a random $s \in_R Z_q^*$ as master key and sets $P_{pub} = sP$ as the public key. The public parameters of the systems are $params : \{q, G_1, G_2, e(\bullet, \bullet), P, P_{pub}, H_1, H_2\}$.

Extract:

1. A user sends his/her identity ID to the PKG and authenticates himself to the PKG.

2. The user chooses a random $r \in_R Z_q^*$ as his long-term secret key and sends $R = rP$ to the PKG.

3. The PKG computes $S_{ID} = sQ_{ID} = sH_1(ID \| T, R)$ and sends it to the user via a secure channel, where T is the life span of the secret key r.

4. The user accepts private key pair (S_{ID}, r) and the public key ID.

Sign:

To sign a message m using the secret key (S_{ID}, r) corresponding to the identity (public key) ID, the following steps are performed by the signer:

1. Choose a $u \in_R Z_q^*$

2. Compute $V = H_2(m, u, R)$

3. Compute $S = uS_{ID} + rV$

The signature δ on the message m: $\delta = \{m, u, S, R, T\}$, which will be discussed later.

Verify:

To verify a signature $\delta = \{m, u, S, R, T\}$ of an identity ID on the message m, the verifier does the following:

1. Compute $Q_{ID} = H_1(ID \| T, R)$

2. Compute $V = H_2(m, u, R)$

3. Accept the signature if and only if the equation $e(S, P) = e(Q_{ID}, P_{pub})^u e(V, R)$ holds.

Trace:

In actually the dishonest PKG can impersonate a signature for an identity ID as follows:

1. The PKG chooses a random $r' \in_R Z_q^*$, computes $R' = r'P$ and lets $Q_{ID} = H_2(ID \| T, R')$. This step means that the PKG can forge the user's private key (S'_{ID}, r') corresponding to identity ID. $r' = r$ is a unlikely event.

2. The PKG then performs the above described sign protocol on a message m to produce a valid signature $\delta' = \{m, u', S', R', T\}$, and the signature δ' passes the verify protocol.

We note that the private key (S_{ID}, r) grasped by the user is different from the private key (S'_{ID}, r') used by the PKG to forge a signature δ', because the PKG want to get r (randomly chosen by the user) from rP (the user sends to the PKG) they are confronted with DLP.

The user can prove the dishonesty of the PKG by providing a "knowledge proof" of his secret key (S_{ID}, r) to an arbiter. If the equation

$$e(S_{ID}, P) = e(H_1(ID \| T, rP), P_{pub})$$ holds, i.e., identity ID corresponds to rP

for a same period T, the arbiter deduces PKG dishonest because the private key S_{ID} includes the master key s, which is only known by the PKG. So if the user can proof the validation of their private key pair (S_{ID}, r), then the PKG is dishonest. The proof is similar to CA-based system in [7].

4 Security Proof

Many paper presented efficient security reduction from the Diffie-Hellman problem to signature scheme [6, 8, 9, 10,11]. Our security reduction is slightly different because the PKG no longer is treated as a trusted party and the signer grasps two private keys (S_{ID}, r). So we must discuss in two cases: forgery with no participation of PKG and forgery with participation of PKG. Our secure proof presented below:

Case 1: Forgery with No Participation of PKG

In this case we assume that the PKG is a trusted parity so the forger F cannot obtain any signer's secret key S_{ID} from the PKG. The signer also masters long-term private key r. We claim theorem below holds.

Theorem 1: *In the random oracle model, if a probabilistic polynomial time (PPT) forger F has an advantage ε in forging a signature in an attack defined in section 2.2 when running in a time t and asking q_{H_1} queries to random oracles H_1, q_{H_2} queries to random oracles H_2, q_E queries to the key extraction oracle and q_S queries to the signature oracle, then the CDHP can be solved with an advantage*

$$\varepsilon' > \frac{\varepsilon - (q_S(q_{H_1} + q_{H_2} + q_S) + 1)/2^k}{e(1 + q_E)}$$

within a time $t' < t + (2q_{H_1} + q_E + q_{H_2} + 2q_S)t_m + (q_S + 1)t_e$ where t_m is the time of computing scalar multiplication in G_1, t_e is the time to computing multi-exponentiation in G_1.

Proof: Suppose the challenger C receives a random instance (P, aP, bP), denoted by (P, A, B), of the CDHP and has to compute the value of abP, both a and b are unknown to C. Let $P_{pub} = A$ as a system overall public key. C solves the CDHP by using a PPT forger F. During the game, F will consult C for answers to the random oracles H_1 and H_2. Roughly speaking, these answers are randomly generated, but to maintain the consistency and to avoid collision, C keeps two lists L_1, L_2 to store the answers used. We assume F will ask for H_1 before ID is used in any other queries. Now F performs a series of queries:

Queries on random oracle H_1: When F asks queries on the hash values of identities, C checks the list L_1. If an entry for the query is found, the same answer will be given to F; otherwise, C randomly chooses $x \in_R Z_q^*$ and computes $R = rP \leftarrow xP$. The oracle input is (ID, R, T), where T is predetermined. C flips a coin $D \in \{0,1\}$ that yields 0 with probability δ and 1 with probability $1 - \delta$. C then picks $y \in_R Z_q^*$. If $D = 0$ then C returns yP as the value of the $H_1(ID \| T, R)$. If $D = 1$ then C returns yB. In both cases, C inserts a tuple (ID, R, T, D, x, y) in a list L_1 to keep track of the way it answered the query.

Queries on key extraction: When F request the private key associated to an identity ID, C recovers the corresponding (ID, R, T, D, x, y) from L_1. If $D = 1$ then C outputs "failure" and aborts because it is unable to coherently answer the queries. Otherwise, C returns $yP_{pub} \leftarrow yA$ and x as a private key associated to ID.

Queries on random oracle H_2: When F sends (ID, R, T, m, u) to the random oracle C checks the corresponding list L_2. If an entry for the query is found, the same answer will be given to F. Otherwise, C randomly chooses $z \in_R Z_q^*$, returns zP as the hash value to F and stores the tuple (ID, R, T, m, u, z) in L_2.

Queries on signature: When F queries the signature oracle on a message m for an identity ID, C randomly chooses $x \in_R Z_q^*$, computes $R = rP = xA \leftarrow xP_{pub}$.

(ID, R, T) is the input of random oracle H_1 and return $Q_{ID} = H_1(ID \| T, R)$ as hash value. It then chooses $\alpha, \beta, \lambda \in_R Z_q^*$, lets $u \leftarrow \alpha$ and $S = uS_{ID} + rH_2 = \beta P_{pub} \leftarrow \beta X$. Then C stores the hash value $H_2 = r^{-1}(S - uS_{ID}) \leftarrow x^{-1}(\beta P - \alpha Q_{ID})$. The pair (u, S) is a valid signature from the F's point of view. C outputs "failure" and aborts when rP (namely H_1) or H_2 is predefined for the input (ID, m, u) because selection on the value of r and H_2 in signature queries is different from in queries on random oracle H_1 or H_2.

Eventually, F output a signature $\delta' = \{m', u', S', R', T\}$ of identity ID', and then C recovers the truple (ID', R', T, D'). If $D' = 0$ then C outputs "failure" and aborts. If $D' = 1$ then C find out the entry of (ID', R', T, H_2') with overwhelming probability.

Hence, Noted that $Q_{ID'} = y'B$ and $H_2' = z'P$ in the list L_1 and L_2, x, y, z is known for C. So it also knows that:

$$e(S', P) = e(Q_{ID'}, A)^{u'} e(H_2', x'P)$$
$$\Leftrightarrow e(S' - x'H_2', P) = e(Q_{ID'}, A)^{u'}$$
$$\Leftrightarrow e(S' - x'H_2', P) = e(u'y'B, A)$$
$$\Leftrightarrow e(S' - x'H_2', P) = e(u'y'abP, P)$$

According to the non-generation of bilinear pairings, C gets $abP = (u'y')^{-1}(S' - x'z'P)$, which is the solution of CDH instance (P, aP, bP). In signature queries the probability of C's abort is at most $q_S(q_{H_1} + q_{H_2} + q_S)/2^k$. A conflict on H_1 is at most $q_S(q_{H_2} + q_S)/2^k$, because the list L_2 stores at most $q_{H_2} + q_S$ entries. In the same way, the conflict on H_1 is at most $q_S q_{H_1}/2^k$. While the probability for F to output a valid forge signature without asking the corresponding H_2 query is at most $1/2^k$.

Similar to the analysis in [6], the probability of failure in query on key extract is δ^{q_E}. The probability that C does not abort during the forge step is $1 - \delta$. Therefore, the probability that C does not fail in the game is $\delta^{q_E}(1 - \delta)$. This value is maximized at $\delta_{opt} = 1 - 1/(q_E + 1)$. Using δ_{opt}, the probability that C does not abort is at least $1/e(1 + q_E)$. Eventually, it comes that C's advantage is at most:

$$\frac{\varepsilon - (q_S(q_{H_1} + q_{H_2} + q_S) + 1)/2^k}{e(1 + q_E)}$$

Case 2: Forgery with Participation of PKG

In this case, the PKG is not a trusted parity, so the forger F can obtain any signer's long-term public key rP and secret key S_{ID} from the PKG. Therefore, the signer only master private key r. For a valid signature $S = S_1 + S_2 = uS_{ID} + rV$, the forger can compute $S_1 = uS_{ID}$ and V while we declaim that the forger cannot output $S_2 = rV = rH_2(m,u,R)$ with non-negligible probability. This kind of signature is similar to [12], We consider the following game as [5] defined:

Queries on oracle H_1 and key extraction are deleted because F knows the accurate secret key S_{ID} and long-term public key rP. F can make queries on oracle H_2 and signature queries at most q_{H_2}, q_S times respectively. For simplicity we only discuss the forgery on S_2. Assumed that the input of i-th $(1 \le i \le q_{S_2})$ query is (m_i, u, R) and then F gets the corresponding signature S_{2i}. Finally, F outputs a new signature (m_i, S_{2i}). We say that the adversary wins the game if rP is not queried. Now we present a concise security proof similar to [5]:

An algorithm A executes an adaptively chosen message attack to our scheme with a non-negligible probability. We can construct an algorithm B as follows:

- Chooses an integer $x \in \{1, 2, \ldots, q_{S_2}\}$. Define $Sign(H_2(m_i, u, R)) = S_{2i}$.
- For $i = 1, 2, \ldots, q_{S_2}$, B responds to A's queries to H_2 and Sign, while for $i = x$, B replaces m_x with m.
- A outputs (m', S_2').
- If $m' = m$ and the signature S_2 is valid, B outputs (m, u, R, S_2); otherwise, outputs "failure".

Note that x is randomly chosen, A knows nothing from the queries result. Also, since H_2 is a random oracle, the probability that the output of A is valid without query of H_2 is $1/2^k$. Let $H_2(m, u, R) = aP$, we obtain $S_2 = raP$ from (P, rP, aP), which means that we solved CDH problem. Actually, from the result of [12], we also can deduce that the probability of the adversary can successfully forge a valid partial signature is negligible.

5   Efficiency

Chen's scheme [5] compare with our proposed scheme is showed in Table 1. We consider the time-exhausting operations. Ga denotes the cost of point addition over

G_1. Gm denotes the cost of point scalar multiplication over G_1. Za denotes the cost of addition over Z_q. Zm denotes the cost of multiplication over Z_q. H_G denotes the cost of hash function which hash $\{0,1\}*$ into G_1 and H_Z denotes the cost of hash function which hash $\{0,1\}*$ into Z_q. e denotes the cost of pairing operation.

Table 1. Comparison with Chen's Scheme

Phase	Chen's scheme	Our scheme
Sign	$3\,Gm + Ga + Za + H_G + H_Z$	$2\,Gm + Ga + H_G$
Verify	$Gm + Ga + 2\,H_G + H_Z + 4\,e$	$Gm + H_G + 3\,e$

From the Table 1, we draw a conclusion that the computational costs of our scheme are lower than previous scheme in the phase of "*sign*" and "*verify*".

Moreover, the length of the signature of proposed scheme is shorter than the Chen's scheme. Except the necessary information, such as $\{m, R(rP), T\}$, the signature of our scheme includes an element of Z_q^* and an element of G_1. On the contrary, Chen's signature includes three elements of G_1. So our scheme is more suitable to low-bandwidth communication and cabined storage space environments. The short length of the proposed signature makes the cryptosystem much more practical.

6 Conclusion

Assumed that the PKG is no longer a trusted party, we present an ID-based signature scheme to solve the inherent problem in ID-based cryptosystem, key escrow. Moreover, we demonstrate that our scheme is secure against existential forgery on adaptively chosen message and *ID* attacks assuming the complexity of Computational Diffie-Hellman (CDH) problem. Basing on our proposed signature scheme, we can furthermore construct group or ring signature scheme eliminating the problem of key escrow.

References

1. Shamir, A.: Identity Based Cryptosystems and Signature Schemes. In: G.R. Blakley, D. Chaum (Eds.): Advances in Cryptology - Crypto' 84. Lecture Notes in Computer Science, Vol. 196. Springer-Verlag, Berlin Heidelberg New York (1984) 47-53
2. Sattam, S., Al-Riyami, S., Paterson, K.G.: Certificateless public key cryptography. In: Advances in Cryptology-Asiacrypt'2003. Lecture Notes in Computer Science, Vol. 2894. Springer-Verlag, Berlin Heidelberg New York (2003) 452-473

3. Gentry, C.: Certificate-based encryption and the certificate revocation problem. In: Biham, E. (eds.): Advances in Cryptology-EUROCRYPT 2003. Lecture Notes in Computer Science, Vol. 2656. Springer-Verlag, Berlin Heidelberg New York (2003) 272-293

4. Jae Choon Cha, Jung Hee Cheon: An Identity-Based Signature from Gap Diffie-Hellman Groups. In: Desmedt, Y.G. (eds.): Proceedings of Public Key Cryptography – PKC'03. Lecture Notes in Computer Science, Vol. 2567. Springer-Verlag, Berlin Heidelberg New York (2003) 18-30

5. Chen, X., Zhang, F.G., Kim, K.: A New ID-based Group Signature Scheme from Bilinear Pairings, In: Kijoon Chae, Moti Yung (Eds.): Proceedings of WISA'03, 585-592, Jeju Island, Korea.   The full   version   appears   in   Cryptology   ePrint   Archive: http://eprint.iacr.org/2003/116

6. Benoıt Libert, Jean-Jacques Quisquater: The Exact Security of an Identity Based Signature and its Applications. The full version appears in Cryptology ePrint Archive: http://eprint.iacr.org/2004/102.pdf

7. Balfanz, D., Durfee, G., Shankar, N., Smentters, D., Staddon, J., Wong, H.: Secret handshakes from pairing-based agreements: Proceeding of the 2003 IEEE Symposiumon Security and Privacy, Berkeley, CA, United States (2003) 180–196

8. Bellare, M., Namprempre, C., Neven, G.: Security Proofs for Identity-Based Identification and Signature Schemes. In: Christian Cachin, Jan Camenisch (eds.): Advances in Cryptology - Eurocrypt'04. Lecture Notes in Computer Science, Vol. 3027. Springer-Verlag, Berlin Heidelberg New York (2004) 268–286

9. Sherman S.M. Chow, Yiu, S.M., Lucas C.K. Hui, Chow, Chow, K.P.: Efficient Forward and Provably Secure ID-Based Signcryption Scheme with Public Verifiability and Public Ciphertext Authenticity. In: Jong In Lim, Dong Hoon Lee (eds.): Proceedings of ICISC'03. Lecture Notes in Computer Science, Vol. 2971. Springer-Verlag, Berlin Heidelberg New York (2001) 352–369

10. Hess F.: Efficient Identity Based Signature Schemes Based on Pairings. In: Nyberg, K., Heys, H. (eds.): Advances in Cryptology-Asiacrypt 2001. Lecture Notes in Computer Science, Vol. 2595. Springer-Verlag, Berlin Heidelberg New York (2003) 310–324

11. Boneh, D., Boyen, X.: Short Signature without Random Oracles. In: Cachin, C., Camenisch, J. (eds.): Advances in Cryptology: EUROCRYTP'04. Lecture Notes in Computer Science, Vol. 3027. Springer-Verlag, Berlin Heidelberg New York (2004) 56–73

12. Boneh, D., Lynn, B., Shacham, H.: Short Signatures from the Weil pairings. In: Boyd C. (eds.): Advances in Cryptology-Asiacrypt 2001. Lecture Notes in Computer Science, Vol. 2248. Springer-Verlag, Berlin Heidelberg New York (2001) 514–532

13. Dae Hyun Yum, Pil Joong Lee: Generic Construction of Certificateless Signature. In: Huaxiong W., Josef P., Vijay V. (eds.): Information Security and Privacy (ACISP 2004). Lecture Notes in Computer Science, Vol. 3108. Springer-Verlag, Berlin Heidelberg New York (2004) 200–211

Specifying Authentication Using Signal Events in CSP

Siraj A. Shaikh[1], Vicky J. Bush[1], and Steve A. Schneider[2]

[1] Department of Computing, UGBS, University of Gloucestershire,
Park Campus, The Park, Cheltenham Spa, GL52 2RH, UK
{Sshaikh, Vbush}@glos.ac.uk
[2] Department of Computing, SEPS, University of Surrey,
Guildford, Surrey, GU2 7XH, UK
{S.schneider}@surrey.ac.uk

Abstract. The formal analysis of cryptographic protocols has firmly developed into a comprehensive body of knowledge, building on a wide variety of formalisms and treating a diverse range of security properties, foremost of which is authentication. The formal specification of authentication has long been a subject of examination. In this paper, we discuss the use of correspondence to formally specify authentication and focus on Schneider's use of signal events in CSP to specify authentication. The purpose of this effort is to strengthen this formalism further. We develop a formal structure for these events and use them to specify a general authentication property. We then develop specifications for recentness and injectivity as sub-properties, and use them to refine authentication further. Our work is motivated by the desire to effectively analyse and express security properties in formal terms, so as to make them precise and clear.

1 Introduction

Schneider [14] uses the process algebra Communicating Sequential Processes (CSP) [6] to model cryptographic protocols. The protocol participants are modelled as independent processes, interacting with each other by exchanging messages. Different roles are modelled as different processes, for example, initiator, responder and server. The use of CSP to model this type of parallel message-passing distributed system has many advantages. The model captures the precise specifications of a cryptographic protocol and is extensible as different aspects of protocol modelling can be included. Schneider [14] takes advantage of this feature and introduces additional control events to help in the analysis. These events, called signals, are introduced in the model in terms of protocol participants and messages. Signals are used to express security properties, especially authentication, which is central to our discussion.

The purpose of this paper is to investigate further into this formalism and strengthen it. We develop the structure of signals and their use within protocol modelling, and use them in CSP trace specifications to express authentication along with further notions of recentness and injectivity.

Our work is motivated by the desire to effectively analyse and express authentication properties in formal terms, so as to make them more precise and clear [3]. Further motivation is provided by Meadows [9], who notes the significance of the specifica-

D. Feng, D. Lin, and M. Yung (Eds.): CISC 2005, LNCS 3822, pp. 63–74, 2005.
© Springer-Verlag Berlin Heidelberg 2005

tion of requirements for formal cryptographic protocol analysis, and suggests three important characteristics for expressing such requirements: they must be firstly, expressive enough to specify useful security properties, secondly, unambiguous and finally, "easy to read and write". In this paper, we present an approach that attempts to satisfy these characteristics.

The rest of this paper is organised as follows. Section 2 discusses the trace semantics in CSP in detail relevant to our usage in this paper. Section 3 discusses correspondence with respect to authentication. Section 4 presents our main contribution where we formalise a structure for signal events to specify properties such as authentication, with recentness and injectivity. The Needham-Schroeder-Lowe [8] protocol is presented, in Section 4.4, as an example of how to use these signal events. Section 5 concludes the paper.

2 CSP Trace Specifications

In this section we briefly go over the trace semantics in CSP. While we discuss this notation in detail relevant to our usage in this paper, we take for granted the reader's basic knowledge of CSP and its use by Schneider [13,14] to model security protocols; in-depth treatments of CSP are provided by Roscoe [11], Schneider [15] and Ryan, et al [12].

The trace semantics in CSP allows us to capture the sequence of events performed by a communicating process as a trace and then use the trace to model the behaviour of the process. A trace is a sequence of events tr. A sequence tr is a trace of a process P if some execution of P performs exactly that sequence of events. This is denoted as $tr \in traces(P)$, where $traces(P)$ is the set of all possible traces of P. An example of a trace could be $\langle a, b \rangle$ where event a is performed followed by event b, whereas $\langle \rangle$ is an empty trace. A concatenation of two traces tr_1 and tr_2 is written as $tr_1 \frown tr_2$, which is the sequence of events in tr_1 followed by the sequence of events in tr_2. A trace tr of the form $\langle a \rangle \frown tr'$ expresses event a followed by tr', the remainder of the trace. A prefix tr' of tr is denoted $tr' \leqslant tr$. The length #tr of a trace is the number of elements that it contains so that for example, #$\langle a,b,d \rangle = 3$. The projection operation, $tr \upharpoonright A$, is the maximal subsequence of tr, all of whose events are drawn from a set of events A.

Schneider [13] uses trace semantics to specify security properties for protocols as trace specifications. This is done by defining a predicate on traces and checking whether every trace of a process satisfies the specification. For a process P and a predicate S, P satisfies S if $S(tr)$ holds for every trace tr of P. More formally, P **sat** S $\Leftrightarrow \forall\, tr \in traces(P) \bullet S(tr)$.

3 Authentication by Correspondence

The notion of signals is inspired by Woo and Lam's [17] use of correspondence assertions to specify authentication. This section describes the notion of correspondence and its relationship with the property of authentication.

We define the notion of correspondence as, for some A and B, if a participant A initiates communication with a corresponding participant B then the correspondence property requires B to have taken part in the communication and indeed been A's correspondent. The idea is used to make explicit a participant's involvement (role) in their run of the protocol with respect to the involvement of a corresponding participant and, therefore, a basis on which the "authenticated-to-authenticator" relationship between the two participants of an authentication protocol is formally expressed.

Authentication is an important security property provided by a family of cryptographic protocols, aptly named authentication protocols. The goal of such protocols is to allow communicating parties to confirm (to varying extent) each other's identities over a public network. There are many attempts at formally defining authentication protocols and expressing their goals in various terms [1], [2], [7]. Over the years, correspondence has emerged as "the concept of choice" [4] for analysing and verifying such authentication goals.

If the goal of an authentication protocol is for A to authenticate B, then B is required to play its intended role in the protocol. While we use correspondence to express A and B's involvement in a protocol run, it merely serves as a means to establish the involvement of participants in protocol runs. For the purpose of authentication, however, we need to formally express the often subtle requirements such as a participant's engagement in the correct sequence of events, i.e. message-exchanges, along with an agreement on a set of data values and/or the number of executed runs between the participants. Consequently, proving correspondence for a protocol seldom proves the authentication goals of a protocol.

The use of correspondence to specify authentication was first attempted by Woo and Lam [20]. They describe correspondence in terms of the participants in an authentication protocol as "when an authenticating principal finishes its part of the protocol, the authenticated principal must have been present and participated in its part of the protocol". Woo and Lam [17] introduced the notion of correspondence assertions as formal instruments to express authentication, defined with respect to protocol executions. A correspondence assertion, using the operator '$\hookleftarrow$' which is read as "is preceded by", is expressed as $(B, EndRespond(A)) \hookleftarrow (A, BeginInit(B))$.

The above assertion states the requirement for a protocol with two participants A (initiator) and B (responder), where the construct $(B, EndRespond(A))$ represents a successful end of B's response with A and $(A, BeginInit(B))$ represents A's beginning of initiating a protocol run with B. The assertion effectively states that B's successful response to A has to be preceded by A's corresponding intent to run the protocol with B. These constructs can be used to specify further details of a protocol, such as any cryptographic keys or data being used or communicated, providing a very simple basis for specifying authentication goals of a protocol (See Gordon and Jeffrey's typing approach [5] as an example that makes use of correspondence assertions to specify authentication).

4 Signal Events in CSP

Schneider [14] makes use of correspondence while expressing authentication in terms of trace specifications. The style of expression and the use formal instruments is very similar to that of Woo and Lam's correspondence assertions above. For an authentication protocol, Schneider's [14] uses signal events of the form *Running* and *Commit* to express the progressive stages of the protocol on behalf of the participants. If two protocol participants A and B are running in parallel, where A is trying to authenticate B, the signal *Commit.A.B* indicates A's authentication of B and *Running.B.A* indicates B's involvement in the run with A. The authentication property is then expressed as whenever *Commit.A.B* appears in a trace *tr* of this system, the corresponding *Running.B.A* signal appears beforehand.

In this section, we introduce Schneider's use in [14] of signal events and demonstrate their use to specify authentication by correspondence. We then proceed to formalise the structure of these events and their use within the protocol modelling in CSP.

We formalise a general definition of authentication as a trace specification. We assume a *System* that comprises of a protocol with two participants A and B running in parallel

$$System = A \parallel B$$

where *tr* is some trace of the *System*, $tr \in traces(System)$. We then formalise authentication in *Definition 1*

Definition 1.

> $Authentication\_A\_to\_B(tr) = tr' \wedge \langle Commit.A.B \rangle \leqslant tr \Rightarrow \langle Running.B.A \rangle$ in tr'

To express B's authentication of A, we simply use *Commit.B.A* to indicate B's authentication of A and *Running.A.B* to indicate A's involvement in the run with B. The *System* is said to satisfy *Authentication_A_to_B* if all its traces satisfy the trace specification above

> $System$ **sat** $Authentication\_A\_to\_B \Leftrightarrow$
>
> $\forall tr \in traces(System) \bullet Authentication\_A\_to\_B(tr)$

4.1 Formalising Signal Structure

This section focuses on signals such as *Commit.B.A* and makes explicit the structures of such signals and the role each part of the signal plays.

A signal event is introduced within a participant's modelled protocol run; the information articulated by the signal is with respect to that participant at that particular stage in the protocol run. In terms of concurrent processes, a signal is strictly local to a process; so it cannot include any information that a participant has not observed or engaged in up to the point the signal is introduced. We divide a signal event into two distinct parts, *Event* and the *Data*, and formally express it as

$$Event.Data$$

The *Event* part is a member of a set of events denoted by *EVENT*

$$Event \in EVENT$$

where $\{Running, Commit, Begin\_Run\} \subseteq EVENT$

The *Running* event indicates that a participant is in a state of execution with perhaps further parameters relevant to that execution defined in the *Data* part of the signal. The *Commit* event indicates the participant's state of agreement regarding some particular execution, details of which are defined in the *Data* part. The

Begin_Run event indicates the start of a protocol run. The set *EVENT* however is not limited to these three events and more events could be added if required for the purpose of analysis. While the *Event* part of the signal signifies the type of occurrence of the signal, the *Data* part simply states the information that is strictly relevant to the occurrence.

The *Data* part of the signal consists of various types of information, such as identifiers for protocol participants, freshly-generated random numbers called nonces and cryptographic keys. The *Data* part indicates the event participants and any critical information relevant to the event and the property being expressed (for example, the nonce being used as part of the challenge and response mechanism in an authentication protocol).

We formalise a set $\mathcal{A}$ of atoms that will be part of the protocol message space and, hence, can be included in the *Data* part. Consider the set of participant identities on the network to be $\mathcal{U}$, the set of nonces used by the participants in protocol runs as $\mathcal{N}$, the set of timestamps used by all participants as $\mathcal{T}$ and a set of encryption keys used as $\mathcal{K}$. The set of all such atoms is $\mathcal{A}$, where atoms are defined as $\mathcal{A} = \mathcal{U} \cup \mathcal{N} \cup \mathcal{T} \cup \mathcal{K}$.

We divide *Data* into two distinct parts. The first part indicates the identities of possible protocol participants while the second part specifies any data such as nonces used within the protocol run, shared or distributed keys that are being used in this involvement or even identities of participants. We write the concatenation of these elements as *Data* $= u_1.u_2.d$, such that $u_1, u_2 \subseteq \mathcal{U}$ and $d \subseteq \mathcal{A}$. The structure of the entire signal can now be unfolded to *Event*.$u_1.u_2.d$

The order of elements u_1 and u_2 is such that the participant process(es) in which the *signal* is introduced is listed first, as u_1, followed by the participant(s) it is intentionally running the protocol with, as u_2. The assertion of the signal with respect to participant processes clarifies the nature of the property being specified.

We define the elements u_1 and u_2 as subsets of $\mathcal{U}$ to accommodate specifications which indicate the involvement of a group of participants. So, for example, the signal *Running.{A}.{B,C}* indicates *A*'s run with participants *B* and *C*. If only one participant is stated, we will overload the notation and write the singleton set without any brackets, such that the signal *Running.A.B* indicates *A*'s run with *B*. We do not imply any strict order for the placing of nonces (or other data) in the data part *d* of signals.

For properties where no (or only one) participant is specified, we indicate the anonymous identity by using a general symbol *u*. So, for example, *Running.B.u* indicates *B*'s run with a participant whose identity *B* is not aware of.

4.2 Signals to Specify Recentness

Recentness is an important property often discussed in the context of authentication (and key establishment) protocols. This property is critical to cryptographic protocols as the use of cryptography serves as means of providing some form of trust between protocol participants. This trust, however, may be valid for some limited time after which it may not hold. Consider the one-step protocol shown in Figure 1 for example. The protocol allows *A* to authenticate itself to *B* by just signing *B*'s identity and sending it to *B*. At a later stage, when an intruder replays the old message to *B* to convince it of *A*'s authenticity, *B* is misled into authenticating *A*. Since the protocol provides no indication on the recentness of A's run, the goal of the protocol is defeated. Due to the very nature of such a trust (subject to deception and manipulation by an intruder in an open environment), it needs to be inextricably tied with some notion of time in the sense of being previous or recent. In this section, we use signal events to specify recentness and express recentness in the context of authentication.

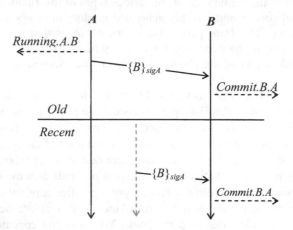

Fig. 1. The problem of recentness

For a protocol to satisfy the property of recentness, we assume that it already satisfies *Definition 1*, that is to say, for every *Commit* event that occurs a corresponding *Running* event precedes it. We consider the entire protocol sequence from the perspective of the current run (a complete single run as intended by the protocol designer) and any signals that are modelled are only meaningful for this run; any *Running* or *Commit* events, for example, occur in this current run. We consider a run to be previous to a current run if it has started before the current run has started. It may or may not have finished before the current has started (so they may overlap).

We introduce an extra signal event, *Begin_Run*, to differentiate between the previous and current run of a protocol. The data part of this signal could include the names of the participants such as A, B, etc. and any other data values used during this run such as a nonce or a timestamp, which acts as a recentness indicator. The signal is used to mark the start of a current run and is the very first event to appear in the trace of this run; any other signal or communication event occurs following this event. The event is (usually) placed in the initiator's run since the very first protocol message naturally appears in an initiator's run.

Now, any *Commit* events that are modelled as part of this protocol are preceded by the corresponding *Running* events. The property of recentness requires that if a participant A commits to a protocol run with a participant B, then B has taken part in the run recently. Since A commits to a current run of the protocol, it requires that B has taken part in the current run as well. While the current run has only started after the *Begin_Run* event, the recentness property requires B's *Running* event to be preceded by *Begin_Run*. We build on the general definition of authentication in *Definition 1* and formalise recent authentication in *Definition 2* below

Definition 2.

$$Recent\_Authentication\_A\_to\_B(tr) = Authentication\_A\_to\_B(tr)$$
$$\wedge \; tr_0 \,^\frown\, \langle Running.B.A \rangle \leqslant tr \Rightarrow \langle Begin\_Run.A.B \rangle \; in \; tr_0$$

In the definition above, the corresponding *Running.B.A* event precedes every *Commit.A.B* event and a corresponding *Begin_Run.A.B* event precedes every *Running.B.A* event, indicating that the *Running.B.A* event occurs after the start of the current run.

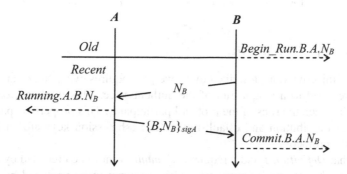

Fig. 2. Modelling recentness using the *Begin_Run* event

To demonstrate our modelling of recentness, consider the simple protocol shown in Figure 2 above. The protocol lets *B* send a fresh nonce N_B to *A*, who responds by signing the nonce along with *B*'s identity and sending it back to *B*. *B* is assured that *A* has only responded after *B* has sent N_B out to *A*. We place a *Begin_Run.B.A.N_B* signal to indicate the start of this run by *B*. For *B*, it acts as a recentness indicator for *A*'s response, as *A* could not have possibly replied before this event.

Note that *Definition 2* does not restrict *Commit.A.B* to appear only once for every *Running.B.A* prior to it. So it is possible for *A* to authenticate *B* more than once while *B* has only run the protocol once. We deal with this issue in the following section. The property provided by *Definition 2*, however, is still useful. Due to the use of *Begin_Run.A.B*, if *A* does authenticate *B* more than once, *A* is still assured that *B* has run the protocol recently. This models precisely the nature of authentication provided by many protocols that use timestamps to serve as a measure of recentness. These protocols are designed so that an authenticator accepts a message (containing a timestamp) within an acceptable window (length of time during which the message is deemed to be recent). If so, then it is possible that an authenticating message from the authenticatee is replayed to the authenticator several times during the acceptable window. As soon as the window expires, however, the authenticator declines any such message to be recent; an example of this is available in [16].

Our approach to recentness is comparable to Lowe's earlier work [7] on specifying recentness. We focus on a single protocol run and use a signal event to mark the start of a recent run. Lowe, on the other hand, uses a unique signal *Begin.ds* [7] to mark the start of every run between two participants, where *ds* indicates the involved participants such as *A* and *B*, along with an extra field for a *run identifier*. The *run identifier* (assigned α, β, etc.) is used to associate the corresponding *Begin* and *Commit* signals with every run. Lowe uses this signal to specify the runs of the involved participants such that they ought to overlap during execution. If the runs of the participants satisfy this overlapping then the recentness of a participant's run is verified. This approach of overlapping runs however may not always hold true; a participant may finish its run of the protocol while the other participant may not even have started by that stage, which is possible in protocols that use trusted servers. Lowe gets around this by suggesting that a server's run may overlap both participants' run, one followed by another; there may still be limitations where more than one server is involved as Lowe highlights [7].

4.3 Signals to Specify Injectivity

The notion of injectivity, as described by Lowe [7], requires every run of an authenticator to correspond to a unique run of the authenticatee. This implies a one-to-one relationship between the runs of the protocol participants. This property is particularly useful for key distribution and establishment as fresh session keys are attributed to each run of the protocol.

Observe that *Definition 1* and *2* require a *Commit* event to be preceded by a *Running* event but they do not require every *Commit* event to be preceded by a unique *Running* event. Consequently, we may have more than one *Commit* event for a single *Running* event. An authenticatee may run the protocol only once but the authenticator may authenticate that run more than once.

To specify injectivity in trace specifications, we require each *Commit* signal to be preceded by a corresponding *Running* signal. The number of *Running* signals is strictly equal to or more than the number of corresponding *Commit* signals. We build further on *Definition 1* and formalise injective authentication in *Definition 3* below

Definition 3.

$$Injective\_Authentication\_A\_to\_B(tr) = Authentication\_A\_to\_B(tr)$$
$$\wedge \ \#(tr\!\restriction Running.B.A) \ \geqslant \ \#(tr\!\restriction Commit.A.B)$$

The above property ensures that every time A authenticates B, B has taken part in a run with A. Observe that the converse is not true, that is to say, B may have attempted to run the protocol with A more times than A has successfully authenticated B.

4.4 Placing Signals

Constructing and placing a signal within a protocol model clearly depends on the nature of the relationship that is being analysed. We use the Needham-Schroeder-Lowe (NSL) protocol as an example to demonstrate the use of signals. It is a good example as it provides both recentness and injectivity along with authentication to both participants.

The NSL protocol was originally presented by Needham and Schroeder [10]. It was later found to have a flaw by Lowe [8] who suggested an amendment, hence the name. The amended protocol is informally specified in Figure 3 below

$$
\begin{array}{llll}
(1) & A \rightarrow B & : & \{A, N_A\}_{pkB} \\
(2) & B \rightarrow A & : & \{N_A, N_B, B\}_{pkA} \\
(3) & A \rightarrow B & : & \{N_B\}_{pkB}
\end{array}
$$

Fig. 3. Needham-Schroeder-Lowe protocol

The goal of the protocol is to authenticate A to B and B to A. A initiates the protocol by sending to B its own identity concatenated with a nonce N_A and encrypted with B's public key. Once B receives the message, it is aware of A and its nonce N_A. B responds by generating a nonce N_B, concatenating it with N_A and its own identity, encrypting it under A's public key and sending it back to A. Once A finds the nonce N_A in B's response, it successfully authenticates B. A finally sends back B's nonce N_B encrypted under B's public key. Upon receipt of this, B successfully authenticates A. The complete execution of the protocol is shown in Figure 4 below.

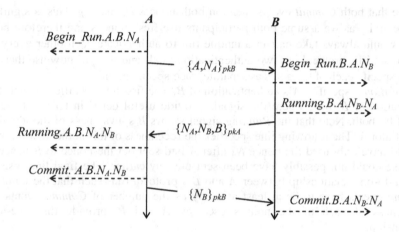

Fig. 4. Complete execution of the NSL protocol

We have placed the signal events in the protocol specification in Figure 4. We have used six signal events, each of which we will explain in detail below in the order as they appear.

Begin_Run.A.B.N_A. The signal indicates the initiation of the protocol on behalf of A with B. We use nonce N_A to identify this particular run on A's behalf and also to act as a recentness indicator for A's authentication of B.

Begin_Run.B.A.N_B. The signal indicates the start of the response from B to A, after it receives the first message from A. The nonce N_B is not only mentioned as a unique identifier for this run of B, but also as a recentness indicator for B's authentication of A.

Running.B.A.N_B.N_A. This signal is important for A's authentication of B. At this stage, B is in possession of all the information that it needs to respond to A: A's identity, A's nonce N_A and B's own nonce N_B. We put N_B before N_A in terms of order, only to show that it is generated by B and therefore more relevant to it. We do the same for N_A in A's signals.

Running.A.B.N_A.N_B. This signal corresponds to the *Running* signal in B's run. It is only after receiving B's response to the first message that A reaches a stage where it has all the information it needs for this protocol, particularly B's nonce N_B.

Commit.A.B.N_A.N_B. B's response also allows A to authenticate B: this signal indicates the successful authentication event. A is assured that B has received its nonce N_A and responded. A can also guarantee B's choice of the nonce N_B for this run.

Commit.B.A.N_B.N_A. The protocol run is completed by A sending the last message to B. Once B receives the last message, it is assured that A is in possession of the nonce N_B and has agreed upon it, allowing B to authenticate A: this signal indicates the successful authentication event and corresponds to A's *Commit* event.

Note that both *Commit* events mention both nonces N_A and N_B. This is significant for injectivity as we assume both participants use fresh nonces and therefore both A and B would always take part in a unique run to authenticate each other every time they do so. The protocol has two authentication goals and we will now use these signals to specify each of the goals as separate trace specifications.

Definition 4 specifies A's authentication of B. The first line specifies the actual authentication of B to A, where the signals provide useful detail in terms of the data agreed by both. Note that the *Running* signal shows B's awareness of the identity of the initiator A. The following line specifies the recentness of this authentication where B could have only used the nonce N_A after A had sent out the nonce to B hence, B's response could not possibly have been sent out any earlier. The final line insists on the one-to-one relationship between A and B's protocol runs such that the number of *Running* events have to be at least as many as the number of *Commit* events – the uniqueness of each of the nonces used by A and B, provide this one-to-one relationship.

Definition 4.

$NSL\_A\_authenticate\_B(tr) =$

$$tr' \wedge \langle Commit.A.B.N_A.N_B \rangle \leqslant tr \Rightarrow \langle Running.B.A.N_B.N_A \rangle \text{ in } tr'$$

$$\wedge\ tr_0 \wedge \langle Running.B.A.N_B.N_A \rangle \leqslant tr \Rightarrow \langle Begin\_Run.A.B.N_A \rangle \text{ in } tr_0$$

$$\wedge\ \#(tr \restriction Running.B.A.N_B.N_A) \geqslant \#(tr \restriction Commit.A.B.N_A.N_B)$$

Definition 5 specifies B's authentication of A. The first line specifies the actual authentication of A to B, followed by the recentness and injectivity conditions. This property is entirely symmetrical to A's authentication of B.

Definition 5.

$NSL\_B\_authenticate\_A(tr) =$

$$tr' \wedge \langle Commit.B.A.N_B.N_A \rangle \leqslant tr \Rightarrow \langle Running.A.B.N_A.N_B \rangle \text{ in } tr'$$

$$\wedge\ tr_0 \wedge \langle Running.A.B.N_A.N_B \rangle \leqslant tr \Rightarrow \langle Begin\_Run.B.A.N_B \rangle \text{ in } tr_0$$

$$\wedge\ \#(tr \upharpoonright Running.A.B.N_A.N_B) \geqslant \#(tr \upharpoonright Commit.B.A.N_B.N_A)$$

The NSL protocol is a good example where authentication is achieved in a strong form, that is, it provides recentness and injectivity to both participants. Note that the use of a fresh nonce by each participant to provide these properties inherently provides agreement on data (nonces) as well, making this protocol feasible for key derivation.

In terms of authentication goals, observe how signals demonstrate the progressive nature of such a protocol and makes explicit how the protocol steps contribute to its goals.

5 Conclusion

In this paper we have developed the notion of signal events, introduced in [14], to make their structure clearer and, at the same time, flexible to accommodate finer notions of authentication in protocols.

We have demonstrated the usefulness of signal events as formal instruments to express the different flavours of authentication, including recentness and injectivity and, used the NSL protocol as an example. A further example of the use of signal events to specify authentication properties for a basic version of Kerberos can be found in [16].

It is interesting to see how formal attempts at defining authentication bring to the surface the subtle variations that exist between related concepts of authentication. We have attempted to highlight some of these diversities using signal events. The main contribution of this paper, however, is the development of a formal approach that is capable of embracing variations of authentication and makes our understanding of the property clearer, while satisfying the three characteristics of expressiveness, unambiguity and simplicity identified by Meadows [9] for such an approach (as discussed in Section 1).

References

1. Gollmann, D.: What do we mean by entity authentication? In Symposium on Security and Privacy, IEEE Computer Society, (1996) 46-54
2. Gollmann, D.: On the Verification of Cryptographic Protocols - A Tale of Two Committees. In Proceedings of the Workshop on Secure Architectures and Information Flow, ENTCS Volume 32 (2000)
3. Gollmann, D.: Analysing Security Protocols. In A.E. Abdullah, P. Ryan and S. Schneider, editors, Formal Aspects of Security, LNCS 2629, Springer-Verlag (2002), 71-80
4. Gollmann, D.: Authentication by Correspondence. IEEE Journal on Selected Areas in Communication, Special Issue on Formal Methods for Security, Volume 21, No. 1 (2003)
5. Gordon, A. D., Jeffrey, A.: Typing correspondence assertions for communication protocols. In Mathematical Foundations of Programming Semantics 17, ENTCS Volume 45, Elsevier (2001)
6. Hoare, C.A.R.: Communicating Sequential Processes. Prentice-Hall International (1985)

7. Lowe, G.: A hierarchy of authentication specifications. In 10th Computer Security Foundations Workshop, IEEE Computer Society Press (1995), 31-43
8. Lowe, G.: An attack on the Needham-Schroeder public key protocol. Information Processing Letters, Volume 56, (1995), 131-133
9. Meadows, C.: What makes a cryptographic protocol secure? The evolution of requirements specification in formal cryptographic protocol analysis. In P. Degano, editor, 12th European Symposium on Programming, Springer-Verlag LNCS 2618 (2003), 10-21
10. Needham, R., Schroeder, M.: Using encryption for Authentication in Large Networks. Communications of the ACM, Volume 21, No. 12, (1978), 993-999
11. Roscoe, A.W.: The Theory and Practice of Concurrency. Prentice-Hall International (1997)
12. Ryan, P., Schneider, S., Goldsmith, M., Lowe, G., Roscoe, B.: Modelling and Analysis of Security Protocols. Addison-Wesley (2001)
13. Schneider, S.: Security Properties and CSP. IEEE Symposium Research in Security and Privacy (1996)
14. Schneider, S.: Verifying Authentication Protocols in CSP. IEEE Transactions on Software Engineering, Volume 24, No. 9 (1998) 741-758
15. Schneider, S.: Concurrent and Real-time Systems: the CSP Approach. Addison-Wesley London (1999)
16. Shaikh, S., Bush, V., Schneider, S.: Kerberos – Specifying authenticity properties using signal events. In Proceedings of the Indonesia Cryptology and Information Security Conference, (2005) 87-93
17. Woo, T. Y. C., Lam, S.S.: A semantic model for Authentication Protocols. In IEEE Symposium on Security and Privacy (1993) 178-194

Modeling RFID Security

Xiaolan Zhang[1] and Brian King[2,*]

[1] University of Illinois
zhang_xiaolan@ieee.org
[2] Indiana Univ. Purdue Univ at Indianapolis
briking@iupui.edu

Abstract. Many security and privacy protocols for RFID systems have been proposed [7] [12] [6] [11]. In most cases these protocols are evaluated in terms of security based on some model. Here we describe several of the security requirements that are needed in an RFID system and model these requirements. They include privacy of tag data, privacy of ownership, integrity of tag data, and availability of tag identity. We also construct less restrictive versions of many of these models to reflect the security needed for some less security-intensive RFID applications and compare them to existing models.

1 Introduction

Security models play an important role, for they provide tools which allows us to measure the security offered by protocols. Often models are developed as an immediate response to evaluate a protocol. The construction of the model could actually borrow parameters and ideas from the protocol that inspired the development of the model. Clearly security would benefit if there was a disconnect between the development of models and the development of protocols. Further, protocols are often developed for specific applications and may require several security services, thus requiring several security models. Consequently, independent development of a set of security models is essential. More important, RFID systems are utilized for economical reasons, the cost of the tags plays an important role in why the tags can be pervasively implemented. These tags have limited resources, one may be intending to use them as low-cost solutions for a low-cost problems. On the other hand, an RFID system may be used in high-security problems like anti-counterfeiting, pharmaceutical integrity, etc. Many of these applications require a high-level of security. The point is that the application often will dictate the security level. So the best models would allow us to adjust the security parameters to fit our needs. Further, an RFID system has a specific set of security vulnerabilities and so the models should address these vulnerabilities. There has already been a discussion concerning the technology for future RFID tags [14], some of these tags will provide greater functionality.

---

* This work has been supported by a grant provided by The Lily Endowment and the Indiana University Pervasive Technology Labs.

D. Feng, D. Lin, and M. Yung (Eds.): CISC 2005, LNCS 3822, pp. 75–90, 2005.

Such tags will have greater range and slightly more resources. If manufacturing costs can be contained then we may find that these tags will be utilized within applications that are more mainstream, applications that will affect the consumer (bearer of the tags). Such applications will be much more sensitive and will require greater security services such as confidentiality, integrity and authentication and it will be even more important to protect the privacy of the consumer. In this paper we describe a set of security requirements that are needed in an RFID system and model these requirements. They include privacy of tag data, privacy of ownership, integrity of tag data, and availability of tag identity.

2   Security Requirements

Generally, current and future RFID applications require one or more of the following of services which we have grouped into three categories: remote identification (tracking/tracing), authentication (anti-counterfeit) and data collection (sensor). Three security service groups are described as follows:

Remote Identification. It refers to systems for which when a reader interrogates a tag for the identity and property information of the item this tag is associated with. The reader wants to remotely identify the item by querying the tag. Examples include: inventory management, distribution, in-store detection, automatic check out, stream-line monitor, Smart House, port inspection, etc.

Authentication. This is one of the basic tracking functions but applications in this category emphasize the need for authenticity of the identity that the RFID tag reports. It refers to systems where the reader interrogates a tag for verifying the information of the item. The reader may already know the information but may not be sure about its authenticity. Examples of applications include RFID-enabled banknotes, pharmaceutical products, ID cards, passports, certificates.

Data Collection. It refers to systems for which when a reader interrogates a tag, updated data is collected from the item. In this category, the reader already knows the item and previous data but wants to monitor the change in the data. Examples include product quality control, advertising notification, security alarm, sensors.

Applications, as discussed above, indicate some of the functional goals that use RFID technology. However, simply integrating RFID technology into some of these applications will not ensure that the needed services are provided adequately, because many RFID systems operate in unknown or untrusted environments, for which adversaries motivated by different purposes may attack the system. Some attacks may cause tags to return wrong information to readers. Some will block readers from hearing tags. Further, attackers may attempt to hide within a group of authorized users in an attempt to eavesdrop private information. Privacy is an issue that could hinder the wider use of RFID. Privacy problems could arise in RFID applications involving banknotes, medicines, cloths, etc. where tags are permanently activated. In such situations if common items are tagged and actively queried in the mainstream, those parties that possess the tagged items will have their privacy compromised. To ensure a wider use of RFID technology, security must be included into any design of applications. In some systems one must make sure the communication between tags and readers is confidential and authenticated, in other systems the information in provided by the tags needs to be authenticated and in other systems the access (read or write) to the RFID systems, including tags, readers and other related equipment should be classified against unauthorized parties. The goals of security, privacy, and performance are contradictory in many ways. The requirements for each application are different and it is hard to find a one-fits-all security model for all RFID systems. In some specific applications, the level of security that is required may need to be as strong as the security required in a networked computing system. How to implement RFID services together with necessary levels of security when designing a protocol becomes a complex problem.

A significant amount of research has focused on the security protocols for various RFID applications. Juels proposed an simple password scheme against cloning tag in [8]. Juels also provided a pseudonym throttling authentication protocol in [7]. Ranasinghe et al. [13] discussed the use of cryptography to solve RFID problems. Feldhofer [6] [5] proposed to use symmetric key encryption to provide authentication solutions. Ohkubo [12] suggested a hash based protocol and Avoine [2] improved its scalability. The Blocking scheme in [10] and kill tag method [1] are other approaches. Some secure RFID solutions for future applications have been developed: [9] proposed a security model and a protocol for RFID enabled Euro banknotes, [4] presented a model of the lifecycle of RFID tags used in the retail sector and a solution through zero-knowledge protocols, and [11] focused on the security in RFID library systems.

With many RFID protocols already designed, a question arises is how to evaluate those protocols. i.e. whether those protocols provide exactly the security as required. To solve this problem, we should first model RFID systems and define those security services for them. Many of the above authors provided a model to evaluate their protocol. The problem is that the protocol tends to be based for a specific application and the model often reflect this.

3   Formal Definitions

In this section, we describe mathematical models for several security services affected by or needing RFID technology. Our security models are constructed with access groups (authorization) in mind. Adversaries are considered as parties (readers) performing operations that they are not authorized for. Such operations can be: interleaving RF communication, querying a tag (impersonating an authorized reader), responding a reader (impersonating a valid tag), tampering a tag physically or performing DOS attacks by any means. Interleaving and querying is modeled as RF signals an adversary obtained from listening RF signals in communication. Adversaries may initiate a session or intercept a session. We consider cloning, disguising or tampering tag problem as an integrity problem. Integrity also deals with the problem for readers to authenticate tags. In our model, we required that an authorized reader will be able to determine the authenticity of tags with a high probability. For an authorized party, the tag should always be available to be identified.

In an applied RFID system, since a tag's resources are limited, it is unfair and impractical to require tags to defend against adversaries with unlimited resources. In our RFID security models, security requirements are conditioned on tag resources and an assumed bound on the adversarial resources as well. We assume adversaries have limited accesses to a tag and computational powers, which are represented by parameters that differ from applications. Our definitions are used to model an RFID system requiring security based on a resource constrained adversary.

We now consider a model for a general remote identification system. We use the term *item* to represent a physical object that will be remotely identified. It can be money, medicine or cloths. It is the authentic individual information, such as identification number, name, origin, property, distribution pedigree, etc. It is conceptual and physically unalterable. A Toshiba laptop M45-S355 is an example. Even if someone alters the manufacturer identification on its label or tag to be an IBM laptop T43, the item is still a Toshiba laptop M45-S355. Therefore one's goal is to track the authentic identity of an item. *Tag* is the concept used to denote a labeling, it provides information about the item associating with it in form of remote signals. *Identity* is the remote identification information for which the queried tag responds with. *Reader* is a device that receives some/none/all information transmitted from a tag. When a reader queries a tag, the information revealed is the identity but not the item. *Authorized party* is a group of people or organizations that are granted certain permissions to access the identity of an item from remote access. Since any individual in a party accesses a tag through a reader, the reader represents and implements the authorization of its user. For integrity, some data can only be modified by authorized parties, and parties authorized for some tags should be able to recognize the authenticity of this data.

Channel is the source that a tag uses to send information. There are two information channels: public and secret. The two channels are designed to deliver data such that when both channels of information are collected by an authorized party, it provides the desired authenticated identity. The information that the channels provide will vary depending on the authorization group (authorized or unauthorized) that the reader belongs to. Informally, we characterize this as a "view" of signals. Given the same channel of the tag at the same time, readers in different authorized groups may have different views of it. We make no formal requirement as to how information is delivered via the secret channel, it could take many forms, for example it could take the form of a ciphertext, or it could take the form of a physical communication that is not available without secret key. In addition to the two remote RF channels of information, the reader could obtain additional information from a third channel when communicating with the tag. For example, the location where the signal is received. The content of this information has a level of uncertainty and varies depending on the situational-aspects of the communication. We define the *environmental channel* as the channel that delivers side information about the tagged item and we will assume that environmental channel itself reveals little information that one can use for identification. Remember that our focus is to construct models to analyze security protocols that are used over remote communication. If the environmental channel alone has provided enough information for identification, it would be meaningless to analyze the security of the protocol as used over the two remote channels. Although the environmental channel exists and can provide identification in real world applications, we carefully construct our models so they do not criticize protocols (during their evaluation) which only yield information where the source comes solely from the environmental channel. The mathematical model is probabilistic. Some variables are defined as follows:

I is a random variable of the identity of a tagged item. It represents any or all of the data pertaining to the tagged item (representation depends on the application).

Θ is a random variable of the information received from an access to the tagged item. It is a tuple of information from three channels $< U, V, W >$. U is the variable representing the remote information received from a public channel. V represents remote information received from a secret channel. The environment channel W is usually omitted if it is not explicitly discussed.

$\mathcal{I}$ the set of all possible tagged items

$\mathcal{AR}_i$ the set of parties authorized to obtain the true identity information of item $i \in \mathcal{I}$

For the identification security model, a suitable level of integrity is assumed. Therefore tag data is authenticated and trusted to represent the identity of the physical item. There is no need to distinguish the terms "item" and "identity".

We say that a protocol is able to identify an item from the tag if the protocol provides identification of the tag from the remote information. Ideally, if a protocol provides the reader the ability to recognize the item with a probability near 1 given the correct remote information and near 0 given the incorrect information, we would consider this identification protocol reliable and accurate. In our definition, we use $\theta =< u, v >$ to represent the correct information of item i, where u belongs to variable U in tuple Θ and v to V. We use θ' to represent an incorrect information of i. The first equation defines the availability of identification and the second defines the correctness in the ideal situation. It is modeled after perfect secrecy.

Definition 1 (Perfect Identification of tag Identity (PII)). *A protocol satisfies PII has the property that:*

1. *a party is able to identify an item i given its correct tag information,*
   $$\Pr(I = i | \Theta = \theta) = 1 \ and$$
2. *a party cannot identify i given the incorrect tag information θ',*
   $$\Pr(I = i | \Theta = \theta') = 0$$

In real world applications, perfect identification will most likely not exist because several factors affect the probability. Hardware failure, inconsistent power supplies, or transmission errors may cause a reader to accept or reject a tag incorrectly. The probability in the first equation defines the tolerance of tag acceptance errors and the one in the second equation defines the tolerance of tag rejection errors. For RFID applications, the tolerance in the model can be adjusted to fit different requirements. This will be discussed in Section 4. On the other hand, the perfect identification model is not sufficient to describe many applications. Security conditions should be added. Perfect identification is the first step for constructing the other definitions that are needed. One of them is *authorized identification*. In remote tracking systems, the security services are provided for authorized parties. Intuitively, it means two things: one is that only a certain group of authorized readers are able to remotely recognize the identity of an item correctly. Another is that unauthorized readers are given so little information about the item that they cannot distinguish it from others remotely. Obviously an authorized reader should be able to identify an item with perfect identification. But given an unauthorized reader, the remote information should not provide any information that improves the chance of identification better than guessing the identity of the item. You can always guess an item based on your knowledge but the remote information should not provide any help. The second part of the definition of perfect authorized identification is required so that an unauthorized reader cannot identify an item better than guessing even when provided a history. The "history" is a finite collection of pairs of information and results obtained from prior remote accesses[1] of a party. For simplicity, we assume that the membership of a reader does not change in one history. A more complex model of various membership history will be discussed in future work.

$\eta(\cdot)$ is a set representing the history information for a party. It consists of finite number of tuples $\{< \Theta(\cdot), J(\cdot) >\}^*$. $J(\cdot)$ represents the result obtained from access the channel $\Theta(\cdot)$ [2]. It is the set of data of the identification information and maintains that $J(\cdot) \in \mathcal{I}$.

A secure protocol will depend on history. If an adversary has unbounded accesses to RFID tags, it may be impractical to expect that the protocol is impervious to attacks. The following definition consists of two parts. The first part states that authorized parties possess perfect identification. It requires availability and correctness for identification. The second states that the remote information does not improve the identification of tag identification for an unauthorized party. It defines the adversary advantage for identification, i.e. the likelihood

---

[1] The access may be such that another party is actually making the query and this party is merely eavesdropping.

[2] In the history, $\Theta(\cdot)$ will be represented using all three channels because past results may be determined together with the information from the environmental channel as well. Although we do not have assumption that W channel contains no identification information over past accesses. But we have that assumption thus do not consider that channel for the current access.

that one can identify the item with remote information will be the same as without the remote information. Otherwise, the party is able to identify it. The history here is $\eta(\cdot) = \{< \theta_1(\cdot), j_1(\cdot) >, < \theta_2(\cdot), j_2(\cdot) >, \ldots, < \theta_k(\cdot), j_k(\cdot) >\}$. We write $|\eta(\cdot)| = k$ to be the size of history. The size of history is a security parameter. We should point out that our Definition 2 only considers adversaries whose access history is bounded by κ (here κ is a nonnegative integer). That is, if a given protocol allows an unauthorized adversary to be able to identify the tag identification using a history of length κ or less, then that protocol violates our model. However, if the number of history accesses exceeds κ, then the model is indifferent to whether such adversaries should be able to identify the tag identification.

Definition 2 (Authorized PII with κ-history (κAPII)). *A protocol satisfies κAPII provided that:*

1. If α is an authorized party of item i, then α has perfect identification of i.

$$\Pr(I = i | \Theta = \theta, \alpha \in \mathcal{AR}_i) = 1, \text{ and } \Pr(I = i | \Theta = \theta', \alpha \in \mathcal{AR}_i) = 0$$

2. for any party α which is NOT an authorized party of i, whenever α's access history $\eta(\alpha)$ satisfies that $|\eta(\alpha)| \leq \kappa$, then α does not have better chance to identify the item i given any θ'' that is not a correct signal of any tag that party α is authorized for,

$$\Pr(I = i | \Theta = \theta'', \eta(\alpha), \alpha \notin \mathcal{AR}_i) = \Pr(I = i | \eta(\alpha), \alpha \notin \mathcal{AR}_i)$$

Equation 2., from the above definition, implies that the probability that party α can identify i will not improve given the current RF channel access. Furthermore this equation addresses the ability of α to use prior accesses to mine information. We know that history may help identification, since history includes the knowledge you possess. Basically, a protocol cannot control the source of previous knowledge. Because history includes the environmental channel, the result (identification) may be obtained through social engineering. The model is constructed so that it will evaluate the security of a protocol based on the present channel not how history will help identification.

In the case of $\kappa = 0$, an adversary is assumed to memorize no previous tag accesses. Observe that a statically encrypted ciphertext transmitted from a tag will be secure enough to prevent tracking in the sense that the adversary cannot compare any previous ciphertexts to the current one. Under this model, even if the ciphertext does not change, the encryption will appear like a one-time-pad to an adversary. In another model, if we set $\kappa > 0$, then a protocol secure in this model must withstand an adversary who is allowed to have κ recordable previous accesses. We must make sure that any encryption algorithm we choose to encrypt the tag should be secure against chosen ciphertext attack of κ ciphertext-plaintext pairs, or an adversary will have a chance to break the encryption after acquired a history of κ length. Usually, the history size in the model should be set to be higher, if the mobility of tags is lower where a reader has more chances to access the same tag. The history size can be safely lowered, if tags have much greater mobility than a reader, since the reader is less likely to encounter the same tag again. The point is that if the application requires stronger privacy of tag identification, then one should increase the κ parameter.

In many applications, we are not only concerned with the information concerning a single item that an unauthorized party can gather from an access, but we are also concerned with whether this adversarial party can distinguish two items without necessarily identifying their identities. Remember if an authorized party can distinguish item i from others, then it is a serious violation of privacy. Indistinguishability is an important security property when we analyze applications. It is derived directly from the definition of authorized identification.

Definition 3 (Indistinguishability of tag Identity with κ-history (κIN DI)). *A protocol satisfies $\kappa INDI$ provided that: for any party α whose access history $\eta(\alpha)$ satisfies that $|\eta(\alpha)| \leq \kappa$, if α is an unauthorized party for items i and i', then α cannot distinguish item i from i'.*

$$\forall i' \in \mathcal{I}, \Pr(I = i'|\Theta = \theta, \eta(\alpha), \alpha \notin \mathcal{AR}_i \cup \mathcal{AR}_{i'})$$
$$= \Pr(I = i'|\eta(\alpha), \alpha \notin \mathcal{AR}_i \cup \mathcal{AR}_{i'})$$

Theorem 1. *If a protocol satisfies $\kappa APII$ then it satisfies $\kappa INDI$*

In an application, some side information is itself enough to violate bearer privacy. Attacks on the confidentiality of bearers could be unauthorized tracking of either an bearer or transaction between two bearers (depending on if the bearer of the tag has just changed). To understand the problem of tracking, one should first consider the identification of a bearer.

O is a random variable as the bearer of item i.

$\mathcal{O}$ is a set of all bearers or owners.

A bearer's information may be available to the adversary in two possible ways.

I. One way is that the bearer information is included as part of the tag identification information. Remember that identification information i, as we have defined earlier, is a set of all data pertaining to a tagged item. Thus, in this case, the security/privacy of the bearer has already incorporated into the analysis of the perfect identification of tag information. For this case, the bearer o of i should satisfy the following equation as a precondition which implies the incorporation of bearer's information in the identification information.

$$\Pr(I = i) \leq \Pr(O = o)$$

II. The second way is such that the bearer is not included as part of the tag identification. Thus, the bearer's information is obtained from RF channels together with the environmental channel. It is possible that the bearer may be derived totally from environmental channel as a social engineering attack. Since the security model will be used to measure the effectiveness of a protocol, the model should reflect the violation of the privacy of a bearer due to the use of both RF and environmental channels. However, a protocol cannot prevent a stand alone successful social engineering attack. Thus in this second case, we assume the environmental channel only provides partial information about the bearer but not all. The party is able to get information from channels $\theta =< u, v, w >$ (this includes the environmental channel w, on condition that the environmental channel only provides partial information about the bearers). To this end

$$\forall o \in \mathcal{O}, 0 \leq \Pr(O = o | \Theta =< w >, \eta(\alpha), \alpha \notin \mathcal{AR}_i) < 1.$$

Observe our use of $\Theta =< w >$, this implies that the only channel used is the environmental channel, i.e. one is only being provided information from the environmental channel.

Definition 4 (API of tag Bearers with κ-history (κAPIB)). *A protocol satisfies $\kappa APIB$ provided that:*

1. all parties α authorized for item i have perfect identification of bearers o.

$$\Pr(O = o | \Theta = \theta, \alpha \in \mathcal{AR}_i) = 1 \ and \ \Pr(O = o | \Theta = \theta', \alpha \in \mathcal{AR}_i) = 0$$

2. all parties α NOT authorized for item i whose access history $\eta(\alpha)$ satisfies that $|\eta(\alpha)| \leq \kappa$, should not have better chance to identify the item i, given any $\theta'' =< u'', v'', w'' >$ that is not a correct information of any tag the party authorized for,

$$\Pr(O = o | \Theta = \theta'', \eta(\alpha), \alpha \notin \mathcal{AR}_i)$$
$$= \Pr(O = o | \Theta =< w'' >, \eta(\alpha), \alpha \notin \mathcal{AR}_i)$$

One can define Indistinguishability of Tag Bearers with κ-history (κINDB), much like we defined Indistinguishability of Tag Identity with κ-history (κINDI). Due to limited space, we omit the formal definition.

Tags normally used today are read-only but many of today's tags have write capabilities. We should consider the integrity whenever a protocol requires modifications on a tag like in privacy protecting anti-counterfeiting protocol Squealing Euros [9]. Modifications on the tag is a modification on the tag data. *Tag data* is the raw format of information stored at the physical tag memory.

Terms defined above are represented more formally in our model as:

$\mathcal{AW}_i$ the set of parties authorized to modify some data of tagged item i.
T_i is tag data of item i.
$\mathcal{T}_i$ is the set of all possible tag data T_i.
B_i is an operation on tag data T_i. $\mathcal{B}_i$ is set of operations on a tag data B_i.

$\mathcal{AUTH}$ is set of all authentic tags, tags whose tag data can be authenticated. Any protocol that modifies the data on a tag should only allow the modification if it is performed in an authorized manner by an appropriate modification function. This is a function that whenever it is utilized, guarantees that the data that maintains its integrity. Modification is a function that uses three inputs: current tag data, operation and authorization. Tag data is the data in the tag before the modification. Operation defines how the tag data is to be modified. Authorization is the authorized group of the party who wishes to perform the modification.

Definition 5 (Modification Function). *The modification function f_M is defined as the mapping $f_M : \mathcal{T}_i \times \mathcal{B}_i \times \mathcal{AW}_i \rightarrow \mathcal{T}_i$.*

If the input data and authorization are valid for the requested operation, then the tag data can be modified in prescribed way. If it is not, then the modification function does not allow any change. Note that authorization here determines whether a party has the write permission on this tag.

A tag T_i may experience many modifications during the course of its life. We denote $M_{T_i} = < m_1, m_2, \ldots, m_n >$ as the sequence of modification history states of T_i. m_x is the state before the xth modification. A state $m_x = (t_x, b_x, \alpha_x)$ reflects the three inputs of the modification function where $t_x \in T_i$ and $b_x \in \mathcal{B}_i$, and α_x is the party attempting to modify the tag. Modifying a tag results in a transfer from the current tag state to the tag data of the next one. One should interpret that modifying a tag by using the modification function is a valid modification and it will not lose integrity. Any physical modification of the tag, which is not supported by the modification function is interpreted as unauthentic, and characterize the tag as "dirty". But we allow operations that clean dirty tags, much like an accountant can rectify an arithmetic error in the books. Informally, a tag is authentic given that: there exists a sequence of states (tag data, operation and party authorization) starting from an authentic original state, such that the modification function, successively applied, results in an "clean" state.

Definition 6 (Authentic tag data). *Given tag data T of modification history M_T, T is authentic if there exists a subsequence $< m_{x_1}, m_{x_2}, \ldots, m_{x_l} > \in M_T$ where $1 \le x_1 < \cdots < x_l = n$ and $f_m(m_{x_j}) = t_{x_{j+1}}$ (notice that in the definition of authentic, the subsequence must conclude with the current state of the tag, i.e. $x_l = n$). We say $T \in \mathcal{AUTH}$.*

For any application that allows modification, there are two possible criterions concerning integrity to consider: first, how well does it protect against unauthorized modification and second, does it allow an authorized party to detect unauthorized modification. Most remote identification systems can be attacked physically and so it is difficult to maintain the first criteria. We focus our definition of integrity on the second criteria. That is, we our definition of integrity is based on whether the protocol supports that any authorized party α of a tagged item i will be able to distinguish an authentic tag from a non-authentic tag given correct remote signals $\theta = < u, v >$.

Definition 7 (Perfect Integrity of tag Data (PID)). *A protocol that satisfies PID provided that:*

1. an authorized party α is able to recognize an authentic tag,

$$\Pr(party\ \alpha\ recognizes\ T\ as\ authentic\ |\Theta = \theta, T \in \mathcal{AUTH}, \alpha \in \mathcal{AR}_T) = 1$$

and

2. an authorized party α is able to recognize a fake tag,

$$\Pr(party\ \alpha\ recognizes\ T\ as\ authentic\ |\Theta = \theta, T \notin \mathcal{AUTH}, \alpha \in \mathcal{AR}_T) = 0$$

The actual definition of what it means for "a party to recognize a tag is authentic" is dependent on the given protocol. For a greater discussion we refer the reader to [18].

4   Security Model for RFID Systems

RFID system imposes additional constraints on tracking. An RFID tag has physical limitations and application constraints. Some of these limitations will enhance the security but others will undermine it. It is not fair to require perfect authorized identification and integrity for all RFID systems. One needs to consider the RFID limitations, and incorporate the limitations within the definition of security services for RFID. First we define:

Tag's access limitation: $\phi_{Ta}(\cdot) =< D_T, B_T(\cdot) >$
  D_T the reader's range (meters).
  $B_T(\cdot)$ resource bound for readers. It is a tuple, one for readability $R_b(\cdot)$, one for writability $W_b(\cdot)$ and another for computational power $C_b(\cdot)$ (number of gates). Readability is the maximal number of inquiries that a party is allowed to utilize on a tag. Writability is the maximal size of memory that a party is allowed to make to one tag. $\forall \alpha \in \mathcal{AR}_T, R_b(\alpha) = \infty, C_b(\alpha) = \infty, \forall \alpha \in \mathcal{AW}_T, W_b(\alpha) =$ modifiable size for this party, $C_b(\alpha) = \infty$. Otherwise $R_b(\alpha), W_b(\alpha), C_b(\alpha)$ are some fixed value.
Tag's resource: $\phi_{Ts} =< P_T, C_T, M_T >$.
  P_T the physical condition (boolean). '0' means that it is physically unremoveable from the host item. '1' means removeable.
  C_T the computational power limitation (number of gates).
  M_T the memory limitation (number of bits).

For most tags, D_T will be a few meters (often this limitation D_T is considered to be a security mechanism that prevents eavesdropping). P_T is assumed to be 0. C_T is often limited to 400-4000 of gates (this hardly meets the requirements to allow one to use symmetric key encryption). M_T is around 1Kbits.

Given a fixed tag, readers may access the tag in various conditions. We define reader's access limitation as a tuple of distance and resources to one tag. $\phi_r(\cdot) =< D, B(\cdot) >$. Our definition is satisfied whenever the reader's access limitation is smaller than tag's. For authorized readers, their B will be always smaller than B_T. However, for unauthorized readers, their B is some set of resources that are mostly affected by money and time available to an adversary. Due to the cost-limitation of tags, it is almost impossible to design a protocol resistant to adversaries with unlimited resource.

In a real-world application, many other factors may affect the ability to recognize an item correctly, such as encryption errors, communication errors, and hardware errors. However, if these errors occur with a small probability, then a final decision would be correct according to an acceptable error rate. Define δ be the acceptable error tolerance for an authorized party to accept an incorrect tag. Define ϵ be the rejection error tolerance for an authorized party to reject a correct tag. A system could still be considered secure, if the maximum advantage an unauthorized party can gain to identify a tag is acceptably small. Define γ to be the maximal adversary advantage that an unauthorized party is allowed to obtain to identify a tag correctly. δ, ϵ, γ are small nonnegative numbers between

0 and 1 (including the endpoints), and the choice of these parameters depend on the application. Our previous security models are now modified to incorporate those parameters.

Suppose the tag of an item i has limitations $\phi_{Ta}(\cdot) = <D_T, B_T(\cdot)>, \phi_{Ts} = <P_T, C_T, M_T>$. The party has a history $\eta(\alpha) = \{<\theta_1(\alpha), j_1(\alpha)>, <\theta_2(\alpha), j_2(\alpha)>, \ldots, <\theta_k(\alpha), j_k(\alpha)>\}$.

Definition 8 $((\delta, \epsilon, \gamma, \kappa)$ RFID APII). *An RFID protocol satisfies $(\delta, \epsilon, \gamma, \kappa)$ APII provided that:*

1. an authorized party α of item i has perfect identification.

$$\Pr(I = i | \Theta = \theta \, \phi_r(\alpha) \leq \phi_{Ta}(\alpha), \phi_{Ts}, \alpha \in \mathcal{AR}_i) \geq 1 - \delta$$
$$\Pr(I = i | \Theta = \theta', \phi_r(\alpha) \leq \phi_{Ta}(\alpha), \phi_{Ts}, \alpha \in \mathcal{AR}_i) \leq \epsilon$$

2. for all parties α not authorized for item i whose access history $\eta(\alpha)$ satisfies that $|\eta(\alpha)| \leq \kappa$, α does not have better chance to identify the item i, given θ'' that is not a correct signal of any tag that party α is authorized for,

$$\Pr(I = i | \Theta = \theta'', \eta(\alpha), \phi_r(\alpha) \leq \phi_{Ta}(\alpha), \phi_{Ts}, \alpha \notin \mathcal{AR}_i)$$
$$\leq \Pr(I = i | \eta(\alpha), \alpha \notin \mathcal{AR}_i) + \gamma$$

Similarly, indistinguishability of tag identity in RFID can be introduced, due to space limitations we omit the definition.

We now consider the privacy of the bearer.

Definition 9 $((\delta, \epsilon, \gamma, \kappa)$ RFID APIB). *An RFID protocol satisfies $(\delta, \epsilon, \gamma, \kappa)$ APIB provided that:*

1. an authorized party α of item i has perfect identification of bearers o.

$$\Pr(O = o | \Theta = \theta, \phi_r(\alpha) \leq \phi_{Ta}(\alpha), \phi_{Ts}, \alpha \in \mathcal{AR}_i) \geq 1 - \delta$$
$$\Pr(O = o | \Theta = \theta', \phi_r(\alpha) \leq \phi_{Ta}(\alpha), \phi_{Ts}, \alpha \in \mathcal{AR}_i) \leq \epsilon$$

2. for all parties α not authorized for item i whose access history $\eta(\alpha)$ satisfies that $|\eta(\alpha)| \leq \kappa$, α does not have better chance to identify the bearer o, given $\theta'' = <u'', v'', w''>$ that is not a correct information of any tag that party α is authorized for,

$$\Pr(O = o | \Theta = \theta'', \eta(\alpha), \phi_r(\alpha) \leq \phi_{Ta}(\alpha), \phi_{Ts}, \alpha \notin \mathcal{AR}_i)$$
$$\leq \Pr(O = o | \Theta = <w''>, \eta(\alpha), \alpha \notin \mathcal{AR}_i) + \gamma$$

Errors are usually caused by hardware failures, weak power supply, or poor transmission. Low quality hardware of tags or readers, high mobility during communication, electromagnetic noisy environment can all increase the error rate. According to [16], tag read or write error rate may range from 0% in a controlled environment to exceeding 5% in a non-controlled environment. On the other hand, some protocols are probabilistic. i.e. They derive a correct result with a certain probability. Error tolerance should vary depending on applications. δ determines the error tolerance for tag acceptance. If a system is very restrictive in accepting tags correctly, then δ should be set smaller in the model. ϵ is the error tolerance for rejection. If a system requires that rejection only occurs when their is clear evidence of improper tag information then ϵ would be smaller. γ is the security bound for adversary advantage. If a system requires higher privacy, γ should be reduced. The parameters in our model should be chosen independently for each system and becomes a guideline that helps determine the quality of hardware, communication environment and algorithm used in protocols.

The following example demonstrates how to apply the apply parameter configuration within our models to assess security of protocols. We assume, within this example, that the hardware, software and all communications are 100% reliable, since our immediate focus is to assess the security protocol only.

Example 1 (Password protection of tag data by authorized parties).

Suppose that the tag data is password protected. The problem is that the password must be transmitted over the RF channel. There are several possible ways to handle this. (i) First suppose that the transmission is made over an unencrypted channel. (ii) Second, suppose we encrypt the channel using a fixed channel key, which is delivered securely to all authorized parties. (iii) Third, suppose that during manufacturing, the manufacturer has prestored k keys, and that the order of the keys order has been set. When the tag is queried with a encrypted password, it will use the current key and then will toggle the next key to be set as the current key.

Clearly Example 1-(i) does not satisfy $(0,0,0,0)$APII since the password is transmitted in the clear. This is a common mechanism that is used today, the argument for its use is that the D_T distance in ϕ_{Ta}, is limited, thus eavesdropping is limited. For example, suppose that an application has been analyzed, and due to the mobility of the tags, authorized readers and the distance D_T, the protocol designers have modeled the probability that an unauthorized reader will be able to get within D_T communication distance between an authorized reader and tag to be q_1. Then the protocol satisfies $(0, 0, q_1, 0, 0)$APII. Example 1-(ii) will violate $(0,0,0,0)$APIB since the key is fixed. Consequently the encrypted password forms a static ciphertext that allows the tracing of the bearer. The analysis for Example 1-(iii) is slightly more complex than the above. If one assumes that an adversary has stored κ accesses where $\kappa \geq k$ and one assumes that the accesses are such that each of the prestored keys weree equally likely then clearly this protocol would violate $(0,0,0,\kappa)$APIB. For the case where κ satisfies $0 < \kappa < k$, and again one assumes that each of the k keys were equally likely to be accessed as the current key, then clearly we would still violate $(0,0,0,\kappa)$APIB. This protocol would only satisfy the security model of $(0,0,\gamma,\kappa)$APIB where γ is suitably large enough.

More examples are provided in the extended version of this paper [19].

5   Previous Work and Comparison

Juels developed models for authentication security and privacy in [7]. Ohkubo et al [12] proposed two security requirements for RFID systems: indistinguishability and forward security. Avoine defined existential and universal untraceability under five kinds of oracle access modes [3] and derived logical implications among them. In some ways Juels' models, Ohkubo's models, Avoine's models and our models are very similar, but they are different in many aspects like building blocks, adversary assumptions and security services provided. We will briefly compare and discuss the merits of each work in this section.

Juels' model focuses on defining the advantage of adversaries in tag authentication and privacy attacks. Similarly, Ohkubo's model also defines the advantage of adversaries in indistinguishability and forward security. Their work all focus on finding the adversary advantage of various security problems. However, definitions in our model cover availability, integrity and confidentiality services that are needed in a RFID protocol. The security goal in Juels', Ohkubo's and Avoine's models are to reduce the advantage of the adversaries to be as low as possible. But our model suggests setting security parameters for specific applications. Moreover, Juels' and Ohkubo's models were constructed closely to their protocols [7] and [12]), respectively. In Juels' models, some parameters in the models are borrowed from his protocol. In contrast, we constructed our models directly from analyzing security services required in a remote identification system (RFID system is a instance) rather than from any current protocol. Avoine's model is constructed from a broader picture of untraceability as well. His model has been applied on many existing protocols from a neutral point of view. Adversary assumptions in four models are similar. Access to RF channels and tag memory are both considered. But Juels', Ohkubo's and Avoine's models do not include the integrity attacks on modifiable tags nor DOS attacks, which are included in our model. Also our model considers multiple authorization party accesses and the relationship between adversaries and tags are more complex. A more detailed comparision will be provided in the extended version of this paper [19].

6   Conclusion

We have discussed the necessary security requirements that current and future RFID systems will need. The security requirements for RFID include: availability of identity information, integrity of tag data, privacy of tag information and privacy of ownership. In order to evaluate whether an RFID application protocol provides the necessary security requirements one measures the protocol against the necessary model. In this work we have developed security models for each of the necessary requirements. The models that we have developed included models for identification, integrity, and perfect identification for tag identity and ownership. Satisfying these models provide services that include confidentiality, integrity and availability. In addition to constructing strong versions of these models, we have constructed versions of many of these models which have less-restrictive requirements, and these models have been developed with security parameters that can be adjusted to fit the application. These models may be more practical for the security within an RFID systems, which use limited resource tags that are low-cost in an application where security needs are not as great. Future work will focus on developing a less restrictive model for integrity that can be used in RFID applications whose integrity requirements are not as strict.

References

1. 860MHzC930MHz Class I Radio Frequency Identification Tag: radio frequency and logical communication interface specification. Technical report, Auto-ID Center (2002)
2. Avoine, G., Oechslin, P.: A scalable and provably secure hash based RFID protocol. In: The 2nd IEEE International Workshop on Pervasive Computing and Communication Security – PerSec 2005 (To appear), Kauai Island, Hawaii, USA, IEEE Computer Society Press (2005)
3. Avoine, G.: Adversarial model for radio frequency identification. Cryptology ePrint Archive, Report 2005/098, http://eprint.iacr.org/ (2005)
4. Engberg, S., Harning, M., Damsgaard Jensen, C.: Zero-knowledge device authentication: Privacy and security enhanced RFID preserving business value and consumer convenience. In: The Second Annual Conference on Privacy, Security and Trust – PST, New Brunswick, Canada (2004)
5. Feldhofer, M., Dominikus, S., Wolkerstorfer, J.: Strong authentication for RFID systems using the AES algorithm. In Joye, M., Quisquater, J.J., eds.: Workshop on Cryptographic Hardware and Embedded Systems – CHES 2004. Volume 3156 of Lecture Notes in Computer Science., Boston, Massachusetts, USA, IACR, Springer-Verlag (2004) 357–370
6. Feldhofer, M.: A proposal for authentication protocol in a security layer for RFID smart tags (2003)
7. Juels, A.: Minimalist cryptography for low-cost RFID tags. In: The Fourth International Conference on Security in Communication Networks – SCN 2004. Lecture Notes in Computer Science, Amalfi, Italia, Springer-Verlag (2004)
8. Juels, A.: Strengthening EPC tags against cloning. Manuscript (2004)
9. Juels, A., Pappu., R.: Squealing euros: Privacy-protection in RFID-enabled banknotes. In: Financial Cryptography, Springer-Verlag (2003) 103–121
10. Juels, A., Rivest, R.L., Szydlo, M.: The blocker tag: selective blocking of RFID tags for consumer privacy. In: Proceedings of the 10th ACM conference on Computer and communication security, ACM Press (2003) 103–111
11. Molnar, D., Wagner, D.: Privacy and security in library RFID: Issues, practices, and architectures. In Pfitzmann, B., Liu, P., eds.: Conference on Computer and Communications Security – ACM CCS, Washington, DC, USA, ACM, ACM Press (2004) 210–219
12. Ohkubo, M., Suzuki, K., Kinoshita, S.: Cryptographic approach to "privacy-friendly" tags. In: RFID Privacy Workshop, MIT, MA, USA (2003)
13. Ranasinghe, D., Engels, D., Cole, P.: Low-cost RFID systems: Confronting security and privacy. In: Auto-ID Labs Research Workshop, Zurich, Switzerland (2004)

14. Sarma, S.E., Engels, D.W.: On the future of RFID tags and protocols. Technical Report MIT-AUTOID-TR-018, AUTO-ID Center (2003)
15. Sarma, S.E., Weis, S.A., Engels, D.W.: RFID systems and security and privacy implications. In: Workshop on Cryptographic Hardware and Embedded Systems, Lecture Notes in Computer Science (2002) 454–470
16. Sutton, G.D.: Radio frequency identification - basics for manufacturing. (1993)
17. Yoshida, J.: Euro bank notes to embed RFID chips by 2005. EE Times (2001)
18. Zhang, X., King, B.: Integrity improvements to an RFID privacy protection protocol for anti-counterfeiting. Information Security Conference. Singapore 2005, 474-481.
19. Zhang, X., King, B.: "Modeling RFID security (extended version)" `http://www.engr.iupui.edu/ briking/papers/model.pdf`

Enforcing Email Addresses Privacy Using Tokens

Roman Schlegel and Serge Vaudenay

EPFL, CH-1015 Lausanne, Switzerland
http://lasecwww.epfl.ch

Abstract. We propose a system which allows users to monitor how their email addresses are used and how they spread over the Internet. This protects the privacy of the user and can reduce the SPAM phenomenon. Our solution does not require changes to the email infrastructure, can be set up by the end user on an individual basis and is compatible with any email client as long as emails are centralized on a server (e.g. an IMAP server). Nevertheless, it requires that people use email messaging quite differently.

1 Towards a Fair Competition Between Humans and Robots

Anyone can send an email to a given address (which is just a simple string) at basically no cost. Those strings used to be systematically exchanged until robots collected them automatically in every public electronic discussion forum and used them for spamming. That is why today "poor" human users have to face armies of well trained robots which are launched by associations of hackers and spammers. This situation is obviously unfair.

Current counter-spam solutions are based on one of the following techniques.

- Deterministic filters using well configured rules.
- Filters based on artificial intelligence or evolutionary processes (which learn to recognize regular email senders).
- Collaborative filtering, e.g. by polling or Bayesian methods.
- Charging policies to render sending emails less cheap.
- More interactive protocols to prove that an email sender is a real sender.

The last two approaches require changes to the current email infrastructure. The first one is obviously limited and the second one leads to false positive and false negative alerts. The third one only works in the case where spam is sent to a large number of email users within the same community. All approaches are eventually defeated by spammers.

On a separate subject, web page addresses — URLs — are widely exchanged, anyone can access a URL for free, but the HTTP server (a kind of a robot itself) can monitor which (human) client is requesting which URL by using cookies. Indeed, cookies are a privacy threat to legitimate (human) web surfers. So it

D. Feng, D. Lin, and M. Yung (Eds.): CISC 2005, LNCS 3822, pp. 91–100, 2005.

seems that machines have powerful audit tools at their disposal which could be used by humans as well. Actually, cookie-like strings could be a solution to strengthen the privacy of email addresses. Indeed, by appending a string (that we actually call a *token*), we can monitor how email addresses spread.

Here is a typical scenario. A user Alice would like to receive emails from another user Bob, so she gives him her email address together with a private token. Incoming emails using this token and not coming from Bob's address can simply be ignored. If a spammer manages to intercept the token and spoof emails as coming from Bob, Alice can easily deactivate the token. Another case is when Bob abuses his privilege to send emails to Alice by sending unsolicited emails. Alice can deactivate the token as well.

In this paper we present an application called XToken[1] which is a first step towards implementing the solution described above. In Section 3 we explain the various possible tokens. Section 4 tells how an email sender should first get a token by using a token distributor. Then Section 5 presents a signature-based alternative which works provided that all users use it. Finally Section 6 proposes an agenda on how to deploy this solution and discusses how spammers may recycle their activities.

2   Previous Works

In recent years a lot of different proposals have been made to defeat spam but none of them proved to be a panacea so far. In addition to that not all proposals have yet been implemented on a larger scale. These include for example (non-exhaustive list):

Filtering: Well-defined deterministic rules or AI techniques can be used to identify unsolicited emails.

Domainkeys: This system uses public key cryptography to sign all messages sent from a specific domain. The recipient can verify the signature by looking up the public key using a DNS query. This system does not prevent abuse of the email system but it makes tracking easier. Domainkeys was submitted as a draft to the IETF [7].

Greylisting: Another technique which has been introduced recently with some success is greylisting. The destination mail server will reject a message for the first 5 minutes. The originating mail server will retry after about 15 minutes and will succeed the second time. The idea behind this technique is that a spam software will not normally try to deliver a message more than once but will move to the next address after a failed attempt. Greylisting was first proposed in 2003 [8].

Micro-payments: This method tries to address the fact which makes spam possible, namely the problem that the cost of sending millions of messages

---

[1] The application is distributed under the GNU General Public License and can be downloaded from http://xtoken.sourceforge.net. A complete manual is available as part of the distribution.

is negligible with the current, widespread broadband technology. Micropayments would charge a small fee for every message sent, making it economically infeasible to send spam. Alternatively the price can be paid in terms of computation resources, meaning the sender has to demonstrate that some energy was spent in order to send the email [4].

Challenge-response: The so-called challenge-response mechanisms are a technique which has been known for quite some time though not necessarily in relation to spam. Applied to email this means that in order to be able to send a message to a recipient, a challenge has to be solved first. Because this normally requires the exchange of three messages (request, challenge, response + email) the concept of pre-challenges has been devised which allows to send messages without requesting a challenge first. The idea is that an already publicly known challenge (which changes periodically) has to be solved to be able to send a message. This reduces the number of required messages between recipient and sender to one like in normal email [6].

SPA: A concept proposed by John Ioannidis from AT&T Labs called SPA (Single-Purpose Address) [9] is in fact quite similar to the concept proposed in this paper. The idea behind SPA is to encode a security policy into an email address. This policy describes the acceptable use of the address and is enforced by the receiver of the message (because the sender cannot be trusted). For a comparison of SPA and XToken see section 7.

Another often mentioned technology in relation to spam is *captcha* (Completely Automated Public Turing Test to Tell Computer and Humans Apart) [3]. It is not a technology to counter spam *per se* but nowadays it is often used to prevent bots from accessing certain information or pages. The idea of captchas is that they present a problem which is easy to solve for a human but very difficult for a computer program. Captchas exist in different forms: they can contain a transformed text on a special background, show different images together with a semantic challenge or they can be based on audio.

Typical examples are web email providers which require the user to solve a captcha when opening a new account to prevent spam bots from using the service.

Captchas in themselves do not solve the problem of spam, but they can be used as one part of a wider system as it will be explained below.

3   Fighting Spam Using XToken

3.1   The Token Concept

XToken uses little pieces of information (so-called tokens) to distinguish legitimate from unsolicited emails. Each user has a collection of tokens which he can distribute to his friends and associates. They can include these tokens when sending emails and thus mark them as legitimate (referred to as "valid" hereafter).

The user can choose whether to create one token per person or send the same token to several people. This is obviously a trade-off: One token per person permits fine-grained control over who can send messages while increasing the time needed for managing the tokens. To give one token to a group of people reduces the management overhead but limits the resolution of control to the whole group.

Technically a token is a combination of identifiers which references a token stored on the local computer of the recipient. The length of a token is usually between 6 and 9 bytes although to be able to transmit the token using the email system it is encoded in base64 which increases the length to at least 8 bytes. The base64 representation is then enclosed in '$' signs and added to a field in the email message. Possible fields include the `To:`, `CC:` and the subject header. A typical token looks as follows:

> `$DAdb12wD$`

The easiest way to use a token received from a friend or associate is by including it in the email address stored in the address book. An entry would then look like this:

> `John Doe $DAdb12wD$ <john.doe@somedomain.net>`

When writing an email message and selecting the address from the address book the token will automatically be included in the message. Temporary tokens are best included in the subject line like this:

> `Subject: Re: Your letter $DAdb12wD$`

3.2   Token Types

XToken uses various types of tokens, each of which offers additional functionality. At the moment there exist four types but new types can be added easily.

SimpleToken: This token can be bound to a specific email address. If the token is received in an email message it is only valid if the sender address matches the address specified when creating the token. It is also possible to use the token without a bound address, in that case the token is always valid, independent of who uses it.

DateToken: As the name implies, this token has a date associated and is considered valid only until the specified date. If the token is used after that date it is considered invalid.

CounterToken: This type of token has an associated counter which is initialized to an arbitrary number when creating the token. Each time the token is received in an email message the counter is decremented until it reaches zero. Once the counter has reached zero the token is no longer considered to be valid.

DateCounterToken: The last token is a combination of a DateToken and a CounterToken and contains a date and a counter. The token can be used in two ways: Either it is valid until the specific date *or* until the counter reaches zero or it can be valid until the specific date *and* until the counter reaches zero.

It is possible to add almost arbitrary functionality by adding new token types. One idea could be to create a token which, if contained in an email, causes this email to be sent to a mobile phone by text message. XToken already supports for example sorting based on tokens, meaning that an email containing a specific token gets automatically moved to a pre-defined IMAP folder.

Tokens can be revoked at any time, rendering them invalid immediately. This is useful if a token has been compromised or should no longer be valid for some other reason.

The XToken interface provides a dialog to manage the token database. The dialog can be used to create, revoke and delete tokens and to display additional information about existing tokens.

3.3   Using Tokens to Process Incoming Emails

XToken can be configured to treat incoming email messages in a multitude of ways depending on whether a message contains a valid token (or a valid signature, see Section 5) or not. The possible actions include:

Move Valid Messages: In this mode XToken will move all messages containing a valid token to a defined folder, separating them from unsolicited messages.

Move Invalid Messages: When using this mode all invalid messages (i.e. without a valid token) will be moved to a defined folder leaving only legitimate messages in the inbox.

Flag Valid Messages: Instead of moving valid or invalid messages this mode leaves all messages in the inbox but flags valid messages with the standard IMAP flag \Flagged. Normally mail applications emphasize flagged messages somehow.

Concerning the technical implementation XToken behaves like a normal IMAP client which can be run in parallel with any other IMAP client. It monitors one or several IMAP mailboxes for incoming messages and handles them according to the configuration (see Figure 1). As a consequence XToken need not interact with the user's favorite email client: it cleans the mailbox directly on the IMAP server.

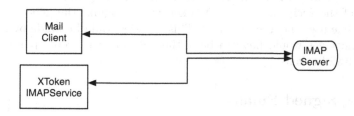

Fig. 1. XToken monitors one or several IMAP mailboxes in parallel with existing mail clients

4   Token Distributor

When using tokens one of the difficulties is the distribution. Clearly it is infeasible to send a token to a person who might potentially send an email at some time in the future. It is therefore necessary to implement mechanisms which allow a person with a legitimate interest to obtain at least a temporary token. It is important to note that all mechanisms described below introduce an additional hurdle when making first contact with a recipient. Possible mechanisms to distribute tokens include:

- SMTP-based distributor: If someone wants to send a message he first sends a specially crafted email to the recipient. An application (presumably XToken) will intercept the message and automatically generate a response with a one-time token (a token which can be used exactly once). The sender can then include this token in the real message. This method is moderately resistant against spam bots as it requires a valid return email address. When using this method it probably makes sense to limit the number of tokens which are generated for a specific email address in a given period of time (e.g. 1 token per hour or per day etc.).
- Web-based distributor: Instead of sending an email message the sender has to fill in a web form (e.g. his name and email address) and an email containing a one-time token will then be sent to the specified address. This mechanism has the same resistance against spam bots as the distributor based on SMTP. A rate-limiting feature would be useful here as well.
- Web-based distributor with captcha: To eliminate the need of sending email messages one could imagine creating a script which directly generates and displays a one-time token but is hidden behind a captcha. Thus only a human can access the script and consequently the token. Unless some mechanism is implemented to prevent the same person from accessing the script again and again an attacker could generate an arbitrary number of tokens although at considerable cost as it would have to be done manually.
- Combination of SMTP-based distributor and captcha: A captcha is sent by email on request and the solution to the captcha is a one-time token. This is basically a normal SMTP-based distributor but with an added layer of security to prevent spam bots from using the distributor.

The disadvantage of the two web-based distributors is that a second mechanism has to be implemented which transfers a copy of the generated tokens to the computer of the recipient so that XToken will recognize the generated tokens when someone uses them in an email. This transfer could be made by email but then the messages would have to be authenticated to prevent spammers from injecting invalid tokens.

5   Using Signed Emails

XToken also implements signatures as another mechanism to mark messages as valid (if used consequently signatures completely replace tokens). While signatures need more effort for the initial set-up, once they are configured they require less intervention than tokens. An important prerequisite though is that both sender and recipient use XToken. On the other hand, when using tokens it suffices if the recipient uses XToken.

The initial set-up when using signatures is more complicated for the following reason: In order for XToken to be able to intercept and sign outgoing messages they have to pass through XToken. This is achieved by using a local SMTP proxy (see also below). The additional effort required by the user is that he has to reconfigure his mail client so that outgoing emails pass through the local proxy. He then also has to configure XToken so it knows to which SMTP server it has to forward the signed emails. Although this reconfiguration is not particularly difficult it does require some basic networking knowledge.

The idea of using signatures in XToken has some similarities with domainkeys mentioned earlier. The main difference is that domainkeys work on whole domains while XToken signatures work on individual email addresses. Furthermore, while domainkeys have to be implemented by the system administrator of a specific domain, XToken signatures can be used by any end-user without being dependent on his ISP.

A signature is calculated over several header fields to make it unique for each message. It is made with the private-key of the sender and then added to the message together with the public-key which allows to verify the signature. For performance reasons the body of the message is not signed. While it is true that including the body when signing would increase the robustness of the signature, the current scheme only needs to retrieve the headers from the server (for the signature verification) which is a very efficient operation on an IMAP server. If the body also had to be retrieved this could significantly degrade the performance of the application, especially if a message contains attachments.

When a user receives a signed message XToken automatically retrieves the public-key from the message and compares it to a list of locally stored public-keys. If the key is not known the user is asked whether he wants to trust it and the key is then added to the local list. If the user decides to trust the key any subsequent message signed with this key will be considered valid.

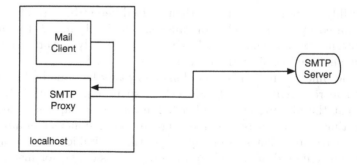

Fig. 2. Outgoing messages are signed using a SMTP proxy

If used consequently, signatures completely automate the process of sending and receiving legitimate messages. The user only has to intervene when a message with a new public-key is received.

The signature algorithm used in XToken is ECDSA (elliptic curve digital signature algorithm) [1, 2] because of the compactness of the keys and the generated signatures, but any other standard signature scheme can be added.

Figure 2 illustrates how outgoing messages are signed using an SMTP proxy running on the local computer.

6   A Proposed Deployment Agenda

In this section we propose an agenda to change the way a user uses email messaging. Eventually, only solicited emails will arrive in his/her mailbox, but unexpected emails from human beings can still be received at the additional cost of human involvement.

1. The user distributes tokens and uses the flag action (legitimate emails get flagged). He/she observes how XToken behaves.
2. As the user begins to trust XToken, invalid messages are moved to quarantine in a specific folder. The user still regularly checks the folder but he/she is no longer distracted by incoming spam.
3. The quarantine folder is less and less regularly checked. Emails are automatically answered and removed after a while. The reply includes a free one-time token.
4. More and more users adopt XToken or equivalent applications. They are all aware of the new healthy way to use email. They are familiar with token distributors and understand they have to get a token first to send an email.
5. Users now automatically sign email headers and tokens are less and less used, except for online services.
6. Invalid messages are automatically answered and removed as soon as they arrive. The answer includes an URL explaining how to reach the user and a link to an online one-time token distributor.

At this stage, spammers can continue their activities in the two following ways:

- sniff (valid) email headers and use them with different bodies. This attack is quite limited by 1- the number of valid emails circulating, 2- the ability to sniff Internet traffic. These attacks can be completely thwarted by signing the full email and not just the headers.
- break one-time token distributors. This can easily be done by humans, but the human requirement is a bottleneck in spamming activities. Let us assume that the distributor is hidden behind a secure captcha. Clearly, the human time of spammers is not enough to get a sufficient number of tokens to make sure that sending spam is still profitable. An alternate way is to use distributed human computation [5]. Assuming, for instance, that spammers create a free pornography web site, they can easily make robots

which collect captchas and have a front screen asking the visitor to solve one of the collected captchas for the robot before entering the web site. A way to thwart this attack consists of using captchas *and* tokens sent by email. If it became harder and harder for spammers to get sufficient valid email addresses, the front screen would require the email address of the visitor. Clearly, this would be dissuasive for the visitor. Should a visitor nevertheless give his email address then human victims of spam will at least have humans to blame for it so the issue will be brought back on a fairer ground.

7   Comparison XToken and SPA

SPA and XToken share the following features:

- Email addresses are augmented by adding additional information
- Modified addresses are given to friends and associates to enforce an acceptable use policy
- Addresses can be made to expire

Despite these similarities there are some significant differences:

- SPAs store all additional information in the email address itself. XToken only stores an identifier and keeps a local database with the complete information (in the case of tokens). Both methods have advantages and disadvantages. The method how the additional information is stored in an email address also differs.
- XToken is completely independent of the email infrastructure while SPAs as described in [9] rely on some specific infrastructure.

While the aim of SPAs and XToken is the same they differ in the approach. SPAs, at least partially, require a special infrastructure whereas an explicit goal of XToken was to make it infrastructure-independent so that it is entirely controlled by the end-user.

When used with signatures XToken also requires less intervention by the user than SPA. There is no need to create new modified addresses and send them to possible associates. The only effort required by the recipient is to occasionally accept or reject a public key.

8   Conclusion

We proposed a way to limit the spam phenomenon which needs neither any corporate involvement nor any changes to the email infrastructure: users can freely install this solution and use it. Our solution requires human email users to expend some additional effort for sending an email, at least the first time they use the email address. A key challenge is to make the token management interface as user-friendly as possible. Depending on whether users will accept this new way of using emails, our solution provides an easy way to limit spam at the user level. Hopefully, when most users adopt healthy ways to use emails, the activities of spammers will become less and less lucrative and can be eradicated throughout the Internet. We invite people to test the first implementation of this approach and welcome further development.

References

1. ANSI X9.62. Public Key Cryptography for the Financial Services Industry: The Elliptic Curve Digital Signature Algorithm (ECDSA). American National Standard Institute. American Bankers Association. 1998.
2. Digital Signature Standard (DSS). *Federal Information Processing Standards* publication #186-2. U.S. Department of Commerce, National Institute of Standards and Technology, 2000.
3. L. von Ahn, M. Blum, N.J. Hopper, J. Langford. CAPTCHA: Using Hard AI Problems for Security. In *Advances in Cryptology EUROCRYPT'03*, Warsaw, Poland, Lecture Notes in Computer Science 2656, pp. 294–311, Springer-Verlag, 2003.
4. C. Dwork, A. Goldberg, M. Naor. On Memory-Bound Functions for Fighting Spam. In *Advances in Cryptology CRYPTO'03*, Santa Barbara, California, U.S.A., Lecture Notes in Computer Science 2729, pp. 426–444, Springer-Verlag, 2003.
5. C. Gentry, Z. Ramzan, S. Stubblebine. Secure Distributed Human Computation. In *Proceedings 6th ACM Conference on Electronic Commerce (EC-2005)*, Vancouver, Canada, pp. 155–164, ACM Press, 2005.
6. R. Roman, J. Zhou, J. Lopez. Protection against Spam using Pre-Challenges. In *Security and Privacy in the Age of Ubiquitous Computing IFIP TC11 20th International Information Security Conference (SEC'05)*, Chiba, Japan, pp. 281–293, Springer-Verlag, 2005.
7. M. Delany (Editor). Domain-based Email Authentication Using Public-Keys Advertised in the DNS (DomainKeys). IETF Draft, 2005
8. E. Harris. The Next Step in the Spam Control War: Greylisting. http://www.greylisting.org/articles/whitepaper.shtml, 2003
9. J. Ioannidis. Fighting Spam by Encapsulating Policy in Email Addresses, Symposium of Network and Distributed Systems Security (NDSS) 2003, San Diego, California, February 2003

Efficient Authentication of Electronic Document Workflow

Yongdong Wu

Information Security Lab,
Institute for Infocomm Research, Singapore
wydong@i2r.a-star.edu.sg

Abstract. In the history of document circulation, many participants may annotate and sign on the document so as to produce a final authentic document. This circulation process requires that a later participant can know the document circulation history, verify all the previous annotations, but can not modify them. To be applicable to devices of limited resources, the document processing approach should be efficient in terms of computational cost and network overhead. This paper extends an aggregate signature scheme so as to combine many signatures into one no matter which kind of circulating route (sequential, parallel, or hybrid) is. Since the proposal enables to manage the documents easily, it is useful and practical in office automation applications.

1 Introduction

In a conventional office, there are many documents (e.g., student examination form, medical leave application forms, purchase forms, ...), which will be circulated daily. A general document process workflow includes following steps:

(1) An employee prepares a document such as medical claim form.
(2) The document is circulated to a senior staff or reviewer.
(3) The senior staff verifies the authenticity of the hand-written signature on the document.
(4) The senior staff reviews the document, comments and signs on the document where applicable, then passes it on to a next reviewer.
(5) Repeat steps (2)-(4), until a completed document is produced. If there are several independent reviewers, several final documents will be generated and stored.

On any stage, a reviewer can read all former comments and verify their hand-written signatures or seals, but can not modify them. An electronic document workflow system should play the same role in a modern paperless office. A simple solution can be as follows: the originator creates a document, signs on it with his private key, and submits the signed document to a reviewer. A reviewer verifies the document, appends his comment at the end of the received document, signs the new document and transmits the new document along with all the signatures.

D. Feng, D. Lin, and M. Yung (Eds.): CISC 2005, LNCS 3822, pp. 101–112, 2005.

In this naïve method, the number of signatures is the same as the number of reviewers, hence the signature verification cost and communication overhead are not satisfactory.

To monitor or authenticate the activities of the participants, Atluri *et al.* [1]-[3] managed the workflow based on some policies. Yuichi *et al.* [4] recorded the circulation history so as to regulate the behaviors. Printz [5] described two complementary tools for the support of cooperative processes: electronic circulation folders and shared workspaces. Circulation folders support structured work processes, shared workspaces provide a working environment for less structured processes. Both approaches are complementary and their combined usage enables telecooperation and cooperative knowledge management.

Mori *et al.* [6] provided a method of editing and circulating documents sequentially with attest patterns such as signets. The data structure of each electronic document is assembled in a data structure that separates the document content data from the attest patterns. If any reviewing person requests to amend the electronic document to which the attest patterns have been added, a display of only the content data of the above electronic document is presented to the reviewing person. The reviewing person then amends the content data of the document, the prior approval of the document is removed and thus amended electronic document is re-circulated. This re-circulation process increases the network traffic and reviewer's load. Mori's approach is not applicable to the situation that the predecessor should not read the successor's comments. For example, an employee may not know the employer's evaluation.

Hiroshi *et al.* [7] proposed an electronic document processing system. An originator produces a document and sends it out. When a reviewer receives it, he can change its content to produce a new version, maintain a version management table, and signature. All the digital signatures, the new version and the version management table are transmitted to a next person. The receiver can verify the latest signature and restore all the former versions with the version management information. In fact, their system was suspected to applicable to general document editors and document formats. It did not address how to circulate and process documents in parallel either. Furthermore, since all the individual signatures are transmitted and verified, the computational cost and communication overhead are heavy.

Shieh *et al.* [8] motivated the need for efficient multisignature schemes in delegated mobile services. With the schemes, delegates can be identified and delegated accesses can be controlled. Based on their message recovery digital signature scheme, two digital multisignature schemes are proposed: the parallel multisignature scheme and the serial multisignature scheme. The parallel multisignature scheme allows each user to sign the same message separately and independently, and then combines all individual signatures into a multisignature. The serial multisignature scheme allows a group of users to sign the message serially, and does not need to predetermine the signing order. However, due to requirement of message recovery, the computational cost of their scheme is unacceptable for mobile devices of limited resources. Worse, it is vulnerable to insider attack [9].

Nowadays, it is usually in desire for the management team to approve the reports in a paperless office. To meet this demand, the present approach describes an efficient document workflow which is an electronic analogy of the conventional office document workflow. Concretely, an original document is produced with an editor such as Microsoft Word, and signed. This signed document is sent to one or more reviewers. When a reviewer receives a document, he can verify all the content generated by the previous reviewers with only one digital signature. Afterwards, he annotates on the document, without altering any earlier comments, and form his version. In the circulating process, if a reviewer receives several documents originated from the source, he combines them and forms a new document before he signs on.

Boneh *et al.* [10] proposed aggregate signature scheme which produces only one signature for many reviewers in parallel. Zhu *et al.* [11] introduced sequential aggregate signatures which allows each reviewer transforms a sequential aggregate into another that includes a signature on a message of his choice.

This paper enables to approve document in sequential, parallel or hybrid manner. Comparing with the conventional workflow, the present scheme produces only one final document no matter which circulating route is, it is preferable to manage documents.

The remainder of this paper is organized as follows. Section 2 introduces the basic structure of workflow. Sections 3 elaborates the authentic workflow. For ease of understanding, a simple example is provided in Section 4. In Section 5, the performance is addressed in terms of computational cost and communication overhead. Section 6 summarizes the paper.

2 Preliminaries

2.1 Notation

P_i : The ith reviewer. P_0 is the originator, P_z is the final receiver. Every participant, either the originator or each subsequent reviewer, has a private key x_i and a corresponding public key v_i which is derived from x_i.

ID_i : The identification of the reviewer P_i.

C_i : The comment from P_i. Especially, comment C_0 is the original document.

T_i : Signing time-stamp of P_i

σ_i : Individual signature generated by P_i. To produce the signature σ_i, P_i calculates the hash value of the signature data, which comprises of ID_i, C_i and T_i, then he signs on the hash value by using his private key according to a public key crypto-system.

ARC: A folder. It includes all the comment C_i, T_i as well as the reviewer identification ID_i.

σ: The folder signature which is aggregated from the individual signatures σ_i of all the participants. It is appended on the folder.

H(.): One-way hash function such as SHA[12].

2.2 Aggregate Signature

A digital signature algorithm (e.g. RSA [13] and DSA [14]) is a cryptographic tool for generating non-repudiation evidence, authenticating the integrity as well as the origin of the signed message. To authenticate multiple messages efficiently in terms of the communication overhead and computational cost, Boneh *et al.* [10] (hereafter referred to as the BGLS scheme) recently proposed a cryptographic primitive called aggregate signature which allows aggregation of multiple individual signatures into one *aggregate* signature. Verification of the unified signature is *equivalent* to verifying individual component signatures. If any of the messages is tampered, the aggregate signature is regarded as invalid.

Specifically, the BGLS scheme is a multi-signer scheme. It aggregates signatures generated by distinct signers on different messages into one short aggregate signature based on elliptic curves [15] and bilinear mappings [16]. A bilinear map is a map $e : \mathbb{G}_1 \times \mathbb{G}_2 \to \mathbb{G}$, where: (a) $\mathbb{G}_1$ and $\mathbb{G}_2$ are two (multiplicative) cyclic groups of prime order p; (b) $|\mathbb{G}_1| = |\mathbb{G}_2| = |\mathbb{G}|$; (c) g_1 is a generator of $\mathbb{G}_1$ and g is a generator of $\mathbb{G}_2$. The bilinear map $e : \mathbb{G}_1 \times \mathbb{G}_2 \to \mathbb{G}$ satisfies the following properties:

1. Bilinearity: for all $\alpha, \beta \in \mathbb{G}_1$, $\gamma \in \mathbb{G}_2$, $\mathbf{e}(\alpha\beta, \gamma) = \mathbf{e}(\alpha, \gamma)\mathbf{e}(\beta, \gamma)$;
2. Non-degenerate: $\mathbf{e}(g_1, g) \neq 1$

The BGLS scheme uses a full-domain hash function $\mathbf{H}: \{0,1\}^* \to \mathbb{G}_1$. Key generation involves picking a random $x \in \mathbb{Z}_p$ as a secret key of a signer, and computing $v = g^x \in \mathbb{G}_2$ as the public key of the signer. Signing a message m involves computing the message hash $h = \mathbf{H}(m)$ and then the individual signature $\sigma_x = h^x$. To verify a signature on message m, one computes $h = \mathbf{H}(m)$ and checks whether $\mathbf{e}(\sigma_x, g) = \mathbf{e}(h, v)$ holds.

2.3 System Structure

Fig.1 is the diagram of system configuration, which includes a database storing all the public keys or certificates (e.g. CCITT X.509 or ISO 9796), network, originator P_0, a plurality of intermediate reviewer P_i and a final reviewer P_z.

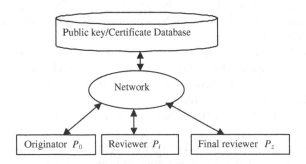

Fig. 1. System structure

Via network, reviewers can transmit messages to each other or access to database to obtain public keys.

Fig.2 is an illustration of document circulating route. The originator P_0 generates a folder, and any reviewer P_k verifies all the previous participants' comments. The dash rectangle frame is a basic cell in the distribution route. At any cell, the first reviewer P_k receives a folder from the network and transmits it to the last reviewer P_n with the help from other intermediate reviewers, e.g. P_{k+1} and $P_{(1)}$. Any reviewer in the path may update the folder. A cell may comprise of two transmission modes, one is a sequential route such as the path from P_{k+1} to $P_{(1)}$. In this mode, a sender gives his document to only one receiver, and another is parallel route such as P_k or P_n. In this parallel mode, P_k distributes his folder to several receivers independently, or P_n receives several folders from different senders. In Fig.2, dash arrow means that there may be nested cells.

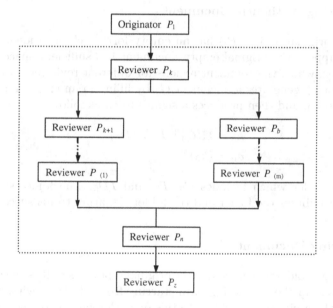

Fig. 2. Circulating path

3 Authentication of Document Workflow

The main objective of the authentic workflow is to enable any reviewer to verify all the previous comments with only one signature. Fig.3 is the processing flowchart of document on each reviewer side. It includes folder receiving, signature verifying, document annotating, and signature generating. After receiving a folder, the reviewer verifies all the comments. Only if all the comments are authentic, he comments on the document and signs on the message including signer's identification, comments, timestamp. Then he inserts the message into the folder. The new folder signature is used to replace the old one.

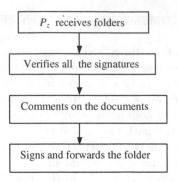

Fig. 3. Folder processing at the reviewer (e.g. P_z) side

3.1   Preparing Authentic Document

Initially, the originator (i.e., P_0) has an empty form such as student examination form. Suppose the original empty document has sufficient space for every comment. Meanwhile, the comment regions for different reviewers are different. The originator P_0 generates a document C_0 by filling in an empty form, inserts his timestamp T_0, and then produces a signature σ_0 as follows

$$h_0 = \mathbf{H}(C_0 \parallel T_0 \parallel ID_0) \tag{1}$$
$$\sigma_0 = (h_0)^{x_0} \tag{2}$$

He creates a folder which includes C_0, T_0, and ID_0. The folder signature is $\sigma = \sigma_0$. P_0 distributes the folder and the folder signature to his successors.

3.2   Verifying Document

After receiving a folder which include the original report, as well as the comments of the reviewers in the circulating path starting from P_0, the reviewer P_i must check the authenticity of the folder. To this end, P_i requests for the public keys or certificates corresponding to the previous reviewers from the database, and extracts all the comments, timestamps and reviewers' identifications from the folder. With the aggregate signature σ, he checks whether the Eq.(3) is true or not.

$$\mathbf{e}(\sigma, g) = \prod_{j=0}^{n-1} \mathbf{e}(h_j^{k_j}, v_j), \tag{3}$$

where n is the number of the ancestors of P_i, and k_j is the number of paths from P_j to P_0 on account of the repetition. For instance, in Section 4, $k_0 = 2$. If Eq.(3) is not true, he rejects the folder ARC and quits.

If P_i received $t > 1$ folders, i.e., more than one parallel reviewer, he checks the authenticity of each folder by checking Eq.(3). If any folder is bogus, he rejects the folder and quits. Otherwise, he aggregates the t BGLS signatures $\sigma_1', \sigma_2', \ldots, \sigma_t'$ into one signature. To this end, P_i computes

$$\sigma = \prod_{j=1}^{t} \sigma_j' \tag{4}$$

where σ_j' corresponds to the signature on each folder. Because $\sigma \in \mathbb{G}$, the aggregate signature σ is of the same size as an individual signature.

3.3   Annotating the Document

Only if all the comments are authentic, the reviewer starts to annotate the document. The reviewer P_i finds the right space to insert his comment C_i, and inputs the comment timestamp T_i. Please note that the data structure of document may be different from the interface of the display. To access to the content for display, data is referenced. At last P_i inserts his data which comprises of ID_i, T_i, and C_i into the folder ARC.

3.4   Generating the Signature

After annotating the document to form a new folder, the reviewer will generate a new signature for the new folder. P_i calculates his own signature $\sigma_i = h_i^{x_i}$, where $h_i = \mathbf{H}(C_0 \parallel T_0 \parallel ID_0 \parallel \ldots \parallel C_i \parallel T_i \parallel ID_i)$. Then, the reviewer updates the old signature as $\sigma \leftarrow \sigma \sigma_i$, which replaces the old one.

4   An Illustrative Example

In this section, we exemplify the authentic workflow with the examination processing of student proposals. For simplicity, we ignore how to comment on a document. The signature is generated with the method introduced in Section 3. The device such as PDA has the common parameters, i.e., g_1, g, and finite field G parameters. In addition, the private key x_i for each reviewer/device is stored in the device. Therefore, the storage requirement for the device is light-weight.

Suppose an empty document is shown in Fig.4, which requires the student name, project name, and the designated examiners, and spaces for comments, signet and date so as to generate a complete document. From the empty form, any participant knows the circulating path which is shown in Fig.5.

For example, a student named John (i.e. P_0) fills in the empty form to generate an original report as shown in Fig.6. In the original report, C_0 is the title "Wireless network security" and timestamp T_0 is "1/1/04". According to Equations (1) and (2), John calculates $h_0 = \mathbf{H}(C_0 \parallel T_0 \parallel John)$ and produces the folder signature $\sigma = \sigma_0 = (h_0)^{x_0}$. John sends to reviewers P_1 and P_2 the folder and its signature σ.

One reviewer P_1 checks the authenticity of the folder, and reviews the works of the student John (how to review the work is beyond the scope of this paper)

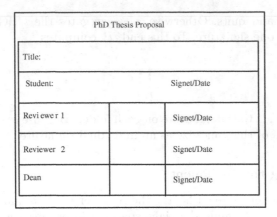

Fig. 4. An example empty form for student examination

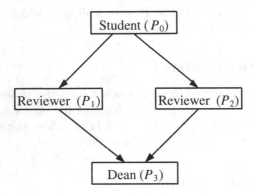

Fig. 5. The circulating path for the student examination

and generates the score (optionally comment) 85, and signs on the examination report as shown in Fig.7. Thus, C_1 is the score 85 and T_1 is "2/2/04". The examiner P_1 calculates $h_1 = \mathbf{H}(C_0 \parallel T_0 \parallel John \parallel C_1 \parallel T_1 \parallel P_1)$ and then produces his individual signature $\sigma_1 = (h_1)^{x_1}$. As a result, $\sigma = \sigma_0 \sigma_1$ is the new folder signature for the folder of P_1. P_1 sends to the dean the new folder and the new folder signature.

A second reviewer P_2 checks the authenticity of the report, and reviews the works of the student John and generates the score (optionally comment) 88, and signs on the examination report as shown in Fig.8. Thus, C_2 is the score 88 and T_2 is "1/2/04". The examiner P_2 computes $h_2 = \mathbf{H}(C_0 \parallel T_0 \parallel John \parallel C_2 \parallel T_2 \parallel P_2)$ and then produces his individual signature $\sigma_2 = (h_2)^{x_2}$. The new folder signature $\sigma = \sigma_0 \sigma_2$ for the folder generated from reviewer P_2. P_2 sends to the dean the new folder and the new folder signature.

After receiving two reviewing reports, the dean (P_3) checks the authenticity of the reports sent from two reviewers. When the reports are genuine, he combines

PhD Thesis Proposal				
Title:	Wireless network security			
Student:	John		Signet/Date	1/1/04
Reviewer 1			Signet/Date	
Reviewer 2			Signet/Date	
Dean			Signet/Date	

Fig. 6. An original report. Here the signature σ_0 is not shown.

PhD Thesis Proposal				
Title:	Wireless network security			
Student:	John		Signet/Date	1/1/04
Reviewer 1	P_1	85	Signet/Date	2/2/04
Reviewer 2			Signet/Date	
Dean			Signet/Date	

Fig. 7. One review report. Here the aggregated report signature is not shown.

the reports and makes his own comment C_3 (here it's the average score 86.5), its stamp T_3 is "1/3/04", and generates a final folder signature. Specifically, the dean computes $h_3 = \mathbf{H}(C_0 \parallel T_0 \parallel John \parallel C_1 \parallel T_1 \parallel P_1 \parallel C_2 \parallel T_2 \parallel P_2 \parallel C_3 \parallel T_3 \parallel P_3)$ then produces his individual signature $\sigma_3 = (h_3)^{x_3}$. The final folder signature is $\sigma = (\sigma_0\sigma_1)(\sigma_0\sigma_2)\sigma_3 \in \mathbb{G}$ which is inserted into the final folder. The final report is as shown in Fig.9. If someone would like to check the authenticity of the final document, she calculates

$$
\begin{aligned}
\mathbf{e}(\sigma, g) &= \mathbf{e}(\sigma_0^2\sigma_1\sigma_2\sigma_3, g) = \mathbf{e}(\sigma_0^2, g)\mathbf{e}(\sigma_1, g)\mathbf{e}(\sigma_2, g)\mathbf{e}(\sigma_3, g) \\
&= \mathbf{e}(h_0^{2x_0}, g)\mathbf{e}(h_1^{x_1}, g)\mathbf{e}(h_2^{x_2}, g)\mathbf{e}(h_3^{x_3}, g) \\
&= \mathbf{e}(h_0^2, v_0)\mathbf{e}(h_1, v_1)\mathbf{e}(h_2, v_2)\mathbf{e}(h_3, v_3)
\end{aligned}
\tag{5}
$$

Clearly, Eq.(5) is in concert with Eq.(3). That is to say, any one can verify the authenticity of the final document with the public keys of the participants P_0, P_1, P_2 and P_3 based on only one aggregate signature. Similarly, both P_1 and P_2

PhD Thesis Proposal				
Title:	Wireless network security			
Student:	John		Signet/Date	1/1/ 04
Reviewer 1			Signet/Date	
Reviewer 2	P_2	88	Signet/Date	1/2/04
Dean			Signet/Date	

Fig. 8. One review report. Here the aggregated report signature is not shown.

PhD Thesis Proposal				
Title:	Wireless network security			
Student:	John		Signet/Date	1/1/ 04
Reviewer 1	P_1	85	Signet/Date	2/2/04
Reviewer 2	P_2	88	Signet/Date	1/2/04
Dean	P_3	86.5	Signet/Date	1/3/04

Fig. 9. The final report which is the unique document to be stored. Here the aggregated report signature is not shown.

can check the authenticity of their received folder. At the same time, no one is able to forge a valid aggregate signature. Interested readers, please refer to the security proof in [10].

5   Performance

In this section, we discuss the performance evaluation of the aggregate signature based authentication scheme by comparing it with the individual signature based authentication scheme from three aspects:

- the computational cost incurred by aggregating multiple signatures;
- the computational cost incurred by verifying the aggregate signature;
- the communication overhead incurred by transmitting the signature.

Table 1 lists the comparison results between the aggregate signature with the individual signature given that there are k participants. In the Table, t_M denotes the computational cost of a modular multiplication, t_B denotes the operation cost of a bilinear mapping and $|\sigma|$ denotes the size of an individual signature in bits. In the Table, the computational cost of individual signature is fixed and ignored.

Table 1. Comparison of individual signature based scheme and aggregate signature

	Individual Signature	Present
Signing time	0	t_M
Verifying time	$(2k)t_B$	$(k-1)t_M + (k+1)t_B$
Overhead	$k|\sigma|$	$|\sigma|$

where the verification time maybe variable with the circulating path in our scheme. From Table 1, we know that our scheme requires one more modular multiplication, while for verification,

- the present scheme requires additional $(k-1)$ modular multiplication operations, but saves $k-1$ bilinear mapping operations. Since a bilinear mapping is much more expensive than a modular multiplication, the total verifying time is reduced greatly.
- the communication overhead of the present method is constant (one signature), whereas that of the individual signature based scheme is linear to the number of reviewers.

Experiment results on the BGLS signature scheme with 512-bit moduli were obtained in [17] using a P3-977Mhz Linux machine with the OpenSSL library for computing the individual operations. From the experiment results in [17], we can derive that $t_M = 0.12ms$ and $t_B = 31ms$, thus $(2k)t_B \gg (k-1)t_M+(k+1)t_B$. Therefore, the present scheme outperforms the individual signature based scheme in terms of computational cost and communication overhead.

6   Conclusion

This paper proposes a processing method of electronic analogy of the conventional office document workflow. In the authentic processing, an originator prepares a document, signs on it, and sends the complete document to one or more reviewers for approval via heterogenous networks. Once a reviewer annotates and signs on the document, a new version is produced. The updated document is forwarded to other reviewers for further processing. The circulating route may be sequential, parallel or hybrid. In parallel circulating, the reviewer has to combine documents generated from the same original document to form a complete document. Therefore, the present scheme produces only one final document no matter which circulating path is. The property is helpful in managing the documents. After a reviewer verifies all the signatures, he can annotate on the document, without altering any earlier comments, and form his version.

References

1. V. Atluri, E. Bertino, E. Ferrari, P. Mazzoleni, "Supporting Delegation in Secure Workflow Management Systems," IFIP WG 11.3 Conference on Data and Application Security, pp.199-212, 2003.
2. V. Atluri, S. Chun and P. Mazzoleni, "A Chinese Wall Security Model for Decentralized Workflow Systems," 8th ACM Conference on Computer and Communication Security, pp.48-57, 2001.
3. V. Atluri and W-K. Huang, "Enforcing Mandatory and Discretionary Security in Workflow Management Systems," J. of Computer Security, 5(4):303-339, 1997.
4. Mori Yuichi, and Suga Kazuhiro, "Digitised document circulating system with circulation history", US patent No. 5,767,847, 1998.
5. Wolfgang Prinz, "Two Complementary Tools for the Co-operation in a Ministerial Environment", Journal of Universal Computing Science, pp 843-864, 1997.
6. Mori Kenjiro, and Nose Toshiro "Method of editing and circulating an electronic draft document amongst reviewing persons at remote terminals attached to a local area network," US patent No. 5,040,142, 1991
7. Matsumoto Hiroshi, and Takaragi Kazuo, "Electronic document processing system and method of forming digital signature," US patent No. 5,465,299, 1995
8. Shiuh-Pyng Shieh, Chern-Tang Lin, Wei-Bon Yang, and Hung-Min Sun, "Digital Multisignature Schemes for Authenticating Delegates in Mobile Code Systems," IEEE Trans. on Vehicular Technology, 49(4)1464-1473, 2000
9. X. Yi, C. K. Siew, "Attacks on Shieh-Lin-Yang-Sun digital multisignature schemes for authenticating delegates in mobile code systems," IEEE Trans. on Vehicular Technology, 51(6):1313-1315, 2002
10. D. Boneh, C. Gentry, B. Lynn, H. Shacham, "Aggregate and verifiably encrypted signatures from bilinear maps", EUROCRYPT, LNCS 2656, pp.416-432, 2003.
11. Huafei Zhu, Feng Bao, Tieyan Li, Yongdong Wu, "Constructing Sequential Aggregate Signatures for Secure Wireless Routing Protocols", IEEE WCNC, 2005.
12. National Institure of Standards and Technology, "Secure Hash Standard (SHS)", FIPS Publication 180-1, 1995.
13. R. L. Rivest, A. Shamir, and L. M. Adleman, "A method for obtaining digital signatures and public-key cryptosystems," *Comm. of the ACM*, 21(2):120-126, 1978.
14. National Institure of Standards and Technology, "Proposed Federal Information Processing Standard for Digital Signature Standard (DSS)," Federal Register, Vol. 56, No. 169, pp. 42980-42982, 1991.
15. I. E. Shparlinski, *Finite Fields: Theory and Computation*, pp.215-239, Kluwer Academic Publishers, ISBN 0-7923-5662-4, 1999.
16. F. Hess, "Efficient Identity based Signature Schemes based on Pairings," Selected Areas in Cryptography 2002, LNCS 2595, pp.310-324, 2003
17. E. Mykletun, M. Narasimha, G. Tsudik, "Authentication and integrity in outsourced databases", NDSS, 2004.

Practical Strong Designated Verifier Signature Schemes Based on Double Discrete Logarithms

Raylin Tso, Takeshi Okamoto[1], and Eiji Okamoto[2]

Department of Risk Engineering,
Graduate School of Systems and Information Engineering,
University of Tsukuba,
1-1-1 Tennodai, Tsukuba, Ibaraki, 305-8573, Japan,
raylin@cipher.risk.tsukuba.ac.jp
{ken[1], okamoto[2]}@risk.tsukuba.ac.jp

Abstract. We notice that a strong designated verifier signature (SDVS) scheme can easily be realized by any secure one-way and two-party authenticated key agreement scheme. So any SDVS scheme without lower communication/computation cost or enhanced security comparing to these one-way and two-party authenticated key agreement schemes may have less advantage in practical use. In this paper, we introduce an SDVS scheme which realizes low communication/computation cost and is more efficient than current one-way key agreement schemes and SDVS schemes. In addition, we show how to remove a hash function used in this scheme where in this modified scheme, an enhanced security will be provided such that the consistency of a signature cannot be ascertained by any third party even if the signer's private key is revealed. We will prove the security of our schemes using random oracle models.

Keywords: CDH assumption, DDH assumption, double discrete logarithm, designated verifier signature, one-way two-party authenticated key agreement, privacy.

1 Introduction

Designated Verifier Signature (DVS) is a new cryptographic signing protocol that enables an entity, *Alice*, to prove the validity of a signature to a specific verifier, *Bob*, in such a way that although *Bob* can verify the validity of the signature, he cannot prove this to any third party. This is due to the fact that *Bob* can also generate a signature intended for himself which is indistinguishable from the original signature.

The first *non-interactive* DVS scheme was proposed by Jakobsson et al. [6] in 1996. This scheme has a weakness that the signature is universally verifiable (i.e., anyone can make sure that there are only two potential signers). Hence, if the signature is captured by a third party under the public channel before arriving at its destination, *Bob*, then one can identify the signer since it is now sure that *Bob* did not forge the signature. To overcome this drawback, an encryption scheme is required for encrypting the signature.

D. Feng, D. Lin, and M. Yung (Eds.): CISC 2005, LNCS 3822, pp. 113–127, 2005.

In [11], Saeednia et al. proposed an extension of DVS scheme and was formalized as the notion of *strong* designated verifier signature (SDVS) scheme. In an SDVS scheme, only the designated verifier is capable of verifying the validity of the signature although an encryption scheme has not been used. This is because the designated verifier's private key is involved in the verification phase.

SDVS schemes are very useful in any situation when a signer hopes to keep privacy of his/her identity to other parties but allows the specified verifier to verify the validity of his/her signature. For example, SDVS allows a spy agent to efficiently send a statement anonymously against his enemies but non-anonymously from a designated verifier's view, thus it provides privacy of sender's identity to other people but authenticity to the designated verifier at the same time. SDVS also provides a way for a merchant and a customer to negotiate for a best price of a purchase without any third party to verify the validity of the negotiated price.

On the other hand, in recent years, many efficient *key agreement protocols* (See Section 3) are proposed. In particular, key agreement protocols proposed in [9] and Scheme II in [7] are one-way and two-party authenticated, which means that both entities' identities can be verified but only one entity (sender) is need to be on-line. We note that using these kinds of one-way two-party authenticated key agreement schemes, SDVS can be realized efficiently. Therefore, any SDVS scheme without higher performance in the cost of communication and computation than using these one-way two-party key agreement schemes may have less significance in practice.

In this paper, firstly we show how a SDVS can be realized efficiently using any one-way and two-party authenticated key agreement scheme. Then we introduce our efficient SDVS scheme. Our scheme is based on the Diffie-Hellman key distribution and double discrete logarithms. Its security can be reduced to the *Computational Diffie-Hellman* (CDH) problem and the *Decision Diffie-Hellman* (DDH) problem. The main trick in our scheme is to make the SDVS generation *deterministic*. The randomization of a signature is depended on the hash of a message. With this technique we can reduce the communication cost of a signature from (at least) 2 of the previously proposed scheme to only 1 and make our SDVS scheme more efficient than current schemes and schemes realized using one-way key agreement protocols described above. The importance is that the security of our scheme has not been affected although it is deterministic. We will show that our scheme has the most serious security consideration. In addition, since a main purpose of a SDVS scheme is to protect the privacy of a signer's identity, in the later half of the paper, we will modify our scheme by replacing the hash function with a random parameter so as to provides an enhanced security. That is, the validity of previously signed signature cannot be verified by any third party even if he/she knows the signer's private key.

Related Works. An SDVS scheme is also called as a *deniable signature scheme* [1, 3, 4, 12] which is due to the property that the signer can later deny his/her signature. We notice that scheme proposed in [4] is also a Diffie-Hellman key based protocol. Our scheme is similar to the scheme in [4] but their scheme is interactive which need key exchanging between signer and verifier before signing a message whereas our scheme is non-interactive. In addition, although our scheme is non-interactive, we have concrete security proofs on our scheme but their scheme has no concrete security proof. Recently, Shao [12] has also pointed out that many schemes (including [4]) have the following weakness:

"*The sender does not know to whom he proves the source of a given message, and then a third party can impersonate the specified receiver to identify the source of a given message.*"

But our scheme can defeat this kind of attack since a receiver's public key is involved in the signing phase and the receiver's private key is required in the verification phase. Furthermore, the hash function of our scheme can be removed by adding only one parameter but scheme [4] has no clear description about the hash function they used. Finally, our scheme can easily be modified into an ID-based SDVS scheme by using the k-resilience technique proposed in [5] or [10] but the same mechanism is not applicable to the scheme in [4].

The rest of this paper is organized as follows. In Section 2, we recall some definitions and give a new complexity assumption which will be used in the later of this paper. In Section 3, we show how a SDVS scheme can be realized using one-way and two-party authenticated key agreement schemes. Section 4 describes our proposed scheme, security proofs and its efficiency. In Section 5, we show a modified scheme based on the proposed scheme in which no hash function is required. Its security is also considered and the efficiency and performance comparison with other SDVS schemes is illustrated. Finally, Section 6 gives a conclusion remark on this paper.

2   Preliminaries

2.1   Complexity Assumptions

We briefly review two well known complexity assumptions where the security of our schemes are based on. In addition, we give a new complexity assumption called μ-*strong exponentiation assumption* in which the security of our modified scheme can be reduced to. The security of this assumption will be discussed in detail in Section 5 in which we will first make a concrete proof to the security of our first scheme and then show that the security of the μ-strong exponentiation assumption implies the security of our first scheme.

Definition 1. Computational Diffie-Hellman (CDH) Assumption: Let G be a cyclic group of prime order p and g be a generator of G, the challenger chooses $a, b \in Z_p$ at random and outputs $(g, A = g^a, B = g^b)$. The adversary then attempts to output $g^{ab} \in G$. An adversary, $\mathcal{B}$, has at least an ϵ advantage if

$$Pr[\mathcal{B}(g, g^a, g^b) = g^{ab}] \geq \epsilon$$

where the probability is over the randomly chosen a, b and the random bits consumed by $\mathcal{B}$.

Definition 2. We say the CDH assumption is (t, ϵ)-secure if there is no t-time adversary with at least ϵ advantage in solving the above game.

Definition 3. Decisional Diffie-Hellman (DDH) Assumption: The challenger picks $a, b, c \in Z_p$ at random and then flips a fair binary coin β. If $\beta = 1$, it outputs the tuple $(g, A = g^a, B = g^b, Z = g^{ab})$. Otherwise, it outputs $(g, A = g^a, B = g^b, C = g^c)$. The adversary must then output a guess β' of β. An adversary $\mathcal{B}$ has at least an ϵ adversary in solving the DDH problem if

$$\left| Pr[\beta(g, g^a, g^b, g^{ab}) = 1] - Pr[\beta(g, g^a, g^b, g^c) = 1] \right| \geq \epsilon$$

where the probability is over the randomly chosen a, b, c and the random bits consumed by $\mathcal{B}$.

Definition 4. We say the DDH assumption is (t, ϵ)-secure if there is no t-time adversary with at least ϵ advantage in solving the above game.

Definition 5. μ-Strong Exponentiation Assumption: Let p be a large prime and $V \in Z_p^*$ be a secret value. Consider the following game played by an adversary.

Phase 1: The adversary is allowed to make a query of $m \in Z_p$, and the challenger responds with (α, s) where $\alpha \xleftarrow{R} Z_p^*$ and $s \leftarrow (m+\alpha)^V$. The adversary can repeat this $\mu_1 (\leq \mu)$ times for different m.

Challenge: The adversary submits a m^* where m^* has not been queried in the previous phase. The challenger responds with $\alpha^* \xleftarrow{R} Z_p^*$.

Phase 2: The adversary repeats Phase 1 $\mu - \mu_1$ times with the restriction that the query of m^* cannot be made.

Find: The adversary output a $s^* \in Z_p^*$ such that $s^* = (m^* + \alpha^*)^V$.

A strong version of Definition 5 can be reduced to the following problem:

Let p be a large prime and $V \in Z_p^*$ be a secret. Given $(m^*, \alpha^*), (m_1, \alpha_1, s_1), \cdots, (m_\mu, \alpha_\mu, s_\mu)$ where α is randomly picked from Z_p^* and m, s are elements of Z_p such that $(m_i + \alpha_i)^V = s_i$ for all $1 \leq i \leq \mu$. Find an $s^* \in Z_p^*$ such that $s^* = (m^* + \alpha^*)^V$.

Definition 6. We say that the μ-Strong Exponentiation Assumption is (t, ϵ)-secure if there is no t-time adversary with at least ϵ advantage in solving the above game.

The hardness of this assumption will be discussed in Section 5.

2.2   Double Exponentiation and Double Discrete Logarithms

Let p be a large prime so that $q = (p-1)/2$ is also a prime, $g \in Z_p^*$ be an element of order q, and h be a generator of Z_p^* so that the computing discrete logarithms to the base g and h are difficult.

By double exponentiation with base h and g, we mean the function:

$$Z_q^* \mapsto Z_p^* : \quad x \mapsto h^{(g^x)}.$$

By the double discrete logarithm to the bases h and g, we mean the following problem:

$$\text{Given } (h^{(g^x)}, h^{(g^y)}). \quad \text{Find } h^{(g^{xy})}.$$

2.3 SDVS Schemes' Model

Definition 7. [11] **Designated Verifier:** Let $P(A, B)$ be a protocol for *Alice* to prove the truth of the statement Ω to *Bob*. We say that *Bob* is a designated verifier if he can produce identically distributed transcripts that are indistinguishable from those of $P(A, B)$.

Definition 8. [11] **Strong Designated Verifier:** Let $P(A, B)$ be a protocol for *Alice* to prove the truth of the statement Ω to *Bob*. we say that $P(A, B)$ is a strong designated verifier proof if anybody can produce identically distributed transcripts that are indistinguishable from those of $P(A, B)$ for everybody, except for *Bob*.

Definition 9. An SDVS scheme with security parameter k consists of the following algorithms:

- **System parameter generation algorithm** *SysGen*: It takes 1^k as input and the outputs are the public parameters.
- **Key generation algorithm** *KeyGen*: It takes the public parameters as input and outputs a public/private key pair (pk_i, sk_i) for each entity P_i in the scheme.
- **Signing algorithm** *Sign*: It takes a message m, a signer P_i's private key sk_i, a verifier P_j's public key pk_j. The output σ is an SDVS of m.
- **Verifying algorithm** *Veri*: It takes (σ, m, pk_i, sk_j) and the public parameters as inputs, outputs "*accept*" if σ is a valid SDVS of m, otherwise, outputs "*reject*".

Definition 10. Security Consideration: An SDVS scheme must satisfy the following properties: [8]

- **Correctness:** A properly formed designated verifier signature must be accepted by the verifying algorithm.
- **Unforgeability:** Given a pair of signing keys (pk_i, sk_i) and a pair of verifying keys (pk_j, sk_j), it is computationally infeasible, without the knowledge of the secret keys (sk_i, sk_j), to produce a valid SDVS σ which will be accepted by the designated verifier P_j with verifying keys (pk_j, sk_j).
- **Non-transferability:** Given a message m and an SDVS σ of this message, it is (unconditionally) infeasible to determine who from the original signer or the designated verifier performed this signature, even if one knows all secrets.

- **Privacy of signer's identity:** Given a message m and an SDVS σ of this message, it is computationally infeasible, without the knowledge of the secret key of P_j or the one of the signer, to determine which pair of signing keys was used to generate σ.

3   SDVS Realized by One-Way Key Agreement Protocols

Key agreement protocols are designed for the purpose of establishing an agreed session key between a sender and a receiver in order to achieve the goal of encrypting a message by the sender and recovering the message by the receiver over an open network. Most of the proposed key agreement protocols are two-pass which need both entities to be on-line. Recently, some one-way key agreement protocols are proposed [7, 9], these protocols are not only efficient but also provide authentications for both the sender and receiver. Using these protocols, SDVS can also be realized efficiently.

Suppose a signer *Alice* wants to sign a message m and designates *Bob* as the verifier, we show how this can be done simply by using an one-way two-party authenticated key agreement protocol with any symmetric key cryptosystem.

Signature:

- Let G be a multiplicative group and g be a generator of G, *Alice* randomly picks $r \in G$ and computes $R = g^r$.
- Input r, *Alice*'s private key and *Bob*'s public key to a pre-determined one-way two-party authenticated key agreement protocol $KeyAgr$, $KeyAgr$ outputs a session key K_{AB} for *Alice*.
- Input the session key K_{AB} and the message m to a pre-determined symmetric encryption algorithm Enc, Enc outputs a ciphertext $C \leftarrow Enc_{K_{AB}}(m)$.
- The SDVS of the message m is $\sigma \leftarrow (R, C)$.

Verification:

- Input R, *Bob*'s private key and *Alice*'s public key to the key agreement protocol $KeyAgr$, $KeyAgr$ outputs a session key K_{BA} for *Bob*.
- Input K_{BA} and m to the encryption algorithm Enc, Enc outputs an other ciphertext $\tilde{C} \leftarrow Enc_{K_{BA}}(m)$.
- Accept σ as a valid signature if and only if $\tilde{C} = C$.

Security: (sketch)

- **Correctness:** Depends on the consistency of the keys K_{AB} and K_{BA}.
- **Unforgeability:** Depends on the secrecy of the session key $K_{AB} = K_{BA}$, and the security of the encryption algorithm E.
- **Privacy of singer's identity:** Depends on the secrecy of the session key.
- **Non-transferability:** Trivial, since *Alice* and *Bob* do the computation in a symmetric way.

Since the encryption and decryption of m use a symmetric cryptosystem and the exclusive key $K_{AB} = K_{BA}$ is shared efficiently using these one-way protocols, if any proposed SDVS scheme does not more superior to previously proposed one-way two-party authenticated key agreement scheme in security or in computational efficiency, then the SDVS may have less significance in practice.

4   Proposed Scheme

In this section, we introduces an efficient SDVS scheme which is based on the double discrete logarithms and can be implemented on any multiplicative group in which the CDH problem and DDH problem are hard.

System parameters generation: A trusted authority (TA) who is trusted by all the entities is responsible for the system parameters generation. On input a security parameter 1^k to the system parameter generation algorithm $SysGen$, $SysGen$ outputs the following public parameters.

- p: a large prime so that $q = (p-1)/2$ is also a prime and the computing discrete logarithm problem in Z_p^* is difficult.
- g: an element in Z_p^* of order q and the computing discrete logarithm to the base g is difficult.
- $\mathcal{H}: \{0,1\}^* \longrightarrow Z_p^*$ a collision resistant hash function.

Key generation: The key generation algorithm $KeyGen$ generates public /private keys by picking up random $\{a,b\} \xleftarrow{R} Z_q^* \times Z_q^*$, and computing $V_a \leftarrow g^a \bmod p$, $V_b \leftarrow g^b \bmod p$. The private/public key pair for participant $Alice$ is (a, V_a), and the private/public key pair for participant Bob is (b, V_b).

Signature generation: When $Alice$ wants to sign a message $m \in \{0,1\}^*$ while the signature is supposed to be verifiable by Bob only. $Alice$ executes the $Sign$ algorithm and does the following steps:

- Given $Alice$'s private key a, and Bob's public key V_b, computes $V_b^a \bmod p$.
- Computes $\mathcal{H}(m)$ and $\mathcal{H}(m)^{V_b^a} \bmod p$.
- The strong designated verifier signature for m is $\sigma \leftarrow \mathcal{H}(m)^{V_b^a}$.

Verification: With the knowledge that the signature σ is signed by $Alice$, then only Bob can verify the validity of the signature. Bob executes the $Veri$ algorithm and does the following steps:

- Given Bob's private key b, and $Alice$'s public key V_a, computes $V_a^b \bmod p$.
- Given the message m, computes $\mathcal{H}(m)$ and $\tilde{\sigma} \leftarrow \mathcal{H}(m)^{V_a^b} \bmod p$.
- Accepts σ as a valid signature if and only if $\sigma = \tilde{\sigma}$.

The correctness of this scheme is straightforward.

4.1   Security

We prove that the proposed scheme (PS) is secure against existential forgery under adaptive chosen message attack (EF-ACMA) in the random oracle model.

Definition 11. Given a security parameter k, the advantage of an forgery algorithm $\mathcal{A}$ in existentially forging a SDVS of our PS, where $\mathcal{A}$ can access to a signing oracle Σ and a random oracle $\mathcal{H}$, is defined as

$$Adv_{PS,A}^{ef-acma} \triangleq$$

$$Prob \left[Veri(pk_i, sk_j, m, \sigma) = accept \; \middle| \; \begin{array}{l} (p,g) \xleftarrow{R} SysGen(1^k), \\ (sk_i, pk_i, sk_j, pk_j) \xleftarrow{R} KenGen(P_i, P_j), \\ (m, \sigma) \xleftarrow{R} \mathcal{A}^{\Sigma, \mathcal{H}}(pk_i, pk_j) \end{array} \right]$$

Theorem 1. (Unforgeability) Suppose there exists an adversary $\mathcal{A}$ which can $(\mathcal{T}, q_{\mathcal{H}}, q_S, \epsilon)$-break the proposed scheme via existential forgery under adaptive chosen message attack, then we can construct an algorithm $\mathcal{B}$ which can $(\mathcal{T}', \epsilon')$-break the CDH problem on Z_p^* where

$$\mathcal{T}' \leq \mathcal{T} + (q_{\mathcal{H}} + q_S)\mathcal{T}_{Exp} + (q_{\mathcal{H}} - q_S)\mathcal{T}_{MC} + 1\mathcal{T}_{Inv} \quad and$$

$$\epsilon' = 1/q_s \cdot (1 - 1/(q_S + 1))^{(q_S+1)}\epsilon.$$

Here $\mathcal{T}_{Exp}$, $\mathcal{T}_{MC}$, and $\mathcal{T}_{Inv}$ denote the time cost of exponential operation, multiplication and inversion on Z_p^*, respectively.

Proof: We utilize the idea in [2] and implement their idea to this proof. We show how a CDH problem can be solved if a signature of our scheme can be forged.

In the following proof, we assume that $\mathcal{A}$ always requests the hash query of a message m before it requests a signature query of m. In addition, $\mathcal{A}$ always requests a hash query of the message m^* that it outputs as its forgery, but it cannot request the singing query of the message m^*. It is trivial to modify $\mathcal{A}$ to have this property. Any of its queries may depend on previous queries and $\mathcal{B}$ is responsible for replying these queries. Also, $\mathcal{B}$ has to record a list of messages, m_i, $|m_i| = q_{\mathcal{H}}$, hash queries HQ_i, $|HQ_i| = q_{\mathcal{H}}$, and signing queries σ_i, $i \in \{1, \cdots, q_{\mathcal{H}}\}$, $|\sigma_i| = q_S$, as the form (m_i, HQ_i, σ_i), on which $\mathcal{A}$ requests in order to make sure that each query has distinct answer. In the following proof, $\mathcal{B}$ is constructed in a series of games. Each $\mathcal{B}$ constructed in the next game is a modification of that in the previous game. The final variant of $\mathcal{B}$ thus is the one for solving the CDH problem. For convenience, we omit the notation of $\bmod p$ in the following games.

- [*Game 0*] $\mathcal{B}$ is given (g, g^a, g^b) and a challenge (h, h^α, h^β) where h is a randomly selected generator of the cyclic group Z_p^*, $\alpha = g^{ab}$, and $\beta \xleftarrow{R} Z_p^*$. In the setup phase, $\mathcal{B}$ assigns $V_a \leftarrow g^a$ to the signer's public key, and $V_b \leftarrow g^b$ to the verifier's public key. It then provides V_a and V_b to $\mathcal{A}$ and allows $\mathcal{A}$ to run. Each time when $\mathcal{A}$ makes a hash query HQ_i of a message m_i, $\mathcal{B}$ feeds HQ_i with h^{r_i} where $r_i \xleftarrow{R} Z_p^*$. Since Z_p^* contains $\phi(p-1) = q$ primitive elements, where ϕ is Euler's function, $r_i \xleftarrow{R} Z_p^*$, and h is a randomly selected primitive element of Z_p^*, therefore, each HQ_i is uniformly distributed in Z_p^*. From the perspective of $\mathcal{A}$, it is indistinguishable from a random oracle to the hash oracle $\mathcal{A}$ simulates. In addition, at any time when a signing query σ_i of a message m_i, $i \in \{1, \cdots, q_{\mathcal{H}}\}$ is requested, $\mathcal{B}$ responds with $\sigma_i \leftarrow (h^\alpha)^{r_i}$. Therefore, σ_i is a valid signature of message m_i. Finally, $\mathcal{A}$ outputs a forged signature (m^*, σ^*). If σ^* is a valid signature of m^*, and $m^* = m_{i^*}$ for some i^* whose signing query has not been queried, then $\mathcal{B}$ outputs "success"; otherwise, it outputs "failure". Since $\mathcal{A}$ outputs a successful forgery in probability ϵ, by Definition 11, we have $Adv_{PS,\mathcal{A}}^{ef-acma} = \epsilon$, thus,

$$Adv_{\mathcal{B}}^{Game\ 0} = Prob\left[\mathcal{B}^{\mathcal{A}}(g, g^a, g^b, h, h^\alpha, h^\beta) = success \left| \begin{matrix} \alpha = g^{ab}, \\ \beta \xleftarrow{R} Z_p^* \end{matrix} \right.\right]$$

$$= Adv_{PS,\mathcal{A}}^{ef-acma} = \epsilon.$$

- [*Game* 1] $\mathcal{B}$ behaves as that in *Game* 0 with a difference that, in this game, $\mathcal{B}$ picks up a random bit $S_i \leftarrow 1$ with probability $1/(q_S + 1)$ and $s_i \leftarrow 0$ with probability $1 - 1/(q_S + 1)$ before its reply to HQ_i of a message m_i. Finally, $\mathcal{B}$ outputs "success" if $\mathcal{A}$ succeeds in outputting a forgery (m^*, σ^*) and $s_{i^*} = 1$ for the message m^*. The change in this game will not affect the behavior of $\mathcal{A}$ since $\mathcal{A}$ has no information about any s_i. Thus we have $Adv_{\mathcal{B}}^{Game\ 1} = Adv_{\mathcal{B}}^{Game\ 0} \cdot Prob[s_{i^*} = 1] = \epsilon/(q_S + 1)$. We define s_0 and s_1 with different probabilities in order to let $\mathcal{B}$ of the following games to have maximal advantages.
- [*Game* 2] In this game, $\mathcal{B}$ functions as that in *Game* 1 but outputs "success" only if $s_{i^*} = 1$ of the message m^* and $s_i = 0$ of the other messages m_i. The same as that in *Game* 1, $\mathcal{A}$ cannot get any information about s_i, so its behavior is independent of any s_i. Since $\mathcal{A}$ makes q_S signing queries and for each signing query of a message m_i, the probability that $s_i = 0$ is $1 - 1/(q_S + 1)$, therefore, we have $Adv_{\mathcal{B}}^{Game\ 2} = Adv_{\mathcal{B}}^{Game\ 1} \cdot Prob[s_{i_j} = 0, 1 \leq j \leq qs] = \epsilon/(q_S + 1) \cdot (1 - 1/(q_S + 1))^{q_S} = 1/q_s \cdot (1 - 1/(q_S + 1))^{(q_S+1)}\epsilon$.
- [*Game* 3] In this game, $\mathcal{B}$ functions as that in *Game* 2 with the difference that if $\mathcal{A}$ requests a signature on a message m_i for which $s_i = 1$, then $\mathcal{B}$ declares failure and halts immediately. If, finally, $\mathcal{A}$ creates a valid forgery (m^*, σ^*) and $\mathcal{B}$ outputs "success" in *Game* 3, then there is no difference between *Game* 2 and *Game* 3. Therefore, $Adv_{\mathcal{B}}^{Game\ 3} = Adv_{\mathcal{B}}^{Game\ 2} = 1/q_s \cdot (1 - 1/(q_S + 1))^{(q_S+1)}\epsilon$. *Game* 3 provides a shortcut for the case of "failure".
- [*Game* 4] In *Game* 4, we modifies the setup phase of *Game* 3. That is, if $s_i = 1$ for some m_i, then $\mathcal{B}$ sets $HQ_i \leftarrow h^\beta h^{r_i}$. But no change will be occurred if $s_i = 0$. Since h is a primitive element in Z_p^* and r_i is randomly picked from Z_p^*, $h^\beta h^{r_i}$ is also uniform distribution in Z_p^*. Therefore, this modification is still indistinguishable from a random oracle and $\mathcal{A}$ will behave under $\mathcal{B}$ exactly as it does in *Game* 3. So we have $Adv_{\mathcal{B}}^{Game\ 4} = Adv_{\mathcal{B}}^{Game\ 3} = 1/q_s \cdot (1 - 1/(q_S + 1))^{(q_S+1)}\epsilon$.
- [*Game* 5] In this final game, whenever $\mathcal{B}$ in *Game* 4 outputs "success", it also outputs "success" in *Game* 5 and, in addition, it outputs $\sigma^*/(h^\alpha)^{r_{i^*}}$, where σ^* is the forged signature of a message m^*. Clearly, $Adv_{\mathcal{B}}^{Game\ 5} = Adv_{\mathcal{B}}^{Game\ 4} = 1/q_s \cdot (1 - 1/(q_S + 1))^{(q_S+1)}\epsilon$.

In *Game* 5, if the forgery (m^*, σ^*) $\mathcal{A}$ made is a valid message/signature pair, then $\sigma^* = QH_{i^*}^\alpha = h^{\alpha\beta} \cdot (h^\alpha)^{r_{i^*}}$. Consequently, we have $\sigma^*/(h^\alpha)^{r_{i^*}} = h^{\alpha\beta}$ which is the solution of the CDH challenge (h, h^α, h^β).

Now, we consider the running time required by $\mathcal{B}$. It is the same as $\mathcal{A}$'s running time plus the time it takes to respond to the q_H hash queries, to the q_S signing queries and the computation cost of the output $h^{\alpha\beta}$ from $\sigma^*/(h^\alpha)^{r_i^*}$.

If $s_i = 0$ for a message m_i, then answering HQ_i costs $1\mathcal{T}_{Exp}$ and answering σ_i costs $1\mathcal{T}_{Exp}$ (if the signing query σ_i has been asked). Totally, it costs at most $2\mathcal{T}_{Exp}$ for m_i with $s_i = 0$. On the other hand, if $s_i = 1$ for a message m_i, since its signing query is not allowed if $\mathcal{B}$ outputs "success" at the end of the game, so it costs $1\mathcal{T}_{Exp} + 1\mathcal{T}_{MC}$ for answering the hash query HQ_i. To consider the most time consuming case, we may assume that for each m_i whose signing query has not been asked, the s_i of that m_i is 1 so that it costs $\mathcal{B}$ $1\mathcal{T}_{Exp} + 1\mathcal{T}_{MC}$ to respond the hash query HQ_i. There are totally q_S signing queries and q_H hash queries. So it costs at most $(q_H - q_S)(1\mathcal{T}_{Exp} + 1\mathcal{T}_{MC})$ for all $s_i = 1$ and $2q_S\mathcal{T}_{Exp}$ for all $s_i = 0$. Totally, for all the queries of $s_i = 0$ and $s_i = 1$, it costs $(q_H + q_S)\mathcal{T}_{Exp} + (q_H - q_S)\mathcal{T}_{MC}$. Further, to compute $h^{\alpha\beta} \leftarrow \sigma^*/(h^\alpha)^{r_i^*}$, it costs $1\mathcal{T}_{Inv} + 1\mathcal{T}_{MC}$. Finally, we have $\mathcal{T}' \leq \mathcal{T} + (q_H + q_S)\mathcal{T}_{Exp} + (q_H - q_S)\mathcal{T}_{MC} + 1\mathcal{T}_{Inv}$. $\square$

Theorem 2. (Privacy of Signer's identity) The proposed scheme provides (computational) indistinguishability of signer's identity. More precisely, given two public keys $(g^a, g^{a'})$ of two signers P_A, $P_{A'}$, respectively, and one public key g^b of a verifier P_B, where a, b, and c are randomly picked from Z_q^*. Then for any randomly picked message $m \leftarrow \{0, 1\}^*$, it is computationally infeasible for an adversary $P_C \notin \{P_A, P_{A'}, P_B\}$ to distinguish whether a signature $\sigma^* = \mathcal{H}(m)^{g^{a^*b}}$ is signed from P_A or $P_{A'}$ (i.e., whether $a^* = a$ or a').

Proof: (sketch). Based on the intractability of the DDH Assumption on Z_p^* and Z_q^*, it is easy to proof that this scheme provides privacy of signer's identity.

- The challenger feeds an adversary $\mathcal{A}$ with three public keys $g^a, g^{a'}$ and g^b.
- For any message m queried by $\mathcal{A}$, the challenger sets $\mathcal{H}(m) \leftarrow h^r$, where $r \xleftarrow{R} Z_q^*$ and h is a generator of Z_p^* with order $p - 1$.
- Denotes $\alpha_0 \leftarrow g^{ab}$, $\alpha_1 \leftarrow g^{a'b}$, the challenger feeds $\mathcal{A}$ with h^{α_0} and h^{α_1}. Because of the intractability of CDH problem in Z_p^*, this additional information will not affect the security of our scheme.
- The challenger outputs $\mathcal{H}(m^*) \leftarrow h^{r'}$ and $\sigma^* \leftarrow \mathcal{H}(m^*)^{\alpha^*}$ where $r' \xleftarrow{R} Z_q^*$ and $\alpha^* \in \{\alpha_0, \alpha_1\}$ as $\mathcal{A}$'s challenge. $\mathcal{A}$ has to distinguish if σ^* is a signature signed using public key g^a or $g^{a'}$ (i.e., $\alpha^* = \alpha_0$ or α_1).
- With the knowledge of $< h^{\alpha_0}, h^{\alpha_1}, h^{r'}, h^{r'\alpha^*} >$, if $\mathcal{A}$ solves its challenge successfully with advantage ϵ, then $\mathcal{A}$ also solves the DDH problem with advantage ϵ. That is, given $< h^{r'}, h^{\alpha^*}, h^\beta >$, $\mathcal{A}$ successfully distinguished whether β equals to $r'\alpha^*$ or not with advantage ϵ. $\square$.

Theorem 3. (Non-transferability) The proposed scheme provides non-transferability of a signature.

This is obvious since the computation of a signature and the corresponding verification is done symmetrically.

4.2   Efficiency

Since the randomize of the SDVS is depended on the hash $\mathcal{H}(m)$ of a message m instead of any random parameter, it realizes the low communication cost. A SDVS consists of only one parameter $\sigma \in Z_p^*$ while previously proposed SDVS schemes consist of at least two parameters. On the other hand, this scheme is very efficient in computation. If we neglect the hashing and modular operations which do not cost a lot of time, then only one exponentiation in Z_q^* (which can be pre-computed off-line) and one exponentiation in Z_p^* are required for both a singer and a verifier in this scheme.

5   Remove the Hash Function

In this section, we show how to remove the hash function from the previous scheme by providing an additional parameter. This modified scheme provides an enhanced security than the previous scheme. That is, the consistency of a signature cannot be verified by any third party even if he/she knows the signer's private key. For easy of description, we denote the scheme in Section 4 as Scheme I and scheme modified in this section as Scheme II.

The system setting phase and key generation phase are the same as those in Scheme I. For convenience, we assume the message m be an element of Z_p in Scheme II (c.f., $m \in \{0,1\}^*$ in Scheme I).

Signature generation: Using *Sign* algorithm, when *Alice* wants to sign a message $m \in Z_p$ while the signature is supposed to be verifiable by *Bob* only:

- Given *Alice*'s private key a, and *Bob*'s public key V_b, compute V_b^a.
- Pick $r \xleftarrow{R} Z_p^*$, compute V_b^r and g^r.
- The SDVS for m is $(Q, \sigma) \leftarrow (V_b^r, (m + g^r)^{V_b^a})$.

Verification: Knowing that the signature σ is originated from *Alice*, then only *Bob* can verify the validity of the signature. Using *Veri* algorithm, *Bob* does the following steps:

- Given *Bob*'s private key b, and *Alice*'s public key V_a, compute V_a^b.
- Given Q, compute $\varsigma \leftarrow Q^{b^{-1}}$.
- Given the message m, compute $\tilde{\sigma} \leftarrow (m + \varsigma)^{V_a^b}$.
- Accept σ as a valid signature if an only if $\sigma = \tilde{\sigma}$.

The correctness of this scheme is straightforward.

5.1   Security

The security of this modified scheme can be reduced to the security of the μ-strong exponentiation assumption defined in Definition 5. We first show that breaking this assumption implies breaking the unforgeability of our Scheme I.

Theorem 4. If there exists an adversary $\mathcal{A}$ which can (t, ϵ)-break (strong version) μ-strong exponentiation assumption, then there exists another algorithm $\mathcal{B}$ which can (t, μ, ϵ)-break the unforgeability of our scheme I proposed in Section 4. Here μ is the maximum number of times $\mathcal{B}$ can access to the signing oracle.

Proof: $\mathcal{B}$'s purpose is to output a valid forgery of Scheme I. In the Setup Phase, the challenger generates all the public parameters and gives them to $\mathcal{B}$. In particular, V_a is the signer's public key and V_B is the designated verifier's public key. In Phase 1, $\mathcal{B}$ can ask a hash query of a message m and a signing query of m at any time and repeat by providing different message m. In Scheme I, $\mathcal{H}(m)$ maps any message string $m \in \{0, 1\}^*$ to an element of Z_p^*. For convenience, we assume m of Scheme I be an element of Z_p [1]. Thus, for each hash query of a message m_i, the response from the hash oracle $\mathcal{H}(\cdot)$ can be described as $\mathcal{H}(m_i) = m_i + \alpha_i$ for some $\alpha_i \in Z_p^*$. On the other hand, for each signing query σ_i of m_i, the response from the signing oracle is $\sigma_i \leftarrow \mathcal{H}(m_i)^{V_b^a} = (m_i + \alpha_i)^{V_b^a}$, $1 \leq i \leq \mu$. In the Challenge Phase, $\mathcal{B}$ submits m^* which $\mathcal{B}$ will use to forge a SDVS of m^*. We assume the hash query of m^*, which is $\mathcal{H}(m^*) = m^* + \alpha^*$, has been queried in Phase 1. If not, then we allow $\mathcal{B}$ to ask at this phase. After the Challenge Phase, $\mathcal{B}$ repeats Phase 1 with the restriction that the signing query of m^* cannot be made. Finally, after enough hash queries and μ signing queries, $\mathcal{B}$ provides $(m^*, \alpha^*), (m_1, \alpha_1, \sigma_1), \cdots, (m_\mu, \alpha_\mu, \sigma_\mu)$ to $\mathcal{A}$ and allows $\mathcal{A}$ to run. Consequently, if $\mathcal{A}$ solves the (strong version) μ-strong exponentiation assumption and finds an s^* such that $(m^* + \alpha^*)^V = s^*$ with ϵ advantage and time t, then (m^*, s^*) is also a valid forgery in Scheme I so $\mathcal{B}$ also solves its challenge with the same advantage and time. $\square$

In fact, the behalf of $\mathcal{B}$ in the proof of Theorem 4 is exactly the same as that of an adversary of Definition 5. Therefore, breaking Definition 5 implies breaking the unforgeability of Scheme I by the same algorithm $\mathcal{B}$. Using similar analysis, one can also reduce the unforgeability of Scheme II to μ-strong exponentiation assumption. Simply speaking, in Scheme II, given $m^*, \alpha^* (= g_i^r = Q^{-b})$, if an adversary who can find an s^* such that (m^*, Q, s^*) being a valid forgery of Scheme II, then s^* is also the solution of the μ-strong exponentiation problem. We believe that it should be much more difficult in solving Scheme II than in solving the μ-strong exponentiation assumption since in Scheme II, each g^{r_i} and $m_i + g^{r_i}$ is a secret to the adversary.

Non-transferability is straightforward. The security of privacy of signer's identity can be reduced to the security of Scheme I.

Theorem 5. Privacy of signer's identity: If there exists an algorithm $\mathcal{A}$ which can (t, ϵ)-break the indistinguishability of signer's identity of Scheme II, then there exists another algorithm $\mathcal{B}$ which can (t, ϵ)-break the privacy of signer's identity of Scheme I.

Proof: (sketch). In Scheme I, the same as that in the proof of Theorem 4, if we set $m \in Z_p$, then the value of $\mathcal{H}(m_i)$ is equal to $m_i + \alpha_i$ for some $\alpha_i \in Z_p^*$. On the

---

[1] It is easy to achieve this goal. For example, add a new hash function $\mathcal{H}' : \{0, 1\} \rightarrow Z_p$, or simply replace the binary notation of m to the decimal notation.

other hand, in Scheme II, since any third party trying to extract g^r from Q suffers the intractability of CDH problem, so g^r is a secret value from the viewpoint of any third party thus $m + g^r$ is also a secret value for any adversary. Consequently, if we omit Q in Scheme II since it gives no (computational) information to the adversary, then a signature of a message m_i using Scheme I is indistinguishable from the signature of m_i using Scheme II. In other words, by given the tuple $(\sigma^*, m^*, V_a, V_b)$ where σ^* is the signature of a message m^* and V_a, V_b are two public keys of a signer and a verifier, respectively, then no adversary is able to distinguish whether σ^* is signed using Scheme I or Scheme II (i.e., $\sigma^* = \mathcal{H}(m_i)^{V_{ab}} = (m_i + \alpha_i)^{V_{ab}}$ in Scheme I or $\sigma^* = (m_i + g^{r_i})^{V_{ab}}$ in Scheme II). The difference between the two schemes is that everyone can learn the values of m_i and α_i from $\mathcal{H}(m_i)$ in Scheme I but no adversary can learn the value of g^{r_i} and $m_i + g^{r_i}$ in Scheme II. Hence, if there exists an algorithm $\mathcal{A}$ which can break the privacy of signer's identity in Scheme II, then by simulating Scheme II using all the information in Scheme I, $\mathcal{B}$ can utilize $\mathcal{A}$ and break the privacy of signer's identity in Scheme I. $\qquad\square$

Furthermore, in Scheme II, the privacy of a signer's identity is protected even if his/her private key is disclosed. This is due to the reason that a signature signed by *Alice* used two secret values: *Alice*'s private key a and a random number $g^r \in G$. Therefore, the validity of a *Bob*-designated verifier signature signed by *Alice* can not be ascertained with only *Alice*'s private key a. With this property, the secrecy of previously signed signatures will not be affected even if the signer, *Alice*'s private key is disclosed. Thus, the privacy of signer's identity can be protected in a higher security.

5.2 Efficiency and Performance Comparison

The time-consuming operations in Scheme II consists of two exponential computation for each signer and verifier whereas one of the two operations can be pre-computed off-line. Table 1 shows the performance comparison of our two schemes with previously proposed (strong) DVS schemes in communicational cost (data flow) and computational cost. Table 2 shows the same performance comparison of our Scheme I with some one-way two-party authenticated key agreement schemes (when they are used as SDVS schemes). For the comparison to be effective, we only consider the operations of **P**airing computation (P), **E**lliptic **C**urve **M**ultiplication (ECM), **Ex**ponential computation (Exp) and **In**versive operation (Inv), which are the most time-consuming operations. In addition, $|n^r| = 111$ according to [8] and we can set $|p| = 512$ and $|G| = |Z_q|$ with $|q| = 160$ in Table 1 so that they can have comparable security. We emphasize that the data-flow size of our schemes can be largely reduced by adapting an elliptic curve setting. In Table 2, the size of data flow in each scheme depends on the encryption scheme to be used, so we only describe them in number.

From the performance comparison, we note that our Scheme I is superior to other schemes in almost every aspects and our Scheme II provides enhanced privacy security than other schemes.

Table 1. Performance Comparison I

	Data Flow	Sign		Verify		Type	Privacy
		off-line	on-line	off-line	on-line		enhanced
Scheme I	1 in Z_p	1 Exp	1 Exp	1 Exp	1 Exp	**SDVS**	No
Scheme II	2 in Z_p	1 Exp	2 Exp	1 Exp	2 Exp	**SDVS**	**Yes**
JIS [6]	3 in Z_q 3 in Z_p	-	4 ECM	-	4 ECM	DVS	No
LV [8]	1 in n_r 1 in Z_q	-	1 P	-	1 P 1 ECM	SDVS	No
SKM [11]	3 in Z_q	-	1 Exp 1 Inv	-	3 Exp	SDVS	No
SZM [13]	2 in Z_q 1 in G	-	1 P 3 ECM	1 P	2 P 2 Exp	SDVS	No

Table 2. Performance Comparison II

	Data Flow	Sign		Verify	
		off-line	on-line	off-line	on-line
Scheme I	1	1 Exp	1 Exp	1 Exp	1 Exp
Scheme II of [7]	2	1 ECM	2 ECM	-	2 ECM
Scheme I of [9]	2	1 P	1 ECM 1 Exp	1 P	1 P
Scheme II of [9]	2	-	1 P 3 ECM	-	1 P 1 ECM

6   Conclusion

In this paper, we showed how a SDVS can be realized efficiently using any one-way and two-party authenticated key agreement scheme, so any secure SDVS scheme without lower communication and computation cost comparing to these key agreement schemes may have less advantage in practical use. For this reason, we proposed our efficient SDVS scheme. We also made a modification of this scheme so as to remove the hash function of the scheme and the modified scheme provides the privacy of signer's identity in a higher security than previously proposed schemes. Finally, the performance comparison of our schemes with other schemes is investigated.

Although our schemes are not ID-based, it is easily to modify our schemes into ID-based SDVS schemes by using the k-resilience technique proposed in [5, 10]. In this case, some efficiency and security will be slightly sacrificed.

References

1. Y. Aumann, and M. Rabin, *Efficient deniable authentication for long messages*, International Conference on Theoretical Computer Science in Honor of Professor Manuel Blum's 60th Birthday (1998), avaible at **http://www.cs.cityu.edu.hk/dept/video.html**.

2. D. Boneh, B. Lynn and H. Shacham, *Short signatures from the Weil pairing*, Advances in cryptology –CRYPTO'01, Lecture Notes in Comput. Sci. **2248** (2001), 514–532.
3. X. Deng, C. H. Lee and H. Zhu, *Deniable authenticaion protocols*, IEE Proceedings –Computers and Digital Techniques **148(2)** (2001), 101–104.
4. L. Fan, C. X. Xu, and J. H. Li, *Deniable authentication protocol based on Diffie-Hellman algorithm*, Electronics Letters **38(4)** (2002), 705–706.
5. S.-H. Heng, K. Kurosawa, *k-resilient identity-based encryption in the standard model*, Advances in cryptology –CT-RSA'04, Lecture Notes in Comput. Sci. **2964** (2004), 67–80.
6. M. Jakkobsson, K. Sako and T. Impagliazzo, *Designated verifier proofs and their applications*, Advances in cryptology –EUROCRYPTO'96, Lecture Notes in Comput. Sci. **1070** (1996), 143–154.
7. L. Law, A. Menezes, M. Qu, J. Solinas and S. Vanstone, *An efficient protocol for authenticated key agreement*, Designs, Codes and Cryptogr. **28** (2003), no. 2, 119–134.
8. F. Laguillaumie, D. Vergnaud, *Designated Verifier Signatures: Anonymity and Efficient Construction from Any Bilinear Map*, SCN'04, Lecture Notes in Comput. Sci. **3352** (2005), 107–121.
9. T. Okamoto, R. Tso and E. Okamoto, *One-way and two-party authenticated ID-based key agreement protocols using pairing*, MDAI'05, Lecture Notes in Artificial Intelligence **3558** (2005), 122–133.
10. T. Okamoto, R. Tso, T. Takagi and E. Okamoto, *k-resilient ID-based key distribution schemes from pairing – three party case*, Proceedings of The International Workshop on Coding and Cryptography 2005 (WCC'05), 402–412.
11. S. Saeednia, S. Kremer and O. Markowitch, *An efficient strong designated verifier signature scheme*, ICISC'03, Lecture Notes in Comput. Sci. **2971** (2003), 40–54.
12. Z. Shao, *Efficient deniable authentication protocol based on generalized ElGamal signature scheme*, Computer Standards & Interfaces, **26** (2004), 449–454.
13. W. Susilo, F. Zhang and Y. Mu, *Identity-based strong designated verifier signature schemes*, ACISP'04, Lecture Notes in Comput. Sci. **3108** (2004), 313–324.

Efficient Group Signatures from Bilinear Pairing

Xiangguo Cheng[1,2], Huafei Zhu[2], Ying Qiu[2], and Xinmei Wang[1]

[1] State Key Laboratory of Integrated Services Network,
Xidian University, Xi'an 710071, P.R. China
{xgcheng, xmwang}@xidian.edu.cn
[2] Institute for Infocomm Research (I²R),
21 Heng Mui Keng Terrace, Singapore 119613
{stuxgc, huafei, qiuying}@i2r.a-star.edu.sg

Abstract. This paper presents two types of group signature schemes from bilinear pairings: the *mini* type and the *improved* type. The size of the group public keys and the length of the signatures in both schemes are constant. An on-line third party is introduced to help the schemes to realize the "join" of group members, the "opening" of group signatures, and the immediate "revocation" of group membership. It is shown that the introduction of this party makes our schemes much more simple and efficient than the previous schemes of this kind. The mini group signature is in fact only a BLS short signature. Unfortunately, it has a drawback of key escrow. A dishonest group manager can forge any group signature at his will. To avoid this drawback, we put forward an improved scheme, which is also very simple and efficient, and satisfies all the security requirements of a group signature scheme.

Keywords: Group signature; Digital signature; GDH group; Bilinear pairing.

1 Introduction

Group signatures, primitively introduced by Chaum and van Heyst [11], allow a group member to sign a message on behalf of the group without revealing his identity. In addition, it is difficult to determine whether two different signatures were generated by the same group member or not. In the case of a dispute, the group manager will be able to "open" a group signature and incontestably show the identity of the original signer.

Group signatures have many practical applications such as *e-voting*, *e-bidding*, *e-cash*, and *fingerprinting systems*. Following the first work by Chaum and van Heyst, many group signature schemes have been proposed. In the early group signature schemes [11, 12, 13], the size of the group public keys and the length of the signatures linearly grew with the number of the group members. Although many of them have been proven to be secure, they are inefficient for large groups. Schemes where the size of the group public keys and the length of the signatures are constant have been proposed in [14, 1, 15, 2, 20, 18]. However, much of them are either insecure or inefficient. In fact, it is still an open problem to design a group signature scheme that is secure and as efficient as the regular signature scheme such as RSA or DSA.

D. Feng, D. Lin, and M. Yung (Eds.): CISC 2005, LNCS 3822, pp. 128–139, 2005.

We note that many group signature schemes [14, 16, 17, 18, 4, 7, 8] are constructed by making use of two different ordinary signatures: One is used to generate the membership certificates as part of the Join protocol and the other one is used to actually generate group signatures as part of the Sign protocol. Consequently, the join of the group members and the generation and verification of the group signatures are very complicated.

Using bilinear pairings as a constructive tool, this paper presents two types of group signature schemes: the *mini* type and the *improved* type. The size of the group public keys and the length of the signatures in both schemes are constant. An on-line third party, called a *security mediator*, is introduced to help our scheme to realize the "join" of group members, the "opening" of group signatures and the immediate "revocation" of group membership. It is shown that the introduction of the *security mediator* makes our schemes much more simple and efficient. The mini type group signature is in fact only the famous BLS short signature from bilinear pairings [9]. but it has a drawback of key escrow and a dishonest group manager can forge any group signature at will since he knows all the private keys of the group members. To avoid the key escrow of the mini scheme, we put forward an improved group signature scheme. Although it is not so efficient as the mini scheme, to our best knowledge, it is still much more simple and efficient than the previous schemes of this kind. We will show that the improved scheme satisfies all the security requirements of a secure group signature scheme.

The rest of this paper is organized as follows. Section 2 does some preliminary work. Section 3 describes the definition and security requirements of a group signature scheme. A mini group signature scheme and its security analysis are presented in Section 4. Section 5 introduces the improved group signature scheme and analyzes its security. Conclusion is drawn in the last section.

2 Preliminaries

2.1 Bilinear Pairing

Let G_1 be a cyclic additive group generated by P, whose order is a prime q, and G_2 a cyclic multiplicative group of the same order q. A bilinear pairing is a *computable* map $e : G_1 \times G_1 \to G_2$ with the following properties:

1. *Bilinear:* $e(aR_1, bR_2) = e(R_1, R_2)^{ab}$ for any $a, b \in \mathbb{Z}_q$ and $R_1, R_2 \in G_1$.
2. *Non-degenerate:* There exists $R_1, R_2 \in G_1$ such that $e(R_1, R_2) \neq 1$. Which means that $e(P, P) \neq 1$ since P is the generator of the cyclic group G_1.

2.2 Gap Diffie-Hellman Group

Assume that the *Discrete Logarithm* (DL) problem in both G_1 and G_2 is hard. Consider *Computational Diffie-Hellman* (CDH) problem (given $P, aP, bP \in G_1$ for all $a, b \in \mathbb{Z}_q^*$, compute abP) and *Decisional Diffie-Hellman* (DDH) problem (distinguish (P, aP, bP, abP) from (P, aP, bP, cP) for all $a, b, c \in \mathbb{Z}_q^*$) in G_1.

They are generally considered to be hard [9, 5]. However, the DDH problem becomes easy with the help of bilinear pairings since (P, aP, bP, cP) is a valid DH tuple (the tuple of the form (P, aP, bP, abP)) if and only if $e(aP, bP) = e(P, cP)$.

We call G a *Gap Diffie-Hellman* (GDH) group if DDH problem is easy while CDH problem is hard in G. The above discussion tells us that bilinear pairings can help us to obtain GDH groups. Such groups can be found on super-singular elliptic curves or hyper-elliptic curves over the finite fields, and the bilinear pairings can be derived from the Weil or Tate pairings [9, 5].

Schemes in this paper can work on any GDH group. Throughout this paper, we define the system parameters in all schemes as follows: G_1, G_2, P and q are as described above. Define a cryptographic hash function: $H : \{0, 1\}^* \rightarrow \mathbb{Z}_q^*$. All these parameters are denoted as $Params = \{G_1, G_2, e, q, P, H\}$ and can be obtained by running a *GDH Parameters Generator* [9].

3   Definition and Security Requirements

In this section, we describe the definition and security requirements of a group signature scheme.

3.1   Definition

A group signature scheme consists of two parties: the *group manager* (GM) and a set of *group members* and comprises a family of at least five procedures described as follows.

1. `Setup`: A probabilistic algorithm that on input a security parameter k and outputs the system parameters, the group public key and the corresponding secret key.
2. `Join`: A protocol between GM and a user to join the group. After running this protocol, the user becomes a member of the group and gets his membership certificate and the membership secret.
3. `Sign`: A probabilistic algorithm that on input a group public key, a membership certificate, a membership secret and a message, and outputs the group signature on the given message.
4. `Verify`: A boolean-valued algorithm used to verify the validity of the group signature generated by the `Sign`.
5. `Open`: An algorithm only run by GM. Given a message, a valid group signature on it, a group public key and the corresponding secret key, determine the identity of the signer.

3.2   Security Requirements

A *secure* group signature scheme must satisfy the following security properties.

1. **Correctness:** A valid group signature generated by a group member using `Sign` must be accepted by `Verify`.

2. **Unforgeability:** None but a group member is able to produce a valid group signature on behalf of the group.
3. **Anonymity:** Given a valid group signature of some message, it is computationally hard to determine the original signer for everyone but GM.
4. **Unlinkability:** Given several group signatures on the same or different messages, it is computationally infeasible to decide whether the signatures were generated by the same or by different group members.
5. **Exculpability:** A group signature generated by a group member cannot be successfully attributed to another. Even GM cannot produce signatures on behalf of other group members.
6. **Traceability:** GM is always able to open a valid group signature and identify the actual signer.
7. **Coalition-resistance:** Even if a coalition of some group members (even a whole set of the entire group) collaborate to generate a valid group signature on some message, can GM attribute the signature to the colluding members.

4   The Mini Group Signature

Apart from GM and a set of group members, we introduce a trusted on-line third party, called a *security mediator* (SEM) in our scheme. The main idea behind our scheme is that the secret key of the group is split into two parts by GM, one part is given to the user as his group membership secret key, and the other one is given to SEM. Neither the group member nor SEM can sign a message without the other's help. To revoke the membership of a group member, GM needs only ask SEM not to provide the group member partial signatures any more. The group membership can therefore be revoked immediately. SEM has the following functionality in our scheme:

(1) Help GM and the users to easily realize the `join` protocol. As a result, the users become group members.
(2) Help the legal group members to produce valid group signatures.
(3) Realize the immediate revocation of group membership.
(4) Help GM to open some group signatures and reveal the identities of the original signers in the case of a later dispute.

In the following, we will show that a very simple and efficient group signature scheme can be constructed with the help of SEM.

4.1   The Proposed Scheme

The mini group signature scheme is described as follows:

1. `Setup`: Given a security parameter κ, GM runs the *GDH Parameters Generator* to obtain the system parameters $Params = \{G_1, G_2, e, q, P, H\}$. It then randomly chooses $x \in \mathbb{Z}_q^*$ and computes $X = xP \in G_1$. The private-public key pair of the group is (x, X).

2. **Join:** Suppose that U_i is a user who wants to join the group. Assume that the communication between GM and users and between SEM and GM is secure. GM randomly chooses $x_i^u \in \mathbb{Z}_q^*$ and computes $x_i^s = (x - x_i^u) \bmod q$. x_i^u is sent to U_i and (x_i^s, U_i) is sent to SEM. After this protocol, U_i becomes a group member and his group membership secret key is x_i^u. When distributing the private keys to the group members, there are some requirements described as follows:
   - $x_i^u \neq x_j^u$ when $i \neq j$.
   - $x_{i_1}^u + x_{i_2}^u + \cdots + x_{i_j}^u \neq x \bmod q$ for any positive integer j.
   - $x_{i_1}^u + x_{i_2}^u + \cdots + x_{i_j}^u \neq x_{i_l}^u \bmod q$ for any positive integers j and l.
3. **Sign:** To generate a group signature on some message M, the group member U_i collaborates with SEM to do the following work:
   - U_i sends $H(M)$ along with his identity to SEM.
   - SEM first checks that the group membership of U_i has not been revoked. It then computes $\sigma_i^s = x_i^s H(M)$, stores $(U_i, H(M))$ and sends σ_i^s back to U_i.
   - U_i computes $\sigma_i^u = x_i^u H(M)$ and $\sigma_i = \sigma_i^s + \sigma_i^u$. He checks whether $e(P, \sigma_i) = e(X, H(M))$ holds. If so, the group signature on message M is set to be $\sigma = \sigma_i$.
4. **Verify:** The verifier accepts the signature σ on message M if $(P, X, H(M), \sigma)$ is a valid DH tuple, *i.e.* $e(P, \sigma) = e(X, H(M))$ holds.
5. **Open:** In the case of a dispute, GM has to open some group signatures. Suppose that he wants to open a signature σ on some message M. He need only send an enquiry to SEM. SEM consults the storage list and sends the original signer U_i back to GM.

Our group signature is in fact the famous BLS short signature from bilinear pairings [9]. This makes our group signature very short. The introduction of SEM makes our scheme very simple and efficient. Note that none of the group member can generate a valid group signature without the help of SEM. The group membership can therefore be immediately revoked if GM ask SEM not to help the group member any more.

4.2   Security Analysis

In the following, we will show that our mini group signature scheme satisfies almost all the security requirements of a secure group signature scheme.

Correctness: The group signature σ on message M given by the group member U_i consists of two parts: the partial signature σ_i^s given by SEM and the partial signature σ_i^u given by U_i. We note that

$$\sigma = \sigma_i^s + \sigma_i^u = x_i^s H(M) + x_i^u H(M) = (x_i^s + x_i^u) H(M) = x H(M)$$

since $x = (x_i^s + x_i^u) \bmod q$. That is to say, σ is a BLS short signature of M under the group public key X. Therefore, $e(P, \sigma) = e(X, H(M))$. Which guarantees the security property of correctness of our mini scheme.

Unforgeability: From the generation of the individual group signature, we know that such a signature can be viewed as a $(2,2)$ threshold signature. It is shown in [9] that the underlying scheme is existential unforgeable in the random oracle model for any GDH group. It is also shown in [10] that the threshold version is as secure as the original one since a forgery on the threshold scheme allows to build a forgery on the original signature scheme. This allows to prove the unforgeability of our group signature scheme.

Anonymity: Given a message M, the group signature generated by the group member U_i is:

$$\sigma_i = \sigma_i^s + \sigma_i^u = x_i^s H(M) + x_i^u H(M) = (x_i^s + x_i^u)H(M) = xH(M);$$

and the group signature generated by the group member U_j is:

$$\sigma_j = \sigma_j^s + \sigma_j^u = x_j^s H(M) + x_j^u H(M) = (x_j^s + x_j^u)H(M) = xH(M).$$

Therefore, the group signatures on the same message generated by different group members are all the same. They are all only the BLS short signatures under the group public key X and any group signature consists of no information of the original signer. In no case can one determine the original signer just from the group signature. That is to say, our group signature scheme satisfies the security property of anonymity.

Unlinkability: As discussed above, anyone (even if GM) can find nothing from the signature about the signer since the group signatures on the same message generated by different group members are all the same and a group signature consists of no information of the original signer. That is, given several group signatures, it is difficult to determine whether they were generated by the same group member or not. Therefore, our group signature scheme has the security property of unlinkability.

Exculpability: Note that none of the group member can generate a group signature without the help of SEM. Once a group member has signed a message, his identity along with the hash value of the message must have been stored by the trusted SEM in the storage list (To assure the security of the scheme, the storage list can only be opened by SEM). Therefore, none of the group members can sign messages on behalf of other group members or attribute a signature generated by a group member to another since $x_i^u \neq x_j^u$ when $i \neq j$ (it is apparent that the group member U_i can sign messages on behalf of U_j or attribute a signature generated by himself to U_j if $x_i^u = x_j^u$). That is, our scheme has the security property of exculpability.

Traceability: In the case of a dispute, GM can easily open any group signature and identify the actual signer with the help of the trusted SEM. We note that all group signatures can be produced only with the help of SEM, and SEM has stored the identities of the original signers at the time it provided the partial signatures.

Coalition-resistance: We note that, without the help of SEM, none of the group members can generate a valid group signature. Even if a coalition of some group members (even a whole set of the entire group) collaborate, they cannot generate a valid group signature since $x_{i_1}^u + x_{i_2}^u + \cdots + x_{i_j}^u \neq x \bmod q$, $x_{i_1}^u + x_{i_2}^u + \cdots + x_{i_j}^u \neq x_{i_l}^u \bmod q$ for any positive integers j and l (Noted that the group members $U_{i_1}, U_{i_2}, \cdots, U_{i_j}$ can collaborate to generate a valid group signature if $x_{i_1}^u + x_{i_2}^u + \cdots + x_{i_j}^u = x \bmod q$ and they can also produce a valid group signature on behalf of the group member U_{i_l} with the help of SEM if $x_{i_1}^u + x_{i_2}^u + \cdots + x_{i_j}^u = x_{i_l}^u \bmod q$). That is, our scheme satisfy the security property of Coalition-resistance.

Compared with the previous schemes of this kind, the advantage of our mini group signature scheme is obvious:

(1) As discussed above, the group signature is in fact the BLS short signature from bilinear pairing.
(2) The introduction of SEM provides a simple and immediate revocation of the group membership since none of the group member can generate a valid signature without the help of SEM.
(3) The introduction of SEM provides an efficient method for the users to join the group.
(4) The storage of the identities of the signers provides a simple and practical method for GM to open the group signatures and identify the original signers.

Unfortunately, there is also a drawback in our mini group signature scheme: *GM can generate valid group signatures on behalf of any group member* since he knows the private keys of all group members.

The following improved group signature scheme gives a satisfactory solution to the aforementioned drawback.

5   The Improved Group Signature

To avoid the drawback of the above mini group signature scheme, we make an adjustment on the scheme and come up with an improved group signature scheme in this section. Although it is not so efficient as the mini group signature scheme, to our knowledge, it is still much more simple and efficient than the previous schemes of this kind.

5.1   The Proposed Scheme

The improved group signature scheme is described as follows:

1. **Setup:** Given a security parameter κ, GM and SEM do the following work, respectively.
    - GM runs the *GDH Parameters Generator* to obtain the system parameters $Params = \{G_1, G_2, e, q, P, H\}$.
    - GM randomly chooses a number $x \in \mathbb{Z}_q^*$ and computes $X = xP$.
    - SEM randomly chooses $y \in \mathbb{Z}_q^*$ and computes $Y = yP$.

    The group public key is (X, Y), while x and y are kept secret by GM and SEM, respectively.

2. **Join:** Suppose that a user U_i wants to join the group. We assume that the communication among GM, SEM and the users is secure. To realize the join of U_i, they collaborate to do as follows:
   - GM randomly chooses $x_i^u \in \mathbb{Z}_q^*$, computes $x_i^s = (x - x_i^u) \bmod q$. x_i^u is sent to U_i and (x_i^s, U_i) is sent to SEM.
   - After receiving (x_i^s, U_i), SEM randomly chooses $y_i^u \in \mathbb{Z}_q^*$ and computes $y_i^s = (y - y_i^u) \bmod q$. It keeps y_i^s secret and sends y_i^u to U_i.

   After this protocol, U_i becomes a group member and his group membership secret key is (x_i^u, y_i^u). When distributing the private shares to the group members, there are some requirements described as follows:
   - $x_i^u \neq x_j^u$ and $y_i^u \neq y_j^u$ when $i \neq j$.
   - $x_{i_1}^u + x_{i_2}^u + \cdots + x_{i_j}^u \neq x \bmod q$ and $y_{i_1}^u + y_{i_2}^u + \cdots + y_{i_j}^u \neq y \bmod q$ for any positive integer j.
   - $x_{i_1}^u + x_{i_2}^u + \cdots + x_{i_j}^u \neq x_{i_l}^u \bmod q$ and $y_{i_1}^u + y_{i_2}^u + \cdots + y_{i_j}^u \neq y_{i_l}^u \bmod q$ for any positive integers j and l.
3. **Sign:** To generate a group signature on some message M, U_i collaborates with SEM to do the following work:
   - U_i sends $H(M)$ along with his identity to SEM.
   - SEM first checks that U_i's membership has not been revoked. It then computes $v_i^s = y_i^u H(M)$ and $\sigma_i^s = x_i^s H(M)$. It stores $(U_i, H(M))$ and sends (v_i^s, σ_i^s) back to U_i.
   - U_i computes $\sigma_i^u = x_i^u H(M)$ and $v_i^u = y_i^u H(M)$. Let

   $$\sigma_i = v_i^s + v_i^u + \sigma_i^s + \sigma_i^u.$$

   He checks whether $e(P, \sigma_i) = e(X + Y, H(M))$ holds. If so, the group signature on message M is set to be $\sigma = \sigma_i$.
4. **Verify:** The verifier accepts the group signature σ on message M if $(P, X + Y, H(M), \sigma)$ is a valid DH tuple, that is, $e(P, \sigma) = e(X + Y, H(M))$ holds.
5. **Open:** To open a group signature, GM needs only to send a enquiry to SEM. SEM can easily identifies the original signer from the storage list.

5.2 Security Analysis

We first show that the drawback existed in the mini scheme have been avoided in our improved scheme: Note that the group signature in our improved scheme depends on not only the private key x of GM but also the private key y of SEM. GM cannot forge the group member to generate a valid signature any more since he does not know y.

In the following, we will show that our improved scheme satisfies all the security requirements of a secure group signature scheme.

Correctness: The property of correctness can be easily derived from the generation of the group signature. Given a valid group signature σ on message M. Note that

$$\begin{aligned}
\sigma &= v_i^s + v_i^u + \sigma_i^s + \sigma_i^u \\
&= y_i^s H(M) + y_i^u H(M) + x_i^s H(M) + x_i^u H(M) \\
&= (y_i^s + y_i^u) H(M) + (x_i^s + x_i^u) H(M) \\
&= y H(M) + x H(M) = (x + y) H(M)
\end{aligned}$$

Therefore,

$$e(P, \sigma) = e(P, (x + y)H(M)) = e(P, xH(M))e(P, yH(M))$$
$$= e(X, H(M))e(Y, H(M)) = e(X + Y, H(M))$$

That is, $(P, X + Y, H(M), \sigma)$ is a valid DH tuple.

Unforgeability: The following proof shows that our scheme satisfies the security property of Unforgeability.

Note that our group signature can be viewed as a multisignature generated by GM and SEM. Suppose that there is a polynomial time adversary $\mathcal{A}$ for our group signature scheme, we will construct an adversary $\mathcal{B}$ for the underlying BLS short signature scheme by making use of $\mathcal{A}$. We give a strong assumption that the adversary $\mathcal{B}$ has corrupted GM or GM is dishonest. The adversary is given the access to the hash and group signature signing oracles. $\mathcal{B}$ simulates GM and interacts with $\mathcal{A}$ as the following.

> **Hash Queries:** $\mathcal{A}$ requests the hash values on some messages of his choice, $\mathcal{B}$ makes the same queries on these messages to its own hash oracle and gives the responses back to $\mathcal{A}$.
>
> **Group Signature Queries:** Proceeding adaptively, $\mathcal{A}$ requests the group signatures on some messages of his choice. $\mathcal{B}$ requests the signatures on these messages to its own group signature oracle and gives the response back to $\mathcal{A}$. For the j-th query, $\mathcal{A}$ supplies a messages M_j, and obtains the response σ_j.
>
> **Outputs:** Eventually algorithm $\mathcal{A}$ halts, outputting a message $\hat{M}$ and its group signature forgery $\hat{\sigma}$, Where $\hat{M}$ must be a message that $\mathcal{A}$ have not required. If $\mathcal{A}$ fails to output a valid forgery, then $\mathcal{B}$ reports failure and terminates. Otherwise, $\mathcal{B}$ computes $\hat{\sigma}_1 = xH(\hat{M})$ and $\hat{\sigma}_2 = \hat{\sigma} - \hat{\sigma}_1$. It is apparent that $\hat{\sigma}_2$ is a valid BLS short signature forgery of $\hat{M}$ under the public key Y.

If there exists an efficient algorithm $\mathcal{A}$ to forge our group signature scheme, then we can construct an algorithm $\mathcal{B}$, with the same advantage, to forge the underlying BLS short signature scheme. However, it is shown in [9] that the BLS short signature scheme is secure against existential forgery under adaptively chosen message attack in the random oracle model with the assumption that G_1 is a GDH group. Therefore, Our group signature scheme is existential unforgeable.

Anonymity: Given a message M, the group signature given by U_i is:

$$\sigma_i = v_i^s + v_i^u + \sigma_i^s + \sigma_i^u = y_i^s H(M) + y_i^u H(M) + x_i^s H(M) + x_i^u H(M) = (x+y)H(M).$$

The group signature generated by the group member U_j $(i \neq j)$ is:

$$\sigma_j = v_j^s + v_j^u + \sigma_j^s + \sigma_j^u = y_j^s H(M) + y_j^u H(M) + x_j^s H(M) + x_j^u H(M) = (x+y)H(M).$$

Thus the group signatures on the same message generated by different group members are all the same. Any group signature consists of no information of the original signer. In no case can one determine the original signer just from the group signature. That is to say, our group signature scheme satisfies the security property of anonymity.

Unlinkability: As discussed above, anyone (even if GM) can find nothing from the signature about the signer since all the group members generate the same group signature on the same message and a group signature consists of no information of the original signer. That is to say, given several group signatures, it is difficult to determine whether they were generated by the same group member or not. Therefore, our group signature scheme has the security property of unlinkability.

Exculpability: We note that, none of the group members can generate a group signature without the help of SEM. Once a group member U_i has signed a message M, $(U_i, H(M))$ must have been stored by SEM in the storage list. Therefore, none of the group members can sign messages on behalf of other group members or attribute a signature generated by a group member to another since $x_i^u \neq x_j^u$ and $y_i^u \neq y_j^u$ when $i \neq j$. If and only if $x_i^u = x_j^u$ and $y_i^u = y_j^u$, can U_i sign messages on behalf of U_j or attribute signatures generated by himself to U_j. The group signature can be viewed as a multisignature generated by GM and SEM. GM cannot produce group signatures on behalf other group members since it has been shown in [10] that such a multisignature is unforgeable in the random oracle model. Therefore, our scheme has the security property of exculpability.

Traceability: Since SEM has stored the identity of the signer at the time it provided the partial signatures, it is easy for GM to open a group signature and identify the actual signer with the help of SEM.

Coalition-resistance: We first show two cases that some group members can collaborate to forge a group signature.

Case 1. $x_{i_1}^u + x_{i_2}^u + \cdots + x_{i_j}^u = x \bmod q$ and $y_{i_1}^u + y_{i_2}^u + \cdots + y_{i_j}^u = y \bmod q$
In this case, the group members $U_{i_1}, U_{i_2}, \cdots, U_{i_j}$ can collaborate to generate a valid group signature and GM cannot identifies those original signers.

Given a message M, U_{i_m} $(1 \leq m \leq j)$ computes $\hat{\sigma}_{i_m} = x_{i_m}^u H(M)$ and $\hat{v}_{i_m} = y_{i_m}^u H(M)$. Let $\hat{\sigma} = \sum_{m=1}^{j}(\hat{\sigma}_{i_m} + \hat{v}_{i_m})$. It is apparent that $\hat{\sigma}$ is a valid group signature on M under public (X, Y).

Case 2. $x_{i_1}^u + x_{i_2}^u + \cdots + x_{i_j}^u = x_{i_l}^u \bmod q$ and $y_{i_1}^u + y_{i_2}^u + \cdots + y_{i_j}^u = y_{i_l}^u \bmod q$
In this case, the group members $U_{i_1}, U_{i_2}, \cdots, U_{i_j}$ can collaborate to generate a valid group signature on behalf of U_{i_l}.

Given a message M, each U_{i_m} $(1 \leq m \leq j)$ computes $\hat{\sigma}_{i_m} = x_{i_m}^u H(M)$ and $\hat{v}_{i_m} = y_{i_m}^u H(M)$. Let $\hat{\sigma}_{i_l}^u = \sum_{m=1}^{j} \hat{\sigma}_{i_m} = \sum_{m=1}^{j} x_{i_m}^u H(M) = x_{i_l}^u H(M)$, $\hat{v}_{i_l}^u = \sum_{m=1}^{j} \hat{v}_{i_m} = \sum_{m=1}^{j} y_{i_m}^u H(M) = y_{i_l}^u H(M)$. Then they send $H(M)$ along with U_{i_l}'s identity to SEM and obtain $\hat{\sigma}_{i_l}^s = x_{i_l}^s H(M)$ and $\hat{v}_{i_l}^s = y_{i_l}^s H(M)$. It is apparent that $\hat{\sigma} = \hat{v}_{i_l}^s + \hat{\sigma}_{i_l}^s + \hat{\sigma}_{i_l}^u + \hat{v}_{i_l}^u$ is a valid group signature generated by $U_{i_1}, U_{i_2}, \cdots, U_{i_j}$ on behalf U_{i_l}. In other cases, none of the group members can generate valid group signatures without the help of SEM and even if some group members (even a whole set of the entire group, including GM) collaborate, they cannot generate valid group signatures. Our scheme satisfy the security property of Coalition-resistance since the aforementioned two cases have been avoided in our scheme.

6 Conclusions

In this paper, we have proposed two types of group signature schemes based on the bilinear pairings. The introduction of the *security mediator* makes some protocols of our schemes such as the join of the group members, the immediate revocation of the membership and the open of the group signatures very simple and practical. To our knowledge, no so simple and efficient group signatures have been proposed so far.

Note that the signatures on the same message signed by different group members are all the same. Once two different group members have signed the same message, SEM will not be able to distinguish between the two original signers. The best solution to this obstacle is that SEM does not allow different group members to sign the same message.

For the future work, we try to give a security proof of our scheme under the strong security notion of group signatures given in [8] and [7].

References

1. G. Ateniese, J. Camenisch , M. Joye and G. Tsudik. A practical and provably secure coalition-resistant group signature scheme. In: *Advances in Crypto'00, LNCS 1880*, pp.255-270, Springer-Verlag, 2000.
2. G. Ateniese and B. de Medeiros. Efficient group signatures without trapdoors. In: *Advances in Asiacrypt'03, LNCS 2894*, pp.246-268, Springer-Verlag, 2003.
3. G. Ateniese and G. Tsudik. Some open issues and new directions in group signature schemes. In: *Financial Cryptography (FC'99), LNCS 1648*, pp.196-211, Springer-Verlag, 1999.
4. D. Boneh, X. Boyen and H. Shacham. Short group signatures. In: *Advances in Crypto'04, LNCS 3152*, pp.41-55, Springer-Verlag, 2004.
5. D. Boneh and M. Franklin. Identity based encryption from the Weil pairing. In: *Advances in Crypto'01, LNCS 2139*, pp.213-229, Springer-Verlag, 2001.
6. D. Boneh, X. Ding, G. Tsudik and C. Wong. A method for fast revocation of public key certifates and security capabilities. In: *Proceedings of the 10th USENIX Security Symposium*, USENIX 2001.
7. M. Bellare, H. Shi and C. Zhang. Foundations of group signatures: the case of dynamic groups. In: *Topics in CT-RSA 2005, LNCS 3376*, pp.136-153. Springer-Verlag, 2005.
8. M. Bellare, D. Micciancio and B. Warinschi. Foundations of group signatures: formal definitions, simplified requirements, and a constructionbased on general assumptions. In: *Advances in Eurocrypt'03, LNCS 2656*, pp.614-629, Springer-Verlag, 2003.
9. D. Boneh, B. Lynn and H. Shacham. Short signatures from the Weil pairing. In: *Advances in Asiacrypt'01, LNCS 2248*, pp.514-532, Springer-Verlag, 2001.

10. A. Boldyreva. Efficient threshold signature, multisignature and blind signature schemes based on the gap-Diffie-Hellman-group signature scheme. In: *Advances in PKC'03, LNCS 2567*, pp.31-46, Springer-Verlag, 2003.
11. D. Chaum and E. van Heyst. Group Signatures. In: *Advances in Eurocrypt'91, LNCS 547*, pp.257-265, Springer-Verlag, 1991.
12. J. Camenisch and M. Stadler. Efficnt and generalized group signatures. In: *Advances in Eurocrypt'97, LNCS 1233*, pp.465-479, Springer-Verlag, 1997.
13. L. Chen and T. P. Pedersen. New group signature schemes. In: *Advances in Eurocrypt'94, LNCS 950*, pp.171-181, Springer-Verlag, 1994.
14. J. Camenisch and M. Stadler. Effient group signature schemes for large groups. In: *Advances in Crypto'97, LNCS 1296*, pp.410-424, Springer-Verlag, 1997.
15. J. Camenisch and M. Michels. A group signature scheme with improved efficiency. In: *Advances in Asiacrypt'98, LNCS 1514*, pp.160-174, Springer-Verlag, 1998.
16. J. Camenisch and M. Michels. A group signature scheme based on an RSA-variant. *Technical Report RS-98-27*, BRICS, University of Aarhus, November 1998. An earlier version appears in [15].
17. J. Camenisch and M. Michels. Separability and efficiency for generic group signature schemes. In: *Advances in Crypto'99, LNCS 1666*, pp.413-430, Springer-Verlag, 1999.
18. X. Ding, G. Tsudik and S. Xu. Leak-free group signatures with immediate revocation. In: *Proceedings of 24th International Conference on Distributed Computing Systems (ICDCS 2004)*, pp.608-615, IEEE Computer Society, 2004.
19. R. Gennaro, S. Jarecki, H. Krawczyk and T. Rabin. Robust Threshold DDS Signatures. In: *Advances in Eurocrypt'96, LNCS 1070*, pp.354-371, Springer-Verlag, 1996.
20. L. Nguyen and R. Safavi-Naini. Efficient and provably secure trapdoor-free group signature schemes from bilinear pairings. In: *Advances in Asiacrypt'04, LNCS 3329*, pp.372-386, Springer-Verlag, 2004.

Enhanced Aggregate Signatures from Pairings

Zuhua Shao

Department of Computer and Electronic Engineering,
Zhejiang University of Science and Technology,
No. 85, XueYuan Road, Hangzhou, Zhejiang,
P.R. of China, 310012
zhshao_98@yahoo.com

Abstract. Recently, Boneh et al. proposed the concept of an aggregate signature, introduced security models for such signatures, and also presented some applications. An aggregate signature scheme is a digital signature that supports aggregation: Given n signatures on n distinct messages from n distinct users, it is possible to aggregate all these signatures into a single short signature. This single signature, along with the n original messages will convince verifiers that the n users did indeed sign the n original messages respectively, i.e., user i signed message M_i for $i = 1, \ldots, n$. In this paper, however, we find that their security model has some defects. The capacity that the adversaries possess was constrained according to the standard security definition of signatures. We propose an improvement of the Boneh's scheme by presenting a new security model and giving a formal proof in random oracle model.

Keyword: Aggregate signature, security model, random oracle model.

1 Introduction

In 2003, Boneh et al. [3] introduced the concept of an aggregate signature AGS. Suppose that there are n signers, each chooses a public-private key pair (PK_i, SK_i) in the same system parameters. Signer u_i signs a message M_i to obtain a signature σ_i. Then there is a public aggregation algorithm that takes as input all of individual signatures σ_1, ..., σ_n and outputs a short compressed signature σ. Anyone can aggregate the signatures. Moreover, the aggregation can be performed incrementally. There is also an aggregate verification algorithm that takes as input $PK_1, \ldots, PK_n, M_1, \ldots, M_n$ and σ, and decides whether the aggregate signature is valid.

Aggregate signatures have many real-world applications involving signatures on many different messages generated by many different users. Boneh et al. provided some examples. In a Public Key Infrastructure (PKI) of depth n, each user is given a chain of n certificates. The chain contains n signatures by n Certificate Authorities (CAs) on n distinct certificates. Similarly, in the Secure BGP protocol (SBGP) [6] each router receives a list of n signatures attesting to a certain path of length n in the network. A router signs its own segment in the path and forwards the resulting list of $n + 1$ signatures to the next router. As a result, the number of signatures in routing messages is linear in the length of the path. Both applications would benefit from a method for compressing the list of signatures on distinct messages issued by distinct parties.

D. Feng, D. Lin, and M. Yung (Eds.): CISC 2005, LNCS 3822, pp. 140–149, 2005.

Specifically, X.509 certificate chains could be shortened by compressing the n signatures in the chain into a single signature. Hence, an aggregate signature scheme enables us to achieve precisely a type of compression, reducing verification load and storage load.

Intuitively, the security requirement for an aggregate signature scheme is that the aggregate signature σ is declared valid only if the aggregator who creates the compressed signature σ was given all of valid individual signature $\sigma_1, ..., \sigma_n$. If so, an aggregate signature provides non-repudiation at once on many different messages signed by many signers.

Boneh et al. constructed an aggregate signature scheme based a short signature, due to Boneh, Lynn, and Shacham [4]. This signature scheme can work in any group, where the Decision Diffile-Hellman problem (DDH) is easy, but the Computational Diffile-Hellman problem (CDH) is hard. Such group is referred as Gap group [9]. However, general gap groups are insufficient for constructing efficient aggregate signatures. Instead, Boneh et al. used a bilinear map [2], called "pairing", to construct aggregate signatures.

In their paper [3], Boneh et al. presented a security model for such signatures. However, the capacity that the adversaries possess was constrained according to the standard security definition of signatures. An adversary is required to forge an aggregate signature for some messages while he is only allowed to request some individual signatures on messages of his choice. Moreover, the adversary would not be considered as wining attack games, although he could derive a new individual signature, if any.

In this paper, we will propose an enhanced aggregate signature scheme from pairings where an explicit entity acts as aggregator who should be held responsibility on behalf of other signers. We also present a new security model and give a formal proof in random oracle models. Our model strengthens security by giving more power to adversaries in attack games and requiring the aggregator to play an active role.

The rest of this paper is organized as follows. Section 2 gives some background definitions for parings, presents the new security model, and then gives a security proof in random oracle model. In Section 3, we analysis the defects in the Boneh's scheme in contrast with our enhanced aggregate signature scheme. Finally, we conclude in Section 4.

2 Enhanced Aggregate Signature Scheme

In this section, we first briefly review bilinear maps and associated computation problems. Then we describe the enhanced aggregate signature scheme. Finally, we show that the enhanced aggregate signature scheme is existential unforgeable against adaptive chosen message attacks (EUF-CMA).

2.1 Review of Pairings

In their pioneer work of Boneh and Franklin [2], a bilinear map, called "pairing", is used. Typically, the pairing used is a modified Weil pairing or Tate pairing on a supersingular elliptic curve or abelian variety. For the reason of brevity, we describe pairings and the related mathematics in a more general format here.

Let G_1 and G_2 be two cyclic groups of the same large prime order q. We write G_1 and G_2 additively and multiplicatively groups, respectively. Let P is a generator of G_1. Assume that the discrete logarithm problems in G_1 and G_2 are hard. Let $e: G_1 \times G_1 \to G_2$ be an admissible pairing which satisfies the following properties:

1. Bilinear: $e(aP, bP') = e(P, P')^{ab}$ for all $P, P' \in G_1$, and $a, b \in Z_q$.
2. Non-degenerate: There exist $P, P' \in G_1$ such that $e(P, P') \neq 1$. This means that if P is a generator of G_1, then $e(P, P)$ is a generator of G_2.
3. Computability: There is an efficient algorithm to compute $e(P, P')$ for all $P, P' \in G_1$.
4. The map $f_P: G_1 \to G_2$ by $f_P(Q) = e(Q, P)$, where $P \in G_1^*$ (G_1^* denotes the set $G_1 \backslash \{O\}$ where O is the identity element in the additive group G_1), is believed to be a one-way isomorphic function.

The Weil pairing and Tate pairing associated supersingular elliptic curve can be modified to create such bilinear pairing.

Bilinear Diffie-Hellman (BDH) Parameter Generator: We say that a randomized algorithm IG is a BDH parameter generator if IG takes a security parameter $k > 0$, runs in time polynomial in k, and outputs the description of two groups G_1 and G_2 of the same large prime order q and the description of an admissible pairing $e: G_1 \times G_1 \to G_2$.

The security model of the aggregate signatures is based on the difficulty of the following assumption.

CDH Assumption. Let IG be a BDH parameter generator. We say that an algorithm A has advantage $\varepsilon(k)$ in solving the CDH problem for IG if for sufficiently large k:

$$\mathrm{Adv}_{IG,A}(k) = \Pr\left\{ A(q, G_1, G_2, e, P, aP, bP) = abP \;\middle|\; \begin{array}{l} < q, G_1, G_2, e > \leftarrow IG(1^k) \\ P \leftarrow G_1, a, b \leftarrow Z_q^* \end{array} \right\} \geq \varepsilon(k)$$

The probability is taken over the choice of P, a, b and A's coin tosses.

We say that IG satisfies the CDH assumption if for any randomized polynomial time (in k) algorithm A we have that $\mathrm{Adv}_{IG;A}(k)$ is a negligible function. When IG satisfies the CDH assumption we say that CDH is hard in groups generated by IG.

However, Boneh et al. use more general case in [3]. They consider bilinear a map $e: G_1 \times G_2 \to G_T$ where all groups are multiplicative and of prime order p and there is a computable isomorphism ψ from G_2 to G_1. To simplicity, we set $G_1 = G_2$ and $\psi = I$, the identity map.

2.2 Enhanced Aggregate Signatures Scheme AGS

We describe enhanced aggregate signatures in our general format. The scheme comprises five algorithms: *KeyGen*, *Sign*, *Verify*, *Aggregate*, and *AggregateVerify*:

KeyGen: Take as input 1^k, run the randomized algorithm IG to generate the system parameters $<q, G_1, G_2, e, P>$ and a full-domain hash function H: $\{0, 1\}^* \rightarrow G_1$. For each signer u_i, picks up at random x_i in Z_q^* as his private key and computes his public key $Y_i = x_i P$. Similarly, the aggregator chooses his key pair $\{x_0, y_0\}$.

Sign: For a message $M_i \in \{0, 1\}^*$, a signer with key pair $\{x_i, y_i\}$ computes his individual signature $\sigma_i = x_i H(M_i)$.

Verify: Each individual signature σ_i can be verified by checking $e(\sigma_i, P) = e(H(M_i), Y_i)$.

Aggregate: Suppose that an aggregator is given n individual signatures $\sigma_1, \ldots, \sigma_n$ for n messages $M_1, \ldots, M_n$ with respect to public keys $Y_1, \ldots, Y_n$. The aggregator first verifies individual signatures by checking $e(\sigma_i, P) = e(H(M_i), Y_i)$, $i = 1, \ldots, n$. If all signatures are valid, the aggregator computes the aggregate signature $\sigma = \sigma_1 + \ldots + \sigma_n + x_0 H(M_1 \| \ldots \| M_n)$.

AggregateVerify: accept the aggregate signature only if $e(\sigma, P) = e(H(M_1\|\ldots\|M_n),$

$$Y_0) \prod_{i=1}^{n} e(H(m_i), Y_i).$$

Consistency: $e(\sigma, P) = e(\sigma_1 + \ldots + \sigma_n + x_0 H(M_1\|\ldots\|M_n), P) = e(x_0 H(M_1\|\ldots\|M_n),$

$$P) \prod_{i=1}^{n} e(x_i H(m_i), P) = e(H(M_1\| \ldots \| M_n), Y_0) \prod_{i=1}^{n} e(H(m_i), Y_i).$$

Therefore, if all of individual signatures are valid, so is the aggregate signature.

2.3 Security of the Enhanced Aggregate Scheme

The standard definition of the security of signature schemes, together with the first construction that satisfies it, was given by Goldwasser et al. [5].

Existential unforgeability against adaptive chosen message attacks (EUF-CMA) is the strongest security model of signature schemes, where the adversary is allowed to ask the signer to sign any message of its choice in an adaptive way, it can adapt its queries according to previous answers. Finally, the adversary could not provide a new message-signature pair with non-negligible advantage. Hence, it is natural to require that aggregate signatures also satisfy this strong security notion. However, the definition of the security for aggregate signatures must be strengthened more. The reason is that there are two types of signatures, aggregate signature and individual signature. Although the adversary would be allowed to ask the signers to sign any message of its choice, either batch message or individual message, he still could not provide a new message-signature pair, whether aggregate signature or individual signature.

We say that an aggregate signature scheme AGS is existential unforgeable against adaptive chosen message attacks (EUF-CMA) if no polynomial bounded adversary A has a non-negligible advantage against the challenger in the following game:

KeyGen: The challenger takes as input 1^k, runs the randomized algorithm IG to generate the system parameters $<q, G_1, G_2, e, P>$ and a full-domain hash function H: $\{0, 1\}^* \rightarrow G_1$. Then the challenger generates $s + 1$ $(s < n)$ public key $Y_0, Y_1, ..., Y_s$ at random. Finally, the challenger gives the results to the adversary.

Phase 1: The adversary issues some signature queries.

- Individual signature query $<M_i, Y_i>$: A requests an individual signature for message M_i of its choice under public key Y_i, $0 \le i \le s$.

-Aggregate signature query $<M_1, ..., M_i, Y_0, Y_1, ..., Y_i>$: A requests an aggregate signature for messages $M_1, ..., M_i$ of its choice under public keys $Y_0, Y_1, ..., Y_i$, $1 \le i \le s$.

Challenge: Once the adversary decides that Phase 1 is over, A outputs $n - s$ additional public keys $Y_{s+1}, ..., Y_n$ of its choice. These public keys, along with the initial public keys $Y_0, Y_1, ..., Y_i$ will be included in A's forged aggregate signatures and aggregate signature queries.

Phase 2: The adversary issues some more signature queries.

- Individual signature query $<M_i, Y_i>$: A requests an individual signature for message M_i of its choice under public key Y_i, $0 \le i \le s$.

- Aggregate signature query $<M_1, ..., M_i, Y_0, Y_1, ..., Y_i>$: A requests an aggregate signature for messages $M_1, ..., M_i$ of its choice under public keys $Y_0, Y_1, ..., Y_i$, $1 \le i \le n$.

Response: Finally, the adversary A outputs an individual signature σ_i for message M_i of its choice under public key Y_i, $0 \le i \le s$, or an aggregate signature σ for messages M_1, ..., M_i of its choice under public keys $Y_0, Y_1, ..., Y_i$, $1 \le i \le n$.

The adversary A wins the game if the output signature is not nontrivial, i.e. if σ_i is an individual signature, A did not requests a signature, either individual or aggregate, on the message M_i; if σ is an aggregate signature, there exists at least a message M_j in M_1, ..., M_i, $1 \le j \le s$ and A did not requests a signature, individual or aggregate, on the message M_j. The probability is over the coin tosses of the key generation algorithm and of A.

Definition: An aggregate signature forger $A(t, q_H, q_{is}, q_{as}, n, \varepsilon)$-breaks an n-signer aggregate signature scheme in the aggregate chosen key model, if after running in time at most t, making at most q_H adaptive queries to the hash function, at most q_{is} adaptive queries to the individual signing oracle and at most q_{as} adaptive queries to the aggregate signing oracle, A outputs a nontrivial forged signature by at most n signers, with probability at least ε. An aggregate signature scheme is $(t, q_H, q_{is}, q_{as}, n, \varepsilon)$-secure against existential forgery in the aggregate chosen-key model if no forger $A(t, q_H, q_{is}, q_{as}, n, \varepsilon)$-breaks it.

Theorem. Let the hash functions H be random oracle. Then the enhanced aggregate signature scheme AGS is existential unforgeable against adaptive chosen message attacks (EUF-CMA) assuming CDH is hard in groups generated by IG. Concretely, suppose there is an EUF-CMA adversary A, that has advantage ε against the AGS scheme and A runs in time at most t. Suppose that A makes at most q_H adaptive queries to the hash function, at most q_{is} adaptive queries to the individual signing oracle and at most q_{as} adaptive queries to the aggregate signing oracle. Then there is a CDH algorithm B that has an advantage ε' for IG with running time t', where:

$$\varepsilon \leq (e(q_{is} + (n + 1)q_{as} + n + 1)\varepsilon' \tag{1}$$

$$t \approx t' - (q_H + 2(q_{is} + (n + 1)q_{as}) + 2n + 4) \, c_{G1} \tag{2}$$

Where e is the base of natural logarithms, and one point scalar on G_1 takes time c_{G1}.

Proof: We show how to construct a CDH adversary B that uses A as a computer program to gain an advantage ε' for IG with running time t'. The challenger runs IG to obtain $<q, G_1, G_2, e, P, aP, bP>$. Its goal is to output $Q = abP \in G_1$. Algorithm B simulates the challenger and interacts with forger A as follows.

KeyGen: Algorithm B takes as input 1^k, run the randomized algorithm IG to generate the system parameters $<q, G_1, G_2, e, P>$, a full-domain hash function $H: \{0, 1\}^* \rightarrow G_1$, $Q_1 = aP$ and $Q_2 = bP$. Algorithm B generates at random $s + 1$ ($s < n$) public key Y_0, Y_1, ..., Y_s by $Y_i = Q_1 + r_i P$, where r_i is a random in Z_q^*. Finally, Algorithm B gives the results to forger A.

Hash Queries. At any time Algorithm A can query the hash oracle H. To response to these queries, B maintains a list of tuples $<M_i, h_i, c_i, coin_i>$ for the hash oracle H. we refer to this list as H-list. The contents of the list are "dynamic" during the attack game. Namely, when the game starts, it is initially empty, but at end of the game, it records all pairs of queries/answers. When A queries the oracle H at some massage $M \in \{0, 1\}^*$, Algorithm B responds as follows:

1. If the query M already appears on the H-list in some tuple $<M, h, c, coin>$, then algorithm B responds with $h = H(M)$.
2. Otherwise, B generate a random $coin \in \{0, 1\}$ so that $\Pr[coin = 0] = \delta$ form some δ that will be determined later.
3. Algorithm B picks a random c in Z_q^*. If $coin = 0$, B computes $h = Q_2 + cP$. If $coin = 1$, B computes $h = cP$.
4. Algorithm B responds with $h = H(M)$ and adds the tuple $<M, h, c, coin>$ to the H-list.

Obviously, either way, h is uniform in G_1 and is independent of A's current view as required.

Individual Signature Queries. When in Phase 1 or 2, algorithm A can request an individual signature on some message M under the challenge public key Y_i, $0 \leq i \leq s$. Algorithm B responds to this query as follows:

1. Algorithm B runs the above algorithm for responding to H-queries on M, obtaining the corresponding tuple $<M, h, c, coin>$ on the H-list. If $coin = 0$, then B reports failure and terminates.
2. If $coin = 1$ holds, we know that $h = cP$. Let $\sigma = cY_i \in G_1$. Observe that $e(\sigma, P) = e(cY_i, P) = e(cP, Y_i) = e(H(M), Y_i)$. Therefore σ is a valid individual signature on M under the public key Y_i. Algorithm B gives σ to algorithm A. The probability of success is $(1 - \delta)$.

Aggregate Signature Queries. When in Phase 1 or 2, algorithm A can request an aggregate signature for messages M_1, ..., M_i of its choice under public keys Y_0, Y_1, ..., Y_i, $1 \le i \le n$.

As individual signature queries, Algorithm B computes i individual signatures σ_j on the message M_j under the challenge public key Y_j, $j = 1$, ..., i. Then Algorithm B computes the individual signatures σ_0 on the message $(M_1\|...\| M_i)$ under the challenge public key Y_0. Finally, Algorithm B computes $\sigma = \sigma_0 + ... + \sigma_i$. If the corresponding $coin_0 = ... = coin_i = 1$, Algorithm B could generate a valid aggregate signature. Otherwise, B reports failure and terminates. The probability of success is at least $(1 - \delta)^{n+1}$.

Output. If B does not report failure, Algorithm A would return a nontrivial individual signature σ_i or an aggregate signature σ with probability ε.

Case 1. σ_i is an individual signature, A did not requests a signature, either individual or aggregate, on the message M_i under the challenge public key $Y_i = Q_1 + r_i P$, $0 \le i \le s$. B runs the above algorithm for responding to the H-list on M_i to obtain the corresponding tuple $<M_i, h_i, c_i, coin_i>$. If $coin_i = 0$, then $H(M_i) = h_i = Q_2 + c_i P$ holds. Hence,

$$e(\sigma_i, P) = e(H(M_i) , Y_i)$$
$$= e(Q_2 + c_i P, Q_1 + r_i P)$$
$$= e((a + r_i)(Q_2 + c_i P), P)$$
$$= e(aQ_2 + r_i Q_2 + c_i Q_1 + r_i c_i P, P)$$

Because the map f_P: $G_1 \to G_2$ by $f_P(Q) = e(Q, P)$, is an isomorphic map,

$$\sigma = aQ_2 + r_i Q_2 + c_i Q_1 + r_i c_i P$$

It implies $D = aQ_2 = abP = \sigma - (r_i Q_2 + c_i Q_1 + r_i c_i P)$.

Therefore, Algorithm B can derive D if $coin_i = 0$. Otherwise B declares failure and halts.

Case 2. σ is an aggregate signature so that $e(\sigma, P) = e(H(M_1\|...\|M_k), Y_0)$ $\prod_{i=1}^{k} e(H(m_i), Y_i)$. There exists at least a message M_j in M_1, ..., M_i, $1 \le j \le s, j \le k$ and A did not request a signature, either individual or aggregate, on the message M_j.

Algorithm B runs its hash algorithm at each M_e, $0 \le e \le k$, obtaining the $(k + 1)$ corresponding tuples $<M_e, h_e, c_e, coin_e>$ on the H-list.

Algorithm B now proceeds only if $coin_j = 0$ and other $coin_e = 1$; otherwise B declares failure and halts. For $e \ne j$, $coin_e = 1$ implies $H(M_e) = h_e = c_e P$. Algorithm B can compute $\sigma_e = c_e Y_e$ so that $e(\sigma_e, P) = e(c_e Y_e, P) = e(c_e P, Y_e) = e(H(M_e), Y_e)$. Finally Algorithm B can compute $\sigma_j = \sigma - \sum_{e=0, e \ne j}^{k} \sigma_e$ so that $e(\sigma_j, P) = e(H(M_1\|...\|M_k),$

$Y_0) \prod_{i=1}^{k} e(H(m_i), Y_i) / \prod_{i=0, i \neq j}^{k} e(H(m_i), Y_i) = e(H(M_j), Y_j)$. Thus, Algorithm B

obtains an individual signature σ_j. As Case 1, Algorithm B can derive D if $coin_j = 0$.

Now, it remains to compute the probability ε' that Algorithm B can derive D in the attack game.

First, we compute the probability that B does not abort during the simulation. To respond an individual signature query, B runs its hash algorithm to obtain $<M_i, h_i, c_i, coin_i>$, if $coin_i = 1$, B does not abort. To respond an aggregate signature query, B runs at most $(n + 1)$ its hash algorithm, if $coin_0 = \ldots = coin_i = 1$, $1 \leq i \leq n$, B does not abort. Hence,

$$\Pr[B \text{ does not abort during the simulation}] = (1 - \delta)^{q_{is} + (n+1)q_{as}}$$

Then, Algorithm A returns a nontrivial individual signature σ_i or an aggregate signature σ with probability ε.

Finally, Algorithm B transforms A's forgery into the CDH solution. If A returns a nontrivial individual signature σ_i on the message M_i, the probability that Algorithm B can derive D is that of $coin_i = 0$, which is δ, since the adversary does not request the signature query, either individual or aggregate, on the message M_i. If A returns a nontrivial aggregate signature σ, the probability that Algorithm B can derive D is that of $coin_j = 0$ and other $coin_e = 1$. Hence, the probability that Algorithm B can derive D form the output of A is at least $\delta(1 - \delta)^n$ in both Case 1 and Case 2.

Therefore, the probability ε' that Algorithm B can derive D is at least

$\varepsilon\delta(1 - \delta)^{q_{is} + (n+1)q_{as} + n}$. This expression is optional for $\delta = 1/(q_{is} + (n+1)q_{as} + n + 1)$.

For a huge value $q_{is} + (n+1)q_{as} + n + 1$, the success probability is approximately $\varepsilon/(e(q_{is} + (n+1)q_{as} + n + 1))$.

Therefore, $\varepsilon \leq (e(q_{is} + (n+1)q_{as} + n + 1)\varepsilon'$.

The running time of Algorithm B is that of Algorithm A plus time taken to respond to q_H hash queries, q_{is} individual signature queries, q_{as} aggregate signature queries and the time to transform A's forgery into the CDH solution. Each hash query requires a point scalar in G_1. Each individual signature requires a point scalar in G_1 and a hash query. An aggregate signature query requires at most $n + 1$ individual signatures. To transform A's forgery into the CDH solution, B requires at most $n + 1$ additional hash queries, $n + 3$ point scalars. Hence,

$$t' \approx t + (q_H + 2(q_{is} + (n+1)q_{as}) + 2n + 4)c_{G1}$$

Notice that we only consider the time taken to compute point scalars in G_1, since it is more time-consuming than point additions in G_1.

3 Comparison with the Aggregate Signature of Boneh et al.

In this section, we point out that there are some defects in the aggregate signature scheme of Boneh et al. compared with our enhanced aggregate signature scheme.

1. There is no aggregate signature query in the security model of Boneh et al., although the adversary is required to forge a new aggregate signature in attack games.

2. If the adversary can forge a new individual signature in an attack game, it is not regarded as that the adversary wins the attack game, although the adversary is allowed to request individual signature for messages of its choice.

3. If there is some dispute, neither the aggregator nor signers could be held responsibility. For example, if n signers compute their individual signatures $\sigma_i' = x_i H(M_i) + d_i$ instead of $\sigma_i = x_i H(M_i)$, $i = 1, 2, \ldots, n$, the verifiers can not find σ_i' is not the valid signature on the message M_i, as long as $d_1 + d_2 + \ldots + d_n = 0 \bmod q$. The individual signers can deny their signatures in the sequel.

4. The aggregator forger A is provided with only one public key rather than multiple public keys in the enhanced aggregate signature scheme.

5. To withstand with false public key attack previously considered in the context of multisignature [1, 8]. Boneh et al. stipulated that the messages aggregate signed are different from each other. However, this is maybe unnecessary, since X.509 protocol stipulates that certificate authority should validate public keys of users to ensure that the public keys in the system are well generated before issuing public key certifications [7].

In our enhanced aggregate signature scheme, the adversary is allowed to issue two types of signature queries, either individual or aggregate. As consequence, the adversary would be regarded as wining in attack games, as long as the adversary can forge a new message-signature pair, whether individual or aggregate.

Contrary to anonymous aggregator in the Boneh's scheme, our enhanced scheme uses active aggregators responsible for the aggregate signatures. Moreover, the individual signature the aggregator generates is on all messages. If there is some dispute, the aggregator should be held responsibility on behalf of other signers. Hence, our enhanced aggregate signature scheme can provide non-repudiation.

4 Conclusions

We enhance the Boneh' aggregate signature scheme by defining more power adversaries in attack games. The adversary can request two types of signature queries, either individual or aggregate. Meanwhile, as long as the adversary can provide anyone kind of forgery, whether individual signature or aggregate signature, the adversary would be considered as wining attack games.

We require that the aggregator to sign all individual messages. This active role would increase the non-repudiation of aggregate signatures.

Acknowledgements

This material is based upon work funded by Zhejiang Provincial Natural Science Foundation of China under Grant No.Y104201.

The author wishes to thank the anonymous referees for their very useful comments and suggestions.

References

1. D. Boneh, C. Gentry, B. Lynn, and H. Shacham. Aggregate and Verifiably Encrypted Signatures from Bilinear Maps, *Advances in Cryptology-Eurocrypt'03*, LNCS 2656, Springer-Verlag, Berlin, pp. 614-629, 2003.
2. S. Kent, C. Lynn, and K. Seo. Secure border gateway protocol (Secure-BGP). *IEEE J. Selected Areas in Comm.*, 18(4), pp.582-92, April 2000.
3. D. Boneh, B. Lynn, and H. Shacham. Short signatures from the Wail pairings, *Advances in Cryptology-Asiscrypt'01*, Gold Coast, Australia, LNCS 2248, Springer-Verlag, Berlin, pp.514-532, 2001.
4. T. Okamoto and D. Pointcheval. The gap problems: A new class of problems for security of cryptographic primitives. *In Proceedings of PKC 2001*, LNCS 1992, Springer-Verlag, pp. 104-118, 2001.
5. D. Boneh and M. Franklin. Identity-based encryption from the Weil pairing, *Advances in Cryptology - CRYPT'01*, LNCS 2139, Springer-Verlag, pp. 213-229, 2001.
6. S. Goldwasser, S. Micali, R. Rivest, A digital signature scheme secure against adaptive chosen-message attacks, *SIAM Journal on Computing*, 17(2), pp.281-308, 1988.
7. S. Micali, K. Ohta, and L. Reyzin. Accountable-subgroup multisignatures (extended abstract), *In Proceedings of CCS 2001*, ACM Press, pp. 245-54, 2001.
8. A. Boldyreva. Efficient threshold signature, multisignature and blind signature schemes based on the gap-Diffie-Hellman-group signature scheme. *In Proceedings of PKC 2003*, LNCS 2567, Springer-Verlag, pp. 31-46, 2003.
9. IEEE P1363 Standard Specifications for Public Key Cryptography, Approved 30 January, 2000.

Constructing Secure Proxy Cryptosystem

Yuan Zhou, Zhenfu Cao, and Zhenchuan Chai

Department of Computer Science and Engineering,
Shanghai Jiao Tong University, Shanghai 200030, P.R. China
zhouyuan@sjtu.edu.cn, zfcao@cs.sjtu.edu.cn,
zcchai@cs.sjtu.edu.cn

Abstract. Proxy cryptosystem was first proposed by Mambo and Okamoto, for the delegation of the power to decrypt ciphertexts. However, to our knowledge, there is no reasonable mode aimed at this cryptographic notion. In this paper, we first present a practical mode: proxy cryptosystem based on time segmentation. Under this mode, a secure model is proposed and a proxy cryptosystem is constructed. Our construction uses ideas from the HIBE scheme of Gentry and Silverberg, the FSPE scheme of Canetti et al. and the scheme of Fujisaki and Okamoto, and is proven to be secure based on the hardness of bilinear Diffie-Hellman assumption. At last, we give an identity based (ID-based) version of the proxy cryptosystem based on time segmentation.

Keywords: Proxy cryptosystem, bilinear Diffie-Hellman, ID-based.

1 Introduction

1.1 Background and Related Work

Recently, e-commerce environments have been paid great attentions. Let us consider an scenario that a president carries a heavy burden. He must deal with many business information encrypted by his partners. He wants to release him from his heavy work. A sensible choice is to delegate his decryption capability to his assistant.

The primitive method of delegating decryption is to "decrypt and re-encrypt". In this method, there are two parties, one is original decryptor, and the other is delegated decryptor. When some ciphertext is sent to the original delegator, he first uses his secret key to compute the corresponding plaintext M, then encrypt it with the delegated decryptor's public key. Apparently, it is inefficient.

Proxy cryptosystem was first introduced by Mambo and Okamoto [1]. It allows an original decryptor to transform the ciphertext into another ciphertext for a delegated decryptor. Once the ciphertext transformation is executed, the delegated decryptor can compute a plaintext in place of the original decryptor. After Mambo and Okamoto's initial work, many scholars have done a lot of work in this field. In 1998, Blaze, Bleumer, and Strauss [5] proposed the notion of atomic proxy cryptography, in which the original decryptor and delegated decryptor

D. Feng, D. Lin, and M. Yung (Eds.): CISC 2005, LNCS 3822, pp. 150–161, 2005.

publish a transformation key that a semi-trusted intermediary to transforms ciphertext encrypted for the original decryptor directly into ciphertext that can be decrypted by the delegated decryptor. Follow on [5], Jakobsson [6] developed a quorum-based protocol where the semi-trusted intermediary is divided into subcomponents, each controlling a share of the transformation key. Although these schemes is more efficient than "decrypt and re-encrypt", they still have a common problem: When original decryptor or a semi-trusted intermediary is off-line and does not to execute transformation, the delegated decryptor cannot decrypt some ciphertext encrypted for the original decryptor. In fact, it is desirable that a delegated decryptor can decrypt the ciphertext without transformation from other entity.

Recently, a transformation-free proxy (TFP) cryptosystem [7] was present. The TFP scheme allows delegated decryptor to do decryption without any ciphertext transformation. However, in the scheme, the encryption keys aimed to different delegated decryptor are not fixed. Moreover, no formal security notion are given.

1.2 Our Contribution

Proxy Cryptosystem Based on Time Segmentation. In this paper, we apply a time segmentation mode to proxy cryptosystem. Our thinking is from the forward-secure schemes [8, 9]. In a proxy cryptosystem based on time segmentation (PCBTS), a original decryptor registers a public key PK and keeps private the corresponding secret key, which we denote SK. The time during which the public key PK is desired to be valid is devided into segmentations, say n of them, numbered t_1, t_2, $\cdots$, t_n. The public key stays fixed throughout the lifetime of the scheme, this is curial for making such a scheme viable. When the original decryptor wants to delegate his decryption capacity of time segmentation t_i, he derive the proxy secret key at t_i from his secret key SK. Then the proxy decryptor obtains the complete decryption capacity during time segmentation t_i. Moveover, a PCBTS scheme should guarantee that even if adversary knows proxy secret key at time segmentation t_i, messages encrypted during all time segmentations except t_i remain secret.

Moveover, We define a rigorous notion of security for PCBTS and ID-based PCBTS.

PCBTS Schemes. We propose a PCBTS scheme, which security is based on computational BDH assumption [13, 14]. Under this scheme, we construct an ID-based PCBTS scheme.

1.3 Organization

In section 2, we first define PCBTS and formally define its security notion, then a PCBTS scheme is provided under the computational BDH assumption in the secure model. In section 3, we define ID-based PCBTS and formally define security notion for ID-based PCBTS. In this section, we also provide a ID-based PCBTS scheme. Section 4 gives conclusions.

2   Proxy Cryptosystem Based on Time Segmentation and Its Security

In this section, we provide definition of proxy cryptosystem based on time segmentation (PCBTS). We first discuss the form of algorithms to specify such schemes, and then discuss security. After that, we present a secure PCBTS scheme.

2.1   Proxy Cryptosystem Based on Time Segmentation

Definition 2.1. A Proxy cryptosystem based on time segmentation (PCBTS) scheme is a 5-tuple of PPT algorithms ($\mathcal{G}$, $\mathcal{PKD}$, $\mathcal{E}$, $\mathcal{D}$, $\mathcal{PD}$) such that:

- The *key generation algorithm* $\mathcal{G}$ takes as input a security parameter 1^k, and possibly other parameters, to return a public key PK, and corresponding secret key SK. The algorithm is probabilistic.
- The *proxy key derivation algorithm* $\mathcal{PKD}$ takes as input the public key PK, the secret key SK, and the time segmentation t, to return the proxy secret key SK_{ts} of the corresponding time segmentation.
- The *encryption algorithm* $\mathcal{E}$ takes as input PK, a time segmentation t, and a message M, to return a ciphertext C.
- The *decryption algorithm* $\mathcal{D}$ takes as input PK, the corresponding time segmentation t, the secret key SK, and a ciphertext C to return a message M.
- The *proxy decryption algorithm* $\mathcal{PD}$ takes as input PK, the secret proxy secret key SK_{ts} of the corresponding time segmentation t, and a ciphertext C, to return a message M.

These algorithms must satify the standard correctness requirements as follows:

1. for any (PK, SK) output by $\mathcal{G}(1^k)$, and any message M, we have $M = \mathcal{D}(PK, t, SK, \mathcal{E}(PK, t, M))$.
2. for any (PK, SK_{ts}) output by $\mathcal{PKD}(PK, SK, t)$, and any message M, we have $M = \mathcal{PD}(PK, SK_{ts}, \mathcal{E}(PK, t, M))$.

2.2   Security Notion for PCBTS

We wish to assess the security of a PCBTS scheme. To do this efficiently we must first pin down an appropriate model, in which, all potential action of the adversary must be considered. We extend the notion of indistinguishability of chosen plaintext attack (IND-CPA) [10] and the notion of indistinguishability of adaptive chosen ciphertext attack (IND-CCA2) [11], and take into account the obtaining of a proxy secret key of some time segmentation. We call this attack scenario a *selective time segmentation* attack.

The adversary knows the user's public key PK. The goal is that even exposure of some proxy secret keys corresponding to some time segmentations it should be computationally infeasible for an adversary to obtain even a bit plaintext information of a given ciphertext of time segmentation t^* (the proxy secret key of t^* have not been obtained by the adversary) with respect to the already obtained proxy secret keys.

Definition 2.2. A PCBTS scheme is secure against *selective time segmentation, chosen plaintext* attacks (STS-CPA) if no polynomially bound adversary $\mathcal{A}$ has a non-negligible advantage against the Challenger in the following game:

1. The challenger takes a security parameter 1^k and runs the $\mathcal{G}$ algorithm. It gives the adversary the public key PK, it keeps the secret key SK to itself.
2. The adversary issues queries $q_1, q_2, \cdots, q_m$ where query q_i is:
   - Proxy secret key query (t_i). The challenger responds by running algorithm $\mathcal{PKD}$ to generate the proxy secret key SK_{ts}^i corresponding to the time segmentation t_i. It sends SK_{ts}^i to the adversary.
3. The adversary generates a request challenge (t^*, M_0, M_1). Here, M_0 and M_1 are equal plaintext, and t^* is a time segmentation and did not appear in any proxy secret key query in the second step. The challenger picks a random bit $b \in \{0, 1\}$ and sets $C^* = \mathcal{E}(PK, t^*, M_b)$. It sends C^* as the challenger to the adversary.
4. The adversary issues more queries $q_{m+1}, q_{m+2}, \cdots, q_n$ where query is:
   - Proxy secret key query (t_i) where $t_i \neq t^*$. Challenger responds as the second step.

At the end of the game the adversary outputs $b' \in \{0, 1\}$ and wins the game if $b' = b$. The adversary's *advantage* is the absolute value of the difference between its success probability and $1/2$.

Definition 2.3. A PCBTS scheme is secure against *selective time segmentation, chosen ciphertext* attacks (STS-CCA) if no polynomially bound adversary $\mathcal{A}$ has a non-negligible advantage against the challenger in the following game:

1. The challenger takes a security parameter 1^k and runs the $\mathcal{G}$ algorithm. It gives the adversary the public key PK, it keeps the secret key SK to itself.
2. The adversary issues queries $q_1, q_2, \cdots, q_m$ where query q_i is one of:
   - Proxy secret key query (t_i). The challenger responds by running algorithm $\mathcal{PKD}$ to generate the proxy secret key SK_{ts}^i corresponding to the time segmentation t_i. It sends SK_{ts}^i to the adversary.
   - Decryption query (C_i, t_i). The challenger runs algorithm $\mathcal{D}$ to decrypt the ciphertext C_i using the secret key SK. It sends the resulting plaintext to the adversary.
3. The adversary generates a request challenge (t^*, M_0, M_1). Here, M_0 and M_1 are equal plaintext, and t^* is a time segmentation and did not appear in any proxy secret key query in the second step. The challenger picks a random bit $b \in \{0, 1\}$ and sets $C^* = \mathcal{E}(PK, t^*, M_b)$. It sends C^* as the challenger to the adversary.

4. The adversary issues more queries $q_{m+1}, q_{m+2}, \cdots, q_n$ where query is one of
   - Proxy secret key query (t_i) where $t_i \neq t^*$. Challenger responds as the second step.
   - Decryption query (C_i, t_i) where $(C_i, t_i) \neq (C^*, t^*)$. Challenger responds as the second step.

At the end of the game the adversary outputs $b' \in \{0, 1\}$ and wins the game if $b' = b$. The adversary's *advantage* is the absolute value of the difference between its success probability and $1/2$.

For proving the security of a PCBTS scheme, we will also adopt a notion called plaintext awareness (PA) [12].

Definition 2.4. Let $\Pi = (\mathcal{G}, \mathcal{PKD}, \mathcal{E}, \mathcal{D}, \mathcal{PD})$ be a STS-CPA PCBTS scheme in random oracle, we say it is secure against PA if for any adversary $\mathcal{B}$, there exists a polynomial time algorithm $\lambda(k)$-knowledge extractor $\mathcal{K}$ for Π in the following game such that $1-\lambda(k)$ is negligible in k:

1. The challenger takes a security parameter 1^k and runs the $\mathcal{G}$ algorithm. It gives the adversary the public key PK and random oracle H, it keeps the secret key SK to itself.
2. The adversary $\mathcal{B}$ issues queries $q_1, q_2, \cdots, q_m$ where query q_i is one of:

   - The challenger runs algorithm $\mathcal{E}$ to encrypt the plaintext M_i using the public key PK and random oracle H. It discards the M_i and sends the result ciphertext C_i to the adversary $\mathcal{B}$.
   - Random oracle queries h_i. The challenger responds by a random value H_i as the answer of $H(.)$.

3. The adversary $\mathcal{B}$ creates a C^*. We say $C^* \neq C_i$. It sends C^* to the challenger. When the challenger receives C^*, it run the $\lambda(k)$-knowledge extractor $\mathcal{K}$, which takes as input results C_i of queries M_i, results (h_i, H_i) of queries h_i and C^*. It try to extract the corresponding plaintext M^*.

When C^* is valid ciphertext, the success probability of $\mathcal{K}$ to extract the corresponding is at least $\lambda(k)$.

2.3   The Computational Bilinear Diffie-Hellman Assumption

Bilinear Diffie-Hellman problem was formalized by Boneh and Franklin [13]. We briefly review the relevant facts as they appear in [13, 14]. Let G_1 and G_2 be two (multiplicative) cycle groups of prime order q. A bilinear pairing is a map $e: G_1 \times G_1 \to G_2$ with the following properties:

1. Bilinear: $e(P^a, Q^b) = e(P, Q)^{ab}$, where $P, Q \in G_1$, and $a, b \in Z_q^*$.
2. Non-degeneracy: There exists $P \in G_1$ and $Q \in G_1$ such that $e(P, Q) \neq 1$.
3. Computability: There exists an efficient algorithm to computer $e(P, Q)$ for $P, Q \in G_1$.

Definition 2.5. Given group G_1 and G_2 of the same prime order q, a bilinear map $e: G_1 \times G_1 \to G_2$ and a generator P of G_1, then the computational Bilinear

Diffie-Hellman (CBDH) Problem is defined as follows: Given (P, P^a, P^b, P^c) for some a, b, $c \in Z_q^*$ as input, compute $e(P,P)^{abc} \in G_2$. The advantage of an algorithm $\mathcal{A}$ solving CBDH is

$$Adv(\mathcal{A}) = Pr[\mathcal{A}(P, P^a, P^b, P^c) = e(P,P)^{abc}]$$

where the probability is over the random choice of a, b,c in Z_q^*, the random choice of $P \in G_1^*$ and the random bits of $\mathcal{A}$.

Definition 2.6. Let $\mathcal{IG}$ is a CBDH parameter generator that takes a security parameter 1^k as input. We say that $\mathcal{IG}$ satisfies the CBDH assumption if $Adv(\mathcal{A})$ is negligible (in k) for all PPT algorithms $\mathcal{A}$.

2.4 A PCBTS Scheme Based on the CBDH Assumption

Now, we present a PCBTS scheme. Our construction uses the ideas from [2, 3, 4]. The scheme is described as follows.
   The algorithm $\mathcal{G}(1^k)$ does the following:

1. Run $\mathcal{IG}(1^k)$ to generate groups G_1, G_2 of prime order q and bilinear map e.
2. Select two random generators P, $G_1 \in G_1$ and a random $s \in Z_q^*$. Set $P_{pub} = P^s$, $Q_{sec} = Q^s$.
3. Choose a cryptographic hash function H_1: $\{0,1\}^* \rightarrow G_1^*$. Choose a cryptographic hash function H_2: $\{0,1\}^n \rightarrow Z_q^*$. Choose a cryptographic hash function H_3: $G_2 \rightarrow \{0,1\}^n$.
4. The public key is $PK = (G_1, G_2, e, P, P_{pub}, Q, H_1, H_2, H_3)$. The secret key is Q_{sec}.

The message space is $\mathcal{M} = \{0,1\}^{n-l}$. Here $0 < l < n$. The ciphertext space is $\mathcal{C} = G_1 \times G_1 \times \{0,1\}^n$.

The algorithm $\mathcal{PKD}(PK, Q_{sec}, t)$ does the following:

   Choose a random $d \in Z_q^*$, Set $S_t = Q_{sec} \cdot H_1(t)^d$, and $T_t = P^d$. The proxy secret key $PSK = (S_t, T_t)$.
The algorithm $\mathcal{E}(PK, t, M)$ does the following:

1. Choose a random $r_1 \in \{0,1\}^l$, Set $C_1 = P^{r_2}$, where $r_2 = H_2(m \parallel r_1)$.
2. Set $C_2 = H_1(t)^{r_2}$.
3. Set $C_3 = (m \parallel r_1) \oplus H_3(g)$, where $g = e(P_{pub}, Q)^{r_2}$.
4. Output $C = (t, C_1, C_2, C_3)$.

The algorithm $\mathcal{D}(PK, Q_{sec}, C)$ does the following:

1. Compute $g' = e(C_1, Q_{sec})$.
2. Compute $M' = C_3 \oplus H_3(g')$.
3. Set $r_2 = H_2(M')$. Test that $C_1 = P^{r_2}$. If not, reject the ciphertext.
4. Output M, where M is the first $n - l$ bits of M'.

We verify that decryption succeeds. During encryption $(m \parallel r_1)$ is bitwise exclusive-ored with the hash of g. During decryption C_3 is bitwise exclusive-ored with the hash of g'. These masks used during encryption and decryption are the same since:

$$g' = e(C_1, Q_{sec}) = e(P^{r_2}, Q^s) = e(P, Q)^{r_2 s} = e(P_{pub}, Q)^{r_2} = g$$

Thus, decryption recovers M.

The algorithm $\mathcal{PD}(PK, PSK, C)$ does the following:

1. Compute $g' = e(C_1, S_t) \cdot e(T_t, C_2)^{-1}$.
2. Compute $M' = C_3 \oplus H_3(g')$.
3. Set $r_2 = H_2(M')$. Test that $C_1 = P^{r_2}$. If not, reject the ciphertext.
4. Output M, where M is the first $n - l$ bits of M'.

We verify that proxy decryption succeeds. During encryption $(m \parallel r_1)$ is bitwise exclusive-ored with the hash of g. During decryption C_3 is bitwise exclusive-ored with the hash of g'. These masks used during encryption and decryption are the same since:

$$g' = e(C_1, S_t) \cdot e(T_t, C_2)^{-1} = e(P^{r_2}, Q_{sec} \cdot H_1(t)^d) \cdot e(P^d, H_1(t)^{r_2})^{-1}$$

$$= e(P^{r_2}, Q^s) \cdot e(P^{r_2}, H_1(t)^d) \cdot e(P^d, H_1(t)^{r_2})^{-1}$$

$$= e(P^{r_2}, Q^s) \cdot e(P^{r_2}, H_1(t)^d) \cdot e(P^{r_2}, H_1(t)^d)^{-1}$$

$$= e(P^{r_2}, Q^s) = e(P, Q)^{r_2 s} = e(P_{pub}, Q)^{r_2} = g$$

Thus, decryption recovers M.

Our main result of this section is the following.

Theorem 2.1. Under the CBDH assumption, the above PCBTS scheme is secure in the sense of STS-CCA.

For prove the main theorem, we will first prove Lemma 2.2 and Lemma 2.3.

Lemma 2.2. Under the CBDH assumption, the above PCBTS scheme is secure in the sense of STS-CPA.

The proof of Theorem 2.1 is our full paper [16].

Lemma 2.3. The PCBTS scheme is PA secure.

The proof of Theorem 2.1 is our full paper [16].

Proof of Theorem 2.1. Due to the work of [12], If a encryption is CPA secure, at the same time it also PA, then it is CCA. So the theorem follows directly from Lemma 2.2 and Lemma 2.3.

3   ID-Based Version of Proxy Cryptosystem Based on Time Segmentation

In this section, we will discuss the ID-based version of PCBTS. Like the discussion order of the PCBTS, we first discuss the form of algorithms to specify such schemes, and then discuss security. After that, we convert the PCBTS proposed into a secure ID-based PCBTS scheme.

3.1 ID-Based PCBTS

Definition 3.1. A ID-based PCBTS scheme is a 6-tuple of PPT algorithms ($\mathcal{S}$, $\mathcal{EXT}$, $\mathcal{PKD}$, $\mathcal{E}$, $\mathcal{D}$, $\mathcal{PD}$) such that:

- The *Setup algorithm* $\mathcal{S}$ takes as input a security parameter 1^k, and possibly other parameters, to return system parameters PM, and master-key MK. The algorithm is probabilistic.
- The *Extract algorithm* $\mathcal{EXT}$ takes as input the system parameters PM, the master key MK, and an arbitrary $ID \in \{0,1\}^*$, to return a secret key SK.
- The *proxy key derivation algorithm* $\mathcal{PKD}$ takes as input PM, ID, and a secret key SK, and the time segmentation t, to return the secret proxy secret key SK_{ts} of the corresponding time segmentation.
- The *encryption algorithm* $\mathcal{E}$ takes as input PM, ID, a time segmentation t, and a message M, to return a ciphertext C.
- The *decryption algorithm* $\mathcal{D}$ takes as input PM, ID, the corresponding time segmentation t, the secret key SK, and a ciphertext C to return a message M.
- The *proxy decryption algorithm* $\mathcal{PD}$ takes as input PM, ID, the secret proxy secret key SK_{ts} of the corresponding time segmentation t, and a ciphertext C, to return a message M.

These algorithms must satify the standard correctness requirements as follows:

1. for any (ID, SK) output by $\mathcal{EXT}(PM, MK, ID)$, and any message M, we have $M = \mathcal{D}(PM, ID, t, SK, \mathcal{E}(PM, ID, t, M))$.
2. for any (ID, SK_{ts}) output by $\mathcal{PKD}(PM, ID, SK, t)$, and any message M, we have $M = \mathcal{PD}(PM, ID, SK_{ts}, \mathcal{E}(PM, ID, t, M))$.

3.2 Security Notion for ID-Based PCBTS

When we access the security of an ID-based PCBTS scheme, selective time segmentation accack and chosen ciphertext attack should also be considered. Moveover, as the general ID-based cryptosystem, the attacker may implement secret key extraction attack, which first appears in [14].

Definition 3.2. An ID-based PCBTS is secure against *secret key extraction, selective time segmentation, chosen ciphertext* attacks (ID-STS-CCA) if no polynomially bound adversary $\mathcal{A}$ has a non-negligible advantage against the Challenger in the following ID-based STS-CCA game:

1. The challenger takes a security parameter 1^k and runs the $\mathcal{S}$ algorithm. It gives the adversary the system parameter PM, It keeps the master key MK to itself.

2. The adversary issues queries q_1, q_2, $\cdots$, q_m where query q_i is one of:
   - Extraction query (ID_i). The challenger responds by running algorithm $\mathcal{EXT}$ to generate the secret key SK_i corresponding to (ID_i). It sends SK_i to the adversary.
   - Proxy secret key query (ID_i, t_i). The challenger first generates the secret key SK_i corresponding to ID_i, then responds by running algorithm $\mathcal{PKD}$ to generate the proxy secret key SK_{ts}^i corresponding to the time segmentation t_i. It sends SK_{ts}^i to the adversary.
   - Decryption query (ID_i, C_i, t_i). The challenger runs algorithm $\mathcal{D}$ to decrypt the ciphertext C_i. It sends the resulting plaintext to the adversary.
3. The adversary generates a request challenge (ID^*, t^*, M_0, M_1). Here, M_0 and M_1 are equal plaintext, ID^* is an identity and did not appear in any extraction query in the second step, (ID^*, t^*) did not appear in any proxy secret key of query in the second step. The challenger picks a random bit $b \in \{0, 1\}$ and sets $C^* = \mathcal{E}(PM, ID^*, t^*, M_b)$. It sends C^* as the challenger to the adversary.
4. The adversary issues more queries q_{m+1}, q_{m+2}, $\cdots$, q_n where query is one of
   - Extraction query (ID_i) where $ID_i \neq ID^*$.
   - Proxy secret key query (ID_i, t_i) where $(ID_i, t_i) \neq (ID^*, t^*)$. Challenger responds as the second step. Challenger responds as the second step.
   - Decryption query (ID_i, C_i, t_i) where $(ID_i, C_i, t_i) \neq (ID^*, C^*, t^*)$. Challenger responds as the second step.

At the end of the game the adversary outputs $b' \in \{0, 1\}$ and wins the game if $b' = b$. The adversary's *advantage* is the absolute value of the difference between its success probability and $1/2$.

3.3   An ID-Based PCBTS Scheme Based on the Computational BDH Assumption

Now, we convert the PCBTS scheme in section 2 into ID-based PCBTS scheme. The scheme is described as follows:

The algorithm $\mathcal{S}(1^k)$ does the following:

1. Run $\mathcal{IG}(1^k)$ to generate groups G_1, G_2 of prime order q and bilinear map e.
2. Select a random generator $P \in G_1$ and a random $s \in Z_q^*$. Set $P_{pub} = P^s$.
3. Choose a cryptographic hash function H_0: $\{0,1\}^* \rightarrow G_1$. Choose a cryptographic hash function H_1: $\{0,1\}^* \rightarrow G_1$. Choose a cryptographic hash function H_2: $\{0,1\}^n \rightarrow Z_q^*$. Choose a cryptographic hash function H_3: $G_2 \rightarrow \{0,1\}^n$.
4. The system parameter is $PM = (G_1, G_2, e, P, P_{pub}, H_0, H_1, H_2, H_3)$. The master key is s.

The message space is $\mathcal{M} = \{0,1\}^{n-l}$. Here $0 < l < n$. The ciphertext space is $\mathcal{C} = G_1 \times G_1 \times \{0,1\}^n$.

The algorithm $\mathcal{EXT}(PM, s, ID)$ does the following:

1. Compute $Q_{ID} = H_0(ID) \in G_1^*$.
2. Set the secret key d_{ID} to be $d_{ID} = sQ_{ID}$ where s is the master key.

The algorithm $\mathcal{PKD}(PM, ID, d_{ID}, t)$ does as follows:

1. Compute $Q_{ID} = H_0(ID)$.
2. Choose a random $d \in Z_q^*$, Set $S_t^{ID} = d_{ID} \cdot H_1(t)^d$, and $T_t^{ID} = P^d$. The proxy secret key $PSK = (S_t^{ID}, T_t^{ID})$.

The algorithm $\mathcal{E}(PM, ID, t, M)$ does as follows:

1. Compute $Q_{ID} = H_0(ID)$.
2. Choose a random $r_1 \in \{0,1\}^l$, Set $C_1 = P^{r_2}$, where $r_2 = H_2(M \| r_1)$.
3. Set $C_2 = H_1(t)^{r_2}$.
4. Set $C_3 = (M \| r_1) \oplus H_3(g)$, where $g = e(P_{pub}, Q_{ID})^{r_2}$.
5. Output $C = (t, C_1, C_2, C_3)$.

The algorithm $\mathcal{D}(PM, ID, t, d_{ID}, C)$ does as follows:

1. Compute $g' = e(C_1, d_{ID})$.
2. Compute $M' = C_3 \oplus H_3(g')$.
3. Set $r_2 = H_2(M')$. Test that $C_1 = P^{r_2}$. If not, reject the ciphertext.
4. Output M, where M is the first $n - l$ bits of M'.

We verify that decryption succeeds. During encryption $(M \| r_1)$ is bitwise exclusive-ored with the hash of g. During decryption C_3 is bitwise exclusive-ored with the hash of g'. These masks used during encryption and decryption are the same since:

$$g' = e(C_1, d_{ID}) = e(P^{r_2}, (Q_{ID})^s) = e(P, Q_{ID})^{r_2 s} = e(P_{pub}, Q_{ID})^{r_2} = g$$

Thus, decryption recovers M.

The algorithm $\mathcal{PD}(PM, ID, PSK, t, C)$ does the following:

1. Compute $g' = e(C_1, S_t^{ID}) \cdot e(T_t^{ID}, C_2)^{-1}$.
2. Compute $M' = C_3 \oplus H_3(g')$.
3. Set $r_2 = H_2(M')$. Test that $C_1 = P^{r_2}$. If not, reject the ciphertext.
4. Output M, where M is the first $n - l$ bits of M'.

We verify that proxy decryption succeeds. During encryption $(m \| r_1)$ is bitwise exclusive-ored with the hash of g. During decryption C_3 is bitwise exclusive-ored with the hash of g'. These masks used during encryption and decryption are the same since:

$$g' = e(C_1, S_t^{ID}) \cdot e(T_t^{ID}, C_2)^{-1} = e(P^{r_2}, d_{ID} \cdot H_1(t)^d) \cdot e(P^d, H_1(t)^{r_2})^{-1}$$

$$= e(P^{r_2}, (Q_{ID})^s) \cdot e(P^{r_2}, H_1(t)^d) \cdot e(P^d, H_1(t)^{r_2})^{-1}$$

$$= e(P^{r_2}, (Q_{ID})^s) \cdot e(P^{r_2}, H_1(t)^d) \cdot e(P^{r_2}, H_1(t)^d)^{-1}$$

$$= e(P^{r_2}, (Q_{ID})^s) = e(P, Q_{ID})^{r_2 s} = e(P_{pub}, Q_{ID})^{r_2} = g$$

Thus, decryption recovers M.

About the security of the scheme, we have the following result.

Theorem 3.1. The ID-PCBTS scheme is secure.

The proof of Theorem 3.1 is our full paper [16].

4   Conclusion

In this paper, we have proposed a practical mode of proxy cryptosystem: proxy cryptosystem based on time segmentation (PCBTS). Under this mode, we presented the security model of PCBTS and ID-based PCBTS. At the same time, the corresponding schemes of PCBTS and ID-based PCBTS are given. Our schemes are practical in e-commence scenario.

References

1. Mambo, M. and Okamoto, E.: Proxy cryptosystem: Delegation of a power to decrypt ciphertexts. IEICE Transaction on Fundaments of Electronics Communications and Computer Science, E80-A/1, 54-63, 1997.
2. Gentry, C. and Silverberg, A.: Hierarchical identity-based cryptography. Asiacrypt 2002, LNCS vol. 2501, 2002, pp. 548-566.
3. Canetti,R., Halevi, S. and Katz, J.: A Forward-Secure Public-Key Encryption Scheme. IEE Proceedings - Computers and Digital Eurocrypt 2003, LNCS vol. 2656, pp. 255-271, Springer-Verlag, 2003.
4. E. Fujisaki, T. Okamoto. How to enhance the security of public-key encryption. IEICE Trans. fundamentals, Vol. E83-A, NO. 1, 2000.
5. Blaze, M., Bleumer, G. and Strauss, M.: Divertible protocol and atomic proxy cryptography. In Proceeding of Eurocrypt'98, LNCS 1403, 1998, pp. 127-144.
6. Jakobsson, M.: On quorum controlled asymmetric proxy re-encryption. In Proceedings of public key cryptography, pp. 112-121.
7. Wang, L., Cao, Z., Okamoto, E., Miao, Y. and Okamoto, T.: Transformation-free Proxy Cryptosystems and Their Applications to Electronic Commerce. Infosecu'04, pp. 92, 2004.
8. Bellare, M. and Miner, S. K.: A forward-secure digital signature scheme. Crypto'99, LNCS vol. 1666, Springer-Verlag, 1999, pp.431-448.
9. Bellare, M., Yee, A.: Forward security in private-key cryptography. CT-RSA 2003, LNCS vol. 2612, Springer-Verlag, 2003, pp.1-18.
10. Goldwasser, S. and Micali, S.: Probabilistic Encryption. J. Computer and System Sciences, Vol. 28, 1984, pp. 270-299.

11. Rackoff, C. and Simon, D.: Non-interactive zero-knowledge proof of knowledge and chosen ciphertext attack. In Advanes in Cryptology - CRYPTO'91, LNCS 576, 1992, pp. 433-444.
12. Bellare, M., Desai, A., Pointcheval, D. and Rogaway, P.: Relations among notions of security for public-key encryption schemes. In Advanes in Cryptology - CRYPTO'98, LNCS 1462, 1998, pp. 26-45.
13. Boneh, D. and Franklin, M.: Identity based encryption from the Weil pairing. Crypto 2001, LNCS vol. 2139, Springer-Verlag, 2001, pp. 213-229.
14. Boneh, D. Lynn, B. and Shacham, H.: Short signatures from the Weil pairing. Asiacrypt 2002, LNCS vol. 2248, Springer-Verlag, 2001, pp. 514-532.
15. Bellare, M. and Rogaway, P.: Random oracle are practical: a paradiam for designing efficient protocols. In First ACM Conference on Computer and Communications Security, ACM, 1993.
16. Zhou, Y. Cao, Z. and Chai, Z.: Constructing Secure Proxy Cryptosystem. http:// tdt.sjtu.edu.cn/YZ/Constructing Secure Proxy Cryptosystem.pdf.

Towards a General RC4-Like Keystream Generator

Guang Gong[1], Kishan Chand Gupta[2], Martin Hell[3], and Yassir Nawaz[1]

[1]Department of Electrical and Computer Engineering, University of Waterloo,
Waterloo, ON, N2L 3G1, Canada
[2]Centre for Applied Cryptographic Research,
University of Waterloo,
Waterloo, ON, N2L 3G1, Canada
[3]Department of Information Technology,
Lund University,
P.O. Box 118, S-221 00 Lund, Sweden
G.Gong@ece.uwaterloo.ca, kgupta@math.uwaterloo.ca,
martin@it.lth.se, ynawaz@engmail.uwaterloo.ca

Abstract. RC4 was designed in 1987 when 8-bit and 16-bit processors were commercially available. Today, most processors use 32-bit or 64-bit words but using original RC4 with 32/64 bits is infeasible due to the large memory constraints and the number of operations in the key scheduling algorithm. In this paper we propose a new 32/64-bit RC4-like keystream generator. The proposed generator produces 32 or 64 bits in each iteration and can be implemented in software with reasonable memory requirements. It has a huge internal state and offers higher resistance to state recovery attacks than the original 8-bit RC4. Further, on a 32-bit processor the generator is 3.1 times faster than original RC4. We also show that it can resist attacks that are successful on the original RC4. The generator is suitable for high speed software encryption.

Keywords: RC4, stream ciphers, random shuffle, keystream generator.

1   Introduction

RC4 was designed by Ron Rivest in 1987 and kept as a trade secret until it leaked out in 1994. In the open literature, there is a very small number of proposed keystream generators that are not based on shift registers. An interesting design approach of RC4 which has originated from the exchange-shuffle paradigm [12], is to use a relatively big array/table that slowly changes with time under the control of itself. As discussed by Golić in [6], for such a generator only a few general statistical properties of the keystream can be measured by statistical tests and several properties of the keystream are hard to establish theoretically. Two recent RC4-like 8-bit stream ciphers are VMPC [26] and RC4A [21]. RC4 consists of a table of all the $N = 2^n$ possible n-bit words and two n-bit pointers. In original RC4 n is 8, and thus has a huge state of $log_2(2^8! \times (2^8)^2) \approx 1700$ bits. It is thus impossible to guess even a small part of this state and almost all

D. Feng, D. Lin, and M. Yung (Eds.): CISC 2005, LNCS 3822, pp. 162–174, 2005.

the techniques developed to attack stream ciphers based on linear feedback shift registers (LFSR) fail on RC4.

In this paper we propose some modifications to the RC4 algorithm so that it can exploit the 32-bit and 64-bit processor architectures without increasing the size of the table significantly. We call the proposed algorithm RC4(n, m), since it is general enough to incorporate different word as well as table sizes. For example with 32-bit word size a table of length 256 words can be used. We try to keep the original structure of RC4 as much as possible, however the proposed changes affect some underlying design principles on which the security of RC4 is based. Therefore we analyze the security of the modified RC4 and compare it to the original RC4. We show that RC4(n, m) is faster than RC4 and also that it is secure against several proposed attacks on RC4.

The rest of the paper is organized as follows. In Section 2 we give a brief description of original RC4. In Section 3 we propose a modified RC4 keystream generator. The security of the proposed generator is analyzed in Section 4 followed by a performance analysis in Section 5. We conclude in Section 6.

1.1 Motivation

When RC4 was developed, 8-bit and 16-bit processors were commercially available. Using $n = 8$ was suitable for these processors and the amount of memory needed was feasible. Today the processors have word lengths of 32 bits or 64 bits but the most common mode for RC4 still uses $n = 8$. Using a larger n requires more memory and longer initialization. For $n = 32$ or $n = 64$, the size of the memory needed and the key initialization time are too high. Still, since the processors can work with 32-bit and 64-bit words it is of interest to investigate if it is possible to take advantage of this. To the best of our knowledge, no serious attempts has been made to investigate modifications to the RC4 algorithm such that it can take full advantage of the 32-bit and 64-bit processors.

There are several other stream ciphers that take advantage of 32-bit processors, but RC4 is interesting due to the simplicity of the algorithm and its wide usage in practical applications, e.g., WEP and SSL.

2   Original RC4

In this section we give a description of the original RC4. We also give a brief description of previous attacks on RC4.

2.1   Description of RC4

The RC4 algorithm consists of two parts: The key scheduling algorithm (KSA) and the pseudo-random generation algorithm (PRGA). The algorithms are shown in Figure 1 where l is the length of the secret key in bytes, and N is the size of the array S or the S-box in words. A common keysize in RC4 is between 5 and 32 bytes. In most applications RC4 is used with a word size

KSA(K, S)	PRGA(S)

for i = 0 to N − 1
 S[i] = i;
 j = 0;
 for i = 0 to N − 1
 j = (j + S[i] + K[i mod l]) mod N;
 Swap(S[i],S[j]);
	i = 0;
	 j = 0;
	 while (1)
	 i = (i + 1) mod N;
	 j = (j + S[i]) mod N;
	 Swap(S[i],S[j]);
	 out = S[(S[i] + S[j]) mod N];

Fig. 1. The Key Scheduling Algorithm (KSA) and Pseudo-Random Generation Algorithm (PRGA) in RC4

$n = 8$ and array size $N = 2^8$. In the first phase of RC4 operation an identity permutation $(0, 1, ..., N − 1)$ is loaded in the array S. A secret key K is then used to initialize S to a random permutation by shuffling the words in S. During the second phase of the operation, the PRGA produces random words from the permutation in S. Each iteration of the PRGA loop produces one output word which constitutes the running keystream. The keystream is bit-wise XORed with the plaintext to obtain the ciphertext. All the operations described in Figure 1 are byte operations ($n = 8$). Most modern processors however operate on 32-bit or 64-bit words. If the word size in RC4 is increased to $n = 32$ or $n = 64$, to increase its performance, the size of array S becomes 2^{32} or 2^{64} bytes which is not practical. Note that these are the array sizes to store all the 32-bit or 64-bit permutations respectively.

2.2   Previous Analysis of RC4

Cryptanalysis of RC4 attracted a lot of attention in the cryptographic community after it was made public in 1994. Indeed numerous significant weaknesses were discovered, including Finney's forbidden states [2], classes of weak keys [23], patterns that appear twice the expected probability (the second byte bias) [14], partial message recovery [14], full key recovery attacks [4], analysis of biased distribution of RC4 initial permutation [17], and predicting and distinguishing attacks [13].

Knudsen et al. have attacked versions of RC4 with $n < 8$ by their backtracking algorithm [11]. The most serious weakness in RC4 was observed by Fluhrer et al. in [4] where RC4 was proved to have a practical attack in the security protocol WEP.

Two variants of RC4 has recently been proposed: RC4A [21] and VMPC [26]. RC4A works with two RC4 arrays and its keystream generation stage is slightly more efficient than RC4's, but initialization stage requires twice the effort of RC4. VMPC has several changes to the KSA, the IV integration, the round operation and the output selection. Note that RC4A and VMPC use $n = 8$ as parameter. Maximov described in [16] a linear distinguisher for both the variants, requiring 2^{58} data for RC4A and requiring 2^{54} data for VMPC. Tsunoo et al. described in [25] a distinguisher for RC4A and VMPC keystream generators, requiring 2^{24} and 2^{23} keystream prefixes respectively. For further weaknesses of RC4, and most of the known attacks on it see [7, 2, 9, 6, 5, 18, 8, 23, 11, 14, 4, 24, 22, 17, 20, 21, 13, 1, 16, 25, 15].

3   Proposed Modification to RC4

We now propose a modification to the original RC4 algorithm which enables us to release 32 bits or 64 bits in each iteration of the PRGA loop. This is done by increasing the word size to 32 or 64 while keeping the array size S much smaller than 2^{32} or 2^{64}. We will denote the new algorithm as RC4(n, m) where $N = 2^n$ is the size of the array S in words, m is the word size in bits, $n \leq m$ and $M = 2^m$. For example RC4$(8, 32)$ means that the size of the array S is 256 and each element of S holds 32-bit words. Also we will use the term Z_{2^λ} to represent the integer ring modulo 2^λ.

3.1   Pseudo-Random Generation Algorithm

If we choose n to be much smaller than m ($m = 32$ or 64) in RC4(n, m), then this results in reasonable memory requirements for the array S. However now the contents of the array S do not constitute a complete permutation of 32-bit or 64-bit words. In RC4, a swap operation is used to update the state between outputs. Using a swap to update the state in RC4(n, m) will not change the elements in the array. Instead, to update the state we add an integer addition modulo 2^{32} (2^{64} for $n = 64$). This way of updating the state is the first difference between RC4 and RC4(n, m). Since the state will be updated by replacing a random element by another random m-bit number, the swap operation is not needed. The index value that is updated is the value used for computing the output value. Updating the array with new values is important since the array is not a permutation and the size of the array is only a small fraction of all the possible numbers in Z_M.

   The second main difference between original RC4 and this variant is the usage of a third variable, k, in addition to i and j. This m-bit variable is used for two reasons. First, to mask the output so that it does not simply represent a value stored in the array. Second, to ensure that the new value in the update step does not depend on just one or a few values in the array. The variable k is initialized in the KSA and is key dependent.

3.2   Key Scheduling Algorithm

The key scheduling algorithm (KSA) in RC4 is used to permute the elements in the array in a key dependent way. Each element is swapped with a random element. In this variant of RC4 the elements will not be a permutation of a small set so a similar modification is made to the KSA as to the PRGA. In order to

KSA(K, S)	PRGA(S)

for i = 0 to N − 1
 S[i] = a_i;
j = k = 0;
Repeat r times
 for i = 0 to N − 1
  j = (j + S[i] + K[i mod l]) mod N;
  Swap(S[i],S[j]);
  S[i] = S[i] + S[j] mod M;
  k = k + S[i] mod M;
	i = 0;
	j = 0;
	while (1)
	 i = (i + 1) mod N;
	 j = (j + S[i]) mod N;
	 k = (k + S[j]) mod M;
	 out = (S[(S[i] + S[j]) mod N] + k) mod M;
	 S[(S[i] + S[j]) mod N] = k + S[i] mod M;

Fig. 2. The modified Key Scheduling Algorithm (KSA) and Pseudo-Random Generation Algorithm (PRGA) for RC4(n, m)

achieve a high degree of randomness in the key scheduling we keep the swap operation in the KSA. In addition to the swap operation each word is updated through an integer addition. We give some initial values, a_i, for RC4(8, 32), in Appendix A. The modified KSA and PRGA are given in Figure 2 where $N = 2^n$, $M = 2^m$, K is a vector of bytes and l is the length of the key K in bytes. RC4(n, m) can use the same flexible span of keysizes as RC4. The value of r in the KSA is motivated below and for a random array with 256 32-bit numbers the value of r is 20.

We take the example of 256 32-bit numbers to motivate the number of steps used in the KSA. The array is initiated with 256 fixed 32-bit numbers and after the key scheduling algorithm the goal is that without knowing any bits of the key an attacker can not guess the number in any array position with probability significantly greater than 2^{-32}. Since the array only contains a small fraction of all 32-bit numbers, the entries need to be updated. We update as the sum of the two swapped entries. After running through the array once, the probability that value i is not updated is

$$\left(\frac{255}{256}\right)^{256} \approx 0.37,$$

so a known value will be in the array with probability ≈ 0.37. The probability that this value is not updated after r rounds is 0.37^r. For a random array with 256 32-bit numbers the probability that a specific number is in the array is

$$1 - (1 - 2^{-32})^{256} \approx 2^{-24}$$

since a value can be present more than once in our case. We run the key initialization a sufficient number of rounds so that any initial value remains unupdated with probability $\leq 2^{-24}$. Hence, the number of rounds, r, we need in the initialization is

$$\left(\frac{255}{256}\right)^{256r} = 2^{-24} \Rightarrow r \approx 16.6.$$

Table 1. The minimum number of rounds in the key scheduling

Mode	r	Mode	r
RC4(8, 32)	16.6	RC4(8, 64)	38.7
RC4(9, 32)	15.9	RC4(9, 64)	38.1
RC4(10, 32)	15.2	RC4(10, 64)	37.4
RC4(11, 32)	14.6	RC4(11, 64)	36.7
RC4(12, 32)	13.9	RC4(12, 64)	36.1

For the case RC4(8, 32) we will take the value of r to be 20. Similarly the value of r can be calculated for different array size and different bit numbers. In Table 1 we list the minimum number of rounds needed in the key scheduling such that no number has significantly higher probability of being in the array than any other number. We suggest to always use 20 rounds in the 32-bit version and always 40 rounds in the 64-bit version, when the array size is between 2^8 and 2^{12}.

4   Security Analysis of RC4(n, m)

In this section we analyze the security of RC4(n, m). We show that RC4(n, m) resists all known significant attacks on RC4. We consider the resistance of the generator against state recovery attacks and the randomness properties of the keystream.

4.1   Statistical Tests on the Keystream

Keystream generated by the RC4(8, 32) stream cipher was tested with NIST statistical tests [19]. No bias was found by any of the 16 tests from the NIST suite. We tested 2^{35} output bits from the generator.

4.2   Security of the Key Scheduling Algorithm

We choose the number of steps in the key scheduling algorithm such that the probability that a specific number is not updated is smaller than the probability that this number is present in a random array of size N with m-bit numbers. This ensures that an attacker can not guess an array entry with probability significantly higher than $N/2^m$ when key generation starts. However, even if r is small it is unclear if an attacker can use the information about the values in the array in an actual attack. This is because the first output is the sum of $20 \cdot 256 + 2$ for RC4($n, 32$) and $40 \cdot 256 + 2$ for RC4($n, 64$) previous and current values in the array.

4.3   Internal State of RC4(n, m)

Like the original RC4, the security of RC4(n, m) comes from its huge internal state. The size of the internal state of original RC4 is approximately 1700 bits. In case of RC4(n, m) the internal state does not consist of a permutation and it may have repetitions of words. The number of ways of putting 2^m elements into N cells where repetitions are allowed is $(2^m)^N$. Note, in RC4(n, m) we are using an m-bit variable k, which can be thought of as another cell. Therefore the size of the internal state is simply given by $N^2 \times (2^m)^{N+1}$. For example for RC4$(8, 32)$ this number is 8240 bits which is much larger than original RC4. Recovering the internal state of RC4(n, m) is therefore much harder than recovering the internal state of RC4.

4.4   Resistance to IV Weakness

Fluhrer, Mantin and Shamir showed in [4] a key recovery attack on RC4 if several IVs were known. The attack will work if the IV precedes or follows the key. In [15], Mantin showed that XORing the IV and the key also allows for a key recovery attack in the chosen IV model. The attack in which the IV precedes the key relies on the fact that the state at some point is in a *resolved* condition, which means that with probability 0.05, we can predict the output and also recover one byte of the key. Repeating the attack recovers another byte of the key etc. In RC4(n, m) this attack will not be possible. In the resolved condition the value i must be such that if $X = S_i[1]$ and $Y = S_i[X]$, then $i \geq 1$, $i \geq X$ and $i \geq X + Y$, where $S_i[V]$ is the entry $S[V]$ at time i. Moreover, $S_i[1]$, $S_i[X]$ and $S_i[X + Y]$ must be known to the attacker. Since the array is iterated 20 times for RC4$(8, 32)$ and the key is used in all iterations, an attacker will not know the state after one iteration. Hence, the attacker can not know the state at a time when $i > 1$ in the last iteration which would be necessary for the attack to work. With similar arguments, we can conclude that the IV weakness in RC4 cannot be used for RC4(n, m) when the IV follows or is XORed with the key either.

Concatenating the IV and the secret key does not seem to introduce an exploitable weakness to the cipher. However, we still consider it better to use a hash function on the secret key and IV and then use the hash value as session key. Then no related keys will be used if the IV is e.g., a counter. This is the mode used in SSL.

4.5   Resistance to Mantin's Distinguishing Attack

In [14] Mantin and Shamir discovered that the second output byte of RC4 is extremely biased, i.e., it takes the value of zero with probability $2/N$ instead of $1/N$. This is due to the fact that if $S_0[2] = 0$ and $S_0[1] \neq 2$, the second output byte of the keystream is zero with probability one. In RC4(n, m) the output is given by out $= (S[(S[i] + S[j]) \bmod N] + k) \bmod M$, where we assume that k is uniformly distributed. Therefore if $S_0[2] = 0$ and $S_0[1] \neq 2$ in RC4(n, m), the output word will still be uniformly distributed due to k. Therefore Mantin's distinguishing attack does not apply to RC4(n, m).

4.6   Resistance to Paul and Preneel's Distinguishing Attack

In [20] Paul and Preneel discovered a bias in the first two output bytes of the RC4 keystream. They observed that if $S_0[1] = 2$, then the first two output bytes of RC4 are always different. Therefore the probability that the first two output bytes are equal is $(1 - 1/N)/N$ which leads to a distinguishing attack. In RC4(n, m) however due to the uniform distribution of k, the above state does not affect the distribution of the first two output bytes. Therefore this attack does not apply to RC4(n, m).

4.7   Probability of Weak States

RC4 has a number of weak states, called Finney states [2]. These states have very short cycles, of length only 65280. The cipher is in a Finney state if $j = i + 1$ and $S[j] = 1$. In this case the swap will be made between $S[i]$ and $S[i + 1]$ and both i and j are incremented by 1. Since the RC4 next state function is an invertible mapping and the starting state is not a Finney state, RC4 will never enter any of these weak states. It is easy to see that RC4(n, m) also has weak states. When all entries are even and k is even, then all outputs as well as all future entries will be even, resulting in a biased keystream. The state update function in RC4(n, m) is not an invertible mapping so it will always be possible to enter one of these weak states. However the probability that all state entries, as well as k are even is very low, 2^{-257}. From this we can conclude that these weak states are of no concern to the security of the cipher.

4.8   Forward Secrecy in RC4(n, m)

Like most of the keystream generators, RC4(n, m) keystream generator can also be represented as a finite state machine. Suppose $N = 2^n$, $M = 2^m$ and $R = Z_N^2 \times Z_M^{N+1}$. The next state function is $f : R \to R$. Let $(i, j, k, x_0, x_1, \cdots, x_{N-1}) \in R$ be any state, and $(e, d, p, y_0, y_1, \cdots, y_{N-1}) \in R$ be the next state of the function f. Then we have $e = i + 1 \bmod N$, $d = j + x_e \bmod N$, $p = k + x_d$, $v = x_e + x_d \bmod M$, $y_{v \bmod N} = k + x_e$ and $y_t = x_t, \forall t \neq v \bmod N$. Output of the cipher is $x_{v \bmod N} + p$. As seen above we can deterministically write down the value of each parameter of the next state. So given a state $(e, d, p, y_0, y_1, \cdots, y_{N-1})$, we can recover $(i, j, k, x_0, x_1, \cdots, x_{N-1})$ except x_v because x_v has been replaced. Therefore, without the knowledge of x_v the state function is non invertible.

4.9   Cycle Property

In original RC4 the state function is invertible. Non invertible state functions are known to cause a significantly shorter average cycle length. If the size of the internal state is s and the next state function is randomly chosen then the average cycle length is about $2^{\frac{s}{2}}$. For a randomly chosen invertible next state function the average cycle length is 2^{s-1}, (see [3]). As s in RC4$(8, 32)$ is huge (i.e., 8240) the reduction in cycle length is not a problem.

4.10   Randomness of the Keystream

To analyze the keystream of RC4(n, m) we first state the security principles underlying the design of original RC4. The KSA intends to turn an identity permutation S into a pseudorandom permutation of elements and PRGA generates one output byte from a pseudorandom location of S in every round. At every round the secret internal state S is changed by the swapping of elements, one in a known location and another pointed to by a random index. Therefore we can say that the security of original RC4 depends on the following three factors.

- Uniform distribution of the initial permutation of elements in S.
- Uniform distribution of the value of index pointer j.
- Uniform distribution of the index pointer from which the output is taken (i.e., $(S[i] + S[j]) \bmod N$).

The above three conditions are necessary but not sufficient. The KSA uses a secret key to provide a uniformly distributed initial permutation of the elements in S. The value of the index pointer j is updated by the statement $j = (j + S[i]) \bmod N$. Since the elements in S are uniformly distributed the value of j is also uniformly distributed. By the same argument $(S[i] + S[j]) \bmod N$ is also uniformly distributed. Note that the internal state of RC4 consists of the contents of array S and the index pointer j. The state update function consists of an update of the value of j and the update of the permutation in S through a swap operation given by the statement $\text{Swap}(S[i], S[j])$. Since j is updated in a uniformly distributed way, the selection of the locations to be swapped is also uniformly distributed. This ensures that the internal state of RC4 evolves in a uniformly distributed way.

We now consider RC4(n, m). The first difference from original RC4 is that whereas the array S in original RC4 is a permutation of all the 256 elements in Z_{2^8}, the array S in RC4(n, m) only contains 2^n m-bit words out of 2^m possible words in Z_{2^m}. Consider the PRGA and assume that the initial permutation of 2^n elements in S is uniformly distributed over Z_{2^m}. Then the index pointer j is update by the statement

$$j = j + S[i] \quad \bmod N$$

where $j \in Z_{2^n}$ and $S[i] \in Z_{2^m}$. If the value of $S[i]$ is uniformly distributed over Z_{2^m}, the value of index pointer j is also uniformly distributed over Z_{2^n}. This implies that the value of the index pointer from which the output is taken (i.e., $S[i] + S[j] \bmod N$) is uniformly distributed over Z_{2^n}. For the above properties to hold during PRGA phase it is essential that the internal state of the RC4(n, m) evolves in a uniformly distributed manner. Recall that in original RC4 the uniform distribution of pointer j was the reason for the state to evolve uniformly since all the 256 elements in Z_{2^8} were present in the state. However in RC4(n, m) this is not the case and the uniform distribution of j over Z_{2^n} is not sufficient. The state update function also consists of the update of an element in S by integer addition modulo M given by the statement

$$S[S[i] + S[j] \quad \bmod N] = k + S[i] \quad \bmod M.$$

Since both k and $S[i]$ are uniformly distributed, the updated element in the state is also uniformly distributed. The internal state of RC4(n, m) evolves in a uniformly distributed manner and therefore the output of the cipher is also uniformly distributed, i.e., all the elements from Z_{2^m} occur with equal probability.

5   Performance of RC4(n, m)

RC4($n, 32$) has been designed to exploit the 32-bit architecture of the current processors. If n is chosen such that the corresponding memory requirements are reasonable, RC4($n, 32$) can give higher throughput than the original 8-bit RC4. We implemented both 8-bit RC4 and RC4($8, 32$) on a PC and computed the ratio of the throughput obtained from both. Our results show that RC4($8, 32$) is approximately 3.1 times faster than the original 8-bit RC4 on a 32-bit machine. On a 64-bit machine RC4($8, 64$) is 6.2 times faster than RC4. This speedup is significant when large files are encrypted.

Though the keystream generation is faster than original RC4, the key scheduling algorithm is slower. This is due to the importance of sufficient randomness in the initial state when keystream generation starts. In a situation where many small packets are encrypted with different keys/IVs, RC4 might still be faster due to its faster KSA.

6   Conclusions and Future Work

In this paper we have investigated a possible extension to the RC4 stream cipher. We motivate this by the fact that modern computers are based on a 32/64-bit architecture. We propose a stream cipher, RC4(n, m), that is similar to RC4 in many ways, but takes advantage of the larger word size in modern processors. In the specific case, RC4($8, 32$), the proposed keystream generator is 3.1 times faster than 8-bit RC4 on a 32-bit machine. Similarly, RC4($8, 64$) is 6.2 times faster on 64-bit machine. The internal state of this generator is much larger than the internal state of original RC4. Moreover given the current internal state of the generator it is not possible to retrieve the previous state in the absence of the keystream. The keystream produced by the proposed generator has good randomness properties and we show that none of the significant attacks on original RC4 can be used on RC4(n, m). The key scheduling algorithm of RC4(n, m) is much slower than that of RC4 since the entries of the array must be sufficiently random before keystream generation starts. An improvement of the KSA would be an interesting future research direction.

Acknowledgements. We wish to thank Palash Sarkar who motivated the problem and Alfred Menezes who gave momentum to it. We also wish to thank Alexander Maximov, Matthew McKague, Souradyuti Paul and Hongjun Wu for providing several useful and valuable suggestions.

References

1. E. Biham, L. Granboulan, and P. Nguyen. Impossible and Differential Fault Analysis of RC4. *Fast Software Encryption 2005.*
2. H. Finney, An RC4 cycle that can't happen, *Post in sci.crypt, September 1994.*

3. P. Flajolet and A. M. Odlyzko. Random Mapping Statistics (Invited), *Eurocrypt '89*, vol. 434 of LNCS, pp. 329-354, Springer-Verlag, 1990.
4. S. Fluhrer, I. Mantin, and A. Shamir. Weaknesses in the Key Scheduling Algorithm of RC4. *SAC 2001*, vol. 2259 of LNCS, pp. 1-24, Springer-Verlag, 2001.
5. S. Fluhrer and D. McGrew. Statistical Analysis of the Alleged RC4 Keystream Generator. *Fast Software Encryption 2000. vol. 1978 of LNCS, pp. 19-30, Springer-Verlag, 2000.*
6. J. Golić. Linear Statistical Weakness of Alleged RC4 Keystream Generator, *Eurocrypt '97 (W. Fumy, ed.), vol. 1233 of LNCS, pp. 226-238, Springer-Verlag, 1997.*
7. J. Dj. Golić. Iterative Probabilistic Cryptanalysis of RC4 Keystream Generator. In *ACISP'2000, Volume 1841 of LNCS, pages 220–233. Springer-Verlag, 2000.*
8. A. Grosul and D. Wallach. A related key cryptanalysis of RC4. *Department of Computer Science, Rice University, Technical Report TR-00-358, June 2000.*
9. R. Jenkins. Isaac and RC4. *Published on the Internet at* http://burtleburtle.net/bob/rand/isaac.html.
10. A. Klimov and A. Shamir, A New Class of Invertible Mappings, *CHES 2002, Vol. 942 of LNCS, pp. 470-483, Springer-Verlag, 2002.*
11. L. Knudsen, W. Meier, B. Preneel, V. Rijmen, and S. Verdoolaege. Analysis Methods for (Alleged) RC4. *Asiacrypt '98, vol. 1514 of LNCS, pp. 327-341, Springer-Verlag, 1998.*
12. M. D. MacLaren and G Marsaglia. Uniform random number generation. *J. ACM, vol. 15, pp. 83–89, 1965.*
13. I. Mantin. Predicting and Distinguishing Attacks on RC4 Keystream Generator. *Eurocrypt Vol. 3494 of LNCS, pp. 491-506, Springer-Verlag, 2005.*
14. I. Mantin and A. Shamir. A Practical Attack on Broadcast RC4. *Fast Software Encryption 2001. Vol. 2355 of LNCS, pp. 152-164, Springer-Verlag, 2001.*
15. I. Mantin. The Security of the Stream Cipher RC4. *Master Thesis (2001) The Weizmann Institute of Science.*
16. A. Maximov. Two Linear Distinguishing Attacks on VMPC and RC4A and Weakness of the RC4 Family of Stream Ciphers. *Fast Software Encryption 2005.*
17. I. Mironov. Not (So) Random Shuffle of RC4. *Crypto Vol. 2442 of LNCS, pp. 304-319, Springer-Verlag, 2002.*
18. S. Mister and S. Tavares. Cryptanalysis of RC4-like Ciphers. *SAC '98, vol. 1556 of LNCS, pp. 131-143, Springer-Verlag, 1999.*
19. NIST statistical tests suite with documentation. *Available on the internet at URL* http://stat.fsu.edu/~geo/diehard.html.
20. S. Paul and B. Preneel. Analysis of Non-fortuitous Predictive States of the RC4 Keystream Generator. *Indocrypt 2003, vol. 2904 of LNCS, pp. 52-67, Springer-Verlag, 2003.*
21. S. Paul and B. Preneel. A New Weakness in the RC4 Keystremeam Generator and an Approach to Improve the Security of thr Cipher. *Fast Software Encryption 2004. Vol. 3017 of LNCS, pp. 245-259, Springer-Verlag, 2004.*
22. M. Pudovkina. Statistical Weaknesses in the Alleged RC4 keystream generator. *Cryptology ePrint Archive 2002-171, IACR, 2002.*
23. A. Roos. Class of weak keys in the RC4 stream cipher. *Post in sci.crypt, September 1995.*
24. A. Stubblefield, J. Ioannidis, and A. Rubin. Using the Fluhrer, Mantin and Shamir attack to break WEP. *Proceedings of the 2002 Network and Distributed Systems Security Symposium, pp. 17-22, 2002.*

25. Y. Tsunoo, T. Saito, H. Kubo, M. Shigeri, T. Suzaki, and T. Kawabata. The Most Efficient Distinguishing Attack on VMPC and RC4A. *SKEW 2005*.
26. B. Zoltak. VMPC One-Way Function and Stream Cipher. *Fast Software Encryption, vol. 3017 of LNCS, pp. 210-225, Springer-Verlag, 2004.*

A   Initial Values

Initial values for RC4(8, 32) in hexadecimal format.

a_0 = 144D4800	a_1 = 32736901	a_2 = 51988B02	a_3 = 6FBEAD03
a_4 = 8DE4CE04	a_5 = AC0AF005	a_6 = CA301206	a_7 = E8553407
a_8 = 067B5508	a_9 = 25A17709	a_{10} = 43C7990A	a_{11} = 61ECBA0B
a_{12} = 7F12DC0C	a_{13} = 9E38FE0D	a_{14} = BC5E1F0E	a_{15} = DA84410F
a_{16} = F9A96310	a_{17} = 17CF8411	a_{18} = 35F5A612	a_{19} = 531BC813
a_{20} = 7240E914	a_{21} = 90660B15	a_{22} = AE8C2D16	a_{23} = CCB24E17
a_{24} = EBD87018	a_{25} = 09FD9219	a_{26} = 2723B31A	a_{27} = 4649D51B
a_{28} = 646FF71C	a_{29} = 8294181D	a_{30} = A0BA3A1E	a_{31} = BFE05C1F
a_{32} = DD067D20	a_{33} = FB2C9F21	a_{34} = 1951C122	a_{35} = 3877E223
a_{36} = 569D0424	a_{37} = 74C32625	a_{38} = 93E84726	a_{39} = B10E6927
a_{40} = CF348B28	a_{41} = ED5AAC29	a_{42} = 0C80CE2A	a_{43} = 2AA5F02B
a_{44} = 48CB112C	a_{45} = 66F1332D	a_{46} = 8517552E	a_{47} = A33C762F
a_{48} = C1629830	a_{49} = E088BA31	a_{50} = FEAEDB32	a_{51} = 1CD4FD33
a_{52} = 3AF91F34	a_{53} = 591F4035	a_{54} = 77456236	a_{55} = 956B8437
a_{56} = B490A538	a_{57} = D2B6C739	a_{58} = F0DCE93A	a_{59} = 0E020A3B
a_{60} = 2D282C3C	a_{61} = 4B4D4E3D	a_{62} = 6973703E	a_{63} = 8799913F
a_{64} = A6BFB340	a_{65} = C4E4D541	a_{66} = E20AF642	a_{67} = 01301843
a_{68} = 1F563A44	a_{69} = 3D7C5B45	a_{70} = 5BA17D46	a_{71} = 7AC79F47
a_{72} = 98EDC048	a_{73} = B613E249	a_{74} = D438044A	a_{75} = F35E254B
a_{76} = 1184474C	a_{77} = 2FAA694D	a_{78} = 4ED08A4E	a_{79} = 6CF5AC4F
a_{80} = 8A1BCE50	a_{81} = A841EF51	a_{82} = C7671152	a_{83} = E58C3353
a_{84} = 03B25454	a_{85} = 21D87655	a_{86} = 40FE9856	a_{87} = 5E24B957
a_{88} = 7C49DB58	a_{89} = 9B6FFD59	a_{90} = B9951E5A	a_{91} = D7BB405B
a_{92} = F5E0625C	a_{93} = 1406835D	a_{94} = 322CA55E	a_{95} = 5052C75F
a_{96} = 6F78E860	a_{97} = 8D9D0A61	a_{98} = ABC32C62	a_{99} = C9E94D63
a_{100} = E80F6F64	a_{101} = 06349165	a_{102} = 245AB266	a_{103} = 4280D467
a_{104} = 61A6F668	a_{105} = 7FCC1769	a_{106} = 9DF1396A	a_{107} = BC175B6B
a_{108} = DA3D7C6C	a_{109} = F8639E6D	a_{110} = 1688C06E	a_{111} = 35AEE16F
a_{112} = 53D40370	a_{113} = 71FA2571	a_{114} = 8F204772	a_{115} = AE456873
a_{116} = CC6B8A74	a_{117} = EA91AC75	a_{118} = 09B7CD76	a_{119} = 27DCEF77
a_{120} = 45021178	a_{121} = 63283279	a_{122} = 824E547A	a_{123} = A074767B
a_{124} = BE99977C	a_{125} = DCBFB97D	a_{126} = FBE5DB7E	a_{127} = 190BFC7F
a_{128} = 37301E80	a_{129} = 56564081	a_{130} = 747C6182	a_{131} = 92A28383
a_{132} = B0C8A584	a_{133} = CFEDC685	a_{134} = ED13E886	a_{135} = 0B390A87
a_{136} = 2A5F2B88	a_{137} = 48844D89	a_{138} = 66AA6F8A	a_{139} = 84D0908B
a_{140} = A3F6B28C	a_{141} = C11CD48D	a_{142} = DF41F58E	a_{143} = FD67178F
a_{144} = 1C8D3990	a_{145} = 3AB35A91	a_{146} = 58D87C92	a_{147} = 77FE9E93
a_{148} = 9524BF94	a_{149} = B34AE195	a_{150} = D1700396	a_{151} = F0952497

a_{152} = 0EBB4698	a_{153} = 2CE16899	a_{154} = 4A07899A	a_{155} = 692CAB9B
a_{156} = 8752CD9C	a_{157} = A578EE9D	a_{158} = C49E109E	a_{159} = E2C4329F
a_{160} = 00E953A0	a_{161} = 1E0F75A1	a_{162} = 3D3597A2	a_{163} = 5B5BB8A3
a_{164} = 7980DAA4	a_{165} = 97A6FCA5	a_{166} = B6CC1DA6	a_{167} = D4F23FA7
a_{168} = F21861A8	a_{169} = 113D83A9	a_{170} = 2F63A4AA	a_{171} = 4D89C6AB
a_{172} = 6BAFE8AC	a_{173} = 8AD409AD	a_{174} = A8FA2BAE	a_{175} = C6204DAF
a_{176} = E5466EB0	a_{177} = 036C90B1	a_{178} = 2191B2B2	a_{179} = 3FB7D3B3
a_{180} = 5EDDF5B4	a_{181} = 7C0317B5	a_{182} = 9A2838B6	a_{183} = B84E5AB7
a_{184} = D7747CB8	a_{185} = F59A9DB9	a_{186} = 13C0BFBA	a_{187} = 32E5E1BB
a_{188} = 500B02BC	a_{189} = 6E3124BD	a_{190} = 8C5746BE	a_{191} = AB7C67BF
a_{192} = C9A289C0	a_{193} = E7C8ABC1	a_{194} = 05EECCC2	a_{195} = 2414EEC3
a_{196} = 423910C4	a_{197} = 605F31C5	a_{198} = 7F8553C6	a_{199} = 9DAB75C7
a_{200} = BBD096C8	a_{201} = D9F6B8C9	a_{202} = F81CDACA	a_{203} = 1642FBCB
a_{204} = 34681DCC	a_{205} = 528D3FCD	a_{206} = 71B360CE	a_{207} = 8FD982CF
a_{208} = ADFFA4D0	a_{209} = CC24C5D1	a_{210} = EA4AE7D2	a_{211} = 087009D3
a_{212} = 26962AD4	a_{213} = 45BC4CD5	a_{214} = 63E16ED6	a_{215} = 81078FD7
a_{216} = 9F2DB1D8	a_{217} = BE53D3D9	a_{218} = DC78F4DA	a_{219} = FA9E16DB
a_{220} = 19C438DC	a_{221} = 37EA5ADD	a_{222} = 55107BDE	a_{223} = 73359DDF
a_{224} = 925BBFE0	a_{225} = B081E0E1	a_{226} = CEA702E2	a_{227} = EDCC24E3
a_{228} = 0BF245E4	a_{229} = 291867E5	a_{230} = 473E89E6	a_{231} = 6664AAE7
a_{232} = 8489CCE8	a_{233} = A2AFEEE9	a_{234} = C0D50FEA	a_{235} = DFFB31EB
a_{236} = FD2053EC	a_{237} = 1B4674ED	a_{238} = 3A6C96EE	a_{239} = 5892B8EF
a_{240} = 76B8D9F0	a_{241} = 94DDFBF1	a_{242} = B3031DF2	a_{243} = D1293EF3
a_{244} = EF4F60F4	a_{245} = 0D7482F5	a_{246} = 2C9AA3F6	a_{247} = 4AC0C5F7
a_{248} = 68E6E7F8	a_{249} = 870C08F9	a_{250} = A5312AFA	a_{251} = C3574CFB
a_{252} = E17D6DFC	a_{253} = 00A38FFD	a_{254} = 1EC8B1FE	a_{255} = 3CEED2FF

HCTR: A Variable-Input-Length Enciphering Mode

Peng Wang[1], Dengguo Feng[1,2], and Wenling Wu[2]

[1] State Key Laboratory of Information Security,
Graduate School of Chinese Academy of Sciences, Beijing 100049, China
w.rocking@gmail.com
[2] State Key Laboratory of Information Security,
Institution of Software of Chinese Academy of Sciences, Beijing 100080, China
{feng, wwl}@is.iscas.ac.cn

Abstract. This paper proposes a blockcipher mode of operation, HCTR, which is a length-preserving encryption mode. HCTR turns an n-bit blockcipher into a tweakable blockcipher that supports arbitrary variable input length which is no less than n bits. The tweak length of HCTR is fixed and can be zero. We prove that HCTR is a strong tweakable pseudorandom permutation ($\widetilde{sprp}$), when the underlying blockcipher is a strong pseudorandom permutation ($sprp$). HCTR is shown to be a very efficient mode of operation when some pre-computations are taken into consideration. Arbitrary variable input length brings much flexibility in various application environments. HCTR can be used in disk sector encryption, and other length-preserving encryptions, especially for the message that is not multiple of n bits.

Keywords: Blockcipher, tweakable blockcipher, disk sector encryption, modes of operation, symmetric encryption.

1 Introduction

Basic encryption modes, such as CBC [27], increase the message length. But in many scenarios, we need a length-preserving encryption (enciphering). For example, in networking application, some packet format was not defined for cryptographic purposes, and can not be altered. So when we want add privacy features, we can not even lengthen one bit. The other example is disk sector encryption. A disk is partitioned into fixed-length sectors. The sector-level encryption is a low-level encryption. The encryption device knows nothing about the information of files or directories. It encrypts or decrypts sectors when they arrive. Suppose the plaintext at the sector location of T is P, and the encryption algorithm is $\widetilde{E}$, then the ciphertext stored in this sector is $C = \widetilde{E}_K^T(M)$, where K is the secret key. Of course we can not expand the message length, so $|M| = |\widetilde{E}_K^T(M)|$. That is why we need the concept of *tweakable blockcipher* in disk sector encryption. The sector location T is call *tweak*, which is also called associated data in [15, 13].

D. Feng, D. Lin, and M. Yung (Eds.): CISC 2005, LNCS 3822, pp. 175–188, 2005.
© Springer-Verlag Berlin Heidelberg 2005

In the above example the message length is not always fixed and the same as, but usually much longer than, that of well known blockciphers such as DES (64 bits) or AES (128 bits) [6]. For example the sector length is typically 512 bytes. So we need wide-block-length enciphering modes based on blockciphers. When we have a wide-block-length enciphering mode, we can easily put the tweak into it using the method in [11] or [8], to get a tweakable enciphering mode.

This paper proposes a tweakable enciphering mode, or an arbitrary-variable-input-length tweakable blockcipher. We name it HCTR, for it makes use of a special universal hash function and the CTR mode. If the underlying blockcipher is $E : \{0,1\}^k \times \{0,1\}^n \rightarrow \{0,1\}^n$, then our mode supports arbitrary variable length of at lest n bits, using a $(k+n)$-bit key and m blockcipher calls to encipher m blocks plaintext. The length of tweak in HCTR is fixed and can be zero. When it is zero, HCTR becomes an enciphering mode, or a arbitrary-variable-input-length blockcipher.

Our HCTR mode is a hash-encipher-hash construction, part of the middle layer uses the CTR encryption mode. HCTR is similar to the XCB mode [13], and also can be viewed as a generalization to the basic construction of $\widetilde{sprp}$ in [11]. The ABL mode [15] and the XCB mode [13] are unbalanced Feistel constructions using universal hash functions as their components. They also support variable input length, but the secret key is very long (4 keys in ABL and 5 keys in XCB) and have to be generated from a main key. The CMC mode [8] and the EME mode [9] are modes without using any universal hash functions. But they only support the message that is multiple of a block. HCTR has great advantage among these modes.

The attack-model is an adaptive chosen plaintext/ciphertext attack: an adversary can choose a tweak T, a plaintext P and get a ciphertext $C = \widetilde{E}_K^T(P)$; or choose a tweak T, a ciphertext C and get a plaintext $P = (\widetilde{E}_K^T)^{-1}(C)$. The current query can base on previous answers. We prove that HCTR is a strong secure tweakable blockcipher ($\widetilde{sprp}$), which is defined as the one indistinguishable from the independently random permutations indexed by the tweak T. If HCTR is used in disk sector encryption, the effect is that each sector is encrypted with a different random permutation independently. This kind of tweakable blockcipher is under standardization [19] by the IEEE Security in Storage Working Group. Our proof method adopts the game-play technique [2,26], which was first used in [10].

We give basic definitions in Section 2. Specification of HCTR is in Section 3. Section 4 discusses some insure modifications and compares HCTR with other modes. The concrete security bound is given in Section 5.

1.1 Related Work

Constructions of large-block-size blockciphers from small-block-size blockciphers can date back to the pioneering work of Luby and Rackoff [12]. They showed that three rounds of the Feistel structure turns n-bit to n-bit random functions into a $2n$-bit secure blockcipher, and four rounds into a strong secure one. Naor and Reingold [18] showed that two rounds Feistel construction with initial and final strong universal invertible hash functions is enough to construct a strong secure blockcipher. In [17], they further used this hash-encipher-hash construction to get a mode of operation, but the hash function is quiet complex. Patel etc. further discussed the function of universal hash functions in the Feistel construction [20]. Bellare and Rogaway [1] used a special pseudorandom function and a special encryption mode to construct a variable-input-length cipher. Patel etc. [21] made some efficiency improvement to this scheme and the other unbalanced Feistel construction by using universal hash functions.

The constructions of tweakable blockciphers from scratch involve HPC [24] and Mercy [5] (although it has been broken by Fluhrer [7]).

Tweakable blockcipher is not only a suitable model for disk sector encryption and useful in length-preserving encryption, but also a good starting point to do design problem [11]. Following this thought, Rogaway [22] made refinement to modes OCB [23] and PMAC [3] using tweakable blockciphers.

2   Basic Definitions

BLOCKCIPHERS AND TWEAKABLE BLOCKCIPHERS. A *blockcipher* is a function $E : \mathcal{K} \times \mathcal{M} \to \mathcal{M}$ where $E_K(\cdot) = E(K, \cdot)$ is a *length-preserving* permutation for all $K \in \mathcal{K}$. $\mathcal{K} \neq \phi$ is a *key space* and $\mathcal{M} \neq \phi$ is a *message space*. A *tweakable blockcipher* is a function $\widetilde{E} : \mathcal{K} \times \mathcal{T} \times \mathcal{M} \to \mathcal{M}$ where $\widetilde{E}_K^T(\cdot) = \widetilde{E}_K(T, \cdot) = \widetilde{E}(K, T, \cdot)$ is a *length-preserving* permutation for all $K \in \mathcal{K}$ and $T \in \mathcal{T}$. $\mathcal{T}$ is a *tweak space*.

We write $s \xleftarrow{R} S$ to denote choosing a random element s from a set S by uniform distribution. Let Perm($\mathcal{M}$) be the set of all length-preserving permutations on $\mathcal{M}$. When $\mathcal{M} = \{0, 1\}^n$, we denote it as Perm(n). Let $\mathrm{Perm}^{\mathcal{T}}(\mathcal{M})$ be the set of all mappings from $\mathcal{T}$ to Perm($\mathcal{M}$). $\mathrm{Perm}^{\mathcal{T}}(\mathcal{M})$ can also be viewed as the set of all blockciphers $E : \mathcal{T} \times \mathcal{M} \to \mathcal{M}$. If $\widetilde{\pi} \xleftarrow{R} \mathrm{Perm}^{\mathcal{T}}(\mathcal{M})$, then for every $T \in \mathcal{T}$, $\widetilde{\pi}^T(\cdot) = \widetilde{\pi}(T, \cdot)$ is a random permutation. When $\mathcal{M} = \{0, 1\}^n$, we denote it as $\mathrm{Perm}^{\mathcal{T}}(n)$.

An *adversary* is a (randomized) algorithm with access to one or more oracles which are written as superscripts. Without loss of generality, we assume that adversaries never ask trivial queries whose answers are already known. For example, an adversary never repeats a query and never asks $(\widetilde{E}_K)^{-1}(T, C)$ after receiving C as an answer to $\widetilde{E}_K(T, M)$, and so forth. Let $A^\rho \Rightarrow 1$ be the event that adversary A with oracle ρ outputs the bit 1.

$\widetilde{prp}$ AND $\widetilde{sprp}$. A tweakable blockcipher $\widetilde{E} : \mathcal{K} \times \mathcal{T} \times \mathcal{M} \to \mathcal{M}$ is a *(strong) pseudorandom tweakable permutation* ($\widetilde{prp}$ or $\widetilde{sprp}$), if it is indistinguishable from a random tweakable permutation $\widetilde{\pi} \xleftarrow{R} \mathrm{Perm}^{\mathcal{T}}(\mathcal{M})$. More specifically, if the advantage function

$$\mathbf{Adv}_{\widetilde{E}}^{\widetilde{prp}}(A) = \Pr[K \xleftarrow{R} \mathcal{K} : A^{\widetilde{E}_K(\cdot, \cdot)} \Rightarrow 1]$$
$$- \Pr[\widetilde{\pi} \xleftarrow{R} \mathrm{Perm}^{\mathcal{T}}(\mathcal{M}) : A^{\widetilde{\pi}(\cdot, \cdot)} \Rightarrow 1]$$

is sufficiently small for any A with reasonable resources, then $\widetilde{E}$ is said to be a *pseudorandom tweakable permutation* ($\widetilde{prp}$), or a secure tweakable blockcipher, or secure against chosen plaintext attack. If the advantage function

$$\mathbf{Adv}_{\widetilde{E}}^{\widetilde{sprp}}(A) = \Pr[K \xleftarrow{R} \mathcal{K} : A^{\widetilde{E}_K(\cdot,\cdot),\widetilde{E}_K^{-1}(\cdot,\cdot)} \Rightarrow 1]$$
$$- \Pr[\widetilde{\pi} \xleftarrow{R} \mathrm{Perm}^{\mathcal{T}}(\mathcal{M}) : A^{\widetilde{\pi}(\cdot,\cdot),\widetilde{\pi}^{-1}(\cdot,\cdot)} \Rightarrow 1]$$

is sufficiently small for any A with reasonable resources, then $\widetilde{E}$ is said to be a *strong pseudorandom tweakable permutation* ($\widetilde{sprp}$), or a strong secure tweakable blockcipher, or secure against chosen ciphertext attack.

prp AND *sprp*. When the tweak space $\mathcal{T} = \phi$, the tweakable blockcipher becomes the blockcipher. A blockcipher $E : \mathcal{K} \times \mathcal{M} \to \mathcal{M}$ is a *(strong) pseudorandom permutation* (*prp* or *sprp*), if it is indistinguishable from a random permutation $\pi \xleftarrow{R} \mathrm{Perm}(\mathcal{M})$. $\widetilde{prp}$ and $\widetilde{sprp}$ correspond to *prp* and *sprp* respectively.

3   Specification of HCTR

3.1   Notations

A *string* is a finite sequence of symbols, each symbol being 0 or 1. A *block* is a string of fixed length. The blockcipher and multiplication of the finite field are operations over blocks. Let $\{0,1\}^*$ be the set of all strings. If $X, Y \in \{0,1\}^*$, then $X\|Y$ is their concatenation. If $X \in \{0,1\}^*$, then the *bit-length* of X, denoted as $|X|$, is the number of bits in X. $|X| = 0$ if and only if X is the empty string ε. If one block is n bits, we can parse X into $m = \lceil |X|/n \rceil$ blocks: $X = X_1, \cdots, X_m$, where $|X_m| \leq n$, and $|X_1| = \cdots = |X_{m-1}| = n$. Let $|X|_n = \lceil |X|/n \rceil$. We say that $|X|$ has $|X|_n$ blocks. $X[s]$ denotes the sth bit of X from left to right. $X[s,t]$ denotes the substring from the sth bit to the tth bit in X from left to right. For example, if $X = 110011$, then $X[2,4] = 100$. If $X, Y \in \{0,1\}^*$, then $X \oplus Y$ is slightly different to $X \oplus Y$. If $|X| < |Y|$ then $X \oplus Y = X \oplus Y[1, |X|]$. If $|X| = |Y|$ then $X \oplus Y = X \oplus Y$. If $|X| > |Y|$ then $X \oplus Y = X \oplus Y0^*$.

3.2   Multiplication in $GF(2^n)$

We interchangeably think of a block $L = (L_1, \cdots, L_n)$ as an abstract point in the finite field $GF(2^n)$ and as a polynomial $L(x) = L_1 + L_2x + \cdots + L_nx^{n-1}$ in $GF(2)[x]/(p(x))$, where $p(x)$ is an irreducible polynomial of degree n in $GF(2)[x]$. The addition in $GF(2^n)$ is bitwise xor $\oplus$. The multiplication of $A, B \in GF(2^n)$ is denoted as $A \cdot B$ which can be calculated as $A(x)B(x)$ in $GF(2)[x]/(p(x))$. If we choose the blockcipher as AES [6], then the bit-length of a block is 128 bits. The corresponding irreducible polynomial can be chosen as $p(x) = 1 + x + x^2 + x^7 + x^{128}$.

3.3   Universal Hash Function

H is a function family: $H = \{H_h : \{0,1\}^* \to \{0,1\}^n | h \in \{0,1\}^n\}$. For any $X \in \{0,1\}^*$, X is padded into complete blocks and then the polynomial evaluation [4] is used. Suppose $|X|_n = m$, we parse X into $X = X_1, \cdots, X_m$. We append 0s, possibly none, at the end of X to complete the block and append $|X|$, which is written as a n-bit string, as the last block. Then we use polynomial evaluation hash function in h on the padding result. More specifically, H_h is defined as:

$$H_h(X) = X_1 \cdot h^{m+1} \oplus \cdots \oplus X_m 0^* \cdot h^2 \oplus |X| \cdot h$$

which can be calculated as following:

> Algorithm $H_h(X)$
> parse X as $X_1, \cdots, X_m$
> $Y_0 \leftarrow 0^n$
> **for** $i \leftarrow 1$ **to** m **do**
> $\quad Y_i \leftarrow (Y_{i-1} \oplus X_i) \cdot h$
> $Y_{m+1} \leftarrow (Y_m \oplus |X|) \cdot h$
> **return** Y_{m+1}

When X is empty string, we define that $H_h(X) = h$. H is a special AXU (Almost Xor Universal) hash function. It has following properties which will be used in the security proof of HCTR.

1. For any $X_1, X_2 \in \{0,1\}^*, Y \in \{0,1\}^n$ and $X_1 \neq X_2$, $H_h(X_1) \oplus H_h(X_2)$ is a nonzero polynomial in h without constant term. So $\Pr[h \xleftarrow{R} \{0,1\}^n : H_h(X_1) \oplus H_h(X_2) = Y] \leq l/2^n$, where $l = max\{|X|_n, |Y|_n\} + 1$. In other words, H is a $l/2^n$-AXU hash function.
2. For any $X, Y, Z \in \{0,1\}^*, |X| = |Y|$, we have $H(X) \oplus H(Y) \oplus H(Z)$ is a nonzero polynomial in h without constant term.

3.4   The CTR Mode

In HCTR we use a special form of the CTR mode:

> Algorithm $\text{CTR}_K^S(N)$
> $Y \leftarrow E_K(S \oplus 1) || \cdots || E_K(S \oplus m - 1)$
> $D \leftarrow N \oplus Y$
> **return** D

where $|N|_n = m - 1$, K is the key and S is the counter.

3.5   The HCTR Mode

The HCTR mode makes use of a blockcipher E and the special universal hash function H. Assume that the blockcipher is $E : \{0,1\}^k \times \{0,1\}^n \to \{0,1\}^n$. Then HCTR$[E, H]$ is

$$\text{HCTR}[E, H] : \{0,1\}^{k+n} \times \{0,1\}^t \times \{0,1\}^{\geq n} \to \{0,1\}^{\geq n}$$

where $\{0,1\}^{\geq n} = \cup_{m \geq n}\{0,1\}^m$ and $t \geq 0$.

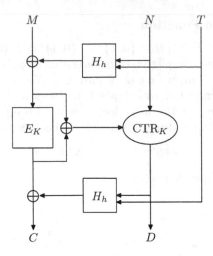

Fig. 1. The HCTR Mode

HCTR$[E, H]$ is illustrated in figure 1. we split the plaintext/ciphertext into two strings. One is the left n bits, and the other is the rest. We assume that plaintext/ciphertext has m blocks. More specifically, HCTR is the following algorithm.

Algorithm $\text{HCTR}_{K,h}^T(M, N)$	Algorithm $(\text{HCTR}_{K,h}^T)^{-1}(C, D)$
$MM \leftarrow M \oplus H_h(N\|T)$	$CC \leftarrow C \oplus H_h(D\|T)$
$CC \leftarrow E_K(MM)$	$MM \leftarrow E_K^{-1}(CC)$
$S \leftarrow MM \oplus CC$	$S \leftarrow MM \oplus CC$
$D \leftarrow \text{CTR}_K^S(N)$	$N \leftarrow \text{CTR}_K^S(D)$
$C \leftarrow CC \oplus H_h(D\|T)$	$M \leftarrow MM \oplus H_h(N\|T)$
return (C, D)	**return** (M, N)

4   Discussions

UNIVERSAL HASH FUNCTION. H in HCTR is a special AXU hash function. We can not substitute H by a general AXU hash function. We define a different universal hash function $H_h'(X)$ base on which HCTR is not secure. The main difference is the padding rule. In the HCTR mode, the padding rule is to append 0s and then the bit-length of X as in H. Now we first append 1 and then 0s to turn the bit-length of X into multiple of n and then use polynomial evaluation hash function. Suppose $X = X_1, \cdots, X_m$ where $|X|_n = m$, and $|X_1| = \cdots = |X_{m-1}| = n$. If $|X_m| = n$, then $H_h'(X) = X_1 \cdot h^{m+1} \oplus \cdots \oplus X_m \cdot h^2 \oplus 10^{n-1} \cdot h$. If $|X_m| < n$, then $H_h'(X) = X_1 \cdot h^m \oplus \cdots \oplus X_m 10^* \cdot h$. We can prove that $\Pr[h \xleftarrow{R} H' : h(X) \oplus h(Y) = Z] \leq \varepsilon$ for all $X, Y \in \{0,1\}^*, Z \in \{0,1\}^n, X \neq Y$. Here $\varepsilon = l/2^n$ where $l = max\{|X|_n, |Y|_n\} + 1$.

We now chose the length of tweak as 0: $T = \phi$. In this situation, we can show that HCTR$[E, H']$ is not even a *prp*. We first make an arbitrary enciphering query (M^1, N^1) such that $|N^1| = n - 1$ and get an answer (C^1, D^1). If $D^1[n - 1] = N^1[n - 1]$, then we do it again until $D^1[n - 1] \neq N^1[n - 1]$. Now we make the other enciphering query (M^2, N^2) such that $M^2 = M^1 \oplus C^1$ and $N^2 = (N^1 \oplus D^1)[1, n - 2]$. We get the answer (C^2, D^2). Then the input to the second blockcipher in the last but one query is the same as the input to the first blockcipher in the last query. Therefore we have that $(N^1 \oplus D^1)[1, n - 2] = (C^2 \oplus H'_h(D^2))[1, n - 2]$ or $(N^1 \oplus D^1)[1, n - 2] = (C^2 \oplus h \cdot D^2 10)[1, n - 2]$. So we can recover h with successful probability of $1/4$ and get rid of the hash function layers. Without the hash function layers, we can easily distinguish HCTR from a random permutation.

LENGTH of TWEAK. The length of tweak is fixed, because in most application environment there is no need for variable length tweak. We can chose the length of tweak according to the practical application environment. If we really need the variable length tweak, we can choose GHASH in [16, 14, 13] which is similar to H and takes two inputs.

MULTIPLICATION. The multiplication in finite field dominates the efficiency of the hash function layers. A simple implement of multiplication is even much slower than one AES call. But notice that the key h is a constant during the enciphering course, therefore we can do some pre-computations before enciphering. This time-memory tradeoffs greatly speeds up the hash function, though a bit more storage is needed. See [16, 25] for specific discussions.

	CMC	EME	ABL	XCB	HCTR
Keys	2	1	4	5	2
Blockciphers	$2m + 1$	$2m + 1$	$2m - 2$	$m + 1$	m
Universal hash	0	0	2	2	2
Variable Input Length	×	Multiple of n bits	√	√	√
Parallelizable	×	Almost	Partially	Partially	Partially

COMPARISONS. We compare HCTR with other enciphering modes, such as CMC, EME, ABL, and XCB, from several aspects. Suppose that we encrypt an message of m blocks. We list the comparisons in the above table. The first is the number of key. The second and third are the invocation number of the blockcipher and universal hash function. The following is whether the mode is parallelizable. In blockciphers, every bit of input bit must effect every bit of output. So there is no full parallelization. Even in the EME mode, the last layer must begin after the first layer is completely finished. In the HCTR mode, the CTR encryption can be parallelizable.

5   Security of HCTR

We prove that HCTR is a $\widetilde{sprp}$. A concrete security bound for HCTR is given in theorem 1. Lemma 1 shows that the random tweakable permutation and its inverse are indistinguishable from oracles that return random bits. This lemma greatly facilitates the proof procedure of lemma 2 which shows the security of HCTR when E_K is replaced by a random permutation.

Lemma 1 (lemma 6 in [8]). *Let $\widetilde{\pi} \overset{R}{\leftarrow} \mathrm{Perm}^T(\mathcal{M})$. Then for any adversary A that makes q queries,*

$$\Pr[A^{\widetilde{\pi}(\cdot,\cdot),\widetilde{\pi}^{-1}(\cdot,\cdot)} \Rightarrow 1] - \Pr[A^{\$(\cdot,\cdot),\$(\cdot,\cdot)} \Rightarrow 1] \leq q^2/2^{N+1}$$

where $\$(T, M)$ returns $|M|$ random bits and N is the bit-length of a shortest string in $\mathcal{M}$.

Let HCTR[Perm$(n), H$] be a variant of HCTR that uses a random permutation on n bits instead of E_K. Specifically, the key generation algorithm returns a random permutation $\pi \overset{R}{\leftarrow} \mathrm{Perm}(n)$ and a random string $h \overset{R}{\leftarrow} \{0,1\}^n$. We first give a concrete security bound for HCTR[Perm$(n), H$].

Lemma 2. *Let $\mathbf{E} = $ HCTR[Perm$(n), H$]. Then for any adversary A that asks enciphering/deciphering queries totalling σ blocks,*

$$\Pr[A^{\mathbf{E}(\cdot,\cdot),\mathbf{E}^{-1}(\cdot,\cdot)} \Rightarrow 1] - \Pr[A^{\$(\cdot,\cdot),\$(\cdot,\cdot)} \Rightarrow 1] \leq ((2+t_0)\sigma^2 + \sigma^3)/2^n$$

where $\$(T, M)$ returns $|M|$ random bits and $t_0 = |T|_n$.

A proof is given in Appendix B.

We now present our result for HCTR$[E, H]$. Our theorem shows that if E is $sprp$, then HCTR$[E, H]$ is a $\widetilde{sprp}$. More specifically, our theorem states that if there is an adversary A attacking the strong pseudorandomness of HCTR$[E, H]$ asking at most σ blocks queries, then there is an adversary B attacking the strong pseudorandomness of E, such that $\mathbf{Adv}_E^{sprp}(B) \geq \mathbf{Adv}_{\mathrm{HCTR}[E,H]}^{\widetilde{sprp}}(A) - q^2/2^{n+1} - ((2+t_0)\sigma^2 + \sigma^3)/2^n$. So when $\mathbf{Adv}_E^{sprp}(B)$ is small for any B with reasonable resources, $\mathbf{Adv}_{\mathrm{HCTR}[E,H]}^{\widetilde{sprp}}(A)$ must be small. This means that the strong security of E implies the strong security of HCTR$[E, H]$. The theorem for HCTR$[E, H]$ is given bellow.

Theorem 1. *For any adversary A that makes q queries totalling σ plaintext/-ciphertext blocks, there is an adversary B that makes σ queries, such that*

$$\mathbf{Adv}_{\mathrm{HCTR}[E,H]}^{\widetilde{sprp}}(A) \leq \mathbf{Adv}_E^{sprp}(B) + q^2/2^{n+1} + ((2+t_0)\sigma^2 + \sigma^3)/2^n$$

where $t_0 = |T|_n$. Furthermore, B runs in approximately the same time as A.

Proof (of theorem 1). Let $\mathbf{E}_1 = \text{HCTR}[E, H]$ and $\mathbf{E}_2 = \text{HCTR}[\text{Perm}(n), H]$. $\tilde{\pi} \xleftarrow{R} \text{Perm}^{\mathcal{T}}(n)$ where $\mathcal{T} = \{0, 1\}^t$. Consider following probabilities:

$$p_1 = \Pr[A^{\mathbf{E}_1, \mathbf{E}_1^{-1}} \Rightarrow 1] - \Pr[A^{\mathbf{E}_2, \mathbf{E}_2^{-1}} \Rightarrow 1],$$

$$p_2 = \Pr[A^{\mathbf{E}_2, \mathbf{E}_2^{-1}} \Rightarrow 1] - \Pr[A^{\$, \$} \Rightarrow 1],$$

$$p_3 = \Pr[A^{\$, \$} \Rightarrow 1] - \Pr[A^{\tilde{\pi}, \tilde{\pi}^{-1}} \Rightarrow 1].$$

Adversary B simulates A and returns whatever A returns. Then $p_1 = \mathbf{Adv}_E^{sprp}(B)$. By lemma 1, we have $p_3 \le q^2/2^{n+1}$. By lemma 2, we have $p_2 \le ((2 + t_0)\sigma^2 + \sigma^3)/2^n$. □

Acknowledgment

We thank the anonymous referees for their many helpful comments. This research is supported by the National Natural Science Foundation Of China (No. 60273027, 60373047, 60025205); the National Grand Fundamental Research 973 Program of China(No. G1999035802, 2004CB318004).

References

1. M. Bellare and P. Rogaway. On the construction of variable-input-length ciphers. In L. Knudsen, editor, *Fast Software Encryption 1999*, volume 1636 of *LNCS*, pages 231–244. Springer-Verlag, 1999.
2. M. Bellare and P. Rogaway. The game-playing technique. Cryptology ePrint Archive, Report 2004/331, 2004. http://eprint.iacr.org/.
3. J. Black and P. Rogaway. A block-cipher mode of operation for parallelizable message authentication. In L. R. Knudsen, editor, *Advances in Cryptology – EUROCRYPT 2002*, volume 2332 of *LNCS*, pages 384–397. Springer-Verlag, 2002.
4. J. L. Carter and M. N. Wegman. Universal classes of hash functions. *Journal of Computer and System Sciences*, 18(2):143–154, 1979.
5. P. Crowley. Mercy: A fast large block cipher for disk sector encryption. In B. Schneier, editor, *Fast Software Encryption 2000*, volume 1978 of *LNCS*, pages 49–63. Springer-Verlag, 2001.
6. FIPS-197. Federal information processing standards publication (FIPS 197). Advanced Encryption Standard (AES), 2001. http://csrc.nist.gov/publications/fips/fips197/fips-197.pdf.
7. S. R. Fluhrer. Cryptanalysis of the Mercy block cipher. In M. Matsui, editor, *Fast Software Encryption 2001*, volume 2355 of *LNCS*, pages 28–36. Springer-Verlag, 2002.
8. S. Halevi and P. Rogaway. A tweakable enciphering mode. In D. Boneh, editor, *Advances in Cryptology – CRYPTO 2003*, volume 2729 of *LNCS*, pages 482–499. Springer-Verlag, 2003.
9. S. Halevi and P. Rogaway. A parallelizable enciphering mode. In T. Okamoto, editor, *The Cryptographers' Track at RSA Conference – CT-RSA 2004*, volume 2964 of *LNCS*. Springer-Verlag, 2004.

10. J. Kilian and P. Rogaway. How to protect DES against exhaustive key search. In N. Koblitz, editor, *Advances in Cryptology – CRYPTO 1996*, volume 1109 of *LNCS*, pages 252–267. Springer-Verlag, 1996.

11. M. Liskov, R. L. Rivest, and D. Wagner. Tweakable block ciphers. In M. Yung, editor, *Advances in Cryptology – CRYPTO 2002*, volume 2442 of *LNCS*, pages 31–46. Springer-Verlag, 2002.

12. M. Luby and C. Rackoff. How to construct pseudorandom permutations from pseudorandom functions. *SIAM Journal on Computing*, 17(2):373–386, 1988. Special issue on cryptography.

13. D. A. McGrew and S. R. Fluhrer. The extended codebook (XCB) mode of operation. Cryptology ePrint Archive, Report 2004/278, 2004. http:// eprint.iacr.org/.

14. D. A. McGrew and J. Viega. The security and performance of the galois/counter mode (GCM) of operation. In A. Canteaut and K. Viswanathan, editors, *Advances in Cryptology – INDOCRYPT 2004*, volume 3348 of *LNCS*, pages 343–355. Springer-Verlag, 2002.

15. D. A. McGrew and J. Viega. The ABL mode of operation, 2004. http://grouper. ieee.org/groups/1619/email/pdf00004.pdf.

16. D. A. McGrew and J. Viega. The galois/counter mode of operation (GCM), 2004. http://csrc.nist.gov/CryptoToolkit/modes/proposedmodes.

17. M. Naor and O. Reingold. A pseudo-random encryption mode. http://wisdom. weizmann.ac.il/ naor/.

18. M. Naor and O. Reingold. On the construction of pseudo-random permutations: Luby-rackoff revisited. In *Proceedings of the 29th Annual ACM Symposium on the Theory of Computing (STOC '97)*, pages 189–199, New York, 1997. Association for Computing Machinery.

19. P1619. IEEE Security in Storage Working Group. http://www.siswg.org/.

20. S. Patel, Z. Ramzan, and G. S. Sundaram. Towards making Luby-Rackoff ciphers optimal and practical. In L. Knudsen, editor, *Fast software encryption 1999*, volume 1636 of *LNCS*, pages 171–185. Springer-Verlag, 1999.

21. S. Patel, Z. Ramzan, and G. S. Sundaram. Efficient constructions of variable-input-length block ciphers. In H. Handschuh and M. A. Hasan, editors, *Selected Areas in Cryptography 2004*, volume 3357 of *LNCS*, pages 326–340. Springer-Verlag, 2005.

22. P. Rogaway. Efficient instantiations of tweakable blockciphers and refinements to modes OCB and PMAC. In P. J. Lee, editor, *Advances in Cryptology – ASIACRYPT 2004*, volume 3329 of *LNCS*, pages 16–31. Springer-Verlag, 2004.

23. P. Rogaway, M. Bellare, J. Black, and T. Krovetz. OCB: a block-cipher mode of operation for efficient authenticated encryptiona. In *Proceedings of the 8th ACM Conference on Computer and Communications Security*, pages 196–205, 2001.

24. R. Schroeppel. The hasty pudding cipher. http://www.cs.arizona.edu/rcs/ hpc/.

25. V. Shoup. On fast and provably secure message authentication based on universal hashing. In N. Koblitz, editor, *Advances in Cryptology – CRYPTO 1996*, volume 1109 of *LNCS*, pages 313–328. Springer-Verlag, 1996.

26. V. Shoup. Sequences of games: a tool for taming complexity in security proofs. Cryptology ePrint Archive, Report 2004/332, 2004. http://eprint.iacr.org/.

27. SP-800-38A. Recommendation for block cipher modes of operation - methods and techniques. NIST Special Publication 800-38A, 2001. http://csrc.nist.gov/ publications/nistpubs/800-38a/sp800-38a.pdf.

A   Intellectual Property Statement

The authors explicitly release any intellectual property rights to the HCTR mode into the public domain. Further, the authors are not aware of any patent or patent application anywhere in the world that cover this mode.

B   Proof of Lemma 2

Proof (of lemma 2). Suppose A makes q queries. Assume that the rth query is (T^r, U^r, V^r), where T^r is the tweak, (U^r, V^r) is the plaintext(ciphertext). Suppose that $m_r = |(U^r, V^r)|_n$. $\sigma = m_1 + \cdots + m_q$ is the total plaintext/ciphertext block number. Furthermore, we split V^r into blocks: $V^r = V_1^r, \cdots, V_{m_r - 1}^r$. We describe the attacking procedure of A as the interaction with games.

Game 1 and **Game 2**. The following Game 1 illustrates how HCTR[Perm(n), H] and its inverse answer A's queries:

$\mathcal{D} \leftarrow \mathcal{R} \leftarrow \phi;\ bad \leftarrow \textbf{false}$

If the rth query (T^r, U^r, V^r) is an enciphering query:
   $UU^r \leftarrow U^r \oplus H_h(V^r \| T^r)$
   $XX^r \xleftarrow{R} \{0, 1\}^n$
   if $UU^r \in \mathcal{D}$ **then** $bad \leftarrow$ **true** $\boxed{XX^r \leftarrow \pi(UU^r)}$

   if $XX^r \in \mathcal{R}$ **then** $bad \leftarrow$ **true** $\boxed{XX^r \xleftarrow{R} \bar{\mathcal{R}}}$
   $\mathcal{D} \leftarrow \mathcal{D} \cup \{UU^r\}$
   $\mathcal{R} \leftarrow \mathcal{R} \cup \{XX^r\}$
   $S^r \leftarrow UU^r \oplus XX^r$
   for $i \leftarrow 1$ **to** $m_r - 1$ **do**
      $YY_i^r \xleftarrow{R} \{0, 1\}^n$
      if $S^r \oplus i \in \mathcal{D}$ **then** $bad \leftarrow$ **true** $\boxed{YY_i^r \leftarrow \pi(S^r \oplus i)}$

      if $YY_i^r \in \mathcal{R}$ **then** $bad \leftarrow$ **true** $\boxed{YY_i^r \xleftarrow{R} \bar{\mathcal{R}}}$
      $\mathcal{D} \leftarrow \mathcal{D} \cup \{S^r \oplus i\}$
      $\mathcal{R} \leftarrow \mathcal{R} \cup \{YY_i^r\}$
   $YY^r \leftarrow YY_1^r \| \cdots \| YY_{m_r - 1}^r$
   $D^r \leftarrow V^r \oplus YY^r$
   $C^r \leftarrow XX^r \oplus H_h(D^r \| T^r)$
   return (C^r, D^r)

If the rth query (T^r, U^r, V^r) is an deciphering query:
   $UU^r \leftarrow U^r \oplus H_h(V^r \| T^r)$
   $XX^r \xleftarrow{R} \{0, 1\}^n$
   if $UU^r \in \mathcal{R}$ **then** $bad \leftarrow$ **true** $\boxed{XX^r \leftarrow \pi^{-1}(UU^r)}$

   if $XX^r \in \mathcal{D}$ **then** $bad \leftarrow$ **true** $\boxed{XX^r \xleftarrow{R} \bar{\mathcal{D}}}$
   $\mathcal{D} \leftarrow \mathcal{D} \cup \{XX^r\}$
   $\mathcal{R} \leftarrow \mathcal{R} \cup \{UU^r\}$

$$S^r \leftarrow UU^r \oplus XX^r$$

for $i \leftarrow 1$ **to** $m_r - 1$ **do**

$\quad YY_i^r \xleftarrow{R} \{0,1\}^n$

$\quad$ **if** $S^r \oplus i \in \mathcal{D}$ **then** $bad \leftarrow$ **true** $\boxed{YY_i^r \leftarrow \pi(S^r \oplus i)}$

$\quad$ **if** $YY_i^r \in \mathcal{R}$ **then** $bad \leftarrow$ **true** $\boxed{YY_i^r \xleftarrow{R} \bar{\mathcal{R}}}$

$\quad \mathcal{D} \leftarrow \mathcal{D} \cup \{S^r \oplus i\}$

$\quad \mathcal{R} \leftarrow \mathcal{R} \cup \{YY_i^r\}$

$YY^r \leftarrow YY_1^r \| \cdots \| YY_{m_r-1}^r$

$N^r \leftarrow V^r \oplus YY^r$

$M^r \leftarrow XX^r \oplus H_h(N^r \| T^r)$

return (M^r, N^r)

Notice that the permutation π is not chosen before the attack, but "on the fly" as needed to answer the queries during the attacking procedure. The sets $\mathcal{D}$ and $\mathcal{R}$, which are multisets in which the element may repeat, keep track of the domain and the range of π respectively. Game 2 is obtained by omitting the boxed statements. Because $XX^r, XY^r (r = 1, \cdots, q)$ are independent random strings, the answers A get, when interacts with Game 2, are also independent random strings. So $A^{\text{Game 2}}$ is the same as $A^{\$,\$}$. In Game 1, each boxed statement is executed if and only if the flag bad is set to be true. Therefor we have

$$\Pr[A^{\mathbf{E},\mathbf{E}^{-1}} \Rightarrow 1] - \Pr[A^{\$,\$} \Rightarrow 1]$$
$$= \Pr[A^{\text{Game 1}} \Rightarrow 1] - \Pr[A^{\text{Game 2}} \Rightarrow 1] \leq \Pr[A^{\text{Game 2}} \text{ set } bad]. \quad (1)$$

Game 3. We make some modifications to Game 2. The answer of each query is directly chosen as random string and the state of bad is set at the end of all queries. Game 3 is the following:

Initialization :
$\mathcal{D} \leftarrow \mathcal{R} \leftarrow \phi$

On the rth query (T^r, U^r, V^r):
$\quad (X^r, Y^r) \xleftarrow{R} \{0,1\}^{m_r \cdot n}$
$\quad$ **return** $(X^r, Y^r)[1, |(U^r, V^r)|]$

Finalization :
for $r \leftarrow 1$ **to** q **do:**

If the rth query (T^r, U^r, V^r) is an enciphering query:
$\quad UU^r \leftarrow U^r \oplus H_h(V^r \| T^r)$
$\quad XX^r \leftarrow X^r \oplus H_h(Y^r[1, |V^r|] \| T^r)$
$\quad \mathcal{D} \leftarrow \mathcal{D} \cup \{UU^r\}$
$\quad \mathcal{R} \leftarrow \mathcal{R} \cup \{XX^r\}$
$\quad S^r \leftarrow UU^r \oplus XX^r$
$\quad$ **for** $i \leftarrow 1$ **to** $m_r - 1$ **do**
$\quad\quad \mathcal{D} \leftarrow \mathcal{D} \cup \{S^r \oplus i\}$
$\quad\quad \mathcal{R} \leftarrow \mathcal{R} \cup \{Y_i^r \oplus V_i^r\}$

If the rth query (T^r, U^r, V^r) is an deciphering query:
$$UU^r \leftarrow U^r \oplus H_h(V^r \| T^r)$$
$$XX^r \leftarrow X^r \oplus H_h(Y^r[1, |V^r|] \| T^r)$$
$$\mathcal{D} \leftarrow \mathcal{D} \cup \{XX^r\}$$
$$\mathcal{R} \leftarrow \mathcal{R} \cup \{UU^r\}$$
$$S^r \leftarrow UU^r \oplus XX^r$$
  for $i \leftarrow 1$ to $m_r - 1$ do
    $\mathcal{D} \leftarrow \mathcal{D} \cup \{S^r \oplus i\}$
    $\mathcal{R} \leftarrow \mathcal{R} \cup \{Y_i^r \oplus V_i^r\}$

$bad \leftarrow$ (there is a repetition in $\mathcal{D}$) **or** (there is a repetition in $\mathcal{R}$)

We have
$$\Pr[A^{\text{Game 2}} \text{ set } bad] = \Pr[A^{\text{Game 3}} \text{ set } bad]. \tag{2}$$

Without lost of generality, suppose that A is a deterministic algorithm. We want to prove that for any fixed $X^r, Y^r (r = 1, \cdots, q)$, the above probability is negligible. But that is not true. For example when $Y_1^1 \oplus V_1^1 = Y_1^2 \oplus V_1^2$, the bad is set to be true. We firstly make some restrictions on the choices of these random strings.

Restrictions on the choices of (X^r, Y^r):

1. X^r, Y_i^r are all distinct.
2. $X^r \neq U^r \oplus X^s \oplus U^s \oplus i \oplus j$ for all $s < r$, $1 \leq i \leq (m_r - 1)$, $1 \leq j \leq (m_s - 1)$.
3. $X^r \neq U^s$ for all $s < r$.
4. $Y_i^r \neq Y_j^s \oplus V_j^s \oplus V_i^r$, for all $s < r$ and for all $s = r, j < i$.

It is easy to calculate that each restriction in the above decreases the choices of (X^r, Y^r) at most $\sigma^2/2^{n+1}$. Totally, the choices of (X^r, Y^r) are decreased at most $2\sigma^2/2^n$.

Game 4. With these restrictions, we fix queries and answers. Suppose that $\{T^r, U^r, V^r, X^r, Y^r | r = 1, \cdots, q\}$ make the probability of setting bad maximum. Now consider the following non-interactive and non-adaptive Game 4:

  for $r \leftarrow 1$ to q do:

If the rth query (T^r, U^r, V^r) is an enciphering query:
$$UU^r \leftarrow U^r \oplus H_h(V^r \| T^r)$$
$$XX^r \leftarrow X^r \oplus H_h(Y^r[1, |V^r|] \| T^r)$$
$$\mathcal{D} \leftarrow \mathcal{D} \cup \{UU^r\}$$
$$\mathcal{R} \leftarrow \mathcal{R} \cup \{XX^r\}$$
$$S^r \leftarrow UU^r \oplus XX^r$$
  for $i \leftarrow 1$ to $m_r - 1$ do
    $\mathcal{D} \leftarrow \mathcal{D} \cup \{S^r \oplus i\}$
    $\mathcal{R} \leftarrow \mathcal{R} \cup \{Y_i^r \oplus V_i^r\}$

If the rth query (T^r, U^r, V^r) is an deciphering query:
$$UU^r \leftarrow U^r \oplus H_h(V^r \| T^r)$$
$$XX^r \leftarrow X^r \oplus H_h(Y^r[1, |V^r|] \| T^r)$$
$$\mathcal{D} \leftarrow \mathcal{D} \cup \{XX^r\}$$
$$\mathcal{R} \leftarrow \mathcal{R} \cup \{UU^r\}$$

$$S^r \leftarrow UU^r \oplus XX^r$$
$$\textbf{for } i \leftarrow 1 \textbf{ to } m_r - 1 \textbf{ do}$$
$$\mathcal{D} \leftarrow \mathcal{D} \cup \{S^r \oplus i\}$$
$$\mathcal{R} \leftarrow \mathcal{R} \cup \{Y_i^r \oplus V_i^r\}$$

$bad \leftarrow$ (there is a repetition in $\mathcal{D}$) **or** (there is a repetition in $\mathcal{R}$)

From the above discussion, we have that

$$\Pr[A^{\text{Game 3}} \text{ set } bad] \leq \Pr[\text{Game 4 set } bad] + 2\sigma^2/2^n. \tag{3}$$

Let $I = \{1, \cdots, q\}$, $I = I_1 \cup I_2$, where $I_1 = \{s \in I | (T^s, U^s, V^s)$ is an enciphering query$\}$ and $I_2 = \{t \in I | (T^t, U^t, V^t)$ is a deciphering query$\}$. Let $l = max\{m_1, \cdots, m_q\}$. We can see that $\mathcal{D} = \mathcal{D}_1 \cup \mathcal{D}_2 \cup \mathcal{D}_3$, where $\mathcal{D}_1 = \{UU^s | s \in I_1\}$, $\mathcal{D}_2 = \{XX^t | t \in I_2\}$, and $\mathcal{D}_3 = \{S^r \oplus i | r \in I, 1 \leq i \leq (m_r - 1)\}$. $\mathcal{R} = \mathcal{R}_1 \cup \mathcal{R}_2 \cup \mathcal{R}_3$, where $\mathcal{R}_1 = \{XX^s | s \in I_1\}$, $\mathcal{R}_2 = \{UU^t | t \in I_2\}$, and $\mathcal{R}_3 = \{Y_i^r \oplus V_i^r | r \in I, 1 \leq i \leq (m_r - 1)\}$.

Any element in $\mathcal{D}$ or $\mathcal{R}$ is a polynomial in h whose degree is at most $(l+t_0)$. We want to prove that for any $X_1, X_2 \in \mathcal{D}$ or $X_1, X_2 \in \mathcal{R}$, the repetition probability $\Pr[X_1 = X_2] \leq (l+t_0)/2^n$. Because the polynomial of degree $(l+t_0)$ has at most $(l+t_0)$ roots in finite field, we only need to prove that $X_1 \oplus X_2$ is a nonzero polynomial in h.

We consider following situations:

- $X_1, X_2 \in \mathcal{D}_1$. (T^s, U^s, V^s), $s \in I_1$ are all distinct, because A never ask trivial query. By property 1 of H, $X_1 \oplus X_2$ is a nonzero polynomial.
- $X_1, X_2 \in \mathcal{D}_2$. By restriction 1, the constant term of $X_1 \oplus X_2$ is nonzero.
- $X_1, X_2 \in \mathcal{D}_3$. By restriction 2, the constant term of $X_1 \oplus X_2$ is nonzero.
- $X_1 \in \mathcal{D}_1$ and $X_2 \in \mathcal{D}_2$. Suppose $X_1 = UU^s$ and $X_2 = XX^t$. If $s < t$, then by restriction 3, the constant term of $X_1 \oplus X_2$ is nonzero. If $s > t$, then $(T^s, U^s, V^s) \neq (T^t, X^t, Y^t[1, |V^t|])$, because A never make trivial query. By property 1 of H, $X_1 \oplus X_2$ is a nonzero polynomial.
- $X_1 \in \mathcal{D}_2$ and $X_2 \in \mathcal{D}_3$. By property 2 of H, $X_1 \oplus X_2$ is a nonzero polynomial.
- $X_1 \in \mathcal{D}_1$ and $X_2 \in \mathcal{D}_3$. The same reason as the above.
- $X_1, X_2 \in \mathcal{R}_1$. By restriction 1, the constant term of $X_1 \oplus X_2$ is nonzero.
- $X_1, X_2 \in \mathcal{R}_2$. (T^t, U^t, V^t), $s \in I_2$ are all distinct, because A never make trivial query. By property 1 of H, $X_1 \oplus X_2$ is a nonzero polynomial.
- $X_1, X_2 \in \mathcal{R}_3$. By restriction 4, $X_1 \oplus X_2$ is a nonzero constant.
- $X_1 \in \mathcal{R}_1$ and $X_2 \in \mathcal{R}_2$. Suppose $X_1 = XX^s$ and $X_2 = UU^t$. If $s > t$, then by restriction 3, the constant term of $X_1 \oplus X_2$ is nonzero. If $s < t$, then $(T^t, U^t, V^t) \neq (T^s, X^s, Y^s[1, |V^s|])$, because A never make trivial query. By property 1 of H, $X_1 \oplus X_2$ is a nonzero polynomial.
- $X_1 \in \mathcal{R}_2$ and $X_2 \in \mathcal{R}_3$. By property 2 of H, $X_1 \oplus X_2$ is a nonzero polynomial.
- $X_1 \in \mathcal{R}_1$ and $X_2 \in \mathcal{R}_3$. The same reason as the above.

There are totally $\sigma(\sigma - 1)/2$ pairs of elements in $\mathcal{D}$ and $\sigma(\sigma - 1)/2$ pairs of elements in $\mathcal{R}$. So the probability of repetition in $\mathcal{D}$ or $\mathcal{R}$ is at most $(l+t_0)\sigma^2/2^n$.

$$\Pr[\text{Game 4 set } bad] \leq (l + t_0)\sigma^2/2^n \leq (t_0\sigma^2 + \sigma^3)/2^n. \tag{4}$$

Combine (1), (2), (3) and (4), we complete the proof.   □

The kth-Order Quasi-Generalized Bent Functions over Ring Z_p

Jihong Teng[1], Shiqu Li[2], and Xiaoying Huang[1]

[1] Department of Mathematics and Physics, Information Engineering University,
Zhengzhou, 450001, PRC
tengjihong@263.net
[2] Department of Information, Research Information Engineering University,
Zhengzhou, 450002, PRC

Abstract. In this paper, we propose a new class of logical functions over residue ring of integers modulo p, where p is a prime. The magnitudes of the *Chrestenson* Spectra for this kind of functions, called as kth-order quasi-generalized Bent functions, take only two values—0 and a nonzero constant. By using the relationships between *Chrestenson* spectra and the autocorrelation functions for logical functions over ring Z_p, we present some equivalent definitions of this kind of functions. In the end, we investigate the constructions of the kth-order quasi-generalized Bent functions, including the typical method and the recursive method from the technique of number theory.

1 Introduction

Logical functions have many applications in computer security practices including the construction of keystream generators based on a set of shift registers. Such functions should possess certain desirable properties to withstand known cryptanalytic attacks. Five such important properties are balancedness, correlation immunity of reasonably high order, good propagation characteristic, high algebraic degree and high nonlinearity. The tradeoffs between the design criteria mentioned above have received a lot of attention in Boolean function literature for some time(see [1], [2]). The more criteria that have to be taken into account, the more difficult it is to generate Boolean functions satisfying those properties. Functions achieving the maximum possible nonlinearity are called Bent functions, and were introduced by Rothaus [3] in 1976. They play an important role in cryptology, as well as in error correcting coding because of their immune to differential attack. But Bent functions are not balanced, not correlation immune which make them invulnerable to statistic analysis and correlation attack. Partially Bent functions and semi-Bent functions are proposed in [4] and [5], respectively. They are interesting in that they can be balanced and also highly nonlinear. The common property of partially Bent functions and semi-Bent functions is that the absolute of the *Walsh* Spectra of these functions take only two values, 0 and a nonzero constant c. But Boolean functions possessing such property are not definitely partially Bent functions, nor semi-Bent functions. Hence a new class of

D. Feng, D. Lin, and M. Yung (Eds.): CISC 2005, LNCS 3822, pp. 189–201, 2005.
© Springer-Verlag Berlin Heidelberg 2005

functions are introduced by [6] and [7] almost at the same time, respectively. [6] named such functions plateaued functions, while [7] called them kth-order quasi-Bent functions, because of their similar cryptographic properties to that of Bent functions. In this paper, we call them kth-order quasi-Bent functions, which take Bent functions, partially-Bent functions and semi-Bent functions as its proper subset. [6] and [7] investigate the properties and construction of such functions by different methods and obtain some different results. [8] study the cryptographic properties of k-order quasi-Bent functions by matrix method, which is quite different from the $Walsh$ spectra method and the autocorrelation method. Nowadays, the application of cryptology and communications has turned to the residue ring of integers modulo m, which enable us to study the cryptographic properties of logical functions over ring Z_m. Then a natural question arises: are there logical functions over ring Z_m, whose $Chrestenson$ spectra has the similar properties with that of kth-order quasi-Bent functions? Furthermore, if there are, what about their cryptographic properties, constructions and enumerate? In this paper, we turn our attention to the case where m is a prime, and present a new class of logical functions over ring Z_p, which take generalized Bent functions ([9]) and generalized partially Bent functions([10]) as its proper subset.

The paper is organized as follows: Sections 2 provides basic definitions, notations, and theory to be needed in this paper. In sections 3, the definition of kth-order quasi-generalized Bent functions is suggested, followed by the equivalent definitions of the kth-order quasi-generalized Bent functions through the relationships between the $Chrestenson$ spectra and the autocorrelations functions of the logical functions over ring Z_p. Section 4 suggests the constructions of kth-order quasi-generalized Bent functions, one of which is the typical method, being a modification of the $Maiorana - McFarland$ method. The other is the recursive construction, which is proved to be different from the typical construction. Section 7 concludes this paper by several problems need to be investigated later.

2   Preliminaries

In this paper, let p be a prime, and u a primitive pth root of unity. The p-valued logical function with n variables is a mapping from Z_p^n to Z_p.

Lemma 1. *[11] Let a_i, $0 \le i \le p-1$, be rational integers. Then*

$$a_0 + a_1 u + a_2 u^2 + \cdots + a_{p-1} u^{p-1} = 0 \Longleftrightarrow a_0 = a_1 = \cdots = a_{p-1}. \qquad (1)$$

The $chrestenson$ spectra and autocorrelation functions are of much importance in the study the cryptographic properties of logical functions over Z_p , defined as follows:

Definition 1. *[12] Let $f(x)$, $x \in Z_p^n$ be a p-valued logical function with n variables. Then*

$$S_{(f)}(w) = \frac{1}{p^n} \sum_{x \in Z_p^n} u^{f(x)-w \cdot x}, \quad w \in Z_p^n,$$

$$r_f(s) = \frac{1}{p^n} \sum_{x \in Z_p^n} u^{f(x+s)-f(x)}, \quad s \in Z_p^n,$$

are called the chrestenson cyclic spectra and autocorrelation functions of $f(x)$, respectively.

The following lemma presents the relationships between the *Chrestenson* spectra and autocorrelation functions of the p-valued logical functions to be employed later in the paper.

Lemma 2. *[12] Let $f(x)$, $x \in Z_p^n$ be a p-valued logical function with n variables. Then*

$$\frac{1}{p^n} \sum_{\alpha \in Z_p^n} r_f(\alpha) u^{-w \cdot \alpha} = |S_{(f)}(w)|^2; \tag{2}$$

$$\sum_{w \in Z_p^n} |S_{(f)}(w)|^2 u^{w \cdot \alpha} = r_f(\alpha). \tag{3}$$

Lemma 3. *[12] (Parseval's Equation) Let $f(x)$, $x \in Z_p^n$ be a p-valued logical function with n variables. Then*

$$\sum_{w \in Z_p^n} |S_{(f)}(w)|^2 = 1. \tag{4}$$

3   The kth-Order Quasi-Generalized Bent Function and Its Equivalent Definition

Now we introduce a new class of p-valued logical functions. Here is the definition.

Definition 2. *Let $f(x)$, $x \in Z_p^n$ be a p-valued logical function with n variables. Then $f(x)$ is said to be a kth-order quasi-generalized Bent function if*

$$|S_{(f)}(w)|^2 = 0 \quad or \quad \frac{1}{p^{n-k}},$$

for all $w \in Z_p^n$.

Obviously, $|S_{(f)}(w)|^2 = 0$ if and only if $S_{(f)}(w) = 0$. $f(x)$ is also called a quasi-generalized Bent function, if the particular order k is ignored.

Definition 3. *Let $f(x)$, $x \in Z_p^n$ be a p-valued logical function with n variables. Denote*

$$Supp(S_{(f)}) = \{w : w \in Z_p^n, \ S_{(f)}(w) \neq 0\},$$

and call it the support of the chrestenson cyclic spectra for $f(x)$.

If $f(x)$ is a kth-order quasi-generalized Bent function. Then due to lemma 3, the number of the elements in $Supp(S_{(f)})$ is p^{n-k}, hence the number of vectors in Z_p^n where the *chrestenson* spectra take value 0 is $p^n - p^{n-k}$.

Remark 1. if $k = 0$, then $f(x)$ is generalized Bent function (see [9]); The generalized partially Bent functions introduced in [10] are also quasi-generalized Bent functions.

A natural question arises that whether there exists quasi-generalized Bent functions but not generalized Bent functions, nor generalized partially Bent functions? we now examine the relations between the quasi-generalized Bent functions and the generalized partially Bent functions.

Lemma 4. *[10] Let $f(x)$, $x \in Z_p^n$ be a p-valued logical function with n variables. Then $f(x)$ is a generalized partially Bent function if and only if there exist $t \in Z_p^n$, such that*

$$|S_{(f)}(w)|^2 = \begin{cases} 0 & t + w \notin E^\perp; \\ \frac{1}{p^{n-m}} & t + w \in E^\perp, \end{cases}$$

where $E = \{s \in Z_p^n : r_f(s) = u^{t \cdot s}\}$ is a linear subspace of Z_p^n with dimension m.

The following theorem can be obtained immediately from lemma 4:

Theorem 1. *Let $f(x)$, $x \in Z_p^n$ be a kth-order quasi-generalized Bent function with n variables. Then $f(x)$ is a generalized partially Bent function if and only if there exists $t \in Z_p^n$, such that $t + Supp(S_{(f)})$ is a linear subspace of Z_p^n with dimension $n - k$.*

Then the question turns to construct quasi-generalized Bent function the support of whose *chrestenson* cyclic spectra is not a linear subspace (when $t = 0$ in theorem 1), nor the shifting of a linear subspace , of Z_p^n. The existence of such functions will be presented in section 4.

Now we give the equivalent definitions of kth-order quasi-generalized Bent functions as follows:

Theorem 2. *Let $f(x)$, $x \in Z_p^n$ be a p-valued logical function with n variables. Then $f(x)$ is a kth-order quasi-generalized Bent function if and only if*

$$r_f(\alpha) = \frac{1}{p^{n-k}} \sum_{w \in Supp(S_{(f)})} u^{w \cdot \alpha} \tag{5}$$

holds for all $\alpha \in Z_p^n$.

Proof. Assume that $f(x)$ is a kth-order quasi-generalized Bent function. Then by lemma 2 and definition 2, we have

$$r_f(\alpha) = \sum_{w \in Z_p^n} |S_{(f)}(w)|^2 u^{w \cdot \alpha} = \frac{1}{p^{n-k}} \sum_{w \in Supp(S_{(f)})} u^{w \cdot \alpha}. \tag{6}$$

Conversely, if the equality holds. Then from lemma 2, we have

$$|S_{(f)}(w)|^2 = \frac{1}{p^n} \sum_{\alpha \in Z_p^n} r_f(\alpha) u^{-w \cdot \alpha}$$

$$= \frac{1}{p^n} \sum_{\alpha \in Z_p^n} \frac{1}{p^{n-k}} \sum_{v \in Supp(S_{(f)})} u^{v \cdot \alpha} u^{-w \cdot \alpha}$$

$$= \frac{1}{p^{2n-k}} \sum_{v \in Supp(S_{(f)})} \sum_{\alpha \in Z_p^n} u^{(v-w) \cdot \alpha}$$

$$= \begin{cases} 0 & w \notin Supp(S_{(f)}); \\ \frac{1}{p^{n-k}} & w \in Supp(S_{(f)}), \end{cases}$$

which yields the conclusion immediately.   □

Lemma 5. *[11] Let a_i, b_i, $1 \le i \le n$, be complex numbers. Then*

$$\sum_{i=1}^{n} a_i b_i \le \sqrt{\sum_{i=1}^{n} |a_i|^2 \sum_{i=1}^{n} |b_i|^2}, \tag{7}$$

where the equality holds if and only if there exists a complex number c, such that $a_i = c \overline{b_i}$, for all $1 \le i \le n$.

Theorem 3. *Let $f(x)$, $x \in Z_p^n$ be a p-valued logical function with n variables. Then*

$$\sum_{\alpha \in Z_p^n} |r_f(\alpha)|^2 \ge \frac{p^n}{|Supp(S_{(f)})|}, \tag{8}$$

where the equality holds if and only if $f(x)$ is a quasi-generalized Bent function.

Proof. Denote $S(\alpha) = \sum_{w \in Supp(S_{(f)})} u^{-w \cdot \alpha}$. Then

$$\sum_{\alpha \in Z_p^n} |S(\alpha)|^2 = \sum_{\alpha \in Z_p^n} \sum_{w \in Supp(S_{(f)})} u^{-w \cdot \alpha} \sum_{v \in Supp(S_{(f)})} u^{v \cdot \alpha}$$

$$= \sum_{w,v \in Supp(S_{(f)})} \sum_{\alpha \in Z_p^n} u^{(v-w) \cdot \alpha}$$

$$= p^n \sum_{w \in Supp(S_{(f)})} 1$$

$$= p^n |Supp(S_{(f)})|. \tag{9}$$

Due to lemma 2, we have

$$\sum_{\alpha \in Z_p^n} S(\alpha) r_f(\alpha) = \sum_{\alpha \in Z_p^n} r_f(\alpha) \sum_{w \in Supp(S_{(f)})} u^{-w \cdot \alpha}$$

$$= \sum_{w \in Supp(S_{(f)})} \sum_{\alpha \in Z_p^n} r_f(\alpha) u^{-w \cdot \alpha}$$

$$= p^n \sum_{w \in Supp(S_{(f)})} |S_{(f)}(w)|^2$$

$$= p^n \sum_{w \in Z_p^n} |S_{(f)}(w)|^2 = p^n.$$

Combining lemma 5 and (9), we have

$$p^n = \sum_{\alpha \in Z_p^n} S(\alpha) r_f(\alpha) \le \sqrt{\sum_{\alpha \in Z_p^n} |S(\alpha)|^2 \sum_{\alpha \in Z_p^n} |r_f(\alpha)|^2}$$

$$= \sqrt{p^n |Supp(S_{(f)})| \sum_{\alpha \in Z_p^n} |r_f(\alpha)|^2}. \tag{10}$$

Therefore

$$\sum_{\alpha \in Z_p^n} |r_f(\alpha)|^2 \ge \frac{p^n}{|Supp(S_{(f)})|}.$$

If $f(x)$ is a kth-order quasi-generalized Bent function, by definition 2 and lemma 2, we obtain

$$\sum_{\alpha \in Z_p^n} |r_f(\alpha)|^2 = \sum_{\alpha \in Z_p^n} \sum_{w \in Z_p^n} |S_{(f)}(w)|^2 u^{w \cdot \alpha} \sum_{v \in Z_p^n} |S_{(f)}(v)|^2 u^{-v \cdot \alpha}$$

$$= \sum_{w \in Z_p^n} |S_{(f)}(w)|^2 \sum_{v \in Z_p^n} |S_{(f)}(v)|^2 \sum_{\alpha \in Z_p^n} u^{(w-v) \cdot \alpha}$$

$$= p^n \sum_{w \in Z_p^n} |S_{(f)}(w)|^4 \tag{11}$$

$$= p^n \sum_{w \in Supp(S_{(f)})} \frac{1}{p^{2n-2k}}$$

$$= \frac{p^n}{p^{n-k}} = \frac{p^n}{|Supp(S_{(f)})|} \tag{12}$$

hence the sufficiency holds.

Conversely assume the equality in (8) holds, that is

$$\sum_{\alpha \in Z_p^n} S(\alpha) r_f(\alpha) = \sqrt{\sum_{\alpha \in Z_p^n} |S(\alpha)|^2 \sum_{\alpha \in Z_p^n} |r_f(\alpha)|^2},$$

by lemma 2, there must be a complex number c, such that

$$r_f(\alpha) = c \cdot \overline{S(\alpha)}. \tag{13}$$

Combining (9) and (13), we have

$$p^n = \sqrt{\sum_{\alpha \in Z_p^n} |S(\alpha)|^2 |c|^2 \sum_{\alpha \in Z_p^n} |S(\alpha)|^2}$$

$$= |c| \sum_{\alpha \in Z_p^n} |S(\alpha)|^2$$

$$= p^n |c| \cdot |Supp(S_{(f)}).|$$

Therefore $|c| \cdot |Supp(S_{(f)})| = 1$, and since $|Supp(S_{(f)})|$ is a integer number, $0 < |c| \leq 1$ is a rational number. While for any $w \in Z_p^n$, from lemma 2 and (13), we have

$$|S_{(f)}(w)|^2 = \frac{1}{p^n} \sum_{\alpha \in Z_p^n} r_f(\alpha) u^{-w \cdot \alpha} = \frac{1}{p^n} \sum_{\alpha \in Z_p^n} c\overline{S(\alpha)} u^{-w \cdot \alpha}$$

$$= \frac{c}{p^n} \sum_{v \in Supp(S_{(f)})} \sum_{\alpha \in Z_p^n} u^{(v-w) \cdot \alpha}$$

$$= \begin{cases} c & w \in Supp(S_{(f)}); \\ 0 & w \notin Supp(S_{(f)}). \end{cases} \tag{14}$$

If $w \in Supp(S_{(f)})$, the left side of the above equality is a real number greater than 0, hence c is a rational number greater than 0. Combining (14), definition 1 and lemma 1, there exists an integer number $r > 0$, such that $1/c = p^r$. Denote $k = n - r$, and $f(x)$ is a kth-order quasi-generalized Bent function.   □

Remark 2. It is easy to conclude from the proof of the theorem 3 that $f(x)$ is a quasi-generalized Bent function if and only if the magnitude of the chrestenson cyclic spectra takes only two values, 0 and a nonzero constant c, without emphasizing that $c = 1/p^{n-k}$.

Corollary 1. *Let $f(x)$, $x \in Z_p^n$ be a p-valued logical function with n variables. Then*

$$\sum_{w \in Z_p^n} |S_{(f)}(w)|^4 \geq \frac{1}{|Supp(S_{(f)})|}, \tag{15}$$

where the equality holds if and only if $f(x)$ is a quasi-generalized Bent function.

Proof. It follows immediately from theorem 3 and (11).   □

4   The Constructions of kth-Order Quasi-Generalized Bent Functions

4.1   The Typical Construction of kth-Order Quasi-Generalized Bent Functions

In this section, we focus on the constructions of k-order quasi-generalized Bent functions, which are not generalized partially Bent functions. Firstly we introduce the typical construction similar to the *Maiorana − McFarland* construction.

Theorem 4. *Let $n \geq 1$, and $0 \leq k \leq n$. Denote $r = \frac{n-k}{2}$, and*

$$x = (x_1, x_2, \cdots, x_r) \in Z_p^r, \qquad y = (y_1, y_2, \cdots, y_{n-r}) \in Z_p^{n-r}.$$

Set

$$f(x, y) = \pi(x) \cdot y + \phi(x), \tag{16}$$

where $\pi(x)$ is a mapping from Z_p^r to Z_p^{n-r}, and $\phi(x)$ is any p-valued logical function with r variables. Then $f(x, y)$ is a kth-order quasi-generalized Bent function if and only if

$$|\{\pi(x) : x \in Z_p^r\}| = p^r,$$

that is, $\pi(x)$ is a epimorphism.

Proof. If $\pi(x)$ is a *epimorphism* from Z_p^r to Z_p^{n-r}. Then for any $w \in Z_p^r$, and $v \in Z_p^{n-r}$, we have

$$S_{(f)}(w, v) = \frac{1}{p^n} \sum_{x \in Z_p^r, y \in Z_p^{n-r}} u^{\pi(x) \cdot y + \phi(x) - w \cdot x - v \cdot y}$$

$$= \frac{1}{p^n} \sum_{x \in Z_p^r} u^{\phi(x) - w \cdot x} \sum_{y \in Z_p^{n-r}} u^{(\pi(x) - v) \cdot y}$$

$$= \begin{cases} \frac{1}{p^r} u^{\phi(x_v) - w \cdot x_v} & \text{such that } \pi(x_v) = v; \\ 0 & v \notin \{\pi(x) : x \in Z_p^r\}. \end{cases}$$

The sufficiency holds immediately.

Otherwise, if $\pi(x)$ is not a epimorphism from Z_p^r to Z_p^{n-r}. Then

$$|\{\pi(x) : x \in Z_p^r\}| < p^r,$$

hence

$$|\{v : v \in Z_p^{n-r}, v \notin \{\pi(x) : x \in Z_p^r\}\}| > p^{n-r} - p^r.$$

while for any $w \in Z_p^r$, and $v \notin \{\pi(x) : x \in Z_p^r\}$, we have $S_{(f)}(w, v) = 0$, that is

$$|\{(w, v) : w \in Z_p^r, v \in Z_p^{n-r}, S_{(f)}(w, v) = 0\}| > p^r(p^{n-r} - p^r) = p^n - p^{n-k},$$

which contradicts to the fact that $f(x)$ is a kth-order quasi-generalized Bent function. □

We call the kth-order quasi-generalized Bent functions in the form of (16) as typical quasi-generalized Bent functions, which is a proper subset of the class of quasi-generalized Bent functions, existing only when $n - k$ is even.

Remark 3. Due to theorem 1 and theorem 4, if $\{\pi(x) : x \in Z_p^r\}$ is neither a linear subspace, nor the shifting of a linear subspace of Z_p^{n-r}, then the typical quasi-generalized Bent functions in the form of (16) can not be generalized partially Bent functions.

4.2 The Recursive Construction of kth-Order Quasi-Generalized Bent Functions

The typical kth-order quasi-generalized Bent functions exist only in the case where $n - k$ is even. Now we introduce another construction which are different from the typical construction in that $n - k$ can be odd here.

To derive our construction, we introduce some notation and lemma on number theory.

Let $\eta = \left(\frac{l}{p}\right)$, where $p \neq 2$ is a prime, be a quadratic character. Then

Lemma 6. *[11] For any $a, b \in Z_p \backslash \{0\}$,*

1. *If $\left(\frac{a}{p}\right) = 1$, and $\left(\frac{b}{p}\right) = 1$. Then $\left(\frac{ab}{p}\right) = 1$;*
2. *If $\left(\frac{a}{p}\right) = 1$, and $\left(\frac{b}{p}\right) = -1$. Then $\left(\frac{ab}{p}\right) = -1$.*

Lemma 7. *[11] Denote $G(p) = \sum\limits_{j=0}^{p-1} u^{j^2}$. Then*

$$G(p) = \begin{cases} \sqrt{p} & if \ p \equiv 1 \ mod \ 4; \\ i\sqrt{p} & if \ p \equiv 3 \ mod \ 4. \end{cases} \tag{17}$$

The following lemma is an immediate consequence of lemma 6 and lemma 1.

Lemma 8. *Denote $G(p) = \sum\limits_{j=0}^{p-1} u^{bj^2}$, where $\left(\frac{b}{p}\right) = -1$. Then*

$$G(p) = \begin{cases} -\sqrt{p} & if \ p \equiv 1 \ mod \ 4; \\ -i\sqrt{p} & if \ p \equiv 3 \ mod \ 4. \end{cases} \tag{18}$$

In this section, we consider the function with $n + 1$ variables concatenated of p's functions over Z_p with n variables in the following form:

Let $f_j(x)$, $x \in Z_p^n$, $0 \leq j \leq p - 1$ all be p-valued logical functions with n variables, and denote

$$f(x, x_{n+1}) = \frac{1}{p} \sum_{j=0}^{p-1} I_{\{j\}}(x_{n+1}) f_j(x), \tag{19}$$

where

$$I_{\{j\}}(x_{n+1}) = \begin{cases} 1 & if \ x_{n+1} = j; \\ 0 & if \ x_{n+1} \neq j. \end{cases}$$

The following theorem is an immediate consequence of definition 1 and equation (19):

Theorem 5. *Let $f(x, x_{n+1})$ be a p-valued function with $n + 1$ variables of the form (19). Then*

$$S_{(f)}(w, w_{n+1}) = \frac{1}{p} \sum_{j=0}^{p-1} u^{-w_{n+1} \cdot j} S_{(f_j)}(w) \tag{20}$$

holds for all $w \in Z_p^n$, and $w_{n+1} \in Z_p$.

Theorem 6. *Let* $f_j(x)$, $x \in Z_p^n$, $0 \leq j \leq p-1$ *all be kth-order quasi-generalized Bent functions with n variables, and for any* $w \in Z_p^n$, *there exists* $t, b \in Z_p$, *such that*

$$S_{(f_j)}(w) = u^{bj^2 + tj} S_{(f_0)}(w),$$

for $j = 0, 1, \cdots, p-1$. *Then the p-valued function in the form of (19) is a kth-order quasi-generalized Bent function with* $n+1$ *variables.*

Proof. Due to theorem 5, for any $w \in Z_p^n$, and $w_{n+1} = l \in Z_p$,

$$S_{(f)}(w, l) = \frac{1}{p} \sum_{j=0}^{p-1} u^{-l \cdot j} S_{(f_j)}(w) = \frac{1}{p} \sum_{j=0}^{p-1} u^{-l \cdot j + bj^2 + t \cdot j} S_{(f_0)}(w)$$

$$= \frac{1}{p} \sum_{j=0}^{p-1} u^{b(j + \frac{b^{-1}(t-l)}{2})^2 - \frac{b^{-1}(t-l)^2}{4}} S_{(f_0)}(w)$$

$$= \frac{1}{p} u^{\frac{-b^{-1}(t-l)^2}{4}} S_{(f_0)}(w) \sum_{j=0}^{p-1} u^{b(j + \frac{b^{-1}(t-l)}{2})^2}.$$

1. If $\left(\frac{b}{p}\right) = 1$, from lemma 8 and lemma 6, we have

$$\sum_{j=0}^{p-1} u^{b(j + \frac{b^{-1}(t-l)}{2})^2} = \begin{cases} \sqrt{p} & \text{if } p \equiv 1 \bmod 4; \\ i\sqrt{p} & \text{if } p \equiv 3 \bmod 4. \end{cases}$$

2. If $\left(\frac{b}{p}\right) = -1$, from lemma 8 and lemma 7, we have

$$\sum_{j=0}^{p-1} u^{b(j + \frac{b^{-1}(t-l)}{2})^2} = \begin{cases} -\sqrt{p} & \text{if } p \equiv 1 \bmod 4; \\ -i\sqrt{p} & \text{if } p \equiv 3 \bmod 4. \end{cases}$$

Therefore

$$|S_{(f)}(w, l)|^2 = \frac{1}{p} |S_{(f_0)}(w)|^2 = 0 \text{ or } \frac{1}{p^{n+1-k}},$$

that is, $f(x, x_{n+1})$ is a kth-order quasi-generalized Bent function with $n+1$ variables. $\qquad \square$

Now we give a class of functions satisfying the conditions offered in theorem 6:

Theorem 7. *Let* $f_0(x)$, $x \in Z_p^n$ *be a kth-order quasi-generalized Bent function. Denote*

$$f_j(x) = f_0(x + j\alpha) + bj^2, \quad j = 1, 2, \cdots, p-1,$$

where $\alpha \in Z_p^n$, $b \in Z_p \backslash \{0\}$. *Then* $f(x, x_{n+1})$ *in the form of (19) is a kth-order quasi-generalized Bent function.*

Proof. It is easy to verify that $f_j(x)$, $j = 1, 2, \cdots, p-1$, are all kth-order quasi-generalized Bent functions. For any $w \in Z_p^n$, we have

$$S_{(f_j)}(w) = \frac{1}{p^n} \sum_{x \in Z_p^n} u^{f_0(x+j\alpha)+bj^2-w\cdot x}$$

$$= \frac{1}{p^n} \sum_{y \in Z_p^n} u^{f_0(y)+bj^2-w\cdot y+jw\cdot\alpha}$$

$$= u^{bj^2+jw\cdot\alpha} \frac{1}{p^n} \sum_{y \in Z_p^n} u^{f_0(y)-w\cdot y}$$

$$= u^{bj^2+jw\cdot\alpha} S_{(f_0)}(w),$$

which satisfy the condition in theorem 6, hence the result holds. $\qquad\square$

Theorem 7 shows that there exists a group of kth-order quasi-generalized Bent functions, the concatenation of which is kth-order quasi-generalized Bent function with $n+1$ variables. Moreover, if $n-k$ is odd, $n+1-k$ must be even, hence the recursive construction is different from the typical construction.

In particular, if $f_0(x)$ in theorem 7 is a generalized Bent function. Then $f(x, x_{x+1})$ in the form of (19) is also a generalized Bent function.

Theorem 8. *Let $f_j(x)$, $x \in Z_p^n$, $0 \le j \le p-1$ all be kth-order quasi-generalized Bent functions with n variables. Then the function in the form of (19) is $(k-1)$th-order quasi-generalized Bent functions if and only if*

$$Supp(S_{(f_j)}) \bigcap Supp(S_{(f_k)}) = \emptyset$$

holds for any $0 \le k, j \le p-1$, and $k \ne j$.

Proof. Due to theorem 5, for any $w \in Z_p^n$, and $w_{n+1} \in Z_p$, we have

$$S_{(f)}(w, w_{n+1}) = \frac{1}{p} \sum_{j=0}^{p-1} u^{-w_{n+1}\cdot j} S_{(f_j)}(w).$$

Then $\left| \bigcup_{j=0}^{p-1} Supp(S_{(f_j)}) \right| = p^{n-k+1}$, since

$$|Supp(S_{(f_j)})| = p^{n-k}, \ and \ Supp(S_{(f_j)}) \bigcap Supp(S_{(f_k)}) = \emptyset$$

.

Thus for any $w \in Z_p^n$, if $S_{(f_j)}(w) = 0$, $0 \le j \le p-1$, we have $S_{(f)}(w, w_{n+1}) = 0$, for any $w_{n+1} \in Z_p$. Otherwise, there exists unique $0 \le j \le p-1$, such that $w \in Supp(S_{(f_j)})$, therefore

$$S_{(f)}(w, w_{n+1}) = \frac{1}{p} u^{-w_{n+1}\cdot j} S_{(f_j)}(w),$$

i.e.

$$|S_{(f)}(w, w_{n+1})|^2 = \frac{1}{p^2}|S_{(f_j)}(w)|^2 = 0 \text{ or } \frac{1}{p^{n+1-(k-1)}}.$$

Hence $f(x, x_{n+1})$ is a $(k-1)$th-order quasi-generalized Bent function with $n+1$ variables.

Conversely if there exists $j \neq k$, such that $Supp(S_{(f_j)}) \bigcap Supp(S_{(f_k)}) \neq \emptyset$. Then

$$|\bigcup_{j=0}^{p-1} Supp(S_{(f_j)})| < p^{n-k} \cdot p = p^{n-k+1},$$

therefore

$$|\bigcap_{j=0}^{p-1} \overline{Supp(S_{(f_j)})}| > p^n - p^{n-k+1}.$$

while

$$\bigcap_{j=0}^{p-1} \overline{Supp(S_{(f_j)})} = \{w : w \in Z_p^n, \text{such that } S_{f_j}(w) = 0, \text{for all } 0 \leq j \leq p-1\}.$$

Then for any $w \in \bigcap_{j=0}^{p-1} \overline{Supp(S_{(f_j)})}$, and any $w_{n+1} \in Z_p$, we have

$$S_{(f)}(w, w_{n+1}) = \frac{1}{p}u^{-w_{n+1} \cdot j}S_{(f_j)}(w) = 0,$$

that is

$$|\overline{Supp(S_{(f)})}| > (p^n - p^{n-k+1}) \cdot p = p^{n+1} - p^{n+1-(k-1)},$$

i.e.

$$|Supp(S_{(f)})| < p^{n+1-(k-1)},$$

which contradicts the assumption that $f(x, x_{n+1})$ is a $(k-1)$th-order quasi-generalized Bent function.   □

5   Conclusion

In this paper, we introduce a class of logical functions over ring Z_p, the magnitudes of whose *Chrestenson* cyclic spectra possess a good property: they take values 0 or a nonzero constant. The further applications of this class of logical functions in the design of Hash functions, stream ciphers, block ciphers and communications need to be examined, and whether the work can be extended to the logical functions over ring Z_m, where m is any integer number is the question to be investigated later.

References

1. J.Seberry, X.M.Zhang, Y.Zheng: Relationships among Nonlinearty Criteria. Advances in Cryptology -EUROCRYPT'94, Springer-Verlag, 950 (1994) 376-388
2. W.Meier, O.Staffelbach: Nonlinearity Criteria for Cryptographic Functions. Advances in Cryptology -EUROCRYPT'89, Springer-Verlag, 434 (1990) 549-562
3. O. S. Rothous: On Bent Functions. J. Comb. Theory, 20A (1976) 300-305
4. C. Carlet: Partially-bent Bunctions. Advance in Cryptoloty-CRYPTO'92, Spring-Verlag (1993) 280-291
5. S.Chee, S. Lee, K. Kim: Semi-bent Functions. Advances in Cryptology-ASIACRYPT'94, Springer-Verlag (1995) 107-118
6. Yuliang Zheng and Xianmo Zhang. On Plateaued Functions, IEEE. Trans. Inform. Theory, Vol. 47, No.3 (2001)
7. Liu Wenfen, Li Shiqu and Teng Jihong: The Properties of k-order Quasi-Bent Functions and its Applications. The 7th communication conference for the youth, Publishing House of Electronic Industry(in Chinese) (2001) 939-943
8. Teng Jihong, Li Shiqu and Zhang Wenying: The Matrix Characteristics of the Cryptographic Properties of a Special Kind of k–order Quasi-Bent Functions. The CCICS'2003(in Chinese), The Science Publishing House (2003) 284-289
9. P. Kumar, R. Scholtz, L.Welch: Generalized Bent functions and their Properties. J.combinatorial Theory (Ser. A) 40 (1985) 90-107
10. Zhao Yaqun: The Properties and Construction of Partially Bent Functionsand Generalized Bent Functions. The doctorate thesis of Information Engineering University(in Chinese) (1998)
11. L. E. Dickson: History of the theory of number. Vol. II Addison-Wesley Publishing Company(1984)
12. Li Shiqu, Zeng Bensheng, Lian Yuzhong, etc: Logical Functions in Cryptoloty. Publishing Company of Software and Eletronic Industry (In chinese) (2003)

A Fast Algorithm for Determining the
Linear Complexity of Periodic Sequences

Shimin Wei[1], Guolong Chen[1], and Guozhen Xiao[2]

[1] Department of Computer Science & Technique, Huaibei Coal Normal College,
Dongshan Road 100, Huaibei 235000, Anhui, China
weism02@yahoo.com.cn
[2] Institute of Information Security, Xidian University,
Xi'an 710071, China
gzxiao@xidian.edu.cn

Abstract. An efficient algorithm for determining the linear complexity and the minimal polynomial of sequence with period $p^m q^n$ over a finite field $GF(q)$ is designed, where p and q are primes, and q is a primitive root modulo p^2. The new algorithm generalizes the algorithm for computing the linear complexity of sequences with period q^n over $GF(q)$ and that for computing the linear complexity of sequences with period p^m over $GF(q)$.

1 Introduction

A fundamental problem in the theory of stream ciphers is the determination of the linear complexity of keystreams. The linear complexity of a sequence is defined as the length of the shortest LFSR which can generate this sequence. There is an elegant and efficient method for determining the linear complexity and the associated connection polynomial of any finite bit string or periodic sequence. This procedure is the well known Berlekamp-Massey LFSR synthesis algorithm [1]. In the special case Games and Chan [2] proposed an extremely efficient method for determining the linear complexity of a binary sequence with period 2^n, which is generalized to an algorithm for determining the linear complexity of a sequence with period p^m over $GF(p^n)$ by Ding [3]. Xiao, Wei, Lam and Imamura [4] proposed an extremely efficient algorithm for determining the linear complexity and the minimal polynomial of a sequence with period p^n over GF(q), which is generalized to an algorithm for determining the linear complexity of a binary sequence with period $2^n p^m$, and to one for determining the linear complexity of a sequence with period $2p^n$ over GF(q) by Wei, Xiao and Chen[5-6]. In this paper, an efficient algorithm for determining the linear complexity and the minimal polynomial of a sequence with period $p^m q^n$ over GF(q) is proposed, where q is a primitive root modulo p^2.

---

[1] This work was supported in part by the Natural Science Foundation of China under Grant 60573026 and 60172015, the Natural Science Foundation of Anhui Province in China under Grant 03042204, the Science Research Project of the Education Department of Anhui Province in China under Grant 2004kj317, the Key Project of Chinese Ministry of Education under Grant 205074, and the Academic and Technical leading scholars Research Project of the Education Department of Anhui Province in China under Grant 2005hbz24.

D. Feng, D. Lin, and M. Yung (Eds.): CISC 2005, LNCS 3822, pp. 202–209, 2005.

Let $s=(s_0, s_1, s_2, s_3, \cdots)$ be a nonzero periodic sequence with digits from $GF(q)$. Then there exists a linear recurrence of least positive order L, such that $s_i=-c_1s_{i-1}-c_2s_{i-2}-\cdots-c_Ls_{i-L}$, $j\geq L$, that may generate s. We shall refer to the characteristic polynomial $x^L+c_1x^{L-1}+c_2x^{L-2}+\cdots+c_L$ of this linear recurrence as the minimal polynomial of the sequence s and shall denote it by $f_s(x)$.

2 Two Fast Algorithms for the Linear Complexity

In this section, we introduce two fast algorithms. One is the algorithm for determining the linear complexity of a sequence with period p^n over $GF(q)$ [6], another is one for determining the linear complexity of a sequence with period p^n over $GF(p^m)$ [3], where p and q are primes, and q is a primitive root modulo p^2.

Algorithm 1. Let $s=(s_0, s_1, s_2, s_3, \cdots)$ be a sequence with period $N=p^n$ over $GF(q)$, $s^N=(s_0, s_1, \cdots, s_{N-1})$ the first period of s, and let q be a primitive root modulo p^2. Denote $a=(a_0, a_1, \cdots, a_{l-1})$. Then the algorithm for computing the linear complexity and the minimal polynomial of s is as follows:

Initial value: $a\leftarrow s^N$, $l\leftarrow p^n$, $c\leftarrow 0, f\leftarrow 1$.

1) If $l=1$, go to 2);otherwise $l\leftarrow l/p, A_i=(a_{(i-1)l}, a_{(i-1)l+1},\cdots, a_{il-1})$, $i=1,2,\cdots,p$, go to 3).
2) If $a=(0)$, stop; otherwise $c\leftarrow c+1, f\leftarrow(1-x)f$, stop.
3) If $A_1=A_2=\cdots=A_p$, $a\leftarrow A_1$, go to 1), otherwise $a\leftarrow A_1+A_2+\cdots+A_p$, $c\leftarrow c+(p-1)l$,

Finally, we have that $c(s)=c$ and $f_s(x)=f$.

Algorithm 2. Let $s=(s_0, s_1, s_2, s_3, \cdots)$ be a sequence with period $N=p^n$ over $GF(p^m)$, $s^N=(s_0, s_1, \cdots, s_{N-1})$ the first period of s. Denote $a=(a_0, a_1, \cdots, a_{l-1})$. Then the algorithm for computing the linear complexity and the minimal polynomial of s is as follows:

Initial value: $a\leftarrow s^N$, $l\leftarrow N, c\leftarrow 0, f\leftarrow 1$.

1) If $l=1$, go to 2); otherwise $l\leftarrow l/p$, $A_i=(a_{(i-1)l}, a_{(i-1)l+1}, \cdots, a_{il-1})$, $i=1, 2, \cdots, p$, $b\leftarrow A_1+A_2+\cdots+A_p$, $r\leftarrow q-1$, go to 3).
2) If $a=(0)$, stop; otherwise $c\leftarrow c+1, f\leftarrow(1-x)f$, stop.
3) If $b=(0, \cdots, 0)$, $A_i\leftarrow A_1+A_2+\cdots+A_i$, $i=1, 2, \cdots, r$, go to 4); otherwise $a\leftarrow b$, $c\leftarrow c+rl, f\leftarrow(1-x)^{rl}f$, go to 1).
4) If $r=1$, $a\leftarrow A_1$, go to 1); otherwise $b\leftarrow A_1+A_2+\cdots+A_r$, $r\leftarrow r-1$, go to 3).

Finally, we have that $c(s)=c$ and $f_s(x)=(1-x)^c$ of s.

3 Mathematical Background of the New Algorithm

Let p and q be primes. Then $\phi(p^n)=p^n-p^{n-1}$, where n is a positive integer, ϕ is the Euler ϕ-function. Let $\Phi_n(x)$ be the n-th cyclotomic polynomial. Then $\Phi_n(x)$ is irreducible over $GF(q)$ if and only if q is a primitive modulo n, i.e. if q has order $\Phi(n)$ modulo n [7]. If q is a primitive root modulo p^2, then q is also a primitive root modulo $p^n(n \geq 1)$, hence, $\Phi_{p^n}(x)\,(n \geq 1)$ is irreducible over $GF(q)$ [8].

Theorem 1. Let $a=(a_0, a_1, \cdots, a_{N-1})$ be a finite sequence over $GF(q)$, and let q be a primitive root modulo p^2, where $N=p^m q^n$ (m, $n>0$). Denote $M=p^{m-1}q^{n-1}$, $A_i=(a_{(i-1)M}, \cdots, a_{iM-1})$, $i=1, 2, \cdots, pq$. Then

1) $\gcd(a(x),1-x^{qM}) = \gcd(1-x^{qM}, \sum\limits_{i=1}^{q}[\sum\limits_{j=0}^{p-1}A_{jq+i}(x)x^{(i-1)M}])$;

2) $\gcd(a(x),1-x^{N}) = \gcd(a(x),1-x^{qM}) \cdot \gcd(a(x),\Phi_{p^m}(x)^{q^n})$.

Proof: 1) Since

$a(x) = A_1(x) + A_2(x)x^{M} + \cdots + A_{qp}(x)x^{(qp-1)M}$

$= (1-x^{qM})\sum\limits_{i=1}^{q}[A_i(x)+(A_i(x)+A_{q+i}(x))x^{qM} +\cdots+(A_i(x)+\cdots+A_{(p-2)q+i}(x))$

$x^{(p-2)qM}]x^{(i-1)M} + \sum\limits_{i=1}^{q}(A_i(x)+A_{q+i}(x)+\cdots+A_{(p-1)q+i}(x))x^{[(p-1)q+i-1]M}$

we have

$\gcd(a(x),1-x^{qM}) = \gcd(1-x^{qM}, \sum\limits_{i=1}^{q}(A_i(x)+A_{q+i}(x)+\cdots+A_{(p-1)q+i}(x))x^{[(p-1)q+i-1]M})$

$= \gcd(1-x^{qM}, \sum\limits_{i=1}^{q}(A_i(x)+A_{q+i}(x)+\cdots+A_{(p-1)q+i}(x))x^{(i-1)M})$

$= \gcd(1-x^{qM}, \sum\limits_{i=1}^{q}[\sum\limits_{j=0}^{p-1}A_{jq+i}(x)x^{(i-1)M}])$.

2) Since $1-x^{N} = (1-x^{qM})(\Phi_{p^m}(x))^{q^n}$ and $\gcd(1-x^{qM},(\Phi_{p^m}(x))^{q^n})=1$, we have

$\gcd(a(x),1-x^{N}) = \gcd(a(x),1-x^{qM}) \cdot \gcd(a(x),(\Phi_{p^m}(x))^{q^n})$.

Theorem 2. Let $a=(a_0, a_1, \cdots, a_{N-1})$ be a finite sequence over $GF(q)$, and let q be a primitive root modulo p^2, where $N=[\,p(q-r)+r]\,p^{m-1}q^{n-1}$, $0 \leq r<q$. Denote $M= p^{m-1}q^{n-1}$, $A_i=(a_{(i-1)M}, \cdots, a_{iM-1})$, $i=1, 2, , p(q-r)+r$,

$$I_{j,r} = \begin{cases} \{r+j, p+r+j, \cdots, (q-r-1)p+r+j\} & if \quad r+j \leq p \\ \{r+j-p, r+j, \cdots, (q-r-1)p+r+j\} & if \quad r+j > p \end{cases}$$

for $j=1, 2, \cdots, p$. Then

1) $(\Phi_{p^m}(x))^{q^{n-1}}|a(x)$ if and only if $\sum\limits_{i \in I_{1,r}}A_i = \sum\limits_{i \in I_{2,r}}A_i = \cdots = \sum\limits_{i \in I_{p,r}}A_i$,

2) If $(\Phi_{p^m}(x))^{q^{n-1}}|a(x)$, then

$$\gcd(a(x), (\Phi_{p^m}(x))^{(q-r)q^{n-1}}) = (\Phi_{p^m}(x))^{q^{n-1}} \gcd((\Phi_{p^m}(x))^{(q-r-1)q^{n-1}},$$

$$\sum_{i=1}^{(q-r-1)p+r+1} (\sum_{j=0}^{\lfloor i/p \rfloor} A_{i-jp}(x) - A_{i-jp-1}(x))x^{(i-1)M}),$$

where $\lfloor x \rfloor$ here and hereafter denotes the largest integer less than or equal to x, and $A_0(x)$ here and hereafter is equal to 0.

3) If $(\Phi_{p^m}(x))^{q^{n-1}} | a(x)$ doesn't hold, then

$$\gcd(a(x), (\Phi_{p^m}(x))^{(q-r)q^{n-1}}) = \gcd(a(x), (\Phi_{p^m}(x))^{q^{n-1}})$$

$$= \gcd((\Phi_{p^m}(x))^{q^{n-1}}, \sum_{j=1}^{p}(\sum_{i \in I_{j,r}} A_i(x))x^{(j-1)M}).$$

Proof: 1) Since $(\Phi_{p^m}(x))^{q^{n-1}} = 1 + x^M + \cdots + x^{(p-1)M}$, and

$$a(x) = A_1(x) + A_2(x)x^M + \cdots + A_{(q-r)p+r}(x)x^{[(q-r)p+r-1]M}$$

$$= A_1(x)(1 + x^M + \cdots + x^{(p-1)M}) + (A_2(x) - A_1(x))(1 + x^M + \cdots + x^{(p-1)M})x^M + (A_3(x) -$$

$$A_2(x))(1 + x^M + \cdots + x^{(p-1)M})x^{2M} + \cdots + (A_{p+1}(x) + A_1(x) - A_p(x))(1 + x^M + \cdots$$

$$+ x^{(p-1)M})x^{pM} + (A_{p+2}(x) + A_2(x) - A_{p+1}(x) - A_1(x))(1 + x^M + \cdots + x^{(p-1)M})x^{pM} + \cdots$$

$$+ (A_{(q-r-1)p+r}(x) + \cdots + A_r(x) - A_{(q-r-1)p+r-1}(x) - \cdots - A_{r-1}(x)) \cdot (1 + x^M + \cdots + x^{(p-1)M})$$

$$x^{[(q-r-1)p+r-1]M} - (A_{(q-r-1)p+r}(x) + \cdots + A_r(x))(1 + x^M + \cdots + x^{(p-1)M})x^{[(q-r-1)p+r]M} +$$

$$[\sum_{j=1}^{p}(\sum_{i \in I_{j,r}} A_i(x))x^{(j-1)M}]x^{[(q-r-1)p+r]M},$$

we have that $(\Phi_{p^m}(x))^{q^{n-1}} | a(x)$ if and only if

$$(\Phi_{p^m}(x))^{q^{n-1}} \text{ divides } \sum_{j=1}^{p}(\sum_{i \in I_{j,r}} A_i(x))x^{(j-1)M},$$

if and only if

$$\sum_{i \in I_{1,r}} A_i(x) = \sum_{i \in I_{2,r}} A_i(x) = \cdots = \sum_{i \in I_{p,r}} A_i(x),$$

if and only if

$$\sum_{i \in I_{1,r}} A_i = \sum_{i \in I_{2,r}} A_i = \cdots = \sum_{i \in I_{p,r}} A_i.$$

2) Suppose that $(\Phi_{p^m}(x))^{q^{n-1}} | a(x)$. Then $\sum_{i \in I_{1,r}} A_i = \cdots = \sum_{i \in I_{p,r}} A_i$. By the expression of $a(x)$ we have that

$$\gcd(a(x),(\Phi_{p^m}(x))^{(q-r)q^{n-1}}) = (\Phi_{p^m}(x))^{q^{n-1}}\gcd((\Phi_{p^m}(x))^{(q-r-1)q^{n-1}},A_1(x)+(A_2(x)-$$
$$A_1(x))x^M + (A_3(x)-A_2(x))x^{2M}+\cdots+(A_{p+1}(x)+A_1(x)-A_p(x))x^{pM}$$
$$+(A_{p+2}(x)+A_2(x)-A_{p+1}(x)-A_1(x))x^{pM}+\cdots+(A_{(q-r-1)p+r}(x)+\cdots$$
$$+A_r(x)-A_{(q-r-1)p+r-1}(x)-\cdots-A_{r-1}(x))x^{[(q-r-1)p+r-1]M}-(A_{(q-r-1)p+r}(x)$$
$$+\cdots+A_r(x))x^{[(q-r-1)p+r]M}+(A_{(q-r-1)p+r+1}(x)+\cdots+A_{r+1}(x))x^{[(q-r-1)p+r]M})$$
$$= (\Phi_{p^m}(x))^{q^{n-1}}\gcd((\Phi_{p^m}(x))^{(q-r-1)q^{n-1}},\sum_{i=1}^{(q-r-1)p+r+1}(\sum_{j=0}^{\lfloor i/p\rfloor}A_{i-jp}(x)-A_{i-jp-1}(x))x^{(i-1)M}).$$

3) If $(\Phi_{p^m}(x))^{q^{n-1}}$ does not divide $a(x)$, by the expression of $a(x)$ we have

$$\gcd(a(x),(\Phi_{p^m}(x))^{(q-r)q^{n-1}}) = \gcd(a(x),(\Phi_{p^m}(x))^{q^{n-1}})$$
$$= \gcd((\Phi_{p^m}(x))^{q^{n-1}},\sum_{j=1}^{p}(\sum_{i\in I_{j,r}}A_i(x))x^{(j-1)M}).$$

Theorem 3. Let s be a sequence with period $N=p^mq^n$ over $GF(q)$, q a primitive root modulo p^2. Denote $M=p^{m-1}q^{n-1}$, $A_i=(s_{(i-1)M},\cdots,s_{iM-1})$, $i=1,2,\cdots,pq$. Then $f_s(x)=f_{(a)}(x)(\Phi_{p^m}(x))^z$, hence, $c(s)=c((a))+(p-1)p^{m-1}z$; where $a=(\sum_{i=0}^{p-1}A_{iq+1},\cdots,\sum_{i=0}^{p-1}A_{iq+q})$, $(\Phi_{p^m}(x))^z = (\Phi_{p^m}(x))^{q^n}/\gcd((\Phi_{p^m}(x))^{q^n},s^N(x))$, (a) denotes the sequence with the first period a; hence, $z=q^n-t$, t is the multiple number of the factor $\Phi_{p^m}(x)$ in $\gcd((\Phi_{p^m}(x))^{q^n},s^N(x))$.

Proof: By Theorem 1 we have

$$f_s(x) = (1-x^N)/\gcd(1-x^N,s^N(x))$$
$$= [(1-x^{qM})/\gcd(1-x^{qM},s^N(x))][(\Phi_{p^m}(x))^{q^n}/\gcd((\Phi_{p^m}(x))^{q^n},s^N(x))]$$
$$= [(1-x^{qM})/\gcd(1-x^{qM},\sum_{i=1}^{q}[\sum_{j=0}^{p-1}A_{jq+i}(x)x^{(i-1)M}])]$$
$$[(\Phi_{p^m}(x))^{q^n}/\gcd((\Phi_{p^m}(x))^{q^n},s^N(x))]$$
$$= [(1-x^{qM})/\gcd(1-x^{qM},a(x))][(\Phi_{p^m}(x))^{q^n}/\gcd((\Phi_{p^m}(x))^{q^n},s^N(x))]$$
$$= f_{(a)}(x)(\Phi_{p^m}(x))^z.$$

The expression of the linear complexity $c(s)$ is obvious.

4   A Fast Algorithm for Computing the Linear Complexity

Let s be a sequence with period $N=p^mq^n$ over $GF(q)$, q a primitive root modulo p^2, and let $s^N=(s_0,s_1,\cdots,s_{N-1})$ be the first period of s. By Theorem 2 we know that the computation of $f_s(x)$ can decompose one of $f_{(a)}(x)$ and one of $(\Phi_{p^m}(x))^z$. Denote $a=(a_0, a_1, \cdots, a_{l-1})$. By Algorithm 1, Theorem 1 and Theorem 2 we have the following algorithm for computing $(\Phi_{p^m}(x))^z$ $(m \geq 1)$. It only needs at most $(q-1)n$ iterations.

Algorithm 3. Let s be a sequence with period $N=p^m q^n$ over $GF(q)$, $s^N=(s_0, s_1, \cdots, s_{N-1})$ the first period of s, and q a primitive root modulo p^2. Denote $k=p^{m-1}$.

Initial value: $a \leftarrow s^N$, $l \leftarrow q^n$, $c \leftarrow 0, f \leftarrow 1$.

1) If $l=1$, $A_i=(a_{(i-1)k}, \cdots, a_{ik-1})$, $i=1, 2, \cdots, p$, go to 2); otherwise $l \leftarrow l/q$,
   $A_i=(a_{(i-1)kl}, \cdots, a_{ikl-1})$, $i=1, 2, \cdots, pq$, go to 3).

2) If $A_1=A_2=\cdots=A_p$, stop; otherwise $c \leftarrow c+(p-1)k$, $f \leftarrow f\Phi_{pk}(x)$, stop.

3) If $\sum_{i=0}^{q-1} A_{ip+1} = \cdots = \sum_{i=0}^{q-1} A_{ip+p}$, then $A_i \leftarrow \sum_{j=0}^{\lfloor i/p \rfloor}(A_{i-jp} - A_{i-jp-1})$, $i=1, 2, \cdots, p(q-1)+1$, $r \leftarrow 1$,

   go to 4); otherwise $a \leftarrow (\sum_{i=0}^{q-1} A_{ip+1}, \cdots, \sum_{i=0}^{q-1} A_{ip+p})$, $c \leftarrow c+(p-1)(q-1)lk$, $f \leftarrow f\Phi_{pk}(x)^{(q-1)l}$,
   go to 1).

4) If $\sum_{i \in I_{1,r}} A_i = \sum_{i \in I_{2,r}} A_i \cdots = \sum_{i \in I_{p,r}} A_i$, then $r \leftarrow r+1$, go to 5); otherwise $a \leftarrow (\sum_{i \in I_{1,r}} A_i, \cdots, \sum_{i \in I_{p,r}} A_i)$,

   $c \leftarrow c+(p-1)(q-r-1)lk$, $f \leftarrow f\Phi_{pk}(x)^{(q-r-1)l}$, $r \leftarrow 0$, go to 1).

5) If $r=q$, stop; otherwise $A_i \leftarrow \sum_{j=0}^{\lfloor i/p \rfloor}(A_{i-jp} - A_{i-jp-1})$ for $i=1, 2, \cdots, p(q-r)+r$, go to 4).

Finally, we have that $(\Phi_{p^m}(x))^z =f$, $(p-1)p^{m-1}z=c$.

Combine Algorithm 1, Algorithm 2 and Algorithm 3, we can give an efficient algorithm for computing the linear complexity and the minimal polynomial of s. The new algorithm only needs at most $(q-1)mn$ iterations.

Algorithm 4. Initial value: $a \leftarrow s^N$, $l \leftarrow q^n$, $k \leftarrow p^m$, $c \leftarrow 0, f \leftarrow 1$.

1) If $k=1$, go to 2); otherwise $k \leftarrow k/p$, go to 6).

2) If $l=1$, go to 3); otherwise $l \leftarrow l/q$, $A_i=(a_{(i-1)l}, \cdots, a_{il-1})$, $i=1, 2, \cdots, q$,
   $b \leftarrow A_1+A_2+\cdots+A_q$, $h \leftarrow q-1$, go to 4).

3) If $a=(0)$, stop; otherwise $c \leftarrow c+1$, $f \leftarrow (1-x)f$, stop.

4) If $b=(0,\cdots,0)$, then $A_i \leftarrow A_1+\ldots+A_i$, $i=1, 2, \cdots, h$, go to 5); otherwise $a \leftarrow b$,
   $c \leftarrow c+hl$, $f \leftarrow (1-x)^{hl}f$, go to 2).

5) If $h=1$, then $a \leftarrow A_1$, go to 2); otherwise $b \leftarrow A_1+A_2+\cdots+A_h$, $h \leftarrow h-1$, go to 4).

6) If $l=1$, $A_i=(a_{(i-1)k}, \cdots, a_{ik-1})$, $i=1, 2, \cdots, p$, go to 7); otherwise $l \leftarrow l/q$,
   $A_i=(a_{(i-1)kl}, \cdots, a_{ikl-1})$, $i=1, 2, \cdots, pq$, $b \leftarrow (\sum_{i=0}^{p-1} A_{qi+1}, \sum_{i=0}^{p-1} A_{qi+2}, \cdots, \sum_{i=0}^{p-1} A_{qi+q})$, go to 8).

7) If $A_1=A_2=\cdots=A_p$, $a \leftarrow A_1$, go to 1); otherwise $a \leftarrow A_1+A_2+\cdots+A_p$, $c \leftarrow c+(p-1)k$,
   $f \leftarrow f\Phi_{pk}(x)$, go to 1).

8) If $\sum_{i=0}^{q-1} A_{ip+1} = \cdots = \sum_{i=0}^{q-1} A_{ip+p}$, then $A_i \leftarrow \sum_{j=0}^{\lfloor i/p \rfloor}(A_{i-jp} - A_{i-jp-1})$ for $i=1, 2, \cdots, (q-1)p+1$,

   $r \leftarrow 1$, go to 9); otherwise $a \leftarrow (\sum_{i=0}^{q-1} A_{ip+1}, \sum_{i=0}^{q-1} A_{ip+2}, \cdots, \sum_{i=0}^{q-1} A_{ip+p})$, $c \leftarrow c+(p-1)(q-1)lk$,

   $f \leftarrow f\Phi_{pk}(x)^{(q-1)l}$, go to 6).

9) If $\sum_{i \in I_{1,r}} A_i = \sum_{i \in I_{2,r}} A_i = \cdots = \sum_{i \in I_{p,r}} A_i$, then $r \leftarrow r+1$, go to 10); otherwise

$a \leftarrow (\sum_{i \in I_{1,r}} A_i, \cdots, \sum_{i \in I_{p,r}} A_i)$, $c \leftarrow c+(p-1)(q-r-1)lk$, $f \leftarrow f\Phi_{pk}(x)^{(q-r-1)l}$, $r \leftarrow 0$, go to 6).

10) If $r=q$, $a \leftarrow b$, go to 1); otherwise $A_i \leftarrow \sum_{j=0}^{\lfloor i/p \rfloor}(A_{i-jp} - A_{i-jp-1})$ for

$i=1, 2, \cdots, (q-r)p+ r$, go to 9).

Finally, we have that $c(s)=c$ and $f_s(x)=f$.

In order to illustrate Algorithm 4, we show the following example.

Example 1. Let s be a sequence with period $N=3^2 5^2 =225$ over $GF(3)$, and let $s^{225}=$
210102211000200,100101212101200,212001222200120,001121112022121,2222101
02112011,010200121021201,000021001220122,112012211011021,21110211120022
1,120111220221201,121201111012102,221002220100102,000010221202200,11002
2101020212,111102011002022, be the first period of s. Then by Algorithm 4 we have
that the algorithm for computing the linear complexity and the minimal polynomial of
s is as follows:

Initial value: $a \leftarrow s^{225}$, $l \leftarrow 3^2$, $k \leftarrow 5^2$, $c \leftarrow 0$, $f \leftarrow 1$

1)$k \leftarrow 5$. A)$l \leftarrow 3$,
$A_1=210102211000200$ $A_2=100101212101200$ $A_3=212001222200120$
$A_4=001121112022121$ $A_5=222210102112011$ $A_6=010200121021201$
$A_7=000021001220122$ $A_8=112012211011021$ $A_9=211102111200221$
$A_{10}=120111220221201$ $A_{11}=121201111012102$ $A_{12}=221002220100102$
$A_{13}=000010221202200$ $A_{14}=110022101020212$ $A_{15}=111102011002022$
$b \leftarrow 001202102002211,002210101220210,102101022220000$
$A_1+A_6+A_{11} \neq A_2+A_7+A_{12}$, $c \leftarrow 120$, $f \leftarrow (\Phi_{25}(x))^6$, $a \leftarrow 01120011000020002112110012$
11210210200211100110222120212122211201200002201.

B) $l \leftarrow 1$. i) $A_1=01120$, $A_2=01100$, $A_3=00200$, $A_4=02112$, $A_5=11001$, $A_6=21121$,
$A_7=02102$, $A_8=00211$, $A_9=10011$, $A_{10}=02221$, $A_{11}=20212$, $A_{12}=12221$, $A_{13}=12012$,
$A_{14}=00000$, $A_{15}=02201$.

$\sum_{i=0}^{2} A_{5i+1} = \sum_{i=0}^{2} A_{5i+2} = \cdots = \sum_{i=0}^{2} A_{5i+5} = 12120$, $r \leftarrow 1$,

ii) $A_1=01120$, $A_2=00010$, $A_3=02100$, $A_4=02112$, $A_5=12222$, $A_6=11210$, $A_7=11021$,
$A_8=00212$, $A_9=12212$, $A_{10}=01102$, $A_{11}=02201$.
$A_1+A_6+A_{11} \neq A_2+A_7$, $a \leftarrow 11201110010020121102110021$, $c \leftarrow 140$, $f \leftarrow (\Phi_{25}(x))^7$, $r \leftarrow 0$.

C) $A_1=11201$, $A_2=11001$, $A_3=02012$, $A_4=11021$, $A_5=10021$,
$A_1 \neq A_2$, $a \leftarrow b$, $c \leftarrow 160$, $f \leftarrow (\Phi_{25}(x))^8$.

2) $k \leftarrow 1$. A) $l \leftarrow 3$;
$A_1=001$, $A_2=202$, $A_3=102$, $A_4=002$, $A_5=211$, $A_6=002$, $A_7=210$, $A_8=101$, $A_9=220$,
$A_{10}=210$, $A_{11}=102$, $A_{12}=101$, $A_{13}=022$, $A_{14}=220$, $A_{15}=000$; $b \leftarrow 112200122$.
$A_1+A_6+A_{11} \neq A_3+A_8+A_{13}$, $a \leftarrow 102210222112121$, $c \leftarrow 184$, $f \leftarrow (\Phi_{25}(x))^8(\Phi_5(x))^6$.

B) $l \leftarrow 1$; $A_1=1$, $A_2=0$, $A_3=2$, $A_4=2$, $A_5=1$, $A_6=0$, $A_7=2$, $A_8=2$, $A_9=2$, $A_{10}=1$, $A_{11}=1$,
$A_{12}=2$, $A_{13}=1$, $A_{14}=2$, $A_{15}=1$;
$A_1+A_6+A_{11} \neq A_2+A_7+A_{12}$, $a \leftarrow 21200$, $c \leftarrow 192$, $f \leftarrow (\Phi_{25}(x))^8(\Phi_5(x))^8$.

C) $A_1=2$, $A_2=1$, $A_3=2$, $A_4=0$, $A_5=0$; $A_1 \neq A_2$, $a \leftarrow b$, $c \leftarrow 196$, $f \leftarrow (\Phi_{25}(x))^8(\Phi_5(x))^9$.

3) A) $l \leftarrow 3$; $A_1=112$, $A_2=200$, $A_3=122$, $b \leftarrow 101$, $h \leftarrow 2$;
$b \neq 000$, $a \leftarrow b$, $c \leftarrow 202$, $f \leftarrow (\Phi_{25}(x))^8 (\Phi_5(x))^9 (1-x)^6$.
   B) $l \leftarrow 1$; $A_1=1$, $A_2=0$, $A_3=1$, $b \leftarrow 2$, $h \leftarrow 2$;
$b \neq 0$, $a \leftarrow b$, $c \leftarrow 204$, $f \leftarrow (\Phi_{25}(x))^8 (\Phi_5(x))^9 (1-x)^8$.
   C) $a \neq 0$, $c \leftarrow 205$, $f \leftarrow (\Phi_{25}(x))^8 (\Phi_5(x))^9 (1-x)^9$.
Finally, $c(s)=c=205$ and $f_s(x)= f=(\Phi_{25}(x))^8 (\Phi_5(x))^9 (1-x)^9$.

5 Conclusion

In this paper, an efficient algorithm for determining the linear complexity and the minimal polynomial of a sequence with period $p^m q^n$ over $GF(q)$ is proposed, where q is a primitive root modulo p^2. The new algorithm generalizes the algorithm for computing the linear complexity of a binary sequence with period $2^n p^m$ and one for computing the linear complexity of a sequence with period p^m over $GF(q)$, where p and q are primes, and q is a primitive root modulo p^2. Comparing the proposed algorithm in this paper with the Berlekamp-Massey algorithm, the former works much faster for a sequence with period $N=p^m q^n$ over $GF(q)$, where p and q are primes, and q is a primitive root modulo p^2. It only needs at most $(q-1)mn$ iterations, but require more storage space. The Berlekamp-Massey algorithm may have to run through more than one period of length $N=p^m q^n$ of the sequence before it stabilizes on the correct connection polynomial and must store a segment of length $2c$ of the sequence, where c is the linear complexity of the sequence, while the algorithm given must always store a period of the sequence.

References

1. Massey, J. L.: Shift register synthesis and BCH decoding. IEEE Trans. on Inform. Theory. 15(1): (1969)122-127
2. Games, R. A., Chan, A. H.: A fast algorithm for determining the complexity of a binary sequence with period 2^n. IEEE Trans on Inform. Theory. 29(1): (1983)144-146
3. Ding, C., Xiao, G., Shan, W.: The Stability Theory of Stream Ciphers. Lecture Notes in Computer Science, Vol. 561. Springer-Verlag, Berlin Heidelberg New York (1991)
4. Xiao, G., Wei, S., Lam, K. Y., Imamura, K.: A fast algorithm for determining the linear complexity of a sequence with period p^n over GF(q). IEEE Trans. on Inform. Theory. 46(6):(2000) 2203-2206
5. Wei, S., Xiao, G., Chen, Z.: A fast algorithm for determining the linear complexity of a binary sequence with period $2^n p^m$. Science in China(Series F). 44(6): (2001)453-460
6. Wei, S., Xiao, G., Chen, Z.: a fast algorithm for determining the minimal polynomial of a sequence with period $2p^n$ over $GF(q)$. IEEE Trans. on Inform. Theory. 48(10)(2002)2754-2758
7. McEliece, R. J.: Finite Fields for Computer Scientists and Engineers. Kluwer Academic, Boston, MA(1987)
8. Rosen, K. H.: Elementary Number Theory and Its Applications. Addision-Wesley, Reading, MA(1988)

An Unbounded Simulation-Sound
Non-interactive Zero-Knowledge Proof System
for NP

Hongda Li and Bao Li

State Key Lab of Information Security,
Graduate School of Chinese Academy of Sciences, Beijing, 100039, China

Abstract. In this paper we use strong one-time signatures schemes and adaptive Non-Interactive Zero-Knowledge (NIZK) proof systems to construct an efficient unbounded simulation-sound NIZK proof system, assuming the existence of one-way permutation and pseudorandom generator. Furthermore, we can obtain an unbounded non-malleable NIZK proof system when replacing the adaptive NIZK proof systems in our construction with adaptive NIZK proof of knowledge.

1 Introduction

Zero-knowledge proof was first defined by Goldwasser, Micali, and Rackoff[GMR89] for use in two-party interactions (between a single prover and a single verifier). It requires that the prover can convince the verifier of some assertion but reveal nothing beyond the validity of the assertion. A great deal of works has been done after its invention, and a well-known fact is that Zero-knowledge proof exists for any NP statement, provided that one-way functions exist[GMW91]. Zero-knowledge proofs has become a fundamental cryptographic tool, and is shown to be useful not only in two-party setting but in a host of situations where multiple parties could be involved. Especially in the secure multi-party computation[GMW87, G02a], it is typically used to force malicious parties according to a predetermined protocol.

Non-interactive zero-knowledge(NIZK) proof was proposed by Blum, three entities: a prover, a verifier and an uniformly selected common reference string which is available to all parties. The Feldman and Micali [BFM88]. The model of NIZK consists of prover sends a single message to the verifier, and all that verifier do is to decide whether to accept or not. It was shown that any NP statement has a NIZK proof[BFM88]. Non-interactive zero-knowledge proof have numerous applications in cryptography, and there are several slightly different definitions. The basic one is about proving a single assertion of a-priori bounded length (may be smaller than the length of common reference string). The literatures [FLS90, BDMP91] considered a natural extension: to prove polynomially many assertions with a single common reference string, where the total length of these assertions is polynomial in length of the common reference string. Adaptive NIZK presented in [FLS90] considered the security of proofs when the assertions

D. Feng, D. Lin, and M. Yung (Eds.): CISC 2005, LNCS 3822, pp. 210–220, 2005.

are adaptively selected based on the common reference string and possibly even based on previous proofs.

NIZK proofs are broadcastable and transferable. It can causes a new problem: a user who have seen an NIZK proof can now prove what he was not able to prove before. That is, NIZK does have malleability. Sahai first introduced non-malleable NIZK in [S99]. His definition states that if after seeing a simulated proof for a statement of its choice, an adversary is able to produce a proof, different from the proof seen by him, for some statement satisfying some polynomial-time verifiable relation, he can do before seeing any proof. Sahai presented an elegant structure to transform any adaptive NIZK into non-malleable NIZK by means of the technique called unduplicatable set selection, assuming that one-way function exists. De Santis, Di Crescenzo, and Ostrovsky in [DDO01] strengthened the notion of non-malleability and introduced unbounded non-malleable NIZK, which requires that any polynomial-time adversary could not prove any new statement if not having any NP witness for the statement, even after seeing any polynomial number of NIZK proofs for statements of its choosing. [DDO01] showed how to transform a NIZK proof of knowledge system into unbounded non-malleable NIZK proof system.

The notion simulation soundness of NIZK proofs related to non-malleability was introduced by Sahai in [S99]. It mixes the zero-knowledge and soundness conditions and is very important in applications of NIZK proofs to the construction of public-key encryption schemes secure against chosen ciphertext attacks [G00]. The simulation soundness requires that a polynomial-bounded adversary can not prove any false theorems even after seeing simulated proofs of any statements of its choosing. Sahai's scheme achieves simulation soundness only with respect to a bounded number of simulated proofs seen by the adversary. Lindell in [L02] considered the problem of one-time simulation soundness, and presented a significant simple construction for CCA2-secure encryption schemes. The authors of [DDO01] extended Sahai's work, and introduced unbounded simulation soundness, in which simulation soundness remains even after the adversary has seen any polynomial number of simulated proofs. They presented a quite complex construction to transform any adaptive NIZK into unbounded simulation-sound NIZK.

Recently, Garay et al considered unbounded simulation soundness and non-malleability of zero-knowledge protocols [GMY03]. They utilize a signature scheme existentially unforgeable against adaptive chosen-message attacks to transform Σ-protocol, a honest-verifier zero-knowledge, into an unbounded simulation sound concurrent zero-knowledge protocol. Furthermore, [GMY03] introduced Ω-protocol, a variant of Σ-protocol, and showed how to transform it into non-malleable and/or universal compassable zero-knowledge protocol. [MY03] studied simulation-sound trapdoor commitment (SSTC), and showed how to construct simulation-sound, non-malleable, and universal compassable zero-knowledge protocol using SSTC scheme.

This paper focuss on unbounded simulation-sound NIZK proof, and aims to construct a more efficient scheme. Under assuming the existence of one-way permutation and pseudorandom generator, we present a new efficient scheme that transforms an adaptive NIZK proof system into an unbounded simulation-sound NIZK proof system. Our construction is both intuitive and simple, and so has a concise proof of correctness. Furthermore, it is also an unbounded non-malleable NIZK proof system if we replace an adaptive NIZK proof system with an adaptive NIZK proof of knowledge in our construction.

The paper is organized as follows. Section 2 mainly contains the definitions of unbounded simulation-sound and unbounded non-malleable NIZK proof system. In section 3 the our scheme is presented.

2   Preliminaries

In this section, we present the cryptographic tools that we use in our construction, and recall the definitions for adaptive non-interactive NIZK and unbounded simulation-sound NIZK. These formal definitions are taken from [S99, DDO01].

We use standard notations for writing probabilistic algorithms and experiments. if $A(\cdot)$ is a probabilistic algorithms, $A(x)$ is the result of running A on input x, and notation $y \leftarrow A(x)$ refers to let y be $A(x)$. For a finite set S, $y \leftarrow S$ denotes that y is uniformly selected from S. For the sake of simplicity, we denote an unspecified negligible function by $\mu(\cdot)$, an unspecified polynomial by $poly(\cdot)$.

Adaptive NIZK: In the general model of NIZK proofs, the prover and verifier both have access to the same uniformly distributed reference string. The soundness of the NIZK proofs is such that if the reference string is indeed uniformly distributed, then the probability that some false theorem can be proved is negligible. The zero-knowledge property is formulated by requiring that there exists a probabilistic algorithm (called simulator), the outputs of which, a reference string and a proof, are computationally indistinguishable form that seen by a verifier in the real setting. The adaptive NIZK proofs is strong forms of NIZK proofs, since its the soundness and zero-knowledge hold when the statement to be proved is chosen by the adversary after the reference string has been fixed.

Definition 1. (adaptive non-interactive zero-knowledge): $\Pi = (poly, P, V, S = (S_1, S_2))$ *is called an adaptive non-interactive zero-knowledge proofs system for a language* $L \in NP$ *with relation* R *if* P, V, S_1 *and* S_2 *are all polynomial-time machines and the following conditions hold:*

- Completeness: *For every* $x \in L$ *and all* w *such that* $R(x,w)=true$, *we have that*

$$V(x, r, P(x, w, r)) = true, \text{ where } r \leftarrow \{0, 1\}^{poly(n)}$$

- Adaptive Soundness: *For any adversary* $A = (A_1, A_2)$, *and* $r \leftarrow \{0, 1\}^{poly(n)}$, *when* $A_1(r) \notin L$, *we have that*

$$Pr[V(A_1(r), r, A_2(r)) = true] < \mu(n)$$

- Adaptive Zero-Knowledge: *For any non-uniform probabilistic polynomial-time adversary $A = (A_1, A_2)$, it holds that*

$$|Pr[Expt_A^S(n) = 1] - Pr[Expt_A(n) = 1]| < \mu(n)$$

where the randomized experiments $Expt_A^S(n)$ and $Expt_A(n)$ are defined as the following:

$Expt_A^S(n):$	$Expt_A(n):$
1. $(r, \tau) \leftarrow S_1(1^n)$.	1. $r \leftarrow \{0,1\}^{poly(n)}$.
2. $(x, w, s) \leftarrow A_1(r)$.	2. $(x, w, s) \leftarrow A_1(r)$.
3. $\pi \leftarrow S_2(x, r, \tau)$.	3. $\pi \leftarrow P(x, w, r)$.
4. Return $A_2(\pi, r, s)$.	4. Return $A_2(\pi, r, s)$.

Adaptive NIZK is first considered in [FLS90]. Under the assumption that one-way permutation exists, [FLS90] gave an adaptive NIZK proof system.

In adaptive NIZK proofs, only one chosen statement is proved. If the zero-knowledge property holds when polynomially many assertions chosen by the adversary are proved, it is called unbounded adaptive NIZK.

Definition 2. (unbounded adaptive NIZK): *$\Pi = (poly, P, V, S = (S_1, S_2))$ is called an unbounded adaptive non-interactive zero-knowledge proofs system for a language $L \in NP$ with relation R if P, V, S_1, S_2 are all polynomial-time machines and the following holds:*

- Completeness: *For every $x \in L$ and all w such that $R(x,w)=true$, we have that*

$$V(x, r, P(x, w, r)) = true, \text{ where } r \leftarrow \{0,1\}^{poly(n)}$$

- Adaptive Soundness: *For any adversary $A = (A_1, A_2)$, and $r \leftarrow \{0,1\}^{poly(n)}$, when $A_1(r) \notin L$, we have that*

$$Pr[V(A_1(r), r, A_2(r)) = true] < \mu(n)$$

- Unbounded adaptive Zero-Knowledge: *For any non-uniform probabilistic polynomial-time adversary $A = (A_1, A_2)$, it holds that*

$$|Pr[Expt_A^S(n) = 1] \text{-} Pr[Expt_A(n) = 1]| < \mu(n)$$

where $Expt_A^S(n)$ and $Expt_A(n)$ denote respectively the following randomized experiments:

$Expt_A^S(n):$	$Expt_A(n):$
1. $(r, \tau) \leftarrow S_1(1^n)$.	1. $r \leftarrow \{0,1\}^{poly(n)}$.
2. Return $A^{S_2(\cdot, r, \tau)}(r)$.	2. Return $A^{P(\cdot, \cdot, r)}(r)$.

Simulation-sound NIZK: The ordinary soundness property of proof systems requires that the prover should be incapable of convincing the verifier of a false statement with overwhelming probability when the reference string is uniformly distributed. The simulation soundness of NIZK proof is one where the soundness holds even with respect to a reference string generated by simulator and after some simulated proofs of chosen statements has been given.

Definition 3. (Unbounded Simulation-Sound NIZK): *Let $\Pi = (poly, P, V, S = (S_1, S_2))$ be an unbounded adaptive non-interactive zero-knowledge proofs system for langauge L. We say that Π is unbounded simulation-sound if for any non-uniform probabilistic polynomial-time adversary A, we have that*

$$\Pr[Expt_{A,\Pi}(n) = true] < \mu(n)$$

where $Expt_{A,\Pi}(n)$ is following experiment:

1. $(r, \tau) \leftarrow S_1(1^n)$.
2. $(x, \pi) \leftarrow A^{S_2(\cdot, r, \tau)}(r)$. (The adversary queries simulator S_2 with statements of its choice, and then obtains simulated corresponding proofs. At last, the adversary outputs a statement x and its proof)
3. *return true iff $(\pi \notin Q$ and $x \notin L$ and $V(x, \pi, r) = true)$, where Q be list of proofs given by S_2.*

Unbounded Non-malleable NIZK: The unbounded non-malleability of NIZK is seek to capture the following requirement: "whatever an adversary can prove after seeing polynomially many NIZK proof for statements of its choosing, it could have proved without seeing it, except for the ability to duplicate the proof[DDO01]." The following definition is taken from [DDO01].

Definition 4. (Unbounded Non-malleable NIZK): *Let $\Pi = (poly, P, V, S = (S_1, S_2))$ be an unbounded adaptive non-interactive zero-knowledge proofs system for the NP langauge L (with relation R). Π is a non-malleable NIZK proof system if there exists a probabilistic polynomial-time oracle machine M such that for all non-uniform probabilistic polynomial-time adversary A and all non-uniform polynomial-time relations R', we have that*

$$\Pr[Expt_{A,R'}^S(n) = true] \leq \Pr[Expt_{M^A}(n) = true] + \mu(n)$$

where $Expt_{A,R'}^S(n)$ and $Expt_A(n)$ are respectively defined as following:

$Expt_{A,R'}^S(n)$:
1. $(r, \tau) \leftarrow S_1(1^n)$.
2. $(x, \pi, aux) \leftarrow A^{S_2(\cdot, r, \tau)}(r)$. (The adversary uses simulator S_2 as an oracle to obtain simulated proof π corresponding to statement of its choice x)
3. *Return true iff $(p \notin Q$ and $R'(x, aux) = true$ and $V(x, p, r) = true)$, where Q be list of proofs given by S_2.*

$Expt_{M^A}(n)$:
1. $(x, w, aux) \leftarrow M^A(1^n)$.
2. *Return true iff $(R(x, w) = true)$ and $R'(x, aux) = true$.*

Strong one-time signatures: Strong one-time signature scheme is defined as a triplet of algorithms (Gen, Sig, Ver), where Gen is a probabilistic generator that outputs a signature-key sk and a verification-key vk, Sig a signature algorithm, and ver a verification algorithm. Except for that for every message m, $Ver(vk, m, Sig(sk, m)) = 1$, where $(vk, sk) \leftarrow Gen(1^n)$, strong one-time signatures schemes requires that no adversary can generate a different valid signature of any message with non-negligible probability when given a signature of a message of its choosing. More formally, for any probabilistic polynomial-time adversary A, it holds that

$$Pr\left[A(vk, \alpha) = (m', \alpha') : (m', \alpha') \neq (m, \alpha) \wedge Ver(vk, m', \alpha') = 1\right] < \mu(n)$$

where $(vk, sk) \leftarrow Gen(1^n), m = A(vk), \alpha = Sign(sk, m)$. Such a signature scheme can be constructed from universal one-way hash functions and one-way permutations[L02].

3   Unbounded Simulation-Sound NIZK

In this section, we first present a construction of unbound simulation-sound NIZK proof scheme for $L \in NP$. Our scheme is based on the existence of adaptive NIZK proof system for some language. Such systems exist under the assumption of existence of trapdoor permutation [FLS90]. In addition, our construction requires the existence of one-way permutation and pseudo-random generator.

Let G be a pseudo-random generator which stretches n bits to $3n$ bits, f: $\{0,1\}^n \rightarrow \{0,1\}^n$ be a one-way permutation, h: $\{0,1\}^* \rightarrow \{0,1\}^n$ be a hush function. The common random reference string of the construction consists of two parts, $\Sigma = (\Sigma_1, \Sigma_2)$, where $|\Sigma_1| = 3n$, $|\Sigma_2| = poly(n)$ (which is decided by a NIZK proof system Π' described below). We define the language L':

$$L' = \{(\sigma_1, \sigma_2, \sigma_3, \sigma_4) : \sigma_1 \in L \text{ or } (\exists s \in \{0,1\}^n, \sigma_2 = f(s) \wedge \sigma_4 = G(h(\sigma_3) \oplus s))\}$$

and assume that Π' is an adaptive NIZK proof system for L'.

Protocol Π for unbounded simulation-sound NIZK

- Prover Algorithm: on input $x \in L$ and a witness w for $x \in L$
  1. $(vk, sk) \leftarrow Gen(1^n)$.
  2. Uniformly selects $u \in \{0,1\}^n$.
  3. Using Σ_2 as the reference string and w as witness, invoke adaptive NIZK proof system Π' to prove $y = (x, u, vk, \Sigma_1) \in L'$. Denote this proof by π'.
  4. $\alpha = Sign(sk, (x, u, \pi'))$.
  5. Output (x, u, vk, π', α).
- Verifier algorithm: on input x and $\pi = (x', u, vk, \pi', \alpha)$
  1. Check $x = x'$ and $Ver(vk, (x, u, \pi'), \alpha) = true$.
  2. Invoke the verifier algorithm of Π' to check that π' is a valid proof for $y = (x, u, vk, \Sigma_1) \in L'$.
  3. Output true if and only if the above two checks succeed.
- Simulation Algorithm:
  1. Simulator S_1:
     - Uniformly selects $\Sigma_2 \in \{0,1\}^{poly(n)}$, $\tau \in \{0,1\}^n$.
     - $\Sigma_1 = G(\tau)$.
     - Output (Σ_1, Σ_2).

2. Simulator S_2:
- $(vk, sk) \leftarrow Gen(1^n)$.
- $u = f(h(vk) \oplus \tau)$.
- Using Σ_2 as the reference string and (τ, vk) as witness, invokes adaptive NIZK proof system Π' to prove $y = (x, u, vk, \Sigma_1) \in L'$. Denote this proof by π'.
- $\alpha = Sign(sk, (x, u, \pi'))$.
- Output (x, u, vk, π', α).

Theorem 1. *Protocol Π is an unbounded simulation-sound NIZK proof system for L if Π' is an adaptive NIZK proof system for L'.*

Proof. We first prove that Protocol Π is an unbounded adaptive NIZK. Completeness is evident. Notice the fact that, if common reference Σ is uniformly chosen at random, the probability that Σ_1 is in the image of G is exponentially small. It shows that $Pr[y = (x, u, vk, \Sigma_1) \in L' : \forall u, vk] < \mu(n)$ when $x \notin L$. Therefor, adaptive soundness follows the property of protocol Π'.

To prove unbounded adaptive Zero-Knowledge property, we define a hybrid random experiment $Expt'_A(n)$, which is different from $Expt_A(n)$ only in the first party of Σ.

$Expt'_A(n)$:
1. $\Sigma_2 \leftarrow \{0, 1\}^{poly(n)}, \tau \leftarrow \{0, 1\}^n, \Sigma_1 = G(\tau), \Sigma = (\Sigma_1, \Sigma_2)$.
2. return $A^{P(\cdot, \cdot, \Sigma)}(\Sigma)$.

If the view of adversary in $Expt_A(n)$ is distinguishable from that in $Expt'_A(n)$, that is, there exist some polynomial $p(n)$ such that

$$|Pr[Expt_A(n) = 1] - Pr[Expt'_A(n) = 1]| > p^{-1}(n)$$

then the adversary is able to distinguishes $\Sigma_1 = G(\tau)$ from uniformly distribution. It is contradictory to the pseudorandom property of $G(\cdot)$. Furthermore, the prover in the experiment $Expt'_A(n)$ and simulator use only different witness to prove the same assertion. From the parallel composition lemma of for witness indistinguishability [G01], we have that

$$|Pr\left[Expt_A^S(n) = 1\right] - Pr\left[Expt'_A(n) = 1\right]| < \mu(n)$$

Thus the unbounded adaptive zero-knowledge follows.

We now begin to prove that protocol Π have unbounded simulation soundness. That is, we are to prove that for any non-uniform probabilistic polynomial-time adversary A, random experiment $Expt_{A,\Pi}(n)$ defined in definition 3 meets with

$$Pr[Expt_{A,\Pi}(n) = true] < \mu(n)$$

Let $Q = \{\pi_s : \pi_s = (x_s, u_s, vk_s, \pi'_s, \alpha_s)\}$ be set of proofs given by simulator. For any vk if there exists a proof $\pi_s = (x_s, u_s, vk_s, \pi'_s, \alpha_s) \in Q$ such that $vk = vk_s$, we say that $vk \in Q$. Suppose that there exist an adversary $A = (A_1, A_2)$ and some polynomial $p(n)$, such that for infinitely many n's,

$$Pr[Expt_{A,\Pi}(n) = true] > p^{-1}(n)$$

In other words, the adversary A, which have seen the simulated proofs for the statements chosen by him, outputs a statement $x \notin L$ and a valid proof $\pi = (x, u, vk, \pi', \alpha) \notin Q$ with non-negligible probability. Then we have that

$$
\begin{aligned}
Pr[Expt_{A,\Pi}(n) = true] &= Pr[(\pi \notin Q) \wedge (x \notin L) \wedge (V(x, \pi, r) = true) \wedge (vk \in Q)] \\
&+ Pr[(\pi \notin Q) \wedge (x \notin L) \wedge (V(x, \pi, r) = true) \wedge (vk \notin Q)] \\
&\leq Pr[(\pi \notin Q) \wedge (x \notin L) \wedge (V(x, \pi, r) = true)|(vk \in Q)] \\
&+ Pr[(\pi \notin Q) \wedge (x \notin L) \wedge (V(x, \pi, r) = true)|(vk \notin Q)]
\end{aligned}
$$

Because G is a pseudorandom generator and f a one-way permutation, the adversary can not get τ from $\Sigma_1 = G(\tau)$ and simulated proofs, and so does not get $f(\tau \oplus h(vk))$ for any $vk \notin Q$. Therefore, the probability that the adversary selects u such that $u = f(\tau \oplus h(vk))$ is 2^{-n}. It is obvious that $x \notin L$ and $(x, u, vk, \Sigma_1) \in L'$ implies $u = f(\tau \oplus h(vk))$. It follows that

$$
\begin{aligned}
&Pr[(\pi \notin Q) \wedge (x \notin L) \wedge (V(x, \pi, r) = true)|(vk \notin Q)] \\
&\leq Pr[(x \notin L) \wedge (V_{\Pi'}((x, u, vk, \Sigma_1), \pi', \Sigma_2) = true)|(vk \notin Q)] \\
&\leq Pr[(x \notin L) \wedge ((x, u, vk, \Sigma_1) \in L'))|(vk \notin Q)] + \mu(n) \\
&\leq Pr[u = f(\tau \oplus h(vk))|(vk \notin Q)] + \mu(n) \leq 2^{-n} + \mu(n)
\end{aligned}
$$

Then, there exist infinitely many n's, satisfying

$$Pr[(\pi \notin Q) \wedge (x \notin L) \wedge (V(x, \pi, r) = true)|(vk \in Q)] > p^{-1}(n) - 2^{-n} + \mu(n)$$

When $vk \in Q$, there exists a proof $\pi_s = (x_s, u_s, vk_s, \pi'_s, \alpha_s) \in Q$, satisfying $vk_s = vk$. Since $\pi \notin Q$, that is $\pi \neq \pi_s$, it must holds that $(x, u, \pi', \alpha) \neq (x_s, u_s, \pi'_s, \alpha_s)$. However, $V(x, \pi, r) = true$ shows that $Ver(vk, (x, u, \pi'), \alpha) = true$. So above equation implies that the adversary can forges a signature with non-negligible probability. It is contradictory to our assumption of the strong one-time signature scheme.

Definition 5. [DP92] $\Pi = (poly, P, V, S = (S_1, S_2), E = (E_1, E_2))$ *is a NIZK proof of knowledge for the language* $L \in NP$ *with witness relation* R *if* Π *is a NIZK proof system for* L *and furthermore* E_1 *and* E_2 *are probabilistic polynomial-time machines such that there exists a negligible function* μ *such that for all n:*

- *The distribution on reference strings produced by* $E_1(1^n)$ *has statistical distance at most* $\mu(n)$ *from the uniform distribution on* $\{0, 1\}^{poly(n)}$.
- *For all adversaries* A, *we have that*

$$Pr[Expt_A(n) = true] \leq Pr[Expt_A^E(n) = true] + \mu(n)$$

where $Expt_A^E(n)$ *and* $Expt_A(n)$ *is respectively defined as following:*

$Expt_A(n)$:	$Expt_A^E(n)$:
1. $r \leftarrow \{0, 1\}^{poly(n)}$.	*1.* $(r, \tau) \leftarrow E_1(1^n)$.
2. $(x, p) \leftarrow A(r)$.	*2.* $(x, p) \leftarrow A(r)$.
3. Return $V(x, p, r)$.	*3.* $w \leftarrow E_2(r, \tau, x, p)$.
	4. Return true if $(x, w) \in R$.

Theorem 2. *If Π' is a NIZK proof of knowledge for L' with witness relation R', protocol Π is a NIZK proof of knowledge system for L with witness relation R.*

Proof. Note that since Π' a proof of knowledge, there are extractor machines E_1' and E_2'. To prove Π a proof of knowledge, we must construct corresponding extractor machines E_1 and E_2.

$E_1(1^n)$:

    1. $\Sigma_2 = E_1'(1^n)$.

    2. $\tau \leftarrow \{0, 1\}^n$, $\Sigma_1 = G(\tau)$.

    3. Return $((\Sigma_1, \Sigma_2), \tau)$

Assuming that $\pi = (x, u, vk, \pi', \alpha)$ is a proof for $x \in L$, we have that π' is a proof for $y = (x, u, vk, \Sigma_1) \in L'$. So we can define E_2 as following:

$E_2(x, u, vk, \pi', \alpha)$:

    1. $w \leftarrow E_2'(\pi')$

    2. Return w.

We define new experiments $Expt_A^*(n), Expt_A^{*E}(n)$ and $Expt_A^{**E}(n)$ by modifying experiments $Expt_A(n)$ and $Expt_A^E(n)$:

$Expt_A^*(n)$:

    1. $\Sigma_1 \leftarrow \{0, 1\}^{3n}$, $\Sigma_2 \leftarrow \{0, 1\}^{polu(n)}$.

    2. $(x, \pi) \leftarrow A(\Sigma)$, where $\pi = (x, u, vk, \pi', \alpha)$.

    3. Return $V'(y, \pi', \Sigma_2)$, where π' is a proof for $y \in L'$ and V' is the verification algorithm of Π'.

$Expt_A^{*E}(n)$:

    1. $(\Sigma, \tau) \leftarrow E_1(1^n)$.

    2. $(x, \pi) \leftarrow A(\Sigma)$, where $\pi = (x, u, vk, \pi', \alpha)$.

    3. $w \leftarrow E_2(\Sigma, \tau, x, p)$.

    4. Return true if $(y, w) \in R'$.

$Expt_A^{**E}(n)$:

    1. $(\Sigma, \tau) \leftarrow E_1(1^n)$.

    2. $(x, \pi) \leftarrow A(\Sigma)$, where $\pi = (x, u, vk, \pi', \alpha)$.

    3. $w \leftarrow E_2(\Sigma, \tau, x, p)$.

    4. Return true if $(y, w) \in R'$ and $(x, w) \notin R$.

Obviously, it holds that

$$\Pr[Expt_A(n) = true] \leq \Pr[Expt_A^*(n) = true]$$

and

$$\Pr[Expt_A^{*E}(n) = true] = \Pr[Expt_A^E(n) = true] + \Pr[Expt_A^{**E}(n) = true]$$

From the fact that Π' is a proof of knowledge, it follows that

$$\Pr[Expt_A^*(n) = true] \leq \Pr[Expt_A^{*E}(n) = true] + \mu(n)$$

Thereby, we obtain that

$$\Pr[Expt_A(n) = true] \leq \Pr[Expt_A^E(n) = true] + \Pr[Expt_A^{**E}(n) = true] + \mu(n)$$

In addition, $Expt_A^{**E}(n) = true$ implies that the adversary knows τ meeting with $\Sigma_1 = G(\tau)$, and so $Pr[Expt_A^{**E}(n) = true] \leq \mu(n)$. Hence, we get that

$$Pr[Expt_A(n) = true] \leq Pr[Expt_A^E(n) = true] + \mu(n)$$

and complete the proof.

Theorem 3. *If the NIZK proof system Π' is a proof of knowledge for L', then protocol Π is an unbounded non-malleable NIZK proof for L.*

Proof. To prove unbounded non-malleability of protocol Π, we must present an oracle machine M^A that can output an instance x, together with a witness w for membership of $x \in L$, satisfying some relation.

We modify experiment $Expt_{A,R'}^S(n)$ in the definition of unbounded non-malleable NIZK by replacing $(\Sigma, \tau) \leftarrow S_1(1^n)$ with $(\Sigma, \tau) \leftarrow E_1(1^n)$. M^A first executes this new experiment, and then invoke E_2 to extract a witness from the proof given by the adversary. The detail of $M^A(1^n)$ is as following:

$M^A(1^n)$:
    1. $\Sigma = ((\Sigma_1, \Sigma_2), \tau) \leftarrow E(1^n)$.
    2. $(x, \pi, aux) \leftarrow A^{S_2(\cdot, \Sigma, \tau)}$.
    3. $w \leftarrow E_2(\pi)$.
    4. Return (x, w, aux) if $(x, w) \in R$.

It is easy to see that

$$Pr[Expt_{A,R}^S(n) = true] \leq Pr[Expt_{M^A}(n) = true] + \mu(n)$$

4 Conclusion

Simulation-sound NIZK proofs, which mixes the zero-knowledge and soundness conditions, is very important in applications of NIZK proofs to the construction of public-key encryption schemes secure against chosen ciphertext attacks. we consider unbounded simulation-sound NIZK proof, and present an efficient scheme based on adaptive NIZK proof system. Our construction is both more simple and efficient than the existing schemes.

References

[BDMP91] M. Blum, A. De Santis, S.Micali and G. Persiano. Non-interactive zero-knowledge proofs. SIAM Journal on Computing, 1991, 20(6):1084-1118.

[BFM88] M. Blum, P. Feldman and S.Micali. Non-interactive zero-knowledge and its applications. In Proceeding of the 19th annual Symposium on Theory of computing, 1988, 103-112.

[DDO01] A. De Santis, G. Di Crescenzo, and R. Ostrovsky et al. Robust non-interactive zero-knowledge. In CRYPTO 2001, Springer-Verlag (LNCS 2139), 566-598.

[DDN98] D. Dolev, C. Dwork, and M. Naor. Non-malleable cryptography. SIAM Journal on Computing, 2000, 30(2):391-437.

[DNS98]   C. Dwork, M. Naor, and A. Sahai. Concurrent zero-knowledge. In Proceeding of the 30th Annual Symposium on Theory of Computing, 1998, 409-418.

[DP92]   A. De Santis, G. persiano. Zero-knowledge proofs of knowledge without interaction. In Proceeding of the 33th Annual Symposium on Foundations of Computer Science, 1992:427-436.

[FLS90]   U. Feige, D. Lapidot, and A. Shamir. Multiple non-interactive zero knowledge proofs based on single random string. In Proceeding of the 31th Annual Symposium on Foundations of Computer Science, 1990, volnme I, 308-317.

[G00]   O. Goldreich. Foundation of cryptography - Volume 2. Draft of a chapter on encryption schemes. http://www.wisdom.weizmann.ac.il/

[G01]   O.Goldreich. Foundation of cryptography - basic tools. Cambridge University Press, 2001.

[G02a]   O. Goldreich. Secure multi-party computation. http://www.wisdom.weizmann.ac.il

[G02b]   O. Goldreich. Zero-knowledge twenty years after its invention. Technical Report. http://citeseer.ist.psu.edu/goldreich02zeroknowledge.html

[GMR89]   S. Goldwasser, S. Macali, and C. Rackoff. The knowledge complexity of interactive proof system. SIAM Journal on Computing, 1989, 18(1):186-208.

[GMW87]   O. Goldreich, S. Micali, and A. Wogderson. How to play any mental game or a completeness theorem for protocols with honest majority. In Proceeding of the 19th annual Symposium on Theory of computing, 1987, 218-229.

[GMW91]   O. Goldreich, S. Micali, and A. Wogderson. Proofs that yoeld nothing but their validity or all languages in NP have zero-knowledge proofs systems. Journal of ACM, 1991, 38(3):691-729.

[GMY03]   J. A. Garay, P. Mackenzie, and K. Yang. Strengthing zero-knowledge protocols using signatures. EUROCTRYPT'03, 2003:177-194.

[L02]   Y. Lindell. A simpler construction of CCA2-secure public-key encryption under general assumptions. http://eprint.iacr.org/2002/057.pdf.

[MY03]   P. Mackenzie, K. Yang. On simulation-sound trapdoor commitments. http://eprint.iacr.org/2003/352.pdf.

[S99]   A. Sahai. Non-malleable non-interactive zero knowledge and adaptive chosen-ciphertext security. In Proceeding of the 40th Annual Symposium on Foundations of Computer Science, 1999, 543-553.

An Improved Secure Two-Party Computation Protocol

Yu Yu, Jussipekka Leiwo, and Benjamin Premkumar

Nanyang Technological University,
School of Computer Engineering, Singapore
yuyu@pmail.ntu.edu.sg, {ASJLeiwo, ASANNAMALAI}@ntu.edu.sg

Abstract. Alice and Bob with their private inputs x_n and y_n respectively, want to compute $f_n(x_n, y_n)$ for some publicly known function f_n without disclosing information regarding their private inputs more than what can be inferred from $f_n(x_n, y_n)$. This problem is referred to as a secure two-party computation and Yao proposed a solution to privately compute f_n using garbled circuits. In this paper, we improve the efficiency of circuit by hardwiring the input of Alice in the circuit without compromising privacy. Using a typical two-party computation problem, namely, the Millionaire Problem, we show that our method reduces circuit size significantly specially for circuits whose fan-in is bounded by 2. We also show that the protocol using the reduced circuit is provably secure.

1 Introduction

Alice and Bob, holding their private x_n and y_n respectively, want to compute $f_n(x_n, y_n)$ without revealing information about x_n and y_n more than what can be inferred from $f_n(x_n, y_n)$. In a secure two-party computation, Alice and Bob engage in such a protocol that both of them learn $f_n(x_n, y_n)$ privately and correctly without a third party. For the sake of simplicity, we only consider the basic setting where Alice and Bob are semi-honest and function f_n is deterministic. This is reasonable because secure computation of probabilistic functions in the malicious model can be reduced to that of deterministic ones [1–Proposition 7.3.4] in the semi-honest model [1–Section 7.4].

Yao [2] first proposed the protocol for secure two-party computation by constructing garbled circuits. The solution in the basic setting can be summarized as follows: Alice represents f_n using Boolean circuit C_n, which computes the same function as f_n, encrypts x_n and garbles C_n to produce $E(x_n)$ and GC_n. Upon receiving $E(x_n)$ and GC_n, Bob executes a 1-out-of-2 Oblivious Transfer (OT) [3] with Alice such that Bob gets his private y_n encrypted to $E(y_n)$ without revealing y_n to Alice. Then Bob evaluates GC_n on $E(x_n)$ and $E(y_n)$ obliviously to produce the encrypted result $E(f_n(x_n, y_n))$ and reveals $f_n(x_n, y_n)$ with the help of Alice. Yao's protocol is efficient in that it needs only constant rounds and one oblivious transfer per input bit of Bob.

D. Feng, D. Lin, and M. Yung (Eds.): CISC 2005, LNCS 3822, pp. 221–232, 2005.
© Springer-Verlag Berlin Heidelberg 2005

Later Goldreich et al. [4] provided solutions for the multi-party case. After that, numerous protocols ([5, 6, 7, 8, 9, 10], just to mention a few) with additional properties for multi-party case were proposed. Garbled circuit construction plays a central role in protocols for secure two-party (multi-party) computation. Since Yao gave no detail on how to construct such a garbled circuit, Goldreich et al. [4], Rogaway et al. [8, 11], Beaver [12], Naor et al [13] and Lindell et al. [14] each proposed a "garbled circuit construction" variant.

In this paper, we propose a protocol as follows: Alice represents x_n and f_n with Boolean circuits $C_n^{x_n}$, where x_n is hardwired in $C_n^{x_n}$ such that (1) $C_n^{x_n}$ and $f_n(x_n, \cdot)$ are functionally equivalent and (2) $Topo(C_n^{x_n})$ (the circuit topology of $C_n^{x_n}$) reveals nothing about x_n. Alice garbles $C_n^{x_n}$ to produce GC_n, which is sent to Bob. After getting y_n encrypted by executing OT with Alice, Bob evaluates GC_n on $E(y_n)$ to produce $E(C_n^{x_n}(y_n))$. Alice decrypts $E(C_n^{x_n}(y_n))$ and sends $C_n^{x_n}(y_n){=}f_n(x_n, y_n)$ to Bob. In the protocol, garbled circuits are constructed using pseudorandom generators (PRGs), which is analogous to Rogaway's construction [11]. We prove that the whole protocol is secure under cryptographic assumptions. We also present the algorithm of construction of such a $C_n^{x_n}$ using C_n (the corresponding circuit of f_n) and x_n. Using the Millionaire Problem [15], we show that the size of $C_n^{x_n}$ is much less than that of the corresponding C_n specially when the fan-in is restricted to the minimal possible value (bounded by 2).

2   The Improved Protocol

2.1   Boolean Circuits

Informally, a standard Boolean circuit is a directed acyclic graph with three types of labeled nodes: inputs, gates and outputs. Inputs are the sources of the graph (i.e. nodes with fan-in 0) and are labeled with input variables. Outputs are the sinks of the graph (i.e. nodes with fan-out 0) and carry the values of the circuit output. Gates are nodes labeled with Boolean functions AND, OR, and NOT with fan-in k ($k{=}1$ in case of NOT gate). The size of a circuit is defined as the number of nodes in the graph. In Fig. 1, we illustrate a Boolean circuit in verbose format. Each node (input, gate or output) is labeled with a node number. For simplicity, we assume that all gates are of fan-in 2 and for each gate $g(a, b)$, its truth table is listed in the fixed order of $[g(0,0),$ $g(0,1), g(1,0), g(1,1)]$. Thus, the function g(a,b) can be other than AND, OR, or NOT as long as their function can be represented using the truth table (e.g. $g(a, b)$ can be $a \vee \bar{b}$ or even degenerate gates such as $g(a, b){=}a$ and $g(a, b){=}0$). Note that NOT gate (gate of fan-in 1) is not necessary since it can be manipulated (using De-Morgan's law) to appear only at the input layer or emulated by XORing with constant 1. Each input/gate node has a field "cp" indicating how many copies of its output are used by other gates. $Topo(C_n)$ is defined as the topology of the node graph of C_n, namely, C_n excluding the "truth table" part (see Fig. 1).

Node no.	Type/Input Node	Truth Table	Cp (Fan-out)
0	INPUT		2
1	INPUT		1
2	INPUT		2
3	GATE / (0, 1)	[0, 1, 1, 0]	2
4	GATE / (0, 2)	[0, 0, 0, 1]	1
5	GATE / (2, 3)	[0, 0, 0, 1]	1
6	GATE / (3, 4)	[0, 1, 1, 1]	1
7	OUTPUT / (5, -)	Equal to the output of node 5	0
8	OUTPUT / (6, -)	Equal to the output of node 6	0

Fig. 1. The verbose format of a 3-input-2-output Boolean circuit, where gates are of fan-in 2 and the function of each gate is defined over $\{0,1\} \times \{0,1\} \mapsto \{0,1\}$

2.2 Obtaining $C_n^{x_n}$ from C_n and x_n

We assume that $f \stackrel{def}{=} \{f_n\}_{n \in \mathbb{N}}$ is a family of polynomial-time computable functions, where $f_n : \{0,1\}^n \times \{0,1\}^n \mapsto \{0,1\}^m$ and C_n is the corresponding polynomial-size circuit of f_n. We describe how to obtain $C_n^{x_n}$ in Algorithm 1. such that Theorem 1 holds.

Theorem 1. *(correctness and privacy regarding x_n): Let C_n compute the same function as $f_n : \{0,1\}^n \times \{0,1\}^n \mapsto \{0,1\}^m$, let $x_n \in \{0,1\}^n$ and let $C_n^{x_n}$ be the resulting circuit of applying Algorithm 1. to C_n and x_n, then for every $y_n \in \{0,1\}^n$, it holds that $C_n^{x_n}(y_n) = C_n(x_n, y_n)$ and $Topo(C_n^{x_n})$ reveals nothing regarding x_n.*

Proof. The correctness (i.e., $C_n^{x_n}(y_n) = C_n(x_n, y_n)$) of Algorithm 1. can be proved by induction, namely, for every node of $C_n^{x_n}$, node j has the same output as node $M(j)$ of C_n. To prove that $Topo(C_n^{x_n})$ discloses nothing regarding x_n, we need only to prove that $Topo(C_n^{x_n})$ is independent of x_n. As shown in Algorithm 1., the topology of $C_n^{x_n}$ is generated in a way regardless of the value of x_n. Thus, the conclusion follows. $\square$

Consider a typical two-party computation problem, the Millionaire Problem, where two millionaires, Alice and Bob want to know who is richer, without revealing their actual wealth x_n and y_n to each other. We assume $x_n = a_{n-1} \cdots a_0$ and $y_n = b_{n-1} \cdots b_0$ are both n-bit unsigned integers with a_{n-1} and b_{n-1} as the most significant bits. Hence, $f_n(x_n, y_n)$ outputs a two-bit value indicating whether $x_n < y_n$, $x_n = y_n$ or $x_n > y_n$. The optimal C_n of fan-in 2 for f_n is as follows:

```
inputs:   a_0, ..., a_{n-1}, b_0, ..., b_{n-1}
gates:    e_0=g_{2n}(a_0,b_0)=a_0⊕b_0⊕1,  lt_0=g_{2n+1}(a_0,b_0)=ā_0∧b_0,
          for i∈{1, ..., n-1}
          be_i=g_{2n+5i-3}(a_i,b_i)=a_i⊕b_i⊕1,  tmp_i=g_{2n+5i-2}(be_i,lt_{i-1})=be_i∧lt_{i-1},
          bl_i=g_{2n+5i-1}(a_i,b_i)=ā_i∧b_i,  e_i=g_{2n+5i}(e_{i-1},be_i)=e_{i-1}∧be_i,
          lt_i=g_{2n+5i+1}(bl_i,tmp_i)=bl_i∨tmp_i
outputs:  lt_{n-1} and e_{n-1} .
```

where $be_i=1$ (resp., $bl_i=1$) iff a_i is equal to (resp., less than) b_i, and $e_i=1$ (resp., $lt_i=1$) iff $a_i \cdots a_0$ is equal to (resp., less than) $b_i \cdots b_0$. Thus, the size of C_n (of fan-in 2) is $2n+(5n-3)+2 = 7n-1$ (see also [16–Table 1] for a similar result 254 when $n=32$). By applying Algorithm 1., we can obtain a $C_n^{x_n}$ as follows:

Algorithm 1. Hardwiring x_n in $C_n(\cdot, \cdot)$ to produce $C_n^{x_n}(\cdot)$.

1: **Inputs:** $x_n=a_{n-1}\cdots a_0$ and C_n, where C_n's input-nodes $(a_0, \cdots, a_{n-1}, b_0, \cdots, b_{n-1})$ are numbered $0, \cdots, 2n-1$ respectively and its gate-nodes are $g_{2n}, \cdots, g_{2n+\Gamma_n-1}$.

2: Number the input-nodes of $C_n^{x_n}$ (i.e. $b_0, \cdots, b_{n-1}$) with $0, \cdots, n-1$ respectively.

3: Define a map M such that node j of $C_n^{x_n}$ corresponds to node $M(j)$ of C_n.

4: Let S_i $(0 \leq i < 2n+\Gamma_n)$ be the set associated to node i of C_n.

5: $M(0)\leftarrow n,\quad \cdots,\quad M(n-1)\leftarrow 2n-1,\quad S_0\leftarrow\phi,\quad \cdots,\quad S_{n-1}\leftarrow\phi,\quad S_n\leftarrow\{n\},\quad \cdots,$
   $S_{2n-1}\leftarrow\{2n-1\}, h\leftarrow n$. {Node h is the next node of $C_n^{x_n}$ to be generated.}

6: $v_0\leftarrow a_0, \cdots, v_{n-1}\leftarrow a_{n-1}$ and mark $v_n, \cdots, v_{2n-1}$ as unknowns. {v_i can be a constant, a unary function or a binary function of other unknowns preceding it.}

7: **for** $i=2n$ to $2n+\Gamma_n-1$, consider gate-node g_i with inputs node l_i and node r_i **do**

8:     **if** $S_{l_i}=\{u, w\}$ and $S_{r_i}=\{y, z\}$ and $S_{l_i}\cup S_{r_i}$ has at least 3 elements **then**

9:         **if** $M^{-1}(l_i)$ is undefined **then**

10:            Represent g'_h (the h-th gate of $C_n^{x_n}$) according to v_{l_i}, $M(h)\leftarrow l_i$, $h\leftarrow h+1$. {namely, if v_{l_i} is a function of node u and node w of C_n, then let g'_h be the same function of node $M^{-1}(u)$ and node $M^{-1}(w)$ of $C_n^{x_n}$.}

11:        **end if**

12:        **if** $M^{-1}(r_i)$ is undefined **then**

13:            Represent g'_h according to v_{r_i}, $M(h)\leftarrow r_i$, $h\leftarrow h+1$.

14:        **end if**

15:        Let g'_h be the same function as g_i with inputs node $M^{-1}(l_i)$ and node $M^{-1}(r_i)$ of $C_n^{x_n}$, $M(h+2)\leftarrow i$, $h\leftarrow h+1$.

16:        $v_i\leftarrow g_i(v_{l_i}, v_{r_i})$, $S_i\leftarrow\{l_i, r_i\}$.

17:     **else if** g_i corresponds to a circuit output of C_n **then**

18:        Suppose $S_{l_i}\cup S_{r_i}=\{u, w\}$, represent g'_h according to $g_i(v_{l_i},v_{r_i})$ with inputs node $M^{-1}(u)$ and node $M^{-1}(w)$ of $C_n^{x_n}$. {note that u may be identical to w}

19:        $M(h)\leftarrow i$, $h\leftarrow h+1$, $v_i\leftarrow g_i(v_{l_i}, v_{r_i})$ and $S_i\leftarrow S_{l_i}\cup S_{r_i}$.

20:     **else if** $S_{l_i}\cup S_{r_i}=\{u, w\}$, or $\{u\}$, or ϕ **then**

21:        $v_i\leftarrow g_i(v_{l_i}, v_{r_i})$ and $S_i\leftarrow S_{l_i}\cup S_{r_i}$.

22:     **end if**

23: **end for**

24: **Output:** $C_n^{x_n}$ of fan-in 2 .

```
inputs:  b_0, ..., b_{n-1}
gates:   e_1=g_n(b_0,b_1)=1 iff a_1a_0=b_1b_0,  lt_1=g_{n+1}(b_0,b_1)=1 iff a_1a_0<b_1b_0
         for i∈{2, ..., n-1}
         e_i=g_{n+2i-2}(e_{i-1},b_i)=e_{i-1}∧(a_i⊕b_i⊕1),
         lt_i=g_{n+2i-1}(lt_{i-1},b_i)=(lt_{i-1}∧(a_i⊕b_i⊕1))∨(ā_i∧b_i)
outputs: lt_{n-1} and e_{n-1} .
```

Therefore, the size of the resulting $C_n^{x_n}$ is only $n+(2n-2)+2=3n$ and $Topo(C_n^{x_n})$ is uniform despite the value of x_n. We stress that for any fixed x_n, $C_n^{x_n}$ is not in the minimal format since it may contain degenerate gates to let $Topo(C_n^{x_n})$ be independent of x_n.

2.3   Construction and Evaluation of Garbled Circuits

Let $\cdot$ denote the concatenation of two binary strings and let $|s|$ be the length of s. For s_1, s_2 of the same length, $s_1 \oplus s_2$ is the bitwise XOR of them. Let Γ_n be the number of Boolean gates of $C_n^{x_n}$. Thus, input-nodes are numbered $0, \cdots, n-1$, gate-nodes are numbered $n, \cdots, n+\Gamma_n-1$ and output-nodes are labeled $n+\Gamma_n$, $\cdots, n+\Gamma_n+m-1$. Let GC_n be the garbled format of $C_n^{x_n}$ and let the security parameter $t=\max\{80, n\}$ (i.e. $t=n$ for sufficiently large n). For $0 \le i < n+\Gamma_n$, W_i^0, W_i^1, c_i are strings associated with node i and cp_i is fan-out of node i (see Fig. 1), where $|W_i^0| = |W_i^1| = t \times cp_i$ and $|c_i| = cp_i$. Let $W_i^{b_i}[j]$ be the $(j+1)$-th t-bit substring of $W_i^{b_i}$ and $c_i[j]$ be the $(j+1)$-th bit of c_i, where $b_i \in \{0,1\}$ and $0 \le j < cp_i$. Let PRG be a pseudorandom generator that expands a t-bit random seed to an $l(t)$-bit pseudorandom string.

We describe how to garble $C_n^{x_n}$ to produce GC_n. First, assign to each node i $(0 \le i < n+\Gamma_n)$ three uniform random strings (W_i^0, W_i^1, c_i) which we call signals with their lengths given above. For each gate k whose inputs are node i and node j, denoted $g_{(b_i,b_j)}$, we first replace the truth table of g by the corresponding signals as follows:

$$[W_k^{g(0,0)} \cdot (c_k \oplus g_{(0,0)}^{cp_k}), W_k^{g(0,1)} \cdot (c_k \oplus g_{(0,1)}^{cp_k}), W_k^{g(1,0)} \cdot (c_k \oplus g_{(1,0)}^{cp_k}), W_k^{g(1,1)} \cdot (c_k \oplus g_{(1,1)}^{cp_k})] \ .$$

where $g_{(b_i,b_j)}^{cp_k}$ denotes a string that has cp_k bits of $g_{(b_i,b_j)}$, gate k is the $(p+1)$-th gate that uses node i as input and $(q+1)$-th gate that uses node j as input. We encrypt and permute the above signal table using the signals of its input nodes $(W_i^0[p], W_i^1[p], c_i[p])$ and $(W_j^0[q], W_j^1[q], c_j[q])$. That is, for each signal $W_k^{g(b_i,b_j)} \cdot (c_k \oplus g_{(b_i,b_j)}^{cp_k})$, XOR it with $(X_{b_j \oplus c_j[q]}^{b_i} \oplus Y_{b_i \oplus c_i[p]}^{b_j})$, where $X_{b_j \oplus c_j[q]}^{b_i}$ and $Y_{b_i \oplus c_i[p]}^{b_j}$ are generated by PRG as follows:

$$PRG(W_i^{b_i}[p]) = \underbrace{x_1...x_{cp_k(1+t)}}_{X_0^{b_i}} \underbrace{x_{cp_k(1+t)+1}...x_{cp_k(2+2t)}}_{X_1^{b_i}} \ ,$$

$$PRG(W_j^{b_j}[q]) = \underbrace{y_1...y_{cp_k(1+t)}}_{Y_0^{b_j}} \underbrace{y_{cp_k(1+t)+1}...y_{cp_k(2+2t)}}_{Y_1^{b_j}} \ .$$

After encryption, permute the resulting table as follows:

$$[W_{00}', W_{01}', W_{10}', W_{11}'] \rightarrow [W_{\pi_k(0,0)}', W_{\pi_k(0,1)}', W_{\pi_k(1,0)}', W_{\pi_k(1,1)}'] \ .$$

where $\pi_k(b_i, b_j) = (b_i \oplus c_i[p]) \cdot (b_j \oplus c_j[q])$. In this way, we garble (encrypt and permute) all Γ_n signal tables to produce GC_n, which differs to $C_n^{x_n}$ in that the truth tables are replaced by the corresponding garbled signal tables.

To evaluate GC_n on input $y_n = b_{n-1} \cdots b_0$, Bob is given $W_0^{b_0} \cdot (b_0^{cp_0} \oplus c_0)$, $\cdots$, $W_{n-1}^{b_{n-1}} \cdot (b_{n-1}^{cp_{n-1}} \oplus c_{n-1})$ and he evaluates GC_n gate by gate as follows: For gate k whose input are node i and node j, Bob uses $W_i^{b_i}$, $W_j^{b_j}$, $(b_i \oplus c_i[p])$, $(b_j \oplus c_j[q])$ to pick up from the garbled truth table the corresponding encrypted signal and decrypt it. Note that p and q are implied by $Topo(C_n)$. Bob picks out the $(b_i \oplus c_i[p]) \cdot (b_j \oplus c_j[q])$-th (e.g., 00-th is the first and 11-th is the fourth) encrypted signal from the truth table, XORs it with it with $(X_{b_j \oplus c_j[q]}^{b_i} \oplus Y_{b_i \oplus c_i[p]}^{b_j})$ and gets $W_k^{b_k} \cdot (b_k^{cp_k} \oplus c_k)$ with $b_k = g_k(b_i, b_j)$.

2.4 The Improved Protocol

Protocol (in semi-honest model)

- **Inputs:** $x_n \in \{0,1\}^n$, $y_n \in \{0,1\}^n$ and C_n, which is polynomial-size in n and computes a polynomial-time function $f_n : \{0,1\}^n \times \{0,1\}^n \mapsto \{0,1\}^m$.
- **Protocol description:**
  1. Alice obtains $C_n^{x_n}$ by applying Algorithm 1. to C_n and x_n, garbles $C_n^{x_n}$ to produce GC_n and sends GC_n to Bob.
  2. Alice and Bob engage in a 1-out-of-2 OT such that Bob gets his input $y_n = b_{n-1} \cdots b_0$ encrypted to $E(y_n) = W_0^{b_0} \cdot (c_0 \oplus b_0^{cp_0})$, $W_1^{b_1} \cdot (c_1 \oplus b_1^{cp_1})$, $\cdots$, $W_{n-1}^{b_{n-1}} \cdot (c_{n-1} \oplus b_{n-1}^{cp_{n-1}})$ without revealing y_n to Alice.
  3. Bob evaluate GC_n on $E(y_n)$ to get $E(f_n(x_n,y_n)) = W_{b_{r_0}}^{b_{r_0}} \cdot (c_{r_0} \oplus b_{r_0}^{cp_{r_0}})$, $\cdots$, $W_{b_{r_{m-1}}}^{b_{r_{m-1}}} \cdot (c_{r_{m-1}} \oplus b_{r_{m-1}}^{cp_{r_{m-1}}})$.
  4. Upon receiving $E(f_n(x_n,y_n))$ from Bob, Alice decrypts it and sends $f_n(x_n,y_n)$ to Bob.
- **Outputs:** Alice and Bob learn $f_n(x_n,y_n) = b_{r_{m-1}} \cdots b_{r_0}$.

3   Proof of the Protocol

In this section, we prove that Alice and Bob can privately compute $C_n^{x_n}$ in the semi-honest model. The proof is given in terms of the simulation paradigm. That is, if the distribution of Alice's (resp., Bob's) view can be simulated by a PPT given only her (his) input and output, then Alice (resp., Bob) gains nothing feasibly more than the output.

3.1   Definition of Privacy

Definition 1. *(privacy w.r.t semi-honest behavior) [1–Definition 7.2.1] : Let f be a family of deterministic functions $\{f_n\}_{n \in \mathbb{N}}$, where $f_n : \{0,1\}^n \times \{0,1\}^n \mapsto \{0,1\}^m$, and let Π be a two-party protocol for computing f. The view of Alice (resp., Bob) during an execution of Π on (x_n,y_n), denoted $VIEW_1^\Pi(x,y)$ (resp., $VIEW_2^\Pi(x,y)$), is $(x_n, r, m_1,...,m_u)$ (resp., $(y_n, r, m_1,...,m_u)$), where r represents the outcome of Alice's (resp., Bob's) internal coin tosses and m_i represents* *the i-th message she (he) has received. We say that Π privately computes f if there exist probabilistic polynomial-time algorithms, denoted S_1 and S_2, such that*

$$\{S_1(x_n, f_n(x_n, \mathbf{y}(x_n)))\}_{x_n \in \{0,1\}^n, n \in \mathbb{N}} \stackrel{c}{\equiv} \{VIEW_1^{\Pi}(x_n, \mathbf{y}(x_n))\}_{x_n \in \{0,1\}^n, n \in \mathbb{N}} \cdot \tag{1}$$

$$\{S_2(y_n, f_n(\mathbf{x}(y_n), y_n))\}_{y_n \in \{0,1\}^n, n \in \mathbb{N}} \stackrel{c}{\equiv} \{VIEW_2^{\Pi}(\mathbf{x}(y_n), y_n)\}_{y_n \in \{0,1\}^n, n \in \mathbb{N}} \cdot \tag{2}$$

where $\mathbf{x}, \mathbf{y} : \{0,1\}^* \mapsto \{0,1\}^*$ are arbitrary length preserving functions.

Eq. 1 and Eq. 2 mean that whatever can be learned from the execution of Π, on every possible input, can be efficiently simulated given only inputs and outputs. In fact, S_1 and S_2 also take C_n as an auxiliary input, which is omitted since f_n is a publicly known function.

3.2 Correctness of the Protocol

Theorem 2. *(correctness w.r.t semi-honest behavior): Let $f \stackrel{def}{=} \{f_n\}_{n \in \mathbb{N}}$ be a family of polynomial-time deterministic functions, where $f_n : \{0,1\}^n \times \{0,1\}^n \mapsto \{0,1\}^m$, then our protocol Π can correctly compute f in the semi-honest model.*

Proof. In the semi-honest model, neither party will deviate from the described protocol. Hence, we only need to prove the correctness of the garbled circuit evaluation. For each Boolean gate k whose input nodes are node i and node j, the (rs)-th item of the table is

$$X_s^{r \oplus c_i[p]} \oplus Y_r^{s \oplus c_j[q]} \oplus (W_k^{g(r \oplus c_i[p], s \oplus c_j[q])} \cdot (c_k \oplus g_{(r \oplus c_i[p], s \oplus c_j[q])}^{cp_k})) \cdot$$

According to the protocol, Bob will pick out the $(b_i \oplus c_i[p]) \cdot (b_j \oplus c_j[q])$-th encrypted signal from the table, XOR it with it with $(X_{b_j \oplus c_j[q]}^{b_i} \oplus Y_{b_i \oplus c_i[p]}^{b_j})$. Since the following equation holds when $r = b_i \oplus c_i[p]$ and $s = b_j \oplus c_j[q]$,

$$X_s^{r \oplus c_i[p]} \oplus Y_r^{s \oplus c_j[q]} = X_{b_j \oplus c_j[q]}^{b_i} \oplus Y_{b_i \oplus c_i[p]}^{b_j} \cdot$$

the resulting value is $W_k^{g(b_i, b_j)} \cdot (c_k \oplus g_{(b_i, b_j)}^{cp_k})$. Therefore, it follows that Π correctly computes f in the semi-honest model. $\qquad\square$

3.3 Privacy of the Protocol

Claim 3. *Assuming the existence of trapdoor permutations, the views of Alice and Bob can be simplified as follows.*

$$VIEW_1^{\Pi}(x_n, \mathbf{y}(x_n)) = \{x_n, C_n^{x_n}, \{W_i^0, W_i^1, c_i\}_{0 \le i < n+\Gamma_n}, f_n(x_n, \mathbf{y}(x_n))\} \cdot \tag{3}$$

$$VIEW_2^{\Pi}(\mathbf{x}(y_n), y_n) = \{y_n, GC_n, \{W_i^{b_i} \cdot (c_i \oplus b_i^{cp_i})\}_{0 \le i < n+\Gamma_n}, f_n(\mathbf{x}(y_n), y_n)\} \cdot \tag{4}$$

where $y_n = b_{n-1} \cdots b_0$, for $n \le i < n+\Gamma_n$ b_i is the result of the i-th node during Bob's evaluation and $f_n(\mathbf{x}(y_n), y_n) = b_{r_{m-1}} \cdots b_{r_0}$.

Proof. Assuming the existence of trapdoor permutations, the 1-out-of-2 OT can be privately computed [1–Proposition 7.3.6] such that Bob gets $y_n = b_{n-1} \cdots b_0$ encrypted to $E(y_n) = W_0^{b_0} \cdot (c_0 \oplus b_0^{cp_0}) \ldots W_{n-1}^{b_{n-1}} \cdot (c_{n-1} \oplus b_{n-1}^{cp_{n-1}})$ while Alice learns nothing about y_n. Hence, the views of Alice and Bob can be written in as in Eq. 3 and Eq. 4. We do not include GC_n and $E(f_n(x_n, \mathbf{y}(x_n)))$ in VIEW_1^{Π} because they are redundant (implied by VIEW_1^{Π}). Regarding Bob, $\{W_i^{b_i} \cdot (c_{b_i} \oplus b_i^{cp_i})\}_{0 \le i < n}$ corresponds to $E(y_n)$ and $\{W_i^{b_i} \cdot (c_{b_i} \oplus b_i^{cp_i})\}_{n \le i < n + \Gamma_n}$ are signals decrypted by Bob during circuit evaluation. For each Boolean gate, Bob will choose one out of four items (encrypted signals) for decryption. We call the item decrypted by Bob on-path item and the other three off-path. Note that the index of the on-path item in each Boolean gate is also implied by VIEW_2^{Π}. Namely, for gate k whose inputs are node i and node j, the index of the on-path item is $(b_i \oplus c_i[p]) \cdot (b_j \oplus c_j[q])$. The XOR string $(X_{b_j \oplus c_j[q]}^{b_i} \oplus Y_{b_i \oplus c_i[p]}^{b_j})$ computed by Bob for decryption is also implied by VIEW_2^{Π}. Therefore, it suffices that Alice's (resp., Bob's) view can be simplified as Eq. 3 (resp., Eq. 4). □

Lemma 1. *Assuming the existence of trapdoor permutations, there exists a probabilistic polynomial-time algorithm S_1 such that Eq. 1 holds.*

Proof. By Claim 3, S_1 needs only to simulate Eq. 3 using x_n, $f_n(x_n, \mathbf{y}(x_n))$. S_1 can obtain $C_n^{x_n}$ using Algorithm 1. and simulate $\{W_i^0, W_i^1, c_i\}_{0 \le i < n + \Gamma_n}$ with uniformly distributed random strings of the same length. □

Lemma 2. *If we replace GC_n of $\text{VIEW}_2^{\Pi}(\mathbf{x}(y_n), y_n)$ with GC_n' to produce*

$$VIEW'_2^{\Pi}(\mathbf{x}(y_n), y_n) = \{y_n, GC_n', \{W_i^{b_i} \cdot (c_i \oplus b_i^{cp_i})\}_{0 \le i < n + \Gamma_n}, f_n(\mathbf{x}(y_n), y_n)\} \ . \tag{5}$$

where GC_n' is constructed by replacing all the off-path[1] items of signal table of GC_n with uniformly distributed random strings of the same length, then the following equation holds

$$\{VIEW'_2^{\Pi}(\mathbf{x}(y_n), y_n)\}_{y_n \in \{0,1\}^n, n \in \mathbb{N}} \overset{c}{\equiv} \{VIEW_2^{\Pi}(\mathbf{x}(y_n), y_n)\}_{y_n \in \{0,1\}^n, n \in \mathbb{N}} \ . \tag{6}$$

assuming the existence of pseudorandom generators (see similar proofs in [11]).

Proof. Note that for each $n \in \mathbb{N}$, $VIEW'_2^{\Pi}$ differs to $VIEW_2^{\Pi}$ only in the off-path items. A hybrid walk [11] is constructed from GC'_n to GC_n,

$$GC_n' = GC_n[0] \to GC_n[1] \to \ldots \to GC_n[\Gamma_n] = GC_n \ .$$

where $GC_n[h_n]$ denotes that the last h_n signal tables (numbered $n + \Gamma_n - h_n, \cdots, n + \Gamma_n - 1$) are from GC_n and the remaining signal tables (numbered $n, \cdots, n + \Gamma_n - h_n - 1$) are from GC_n'. We define $V[n][h_n]$ as

---

[1] For each Boolean gate, Bob will choose one out of four items (encrypted signals) for decryption. We call the item chosen by Bob on-path item and the other three off-path.

$$V[n][h_n] = \{y_n, GC_n[h_n], \{W_i^{b_i} \cdot (c_i \oplus b_i{}^{cp_i})\}_{0 \leq i < n + \Gamma_n}, f_n(\mathbf{x}(y_n), y_n)\} \ . \tag{7}$$

where $0 \leq h_n \leq \Gamma_n$ and $n \in \mathbb{N}$. Hence, it holds that

$$\{VIEW'^{\Pi}_2(\mathbf{x}(y_n), y_n)\}_{y_n \in \{0,1\}^n, n \in \mathbb{N}} = \{V[n][0]\}_{y_n \in \{0,1\}^n, n \in \mathbb{N}} \ . \tag{8}$$

$$\{VIEW^{\Pi}_2(\mathbf{x}(y_n), y_n)\}_{y_n \in \{0,1\}^n, n \in \mathbb{N}} = \{V[n][\Gamma_n]\}_{y_n \in \{0,1\}^n, n \in \mathbb{N}} \ . \tag{9}$$

For contradiction, we assume that Eq. 8 and Eq. 9 are polynomial-time distinguishable. Due to the transitivity of computational indistinguishability [11–Proposition 4.2.1], there exists a sequence, $\{h_n\}_{n \in \mathbb{N}}$, where $0 < h_n \leq \Gamma_n$, so that $\{V[n][h_n - 1]\}_{y_n \in \{0,1\}^n, n \in \mathbb{N}}$ and $\{V[n][h_n]\}_{y_n \in \{0,1\}^n, n \in \mathbb{N}}$ (see also Table 1) are polynomial-time distinguishable.

Table 1. Ensemble $\{V[n][h_n]\}_{y_n \in \{0,1\}^n, n \in \mathbb{N}}$ with $0 \leq h_n \leq \Gamma_n$

Ensemble	1	2	$\cdots$	n $\cdots$
$\{V[n][0]\}_{y_n \in \{0,1\}^n, n \in \mathbb{N}}$	$V[1][0]$	$V[2][0]$	$\cdots$	$V[n][0] \cdots$
$\vdots$	$\vdots$	$\vdots$	$\cdots$	$\vdots$ $\cdots$
$\{V[n][h_n - 1]\}_{y_n \in \{0,1\}^n, n \in \mathbb{N}}$	$V[1][h_1 - 1]$	$V[2][h_2 - 1]$	$\cdots$	$V[n][h_n - 1] \cdots$
$\{V[n][h_n]\}_{y_n \in \{0,1\}^n, n \in \mathbb{N}}$	$V[1][h_1]$	$V[2][h_2]$	$\cdots$	$V[n][h_n] \cdots$
$\vdots$	$\vdots$	$\vdots$	$\cdots$	$\vdots$ $\cdots$
$\{V[n][\Gamma_n]\}_{y_n \in \{0,1\}^n, n \in \mathbb{N}}$	$V[1][\Gamma_1]$	$V[2][\Gamma_2]$	$\cdots$	$V[n][\Gamma_n] \cdots$

By definition, these two ensembles only differ between the k-th signal table of $GC_n[h_n - 1]$ and that of $GC_n[h_n]$ with $k = n + \Gamma_n - h_n$. Without loss of generality, suppose that gate k is an XOR gate whose inputs are node i and node j, $c_i[p] = 1$, $b_i = 0$, $c_j[q] = 0$ and $b_j = 1$, the k-th signal table of $GC_n[h_n - 1]$ and $GC_n[h_n]$ (according to the garbled circuit construction) will be something like Table 2.

Table 2. The k-th signal table of $GC_n[h_n - 1]$ and $GC_n[h_n]$

Index	gate k ($GC_n[h_n - 1]$)	gate k ($GC_n[h_n]$)
00	uniform random string	$X_0^1 \oplus Y_0^1 \oplus (W_k^1 \cdot (c_k \oplus 1^{cp_k}))$
01	uniform random string	$X_1^1 \oplus Y_0^1 \oplus (W_k^0 \cdot (c_k \oplus 0^{cp_k}))$
10	uniform random string	$X_0^0 \oplus Y_1^1 \oplus (W_k^0 \cdot (c_k \oplus 0^{cp_k}))$
11	$X_1^0 \oplus Y_1^1 \oplus (W_k^1 \cdot (c_k \oplus 1^{cp_k}))$	$X_1^0 \oplus Y_1^1 \oplus (W_k^1 \cdot (c_k \oplus 1^{cp_k}))$

Denote $A_1^n, A_2^n, A_3^n, A_4^n, B_1^n, B_2^n, B_3^n, B_4^n$ eight $cp_k(1+n)$-bit strings, where $A_1^n, A_2^n, A_3^n, A_4^n$ are all $U_{cp_k(1+n)}$ distributed and both $B_1^n \cdot B_2^n$ and $B_3^n \cdot B_4^n$ are $PRG(U_n)$ distributed. Thus, $\{A_1^n \cdot A_2^n\}_{n \in \mathbb{N}}$ and $\{B_1^n \cdot B_2^n\}_{n \in \mathbb{N}}$ are computationally indistinguishable and so are $\{A_3^n \cdot A_4^n\}_{n \in \mathbb{N}}$ and $\{B_3^n \cdot B_4^n\}_{n \in \mathbb{N}}$. It follows that

$\{A_1^n \cdot A_2^n \cdot A_3^n \cdot A_4^n\}_{n \in \mathbb{N}}$ and $\{B_1^n \cdot B_2^n \cdot B_3^n \cdot B_4^n\}_{n \in \mathbb{N}}$ are computationally indistinguishable [11–Proposition 4.2.2]. Nevertheless, we can find a contradiction using the following steps: For each $n \in \mathbb{N}$, we replace $GC_n[h_n]$'s $X_0^{b_i \oplus 1}, X_1^{b_i \oplus 1}, Y_0^{b_j \oplus 1}, Y_1^{b_i \oplus 1}$ (e.g., $X_0^1, X_1^1, Y_0^0, Y_1^0$ in Table 2) by $A_1^n, A_2^n, A_3^n, A_4^n$ (resp., $B_1^n, B_2^n, B_3^n, B_4^n$) to produce $GC_n'[h_n-1]$ (resp., $GC_n'[h_n]$) and define $V'[n][h_n-1]$ (resp., $V'[n][h_n]$) as:

$$V'[n][h_n-1] = \{y_n, GC_n'[h_n-1], \{W_i^{b_i} \cdot (c_i \oplus b_i{}^{cp_i})\}_{0 \le i < n + \Gamma_n}, f_n(\mathbf{x}(y_n), y_n)\} \tag{10}$$

$$V'[n][h_n] = \{y_n, GC_n'[h_n], \{W_i^{b_i} \cdot (c_i \oplus b_i{}^{cp_i})\}_{0 \le i < n + \Gamma_n}, f_n(\mathbf{x}(y_n), y_n)\} \tag{11}$$

By Claim 4, $\{V'[n][h_n-1]\}_{y_n \in \{0,1\}^n, n \in \mathbb{N}}$ and $\{V'[n][h_n]\}_{y_n \in \{0,1\}^n, n \in \mathbb{N}}$ are also polynomial-time distinguishable and hence are $A_1^n A_2^n A_3^n A_4^n$ and $B_1^n B_2^n B_3^n B_4^n$, which is a contradiction. □

Claim 4.

$$\{V'[n][h_n-1]\}_{y_n \in \{0,1\}^n, n \in \mathbb{N}} \equiv \{V[n][h_n-1]\}_{y_n \in \{0,1\}^n, n \in \mathbb{N}} . \tag{12}$$

$$\{V'[n][h_n]\}_{y_n \in \{0,1\}^n, n \in \mathbb{N}} \equiv \{V[n][h_n]\}_{y_n \in \{0,1\}^n, n \in \mathbb{N}} . \tag{13}$$

Proof. It is obvious that Eq. 12 (resp., Eq. 13) holds if Eq. 14 (resp., 15) holds.

$$\{GC_n'[h_n-1]\}_{n \in \mathbb{N}} \equiv \{GC_n[h_n-1]\}_{n \in \mathbb{N}} . \tag{14}$$

$$\{GC_n'[h_n]\}_{n \in \mathbb{N}} \equiv \{GC_n[h_n]\}_{n \in \mathbb{N}} . \tag{15}$$

Without loss of generality, we use Table 2 to discuss whether the distribution will change after replacing $GC_n[h_n]$'s $X_0^{b_i \oplus 1}, X_1^{b_i \oplus 1}, Y_0^{b_j \oplus 1}, Y_1^{b_i \oplus 1}$ by $A_1^n, A_2^n, A_3^n, A_4^n$ (resp., $B_1^n, B_2^n, B_3^n, B_4^n$). First, when we replace $X_0^1, X_1^1, Y_0^0, Y_1^0$ of $GC_n[h_n]$ by $A_1^n, A_2^n, A_3^n, A_4^n$ to produce $GC_n'[h_n-1]$, since $A_1^n \oplus A_3^n$, A_2^n and A_4^n are all uniformly distributed and are not correlated with other items in $GC_n'[h_n-1]$, the resulting items $A_1^n \oplus A_3^n \oplus (W_k^1 \cdot (c_k \oplus 1^{cp_k}))$, $A_2^n \oplus Y_0^1 \oplus (W_k^0 \cdot (c_k \oplus 0^{cp_k}))$ and $X_0^0 \oplus A_4^n \oplus (W_k^0 \cdot (c_k \oplus 0^{cp_k}))$ are all uniformly distributed. Thus, it follows that $GC_n[h_n-1]$ and $GC_n'[h_n-1]$ are identically distributed (Eq. 14 and Eq. 12 hold). Second, we proceed to prove that $GC_n[h_n]$ and $GC_n'[h_n]$ are identically distributed, namely, replacing $X_0^1, X_1^1, Y_0^0, Y_1^0$ of $GC_n[h]$ by $B_1^n, B_2^n, B_3^n, B_4^n$ will not change the distribution. Since $X_0^1 \cdot X_1^1$, $Y_0^0 \cdot Y_1^0$, $B_1^n \cdot B_2^n$ and $B_3^n \cdot B_4^n$ are all $PRG(U_n)$ distributed, it suffices to show that neither $X_0^1 \cdot X_1^1$ nor $Y_0^0 \cdot Y_1^0$ is correlated with the other parts of $GC_n[h_n]$. Note that $X_0^1 \cdot X_1^1$ is generated by PRG using seed $W_i^1[p]$ (i.e., $W_i^{b_i \oplus 1}[p]$), which represents semantics 1 (complement of $b_i = 0$). Thus, if node i is an input, $W_i^1[p]$ is not included in $GC_n[h_n]$ or $E(y_n)$, otherwise, node i is a gate, $W_i^1[p]$ resides in the off-path item(s) of GC_n and the corresponding item(s) in $GC_n[h_n]$ are replaced by uniform random strings since $i < k$. For other gates whose input is also node i, they will use other parts of W_i^1 for encryption, namely, $W_i^1[p']$ with $p' \ne p$. Analogously, we can prove that there are no correlations between $Y_0^0 \cdot Y_1^0$ and other parts of $GC_n[h_n]$. Therefore, $GC_n[h_n]$ and $GC_n'[h_n]$ are also identically distributed, namely, Eq. 15 and Eq. 13 hold. □

Lemma 3. *Assume the existence of trapdoor permutations, there exists a probabilistic polynomial-time algorithm S_2 such that Eq. 2 holds.*

Proof. By Claim 3 and Lemma 2, it suffices to simulate $\{W_i^{b_i} \cdot (c_i \oplus b_i^{cp_i})\}_{0 \leq i < n + \Gamma_n}$ and GC_n' using y_n and $f_n(\mathbf{x}(y_n), y_n)$. S_2 can simulate $W_i^{b_i}$ and $c_i \oplus b_i^{cp_i}$ using uniformly distributed strings W_i' and cb'_i, where $|W_i'| = |W_i^{b_i}|$ and $|cb'_i| = cp_i$. To simulate GC_n', S_2 first computes $Topo(C_n^{x_n})$ by invoking Algorithm 1. on C_n and an n-bit zero string (fake x_n) and the topology of the resulting circuit is identical to $Topo(C_n^{x_n})$. Then, fill in the signal tables with on-path and off-path items. For each gate k whose inputs are node i and node j, let the $(cb'_i[p] \cdot cb'_j[q])$-th item be $X_{cb'_j[q]} \oplus Y_{cb'_i[p]} \oplus (W_k' \cdot cb'_k)$ and other three items be uniformly distributed strings of the same length, where p, q are implied by $Topo(C_n)$ and $X_{cb'_j[q]}$ (resp., $Y_{cb'_i[p]}$) is computed by applying PRG to $W_i'[p]$ (resp., $W_j'[q]$) according to Sect. 2.3. The resulting ensemble is identically distributed as Eq. 5. By Eq. 6, it follows that there exists such a S_2 satisfying Eq. 2.   □

Theorem 5. *(privacy w.r.t semi-honest behavior): Assuming the existence of trapdoor permutations and let f be as in Theorem 2, then the protocol Π privately computes f in the semi-honest model.*

Proof. By Lemma 1 and Lemma 3, there exists PPT S_1 and S_2 such that Eq. 1 and Eq. 2. It follows that Π privately computes f in the semi-honest model (see Definition 1).   □

4   Concluding Remarks

We carry out the two-party computation by hardwiring Alice's input in the circuit while preserving the security of the protocol. In practice (cf. the compiler design part of [16]), it would be optimal to lower bound the fan-in [2] by 3 for most basic operations (e.g. addition with carry, comparison, conditional value assignment). Our result is that this lower bound of fan-in can be reduced to 2 (i.e. the minimal possible value) in case of the two-party computation scenario by hardwiring each a_i in circuit efficiently.

References

1. Goldreich, O.: Foundations of Cryptography: Basic Applications. Volume 2. Cambridge University Press (2004)
2. Yao., A.: How to generate and exchange secrets. In: Proc. 27rd Annual IEEE Symp. Found. Comput. Sci. (1986) 162–167

---

[2] Consider a subtraction/comparison operation where we need to compute the bitwise carry with a gate of fan-in 3, i.e., $c_i = carry(a_i + \bar{b}_i + c_{i-1})$, it needs at least three gates if represented using gates of fan-in 2.

3. Rabin, M.: How to exchange secrets by oblivious transfer. Technical report, Tech. Memo TR-81, Aiken Computation Laboratory, Harvard U. (1981)
4. Goldreich, O., Micali, S., Wigderson, A.: How to play any mental game or a completeness theorem for protocols with honest majority. In: Proc. 19th Annual STOC. (1987) 218–229
5. Ben-Or, M., Goldwasser, S., Wigderson, A.: Completeness theorems for non-cryptographic fault-tolerant distributed computation. In: Proc. 20th Annual STOC. (1988) 1–10
6. Chaum, D., Crépeau, C., Damgård, I.: Multiparty unconditionally secure protocols. In: Proc. 20th Annual STOC. (1988) 11–19
7. Rabin, T., Ben-Or, M.: Verifiable secret sharing and multiparty protocols with honest majority. In: Proc 21st Annual STOC. (1989) 73–85
8. Beaver, D., Micali, S., Rogaway, P.: The round complexity of secure protocols. In: Proc. 22th Annual STOC, ACM Press (1990) 503–513
9. Canetti, R., Feige, U., Goldreich, O., Naor, M.: Adaptively secure multiparty computation. In: Proc. 28th Annual STOC. (1996) 639–648
10. Canetti, R., Lindell, Y., Ostrovsky, R., Sahai, A.: Universally composable two-party and multi-party secure computation. In: 34th Annual STOC. (2002) 494–503
11. Rogaway, P.: The round complexity of secure protocols. PhD thesis, Laboratory for Computer Science, MIT (1991)
12. Beaver, D.: Correlated pseudorandomness and the complexity of private computations. In: Proc. 28th Annual STOC. (1996) 479–488
13. Naor, M., Pinkas, B., Sumner, R.: Privacy preserving auctions and mechanism design. In: Proc. 1st ACM Conf. On Electronic Commerce. (1999) 129–139
14. Lindell, Y., Pinkas, B.: A proof of yao's protocol for secure two-party computation. Cryptology ePrint Archive (2004) http://eprint.iacr.org/2004/175/.
15. Yao., A.: Protocols for secure computations. In: Proc. 23rd Annual IEEE Symp. Found. Comput. Sci. (1982) 160–164
16. Malkhi, D., Nisan, N., Pinkas, B., Sella, Y.: Fairplay - a secure two-party computation system. In: Proc. Usenix Security 2004. (2004)

Security Analysis of Some Threshold Signature Schemes and Multi-signature Schemes

Tianjie Cao[1,2] and Dongdai Lin[2]

[1] School of Computer Science and Technology,
China University of Mining and Technology, Xuzhou 221008, China
tjcao@cumt.edu.cn
[2] Institute of Software of Chinese Academy of Sciences, Beijing 100080, China
ddlin@is.iscas.ac.cn

Abstract. Digital signature scheme allows a user to sign a message in such a way that anyone can verify the signature, but no one can forge the signature on any other message. In this paper, we show that Xie and Yu's threshold signature scheme, Huang and Chang's threshold proxy signature scheme, Qian, Cao and Xue's pairing-based threshold proxy signature scheme, Xue and Cao's multi-proxy signature scheme and Zhou et al.'s proxy multi-signature scheme are all insecure against the forgery attacks.

1 Introduction

Threshold signatures are closely related to the concept of threshold cryptography, first introduced by Desmedt [1][2]. In [2], Desmedt and Frankel proposed the first (t, n) threshold digital signature scheme based on the RSA system. In (t, n) threshold signature scheme, any subgroup of t or more shareholders of the designated group can generate a valid group signature in such a way that the verifier can check the validity of the signature without identifying the identities of the signers.

The concept of proxy signature was first introduced by Mambo, Usuda and Okamoto [6][7]. In a proxy signature scheme, original signer delegates his signing capability to proxy signer, and then the proxy signer can sign messages on behalf of the original signer. In a secure proxy signature scheme, only the proxy signer can create a valid proxy signature and anyone else, even the original signer, can not generate a valid proxy signature. Thus, for a valid proxy signature, the actual proxy signer cannot deny that he/she has signed the message and the original signer cannot deny that he/she has delegated the signing authority to the actual proxy signer. That is, the proxy signature scheme holds the security property non-repudiation.

Threshold proxy signature schemes are designed to delegate the signing power to a proxy group of proxy signers [5][13]. In a (t, n) threshold proxy signature scheme, the proxy signature key is shared among a group of n proxy signers delegated by the original signer. Any t or more proxy signers can cooperatively sign messages on behalf of the original signer.

D. Feng, D. Lin, and M. Yung (Eds.): CISC 2005, LNCS 3822, pp. 233–241, 2005.

Multi-signature was first introduced by Itakura and Nakamura in [4]. In a multi-signature scheme, plural signers generate a signature for an identical message. In multi-proxy signatures, the original signer can delegate its signing power to the specified proxy group while ensuring individual accountability of each participant signer. Proxy multi-signature schemes were proposed in [12]. In a proxy multi-signature scheme, a proxy signer is allowed to generate a proxy multi-signature on behalf of two or more original signers. Multi-proxy multi-signature scheme was proposed in [9]. This scheme allows the group of original signers to delegate the signing capability to the designated group of proxy signers.

Recently, many signature variants were proposed. In this paper, we show that Xie and Yu's threshold signature scheme (Xie-Yu scheme) [10], Huang and Chang's threshold proxy signature scheme (Huang-Chang scheme) [3], Qian, Cao and Xue's pairing-based threshold proxy signature schemes (Qian-Cao-Xue schemes) [8], Xue and Cao's multi-proxy signature scheme (Xue-Cao scheme) [11] and Zhou et al.'s proxy multi-signature scheme [14] are all insecure against the forgery attacks.

2   Security Analysis of Xie-Yu's Threshold Scheme

2.1   Brief Review of Xie-Yu Scheme

In [10], Xie-Yu proposed a threshold signature scheme. Xie-Yu schene can be divided into the following four phases:

The system initialization: The trusted center randomly chooses two large primes p and q such that $q|(p-1)$. Let g is a generator with order q in Z_p^*. h is a secure one-way hash function. There are N members U_i with public identity ID_i. The trusted center computes U_i's secret key d_i and public key $y_i = g^{d_i} \bmod p$. Then, the trusted center send d_i to U_i via a secure channel.

The individual signature generation: Without loss of generality, assume that there are T group members want to sign a message M on behalf of the group, the T group member can be denoted as $\{U_1, U_2, \ldots, U_T\}$. Every member U_i generates individual signature and sends it to designated clerk.

The individual signature batch verification and the threshold signature generation: On receiving the individual signature from $U_i(1 \le i \le T)$, the clerk authenticates the individual signatures. If the individual signatures are valid the clerk generates a threshold signature (s, R, E_j) of message M.

The threshold signature verification: Any outsider can use the group public key y to verify the threshold signature (s, R, E_j) of message M by checking the following equation.

$$g^s E_j^{h(M,R,E_j)} = R^R y^{h(M,R,E_j)} \bmod p$$

2.2   Security Analysis

In this subsection, we will show that Xie-Yu scheme is universally forgeable. An adversary can forge a valid threshold signature for any message.

For any message M, the adversary randomly chooses two numbers $r_1, r_2 \in Z_q^*$, computes $E_j = yg^{r_1}(\bmod p), R = g^{r_2} \bmod p$ and $s = r_2 R - r_1 h(M, R, E_j)$. Now we show that (s, R, E_j) is a valid signature of M.

$$g^s E_j^{h(M,R,E_j)} \equiv g^{r_2 R - r_1 h(M,R,E_j)} (yg^{r_1})^{h(M,R,E_j)}$$

$$\equiv g^{r_2 R} y^{h(M,R,E_j)}$$

$$\equiv R^R y^{h(M,R,E_j)} \bmod p$$

3 Security Analysis of Huang-Chang's Threshold Proxy Signature Scheme

3.1 Brief Review of Huang-Chang Scheme

In this sub-section, we will review Huang-Chang's (t, n) threshold proxy signature scheme, in which any t of n proxy signers can sign messages on behalf of the original signer.

Huang-Chang's threshold proxy signature scheme [3] defines the following notations. Let P_0 be the original signer and $PG = \{P_1, P_2, \ldots, P_n\}$ be the proxy group of n proxy signers in such a way that a proxy signature can be created by any subset of t or more proxy signers from PG. First, P_0 chooses two public large primes p and q such that $q|(p-1)$. The integer g is a generator with order q in Z_p^* and h is a secure one-way hash function. Each user P_i owns a private key $x_i \in_R Z_q^*$ and a public key $y_i = g^{x_i} \bmod p$. m_w is a warrant which records the identities of the original signer and the proxy signers of the proxy group, parameters t and n, the valid delegation time.

There are two types of signers in Huang-Chang scheme: the original signer and the n proxy signers. The original signer allows proxy signers in the group PG to sign a message.

Huang-Chang's scheme consists of three stages: the proxy sharing, the proxy signature generation, and the proxy signature verification.

Secret share generation: Let m_w be the warrant that is composed of the identifiers of the original signer and the proxy signers, the threshold value t, and the valid delegation time. In this stage, P_0 firstly generates the group proxy signature key $d = h(x_0, m_w) \bmod q$ and its corresponding proxy verification key e, where $e = g^d \bmod p$. Then P_0 selects a random integer k and computes $R = g^k \bmod p, z = h(m_w, e, R) \bmod q$ and $v' = k - x_0 z \bmod q$. Then, P_0 publishes (m_w, e, v', z). To verify m_w and e are published from P_0, one can compute $R' = g^{v'} y_0^z \bmod p$ by using P_0's public key y_0. If the equation $z = h(m_w, e, R') \bmod q$ holds, one can conclude that (v', z) is a valid signature for (m_w, e). Then, the original signer P_0 computes the partial proxy signing keys from his secret key and delivers them to each proxy signer. In this stage, P_0 delegates the signing capability to PG.

Proxy share generation: Without loss of generality, let B be any subset of indices of t or more proxy signers from PG. Suppose that these members of B want to cooperatively sign a message M on behalf of the original signer P_0.

In this stage, the proxy signature of M generated by members of B is 3-tuple (s, v, B).

Proxy signature verification: To verify the proxy signature actually created by the signers in B, the verifier examines the following steps with the parameters p, q, g, y_i, m_w, e, and hash function h. The verifier confirms m_w and e and checks the valid period of delegation for signing power. If it has expired, the proxy verification key e is invalid. To make sure the proxy signature (s, v, B) of M is indeed signed by the signers in B, the verifier computes $r' = g^s(\prod_{j \in B} y_j)^v e$ mod p. If the equation $v = h(m_w, M, r')$ mod q is satisfied, the receiver concludes that the proxy signature (s, v, B) of M is equivalent to the signature from the original signer and B is the set of actual proxy signers.

3.2   Security Analysis

We show that Huang-Chang's threshold proxy signature scheme is insecure against the original signer's forgery. The detail attacks are described as follows.

P_0 selects a set of actual proxy signers B, a proxy warrant m_w, a message M and a random numbers $r, s \in Z_q^*$. P_0 computes $v = h(m_w, M, r)$ mod q and $e = r(g^s(\prod_{j \in B} y_j)^v)^{-1}$ mod p.

Then, P_0 performs the following steps to create a signature on (m_w, e). P_0 selects a random integer k and computes $R = g^k$ mod $p, z = h(m_w, e, R)$ mod q and $v' = k - x_0 z$ mod q. Then, P_0 publishes (m_w, e, v', z).

Since (m_w, e, v', z) is a signature created by the original signer P_0, any verifier can be convince that (m_w, e) is valid though the verification equations. Now we show that (s, v, B) is a valid signature of M. We have $r' = g^s(\prod_{j \in B} y_j)^v e = r$ mod p, then $v = h(m_w, M, r) = h(m_w, M, r')$ mod q.

4   Security Analysis of Qian-Cao-Xue's Pairing-Based Threshold Proxy Signature Scheme

4.1   Brief Review of Qian-Cao-Xue Schemes

Recently, Qian-Cao-Xue proposed a threshold proxy signature scheme from bilinear pairings [8].

Qian-Cao-Xue's threshold proxy signature scheme [8] defines the following notations. Let $\mathbf{G}_0$ and $\mathbf{G}_1$ denote cyclic groups of prime order q, let P be a generator of $\mathbf{G}_0$ and the bilinear pairing is given as $e: \mathbf{G}_0 \times \mathbf{G}_0 \to \mathbf{G}_1$. Choose two cryptographic hash function $H_1 : \{0,1\}^* \times \mathbf{G}_0* \to Z_q^*, H_2 : \{0,1\}^* \to \mathbf{G}_0^*$. The original signer has a secret key $sk = x_o$, randomly chosen from Z_q^* and a public key $pk = Y_o = x_o P$ which is certified by CA (Certificate Authority).Let $\{P_1, P_2, \ldots, P_n\}$ be the proxy group of n proxy signers in such a way that a proxy signature can be created by any subset of t or more proxy signers. Each proxy signer has a secret key $sk_i = x_i$ randomly chosen from Z_q^* and a public key $pk_i = Y_i = x_i P$ which is certified by CA as well.

Qian-Cao-Xue's scheme consists of three stages: the proxy sharing, the proxy signature generation, and the proxy signature verification.

Secret share generation: Let m_w be the warrant that is composed of the identifiers of the original signer and the proxy signers, the threshold value t, and the valid delegation time. In this stage, the original signer computes the partial proxy signing keys from his secret key and delivers them to each proxy signer.

Proxy share generation: Let m be a message to be signed, any t or more proxy signers cooperate and sign the message m on behalf of the proxy group. Without loss of generality, let $D = \{P_1, P_2, \dots, P_t\}$ be the actual proxy signers and $ASID$ (Actual Signers' ID) be the collection of identities of all the users in D. The proxy signature of m generated by this scheme is 6-tuple $(m, U, m_w, \sigma, K, ASID)$.

Proxy signature verification: To make sure the proxy signature $(m, U, m_w, \sigma, K, ASID)$ is indeed signed by the signers in D, the recipient can verify the validity of the proxy signature by checking if the following equation holds or not.

$$e(P, \sigma) = e(U + (H_1(m_w, U))Y_o + K + \sum_{i=1}^{n} Y_i + \sum_{i=1}^{t} Y_i, H_2(m))$$

If it holds, the recipient accepts the signature, otherwise rejects.

4.2 Security Analysis

We show that Qian-Cao-Xue's threshold proxy signature scheme is universally forgeable. An adversary can forge a valid threshold signature for any message on behalf of the proxy signers and the original signer.

In Qian-Cao-Xue's scheme, the adversary selects a set of actual signers' identities $\{P_1, P_2, \dots, P_t\}$, a proxy warrant m_w, a message m, a random numbers $r \in Z_q^*$ and $U \in \mathbf{G}_0^*$. He/she computes $K = rP - (U + (H_1(m_w, U))Y_o + \sum_{i=1}^{n} Y_i + \sum_{i=1}^{t} Y_i)$ and $\sigma = rH_2(m)$. Then, the 6-tuple $(m, U, m_w, \sigma, K, ASID)$ satisfies the verification equation where $ASID$ be the collection of identities $\{P_1, P_2, \dots, P_t\}$.

5 Security Analysis of Xue-Cao's Multi-proxy Signature Scheme

5.1 Brief Review of Xue-Cao Scheme

There are four roles involved in Xue-Cao scheme [11]: the a system authority SA, the original signer U_o, a group of proxy signers $\{P_1, P_2, \dots, P_n\}$ delegate by U_o, and a clerk trusted by the proxy signers. The SA initializes the system and issues public key certificates for U_o and all of P_i. The clerk is arranged to authenticate the individual proxy signature by each P_i, and produces a muti-proxy signature for the signing message. Initially, the SA selects and publishes the following parameters: p and q are two large primes with $q|(p-1)$ and g is a generator with order q in Z_p^*. h is a secure one-way hash function.

The original signer U_o has a secret key x_o and corresponding public key $y_o = g^{x_o} \bmod p$, each of proxy signer P_i prepares a secret $x_i \in_R Z_q^*$ and a public key $y_i = g^{x_i} \bmod p$, which is certified by the SA.

The Xue-Cao scheme can be divided into three phases:

Proxy key generation: U_o delegates the signing capability to $\{P_1, P_2, \ldots, P_n\}$.

Multi-proxy signature generation: Let m be the message to be signed by all the specified proxy signers $\{P_1, P_2, \ldots, P_n\}$ with the assistance of the clerk. The proxy signature of m for U_o generated by Xue-Cao scheme is 3-tuple $\{R, S, D\}$.

Multi-proxy signature verification: The verifier checks the validity of the proxy signature of the message m through the following equation:

$$g^S = DY(y_o)^{nD} R^{h(m,R)} (\bmod p)$$

where $Y = \prod_{i=1}^n y_i (\bmod p)$. If it holds, the multi-proxy signature $\{R, S, D\}$ of m is valid.

5.2   Security Analysis

We show that Xue-Cao's multi-proxy signature scheme is insecure against the original signer's forgery.

For any message m, the original signer U_o selects $r \in Z_q^*, R \in Z_p^*$ at random and computes $Y = \prod_{i=1}^n y_i (\bmod p), D = (YR^{h(m,R)})^{-1} g^r (\bmod p)$ and $S = r + x_o nD (\bmod q)$.

Now we show that $\{R, S, D\}$ is a valid multi-proxy signature of m.

$$DY(y_o)^{nD} R^{h(m,R)} \equiv (YR^{h(m,R)})^{-1} g^r Y(y_o)^{nD} R^{h(m,R)}$$
$$\equiv g^r (y_o)^{nD}$$
$$\equiv g^S (\bmod p)$$

6   Security Analysis of Zhou et al.'s Proxy Multi-signature Scheme

6.1   Brief Review of Zhou et al. Scheme

In Zhou et al.'s scheme [14], p and q are two large prime integers such that $q|p-1$ and g is a generator with order q in Z_p^*. Let $A_1, A_2, \ldots, A_L$ be L original signers and $B_1, B_2, \ldots, B_L$ be the designated proxy signer. Every original signer $A_i (1 \le i \le L)$ has a private key x_{A_i} and the corresponding public key y_{A_i}, where $x_{A_i} \in_R Z_q^*$ and $y_{A_i} = g^{x_{A_i}} (\bmod p)$. Proxy signer B_i also holds his own key pair (x_{B_i}, y_{B_i}), where $x_{B_i} \in_R Z_q^*$ is the private one, and $y_{B_i} = g^{x_{B_i}} (\bmod p)$ the public one. Furthermore, $h(\cdot)$ is a universal secure hash functions. w_i is the designated proxy warrant negotiated by original signer A_i and proxy signer B_i, which records the delegation policy including limits of authority, valid periods. There is a clerk trusted by the proxy signers.

The Zhou et al.'s scheme can be divided into three phases:

Proxy key generation: A_i delegates the signing capability to B_i.

Proxy multi-signature generation: Let m be the message to be signed by all the specified proxy signers $\{B_1, B_2, \ldots, B_L\}$ with the assistance of the clerk. The proxy multi-signature of m for $\{A_1, A_2, \ldots, A_L\}$ generated by Zhou et al's scheme is $\{R, K_1, K_2, \ldots, K_L, w_1, w_2, \ldots, w_L, s, y_{A_1}, y_{A_2}, \ldots, y_{A_L}, y_{B_1}, y_{B_2}, \ldots, y_{B_L}\}$.

Proxy multi-signature verification: The verifier checks the validity of the proxy multi-signature of the message m through the following equation:

$$\left(\prod_{i=1}^{L}(y_{A_i}^{h(w_i,K_i)}K_i)\right)^m = g^s R^R \left(\prod_{i=1}^{L} y_{B_i}\right)^m (\bmod p)$$

If it holds, the proxy multi-signature $\{R, K_1, K_2, \ldots, K_L, w_1, w_2, \ldots, w_L, s, y_{A_1}, y_{A_2}, \ldots, y_{A_L}, y_{B_1}, y_{B_2}, \ldots, y_{B_L}\}$ of m is valid.

6.2   Security Analysis

We show that Zhou et al.'s proxy multi-signature scheme is insecure against the original signer's forgery.

We assume that the original signer A_i is an attacker. For any message m, the original signer A_i selects $w_j (1 \leq j \leq L), K_j (j \neq i), r_1, r_2 \in Z_q^*$ at random and computes $K_i = g^{r_1}(\prod_{j \neq i} y_{A_j}^{h(w_j, K_j)} K_j)^{-1} \prod_{j=1}^{L} y_{B_i} (\bmod p), R = g^{r_2} \bmod p$ and $s = m(r_1 + x_{A_i} h(w_i, K_i)) - r_2 R (\bmod q)$.

Now we show that $\{R, K_1, K_2, \ldots, K_L, w_1, w_2, \ldots, w_L, s, y_{A_1}, y_{A_2}, \ldots, y_{A_L}, y_{B_1}, y_{B_2}, \ldots, y_{B_L}\}$ is a valid proxy multi-signature of m.

$$g^s R^R \left(\prod_{j=1}^{L} y_{B_j}\right)^m \equiv g^{m(r_1 + x_{A_i} h(w_i, K_i)) - r_2 R}(g^{r_2})^R \left(\prod_{j=1}^{L} y_{B_j}\right)^m$$

$$\equiv g^{m(r_1 + x_{A_i} h(w_i, K_i))}\left(\prod_{j=1}^{L} y_{B_j}\right)^m$$

$$\equiv \left(g^{(r_1 + x_{A_i} h(w_i, K_i))} \prod_{j=1}^{L} y_{B_j}\right)^m$$

$$\equiv \left(g^{r_1} y_{A_i}^{h(w_i, K_i)} \prod_{j=1}^{L} y_{B_j}\right)^m$$

$$\equiv \left(g^{r_1} \prod_{j=1}^{L}(y_{A_j}^{h(w_j, K_j)} K_j)\left(\prod_{j=i}^{L}(y_{A_j}^{h(w_j, K_j)} K_i)\right)^{-1}(K_i)^{-1} \prod_{j=1}^{L} y_{B_j}\right)^m$$

$$\equiv \left(\prod_{j=1}^{L}(y_{A_j}^{h(w_j, K_j)} K_j)\right)^m (\bmod p)$$

7   Conclusion

In this paper, we presented a security analysis of five signature schemes newly published. Our results show that Xie and Yu's threshold signature scheme, Huang and Chang's threshold proxy signature scheme, Qian, Cao and Xue's pairing-based threshold proxy signature scheme, Xue and Cao's multi-proxy signature scheme and Zhou et al.'s proxy multi-signature scheme are all insecure against the forgery attacks.

Acknowledgments

We thank the support of the National Grand Fundamental Research 973 Program of China (No.2004CB318004), the National Natural Science Foundation of China (NSFC90204016) and the National High Technology Development Program of China under Grant (863, No.2003AA144030).

References

1. Desmedt, Y.: Society and group oriented cryptography. Proceedings of Advances in Cryptology -Crypto -87, New York: Springer Verlag (1988)457-469
2. Desmedt, Y., Frankel, Y.: Shared Generation of Authenticators and Signatures. Proceedings of Advances in Cryptology-Crypto -91, New York: Springer Verlag (1991)457-469
3. Huang, H.-F., Chang, C.-C.: A novel efficient (t, n) threshold proxy signature scheme, Information Sciences, In Press, Corrected Proof, Available online 8 April 2005, http://www.sciencedirect.com/
4. ItaKura, K., Nakamura, K.: A Public Key Cryptosystem Suitable for Digital Multi-Signature, NEC Research and Development, Vol.71, (1983)1-8
5. Kim, S., Park, S., Won, D.: Proxy Signatures, Revisited, Proceedings of Information and Communications Security (ICICS'97), Lecture Notes in Computer Science, Vol.1334, Springer-Verlag (1997)223-232
6. Mambo, M., Usuda, K. , Okamoto, E.: proxy signature: Delegation of the power to sign messages, IEICE Transaction Fundamentals, Vol. E79-A(9), (1996)1338-1353
7. Mambo, M., Usuda, K. , Okamoto, E.: Proxy signatures for delegating signing operation, Proceedings of of 3rd ACM Conference on Computer and Communications Security (CCS'96). ACM Press (1996)48-57
8. Qian, H., Cao, Z. Xue, Q.: Efficient Pairing-Based Threshold Proxy Signature Scheme with Known Signers, INFORMATICA, Vol.16(2),(2005)261-274
9. Tzeng, S.-F., Yang, C.-Y., Hwang, M.-S.: A new multi-proxy multi-signature scheme, Technical Report No. CYUT-IM-TR-2002-004, CYUT, 2002.
10. Xie, Q., Yu, X.: Improvement of WPL's (T, N) threshold signature scheme, Proceedings of the 16th International Conference on Computer Communication (ICCC 2004), (2004)1032-1035
11. Xue, Q., Cao, Z.: Improvement of multi-proxy signature scheme, Proceedings of The Fourth International Conference on Computer and Information Technology (CIT 2004), (2004)450-455

12. Yi, L., Bai, G., Xiao, G.: Proxy multi-signature scheme: a new type of proxy signature scheme, Electronics Letters, Vol.36(6) (2000)527-528.
13. Zhang, K.: Threshold Proxy Signature Schemes, Proc. Information Security Workshop (ISW'97), Lecture Notes in Computer Science, Vol.1396, Springer-Verlag (1997)282-290
14. Zhou, H.-S., Tie, L., Li, J.-H., Ni, Y.-S.: Improved proxy multi-signature scheme, Journal of Shanghai Jiaotong University, Vol.38(1), (2004)83-86

ID-Based Threshold Unsigncryption Scheme from Pairings

Fagen Li, Juntao Gao, and Yupu Hu

Key Laboratory of Computer Networks and Information Security,
Ministry of Education, Xidian University,
Xi'an, Shaanxi 710071, P.R. China
fagenli@hotmail.com, {jtgao, yphu}@mail.xidian.edu.cn

Abstract. An identity-based threshold unsigncryption scheme is proposed, which is the integration of the signcryption scheme, the (t, n) threshold scheme and zero knowledge proof for the equality of two discrete logarithms based on the bilinear map. In this scheme, a signcrypted message is decrypted only when more than t members join an unsigncryption protocol and the signature can be verified by any third party. A formal proof of security of this scheme is provided in the random oracle model, assuming the Decisional Bilinear Diffie-Hellman problem is computationally hard.

Keywords: Identity-based cryptography, signcryption, (t, n) threshold, zero knowledge proof.

1 Introduction

Identity-based (ID-based) cryptography (for examples, [4] and [12]) is rapidly emerging in recent years. The distinguishing property of ID-based cryptography is that a user's public key can be any binary string, such as an email address that can identify the user. This removes the need for senders to look up the recipient's public key before sending out an encrypted message. ID-based cryptography is supposed to provide a more convenient alternative to conventional public key infrastructure.

Signcryption, first proposed by Zheng [15] in 1997 , is a new cryptographic primitive that performs encryption and signature in a single logical step in order to obtain confidentiality, integrity, authentication and non-repudiation more efficiently than the traditional "sign-then-encrypt" approach. One of the shortcomings of Zheng's original schemes is that its non-repudiation procedure is more inefficient since they are based on interactive zero-knowledge proofs. To achieve simple and safe non-repudiation procedure, Bao and Deng [3] introduced a signcryption scheme that can be verified by a sender's public key. Furthermore, Steinfeld and Zheng [13] and Malone-Lee and Mao [10] proposed efficient signcryption schemes based on integer factorization and using RSA, respectively. The formal models and security proofs for signcryption schemes have been studied in [1]. In 2002, Malone-Lee [9] gave the first ID-based signcryption scheme. Libert and Quisquater [8] pointed out that Malone-Lee's scheme is not semantically secure and proposed a provably secure ID-based signcryption schemes.

D. Feng, D. Lin, and M. Yung (Eds.): CISC 2005, LNCS 3822, pp. 242–253, 2005.

All of the above schemes consist of only single recipient. However, In many cases, we need to prohibit a single recipient from recovering a signcrypted message. For example, in a sealed-bid auction scheme [7], the bids of bidders are opened by service providers only after all bids are deposited, and then the bidder who bids the highest price wins in the auction. For a secure auction, the non-repudiation must be provided because a bidder may deny his bid after the auction is ended. This can be prevented by a signature scheme. Next for the confidentiality of the bid, it must be encrypted. Finally the coalition between the service providers and some bidders must be prevented. This can be guaranteed by (t, n) threshold scheme where any coalition of service providers, of which size is less than t, can not get any information about the bid of a bidder. In 2001, Koo et al. [6] proposed a new signcryption scheme in which at least t recipients must participate in an unsigncryption process. Zhang et al. [14] also proposed a similar scheme. However, both of their scheme is based on discrete logarithm problem, not ID-based. In their scheme, only the recipients can verify the signature because the unsigncryption needs the recipients' private keys. That is, the non-repudiation of their scheme is not efficient. In addition, the formal models and security proofs for their schemes are also not considered.

In this paper, an ID-based threshold unsigncryption scheme is proposed, which is the integration of the Libert and Quisquater's signcryption scheme [8], the Shamir's (t, n) threshold scheme [11], and Baek and Zheng's zero knowledge proof for the equality of two discrete logarithms based on the bilinear map [2]. In our scheme, a signcrypted message is decrypted only when more than t members join an unsigncryption protocol and the signature can be verified by any third party. A formal proof of security of our scheme is provided in the random oracle model, assuming the Decisional Bilinear Diffie-Hellman problem is computationally hard.

The rest of this paper is organized as follows. Some definitions and preliminary works are given in Section 2. The formal model of ID-based threshold unsigncryption schemes are given in Section 3. Our ID-based threshold unsigncryption scheme is given in Section 4. The formal security proof of our scheme is provided in Section 5. Finally, the conclusions are given in Section 6.

2   Preliminaries

In this section, we briefly describe the basic definition and properties of the bilinear pairings. The Shamir's (t, n) threshold scheme [11] and Baek and Zheng's zero knowledge proof for the equality of two discrete logarithms based on the bilinear map [2] are also briefly described. They are the basic tools to construct our scheme.

2.1   Bilinear Pairings

Let G_1 be a cyclic additive group generated by P, whose order is a prime q, and G_2 be a cyclic multiplicative group of the same order q. Let a, b be elements of Z_q^*. A bilinear pairings is a map $\hat{e} : G_1 \times G_1 \to G_2$ with the following properties:

1. Bilinearity: $\hat{e}(aP, bQ) = \hat{e}(P, Q)^{ab}$.
2. Non-degeneracy: There exists P and $Q \in G_1$ such that $\hat{e}(P, Q) \neq 1$.
3. Computability: There is an efficient algorithm to compute $\hat{e}(P, Q)$ for all $P, Q \in G_1$.

The modified Weil pairing and the Tate pairing [4] are admissible maps of this kind. The security of our scheme described here relies on the hardness of the following problems.

Definition 1. *Given two groups G_1 and G_2 of the same prime order q, a bilinear map $\hat{e} : G_1 \times G_1 \rightarrow G_2$ and a generator P of G_1, the Decisional Bilinear Diffie-Hellman problem (DBDHP) in $(G_1, G_2, \hat{e})$ is to decide whether $h = \hat{e}(P, P)^{abc}$ given (P, aP, bP, cP) and an element $h \in G_2$.*

Definition 2. *Given two groups G_1 and G_2 of the same prime order q, a bilinear map $\hat{e} : G_1 \times G_1 \rightarrow G_2$ and a generator P of G_1, the Computational Bilinear Diffie-Hellman problem (CBDHP) in $(G_1, G_2, \hat{e})$ is to compute $h = \hat{e}(P, P)^{abc}$ given (P, aP, bP, cP).*

The decisional problem is of course not harder than the computational one. However, no algorithm is known to be able to solve any of them so far.

2.2 Shamir's (t, n) Threshold Scheme

In order to share a private key D_{ID}, we need the Shamir's (t, n) threshold scheme. Suppose that we have chosen integers t (a threshold) and n satisfying $1 \leq t \leq n < q$. First, we pick $R_1, R_2, \ldots, R_{t-1}$ at random from G_1^*. Then we construct a function $F(u) = D_{ID} + \sum_{j=1}^{t-1} u^j R_j$. Finally, we compute $D_{ID_i} = F(ID_i)$ for $1 \leq i \leq n$ and send (ID_i, D_{ID_i}) to the i-th member of the message recipient group. When the number of shares reaches the threshold t, the function $F(u)$ can be reconstructed by computing $F(u) = \sum_{j=1}^{t} D_{ID_j} N_j$, where $N_j = \prod_{i=1, i \neq j}^{t} \frac{u - ID_i}{ID_j - ID_i}$ mod q. The private key D_{ID} can be recovered by computing $D_{ID} = F(0)$.

2.3 Baek and Zheng's Zero Knowledge Proof for the Equality of Two Discrete Logarithms Based on the Bilinear Map

To ensure that all unsigncryption shares are correct, that is, to give robustness to threshold unsigncryption, we need a certain checking procedure. we use the Baek and Zheng's zero knowledge proof for the equality of two discrete logarithms based on the bilinear map. We construct a zero-knowledge proof of membership system for the language $L_{EDLog_{P,\tilde{P}}^{G_2}} \overset{def}{=} \{(\mu, \tilde{\mu}) \in G_2 \times G_2 \mid \log_g \mu = \log_{\tilde{g}} \tilde{\mu}\}$ where $g = \hat{e}(P, P)$ and $\tilde{g} = \hat{e}(P, \tilde{P})$ for generators P and $\tilde{P}$ of G_1 as follows.

Suppose that $(P, \tilde{P}, g, \tilde{g})$ and $(k, \tilde{k}) \in L_{EDLog_{P,\tilde{P}}^{G_2}}$ are given to the Prover and the Verifier, and the Prover knows a secret $S \in G_1^*$. The proof system works as follows.

1. The Prover chooses T from G_1 randomly and computes $r = \hat{e}(T, P)$ and $\tilde{r} = \hat{e}(T, \tilde{P})$. The Prover sends r and $\tilde{r}$ to the Verifier.
2. The Verifier chooses h from Z_q^* randomly and sends it to the Prover.
3. On receiving h, the Prover computes $W = T + hS$ and sends it to the Verifier.
4. The Verifier checks if $\hat{e}(W, P) = rk^h$ and $\hat{e}(W, \tilde{P}) = \tilde{r}\tilde{k}^h$. If the equality holds then the Verifier returns *"Accept"*, otherwise, returns *"Reject"*.

As claimed in [2], the above protocol can be easily converted a non-interactive knowledge proof.

3 Formal Model of ID-Based Threshold Unsigncryption

3.1 Description of Generic ID-Based Threshold Unsigncryption

An ID-based threshold unsigncryption scheme consists of the following eight algorithms.

Setup: Given a security parameter k, the private key generator (PKG) generates the system's public parameters *params*. Among the parameters produced by **Setup** is a key P_{pub} that is made public. There is also corresponding master key s that is kept secret.

Extract: Given an identity ID, the PKG computes the corresponding private key D_{ID} and transmits it to its owner in a secure way.

Keydis: Given a private key D_{ID}, the number of unsigncryption members n and a threshold parameter t, an authorized dealer can runs the private key distribution algorithm **Keydis** to distribute the unsigncryption private key D_{ID} into n member in the recipient group. **Keydis** makes use of an appropriate secret-sharing technique to generate shares of the private key $D_{ID_i}(1 \le i \le n)$ as well as verification key $y_i(1 \le i \le n)$ that will be used for checking the validity of unsigncryption shares. Then, each private/verification key pair (D_{ID_i}, y_i) is sent to an appropriate unsigncryption member. The unsigncryption member keep their private key share D_{ID_i} secret and publish the verification key y_i. The authorized dealer would be a normal user or PKG.

Signcrypt: If ID_A wishes to send a message m to group ID_B , ID_A computes **Signcrypt**(m, D_{ID_A}, ID_B) to obtain the ciphertext σ.

Sigver: Given a ciphertext σ, the validity of the message (signature) can be verified by running the signature verification algorithm **Sigver**.

Sharegen: If a legitimate user wants to unsigncrypt a ciphertext σ, he gives it to the each member in group ID_B and requests unsigncryption shares. These members in group ID_B run the unsigncryption share generation algorithm **Sharegen** taking the ciphertext as input and send the resulting unsigncryption shares $\sigma_i(1 \le i \le n)$ to the user. The user can be a normal member in group ID_B.

Sharever: Given a unsigncryption share $\sigma_i (1 \leq i \leq n)$, the validity of the share can be checked by running the unsigncryption share verification algorithm **Sharever**.

Sharecom: When the user collects valid unsigncryption shares from at least t member in group ID_B, the plaintext m can be reconstructed by running the share combining algorithm **Sharecom**.

3.2   Security Notions

Malone-Lee [9] defines the security notions for ID-based signcryption schemes (IDSC). These notions are semantical security (i.e. indistinguishability against adaptive chosen ciphertext attacks and unforgeability against adaptive chosen messages attacks). We modify this definition slightly to adapt for our ID-Based threshold unsigncryption scheme.

Definition 3. *We say that an ID-based threshold unsigncryption scheme (ID-TUSC) has the indistinguishability against adaptive chosen ciphertext attacks property (IND-IDTUSC-CCA) if no polynomially bounded adversary has a non-negligible advantage in the following game.*

1. The challenger $\mathcal{C}$ runs the **Setup** algorithm with a security parameter k and obtains public parameters *params* and a master key s. He sends *params* to the adversary $\mathcal{A}$ and keeps s secret.
2. $\mathcal{A}$ corrupts $t-1$ out of n members in the recipient group.
3. The adversary $\mathcal{A}$ performs a polynomially bounded number of queries(These queries may be made adaptively, i.e. each query may depend on the answer to the previous queries).
   - Key extraction queries: $\mathcal{A}$ produces an identity ID and receives the extracted private key $D_{ID} = $ **Extract**(ID).
   - Signcryption queries: $\mathcal{A}$ produces two identities ID_i, ID_j and a plaintext m. $\mathcal{C}$ computes $D_{ID_i} = $ **Extract**(ID_i) and $\sigma = $ **Signcrypt**(m, D_{ID_i}, ID_j) and sends σ to $\mathcal{A}$.
   - Unsigncryption share queries to the uncorrupted member: $\mathcal{A}$ produces two identities ID_i and ID_j, and a ciphertext σ. $\mathcal{C}$ generates the private key $D_{ID_j} = $ **Extract**(ID_j). Subsequently, $\mathcal{C}$ runs the private key distribution algorithm **Keydis** taking D_{ID_j} as input to share it among n member in the recipient group. Then, $\mathcal{C}$ runs the unsigncryption share generation algorithm **Sharegen** taking σ as input to obtain a corresponding unsigncryption share and returns it to $\mathcal{A}$.
4. $\mathcal{A}$ chooses two plaintexts, m_1 and m_2, and two identities, ID_A and ID_B, on which he wishes to be challenged. The challenger $\mathcal{C}$ picks a random bit b from $\{0, 1\}$ and computes $\sigma^* = $ **Signcrypt**(m_b, D_{ID_A}, ID_B) which is sent to $\mathcal{A}$.
5. $\mathcal{A}$ produces the target identity ID_B. $\mathcal{C}$ generates the private key $D_{ID_B} = $ **Extract**(ID_B). $\mathcal{C}$ then runs the private key distribution algorithm **Keydis** on input D_{ID_B} with parameter (t, n) and obtains a set of private/verification

key pairs $\{(D_{ID_{B_i}}, y_{B_i})\}$, where $1 \leq i \leq n$. Next, $\mathcal{C}$ gives $\mathcal{A}$ the private keys of corrupted members and the verifications keys of all the member. However, the private keys of uncorrupted members are kept secret from $\mathcal{A}$.

6. The adversary $\mathcal{A}$ can ask a polynomially bounded number of queries adaptively again as in the first stage with the restriction that he cannot make the key extraction query on ID_B and cannot make the unsigncryption share query on σ^*.

7. Finally, $\mathcal{A}$ produces a bit b' and wins the game if $b' = b$.

The advantage of $\mathcal{A}$ is defined as $Adv(\mathcal{A}) =| 2P[b' = b] - 1 |$ where $P[b' = b]$ denotes the probability that $b' = b$.

Definition 4. *An ID-based threshold unsigncryption scheme (IDTUSC) is said to be secure against an existential forgery for adaptive chosen messages attacks (EF-IDTUSC-ACMA) if no polynomially bounded adversary has a non-negligible advantage in the following game.*

1. The challenger $\mathcal{C}$ runs the **Setup** algorithm with a security parameter k and obtains public parameters *params* and a master key s. He sends *params* to the adversary $\mathcal{A}$ and keeps s secret.

2. The adversary $\mathcal{A}$ performs a polynomially bounded number of queries(These queries may be made adaptively, i.e. each query may depend on the answer to the previous queries).
   - Key extraction queries: $\mathcal{A}$ produces an identity ID and receives the extracted private key $D_{ID} = \textbf{Extract}(ID)$.
   - Signcryption queries: $\mathcal{A}$ produces two identities ID_i, ID_j and a plaintext m. $\mathcal{C}$ computes $D_{ID_i} = \textbf{Extract}(ID_i)$ and $\sigma = \textbf{Signcrypt}(m, D_{ID_i}, ID_j)$ and sends σ to $\mathcal{A}$.
   - Unsigncryption share queries to the uncorrupted member: $\mathcal{A}$ produces two identities ID_i and ID_j, and a ciphertext σ. $\mathcal{C}$ generates the private key $D_{ID_j} = \textbf{Extract}(ID_j)$. Subsequently, $\mathcal{C}$ runs the private key distribution algorithm **Keydis** taking D_{ID_j} as input to share it among n member in the recipient group. Then, $\mathcal{C}$ runs the unsigncryption share generation algorithm **Sharegen** taking σ as input to obtain a corresponding unsigncryption share and returns it to $\mathcal{A}$.

3. Finally, $\mathcal{A}$ produces a new triple (σ^*, ID_A, ID_B)(i.e. a triple that was not produced by the signcryption oracle) where the private key of ID_A was not asked in the second stage and wins the game if the result of **Sigver** is not the $\perp$ symbol.

The advantage of $\mathcal{A}$ is defined as the probability that he wins.

4   The Proposed Scheme

In this section, we propose an ID-based threshold unsigncryption scheme. The proposed scheme involves four roles: the PKG, the sender Alice, a legitimate user U that wants to unsigncrypt the ciphertext and the message recipient group $B = \{B_1, B_2, \ldots, B_n\}$. It consists of the following eight algorithms.

Setup: Given a security parameter k, the PKG chooses groups G_1 and G_2 of prime order q (with G_1 additive and G_2 multiplicative), a generator P of G_1, a bilinear map $\hat{e} : G_1 \times G_1 \to G_2$ and hash functions $H_1 : \{0,1\}^* \to G_1$, $H_2 : G_2 \to \{0,1\}^n$, $H_3 : \{0,1\}^* \times G_2 \to Z_q^*$ and $H_4 : G_2 \times G_2 \times G_2 \to Z_q^*$. It chooses a master-key $s \in Z_q^*$ and computes $P_{pub} = sP$. It also chooses a secure symmetric cipher (E, D). The PKG publishes system's public parameters $\{G_1, G_2, n, \hat{e}, P, P_{pub}, H_1, H_2, H_3, H_4, E, D\}$ and keeps the master-key s secret.

Extract: Given an identity ID, the PKG sets the user's public key $Q_{ID} = H_1(ID)$, computes the user's private key $D_{ID} = sQ_{ID}$. The sender Alice has a public key Q_{ID_A} and a corresponding private key $D_{ID_A} = sQ_{ID_A}$. The message recipient group B has a public key Q_{ID_B} and a corresponding private key $D_{ID_B} = sQ_{ID_B}$.

Keydis: Suppose that we have chosen integers t (a threshold) and n satisfying $1 \le t \le n < q$. The PKG picks $R_1, R_2, \ldots, R_{t-1}$ at random from G_1^* and constructs a function $F(u) = D_{ID_B} + \sum_{j=1}^{t-1} u^j R_j$. Then, the PKG computes the private key $D_i = F(ID_i)$ and the verification key $y_i = \hat{e}(D_i, P)$ for recipient $B_i (1 \le i \le n)$. Subsequently, the PKG secretly sends the private key D_i and the verification key y_i to B_i. B_i then keeps D_i as secret while making y_i public.

Signcrypt: To send a message m to the recipient group B, the Alice chooses x from Z_q^* randomly and computes the ciphertext $\sigma = (c, r, S)$ as follows:

1. Compute $k_1 = \hat{e}(P, P_{pub})^x$ and $k_2 = H_2(\hat{e}(P_{pub}, Q_{ID_B})^x)$.
2. Compute $c = E_{k_2}(m)$.
3. Compute $r = H_3(c, k_1)$.
4. Compute $S = xP_{pub} - rD_{ID_A}$.

Sigver: Suppose that a legitimate user U that wants to unsigncrypt the ciphertext σ. He computes $k_1' = \hat{e}(P, S)\hat{e}(P_{pub}, Q_{ID_A})^r$ and accept the message if and only if $r = H_3(c, k_1')$. Otherwise, he returns *Invalid Ciphertext*.

Sharegen: U sends σ to each member in group B and requests unsigncryption shares. Each $B_i (1 \le i \le n)$ checks the validity of σ by running **Sigver** as U does. If it is valid, Each $B_i (1 \le i \le n)$ computes $\tilde{y}_i = \hat{e}(D_i, Q_{ID_A})$, $\tilde{u}_i = \hat{e}(T_i, Q_{ID_A})$, $u_i = \hat{e}(T_i, P)$, $v_i = H_4(\tilde{y}_i, \tilde{u}_i, u_i)$ and $W_i = T_i + v_i D_i$ for random $T_i \in G_1$ and send $\sigma_i = (i, \tilde{y}_i, \tilde{u}_i, u_i, v_i, W_i)$ to the user U. Otherwise, B_i returns *Invalid Ciphertext*.

Sharever: U firstly compute $v_i' = H_4(\tilde{y}_i, \tilde{u}_i, u_i)$ and then check if $v_i' = v_i$, $\hat{e}(W_i, Q_{ID_A})/\tilde{y}_i^{v_i'} = \tilde{u}_i$, and $\hat{e}(W_i, P)/y_i^{v_i'} = u_i$. If this test above holds, the σ_i from B_i is a valid unsigncryption share. Otherwise, U returns *Invalid Share*.

Sharecom: When U collects valid unsigncryption shares from at least t member in group B, U computes $k_2' = H_2(\hat{e}(S, Q_{ID_B})(\prod_{j=1}^t \tilde{y}_j^{N_j})^r)$, where $N_j = \prod_{i=1, i \ne j}^t \frac{-ID_i}{ID_j - ID_i} \bmod q$ and recover $m = D_{k_2'}(c)$.

5   Analysis of the Scheme

5.1   Correctness

The correctness can be easily verified by the following equations.

$$k'_1 = \hat{e}(P, S)\hat{e}(P_{pub}, Q_{ID_A})^r$$
$$= \hat{e}(P, xP_{pub})\hat{e}(P, D_{ID_A})^{-r}\hat{e}(P_{pub}, Q_{ID_A})^r$$
$$= \hat{e}(P, P_{pub})^x$$

$$k'_2 = H_2(\hat{e}(S, Q_{ID_B})(\prod_{j=1}^{t} \tilde{y_j}^{N_j})^r)$$

$$= H_2(\hat{e}(S, Q_{ID_B})\hat{e}(\sum_{j=1}^{t} N_j D_j, Q_{ID_A})^r)$$

$$= H_2(\hat{e}(xP_{pub}, Q_{ID_B})\hat{e}(D_{ID_A}, Q_{ID_B})^{-r}\hat{e}(D_{ID_B}, Q_{ID_A})^r)$$

$$= H_2(\hat{e}(P_{pub}, Q_{ID_B})^x)$$

5.2   Security

Theorem 1. *In the random oracle model, we assume we have an IND-IDTUSC-CCA adversary called $\mathcal{A}$ that is able to distinguish ciphertext during the game of definition 3 with an advantage ϵ when running in a time t and asking at most q_{H_1} identity hashing queries, at most q_R H_3 queries, q_R signcryption queries and q_U unsigncrypt share queries. Then, there exists a distinguisher $\mathcal{B}$ that can solve the Decisional Bilinear Diffie-Hellman problem in a time $O(t + (8q_R^2 + 4q_U)T_\epsilon)$ with an advantage*

$$Adv(\mathcal{B})^{DBDH(G_1, P)} > \frac{\epsilon 2^{k-1} - q_U}{q_{H_1}^4 2^{k-2}}$$

where T_ϵ denotes the computation time of the bilinear map.

Proof. We assume the distinguisher $\mathcal{B}$ receives a random instance (P, aP, bP, cP, h) of the Decisional Bilinear Diffie-Hellman problem. His goal is to decide whether $h = \hat{e}(P, P)^{abc}$ or not. $\mathcal{B}$ will run $\mathcal{A}$ as a subroutine and act as $\mathcal{A}$'s challenger in the IND-IDTUSC-CCA game. During the game, $\mathcal{A}$ will consult $\mathcal{B}$ for answers to the random oracles H_1, H_2, H_3 and H_4. Roughly speaking, these answers are randomly generated, but to maintain the consistency and to avoid collision, $\mathcal{B}$ keeps four lists L_1, L_2, L_3, L_4 respectively to store the answers used. The following assumptions are made.

1. $\mathcal{A}$ will ask for $H_1(ID)$ before ID is used in any key extraction queries, signcryption queries and unsigncryption share queries.
2. Ciphertext returned from a signcryption query will not be used by $\mathcal{A}$ in an unsigncryption share query.

3. $\mathcal{A}$ corrupts $t - 1$ unsigncryption members during the attack. That is, $\mathcal{A}$ obtains private keys $\{S_i\}_{1 \leq i \leq t-1}$ of corrupted unsigncryption members.

At the beginning of the game, $\mathcal{B}$ gives $\mathcal{A}$ the system parameters with $P_{pub} = cP$. Note that c is unknown to $\mathcal{B}$ and simulates the master key value for the PKG in the game. Then, $\mathcal{B}$ chooses two distinct random numbers $i, j \in \{1, 2, \ldots, q_{H_1}\}$. $\mathcal{A}$ asks a polynomially bounded number of H_1 queries on identities of his choice. At the i-th H_1 query, $\mathcal{B}$ answers by $H_1(ID_i) = aP$. At the j-th query, he answers by $H_1(ID_j) = bP$. Since aP and bP belong to a random instance of the DBDH problem, $\mathcal{A}$'s view will not be modified by these changes. Hence, the private keys D_{ID_i} and D_{ID_j} (which are not computable by $\mathcal{B}$) are respectively acP and bcP. Thus the solution $\hat{e}(P, P)^{abc}$ of the DBDH problem is given by $\hat{e}(Q_{ID_i}, D_{ID_j}) = \hat{e}(D_{ID_i}, Q_{ID_j})$. For queries $H_1(ID_e)$ with $e \neq i, j$, $\mathcal{B}$ chooses b_e from Z_q^* randomly, puts the pair (ID_e, b_e) in list L_1 and answers $H_1(ID_e) = b_e P$.

We now explain how the other kinds of queries are treated by $\mathcal{B}$.

H_2 queries: On a $H_2(g_e)$ query, $\mathcal{B}$ searches a pair (g_e, R_e) in the list L_2. If such a pair is found, $\mathcal{B}$ answers by R_e, otherwise he answers $\mathcal{A}$ by a random binary sequence $R \leftarrow_R \{0, 1\}^n$ such that no entry $(., R)$ exists in L_2 (in order to avoid collisions on H_2) and puts the pair (g_e, R) into $L2$.

H_3 queries: For a query $H_3(c_e, k_e)$, $\mathcal{B}$ first ensures the list L_3 does not contain a tuple (c_e, k_e, r_e). If such a tuple is found, $\mathcal{B}$ answers r_e, otherwise he chooses $r \leftarrow_R F_q$, gives it as an answer to the query and puts the tuple (c_e, k_e, r) into $L3$.

H_4 queries: For a query $H_4(\tilde{y}_e, \tilde{u}_e, u_e)$, $\mathcal{B}$ first ensures the list L_4 does not contain a tuple $(\tilde{y}_e, \tilde{u}_e, u_e, v_e)$. If such a tuple is found, $\mathcal{B}$ answers v_e, otherwise he chooses $v \leftarrow_R Z_q$, gives it as an answer to the query and puts the tuple $(\tilde{y}_e, \tilde{u}_e, u_e, v)$ into $L3$.

Key extraction queries: When $\mathcal{A}$ asks a question **Extract**(ID_A), if $ID_A = ID_i$ or $ID_A = ID_j$, then $\mathcal{B}$ fails and stops. If $ID_A \neq ID_i, ID_j$ then the list L_1 must contain a pair (ID_A, d) for some d (this indicates $\mathcal{B}$ previously answered $H_1(ID_A) = dP$ on a H_1 query on ID_A). The private key corresponding to ID_A is then $dP_{pub} = cdP$. It is computed by $\mathcal{B}$ and returned to $\mathcal{A}$.

Signcryption queries: When $\mathcal{A}$ perform a signcryption query for a plaintext m and identities ID_A and ID_B. If ID_A and ID_B are not the identities ID_i and ID_j, $\mathcal{B}$ computes the private key D_{ID_A} correspondingly and the query can be answered by running the algorithm **Signcrypt**(m, D_{ID_A}, Q_{ID_B}). In the case $ID_A = ID_i$ or $ID_A = ID_j$ and $ID_B \neq ID_i, ID_j$, $\mathcal{B}$ has to simulate the execution of **Signcrypt**(m, D_{ID_A}, Q_{ID_B}) as follows. He chooses $r \leftarrow_R F_q$ and $S \leftarrow_R G_1^*$. He computes $k' = \hat{e}(P, S)\hat{e}(P_{pub}, Q_{ID_A})^r$ and $\tau = \hat{e}(S, Q_{ID_B})\hat{e}(Q_{ID_A}, D_{ID_B})^r$ where D_{ID_B} is the private key corresponding to ID_B. He find $k_2 = H_2(\tau)$ by running the H_2 simulation algorithm and computes $c = E_{k_2}(m)$. He then checks if L_3 already contains a tuple (c, k', r') with $r' \neq r$. In this case, $\mathcal{B}$ repeats the process with another random pair (r, S) until finding a tuple (c, k', r) whose first two elements do not figure in a tuple of the list L_3. Before obtaining an admissible tuple (c, k', r), $\mathcal{B}$ must repeat the process at most $2q_R$ times. Once an admissible tuple (c, k', r) is found, $\mathcal{B}$ puts (c, k', r) into L_3 before returning the ciphertext (c, r, S) which will appear to be valid from $\mathcal{A}$ point of view. If ID_A and ID_B are the identities ID_i and ID_j, $\mathcal{B}$ signcrypts m like this. He chooses $r^* \leftarrow_R F_q^*$ and $S^* \leftarrow_R G_1$ and computes $k' = \hat{e}(P, S^*)\hat{e}(P_{pub}, Q_{ID_A})^{r^*} = \hat{e}(P, S^*)\hat{e}(cP, aP)^{r^*}$. $\mathcal{B}$ chooses $\tau^* \in_R G_2$ and $k_2' \in_R \{0,1\}^n$ such that no entry $(., k_2')$ is in L_2 and computes $c^* = E_{k_2'}(m)$. He then verifies if the list L_3 already contains an entry (c^*, k_1', r') such that $r' \neq r^*$. If not, he puts the tuple (c^*, k_1', r^*) into L_3 and and (τ^*, k_2') into L_2. In the opposite case, $\mathcal{B}$ chooses another random pair (r^*, S^*) and repeats the process as above until he finds a tuple (c^*, k_1', r^*) whose first two elements do not figure in an entry of L_3. Once he has admissible elements (r^*, S^*), $\mathcal{B}$ gives the ciphertext $\sigma^* = (c^*, r^*, S^*)$. A will never see that σ^* is not a valid signcrypted text of the plaintext m for identities ID_i and ID_j since he will not ask the unsigncryption share of σ^*.

Unsigncryption share queries to the uncorrupted member: When $\mathcal{A}$ observes a ciphertext $\sigma' = (c', r', S')$ for identities ID_i and ID_j, he may want to ask $\mathcal{B}$ for the unsigncryption share of σ'. In such a case, $\mathcal{B}$ always notifies $\mathcal{A}$ that the ciphertext is invalid: if $\mathcal{A}$ previously asked the hash value $H_3(c', \hat{e}(P, S)\hat{e}(P_{pub}, Q_{ID_A})^{r'})$, there is a probability of at most $1/2^k$ that $\mathcal{B}$ answered r' (and that σ' was actually valid from $\mathcal{A}$'s point of view). The simulation fails if L_3 contains a tuple $(c', \hat{e}(P, S)\hat{e}(P_{pub}, Q_{ID_A})^{r'}, r')$. When receiving an unsigncryption share query for a ciphertext $\sigma' = (c', r', S')$ for identities ID_A and ID_B that are not ID_i and ID_j, $\mathcal{B}$ first runs **Keydis** to obtain private/verification key pairs $\{D_l, y_l\}$, where $1 \leq l \leq n$ and computes $\tilde{y}_t = \hat{e}(D_t, Q_{ID_A})$(Suppose that the t-th member has not been corrupted by $\mathcal{A}$). Next, he chooses W_t and v_t uniformly at random from G_1 and Z_q^* respectively, and computes $\tilde{u}_t = \hat{e}(W_t, Q_{ID_A})/\tilde{y}_t^{v_t}$ and $u_t = \hat{e}(W_t, P)/y_t^{v_t}$. Then, $\mathcal{B}$ set $v_t = H_4(\tilde{y}_t, \tilde{u}_t, u_t)$. Finally, he check if L_4 contains a tuple $(\tilde{y}_t, \tilde{u}_t, u_t, v_t')$ with $v_t' \neq v_t$. In this case, $\mathcal{B}$ repeats the process with another random pair (W_t, v_t) until finding a tuple $(\tilde{y}_t, \tilde{u}_t, u_t, v_t)$ whose first three element do not figure in a tuple of the list L_4. Otherwise, $\mathcal{B}$ return the simulated value $\sigma_t = (t, \tilde{y}_t, \tilde{u}_t, u_t, v_t, W_t)$ as a unsigncryption share corresponding to σ' and save $(\tilde{y}_t, \tilde{u}_t, u_t, v_t)$ to L_4.

It is easy to see that, for all queries, the probability to reject a valid ciphertext does not exceed $q_U/2^k$.

After a polynomially bounded number of queries, $\mathcal{A}$ chooses a pair of identities on which he wishes to be challenged. With a probability at least $2/q_{H_1}(q_{H_1} - 1)$ this pair of target identities will be (ID_i, ID_j) (we assume that after the first stage of the game, $\mathcal{A}$ chooses to be challenged on a pair of identities of which he asked the hashing). Notice that, if $\mathcal{A}$ asks the private key of ID_i or ID_j before choosing his target identities, then $\mathcal{B}$ fails because he is unable to answer the question (we recall that, if $\mathcal{A}$ actually chooses to be challenged on ID_i and ID_j, then he cannot ask ID_i nor ID_j's private keys in the second stage). If A does not choose ID_i and ID_j as target identities, then $\mathcal{B}$ fails.

When $\mathcal{A}$ produces his two plaintexts m_0 and m_1, $\mathcal{B}$ chooses a random bit $b \in_R \{0,1\}$ and signcrypts m_b. To do so, he chooses $r^* \leftarrow_R Z_q^*$ and $S^* \leftarrow_R G_1$. He computes $k_1' = \hat{e}(P, S^*)\hat{e}(P_{pub}, Q_{ID_A})^{r^*} = \hat{e}(P, S^*)\hat{e}(cP, aP)^{r^*}, \tau^* =$

$\hat{e}(S^*, Q_{ID_B})h^{r^*}$(where h is $\mathcal{B}$'s candidate for the DBDH problem) to obtain $k_2' = H_2(\tau^*)$(from the H_2 simulation algorithm) and $c_b = E_{k_2'}(m_b)$. He then verifies as above if L_3 contains an entry (c_b, k_1', r') such that $r' \neq r^*$. If not, he puts the tuple (c_b, k_1', r^*) into L_3. In the opposite case, $\mathcal{B}$ chooses another random pair (r^*, S^*) and repeats the process until finding a tuple (c_b, k_1', r^*) whose first two elements do not figure in an entry of L_3. Once he has admissible elements (r^*, S^*), $\mathcal{B}$ just has to send the ciphertext $\sigma = (c_b, r^*, S^*)$ to $\mathcal{A}$.

$\mathcal{A}$ then performs a second series of queries which is treated in the same way as the first one. At the end of the simulation, he produces a bit b' for which he believes the relation $\sigma = \mathbf{Signcrypt}(m_b', D_{ID_i}, ID_j)$ holds. At this moment, if $b = b'$, $\mathcal{B}$ then answers 1 as a result because his candidate h allowed him to produce σ that appeared to $\mathcal{A}$ as a valid signcrypted text of m_b. If $b \neq b'$, $\mathcal{B}$ then answers 0.

We now have to assess $\mathcal{B}$'s probability of success. We saw that $\mathcal{B}$ fails if $\mathcal{A}$ asks the private key associated to ID_i or ID_j during the first stage. We know that there are $q_{H_1}(q_{H_1} - 1)/2$ ways to choose the pair (ID_i, ID_j). Among those $q_{H_1}(q_{H_1} - 1)/2$ pairs of identities, at least one of them will never be the subject of a key extraction query from $\mathcal{A}$. Then, with a probability greater than $2/q_{H_1}(q_{H_1} - 1)$, $\mathcal{A}$ will not ask the questions $\mathbf{Extract}(ID_i)$ and $\mathbf{Extract}(ID_j)$. Further, with a probability exactly $2/q_{H_1}(q_{H_1} - 1)$, $\mathcal{A}$ chooses to be challenged on the pair (ID_i, ID_j) and this must allow $\mathcal{B}$ to solve his decisional problem if $\mathcal{A}$ wins the IND-IDTUSC-CCA game. The value of $\mathrm{Adv}(\mathcal{B})$ is calculated as follows.

$$Adv(\mathcal{B}) = |P_{a,b,c \in_R Z_q}[1 \leftarrow \mathcal{B}(aP, bP, cP, \hat{e}(P,P)^{abc})]$$
$$- P_{a,b,c \in_R Z_q, h \in_R G_2}[1 \leftarrow \mathcal{B}(aP, bP, cP, h)]|$$
$$= \frac{\epsilon - q_U/2^{k-1}}{2(q_{H_1}(q_{H_1}-1)/2)^2} > \frac{\epsilon 2^{k-1} - q_U}{q_{H_1}^4 2^{k-2}}$$

$\square$

The unforgeability against adaptive chosen messages attacks derives from the security of Hess's identity based signature scheme [5] under the Computational Diffie-Hellman assumption. One can show that an attacker that is able to forge a signcrypted message must be able to forge a valid Hess's signature.

Any third party can run $\mathbf{Sigver}$ and check the validity of a signcrypted message. Therefor, our scheme provides the public verifiability.

6   Conclusions

We have successfully integrated the design ideas of the ID-based signcryption scheme, the (t, n) threshold scheme and zero knowledge proof for the equality of two discrete logarithms based on the bilinear map, and have proposed an ID-based threshold unsigncryption scheme. In the proposed scheme, any third party can verify the validity of the signature, but only more than t members in the recipient group can cooperatively recover the message m. As compared to the koo et al. and Zhang et al.'s scheme based on discrete logarithms, the proposed scheme has the following advantages: it provides public verifiability; the key management problem is simplified because of using ID-based cryptosystem; a formal proof of security is provided in the random oracle model, assuming the Decisional Bilinear Diffie-Hellman problem is computationally hard.

Acknowledgements

We would like to thank the anonymous reviewers for their valuable comments and suggestions. This work is supported by NSFC under contract no. 60473029.

References

1. J. Baek, R. Steinfeld, and Y. Zheng. Formal proofs for the security of signcryption. In *Proceedings of PKC'02*, LNCS 2274, pp. 80–98, Springer, 2002.
2. J. Baek and Y. Zheng. Identity-based threshold decryption. In *Proceedings of PKC 2004*, LNCS 2947, pp. 262–276, Springer, 2004.
3. F. Bao and R.H. Deng. A signcryption scheme with signature directly verifiable by public key. In *Proceedings of PKC'98*, LNCS 1431, pp. 55–59, Springer, 1998.
4. D. Boneh and M. Franklin. Identity-based encryption from the weil pairing. In *Advances in Cryptology-CRYPTO 2001*, LNCS 2139, pp. 213–229, Springer, 2001.
5. F. Hess. Efficient identity based signature schemes. In *SAC 2002*, LNCS 2595, pp. 310–324, Springer, 2003.
6. J.H. Koo, H.J. Kim, and I.R. Jeong. Jointly unsigncryptable signcryption schemes. In *Proceedings of WISA 2001*, pp. 397–407, 2001.
7. M. Kudo. Secure electronic sealed-bid auction protocol with public key cryptography. *IEICE Trans. Fundamentals*, E81-A(1): 20–26, 1998.
8. B. Libert and J. Quisquater. New identity based signcryption schemes from pairings. In *Proceedings of 2003 IEEE information theory workshop*, pp. 155–158, 2003.
9. J. Malone-Lee. Identity based signcryption. *Cryptology ePrint Archive*, Report 2002/098, 2002. Available from: http://eprint.iacr.org/2002/098.
10. J. Malone-Lee and W. Mao. Two birds one stone: signcryption using RSA. In *Topics in Cryptology-CT-RSA 2003*, LNCS 2612, pp. 211–225, Springer, 2003.
11. A. Shamir. How to share a secret. *Communications of the ACM*, 24(11):612–613, 1979.
12. A. Shamir. Identity-based cryptosystems and signature schemes. In *Advances in Cryptology-CRYPTO'84*, LNCS 196, pp. 47–53, Springer, 1984.
13. R. Steinfeld and Y. Zheng. A signcryption scheme based on integer factorization. In *Proceedings of ISW'00*, LNCS 1975, pp. 308–322, Springer, 2000.
14. Z. Zhang, C. Mian, and Q. Jin. Signcryption scheme with threshold shared unsigncryption preventing malicious receivers. In *Proceedings of IEEE TENCON'02*, pp. 196–199, 2002.
15. Y. Zheng. Digital signcryption or how to achieve cost (signature & encryption) ≪ cost (signature) + cost(encryption). In *Advances in Cryptology-CRYPTO'97*, LNCS 1294, pp. 165–179, Springer, 1997.

Improvement of Detection Ability According to Optimum Selection of Measures Based on Statistical Approach*

Gil-Jong Mun[1], Yong-Min Kim[2], DongKook Kim[3], and Bong-Nam Noh[3],**

[1] Interdisciplinary Program of Information Security,
Chonnam National University, 500-757, Gwangju, Korea
alcor@lsrc.chonnam.ac.kr
[2] Div. of Information Technology,
Yeosu National Unviersity, 550-749, Yeosu, Korea
bluearain@yosu.ac.kr
[3] Div. of Electronics Computer & Information Engineering,
Chonnam National University, 500-757, Gwangju, Korea
{dkim, bbong}@chonnam.ac.kr

Abstract. A selection of useful measures and a generation of rules for detecting attacks from network data are very difficult. Expert's experiences are commonly required to generate the detection rules. If the rules are generated automatically, we will reduce man-power, management expense, and complexity of intrusion detection systems. In this paper, we propose two methods for generating the detection rules. One method is the statistical method based on relative entropy that uses for selecting the useful measures for generating the accurate rules. The other is decision tree algorithm based on entropy theory that generates the detection rules automatically. Also we propose a method of converting the continuous measures into categorical measures because continuous measures are hard to analyze. As the result, the detection rules for attacks are automatically generated without expert's experiences. Also, we selected the useful measures by the proposed method.

1 Introduction

As the information technology is advanced, many people have easily access to Internet and get much information from it. But many behaviors of abuse are happened as growth of network technique. The biggest problem among them is the attacks of network that misuse weakness of network and systems. Destructions of system resources and unlawful leakage of data occur by attacks of network. An intrusion detection technology is required necessarily to prevent them.

IDS (Intrusion Detection System) is a very useful system that detects misuse behaviors and illegal accesses, and records various behaviors of intrusion, and reports to an administrator in computer systems [1]. Mostly the current IDSs use both anomaly and misuse detection for the real-time detection of a lot of network packets. The tech-

---

* This work was supported (in part) by the Ministry of Information & Communications, Korea, under the Information Technology Research Center (ITRC) Support Program.
** Correspondent author.

D. Feng, D. Lin, and M. Yung (Eds.): CISC 2005, LNCS 3822, pp. 254–264, 2005.

nique of misuse detection detects misuse behavior using rules that are generated by classification and analysis of packets. Network packets have a lot of measures such as *protocol, sequence number, flag, window size, packet size,* and so on. However, the information that is extracted from packets is difficult to analyze and classify into attacks, because it has simpler measures than those of network connections.

In this paper, we extracted the measures of network connections, and selected the useful measures among them by a statistical method. Also this paper presents a method that generates detection rules for intrusion detection based on the selected measures. And we evaluate the performance of the proposed algorithm using KDD (Knowledge Discovery in Database) CUP 99 data set [2].

2 Related Work

A lot of universities and institutions analyzed the packets based on network protocol and studied the detection of attack behaviors on network. Florida University analyzed the absurd distribution of packet headers [3, 4] and U.C Davis University studied the host-based detection and routing-based detection for detecting forged packets [5]. Moreover, Ohio University estimated the meaning of doubtful packets and effect of packets by analyzing IP and TCP's packets [6, 7]. The Boeing Company developed the identification system of *DDoS* (Distributed DoS) by calculating the entropy of attributes of selected packets and frequency-sorted distribution [8]. New Mexico University studied the SVM (Support Vector Machine) to detect the attacks after extracting useful measures from the KDD CUP 99 data set [9].

Various techniques such as data mining, machine learning and artificial intelligence have been studied for the intrusion detection, and used for analyzing enormous data of network. And the approaches to generate rule or pattern have been studied because they are very easy to understand and analyze process of intrusion. One of them is ARL:UT (Applied Research Laboratories of University of Teas at Austin)[10] that achieved the intrusion detection by using the decision tree algorithm and genetic algorithm. Florida University generated the detection rules from the training data based on TCP/IP protocol using LERAD (Learning Rules for Anomaly Detection). Also neural network [11] and Bayesian network [12, 13] have been used for intrusion detection.

This paper presents the method to generate detection rules that use *C4.5* [14] among various decision tree algorithms such as *CHID, CART, QUEST, C4* and *BOAT* [15].

3 RBIDS (Rule-Based Intrusion Detection System)

In this chapter, we propose a detection method based on the statistical method to choose the useful measures and generate the detection rule using decision tree algorithm. After studying the composition of KDD CUP 99 dataset and the model for RBIDS, we present the statistical method and decision tree algorithm.

3.1 KDD CUP 99 Data Set

KDD CUP 99 data set is a dump data offered by KDD CUP 99 to extract the specific measures for intrusion detection from DARPA in1998 [16]. The data set is classified into four attack types such as DoS (Denial of Service), R2L (Remote to Local), U2R (User to Root), probes and normal.

KDD CUP 99 data set consists of the information of network connection, and they can be divided into three types that are basic measures of TCP session such as *duration, protocol type, flag,* etc., contents measures such as *logged in, Su attempted, hot,* etc., and traffic measures such as *packet count, syn error rate,* and so on. And these measures are divided again into two attributes that are discrete measures and continuous measures. While *duration, urgent,* etc., have the continuous attribute, and others such as *protocol type, service,* etc., have discrete one.

3.2 Model for Rule-Based Intrusion Detection System

Figure 1 shows the diagram for rule-based intrusion detection system, and it is consisted of three steps as follows. The first step, data processing and selection of measures, is the process that stores from packets of network to dump data, and after converting dump data into processing data that is necessary in an experiment, we select the useful measures from them using the distance based on a statistical method. The selected measures are consisted of the features to differentiate the normal from the attacks. The second step, training, is the process that creates tree and detection rules using decision tree algorithm based on the selected measures at first step for intrusion detection. The third step, detecting of network intrusions, is the process that compares detection rules created at second step with input data.

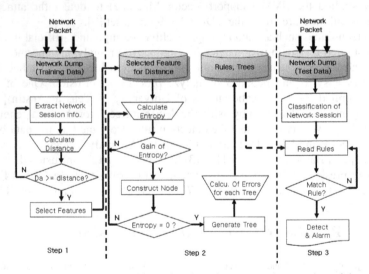

Fig. 1. This diagram is rule-based intrusion detection system that consists of three steps

3.3 Analysis of the Measures

This paper proposes the statistical method to choose the useful measures from training data for intrusion detection. To do this, firstly we calculate the probability distribution for selecting measures. Measures that have values of discrete attribute can calculate easily the probability distribution by themselves. But it is not easy for the continuous measures by themselves because they have irregular values. So we use the interval that is divided by fixed space among the smallest values and the biggest values in the continuous measure. Therefore we can calculate the probability distribution using the interval. Moreover, if there are continuous measures that have fixed value, we calculate the probability distribution like the discrete attributes without dividing intervals. Therefore, we can calculate the probability distribution of all measures about each attack and normal from KDD CUP 99 data set according to above conditions. Table 1 shows the list of measures that revises KDD CUP 99 data set and the bold font are to change from continuous measures to discrete.

We can select to useful measures to differentiate the attacks from the normal by analyzing the probability distributions. Figure 2 shows the probability distribution of *logged_in* that is one of the measures of discrete attribute. *logged_in* is 12th measure among 41 measures. It has the binary value of 0 or 1. We can select the features of 100 percent success to log-in through the distribution of *back* attack in Figure 2. And attacks such as *phf, teardrop, smurf, satan* and *portsweep* appears to be the features of 100 percent fail to log-in 100 percent.

Table 1. The revised list of KDD CUP 99 data set

Type	Attribute	Name
Basic feature	discrete	protocol_type, service, flag, land, **wrong_fragment, urgent**
	continuous	duration, src_byte, dst_byte
Contents feature	discrete	logged_in, root_shell, su_attempted, is_hot_login, is_guest_login, **hot, num_failed_logins, num_file_creations, num_shells, num_access_files ,num_outbound_cmds**
	continuous	num_compromised, num_root
Traffic feature	discrete	-
	continuous	count, serror_rate, rerror_rate, srv_rerror_rate, same_srv_rate,diff_srv_rate, srv_diff_host_rate, dst_host_count,dst_host_srv_count, dst_host_same_srv_rate, dst_host_diff_srv_rate, dst_host_same_src_port_rate, dst_host_srv_diff_host_rate, st_host_serror_rate, dst_host_srv_serror_rate. dst_host_rerror_rate, dst_host_srv_rerror_rate

Figure 3 shows the probability distribution of *serror_rate* that is one of the continuous measures. It is the twenty-fourth measure in all continuous attributes. The value of the measure is error ratio of "SYN" during network connection. We could observe that *smurf* has 100 percent error rate, and normal and the attacks such as *imap, neptune, teardrop,* etc., have low error ratio. Although figure 3 does not show, the attacks such as *spy, rootkit,* etc., do not have the error ratio. Also after observing

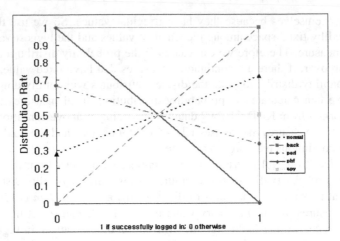

Fig. 2. The probability distribution about logged_in that is the discrete measure, 1 if sussefully logged in; 0 otherwise

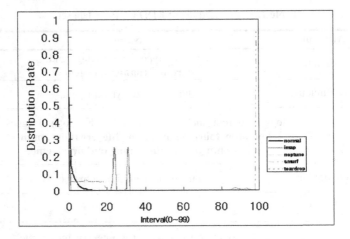

Fig. 3. The probability distribution about serror_rate that is the continuous measure

the probability distribution of other measures, we find that others have features to differentiate the attacks from the normal.

3.4 Selecting Measures Based on Statistical Method

We used *kddcup.data_10_percent.data* that is training data in KDD CUP 99 data set. The *kddcup.data_10_percent.data* which includes the normal and twenty-two attacks is 10 percent of *kddcup.data* to provide forty-one measures in network connection. However, all of the measures do not have features that are able to differentiate between the normal and each attack.

Relative entropy measures the distance of the regularities between two datasets. For example, if $p=q_j$, then the distance is 0, indicating that the two datasets have same regularity [17]. In order to select the useful measures that can classify measures into normal and attacks because we propose a statistical approach based on *relative entropy*. It calculates *distance* between two discrete probability distributions $p(X)$ and $q(X)$ over the same variable vector X. An expression for *relative entropy* is given by

$$D_j = D_{KL}(p(X), q_j(X)) + D_{KL}(q_j(X), p(X)) \tag{1}$$

$$D_{KL}(p(X), q_j(X)) = \sum_X q_j(X) \ln\left(\frac{q_j(X)}{p(X)}\right) \tag{2}$$

where $j \in \{ 1, 2, \ldots, m\}$ is the index of each attack, $X \in \{ x_1, x_2, \ldots, x_N\}$ is a measure vector of random variable(N is the number of all measures and m is the number of attacks). Also $p(X)$ and $q_j(X)$ represent the probability distribution for the normal and the jth attack respectively. It is assumed that the vector X has the independent elements. Equation (1) calculates relative entropy for calculating *distance* between the measure of the normal and that of each attack. According to the values of the D_j, we can select it as the measure of jth attack that is useful for classification. The higher value of D_j represents that the measure X has the different probability distribution between the normal and each attack such that it means a useful measure for jth attack. We discard the measure of low value of D_j because it does not contain the discriminative information. By varying the threshold value of D_j, we can control the total number of the useful measure for jth attack.

3.5 Generation of Detection Rule Using Decision Tree Algorithm

These are methods that generate rules and detect attacks using decision tree algorithm modifying the *C4.5* to process network data based on TCP connections.

To generate detection rules, it extracts and selects information of each session from training data and then constructs nodes by calculating IGs(Information Gains) according to entropy reduction. After construct trees by repeating these processes, the rules generated by calculating errors until final nodes of each tree so that it is used to detection processing.

3.5.1 Discrete Measure
Construction of efficient trees for discrete measures is what calculates values of entropy and constructs into the upper node for measures obtained the highest IGs according to entropy reduction. First, in equation (3), entropy for all class calculated

$$Entropy(D) = \sum_{j=1}^{m} -(p_j) \log(p_j) \tag{3}$$

where m and p_i represent the number of classes, and a probability that one class appeared in all classes.

Next, to construct each node of trees, an entropy reduction among measures is estimated. Reduction of entropy is method to the most easy distinguish among classes and calculated equation (4).

$$IGs(D, A) = Entropy(D) - \sum_{f \in value(A)} \frac{|D_f|}{|D|} Entropy(D_f) \tag{4}$$

where A and D_f represent each measure and the frequency of each value in the measure A, respectively. After calculating IGs of each measure, the measure that has the maximum IGs constructs the most upper node. After the most upper node decided, a tree of *level-1* is completed. It is progressed iteratively until the entropy of the most upper node becomes 0 that a process calculates entropy for total classes and constructs each node of trees.

A classification for continuous measures applied a threshold. That is, it finds a threshold that could get the largest entropy reduction by calculating entropy when a set of variables divided by threshold. A calculating method of entropy is the same as presented previous and need a large of time for calculation to find accurate limits [18].

Figure 4 shows composition of rules that compose rule no., rule name (class) and several conditions. It is converted from decision tree that is generated by C4.5 to rules. The conditions of the rule have the irregular number.

Rule No.	Rule Name (Class)	1st Rule Condition	2nd Rule Condition	...	nth Rule Condition

4   :   warezclient   ; dst_host_srv_diff_host_rate <= 0.48 ; service = ftp ; hot > 24 ; hot <= 28;

Fig. 4. The composition of the detection rule

4 Experiment and Result

This chapter shows the results of the test that experiment with KDD CUP 99 data set using the methods of the chapter 3. In these experiments, we selected useful measures and generated detection rules. Finally, this paper presents the result of the detection. The Experiments used *kddcup.data_10_percent.data* of KDD CUP 99 data set for selecting measures and generating rules and *corrected.data* for testing.

4.1 Selecting Measures

Table 2 shows the selected measures that satisfy condition that is $D_j \geq dist$(where, *dist* = { 0.0, 1.0, ..., 45.0}) using *relative entropy*. And it shows that measures were decreased by the increases of the distance.

We have known that 2 ~ 4 measures were not chosen when the distance increases in table 2. The detection rules were not generated when the condition, $D_j \geq 46.0$, is satisfied, because the selected measures were not existed. So the above condition of the experiments was excepted.

4.2 Generating the Detection Rule

The Experiment was required to generate detection rules using selected measures. Table 5 shows the number of the detection rules of each attack by the increase of the

Table 2. The selected measures by the increases of the distance

No. of meas. \ distance	0	1	2	5	14	16	21	25	29	31	40	45
1	O	O										
2	O	O	O	O	O	O						
3	O	O	O	O	O	O	O	O	O	O	O	
4	O	O	O	O	O	O	O	O	O			
5	O											
35	O	O	O	O	O	O	O					
36	O	O	O	O	O	O	O					
37	O	O	O	O	O							
38	O	O	O	O	O	O	O	O	O	O		
39	O	O	O	O	O	O	O	O	O	O		
40	O	O	O	O								
41	O	O	O	O								

Omitted distance's number :
3, 4, 6 ~ 13, 15, 17~ 20, 22 ~ 24, 26 ~ 28, 30, 32 ~ 39, 41 ~ 44
Omitted measure's number :
6 ~ 34

Table 3. The number of generating detection rules of each attack by the increase of distance

attacks \ distance	0	1	2	5	14	16	21	25
Back	5	8	137	74	78			
buffer_overflow	71	7	7	6	5	2		
ftp_write	4	3	5	4	3			
guess_passwd	1	3	1	2	2	4		
Imap	73	72	8	6	5	1		
Pod	2	2	2	2	4	2	2	1
Portsweep	11	21	149	87	91	5	1	
Satan	11	21	149	87	91	5	1	
Smurf	74	8	8	7	71	5	5	1
Spy	0	0	1	1	1	1		
Teardrop	2	70	4	5	140	1	1	1
Ipsweep	8	77	137	11	13	1	1	
Warezclient	85	78	87	16	75	6		
Warezmaster	2	2	2	3	2			

Omitted distance's number : 2 ~ 13, 15, 17 ~ 20, 22 ~ 30, 32 ~ 39, 41 ~ 44
Omitted attacks : land, loadmodule, multihop,netpune, nmap, perl, phf, rootkit, ipsweep

distance. According to the increase of the distance, we have known a lot of changes that are the number of the detection rules of each attack as well as the number of the whole detection rules in table 3.

4.3 The Result of Test

We executed the test is detects attacks using generated the detection rules. The result is shown in figure 5 that shows high detection rate more than 97 percent in the distance between 10.0 and 20.0. Figure 5 shows that the false positive rate in the distance between 10.0 and 30.0 is lower than other distances. We have known that there are many changes of the detection rules, the detection rate, and the false positive rate through figure 5.

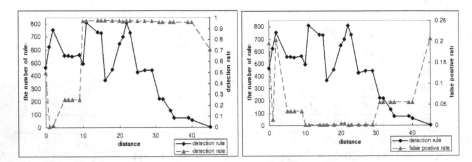

Fig. 5. The first figure is the number of the rules and detection rate by the changes of the distance. The second thing is the number of the rules and False Positive Rate by the changes of the distance.

Table 4. The selected main measures of all attacks when the codition is $D_j \geq 16.0$

No.	Name	Attribute	Distance
2	protocol_type	discrete	19.226
3	service	discrete	44.695
4	flag	discrete	30.334
7	land	discrete	34.510
8	wrong_fragment	continuous	45.999
10	hot	continuous	30.740
12	logged_in	discrete	17.229
14	root_shell	continuous	31.368
19	num_access_files	continuous	28.354
23	count	continuous	20.871
24	srv_count	continuous	20.609
26	srv_serror_rate	continuous	30.907
31	srv_diff_host_rate	continuous	22.423
32	dst_host_count	continuous	26.183
34	dst_host_same_srv_rate	continuous	24.213
37	dst_host_srv_diff_host_rate	continuous	33.553
38	dst_host_serror_rate	continuous	39.335

Omitted measures : 17, 18, 25, 33, 35

If many detection rules that are consisted of many nodes are generated, many computing time, processing time, cost, etc., will be consumed. If the generated rules are very accurate, they are equal to the training data. So, we will see many false alarms in test. Useful and accurate detection rules that have the small number of node are required for satisfactory results. When the condition is $D_j \geq 16.0$, it is the optimum distance.

Also we have known that the rules that are generated by the condition are most suitable. Table 4 shows the measure names, the types and the distance value of all attack. They are the optimum when the distance is 16.0. And we have understood easily the features of each attack when we analyzed the results that show the detection rules, the selected measures in the experiments.

5 Conclusion and Future Work

In this paper, we proposed two methods that are the statistical method and decision tree algorithm for generating the detection rules. The statistical method is used to choose useful measures in whole measures, and decision tree algorithm is used to generate detection rule for the accurate detection. We used KDD CUP 99 data set in this experiment. In the result of the experiments, the number of the selected measures was decreased by the increase of the distance. And the generating detection rules were changed by the selected measures. Because very accurate rules that are similar to training data generate many nodes in tree, the high false positive rate and the low detection rate are occurred in this experiment. In addition to, the useful and accurate detection rules are required for satisfactory results. Therefore, in this paper, we have known the useful distance and measures that are the high detection rate, the low false positive rate and the small detection rules in the experiment. Also, the generated detection rules based on decision tree algorithm is more efficient than expert's system because it is easy for detection rules to generate and understand. As well as, it cut down waste of time, cost, etc.

In future, we will apply the methods in real-time network and get attack data of bulk for generating accurate detection rules of large quantity. And, we will generate detection rules for attacks with ICMP and UDP protocols using decision tree algorithm and progress wide experiments.

Reference

1. Denning, D. E.: An Intrusion-Detection Model. IEEE Trans. on Software Engineering. No.2. (1987)
2. The third international Knowledge discovery and data mining tools competition dataset KDD99 CUP, http://kdd.ics.uci.edu/databases/kddcup99/kddcup99.html. (1998)
3. Mahoney, M., Chan, P.: PHAD: Packet Header Anomaly Detection for Identifying Hostile Network Traffic. Florida Institute of Tech. Technical Report CS-2001-4. (2001)
4. Mahoney, M., Chan, P.: Learning Models of Network Traffic for Detecting Novel Attacks. Florida Institute of Tech. Technical Report CS-2002-08. (2002)
5. Templeton, S., Levitt, K.: Detecting Spoofed Packets. Proc. of the DARPA Information Survivability Conferences and Exposition. (2003)

6. Bykova, M.: Detecting Network Intrusions via a Statistical Analysis of Network Packet Characteristics. the 33rd Southeastern Symposium on System Theory(SSST2001). Ohio Univ. (2001) 18-20
7. Bykova, M., Ostermann, S.: Statistical Analysis of Malformed Packets and Their Origins in the Modern Internet. 2nd IMW 2002. (2002)
8. Feinstein, L., Schnackenberg, D., Balupari, R., Kindred, D.: statistical Approaches to DDos Attack Detection and Response. Proc. of the DARPA Information Survivability Conferences and Exposition (DISCEX'03) (2003)
9. Mukkamala, S., Sung, A.: Identifying Significant Features for Network Forensic Analysis Using Artificial Intelligent Techniques. Intl. of Digital Evidence. Vol. 1. (2003)
10. Chris, S., Lyn, P., Sara, M.: An Application of Machine Learning to Network Intrusion Detection. 54th Annual Computer Security application Conference. (1999)
11. Bigus, J.: Data Mining with Neural Networks. McGraw-Hill. (1996)
12. Pearl, J.: Probabilistic Reasoning in Intelligent System. 2nd edn. Morgan Kaufmann. Networks of Plausible Inference. (1997)
13. Barbara, D., Wu, N., Jajodia, S.: Detecting Novel Network Intrusions using Bayes Estimators. 1st SIA International Conf. on Data Mining. (2001)
14. Ross Quinlan, J.: C4.5:Programs for Machine Learning. Morgan Kaufmann. San Mateo. California. (1993)
15. Mitchell, T.: Machine Learning. McGraw-Hill. (1997)
16. Richard, P., David Freid, J.: Evaluating Intrusion Detection System: The 1998 DARPA off-line Intrusion Detection Evaluation.
17. Lee, W., Xiang, D.: Information-Theoretic Measures for Anomaly Detection. IEEE Symposium on Security and Privacy. (2001)
18. Yoh-Han P.: Adaptive Pattern Recognition and Neural Networks, Addison-Wesley (1989)

The Conflict Detection Between Permission Assignment Constraints in Role-Based Access Control*

Chang-Joo Moon[1], Woojin Paik[1], Young-Gab Kim[2], and Ju-Hum Kwon[3],**

[1] Department of Computer Science, Konkuk University,
322 Danwol-dong, Chungju-si, Chungcheongbuk-do, 380-701, Korea
{cjmoon, wjpaik}@kku.ac.kr
[2] Department of Computer Science and Engineering, Korea University,
Anam-dong 5-ga, Seongbuk-gu, 136-701, Seoul, Korea
ygkim@software.korea.ac.kr
[3] Korea Air Force Central Computer Center, P.O.Box 501-329, Bunam-ri,
Namseon-myeon, Gyeryong-si, Chungcheongnam-do, 321-929, Korea
jkweon@gmail.com

Abstract. Assuring integrity of permission assignment (PA) constraints is a difficult task in role-based access control (RBAC) because of the large number of constraints, users, roles and permissions in a large enterprise environment. We provide solutions to this problem using the conflict concept. This paper introduces the conflict model in order to understand the conflicts easily and to detect conflicts effectively. The conflict model is classified as a permission-permission model and a role-permission model. This paper defines two type conflicts using the conflict model. The first type is an inter-PA-constraints (IPAC) conflict that takes place between PA constraints. The other type is a PA–PAC conflict that takes place between a PA and a PA constraint (PAC). Also, the conditions of conflict occurrence are formally specified and proved. We can assure integrity on permission assignment by checking conflicts before PA and PA constraints are applied.

1 Introduction

The principle motivations behind RBAC are the ability of specify and enforce enterprise-specific access control policies and to streamline the typically burdensome process of authorization management [1]. The main idea of RBAC is that permissions are associated with appropriate roles, and users are assigned to roles, thereby acquiring the users' permissions. In a large enterprise the management of RBAC is a very difficult task due to the number of roles can be up to thousands; the number of users can be up to hundreds of thousands; and the number of permissions can easily exceed a million. Moreover the business processes and the security requirements change as the business environment changes. Because of this change, the authorization information, the user assignment (UA) and the permission assignment (PA) [1] information, also needs to be changed. In spite of these difficult conditions, the security managers should make sure that the RBAC server must safely authorize permissions.

---

* This work was supported by the faculty research fund of Konkuk University in 2005.
** Corresponding author.

D. Feng, D. Lin, and M. Yung (Eds.): CISC 2005, LNCS 3822, pp. 265–278, 2005.

The constraints specify the rules which must be observed during UA and PA. The permission assignment which only depends on the judgment of the security manager without constraint is not desirable considering the large number of permissions, users, roles and constraints. Therefore the constraints are the core aspect of safe permission assignment. But the conflicts between constraints decidedly exist in a large enterprise, because PA and UA constraints are prepared by multiple security managers and many constraints exist. These conflicts need to be solved in order to assure integrity of UA and PA. If there are two conflicting PA constraints, no the permission assignment can satisfy both two constraints, and thus integrity on permission assignment is broken.

Previous studies [2, 3, 4, 5] defined the conflicts of the interest using separation of duty, which ensure that critical operations are divided among two or more people, so that no single person can compromise security. If a security manager implements UA and PA constraints which satisfy separation of duty concept and observe the constraints, the safe permission authorization can be achieved. But the separation of duty is just one among various constraints and previous studies are under a bias toward UA part. There has been no study on the conflicts between various constraints and the work on formal specification of conflicts was also lacking. This paper concentrates on conflicts between PA constraints because the integrity on user assignment is meaningless if the conflicts between PA constraints are detected. Even though, a user has been correctly assigned a role, the user cannot have the proper permissions if the role has improper permissions. Therefore, it is challenging to avoid the conflicts between PA constraints.

This paper introduces the PA constraints [6, 7] which are absolutely necessary in order to understand the conflicts. The proposed conflict model can be used by the security managers to understand the conflicts easily and to detect conflicts effectively. The conflict model is classified as a permission-permission model and a role-permission model. The former defines a conflict based on relationships between permissions. The latter defines a conflict based on relationships between role and permission. We defines two types conflicts using the conflict model, one is an inter-PA-constraints (IPAC) conflict that takes place between PA constraints, and the other is a PA–PAC conflict that takes place between a PA and a PA constraint(PAC). Also, the conflict occurrence conditions are formally specified and proved. A security manager can assure integrity on permission assignment by checking the conflicts before PA and PA constraints are applied.

In the Chapter 2, the RBAC model and the PA constraints are described. In the chapter 3, the conflict model is proposed. In the Chapter 4, IPAC conflict and PA-PAC conflict based on the conflict model is discussed. Lastly in the Chapter 5, the conclusion to this paper is described.

2 Background

2.1 RBAC Model

The concept of RBAC began with multi-user and multi-application on-line systems pioneered in the 1970s [8, 9]. Fig. 1 is a conceptual diagram of the RBAC96 model [8].

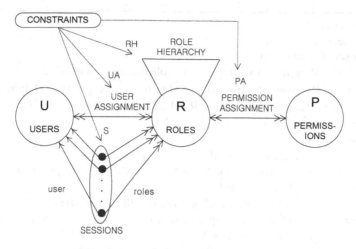

Fig. 1. RBAC model

The RBAC model can effectively manage users and permissions by using role concept. The central notation of RBAC is that permissions are associated with roles, and users are assigned to appropriate roles. This basic concept has the advantage of simplifying the understanding and management of permissions. The model has four elements: users, roles, permissions and sessions. A user (U) represents a human activity or an autonomous agent, while a role (R) is a job function or job title within the organization with some associated semantics regarding the authority and responsibility conferred on a member of the role [6]. A permission (P) is an approval of a particular mode of access to one or more objects in the system. Fig 1 shows UA and PA relations. Both relations are many-to-many relations. The constraint specifies the rules which must be observed during UA and PA. Role Hierarchy (RH) specifies hierarchical structure of the roles. RH is a specific form of the constraints. A senior role inherits the permissions of its junior ones through the hierarchy.

2.2 Constraint on Permission Assignment

This section shows the representative PA constraints, which had been studied previously [6] as preceding work for this paper. These PA constraints are necessary in order to understand the conflicts between PA constraints. Fig. 2 shows the basic elements [6, 7] and the functions, which are necessary to specify the PA constraints and the conflict model.

1) Disjoint Permission (DP) Constraint
The DP constraints prevent that critical permission is assigned two roles which are declared separation of duty. If the DP constraints are not applied, the two roles have the critical permission and then conflict of interest is occurred. Fig. 3 shows the elements of the DP constraints. The static separation of duty (SSD) [1,4] which is essential for the understanding of the DP constraints are defined as shown in the following at first.

$\mathbf{R}$ = a set of roles, $\{r_1, \ldots, r_n\}$

$\mathbf{U}$ = a set of users, $\{u_1, \ldots, u_m\}$

$\mathbf{P}$ = a set of permissions, $\{p_1, \ldots, p_o\}$

$\mathbf{UA} \subseteq \mathbf{U} \times \mathbf{R}$, a many-to-many user-to-role assignment relation.

$\mathbf{PA} \subseteq \mathbf{P} \times \mathbf{R}$, a many-to-many permission-to-role assignment relation.

$\mathbf{RH} \subseteq \mathbf{R} \times \mathbf{R}$ is a partial order on R called the role hierarchy.

$\mathbf{users} : \mathbf{R} \to 2^{\mathbf{U}}$, a function mapping each role r_a to a set of users. ($1 \le a \le n$)

$\mathbf{users}(r_a) = \{u \in \mathbf{U} \mid (u, r_a) \in \mathbf{UA}\}$,

   a function returns all users that are assigned r_a.

$\mathbf{perms} : \mathbf{R} \to 2^{\mathbf{P}}$, a function mapping each role r_a to a set of permissions.

$\mathbf{perms}(r_a) = p \in \mathbf{P} \mid (p, r_a) \in \mathbf{PA}\}$,

   a function returns all permissions that are assigned r_a.

$\mathbf{roles} : \mathbf{P} \to 2^{\mathbf{R}}$, a function mapping each role p_b to a set of roles. ($1 \le b \le o$)

$\mathbf{roles}(p_b) = \{r \in \mathbf{R} \mid (p_b, r) \in \mathbf{PA}\}$,

   a function returns all roles that p_b is assigned.

$\mathbf{juniors} : \mathbf{R} \to 2^{\mathbf{R}}$, a function mapping each role r_a to a set of roles that are junior role of r_a.

$\mathbf{juniors}(r_a) = \{r \in \mathbf{R} \mid (r_a, r) \in \mathbf{RH}\}$,

   a function returns all roles that are junior role of r_a.

$\mathbf{seniors} : \mathbf{R} \to 2^{\mathbf{R}}$, a function mapping each role r_a to a set of roles that are senior role of r_a.

$\mathbf{seniors}(r_a) = \{r \in \mathbf{R} \mid (r_a, r) \in \mathbf{RH}\}$,

   a function returns all roles that are senior role of r_a.

Fig. 2. Basic elements and functions for PA constraints

$\mathbf{ssd}$ = a set of roles that are declared static separation of duty, $\{sr_1, \ldots, sr_q\}$, $\mathbf{ssd} \subseteq \mathbf{R}$

$\mathbf{SSD}$ = a set of $\mathbf{ssd}$, $\{ssd_1, \ldots, ssd_p\}$

$\mathbf{dp}$ = a set of permissions that are applied DP constraint, $\mathbf{dp} \subseteq \mathbf{P}$

$\mathbf{DP}$ = a set of $\mathbf{dp}$, $\{dp_1, \ldots, dp_p\}$

   dp_c and ssd_c form a pair. ($1 \le c \le p$)

Fig. 3. Elements of DP constraint

Definition 1. (SSD constraint).

No user can be assigned with two or more roles that belong to **ssd**.

The formal specification for **Definition 1** is as follows.

$$\forall \mathbf{ssd} \ \left(\bigcap_{d=1}^{q} \mathbf{users}(sr_d) = \varnothing \right)$$

Lemma 1. There exists no senior role common to roles belonging to **ssd**.

Proof. Suppose the role r_1 and r_2 specifying the static separation of duty is declared and the role r_3 is a senior role with respect to r_1 and r_2. The user, who is assigned r_3, causes problems of security, because the user has both permissions of r_1 and r_2. Therefore, the senior role is not allowed for the roles, which are declared static separation of duty.

The formal specification for **Lemma 1** is as follows.

$$\forall \, \textbf{ssd} \; (\bigcap_{d=1}^{q} \textbf{seniors}(sr_d) = \varnothing \,)$$

Definition 2 (DP Constraint).
The permissions belonging to **dp** cannot be assigned to two or more roles belonging to **ssd**.

The formal specification for **Definition 2** is as follows.

$$\forall \, \textbf{ssd} \; (\bigcap_{d=1}^{q} (\textbf{perms}(sr_d) \cap \textbf{dp}) = \varnothing \,)$$

2) Conflicting Permissions (CP) Constraint
This constraint describes the conflict of interest between permissions. If a user has conflicting permissions, the user has permission which exceeds his/her authority and can compromise security. Fig. 4 shows the elements of the CP constraint.

> **cp** = a set of conflict permissions,
> $\{cp\_p_1, \ldots, cp\_p_u\}$, **cp** $\subseteq$ **P**
> **CP** = a set of cp, $\{cp_1, \ldots, cp_t\}$,
> **RC** = **R** × **CP**, $\{(r, cp) \in \textbf{RC} \mid r \in \textbf{R} \land cp \in \textbf{CP}\}$
> **counts**(S) : returns the number of elements in the set S

Fig. 4. Elements of CP constraint

Definition 3 (CP constraint).
Two or more permissions belonging to a **cp** cannot be assigned to the same role.

The formal specification for **Definition 3** is as follows.

$$\forall (r, cp) \, (\, \textbf{count} \, (\textbf{perms}(r) \cap cp) \leq 1)$$

3) Prerequisite Permission (PP) Constraint
Permission p can be assigned to a role only if that role already possesses permission q. The PP constraint is useful to define permissions which should coexist in a role. Fig. 5 shows the elements of the PP constraints. The PP constraints are specified as a structure in the form of [permissions (tp), relations (ao), set of prerequisite permission (pps)]. The permission tp requires a prerequisite permission, and ao is either 'AND' or 'OR'. The pps is a set of prerequisite permission with respect to tp.

Definition 4 (PP constraint).

(i) If *ao* is an 'AND', then all the permissions of *pps* should have been already assigned to the roles, in order for *tp* to be assigned to a role.

(ii) If *ao* is an 'OR', then one or more permissions of *pps* should have been already assigned to the roles, in order for *tp* to be assigned to a role.

---

tp = a permission that requires a prerequisite permission, $tp \in \mathbf{P}$

pps = a set of prerequisite permission, $\{pps\_p_1, \ldots, pps\_p_w\}$, $pps \subseteq \mathbf{P}$

pp = a structure consisting of permissions (*tp*), relations (*ao*) and set of prerequisite permissions (*pps*), [*tp, ao, pps*], *ao* = 'AND' or 'OR'

PP = a set of **pp**, $\{pp_1, \ldots, pp_v\}$

Fig. 5. Elements of PP constraint

The formal specification for **Definition 4** is as follows.

(i) $\forall r \forall pp(((tp \in \mathbf{perms}(r)) \wedge (ao=\text{'AND'})) \rightarrow pps \subseteq \mathbf{perms}(r))$

(ii) $\forall r \forall pp(((tp \in \mathbf{perms}(r)) \wedge (ao=\text{'OR'})) \rightarrow pps\_p_i \in \mathbf{perms}(r))$ $(1 \leq i \leq w)$

4) Permission Assigned to Single Role (PASR) Constraint

The PASR constraints are used when a particular permission is only assigned to a single role for business specific or security reasons. Fig. 6 shows the elements of the PASR constraints. These constraints are specified as a structure of [roles (*pasr_r*), permission set (*pasr_ps*)].

---

pasr = a structure consisting of role (*pasr_r*) and set of permission (*pasr_ps*),
   [*pasr_r, pasr_ps*], *pasr_r* $\in \mathbf{R}$, *pasr_ps* $\subseteq \mathbf{P}$

PASR = a set of **pasr**, $\{pasr_1, \ldots, pasr_x\}$

cop = A set of all the roles with *pasr_r* and its senior roles excluded,
   $\mathbf{R} - (\{pasr\_r\} \cup \mathbf{seniors}(pasr\_r))$, $\{cop\_r_1, \ldots, cop\_r_y\}$

Fig. 6. Elements of PASR constraint

Definition 5 (PASR constraint).

Permissions included in *pasr_ps* are assigned to role *pasr_r* and roles belonging to seniors (*pasr_r*) only.

The formal specification for Definition 5 is as follows.

$$\forall pasr ((pasr\_ps \subseteq \mathbf{perms}(pasr\_r)) \wedge$$

$$(pasr\_ps \cap \bigcup_{k=1}^{y} \mathbf{perms}(cop\_r_k) = \varnothing)).$$

3 Conflict Model

The conflict model is used by the security managers to understand the conflicts easily and to detect conflicts effectively. The conflict model is classified as a permission-permission model and the role-permission model as shown in Fig. 7 and the basic elements in Fig.2 are used to explain two models.

In a permission-permission model, we represented a permission with a circle and a relationship with a directed line. The relationship exists between permissions and connects permissions. An *association* and *disjoint* relationships are possible. If an *association* relationship is set between two permissions, these permissions should be assigned to a role of the pair. Therefore the *association* relationship expresses dependency relation between two permissions. If a *disjoint* relationship is set between two permissions, these permissions should not be assigned to the same role. Therefore *disjoint* relationship expresses expulsive relation between two permissions. If any relationship is not set between two permissions, two permissions can be assigned to the role in pair or otherwise. The PA constraints are divided into association constraint and disjoint constraint according to their own characteristics. The former sets *association* relationship between permissions and the later sets *disjoint* relationship between permissions. If the constraint is deleted, *association* or *disjoint* relationship is also removed.

In the role-permission model, a permission is represented with a circle, and a role is showed as a rounded rectangle, and a relationship expressed by a directed line. The relationship exists between roles and permissions. An *inclusion* and *exclusion* relationships are possible. If an *inclusion* relationship is set between a role and a permission, the permission should be assigned to the role. If an *exclusion* relationship is set between a role and a permission, the permission should have not been assigned to the role. Therefore two relationships express dependency and expulsive relation between role and permission. If any relationship is not set between a role and a permission, the permission can be assigned to the role or otherwise. Also the PA constraints are divided into an inclusion constraint and an exclusion constraint according to its own characteristics. The former sets *inclusion* relationship between the role and the permission. The later sets *disjoint* relationship between the role and the permission.

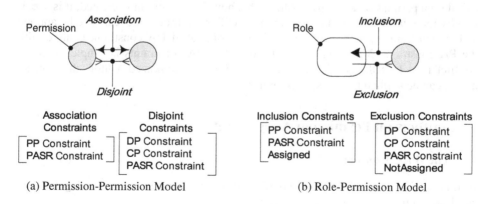

(a) Permission-Permission Model   (b) Role-Permission Model

Fig. 7. Conflict model

The association and inclusion constraint are the PP constraint and the PASR constraint. The PP constraint requires that both the permission and its prerequisite permissions are assigned to the same role. Therefore, the PP constraint sets *association* relationship between these permissions. In addition, if the permission belongs to a specific role, the prerequisite permissions have to belong to the same role. Therefore, the PP constraint also sets an *inclusion* relationship between a specific role and the prerequisite permissions. The PASR constraint requires that the permissions, elements of *pasr_ps*, be assigned to an only specific role which is *pasr_r* role. Because the permissions must always coexist in to the specific role, the PASR constraint sets an *association* relationship between the permissions. In addition, the PASR constraint directly sets *inclusion* relationship between the specific role and the permissions.

The disjoint and exclusion constraints are DP, CP and PASR constraints. The DP constraint sets *disjoint* relationship in the course of restricting permission assignment. For instance, if **ssd**=$\{r_1, r_2, r_3\}$ and **dp**=$\{p_3, p_4, p_5\}$, then permissions p_3, p_4 and p_5 cannot be assigned to roles r_1, r_2 and r_3 more than once. Therefore assignments such as **perms**(r_1)=$\{p_1, p_3\}$, **perms**(r_2)=$\{p_2, p_4\}$ and **perms**(r_3)=$\{p_1, p_2, p_5\}$ are possible. Once the assignment has been made as shown previously, it is impossible to assign p_4 and p_5 to r_1. So DP constraint sets *disjoint* relationship between p_1 and p_4 or p_1 and p_5 in r_1. Also the DP constraint sets *exclusion* relationship between r_1 and p_4 or r_1 and p_5. The CP constraint represents that the permissions, which are the elements of **cp**, cannot coexist in same role due to conflicts of interest. It sets *disjoint* relationship between the permissions. Besides, since if one of the permissions, which are an element of **cp**, is assigned to a specific role, the CP constraint sets an *exclusion* relationship between the other permissions in **cp** and a specific role. For example, if a constraint is defined CP=$\{\{p_1, p_2\}, \{p_3, p_4\}\}$, p_1 and p_2 cannot coexist in the role and thus a *disjoint* relationship is set between p_1 and p_2. If p_1 is assigned to r_1, an *exclusion* relationship is set between p_2 and r_1. In case the PASR constraint is declared, the permissions, which are the elements of *pasr_ps*, have to be assigned to the only specific role which is *pasr_r* role and thus *disjoint* relationship is set between element of *pasr_ps* and elements of *pasr_ps'* that have to be assigned to the other specific role which is *pasr_r'*. So, the PASR constraint can set an *association* and a *disjoint* relationship.

The conflict model can be accommodated to the newly added PA constraints hereafter because it handles basic relationship (*association, disjoint, inclusion, exclusion*) based on a permission and a role. Although a new PA constraint is created, it is specified by the relationships of the conflict model. The conflict model can also be applied to UA constraint symmetrically, because the concept of UA constraint is alike with the PA constraint. Maybe the conflict model for UA constraints is simpler than the conflict model. If the conflict model is modified or minimized a little, the conflict model can be applied to the user assignment.

4   Conflicts on Permission Assignment

4.1 The IPAC Conflicts

In this section, we define IPAC conflicts using the conflict model and generalize condition of the IPAC conflict occurrence.

Definition 6. The IPAC conflict occurs if an *association* relationship and a *disjoint* relationship are set to the same permission-permission relation link.

Definition 7. The IPAC conflict occurs if an *inclusion* relationship and an *exclusion* relationship are set to the same role-permission relation link.

Definition 8. If an *association* relationship is released by an *exclusion* relationship, then the IPAC conflict takes place and vice versa.

Definition 9. If an *inclusion* relationship is released by a *disjoint* relationship, then the IPAC conflict takes place and vice versa.

Table 1 shows the possible combinations of four PA constraints mentioned in the Chapter 2. Since the sequence is disregarded, there are ten possible combinations, and each combination has IPAC conflict value among *No*, *Maybe* and *Yes*. *No* means that no IPAC conflict arises regardless of the contents of the constraints. *Maybe* means that IPAC conflict cannot be determined definitely from only the contents of the constraints. In this case, if additional contents of the assignment are checked, it is possible to judge IPAC conflict. In case of *Yes*, IPAC conflict can be determined from the contents of only the PA constraints.

To define the IPAC conflict, the basic elements of each constraint in the Chapter 2 are used. We will use "." as accessor to access elements of the structure in PP and PASR constraint. We show the generalized conditions of IPAC conflict occurrence and the method of IPAC conflict detection using the conflict model.

Table 1. IPAC conflict value

Constraint	DP	CP	PP	PASR
DP	*No*	-	-	-
CP	*No*	*No*	-	-
PP	*Maybe*	*Yes*	*No*	-
PASR	*No*	*Yes*	*Maybe*	*Yes*

1) IPAC conflict between DP and PP constraint

Theorem 1. With regard to arbitrary **dp**, **pp**, **pp'**, if **count**$(pp.pps \cap pp'.pps) \geq 1$ and $pp.pps \cap pp'.pps \subseteq$ **dp**, then the IPAC conflict value is *Maybe*. If assignment information such that $pp.tp \in r$, $pp'.tp \in r'$, and $\{r, r'\} \subseteq$ **ssd** is confirmed, then the IPAC conflict value is *Yes*.

Proof. Permission p, which is an element of $pp.pps \cap pp'.pps$ is assigned to an arbitrary role according to the assignment information of permissions $pp.tp$ and $pp'.tp$. At this time, the PP constraint sets an *inclusion* relationship between permission p and specific roles that include $pp.tp$ or $pp'.tp$. However, this permission is assigned to only one of the roles which are elements of **ssd** because the p is an element of **dp**. At this time the DP constraint sets an *exclusion* relationship between the roles and p. Since the IPAC conflict may arise depending on the assignment of $pp.tp$ and $pp'.tp$ permissions, the IPAC conflict value is *Maybe*. If assignment information such as $pp.tp \in r$, $pp'.tp \in r'$ and $\{r, r'\} \subseteq$ **ssd** is confirmed, p should be assigned to one role among r, r', and others element of **ssd** by the DP constraint. Consequently, the IPAC conflict value is *Yes* by **Definition 7**.

Example 1. Fig. 8 has constraints PP={*[p₁, AND, {p₃}], [p₂, AND, {p₃}]*}, DP={*{p₁, p₂, p₃}*} and SSD={*{r, r'}*}. By the DP constraint, permission p_1, p_2, and p_3 should be assigned to one of roles r and r'. So the DP constraint can set *exclusion* relationship between p_3 and r. However owing to the PP constraint, prerequisite permission p_3 should be assigned to both of r and r' in order for p_1 to be assigned to r and p_2 to be assigned to r'. The PP constraint sets *inclusion* relationship between p_3 and r. Consequently, a conflict arises between the two constraints because an *inclusion* relationship and an *exclusion* relationship are set between p_3 and r. But if assignment information about p_1 and p_2 is not confirmed, we can merely mention the possibility of a conflict.

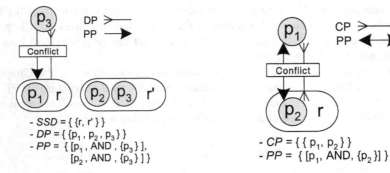

Fig. 8. IPAC conflict between DP and PP constraints

Fig. 9. IPAC conflict between CP and PP constraints

2) IPAC conflict between CP and PP constraint

Theorem 2. With regard to arbitrary **cp** and **pp**, if $pp.tp \in$ **cp** and **count(** $pp.pps$ $\cap$ cp **)** ≥ 1 is confirmed, then the IPAC conflict value is *Yes*.

Proof. The PP constraint sets *association* relationship between permission $pp.tp$ and permission p which is an element of $pp.pps$. However, because $pp.tp$ and p are elements of **cp**, these cannot coexist in the same role. So, the CP constraint sets *disjoint* relationship between $pp.tp$ and p. Consequently, the IPAC conflict takes place between the two constraints by **Definition. 6** and the IPAC conflict value is *Yes*.

Example 2. In Fig. 9, owing to PP={*[p₁, AND, {p₂}]*}, in order for permission p_1 to be assigned to role r, permission p_2 is needed indispensably. So the PP constraint sets *association* relationship between p_1 and p_2. However, by CP={*{p₁, p₂}*}, both p_1 and p_2 cannot be assigned to the r. So the CP constraint sets *disjoint* relationship between p_1 and p_2. Consequently, the IPAC conflict arises between the two constraints because an *association* relationship and a *disjoint* relationship are set between p_1 and p_2.

3) IPAC conflict between PP and PASR constraint

Theorem 3. With regard to arbitrary **pp** and **pasr**, if **count**(*pasr.pasr_ps* ∩ *pp.pps*) ≥ 1, then the IPAC conflict value is *Maybe*. If assignment information such that **count**(**roles**(*pp.tp*) ∩ **cop**) ≥ 1, then the IPAC conflict value is *Yes*.

Proof. By the PP constraint, permission *pp.tp* and permission *p* which is an element of *pasr.pasr_ps* ∩ *pp.pps* should be assigned together to an arbitrary role *r*. The PP constraint sets *association* relationship between *pp.tp* and *p*. Meanwhile, by the PASR constraint, *p* should be only assigned to role *pasr.pasr_r*. Therefore the IPAC conflict may arise depending on the assignment of *pp.tp* and the IPAC conflict value is *Maybe*. If *r* and *pasr.pasr_r* are the same role, the IPAC conflict does not take place. But unless *r* and *pasr.pasr_r* are the same role that is **count**(**roles**(*pp.tp*) ∩ **cop**) ≥ 1, the PASR constraint sets *exclusion* relationship between *p* and *r* and the IPAC conflict takes place between the two constraints by **Definition 8** and the IPAC conflict value is *Yes*.

Example 3. Fig. 10 shows the IPAC conflict between PP and PASR constraint using the conflict model. Owing to PP={*[p₁, AND, {p₂}]*}, in order for permission *p₁* to be assigned to role *r*, permission *p₂* must be indispensable. So the PP constraint sets *association* relationship between *p₁* and *p₂*. On the other hand, by PASR={*[r', {p₂}]*}, *p₂* should be only assigned to role *r'*. So the PASR constraint sets *exclusion* relationship between *r* and *p₂*. Consequently, the IPAC conflict arises between the two constraints because *association* relationship is released by an *exclusion* relationship. But, if assignment information about *p₁* is not confirmed, we can merely mention the possibility of the IPAC conflict.

4) IPAC conflicts between CP and PASR constraint

Theorem 4. With regard to arbitrary *cp* and *pasr*, if **count**(*pasr.pasr_ps* ∩ **cp**) ≥ 2, then the IPAC conflict value is *Yes*.

Proof. Let permissions *p₁* and *p₂* be {*p₁, p₂*} ⊂ (*pasr.pasr_ps* ∩ **cp**) holds true. The PASR constraint sets *association* relationship between *p₁* and *p₂*. However, since they are also elements of **cp**, they cannot coexist in the role *pasr.pasr_r*. So, the CP constraint sets *disjoint* relationship between *p₁* and *p₂*. Consequently, the IPAC conflict takes place between the two constraints by **Definition 7** and the IPAC conflict value is *Yes*.

Example 4. In Fig.11, owing to PASR={*[r, { p₁,p₂}]*}, permissions *p₁* and *p₂* should be assigned role *r* so the PASR constraint sets *association* relationship between *p₁* and *p₂*. However, by CP={{*p₁, p₂*}}, both *p₁* and *p₂* cannot be assigned to the *r* therefore the CP constraint sets *disjoint* therefore between *p₁* and *p₂*. Consequently, the IPAC conflict arises between the two constraints because an *association* relationship and a *disjoint* relationship are set between *p₁* and *p₂*.

5) IPAC Conflicts between PASR constraints

Theorem 5. With regard to arbitrary *pasr* and *pasr'*, if roles *pasr.pasr_r* and *pasr'.pasr_r* are not in hierarchical relationship and **count**(*pasr.pasr_ps* ∩ *pasr'.pasr_ps*) ≥ 1, then the conflict value is *Yes*.

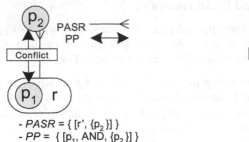

- $PASR = \{ [r', \{p_2\}] \}$
- $PP = \{ [p_1, AND, \{p_2\}] \}$

Fig. 10. IPAC conflict between PP and PASR constraints

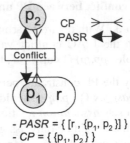

- $PASR = \{ [r, \{p_1, p_2\}] \}$
- $CP = \{ \{p_1, p_2\} \}$

Fig. 11. IPAC conflicts between CP and PASR constraints

Proof. Permission p, which is an element of *pasr.pasr_ps* ∩ *pasr'.pasr_ps* should be assigned to both of *pasr.pasr_r* and *pasr'.pasr_r*, which is not possible owing to the PASR constraint. In this case, the PASR constraint sets an *inclusion* relationship and an *exclusion* relationship between *pasr.pasr_r* and p_1 . Therefore the IPAC conflict takes place between two PASR constraints by **Definition 7** and the conflict value is *Yes*.

The example is skipped because the IPAC conflict between PASR constraints is simple.

4.2 PA-PAC Conflicts

The PA-PAC conflict arises when the permission assignments do not satisfy the PA constraint. The PA-PAC conflict takes place in the following two cases. The first is the case in which a constraint is newly created or changed so that existing permission assignment cannot satisfy the new constraint. The second is the case in which a permission assignment is newly created or changed so that existing constraints is not satisfied by the new permission assignment. In both of the cases, the PA-PAC conflict is detected by checking that whether an assignment information satisfies the PA constraints. We can use formal definition of the PA constraint in order to detect the PA-PAC conflict. If the permission assignment satisfies the formal definitions, PA-PAC conflict will not occur.

In the role-permission model, as the states, in which a permission is assigned to a role and otherwise, are specified as 'Assigned' and 'NotAssigned'. The PA-PAC conflicts can be shown as shown Fig. 12.

Since the contents of assignment are represented as an *inclusion* relationship and *exclusion* relationship by the conflict model, the Definition 7, 8, 9 are applied to PA-PAC conflicts. On the other hand, since in no case 'Assigned' and 'NotAssigned' are applied to the same role-permission link, the two states only conflict with the PA constraints. For instance, permission p_1 has been prevented from getting assigned to role r by a DP constraint which sets an *exclusion* relationship in Fig.12 (a). However, a PA-PAC conflict takes place because an *inclusion* relationship and an *exclusion* relationship are applied to the same role-permission link if p_1 is assigned to r.

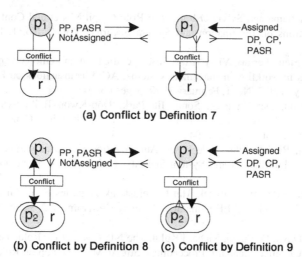

(a) Conflict by Definition 7

(b) Conflict by Definition 8   (c) Conflict by Definition 9

Fig. 12. The PA-PAC conflict

5 Conclusion

We have presented the conflict model that can efficiently visualize the PA constraints and define the conflicts. The conflict model provides good understanding about the conflicts and can detect the conflict effectively. Also we formally specified and proved the conditions of conflict occurrence. This work provides clear criteria to determine whether the conflict is occurred. Consequently we can assure integrity on permission assignment by checking the conflicts before the permission assignment and the PA constraints are applied. The integrity on permission assignment is core part in RBAC research field.

The value of this paper might be diminished if a talented security manager can create PA constraints and conduct precise permission assignment. However, it is a dangerous attempt for the security manager to check the conflict purely depending on the personal judgment in a large enterprise environment. Thus, our works make it possible for the security manager to reduce mistakes and also to prevent improper permission assignment.

References

1. David F.Ferraiolo et al. Role-Based Access Control, Artech House, 2003
2. D.R. Kuhn, Mutual Exclusion of Roles as a Means of Implementing Separation of Duty in Role-Based Access Control Systems, Second ACM Workshop on Role-Based Access Control, 1997.
3. Gligor, V.D., S.I. Gavrila, and D. Ferraiolo. On the formal definition of separation-of-duty policies and their composition, IEEE Symposium on Security and Privacy, May 1998, Oakland, California.

4. Matunda Nyanchama and Sylvia Osborn, The Role Graph Model and Conflict of Interest, ACM Transactions on Information and System Security, Vol. 2, No. 1, February 1999, Pages 3–33.
5. Elisa Bertino, Elena Ferrari, Vijay Atluri, The specification and enforcement of authorization constraints in workflow management systems, ACM Transactions on Information and System Security, Vol. 2, No. 1, February 1999, pages 65-104.
6. Chang-Joo Moon, Dae-Ha Park, Soung-Jin Park, Doo-Kwon Baik, Symmetric RBAC Model that Takes the Separation of Duty and Role Hierarchies into Consid-eration, Computers & Security, Vol.23, No.2, 2004 March, 126~136.
7. Gail-Joon Ahn, Ravi Sandhu, Role-Based Authorization Constraints Specification, ACM Transactions on Information and System Security, Vol. 3, No. 4, November 2000, pages 207-226.
8. Ravi S. Sandhu, Edward J. Coynek, Hal L. Feinsteink , Charles E. Youmank, Role-Based Access Control Models , IEEE Computer, Volume 29, Number 2, February 1996, pages 38-47.
9. Ravi Sandhu, David Ferraiolo, Richard Kuhn, The NIST Model for Role-Base Access Control: Toward A Unified Standard, Proceedings, 5th ACM Workshop on Role Based Access Control, July 26-27, 2000.

Toward Modeling Lightweight Intrusion Detection System Through Correlation-Based Hybrid Feature Selection

Jong Sou Park, Khaja Mohammad Shazzad, and Dong Seong Kim

Computer Engineering Department, Hankuk Aviation University
{jspark, khaja, dskim}@hau.ac.kr

Abstract. Modeling IDS have been focused on improving detection model(s) in terms of (i) *detection model design* based on classification algorithm, clustering algorithm, and soft computing techniques such as Artificial Neural Networks (ANN), Hidden Markov Model (HMM), Support Vector Machines (SVM), K-means clustering, Fuzzy approaches and so on and (ii) *feature selection* through wrapper and filter approaches. However these approaches require large overhead due to heavy computations for both feature selection and cross validation method to minimize generalization errors. In addition selected *feature set* varies according to detection model so that they are inefficient for modeling lightweight IDS. Therefore this paper proposes a new approach to model lightweight Intrusion Detection System (IDS) based on a new feature selection approach named Correlation-based Hybrid Feature Selection (CBHFS) which is able to significantly decrease training and testing times while retaining high detection rates with low false positives rates as well as stable feature selection results. The experimental results on KDD 1999 intrusion detection datasets show the feasibility of our approach to enable one to modeling lightweight IDS.

1 Introduction

Previous approaches for modeling Intrusion Detection System (IDS) have been focused on proposing new techniques so as to improve existing IDS in terms of both (i) classification algorithm and (ii) feature selection. Firstly, on the perspective of modeling of IDS, many studies have been proposed the intrusion detection model based on various kinds of classification algorithm, clustering algorithm, and soft computing techniques such as Artificial Neural Networks (ANN), Hidden Markov Model (HMM), Support Vector Machines (SVM), K-means clustering, Fuzzy approaches and so on. Ourston *et al.* [1] has modeled the multi-stage intrusion using HMM and they have showed that HMM outperforms two classic machine learning techniques such as decision tree and artificial neural network. The main disadvantage of modeling IDS by HMM is the requirement of huge computation resource. Nevertheless this technique shows promising results in rare example problem and detecting coordinated attacks. Many researchers have adopted SVM [17] technique

D. Feng, D. Lin, and M. Yung (Eds.): CISC 2005, LNCS 3822, pp. 279–289, 2005.

for IDS. Fugate *et al.* [6] and D. Kim *et al.* [22] exploited SVM for anomaly detection. Nguyen [7] has shown that one class SVM can differentiate between normal and abnormal network traffic. He has demonstrated that abnormal behavior can be predicted by training the unsupervised SVM with normal or attack free data. Hu *et al.* [8] utilized robust SVM (RSVM) for intrusion detection and compared it with traditional SVM and k-nearest neighbor.

Secondly, many literatures have tried to figure out important features or feature sets in order to not only minimize overhead of detection model but also maximize detection rates. In terms of feature selection, several researches have proposed *identifying important intrusion features* through wrapper and filter approaches. Wrapper method exploits a machine learning algorithm to evaluate the goodness of features or feature set. It provides better performance of selecting suitable features since it employs performance of learning algorithm as an evaluation criterion. On the other hand, Filter method does not use any machine learning algorithm to filter out the irrelevant and redundant features rather it utilizes the underlying characteristics of the training data to evaluate the relevance of the features or feature set by some independent measures such as distance measure, correlation measures, consistency measures [3, 4]. Even though a number of feature selection techniques have been utilized in the fields of web and text mining, and speech recognition, however, there are very few analogous studies in intrusion detection field. Sung and Mukkamala [15] have tried to identify and categorize features according to their importance to detect a specific kind of attacks such as probe, dos, Remote to Local (R2L), and User to Root (U2R). It has used backward feature selection method and SVM [17] and neural network (NN) as feature selection algorithm. They proposed a rule base to rank features according to their weights on classification accuracy, training and testing rate. In addition, Kim *et al.* also have proposed feature selection method based on Genetic Algorithm (GA) [16]. Besides this some PCA and ICA approach also have been proposed to decrease overhead of IDS and increase the detection rates [20].

However those approaches still imposes large overhead due to heavy computations needed both for classification and cross validation method required to minimize generalization errors. They try to improve the performance of the system only by improving the performance of classification algorithm in terms of changing parameters and initial conditions. But it incurs higher computation as it has to deals with the entire given features that are relevant and irrelevant. Moreover selected feature set as the result of feature selection varies according to detection model so that they are inefficient for modeling lightweight IDS.

Therefore in this paper we propose a new approach to help one to model lightweight IDS based on a new feature selection approach named Correlation-based Hybrid Feature Selection (CHFS) which is able to significantly decrease training and testing times while retaining high detection rates with low false positives rates as well as stable feature selection results. The experimental results on KDD 1999 intrusion detection datasets indicate the feasibility of our approach.

This paper is organized as follows. In section 2, proposed approach is presented. In section 3, experiments and their results are introduced. Finally, section 4 concludes our work.

2 Proposed Approach

2.1 Overall Architecture

The overall architecture of our approach is depicted in figure 1. The pre-processed audit data is divided into two datasets: training and testing dataset. Training dataset is further segregated into three sets feature-selection, model building and validation dataset. Feature-selection dataset is passed through our Correlation-based Hybrid Feature Selection process which results in a set of selected features. The model building dataset is then used to build the intrusion detection model using selected features and the model is validated by the validation set. The model is then tested by testing dataset. Next subsections describe Correlation-based Feature Selection (CFS) and Correlation-based Hybrid Feature Selection, respectively.

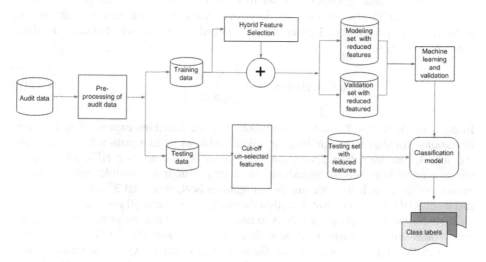

Fig. 1. Overall Architecture of Proposed Approach

2.2 Correlation-Based Feature Selection

Correlation-based Feature Selection (CFS) belongs to filter method and is to find the subset of features, which is best relevant to a class, having no redundant feature. It evaluates merit of the feature subset on the basis of hypothesis: "Good feature subsets contain features highly correlated with the class, yet uncorrelated to each other [2]". This hypothesis gives rise to two definitions. One is feature-class correlation and another is feature-feature correlation. Feature-class correlation indicates how much a feature is correlated to a specific class while feature-feature correlation is the correlation between two features. Equation 1, also known as Pearson's correlation gives the merit of a feature subset consisting of k number of features.

$$Merit_s = \frac{k\overline{r}_{cf}}{\sqrt{k + k(k-1)\overline{r}_{ff}}} \qquad (1)$$

In equation 1, $\bar{r}_{cf}$ is average feature-class correlation, and $\bar{r}_{ff}$ is average feature-feature correlation. For the estimation of $\bar{r}_{cf}$ and $\bar{r}_{ff}$, we need to calculate correlations between features and between features and classes. For discrete class problem, CFS first dicretizes numeric features using technique Fayyad and Irani [18] and then use symmetrical uncertainty (a modified information gain measure) to estimate the degree of association between discrete features [19].

$$\text{Symmetrical Uncertainty (SU)} = \left[\frac{H(X) + H(Y) - H(X, y)}{H(Y) + H(Y)} \right] \qquad (2)$$

In equation 2, $H(X)$ and $H(Y)$ represent entropy of feature X and Y. Symmetrical uncertainty is used because it is a symmetric measure and can therefore be used to measure feature-feature correlation where there is no notion of one attribute being "class" as such[2]. For continuous class data, the correlation between attribute is standard linear correlation. This is straightforward when the two attributes involved are both continuous.

$$\text{Linear Correlation, } r_{XY} = \left[\frac{\sum xy}{\eta \sigma_x \sigma_y} \right] \qquad (3)$$

In equation 3, X and Y are two continuous feature variables expressed in terms of deviations. Another important thing to calculate the merit in equation 1 is to generate the subset. Feature subset generation from given feature set is a NP-hard problem, which can be best solved by exhaustive search. But it is possible only for small number of features. If the total number of features is N, then total 2^N subset exists. For instance, KDD 1999 intrusion detection dataset [12] contains all together 41 features, so here 2.199e+12 number of subset exists and it is a huge number. Therefore, we need some heuristic search method such as simulated annealing, hill climbing, best first, genetic algorithm and so on. Genetic Algorithm (GA) is stochastic search algorithms based on evolutionary ideas of natural selection and genetics [5]. Though GA uses random search technique, yet it is not random. It converges towards the optimal solution by exploiting fitness function of the search. It also exhibits the diversity of locating global optima by using genetic operators such as mutation and crossover. Therefore we use GA for generating feature subset. The subsection describes GA.

2.3 Genetic Algorithm

GA works on a population of solutions and finds an optimal solution out of it. For searching using GA, we need to initialize or build a population of candidate solutions. Each candidate solution is represented as a chromosome. A chromosome consists of one or more genes. Each gene represents a feature. In KDD 1999 intrusion detection datasets [12], each instance consists of 41 features. Therefore each chromosome would consist of 41 genes where each gene is a binary bit indicating the presence or absence of a feature in that chromosome. If the value of a specific gene is 1, it indicates the presence of that feature in that chromosome or feature vector. Figure 2

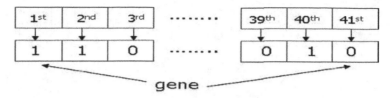

Fig. 2. Structure of a chromosome representing a feature vector

illustrates a chromosome which represents a feature vector or a set of selected features.

Each chromosome is needed to be evaluated against an evaluation function. The selection of evaluation function depends on the problem domain. In our case, Correlation-based Feature Selection (CFS) acts as an evaluation function. It evaluates each chromosome using the merit (discussed in previous section) of the chromosome (feature set). As GA is based on philosophy 'Survival for the fittest', putative chromosomes (feature sets) are selected through *Roulette Wheel Selection*. After selection process, genetic operations – crossover and mutation, are performed to build a population of better chromosomes as next generation. In general, GA can be expressed below:

```
Initialize the population
Evaluate initial population
Do
   Perform selection
   Alteration (crossover and mutation) for new solutions
   Evaluate solutions in the population
While termination criterion is not satisfied
```

And more detailed description for GA is presented in [23, 24].

2.4 Correlation-Based Hybrid Feature Selection

Our hybrid feature selection algorithm is a crafted combination of CFS and Support Vector Machines (SVM). We adopt SVM which have been shown a good performance pattern recognition as well as intrusion detection problems [6, 7, 22]. Our hybrid feature selection algorithm is depicted in figure 3.

As stated earlier, GA is used to generate subsets of features from given feature set. Our algorithm takes full feature set as input and returns the optimal subset of feature after being evaluated by CFS and SVM. Each chromosome represents a feature vector. The length of the chromosome is 41 genes where each gene (bit) may have values 1 or 0 which indicates whether corresponding feature is included or not in the feature vector respectively. Like every stochastic algorithm, the initial population of chromosomes is generated randomly. Merit [2] of each chromosome (Equation 1) is calculated by CFS (see section 2.2). The chromosome having highest merit, γ_{best} represents the best feature subset, S_{best} in population. This subset is then evaluated by SVM classification algorithm and the value is stored in θ_{best} which represents metric of evaluation. Here we have chosen intrusion detection rates as a metric although a complex criterion such as a combination of detection rate and false positive rate or a rule based criterion like [15] could be used.

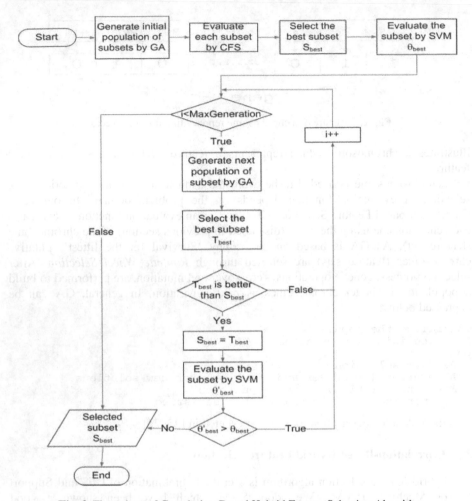

Fig. 3. Flow chart of Correlation-Based Hybrid Feature Selection Algorithm

Then genetic operations, selection, crossover and mutation, are performed and a new population of chromosomes is generated. In each generation, best chromosome or feature subset is compared by previous best subset, S_{best}. If newer subset is better than previous one, it is assigned as the best subset. This subset is then evaluated by SVM. If new detection rate is higher than previous one, this value is to θ_{best} and algorithm goes forward. Otherwise the S_{best} is returned as the optimal subset of features. The algorithm stops if better subset is not found in next generation or when maximum number of generation is reached. The experiments and their results will be presented in next section.

3   Experiments and Results

The overall structure of our approach is depicted in figure 1 as stated in section 2.1. In order to verify the feasibility of our approach, we carry out several experiments on

KDD 1999 intrusion detection dataset [12]. Our approach is divided into three parts –
1) feature selection, 2) training and 3) testing. Next section describes experimental
dataset, environments, and experimental results.

3.1 Experimental Dataset

We have preprocessed the KDD 1999 CUP labeled dataset [12] to make it two class
dataset - normal and attack. The dataset contains total 494,021 instances among these
97,278 (19.69%) instances are normal and 396,743 (80.31%) belongs to attacks. The
dataset contains 24 different types of attacks that are broadly categorized in four
groups: probes, DoS (Denial of Service), U2R (User to Root), and R2L (Remote to
Local). We have sampled 15 different dataset having 20995 instances from the corpus
by uniform random distribution so that the distribution of the dataset should remain
unchanged. Each instance of data consists of 41 features which we have labeled as x1,
x2, x3, x4 and so forth. We only use DoS type of attacks since other attack types have
very small numbers of instance so that they are not suitable for our experiments [21].

3.2 Experimental Environments

All experiments were performed in a Linux (Fedora core 3) machine having
configurations Intel™ Pentium 4, 2.0 GHz, 512 MB RAM and kernel version 2.6.9-
1.667. We have used open source WEKA [13] library for SVM and CFS algorithm.
For implementing our algorithm, we have modified several classes of WEKA library
such as "weka.attributeSelection.GeneticSearch".

3.3 Feature Selection

For feature selection, we have selected a data set randomly from 15 datasets and
applied our algorithm which was described in previous section. We have applied 10
fold cross validation to achieve low generalization error and to determine the
intrusion detection rate. The optimal subset selected has shown 99.56% detection rate.
The indices of feature selected are x1, x6, x12, x14, x23, x24, x25, x31, x32, x37, x40
and x41. The dimension of feature vector is reduced from 43 to 12 that is a significant
gain while the classification rate is above 99%.

3.4 Training and Testing

We have carried out 15 experiments on different datasets having full features and
selected features. Each dataset is divided into training and testing set consisting of
15740 and 5255 instances respectively. The figures from 4 to 7 show the comparisons
between different performance indicators. Figure 4 reveals the dramatic reduction of
model building time with reduced features as expected because the feature selection
process has cut the 70% of total number of features. Testing time depicted in figure 5
also accedes with model training time.

For selected features, though the detection rate is lower than that of having full
features the decrement is very small, in other words, around 0.83% in average (see
figure 6). But the significant performance is achieved in the reduction of false positive
rate (see figure 7), which is 37.5% in average. For all above experiment, we used

polynomial kernel of exponent 1 and c =1 that are default value for SVM classifier in WEKA. It is noteworthy that we have not taken any measure of optimizing the kernel and SVM parameters as our main goal is to investigate that how hybrid feature selection reduced the computational resource while maintaining the detection and false positive rate within tolerable range.

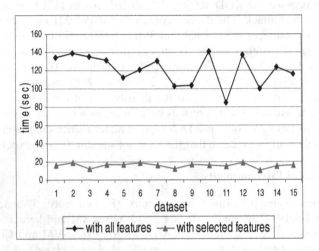

Fig. 4. Model building time vs. dataset index

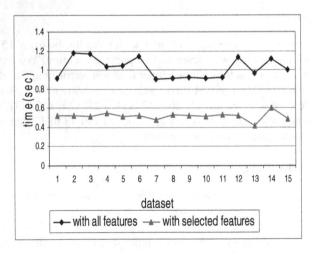

Fig. 5. Model testing time vs. dataset index

Enhancement of detection rate and optimization between false positive and detection rate can be improved further by parameter tuning, exploiting better kernel function and improving classification algorithm [10, 11]. Feature selection, however augments to this optimization.

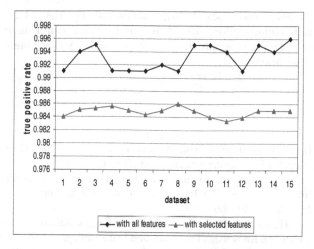

Fig. 6. Detection rates vs. dataset index

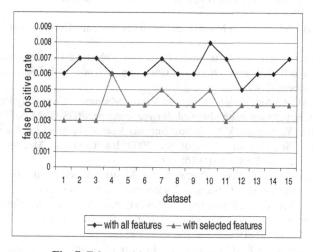

Fig. 7. False positive rates vs. dataset index

4   Conclusions

This paper has proposed a novel approach to model lightweight Intrusion Detection System through Correlation-based Hybrid Feature Selection (CHFS). Our approach has shown the reduction of training and testing time by an order of magnitude while precluded the reduction of detection rate. It has also demonstrated uniformity of the detection and false positive rates among different datasets. Faster training and testing helps to build lightweight IDS as well as provide ease of retrain or modification of model. In our future research, we will investigate the feasibility of implementing the technique in real time intrusion detection environment as well as characterizing type of attacks such as DOS, probes, U2R and R2L which enhance the capability and performance of IDS.

Acknowledgements. This research was supported by the MIC (Ministry of Information and Communication), Korea, under the ITRC (Information Technology Research Center) support program supervised by the IITA (Institute of Information Technology Assessment).

References

1. Ourston, D., Matzner, S., Stump, W., Hopkins, B.: Applications of Hidden Markov Models to Detect Multi-Stage Network Attacks. In: Proc. of the 36th Hawaii Int. Conf. on System Science, IEEE Computer Society Press (2002) 334–343
2. Hall, M.A.: Correlation-based Feature Selection for Discrete and Numeric Class Machine Learning. In: Proc. of the 17th Int. Conf. on Machine Learning. Morgan Kaufmann Publishers Inc. (2000) 359–366
3. Dash, M., Liu, H., Motoda, H.: Consistency Based Feature Selection. In: Proc. of the 4th Pacific Asia Conf. on Knowledge Discovery and Data Mining. (2000) 98–109
4. Almuallim, H., Dietterich, T.G.: Learning Boolean Concepts in the Presence of Many Irrelevant Features. Artificial Intelligence, Vol. 69, Elsevier Science Publishers Ltd. (1994) 279–305
5. Holland, J.H.: Adaptation in Natural and Artificial Systems. University of Michigan Press, Ann Arbor, (1975)
6. Fugate, M., Gattiker, J.R.: Anomaly Detection Enhanced Classification in Computer Intrusion Detection. Lecture Notes in Computer Science, Vol. 2388. Springer-Verlag, Berlin Heidelberg (2002)
7. Nguyen, B.V.: An Application of Support Vector Machines to Anomaly Detection. (2002) available at. http://www.math.ohiou.edu/~vnguyen/papers/IDS_SVM.pdf
8. Hu, W., Liao, Y., Vemuri, V.R.: Robust Support Vector Machines for Anomaly Detection in Computer Security. In: Proc. of the 2003 Int. Conf. on Machine Learning and Application, CSREA Press (2003) 168–174
9. Cannady, J.: Artificial Neural Network for Misuse detection, In: Proc. of the 1998 National Information System Security Conference. (1998) 443–356
10. Chapelle, O., Vapnik, V., Bousquet, O., Mukherjee, S.: Choosing Multiple Parameters for Support Vector Machines. Machine Learning, Vol. 46, Issue 1, Kluwer Academic Publishers. (2002) 131–159
11. Duan, K., Keerthi, S.S., Poo, A.N.: Evaluation of Simple Performance Measures for Tuning SVM Hyperparameters. Neurocomputing, 51 (2003) 41–59
12. KDD Cup 1999 Data. available. http://kdd.ics.uci.edu/databases/kddcup99/kddcup99.html
13. Open Source WEKA Project.: available http://www.cs.waikato.ac.nz/ml/weka/index.html
14. Liu, H., Yu, L.: Toward Integrating Feature Selection Algorithms for Classification and Clustering. IEEE Trans. on Knowledge and Data Engineering, 17(3), (2005) 1–12
15. Sung, A.H., Mukkamala, S.: Identifying Important Features for Intrusion Detection Using Support Vector Machines and Neural Networks. In: Proc. of the 2003 Int. Sym. on Applications and the Internet Technology, IEEE Computer Society Press. (2003) 209–216
16. Kim, D.S., Nguyen, H.-N., Ohn, S.-Y., Park, J.S.: Fusions of GA and SVM for Anomaly Detection in Intrusion Detection System. Lecture Notes in Computer Science, Vol. 3498. Springer-Verlag, Berlin Heidelberg (2005) 415–420
17. Vapnik, V.: The Nature of Statistical Learning Theory. Springer, Berlin Heidelberg New York (1995)

18. Fayyad, U., Irani, K.: Multi-interval discretization of continuos attributes as preprocessing for classification learning. In: Proc. of the 13th Int. Join Conf. on Artificial Intelligence, Morgan Kaufmann Publishers (1993) 1022–1027
19. Press, W.H., Flannery, B. P., Teukolsky, S. A., Vetterling, W.T.: Numerical recipes in C. Cambridge University Press, Cambridge. (1988)
20. Chebrolu, S., Abraham, A., Thomas, J.P.: Data Reduction and Data Classification in an Intrusion Detection System, In: Proc. of 2004 South Central Information Security Symposium. (2004)
21. Sabhnani, M., Serpen, G.: On Failure of Machine Learning Algorithms for Detecting Misuse in KDD Intrusion Detection Data Set. J. of Intelligent Data Analysis. (2004)
22. Kim, D.S., Park, J.S.: Network-based Intrusion Detection with Support Vector Machines, Lecture Notes in Computer Science, Vol. 2662, Springer-Verlag, Berlin Heidelberg (2003) 747–756
23. Melanie Mitchell.: Introduction to Genetic Algorithms, MIT press (1999)
24. Michalewicz, Z.: Genetic Algorithms + Data Structures = Evolution Programs. 3rd edn. Springer-Verlag, Berlin Heidelberg New York (1996)

Security Analysis of Three Cryptographic Schemes from Other Cryptographic Schemes

Sherman S.M. Chow[1], Zhengjun Cao[2], and Joseph K. Liu[3]

[1] Department of Computer Science,
Courant Institute of Mathematical Sciences,
New York University, NY 10012, USA
schow@cs.nyu.edu

[2] Key Lab of Mathematics Mechanization,
Academy of Mathematics and Systems Science,
Chinese Academy of Sciences, Beijing, P.R. China
zjcamss@hotmail.com

[3] Department of Computer Science,
University of Bristol, Bristol, UK
liu@cs.bris.ac.uk

Abstract. Relations between various cryptographic schemes make it possible to build a new cryptographic scheme from (some components of) other kinds of cryptographic schemes. Recently, three new schemes are proposed by exploiting these relationships: a group signature scheme from identity-based signature, another group signature scheme from proxy signature and a signcryption scheme from secret sharing. Unfortunately, we show that these schemes are insecure. These group signature schemes cannot satisfy at least half of the standard security requirements while the signcryption scheme does not even satisfy the basic requirement of a secure signcryption scheme. We hope this work can exhibit the precautions one should take when making schemes with a similar approach.

Keywords: Group signature, signcryption, identity-based signature, proxy signature, secret sharing, bilinear pairings.

1 Introduction

Apart from designing new cryptographic schemes from scratch to achieve more security features or to obtain better performance when compared with existing schemes, another central line of cryptographic research is to identify which cryptographic primitive is sufficient to build another scheme. For examples, the existence of trapdoor permutations implies the existence of group signature schemes [6, 3], and group signature schemes implies both the public key encryption schemes [1] and the one-way function [14].

Some of these constructions are of the theoretical interests only but some of them may result in a new and efficient cryptographic scheme. If we can build a new scheme by using another as a black box with a certain set of security properties, it is possible to have a space-efficient and rapid implementation of multifunctional cryptographic system, which is especially desirable in the paradigm

D. Feng, D. Lin, and M. Yung (Eds.): CISC 2005, LNCS 3822, pp. 290–301, 2005.

of embedded and ubiquitous computing. Recently, there are three schemes proposed following this direction. They are a group signature scheme from identity-based signature [8], a group signature scheme from proxy signature [9] and a signcryption scheme from secret sharing [2].

Our Contributions. We describe concrete attack to show that the group signature scheme proposed in [8] cannot satisfy all of the requirements of a secure group signature, namely, unforgeability, anonymity, linkability, exculpability, traceability and coalition-resistance. We also show that the group signature proposed in [9] cannot satisfy traceability, exculpability and unlinkability; while the signcryption scheme in [2] does not satisfy the ciphertext indistinguishability.

Organization. The next section contains the preliminaries of this paper, which includes the complexity assumptions used by the schemes we review and the security requirements of group signature schemes and signcryption schemes. Section 3, 4, 5 review these schemes mentioned above respectively together with our security analysis. We conclude the paper in Section 6.

2 Preliminaries

2.1 Complexity Assumptions

Definition 1. *Let p be a prime such that $p-1$ has a large prime divisor, given a generator g of a multiplicative group $\mathbb{Z}_p^*$ and a value $g^a \in \mathbb{Z}_p^*$ where $a < p-1$, the Discrete Logarithm problem is to compute a.*

Definition 2. *Given a generator P of an additive group $\mathbb{G}$ and a 3-tuple (aP, bP, cP), the Decisional Diffie-Hellman problem (DDHP) is to decide whether $c = ab$.*

Definition 3. *Given a generator P of an additive group $\mathbb{G}$ and a 2-tuple (aP, bP), the Computational Diffie-Hellman problem (CDHP) is to compute abP.*

Definition 4. *If $\mathbb{G}$ is an additive group such that DDHP can be solved in polynomial time but no probabilistic algorithm can solve CDHP with non-negligible advantage within polynomial time, then we call $\mathbb{G}$ a Gap Diffie-Hellman group.*

2.2 Group Signature

Group signatures, introduced by Chaum and Heyst [6], allow individual members to make signatures on behalf of the group while the verifier only knows that the signer is one of the member of the group, yet cannot compute his identity.

A secure group signature scheme must satisfy the following properties [3]:

– Unforgeability: Only members are able to sign on behalf of the group.
– Anonymity: Given a valid signature of some message, identifying the actual signer is computationally hard for everyone but the group manager.

- Unlinkability: Deciding whether two different valid signatures were produced by the same group member is hard for everyone but the group manager.
- Exculpability: Neither a group member nor the group manager can sign on behalf of other group member, but it precludes the group manager from creating fraudulent signers and then producing group signatures.
- Traceability: The group manager is always able to open a valid signature and identify the actual signer.
- Coalition-resistance: Even a colluding subset of group members (up to the entire group) cooperate together to generate a valid signature, the group manager is still able to revoke one of the colluding group members.

2.3   Signcryption

We want to enjoy confidentiality, authenticity and non-repudiation of message simultaneously in many situations. A traditional approach to achieve this objective is to "sign-then-encrypt" the message, or employing special schemes.

An example of the encryption schemes that provide more than confidentiality is *authenticated encryption* (e.g. [11, 12]). Authenticated encryption provides data integrity in addition to the confidentiality provided by normal encryption. In 1997, Zheng proposed the notion of *signcryption* [18, 19] that combines encryption and signing in one step at a lower computational cost.

Depending on applications, signcryption schemes may have different security features. For examples, public ciphertext authenticity, public verifiability, and forward security [7]. But ciphertext indistinguishability is essential to most encryption (and also signcryption) schemes for common usage.

This notion of confidentiality was proposed together with the probabilistic encryption scheme in [10]. Note that the essential property of the probabilistic algorithm is that even the same plaintext is encrypted under an encryption key twice, two resultant ciphertexts will be different with an overwhelming probability. Probabilistic encryption algorithm challenges the adversary by the following "game", which also defines indistinguishability. At the start of the game, the adversary first prepares two distinct message of equal length and sends them to the encryption oracle, then the challenger tosses a fair coin and encrypts either one of the plaintexts according to the face of the coin appeared. The resultant ciphertext is then presented to the adversary. If the adversary is unable to guess the face of the coin seen by the challenger (i.e. which plaintext is encrypted) with probability significantly greater than $\frac{1}{2}$, then the encryption scheme is considered to be indistinguishable.

This security notion is named as *semantic security* in [10]: whatever is efficiently computable about the plaintext given the ciphertext, is also efficiently computable without the ciphertext. This level of confidentiality is indeed essential, since many message contain certain "non-secret partial information". For example, consider the ciphertext encrypting the name of the candidate/option chosen in an e-voting event, there is no need for the adversary to decrypt the ciphertext if the adversary is fully capable to distinguish the ciphertexts. Most direct applications of one-way trapdoor function (e.g. RSA [13]) are very weak in hiding such kind of semantic information [10].

3   Group Signature from Identity-Based Signature

Recently, Deng and Zhao proposed a new group signature scheme from Gap Diffie-Hellman groups, groups where computational Diffie-Hellman problem is intractable but decisional Diffie-Hellman problem is easy. Their scheme can be seen as a combination of the identity-based signature in [5] and the short signature scheme in [4]. These two building blocks are shown to be existential unforgeable against adaptive chosen-message attacks. However, their adapt to combine them as a group signature is not secure. It is universally forgeable, linkable, untraceable, not anonymous, not exculpable and not coalition-resistant.

3.1   Review

For the sake of completeness we review the group signature scheme proposed by Deng and Zhao here. Their group signature scheme consists of five algorithms, namely, Setup, Join, Sign, Verify and Open.

Setup. Setup generates the public parameter of the group signature scheme, the group manager's private key and the group's public key.

Let E/F_{k^n} be a supersingular elliptic curve whose order has large prime factor q. Let $P \in E/F_{k^n}$ be a point of order q. The subgroup $< P >$ generated by P is defined as $\mathbb{G}_1$. According to the isomorphism ϕ on the curve, define a bilinear map: $\hat{e} : \mathbb{G}_1 \times \mathbb{G}_1 \to \mathbb{G}_2$, where $\mathbb{G}_2$ is a subgroup of $F_{k^{\alpha n}}^*$. Such a bilinear pairing is the key primitive for solving decisional Diffie-Hellman problem of $\mathbb{G}_1$. To map a string to a point on curve, we define $H_1 : \{0,1\}^* \to \mathbb{G}_1$ as a cryptographic hash function using the algorithm MapToGroup [4]. We also define $H_2 : \{0,1\}^* \times \mathbb{G}_1 \to \mathbb{Z}_q^*$ be another cryptographic hash function. The group manager chooses a random number $s \in \mathbb{Z}_q^*$ and computes $P_{pub} = sP$. The public parameter is $(P, P_{pub}, H_1(\cdot), H_2(\cdot, \cdot), \hat{e}(\cdot, \cdot), \alpha, q, n)$. The master secret key and the group's public key is $SK = s$ and $PK = (P, P_{pub})$ respectively.

Join. Join is an interactive protocol between the group manager and a user, which is executed when a user wants to join the group. The input of the protocol contains the group manager's private key and the output of the protocol contains the private-public key pair for the user.

Suppose now that a user u_i wants to join the group. First, u_i randomly chooses $x_i \in \mathbb{Z}_q^*$. Then he/she computes $R_i = x_i P$. To obtain his/her membership certificate, each user must perform the following protocol with the manager:

1. The user u_i sends R_i to the group manager.
2. The group manager regards R_i as an identifier and computes $D_i = sR_i$.

Then D_i is communicated secretly to the user u_i as the group member's secret key. R_i is u_i's public key.

Sign. Sign is a probabilistic algorithm which takes the private key of any arbitrary user who joined the group to produce an anonymous group signature on behalf of the group on a certain message. If user u_i wants to sign a message m on behalf of the group, he/she proceeds as follows:

1. Pick a random $r \in \mathbb{Z}_q^*$, compute $U = rR_i$, $h = H_2(m, U)$, $V = (r + h)D_i$. Then the first part of the signature is $\sigma_1 = (U, V)$.
2. Compute $P_m = H_1(m)$, $S_m = x_i P_m$, and σ_2 being the x-coordinate of S_m.

The final signature of user is $(\sigma_1, \sigma_2, R_i)$, R_i can be treated as a traceability tag.

Verify. Verify is a deterministic algorithm which takes the public key of the group and the message as the input to check whether the signature is a valid one. Given $(\sigma_1, \sigma_2, R_i)$ and m, verification can be divided into two parts:

1. The verifier makes sure that the signature is generated by a group member by checking that $\hat{e}(P_{pub}, \phi(U + hR_i)) = \hat{e}(P, \phi(V))$, using σ_1.
2. The verifier checks that the signature is definitely generated by u_i rather than other members of the group. He/she does the following :
   (a) Find a point $S \in E/F_{k^n}$ of order q whose x-coordinate is σ_2 and whose y-coordinate is some $y \in F_{k^n}$. If no such point exists, reject the signature.
   (b) Set $c = \hat{e}(P, \phi(S))$ and $d = \hat{e}(R_i, \phi(H_1(m)))$
   (c) If either $c = d$ or $c^{-1} = d$, accept the signature. Otherwise, reject it.

Open. Open is the algorithm executed by the group manager when the anonymity of the group signature should be revoked. The group manager knows the identity of the member for each u_i. As a result, it is easy for the group manager, given a message m and a valid group signature, to determine the identity of the signer corresponding to the public key R_i.

3.2   Analysis

Unforgeability. We show the scheme is universally forgeable by describing a way that everyone can generate a private key by his/her own without the execution of Join protocol with the group manager.

Autonomous Join Procedure:

1. Randomly choose $\hat{x} \in \mathbb{Z}_q^*$.
2. Compute the public key by $\hat{R} = \hat{x}P$.
3. Compute the corresponding private key by $\hat{D} = \hat{x}P_{pub}$.

It is easy to see $\hat{D}$ produced is a valid private key since $\hat{D} = \hat{x}P_{pub} = \hat{x}sP = s\hat{x}P = s\hat{R}$. With the help of this autonomous join procedure, anyone outside the group can sign on behalf of the group.

A simple fix to this flaw is to require the user to choose an identifier $ID \in \{0,1\}^*$ and send ID instead of R_i to group manager in Join phase. R_i will be set to $H_1(ID)$. Then, every signature should include ID as the traceability tag instead of R_i. However, after such fix, x_i where $R_i = x_iP$ cannot be easily deduced. To remedy this problem, we can employ another pair of key x_i' and $R_i' = x_i'P$, while x_i' is randomly generated by the user and R_i is set to $H_1(ID\|R')$ in order for this new pair of key to be "certified" by the group manager.

Anonymity. In the Join protocol, the user first generates R_i and requests for the corresponding private key, and the private key is subsequently sent to the user in a secure way. Any eavesdropper in this process can associate the R_i to the identity of the user. Since the user's public key R_i is to be included in every signature he/she produced, the anonymity of the group signature is lost. A simple fix is to employ an anonymous and encrypted key issuing protocol [16].

Unlinkability. It is obvious that the scheme is linkable because a user u_i must use his/her key R_i to make a valid group signature $(\sigma_1, \sigma_2, R_i)$. To overcome the flaw, the authors proposed a modification that each user uses different private-public key pair for each signature [8]. In a sense, such scheme is not practical.

Exculpability. We first show how the group manager can generate a valid group signature, then we describe how this attack affect the exculpability of the scheme.

A key observation on the Sign phase in the original scheme is that user u_i has to use his/her key triple (x_i, R_i, D_i), where x_i is a random number picked by user u_i in $\mathbb{Z}_q^*$, $R_i = x_iP$ and $D_i = sR_i$.

Intuitively, we know that the group manager has absolute superiority in Join phase in the scheme because he/she can generate an arbitrary $R_0 = x_0P$ ($x_0 \in_R \mathbb{Z}_q^*$) solely, then he/she can compute $D_0 = sR_0$ using the master key s. Therefore, he/she obtains a valid key triple (x_0, R_0, D_0) for signing like any group member.

Group Manager's Attack:

If group manager wants to give a message m that is supposed to be signed by someone on behalf of the group, he/she performs the following steps:

1. Pick a random $r \in \mathbb{Z}_q^*$, compute $U = rR_0$, $h = H_2(m, U)$, $V = (r + h)D_0$. Then the first part of the signature is $\sigma_1 = (U, V)$.
2. Compute $P_m = H_1(m)$, $S_m = x_0P_m$, where σ_2 is the x-coordinate of S_m.

The correctness of this forged group signature $(\sigma_1, \sigma_2, R_0)$ is obvious.

Now we analyze the scheme's exculpability. The Open procedure uses only the secret knowledge held by the group manager and is not publicly verifiable. From the above attack, any user can be framed to be the "actual signer".

It is true that the user can provide a knowledge proof of sR_i and try to claim that the secret key sR_0 is not the real private key. Unfortunately, this knowledge proof cannot be used as a proof of treachery of the group manager. Note that for the scheme to achieve anonymity, the user's key R_i (and also x_i) should not be related to the identity of the user, i.e. they should be some binary strings that look like random. The knowledge proof of sR_i where $sR_i \neq sR_0$ does not imply sR_i is the real secret key of the user (e.g. sR_i is a key from conspiracy).

A simple fix is to employ a trusted authority (not the group manager) to certify the relationship between the user and the public key.

Traceability. With the help of the autonomous join procedure described previously, anyone outside the group can sign on behalf of the group without fearing the tracing of the group manager since the Open procedure of the original scheme requires the group manager's knowledge of the real identity of the person invoking the Join protocol.

Even without the help of the autonomous join procedure, any real member of the group (i.e. those who have executed the Join protocol with the group manager) can still generate a untraceable but valid group signature.

Untraceable Signing Procedure:

1. Pick a random $r \in \mathbb{Z}_q^*$ and a random untraceable factor $y \in \mathbb{Z}_q^*$, compute $R_i' = yR_i$. Then compute $U = rR_i'$, $h = H_2(m, U)$, $V = (r + h)yD_i$. Then the first part of the signature is $\sigma_1 = (U, V)$.
2. Compute $P_m = H_1(m)$, $S_m = x_iyP_m$, where σ_2 is the x-coordinate of S_m.

Again, it is easy to see the signature $(\sigma_1, \sigma_2, R_i')$ is valid.

However, since the traceability tag R_i of the signature is spoiled by the random untraceable factor, the signature produced is thus information theoretically untraceable, even the group manager cannot help.

We note that the previous simple fix can be used to prevent this attack.

Coalition-Resistance. Our attack can be carried out by colluding signers group of arbitrary size. For simplicity we show the case for two (u_i and u_j).

Untraceable Coalition Signing Procedure:

1. Pick a random $r \in \mathbb{Z}_q^*$, compute $U = r(R_i + R_j)$, $h = H_2(m, U)$, $V = (r + h)(D_i + D_j)$. Then the first part of the signature is $\sigma_1 = (U, V)$.
2. Compute $P_m = H_1(m)$, $S_m = (x_i + x_j)P_m$ and $R = (R_i + R_j)$.

The final signature of user is (σ_1, σ_2, R), where σ_2 is the x-coordinate of S_m.

It is easy to see that the signature is valid and untraceable. Without knowing the group size of the coalition, the group manager needs to try $O(2^z)$ combinations of R_is (where z is the size of the group) to trace the identities of the colluding signers. If untraceable factor is used, the group manager cannot trace at all even exhausted all of the $O(2^z)$ possibilities. Again, we note that the simple fix described previous can be used to prevent this attack.

4   Group Signature from Proxy Signature

A new group signature scheme with unlimited group size was proposed in [9], using a proxy signature with identity blindness. Unfortunately, we find that the scheme is insecure. It is linkable, untraceable and not exculpable.

4.1 Review

Their group signature scheme consists of five algorithms, namely, `Setup`, `Join`, `Sign`, `Verify` and `Open`.

Setup. Let p, q be two large primes such that $q|(p-1)$ and $\mathbb{G}_q =< g >$ is a q-order multiplicative subgroup of $\mathbb{Z}_p^*$ generated by an element $g \in \mathbb{Z}_p^*$. Let H be a cryptographic hash function defined as $H : \{0,1\}^* \rightarrow \mathbb{Z}_p^*$. The group manager randomly chooses a number $x \in_R \mathbb{Z}_q^*$ as the group's private key. The corresponding group public key is $y = g^x$.

Join. Suppose now that a user u_i wants to join the group. First, u_i randomly chooses $x_i \in \mathbb{Z}_q^*$. Then he/she computes $y_i = g^{x_i}$. To obtain his/her membership certificate, each user must perform the following protocol with the manager:

1. The user u_i sends y_i and his/her identity u_i to the group manager.
2. The group manager blinds the user's identity by choosing a random number $b_i \in_R \mathbb{Z}_q^*$, and computing $u_i' = H(b_i||u_i)$.
3. The group manager chooses a randomly number $k_i \in \mathbb{Z}_q^*$, and creates a warrant message m_i stating that the blind identity u_i' is a legitimate member of the group.
4. The group manager computes $r_i = g^{k_i} \bmod p$ and $s_i = xH(y_i||u_i'||m_i||r_i) + k_i \bmod q$.
5. The group manager records $(y_i, u_i', b_i, u_i, m_i)$ in the group's database.

Then (r_i, s_i, u_i', m_i) is sent to the user u_i. The group member's secret key will be x_i and y_i is the corresponding public key.

Sign. If user u_i wants to sign a message m on behalf of the group, he/she simply use x as the private key to sign the message m using any discrete-logarithm-based signature scheme to give the signature σ, and sends together $(y_i, r_i, s_i, u_i', m_i)$.

Verify. Given a signature $(\sigma, y_i, r_i, s_i, u_i', m_i)$ and a message m, verification can be divided into two parts:

1. The verifier makes sure that the signature is generated by a group member by verifying whether the equation $g^{s_i} = y^{H(y_i||u_i'||m_i||r_i)} \cdot r_i$ holds.
2. The verifier checks that the signature is definitely generated by u_i rather than other members of the group by checking that σ is a valid signature corresponding to the public key y_i.

Open. The group manager knows the relationship of the actual identity and the blinded identity for each member. As a result, it is easy for the group manager, given a message m and a valid group signature, to determine the identity of the signer u_i corresponding to the public key y_i. The group manager can show b_i to the public. Anyone can verify $u_i' = H(b_i||u_i)$ and know the real identity of the signer. The anonymity comes from the one-way property of the hash function.

4.2   Analysis

Traceability. From the first glance, it seems trivial that the group manage can always open a group signature. However, the original paper [9] does not addressed the issue that the user u_i repudiates he/she has joined the group. A key observation on the `Sign` phase is that user u_i just use his/her key to sign the message and simply *append* the group credential $(y_i, r_i, s_i, u'_i, m_i)$ to the signature. It is possible for a malicious group manager to append the group credential to the *normal* signature generated by the private-public key pair (x_i, y_i) and falsely claimed that the resulting signature is a group signature.

From the above weakness, even when the group manager wants to open the signature to revoke its anonymity, no one will trust the group manager as it is possible for the group manager to frame anyone that he/she has joined the group by creating fraudulent signer records and using the above attack.

A correct implementation should use *both* the group credential and the user's secret key x_i to sign the message instead of only using x_i. It can be done by using the new signing key $x'_i = x_i + s_i$ to sign the message and use the corresponding public key $y'_i = y^{H(y_i||u'_i||m_i||r_i)} \cdot r_i \cdot y_i$ to verify. It is easy to see that $y'_i = g^{x'_i}$.

Exculpability. After the above modification, it seems that the group manager cannot "sign on behalf" of other as the group manager does not know x_i. However, we show that the scheme's exculpability is still in question.

Group Manager's Attack:

If group manager wants to give a message m that is supposed to be signed by someone on behalf of the group, after received the public key y_i from the user, he/she performs the following steps:

1. Pick a random $c \in \mathbb{Z}_q^*$, compute $\hat{r}_i = y_i^{-1} \cdot g^c$.
2. Compute $\hat{x}'_i = c + x \cdot H(y_i||u'_i||m_i||\hat{r}_i) \bmod q$ and $\hat{y}'_i = g^{\hat{x}'_i}$.

It is easy to see that $(\hat{x}'_i, \hat{y}'_i)$ is a valid private-public key pair as $\hat{y}'_i = y^{H(y_i||u'_i||m_i||\hat{r}_i)} \cdot \hat{r}_i \cdot y_i$. So the group manager can still sign on behalf of any group member even he/she does not know the user's secret key x_i; the traceability and the exculpability of the scheme are still in question. Indeed, the above attack follows the idea of the attack in [17].

Unlinkability. It is trivial that anyone can link two group signature produced by the same member as he/she must need to provide the same values for $(y_i, r_i, s_i, u'_i, m_i)$ each time. However, we remark that the original paper [9] does not addressed the unlinkability requirement of a group signature.

5   Signcryption from Secret Sharing

The signcryption scheme in [2] makes use of an asymmetric encryption scheme $(E.(\cdot), D.(\cdot))$ satisfying the following properties:

1. $D_{S_i}(E_{P_i}(m)) = m$ for any message m and any key pair (S_i, P_i).
2. $D_{P_i}(E_{S_i}(m)) = m$ for any message m and any key pair (S_i, P_i).
3. The ciphertext domain is a certain group, says $\mathbb{Z}_p^*$, where p is a large prime.

RSA encryption scheme [13] is an example of asymmetric encryption scheme satisfying these properties.

5.1 Review

Setup. Both the signcryptor (user A) and the de-signcryptor (user B) use the key generation algorithm of the above asymmetric encryption scheme to generate their respective private-public key pair $((S_A, P_A)$ and (S_B, P_B) respectively).

Signcrypt. To signcrypt any message m, user A performs the following steps.

1. Compute $h = H(m)$.
2. Compute $s = E_{S_A}(h)$.
3. Compute $c = E_{P_B}(m)$.
4. Compute $\sigma = f(2)$, where $f(x) = c + sx$.
5. Send (s, σ) to user B.

De-Signcrypt. To de-signcrypt any ciphertext (s, σ), user B performs the following steps.

1. Use Lagrange interpolation [15] (of the points $(0, c)$ and $(2, \sigma)$) to recover c.
2. Compute $m = D_{S_B}(c)$.
3. Verify whether $H(m) = D_{P_A}(s)$.

5.2 Analysis

Ciphertext Indistinguishability. Recall that in the definition of ciphertext indistinguishability, the adversary first prepares two distinct message of equal length (m_1 and m_2) and sends them to the challenger. Then the challenger will return the ciphertext given by the encryption of either one. In the above scheme, since s is sent in plaintext, the adversary can use the public key P_A of the sender to compute $h' = D_{P_A}(s)$, and checks whether $h' = H(m_1)$ or $h' = H(m_2)$ to win the game. The probability for the adversary to win this game is 1, which is well over the ideal security level $\frac{1}{2}$.

Notice that the scheme is still vulnerable even the function $f(x)$ used in the Signcrypt algorithm is changed to $f(x) = c + \sigma x$. This modification would not hide s as anyone (with no secret knowledge) can recover it by using Lagrange polynomial interpolation (of the points $(0, c)$ and $(1, \sigma + 1)$).

6 Conclusion

It is interesting to see that the functionalities provided by one cryptographic scheme can be used to build another cryptographic scheme. Recently, there are three schemes proposed following this idea. They are a group signature scheme from identity-based signature [8], another group signature scheme from proxy signature [9] and a signcryption scheme from secret sharing [2]. In this paper, we show that the insecurity of [8] and [9] from different aspects. We also show that a simple adaption [2] of secret sharing cannot be used to build a semantically secure signcryption scheme.

The lessons we learn from these analysis are summarized as follows.

1. The combination of secure cryptographic schemes does not necessarily give a secure cryptographic scheme.
2. The security properties of the building block should be clearly investigated before using it to build a secure cryptographic scheme.
3. The cost of achieving a set of properties may be actually the compromise of other security properties.

We hold that it is not easy to design cryptographic scheme from other schemes.

References

1. Michel Abdalla and Bogdan Warinschi. On the Minimal Assumptions of Group Signature Schemes. In Javier Lopez, Sihan Qing, and Eiji Okamoto, editors, *Information and Communications Security, 6th International Conference, ICICS 2004, Malaga, Spain, October 27-29, 2004, Proceedings*, volume 3269 of *Lecture Notes in Computer Science*, pages 1–13. Springer-Verlag, 2004.
2. Mohamed Al-Ibrahim. A Signcryption Scheme Based on Secret Sharing Technique. In Vladimir Gorodetsky, Leonard J. Popyack, and Victor A. Skormin, editors, *Computer Network Security, Second International Workshop on Mathematical Methods, Models, and Architectures for Computer Network Security, MMM-ACNS 2003, St. Petersburg, Russia, September 21-23, 2003, Proceedings*, volume 2776 of *Lecture Notes in Computer Science*, pages 279–288. Springer, 2003.
3. Mihir Bellare, Daniele Micciancio, and Bogdan Warinschi. Foundations of Group Signatures: Formal Definitions, Simplified Requirements, and a Construction Based on General Assumptions. In Eli Biham, editor, *Advances in Cryptology - EUROCRYPT 2003, International Conference on the Theory and Applications of Cryptographic Techniques, Warsaw, Poland, May 4-8, 2003, Proceedings*, volume 2656 of *Lecture Notes in Computer Science*, pages 614–629. Springer, 2003.
4. Dan Boneh, Ben Lynn, and Hovav Shacham. Short Signatures from the Weil Pairing. In Colin Boyd, editor, *Advances in Cryptology - ASIACRYPT 2001, 7th International Conference on the Theory and Application of Cryptology and Information Security, Gold Coast, Australia, December 9-13, 2001, Proceedings*, volume 2248 of *Lecture Notes in Computer Science*, pages 514–532. Springer, 2001.
5. Jae Choon Cha and Jung Hee Cheon. An Identity-Based Signature from Gap Diffie-Hellman Groups . In Yvo Desmedt, editor, *Public Key Cryptography - PKC 2003, Sixth International Workshop on Theory and Practice in Public Key Cryptography, Miami, FL, USA, January 6-8, 2003, Proceedings*, volume 2567 of *Lecture Notes in Computer Science*, pages 18–30. Springer, 2002.
6. David Chaum and Eugène van Heyst. Group Signatures. In Donald W. Davies, editor, *Advances in Cryptology - EUROCRYPT '91, Workshop on the Theory and Application of of Cryptographic Techniques, Brighton, UK, April 8-11, 1991, Proceedings*, volume 547 of *Lecture Notes in Computer Science*, pages 257–265. Springer, 1991.

7. Sherman S.M. Chow, S.M. Yiu, Lucas C.K. Hui, and K.P. Chow. Efficient Forward and Provably Secure ID-Based Signcryption Scheme with Public Verifiability and Public Ciphertext Authenticity. In Jong In Lim and Dong Hoon Lee, editors, *Information Security and Cryptology - ICISC 2006, 6th International Conference Seoul, Korea, November 27-28, 2003, Revised Papers*, volume 2971 of *Lecture Notes in Computer Science*, pages 352–369. Springer-Verlag, 2004.

8. Donghua Deng and Yiming Zhao. An Efficient Group Signature from Gap Diffe-Hellman Groups. In *ChinaCrypt 2004 (in English)*, pages 186–194, 2004.

9. Ciaotong Fu and Chunxiang Xu. A New Group Signature Scheme with Unlimited Group Size. In Kefei Chen, editor, *Progress on Cryptography, 25 Years of Cryptography in China*, pages 89–96. Kluwer Academic Publishers, 2004.

10. Shafi Goldwasser and Silvio Micali. Probabilistic Encryption. *Journal of Computer and System Sciences*, 28(2):270–299, 1984.

11. Patrick Horster, Markus Michels, and Holger Petersen. Authenticated Encryption Schemes with Low Communication Costs. *Electronics Letters*, 30(15):1212–1213, 1994.

12. Wei-Bin Lee and Chin-Chen Chang. Authenticated Encryption Schemes Without Using a One Way Function. *Electronics Letters*, 31(19):1656–1657, 1995.

13. Ronald L. Rivest, Adi Shamir, and Leonard Adleman. A Method for Obtaining Digital Signatures and Public-Key Cryptosystems. *Communications of the ACM*, 21(2):120–126, February 1978.

14. J. Rompel. One-Way Functions are Necessary and Sufficient for Secure Signatures. In *Proceedings of the Twenty-Second Annual ACM Symposium on Theory of Computing (STOC '90)*, pages 387–394. ACM Press, 1990.

15. Adi Shamir. How to Share A Secret. *Communications of the ACM*, 22(11):612–613, 1979.

16. Ai fen Sui, Sherman S.M. Chow, Lucas C.K. Hui, S.M. Yiu, K.P. Chow, W.W. Tsang, C.F. Chong, K.H. Pun, and H.W. Chan. Separable and Anonymous Identity-Based Key Issuing. In *1st International Workshop on Security in Networks and Distributed Systems (SNDS 2005), in conjunction with 11th International Conference on Parallel and Distributed Systems (ICPADS 2005), July 20-22, 2005, Fukuoka, Japan*, 2005. Full version available at Cryptology ePrint Archive, Report 2004/322.

17. Guilin Wang, Feng Bao, Jianying Zhou, and Robert H. Deng. Security Analysis of Some Proxy Signatures. In Jong In Lim and Dong Hoon Lee, editors, *Information Security and Cryptology - ICISC 2003, 6th International Conference, Seoul, Korea, November 27-28, 2003, Revised Papers*, volume 2971 of *Lecture Notes in Computer Science*, pages 305–319. Springer, 2004.

18. Yuliang Zheng. Digital Signcryption or How to Achieve Cost (Signature & Encryption) << Cost(Signature) + Cost(Encryption). In Burton S. Kaliski Jr., editor, *Advances in Cryptology: Proceedings of CRYPTO 1997 5th Annual International Cryptology Conference, Santa Barbara, California, USA, August 17-21, 1997*, volume 1294 of *Lecture Notes in Computer Science*, pages 165–179.

19. Yuliang Zheng. Signcryption and Its Applications in Efficient Public Key Solutions. In Eiji Okamoto, George I. Davida, and Masahiro Mambo, editors, *Information Security, First International Workshop, ISW '97, Tatsunokuchi, Japan, September 17-19, 1997, Proceedings*, volume 1396 of *Lecture Notes in Computer Science*, pages 291–312. Springer, 1998. Invited Lecture.

An Effective Attack on the Quantum Key Distribution Protocol Based on Quantum Encryption

Fei Gao[1,2], Su-Juan Qin[1], Qiao-Yan Wen[1], and Fu-Chen Zhu[3]

[1] School of Science, Beijing University of Posts and Telecommunications,
Beijing, 100876, China
hzpe@sohu.com
[2] State Key Laboratory of Integrated Services Network, Xidian University,
Xi'an, 710071, China
[3] National Laboratory for Modern Communications, P.O.Box 810,
Chengdu, 610041, China

Abstract. We come up with a special attack strategy to the quantum key distribution protocol based on quantum encryption. With our strategy an eavesdropper can elicit about half of the key bits without being detected by the legal communication parties. Furthermore, the eavesdropping needs only facilities similar to that of the legal parties. Therefore, we draw a conclusion that the original protocol is insecure and, at last, a feasible improvement of the protocol is proposed.

1 Introduction

In Ref.[1], Zhang, Li and Guo proposed a quantum key distribution (QKD) protocol based on quantum encryption. This protocol employs previously shared EPR pairs as a quantum key to encode and decode the classical cryptography key, and the quantum key is reusable. However, here we will show that, this protocol would become insecure if the quantum key is reused for more than two times.

For convenience, except for especial declarations, we use the same notations as in Ref.[1]. Let us give a brief description of the Zhang-Li-Guo protocol firstly (see Fig. 1). At the beginning, Alice and Bob share some quantity of EPR pairs serving as the quantum key: $|\Phi^+\rangle = 1/\sqrt{2}(|00\rangle + |11\rangle)$. To send the key bit (0 or 1) to Bob, Alice prepares a carrier particle γ in the corresponding state $|\psi\rangle$ ($|0\rangle$ or $|1\rangle$), performs a controlled-NOT (CNOT) operation on γ and thus entangles this qubit to the previously shared Bell state. Then she transmits this qubit to Bob, from which Bob can obtain the key bit ψ by performing a CNOT operation and a measurement on it. Because every sending qubit is in a completely mixed state, Eve cannot extract information about the key bit. Furthermore, to strengthen the security of this protocol, Alice and Bob perform a rotation on their respective shared particles before encrypting each $|\psi\rangle$.

$$R(\frac{\pi}{4}) = \frac{1}{\sqrt{2}} \begin{pmatrix} 1 & 1 \\ -1 & 1 \end{pmatrix} \tag{1}$$

D. Feng, D. Lin, and M. Yung (Eds.): CISC 2005, LNCS 3822, pp. 302–312, 2005.
© Springer-Verlag Berlin Heidelberg 2005

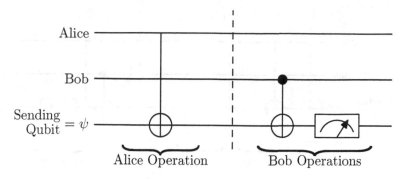

Fig. 1. The Zhang-Li-Guo protocol. Note that in this paper, for simplicity, the operation $R(\pi/4) \otimes R(\pi/4)$ or $R(\pi/4)^{\otimes 3}$ is not included in our figures.

It is well known that the shared particles in Bell state have strong quantum correlation (i.e., entanglement). It is this correlation that makes the quantum encryption secure. The authors of Ref.[1] argues that, because this correlation cannot be produced by LQCC and the eavesdropper cannot establish this correlation with the sender, the quantum key is reusable. However, they overlooked a fact that the sending qubit would bring Eve the chance to entangle her ancilla to the shared Bell state, which means that the eavesdropper can establish this correlation with the sender. As a result, this protocol becomes insecure when the quantum key is reused.

In this paper we propose an effective attack strategy to the Zhang-Li-Guo protocol, with which Eve can obtain about half of key bits without being detected. See Section 2 for the details of this attack strategy. A feasible improvement of the Zhang-Li-Guo protocol is presented in Section 3 and a conclusion is given in Section 4.

2   The Attack Strategy

Now we come to Eve's eavesdropping strategy. Consider a certain EPR pair shared by Alice and Bob, which will be used to encrypt $\gamma_1, \gamma_2, \gamma_3, \ldots$ (the corresponding states are $|\psi_1\rangle, |\psi_2\rangle, |\psi_3\rangle, \ldots$ respectively, where $\psi_i = 0$ or 1). Hereafter we use the term "the i-th round" to denote the processing procedures of γ_i, and Alice and Bob's operation $R(\pi/4) \otimes R(\pi/4)$ is taken as the beginning of each round. Furthermore, we use $|\phi_{i0}\rangle_{A,B,E}$ and $|\phi_{i1}\rangle_{A,B,E}$ to denote the states shared by Alice, Bob and Eve at the beginning and the end of the i-th round, respectively. In addition, the subscripts A, B and E represent the particles belonging to Alice, Bob, and Eve respectively, and γ represents the sending particle. Suppose Eve prepares $|0\rangle$ as her ancilla, the eavesdropping strategy can be described as follows:

(i) In the first round, Eve entangles her ancilla into the Bell state shared by Alice and Bob. More specifically, Eve intercepts the sending qubit and performs

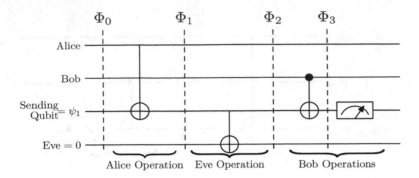

Fig. 2. Eve's attack in the first round

a CNOT operation on her ancilla, then resends the sending qubit to Bob (see Fig. 2). The initial state of Alice, Bob and Eve's particles can be represented as

$$|\phi_{10}\rangle_{A,B,E} = \frac{1}{\sqrt{2}}(|0,0,0\rangle + |1,1,0\rangle)_{A,B,E}. \tag{2}$$

Then the states at various stages in Fig. 2 are as follows:

$$|\Phi_0\rangle = \frac{1}{\sqrt{2}}(|0,0,\psi_1,0\rangle + |1,1,\psi_1,0\rangle)_{A,B,\gamma,E}, \tag{3}$$

$$|\Phi_1\rangle = \frac{1}{\sqrt{2}}(|0,0,\psi_1,0\rangle + |1,1,\overline{\psi}_1,0\rangle)_{A,B,\gamma,E}, \tag{4}$$

$$|\Phi_2\rangle = \frac{1}{\sqrt{2}}(|0,0,\psi_1,\psi_1\rangle + |1,1,\overline{\psi}_1,\overline{\psi}_1\rangle)_{A,B,\gamma,E}, \tag{5}$$

$$|\Phi_3\rangle = \frac{1}{\sqrt{2}}(|0,0,\psi_1,\psi_1\rangle + |1,1,\psi_1,\overline{\psi}_1\rangle)_{A,B,\gamma,E}, \tag{6}$$

where the overline expresses bit flip, for example, $\overline{\psi}_1 = \psi_1 + 1$ modulo 2.

In the last stage, when Bob performs his CNOT operation, he disentangles the sending qubit $|\psi_1\rangle$ and correctly gets the value of ψ_1, while the original Bell state has now been entangled with the state of Eve in the form of

$$|\phi_{11}\rangle_{A,B,E} = \frac{1}{\sqrt{2}}(|0,0,\psi_1\rangle + |1,1,\overline{\psi}_1\rangle)_{A,B,E}. \tag{7}$$

(ii) In the second round, Eve tries to avoid the detection and, at the same time, retain her entanglement with Alice and Bob. As was proved in Ref.[1], Eve can not obtain information in this round. However, we will show that she can take some measures to avoid the detection.

Firstly, when Alice and Bob perform the operations $R(\pi/4) \otimes R(\pi/4)$ on their "Bell state", Eve also performs $R(\pi/4)$ on her ancilla. As a result, the entangled state of Alice, Bob and Eve will be converted into

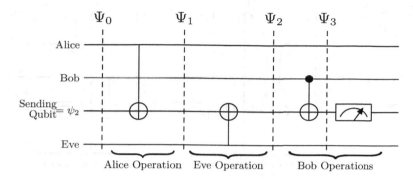

Fig. 3. Eve's attack in the second round

$$|\phi_{20}\rangle_{A,B,E} = R(\frac{\pi}{4})^{\otimes 3}|\phi_{11}\rangle_{A,B,E}$$

$$= \frac{1}{2}\left[|0,0,0\rangle + (-1)^{\psi_1}|0,1,1\rangle + (-1)^{\psi_1}|1,0,1\rangle + |1,1,0\rangle\right]_{A,B,E}, \quad (8)$$

where the identity $R(\frac{\pi}{4})|\psi\rangle = 1/\sqrt{2}[|0\rangle + (-1)^{\overline{\psi}}|1\rangle]$ was used.

Afterwards, Eve intercepts the sending qubit, performs a CNOT operation on it, and then resends it to Bob (see Fig. 3). The states at various stages in Fig. 3 are as follows:

$$|\Psi_0\rangle = \frac{1}{2}\left[|0,0,\psi_2,0\rangle + (-1)^{\psi_1}|0,1,\psi_2,1\rangle\right.$$
$$\left. + (-1)^{\psi_1}|1,0,\psi_2,1\rangle + |1,1,\psi_2,0\rangle\right]_{A,B,\gamma,E}, \quad (9)$$

$$|\Psi_1\rangle = \frac{1}{2}\left[|0,0,\psi_2,0\rangle + (-1)^{\psi_1}|0,1,\psi_2,1\rangle\right.$$
$$\left. + (-1)^{\psi_1}|1,0,\overline{\psi}_2,1\rangle + |1,1,\overline{\psi}_2,0\rangle\right]_{A,B,\gamma,E}, \quad (10)$$

$$|\Psi_2\rangle = \frac{1}{2}\left[|0,0,\psi_2,0\rangle + (-1)^{\psi_1}|0,1,\overline{\psi}_2,1\rangle\right.$$
$$\left. + (-1)^{\psi_1}|1,0,\psi_2,1\rangle + |1,1,\overline{\psi}_2,0\rangle\right]_{A,B,\gamma,E}, \quad (11)$$

$$|\Psi_3\rangle = \frac{1}{2}\left[|0,0,\psi_2,0\rangle + (-1)^{\psi_1}|0,1,\psi_2,1\rangle\right.$$
$$\left. + (-1)^{\psi_1}|1,0,\psi_2,1\rangle + |1,1,\psi_2,0\rangle\right]_{A,B,\gamma,E}. \quad (12)$$

In the last stage, when Bob performs his CNOT operation, he disentangles the sending qubit $|\psi_2\rangle$ and correctly gets the value of ψ_2, while leaving the state

$$|\phi_{21}\rangle_{A,B,E} = \frac{1}{2}\left[|0,0,0\rangle + (-1)^{\psi_1}|0,1,1\rangle\right.$$
$$\left. + (-1)^{\psi_1}|1,0,1\rangle + |1,1,0\rangle\right]_{A,B,E}. \quad (13)$$

(iii) In the third round, Eve eavesdrops the key bit. Firstly, as in step (ii), Eve also performs $R(\pi/4)$ on her ancilla when Alice and Bob perform $R(\pi/4)$ on their respective particles. The entangled state will be changed into

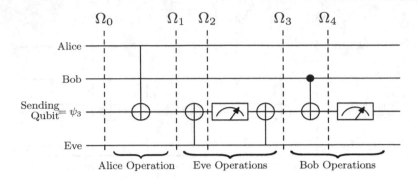

Fig. 4. Eve's attack in the third round

$$|\phi_{30}\rangle_{A,B,E} = R(\frac{\pi}{4})^{\otimes 3}|\phi_{21}\rangle_{A,B,E}$$
$$= \frac{1}{2\sqrt{2}}\left[\alpha\left(|0,0,0\rangle - |1,1,1\rangle\right) - \beta\left(|0,0,1\rangle - |1,1,0\rangle\right)\right]_{A,B,E}, \quad (14)$$

where $\alpha = 1 + (-1)^{\psi_1}$, $\beta = 1 - (-1)^{\psi_1}$.

Afterwards, Eve intercepts the sending qubit, performs a CNOT operation, a measurement and another CNOT operation on it, and then resends it to Bob (see Fig. 4). The states at various stages in Fig. 4 are as follows:

$$|\Omega_0\rangle = \frac{1}{2\sqrt{2}}\left[\alpha\left(|0,0,\psi_3,0\rangle - |1,1,\psi_3,1\rangle\right)\right.$$
$$\left. - \beta\left(|0,0,\psi_3,1\rangle - |1,1,\psi_3,0\rangle\right)\right]_{A,B,\gamma,E}, \quad (15)$$

$$|\Omega_1\rangle = \frac{1}{2\sqrt{2}}\left[\alpha\left(|0,0,\psi_3,0\rangle - |1,1,\overline{\psi}_3,1\rangle\right)\right.$$
$$\left. - \beta\left(|0,0,\psi_3,1\rangle - |1,1,\overline{\psi}_3,0\rangle\right)\right]_{A,B,\gamma,E}, \quad (16)$$

$$|\Omega_2\rangle = \frac{1}{2\sqrt{2}}\left[\alpha\left(|0,0,\psi_3,0\rangle - |1,1,\psi_3,1\rangle\right)\right.$$
$$\left. - \beta\left(|0,0,\overline{\psi}_3,1\rangle - |1,1,\overline{\psi}_3,0\rangle\right)\right]_{A,B,\gamma,E}, \quad (17)$$

$$|\Omega_3\rangle = \frac{1}{2\sqrt{2}}\left[\alpha\left(|0,0,\psi_3,0\rangle - |1,1,\overline{\psi}_3,1\rangle\right)\right.$$
$$\left. - \beta\left(|0,0,\psi_3,1\rangle - |1,1,\overline{\psi}_3,0\rangle\right)\right]_{A,B,\gamma,E}, \quad (18)$$

$$|\Omega_4\rangle = \frac{1}{2\sqrt{2}}\left[\alpha\left(|0,0,\psi_3,0\rangle - |1,1,\psi_3,1\rangle\right)\right.$$
$$\left. - \beta\left(|0,0,\psi_3,1\rangle - |1,1,\psi_3,0\rangle\right)\right]_{A,B,\gamma,E}. \quad (19)$$

It can be seen that Eve disentangles the key qubit by a CNOT operation, and then restores the entangled state by another CNOT operation after a measurement. As a result, Eve obtains the measurement result $\psi_3 + \psi_1$ (modulo 2) and Bob

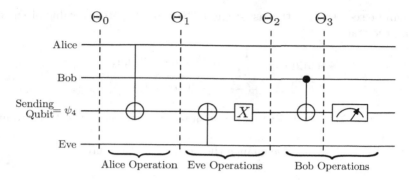

Fig. 5. Eve's attack in the fourth round

correctly gets the value of ψ_3. At last, the entangled state of Alice, Bob and Eve can be written as

$$|\phi_{31}\rangle_{A,B,E} = \frac{1}{2\sqrt{2}} \left[\alpha \left(|0,0,0\rangle - |1,1,1\rangle \right) - \beta \left(|0,0,1\rangle - |1,1,0\rangle \right) \right]_{A,B,E}. \quad (20)$$

(iv) In the fourth round, Eve uses a similar strategy as in the second round to avoid the detection, the only difference is that Eve has to perform an additional $X = \begin{pmatrix} 0 & 1 \\ 1 & 0 \end{pmatrix}$ operation on the sending qubit here (see Fig. 5). After their operation $R(\frac{\pi}{4})^{\otimes 3}$, Alice, Bob and Eve change the entangled state into

$$|\phi_{40}\rangle_{A,B,E} = R(\frac{\pi}{4})^{\otimes 3}|\phi_{31}\rangle_{A,B,E}$$

$$= -\frac{1}{2} \big[|0,0,1\rangle + (-1)^{\psi_1}|0,1,0\rangle$$

$$+ (-1)^{\psi_1}|1,0,0\rangle + |1,1,1\rangle \big]_{A,B,E}. \quad (21)$$

Then Eve performs the operations as described in Fig. 5. The states at various stages are as follows:

$$|\Theta_0\rangle = -\frac{1}{2} \big[|0,0,\psi_4,1\rangle + (-1)^{\psi_1}|0,1,\psi_4,0\rangle$$

$$+ (-1)^{\psi_1}|1,0,\psi_4,0\rangle + |1,1,\psi_4,1\rangle \big]_{A,B,\gamma,E}, \quad (22)$$

$$|\Theta_1\rangle = -\frac{1}{2} \big[|0,0,\psi_4,1\rangle + (-1)^{\psi_1}|0,1,\psi_4,0\rangle$$

$$+ (-1)^{\psi_1}|1,0,\overline{\psi}_4,0\rangle + |1,1,\overline{\psi}_4,1\rangle \big]_{A,B,\gamma,E}, \quad (23)$$

$$|\Theta_2\rangle = -\frac{1}{2} \big[|0,0,\psi_4,1\rangle + (-1)^{\psi_1}|0,1,\overline{\psi}_4,0\rangle$$

$$+ (-1)^{\psi_1}|1,0,\psi_4,0\rangle + |1,1,\overline{\psi}_4,1\rangle \big]_{A,B,\gamma,E}, \quad (24)$$

$$|\Theta_3\rangle = -\frac{1}{2} \big[|0,0,\psi_4,1\rangle + (-1)^{\psi_1}|0,1,\psi_4,0\rangle$$

$$+ (-1)^{\psi_1}|1,0,\psi_4,0\rangle + |1,1,\psi_4,1\rangle \big]_{A,B,\gamma,E}. \quad (25)$$

It can be seen that, in the last stage, Bob correctly gets the value of ψ_4, while leaving the state

$$|\phi_{41}\rangle_{A,B,E} = -\frac{1}{2}\big[|0,0,1\rangle + (-1)^{\psi_1}|0,1,0\rangle$$
$$+(-1)^{\psi_1}|1,0,0\rangle + |1,1,1\rangle\big]_{A,B,E}. \tag{26}$$

(v) In the fifth round, Eve uses the same strategy as in the third round to eavesdrop the key bit, that is, the strategy in step (iii). After their operation $R(\frac{\pi}{4})^{\otimes 3}$, Alice, Bob and Eve change the entangled state into

$$|\phi_{50}\rangle_{A,B,E} = R(\frac{\pi}{4})^{\otimes 3}|\phi_{41}\rangle_{A,B,E}$$
$$= -\frac{1}{2\sqrt{2}}\big[\alpha(|0,0,0\rangle + |1,1,1\rangle) + \beta(|0,0,1\rangle + |1,1,0\rangle)\big]_{A,B,E}. \tag{27}$$

Then Eve performs the operations as described in Fig. 4. The states at various stages are as follows:

$$|\Upsilon_0\rangle = -\frac{1}{2\sqrt{2}}\big[\alpha\,(|0,0,\psi_5,0\rangle + |1,1,\psi_5,1\rangle)$$
$$+\beta\,(|0,0,\psi_5,1\rangle + |1,1,\psi_5,0\rangle)\big]_{A,B,\gamma,E}, \tag{28}$$

$$|\Upsilon_1\rangle = -\frac{1}{2\sqrt{2}}\big[\alpha\,(|0,0,\psi_5,0\rangle + |1,1,\overline{\psi}_5,1\rangle)$$
$$+\beta\,(|0,0,\psi_5,1\rangle + |1,1,\overline{\psi}_5,0\rangle)\big]_{A,B,\gamma,E}, \tag{29}$$

$$|\Upsilon_2\rangle = -\frac{1}{2\sqrt{2}}\big[\alpha\,(|0,0,\psi_5,0\rangle + |1,1,\psi_5,1\rangle)$$
$$+\beta\,(|0,0,\overline{\psi}_5,1\rangle + |1,1,\overline{\psi}_5,0\rangle)\big]_{A,B,\gamma,E}, \tag{30}$$

$$|\Upsilon_3\rangle = -\frac{1}{2\sqrt{2}}\big[\alpha\,(|0,0,\psi_5,0\rangle + |1,1,\overline{\psi}_5,1\rangle)$$
$$+\beta\,(|0,0,\psi_5,1\rangle + |1,1,\overline{\psi}_5,0\rangle)\big]_{A,B,\gamma,E}, \tag{31}$$

$$|\Upsilon_4\rangle = -\frac{1}{2\sqrt{2}}\big[\alpha\,(|0,0,\psi_5,0\rangle + |1,1,\psi_5,1\rangle)$$
$$+\beta\,(|0,0,\psi_5,1\rangle + |1,1,\psi_5,0\rangle)\big]_{A,B,\gamma,E}, \tag{32}$$

where Υ_p corresponds to the state Ω_p in Fig. 4 ($p = 0,1,2,3,4$). It can be seen that Eve's measurement result in this round is $\psi_5 + \psi_1$ (modulo 2).

Obviously, in the last stage, Bob correctly gets the value of ψ_5, while leaving the state

$$|\phi_{51}\rangle_{A,B,E} = -\frac{1}{2\sqrt{2}}\big[\alpha(|0,0,0\rangle + |1,1,1\rangle) + \beta(|0,0,1\rangle + |1,1,0\rangle)\big]_{A,B,E}. \tag{33}$$

Comparing the state $|\phi_{51}\rangle_{A,B,E}$ with $|\phi_{11}\rangle_{A,B,E}$, we can verify that the two states is equivalent except for a global phase factor (i.e., -1). That is, from an observational point of view these two states are identical [2]. Therefore, in the following rounds, Eve can use the same strategy as in the steps from (ii) to (v) repeatedly.

Now let us give a concretely description of our eavesdropping strategy:

1. In the first round, Eve performs the operations as described in Fig. 2;
2. When Alice and Bob perform $R(\frac{\pi}{4})$ on their respective particles at the beginning of every round (except for the first round), Eve also performs $R(\frac{\pi}{4})$ on her ancilla;
3. From the second round to the fifth round, Eve performs the operations as described in Fig. 3, Fig. 4, Fig. 5 and Fig. 4 in turn;
4. In the following rounds, Eve performs the operations as described in item 3 repeatedly.

From the above analysis, we can see that in our eavesdropping strategy no error will be introduced to the key distribution between Alice and Bob, and Eve will obtain exactly the result of

$$\psi_3 + \psi_1, \psi_5 + \psi_1, \psi_7 + \psi_1, \psi_9 + \psi_1, \ldots$$

from which she can infer about half of the key bits by checking two possible values for ψ_1.

It should be emphasized that there is another profitable fact for Eve. That is, at the end of QKD procedure, Alice and Bob will compare a subsequence of the key bits publicly to detect eavesdropping, which obviously leak useful information to Eve. More specifically, as long as any odd numbered data bit is announced, Eve can determine which of the two possible results is true. By this means Eve can obtain the odd numbered data bits completely except for the little-probability event that all the compared bits are even numbered.

It looks like that Eve can only get the odd numbered key bits which is a fixed subset (of the key) known to the legitimate parties. But this is not the fact. In this paper we suppose Eve begins her attack in Alice and Bob's first round when we describe our strategy. In this condition, Eve can obtain ψ_1, ψ_3, ψ_5, ψ_7,... (i.e., the odd numbered key bits). However, this is not always the case. Alternatively, if Eve begins her attack in Alice and Bob's second round, Eve will elicit the value of ψ_2, ψ_4, ψ_6, ψ_8,... (i.e., the even numbered key bits). Furthermore, if she want, Eve can obtain partial odd numbered key bits and partial even numbered key bits in her attack, which can be achieved by the additional parity-switching operations. That is, Eve disentangles her ancilla out from the carrier (i.e., stop the attack) by CNOT operation and begins a new attack in the next rounds. For example, suppose the key bits Alice and Bob want to distribute is ψ_1, ψ_2, ψ_3, ..., ψ_{2k}, ψ_{2k+1}, ψ_{2k+2}, ..., ψ_n (where k is an integer and $2k + 2 < n$), Eve begins her attack when Alice and Bob distribute ψ_1 and stops the attack when Alice and Bob distribute ψ_{2k+1}, then Eve begins a new attack when ψ_{2k+2} is distributed. As a result, Eve can obtain ψ_1, ψ_3, ψ_5, ..., ψ_{2k+1}; ψ_{2k+2}, ψ_{2k+4}, ψ_{2k+6}, ... in favorable circumstances. In a case when the total number of qubits, which Alice send to Bob, is unknown and unpredictable (what is the most typical situation), Eve can balance number of the odd numbered and the even numbered key bits eavesdropped during the attack just by more frequent switching of the parity of the detected qubits. Therefore, Eve can obtain either the odd numbered key bits or the even numbered key bits as she will. It is a random sequence of key bits instead of a fixed subset known to the legitimate parties.

Now it is worthwhile to inspect the basic idea of our attack strategy. Though Eve cannot get information about the key bit in every even round (as proved in Ref.[1]), she can take some more clever measures to avoid the detection and retain her entanglement with Alice and Bob so that she can eavesdrop the key bit in the next round. Our attack strategy is exactly based on this fact. By our strategy, if the shared Bell states are reused for many times, Eve can obtain about half of the key bits without being detected by Alice and Bob. One may argue that the shared Bell states would not be reused for too many times without special treatments by Alice and Bob, such as quantum privacy amplification and entanglement purification [1]. However, from above analysis it can be seen that Eve needs only three rounds to elicit partial information about the key bits, which definitely forms a serous threaten to the Zhang-Li-Guo protocol. In fact, the QKD protocols in Refs.[3, 4] have the same hidden troubles, in which Eve can succeed in eavesdropping the key bits with similar strategy.

3   The Improvement

Before we conclude, let us give a discussion about the rotation

$$R(\theta) = \begin{pmatrix} \cos\theta & \sin\theta \\ -\sin\theta & \cos\theta \end{pmatrix}, \tag{34}$$

which plays an important role in the Zhang-Li-Guo protocol. Without Alice and Bob's rotations at the beginning of every round, this QKD protocol would be insecure. For example, in this condition Eve can entangle her ancilla into the Bell state in the first round (as described in Fig. 2), and then elicit information about the key bits in the following rounds (as described in Fig. 4). As a result, Eve will obtain the result of

$$\psi_2 + \psi_1, \psi_3 + \psi_1, \psi_4 + \psi_1, \psi_5 + \psi_1, \ldots.$$

(To avoid confusion we call this attack strategy S_1, and call the strategy we showed in above paragraphs S_2.) Therefore, the rotations are necessary, and $\pi/4$ is selected as the rotation angle because it leads to the maximum error rate (i.e., $1/2$) caused by Eve when she uses the strategy S_1 [1]. However, it is the selection of $\theta = \pi/4$ that makes the Zhang-Li-Guo protocol insecure against S_2. That is, the error rate caused by Eve is 0 when she uses the strategy S_2. Hereafter we use d_1 and d_2 to denote the error rate corresponding to S_1 and S_2, respectively. In fact, it is not difficult to prove that, if $\theta \neq k\pi \pm \pi/4$ ($k = 0, \pm1, \pm2, \ldots$), it is impossible for Eve to elicit information about the key bits without introducing disturbance (See the Appendix for details). Consequently, by altering θ, we can modify the Zhang-Li-Guo protocol so that it can resist both S_1 and S_2.

As was given in Ref.[1], when Eve uses S_1 to attack, the error rate is $d_1 = 2\cos^2\theta\sin^2\theta$. By similar deduction we can obtain the error rate when S_2 is used, i.e., $d_2 = \frac{1}{2}(\sin^2\theta - \cos^2\theta)^2$. Clearly, there is a trade-off between d_1 and d_2, which satisfy the relation of $d_1 + d_2 = 1/2$. That is, a greater d_1 results in a smaller d_2, and vice versa. It can be seen that $\theta = \pi/4$ is an extreme instance, where d_1 reaches its maximum value $1/2$ but $d_2 = 0$. Therefore, if we do not consider the different extent to which the two strategies threaten the QKD protocol, we can select such a rotation angle (denoted as θ_0) that $d_1 = d_2 = 1/4$, i.e., $2\cos^2\theta_0\sin^2\theta_0 = 1/4$. As a result, when we use θ_0 instead of $\pi/4$ in the Zhang-Li-Guo protocol, it can resist both attack strategies (because either strategy will introduce an error rate of $1/4$). We have to confess that this modification decreases the efficiency of eavesdropping detection. However, $1/4$ is still a sufficient value for a detection probability. In fact, as far as the general intercept-resend strategy is concerned, the detection probability in BB84 protocol [5] is $1/4$, too.

4 Conclusion

In summary, we have presented a special attack strategy to the Zhang-Li-Guo protocol [1], in which Eve can elicit about half of the key bits without being detected and needs only facilities similar to that of the legal parties. Furthermore, this attack also threatens other QKD protocols which are based on reused quantum key, such as [3, 4]. Finally we discussed about the ralation between the security and the value of θ, and pointed out that this QKD protocol would be secure if we use θ_0 instead of $\pi/4$.

Acknowledgement

This work is supported by the National Natural Science Foundation of China, Grant No. 60373059; the National Laboratory for Modern Communications Science Foundation of China, Grant No. 51436020103DZ4001; the National Research Foundation for the Doctoral Program of Higher Education of China, Grant No.20040013007; the Graduate Students Innovation Foundation of BUPT; and the ISN Open Foundation.

References

1. Y-S. Zhang, C-F. Li and G-C. Guo, Phys. Rev. A **64**, 024302 (2001).
2. M. A. Nielsen, and I. L. Chuang, *Quantum computation and quantum information*, (Cambridge University Press, Cambridge, 2000).
3. V. Karimipour, Alireza Bahraminasab, and S. Bagherinezhad, Phys. Rev. A **65**, 052331 (2002).
4. S. Bagherinezhad and V. Karimipour, Phys. Rev. A **67**, 044302 (2003).
5. C. H. Bennett and G. Brassard, in *Proceedings of the IEEE International Conference on Computers, Systems, and Signal Processing, Bangalore, India, 1984* (IEEE, New York, 1984), p. 175.

Appendix

In this appendix we will show that when $\theta \neq k\pi \pm \pi/4$ ($k = 0, \pm 1, \pm 2, ...$), it is inevitable for Eve to introduce disturbance if she has entangled her ancilla into the Bell state in the first round.

Without loss of generality, suppose that in the first round Eve's system has entangled with Alice and Bob's key in the state

$$|\Lambda\rangle = \frac{1}{\sqrt{2}}(|00\rangle|\varphi_0\rangle + |11\rangle|\varphi_1\rangle)_{A,B,E}, \tag{35}$$

where there is no restriction on the form of $|\varphi_0\rangle$ and $|\varphi_1\rangle$. After Alice and Bob do a bilateral rotation $R(\theta)$, Alice does a CNOT operation on the sending qubit $|\psi_2\rangle$ and sends it out. Then Eve does a unitary transformation on the sending qubit and her own system. She expects that Alice and Bob cannot detect her existence (i.e., the error rate caused by her is 0). Assume that the unitary transformation has the universal form

$$U_{\gamma,E}|i\rangle_\gamma|\varphi_j\rangle_E = (a_{ij}|0\rangle|\varphi_{aij}\rangle + b_{ij}|1\rangle|\varphi_{bij}\rangle)_{\gamma,E}, \tag{36}$$

where $i, j = 0, 1$ and there is no restriction on the final state of $|\varphi\rangle_E$. At last, Bob receives the sending qubit and uses a CNOT operation to disentangle it from the shared state.

Suppose that the composite system $|\Lambda\rangle_{A,B,E} \otimes |\psi_2\rangle_\gamma$ is changed into $|\Delta\rangle$ after all the above operations, we can easily write the form of the state $|\Delta\rangle$. If the attack is successful, it requires that the sending qubit $|\psi_2\rangle$ is correctly disentangled by Bob. To satisfy this requirement, we obtain the following results:

When $\psi_2 = 0$, we get

$$b_{00} \cos^2 \theta |\varphi_{b00}\rangle + b_{01} \sin^2 \theta |\varphi_{b01}\rangle = 0, \tag{37}$$

$$-a_{00} \sin \theta \cos \theta |\varphi_{a00}\rangle + a_{01} \sin \theta \cos \theta |\varphi_{a01}\rangle = 0, \tag{38}$$

$$-b_{10} \sin \theta \cos \theta |\varphi_{b10}\rangle + b_{11} \sin \theta \cos \theta |\varphi_{b11}\rangle = 0, \tag{39}$$

$$a_{10} \sin^2 \theta |\varphi_{a10}\rangle + a_{11} \cos^2 \theta |\varphi_{a11}\rangle = 0. \tag{40}$$

When $\psi_2 = 1$, we get

$$a_{10} \cos^2 \theta |\varphi_{a10}\rangle + a_{11} \sin^2 \theta |\varphi_{a11}\rangle = 0, \tag{41}$$

$$b_{00} \sin^2 \theta |\varphi_{b00}\rangle + b_{01} \cos^2 \theta |\varphi_{b01}\rangle = 0, \tag{42}$$

where we omit two equations the same as Eqs.(38) and (39).

With the help of Eqs.(35)~(42), we then obtain two possible conditions: either (1) $|\varphi_0\rangle = |\varphi_1\rangle$, which means $|\Lambda\rangle$ is a product state of Eve's ancilla and Alice and Bob's Bell state; or (2) $\theta = k\pi \pm \pi/4$. This result implies that only when $\theta = k\pi \pm \pi/4$ Eve can entangle her ancilla into the Bell state without introducing any disturbance, which is the exact conclusion we want to prove.

A Remark on Implementing the Weil Pairing

Cheol Min Park[1,*], Myung Hwan Kim[1], and Moti Yung[2]

[1] ISaC and Department of Mathematical Sciences,
Seoul National University, Korea
{mpcm, mhkim}@math.snu.ac.kr
[2] RSA Labs and Department of Computer Science,
Columbia University, USA
moti@cs.columbia.edu

Abstract. We propose an improved implementation of modified Weil pairings. By reduction of operations in the extension field to those in the base field, we can save some operations in the extension field when computing a modified Weil pairing. In particular, computing $e_\ell(P, \phi(P))$ is the same as computing the Tate pairing without the final powering. So we can save about 50% of time for computing $e_\ell(P, \phi(P))$ compared with the standard Miller's algorithm.

Keywords: Pairing-based cryptosystem, Weil pairing, modified Weil pairing, separable endomorphism, distortion map.

1 Introduction

Since Joux [16] proposed the one-round tripartite Diffie-Hellman protocol using pairings in 2000, a great deal of work on pairing-based cryptography has been done. An excellent reference to those work is Barreto's 'Pairing-Based Crypto Lounge' [3]. Due to the fact that pairings are now prevalent and applicable to many aspects of cryptography, it becomes important to implement pairings efficiently. The main strength of the Weil and the Tate pairings in cryptography is their bilinearity. In many cryptographic applications, however, another strong property, called non-degeneracy, is required. But the Weil and Tate pairings are trivial when applied to two dependent points. This problem can be solved using distortion maps, suggested by Verheul [25]. The pairings with distortion maps are called *modified pairings*.

Modified pairings are used in most pairing-based cryptography: tripartite Diffie-Hellman [16], identity-based encryption [5], identity-based signatures [9],[15], [22]; short signatures [6, 27], identity-based chameleon hash [26], identification scheme [18], and so on. In particular, many pairing-based cryptographic applications require to compute special values of modified Weil pairing, namely, $e(P, \phi(P))$'s. See [15],[22],[18],[26],[27].

The methods that are employed in cryptography till now are the Weil and the Tate pairing algorithms whose implementations require quite extensive compu-

---

* Part of this work was done while the first author was visiting Columbia University in 2004.

D. Feng, D. Lin, and M. Yung (Eds.): CISC 2005, LNCS 3822, pp. 313–323, 2005.

tations. To date, there are a few papers about implementing the Weil and Tate pairings. For examples,

- Miller's algorithm [21]
- Galbraith et al. on implementing the Tate pairing [14, 2]
- Barreto et al. on computing the Tate pairing [1, 2]
- Eisenträger et al. on improved Weil pairing evaluation [10] and on the squared Weil and Tate pairings [11]

Most works focused on speeding up the computation of the Tate pairing because the Weil pairing is more time-consuming. We need two Miller steps for computing the Weil pairing while computing the Tate pairing requires only one Miller step. One Miller step is called the Miller lite part and the other Miller step is called the full Miller part[24]. By comparing the exponentiation of the Tate pairing with the computation of the full Miller part, one can see a proper power of the Weil pairing can be computed faster than the Tate pairing at high security levels [19].

Our contribution: In this paper, we present an improved implementation of modified Weil pairings using distortion maps. When computing $e_\ell(P, \phi(Q))$, the full Miller part becomes the same as the Miller lite part. In particular, when computing $e_\ell(P, \phi(P))$, we just need to evaluate the Miller lite part. Computing $e_\ell(P, \phi(P))$ is the same as computing the Tate pairing without the final powering. So, we can save about 50% of time for computing $e_\ell(P, \phi(P))$ compared with the standard Miller's algorithm.

Outline of the paper: In Section 2, we review the definitions and basic properties of the Weil pairing and modified Weil pairings. In Section 3, we give definitions, propositions and examples of injective, separable distortion maps. In Section 4, we propose our methods computing general values and special values of a modified Weil pairing. Finally we conclude in Section 5.

2 The Weil Pairing and Modified Weil Pairings

2.1 The Weil Pairing

Let $\mathbb{F}_q$ denote the finite field containing q elements, where q is a prime power, and $\overline{\mathbb{F}}_q$ be an algebraic closure of $\mathbb{F}_q$. An *elliptic curve* $E(\mathbb{F}_q)$ is the set of all solutions (x, y) over $\mathbb{F}_q$ to an equation

$$y^2 + a_1 xy + a_3 y = x^3 + a_2 x^2 + a_4 x + a_6,$$

where $a_i \in \mathbb{F}_q$ for all i, together with the point at infinity O.

A *divisor* D on $E(\overline{\mathbb{F}}_q)$ is a finite linear combination of symbols (P) with integer coefficients:

$$D = \sum_{P \in E(\overline{\mathbb{F}}_q)} n_P(P), \ n_P \in \mathbb{Z}.$$

The set $Div(E)$ of divisors is the free abelian group generated by the symbols (P). The *support* of a divisor $D = \sum_P n_P(P)$ is the set of points P with $n_P \neq O$. Let f be a nonzero rational function on $E(\overline{\mathbb{F}}_q)$. The *divisor* of a function f is

$$div(f) = \sum_P ord_P(f)(P),$$

where $ord_P(f) \in \mathbb{Z}$ is the order of zero or pole of f at P. Given a divisor $D = \sum_P n_P(P)$, we define

$$f(D) = \prod_P f(P)^{n_P}$$

For two divisors $D_1, D_2 \in Div(E)$, we say that D_1 and D_2 are *equivalent* (write $D_1 \sim D_2$) if $D_1 - D_2 = div(f)$ for some rational function f. The relation $\sim$ is an equivalence relation on $Div(E)$.

Let ℓ be a positive integer which is prime to $p = char(\mathbb{F}_q)$ and

$$E[\ell] = \{P \in E(\overline{\mathbb{F}}_q) | \ell P = O\}.$$

For $P, Q \in E[\ell]$, let A_P and A_Q be divisors which are equivalent to $(P) - (O)$ and $(Q) - (O)$, respectively, and have disjoint support. Then there exist rational functions f_{A_P} and f_{A_Q} such that $div(f_{A_P}) = \ell A_P$ and $div(f_{A_Q}) = \ell A_Q$. The Weil pairing of order ℓ is the map

$$e_\ell : E[\ell] \times E[\ell] \longrightarrow \mu_\ell$$

defined by

$$e_\ell(P, Q) = \frac{f_{A_P}(A_Q)}{f_{A_Q}(A_P)},$$

where μ_ℓ is the set of ℓ-th roots of unity.

2.2   Modified Weil Pairings

Let $P \in E[\ell]$. Then the value of $e_\ell(P, P)$ is 1. If the point P and Q are linearly dependent, the value of $e_\ell(P, Q)$ is still 1 by the bilinearity of the Weil pairing. In many cryptographical applications, this causes some trouble. We can avoid this trouble using distortion maps of Verheul. A *distortion map* ϕ with respect to the point $P \in E(\mathbb{F}_q)$ is an endomorphism that maps P to $\phi(P) \in E(\mathbb{F}_{q^k})$ for some k which is linearly independent from P. By [25], distortion maps always exist on supersingular curves with only a finite number of exceptions but not on most non-supersingular curves. Examples of distortion maps on supersingular curves are given in [17]. With respect to a distortion map ϕ, we define a modified Weil pairing $\hat{e}_\ell$ as follows:

$$\hat{e}_\ell(P, Q) = e_\ell(P, \phi(Q)).$$

Note that with a given point P, one can obtain a pair $(P, \phi(P))$ of points that are linearly independent. In many pairing-based cryptographic settings, a modified Weil pairing is defined on $G \times G$, where G is a cyclic group $\langle P \rangle$.

2.3   Miller's Algorithm

The main part of computing the Weil/Tate pairing is to find the rational function f_{A_P} and evaluate $f_{A_P}(A_Q)$. We need to evaluate $f_{A_P}(A_Q)$ and $f_{A_Q}(A_P)$ for computing the Weil pairing. The evaluation of $f_{A_P}(A_Q)$, is called Miller lite part and the evaluation of $f_{A_Q}(A_P)$, is called the full Miller part. Let $g_{U,V}$ be the line passing through points $U, V \in E$ and g_U be the vertical line passing through points $U, -U$.

Theorem 1. *(Miller's formula). Let P be a point on elliptic curve and f_c be a rational function with divisor $(f_c) = c(P) - (cP) - (c-1)(O), c \in \mathbb{Z}$. For all $a, b \in \mathbb{Z}$ and $Q \in E$,*

$$f_{a+b}(Q) = f_a(Q) \cdot f_b(Q) \cdot g_{aP,bP}(Q)/g_{(a+b)P}(Q)$$

If $P \in E[\ell]$ and we choose $A_P = (P) - (O)$, then $f_{A_P} = f_l$. Hence we can compute the Weil pairing by combining the above formulas with the double-and-add method to compute lP. Note that if $P \in E(\mathbb{F}_q)$, then f_{A_P} is a rational function over the base field $\mathbb{F}_q$ and if $P \in E(\mathbb{F}_{q^k})$, then f_{A_P} is a rational function over the extension field $\mathbb{F}_{q^k}$. Since $P \in E(\mathbb{F}_q)$ and $Q \in E(\mathbb{F}_{q^k})$, the full Miller part is more time-consuming than the Miller lite part.

3   Injective and Separable Distortion Maps

Before we propose our methods computing modified Weil pairings, we need several definitions and propositions. Many of them are from [7].

3.1   A Separable Endomorphism

Let ϕ be an endomorphism and $P \in E(\mathbb{F}_q)$.

Definition 1. *The ramification index of ϕ at P is $e_\phi(P) = ord_P(u \circ \phi)$, where u is a uniformizing variable at $\phi(P)$.*

For the definition of the uniformizing variable, we refer the readers to [7]. It is well known that the values of $e_\phi(P)$ remains the same for all $P \in E(\mathbb{F}_q)$. We call this value the *ramification index* of ϕ, denoted by e_ϕ.

Definition 2. *For an endomorphism ϕ, we define $\phi^* : Div(E) \to Div(E)$ to be the homomorphism satisfying*

$$\phi^*((Q)) = \sum_{\phi(P)=Q} e_\phi(P).$$

Definition 3. *An endomorphism ϕ is called separable if $e_\phi = 1$, and inseparable if $e_\phi > 1$.*

Proposition 1. *Assume that ϕ is an endomorphism and that r is a nonzero rational function. Then*

$$div(r \circ \phi) = \phi^*(div(r))$$

Proof. See Proposition 11.9 of [7] or proposition 3.6(b) of [23].

From this proposition, we obtain the following.

Proposition 2. *Let $Q = \phi(P)$ and*

$$div(f_P) = \ell(P) - \ell(O) \quad div(f_Q) = \ell(Q) - \ell(O).$$

If ϕ is injective and separable, then

$$div(f_P) = div(f_Q \circ \phi).$$

Proof. By Proposition 1, the definition of ϕ^*, and the injectivity and separability of ϕ, we have

$$
\begin{aligned}
div(f_Q \circ \phi) &= \phi^*(div f_Q) \\
&= \phi^*(\ell(Q) - \ell(O)) \\
&= \ell\phi^*(Q) - \ell\phi^*(O) \\
&= \ell\left(\sum_{\phi(X)=Q} e_\phi(X)\right) - \ell\left(\sum_{\phi(Y)=O} e_\phi(Y)\right) \\
&= \ell(P) - \ell(O) \\
&= div(f_p).
\end{aligned}
$$

3.2 Examples of Injective Separable Distortion Maps

The following proposition helps finding injective separable distortion maps that are necessary in our algorithm.

Proposition 3. *An endomorphism ϕ is inseparable if and only if*

$$\phi(x, y) = (u(x^p, y^p), v(x^p, y^p))$$

for some rational functions u and v, where p is the characteristic of $\mathbb{F}_q$.

Proof. See Corollary 12.10 of [7].

The following are examples of injective separable distortion maps.

$\phi_1(x, y) = (\zeta x, y),$	where $\zeta^2 + \zeta + 1 = 0$
$\phi_2(x, y) = (x + s^2, y + sx + t),$	where $s^4 + s = 0$, $t^2 + t + s^6 + s^2 = 0$
$\phi_3(x, y) = (-x + r, iy),$	where $r^3 + 2r + 2 = 0$, $i^2 + 1 = 0$
$\phi_4(x, y) = (-x + r, iy),$	where $r^3 + 2r - 2 = 0$, $i^2 + 1 = 0$
$\phi_5(x, y) = (\zeta x, y),$	where $\zeta^2 + \zeta + 1 = 0$
$\phi_6(x, y) = (-x, iy),$	where $i^2 + 1 = 0.$

It can be easily checked that these distortion maps are indeed injective and separable by Proposition 3. Note that ϕ_1 is used in [5].

Table 1. Examples of distortion maps

Char.	Ext. Deg. ($q = p^m$)	Curve	Emb. Deg	ϕ
$p = 2$	Odd m	$y^2 + y = x^3$	2	ϕ_1
$p = 2$	$m \equiv \pm 1(8)$ $m \equiv \pm 3(8)$	$y^2 + y = x^3 + x + b$	4	ϕ_2
$p = 3$	$m \equiv \pm 1(12)$ $m \equiv \pm 5(12)$	$y^2 = x^3 + 2x + 1$	6	ϕ_3
$p = 3$	$m \equiv \pm 1(12)$ $m \equiv \pm 5(12)$	$y^2 = x^3 + 2x - 1$	6	ϕ_4
$p > 3$ $(p \equiv 2(3))$	$m = 1$	$y^2 = x^3 + a$	2	ϕ_5
$p > 3$ $(p \equiv 3(4))$	$m = 1$	$y^2 = x^3 + ax$	2	ϕ_6

4   Computation of Modified Weil Pairings

In this section, we propose a method of computing modified Weil pairings more efficiently than existing algorithms.

4.1   Computing $e_\ell(P, \phi(Q))$

Before we apply our algorithm to the Weil pairing, we need a new definition of the Weil pairing.

Proposition 4. *Let D_P and D_Q be divisors $(P) - (O)$ and $(Q) - (O)$, respectively, and f_P, f_Q be rational functions such that $div(f_P) = \ell D_P$, $div(f_Q) = \ell D_Q$. Then for random point R,*

$$e_\ell(P, Q) = \frac{f_P(Q + R)}{f_P(R)} \frac{f_Q(-R)}{f_Q(P - R)}.$$

Proof. Let $A_P = (P + S_1) - (S_1)$ and $A_Q = (Q + S_2) - (S_2)$ which have disjoint supports, where S_1 and S_2 are points of the underlying elliptic curve. Then

$$e_\ell(P, Q) = \frac{f_{A_P}(Q + S_2)}{f_{A_P}(S_2)} \frac{f_{A_Q}(S_1)}{f_{A_Q}(P + S_1)}.$$

Let $g(X) = f_p(X - S_1)$. Then

$$div(g) = \ell(P + S_1) - \ell(S_1) = \ell A_P = div(f_{A_P}).$$

Hence $f_{A_P}(X) = \lambda_1 g(X)$ for some constant λ_1. So

$$\frac{f_{A_P}(Q + S_2)}{f_{A_P}(S_2)} = \frac{\lambda_1 g(Q + S_1)}{\lambda_1 g(S_2)} = \frac{f_P(Q + S_2 - S_1)}{f_P(S_2 - S_1)}.$$

Similarly,

$$\frac{f_{A_Q}(S_1)}{f_{A_Q}(P + S_1)} = \frac{f_Q(S_1 - S_2)}{f_Q(P + S_1 - S_2)}.$$

Let $S_2 - S_1 = R$. Then the proposition is followed.

Corollary 2. *For an injective, separable distortion map ϕ,*

$$e_\ell(P, \phi(Q)) = \frac{f_P(\phi(Q) + R)}{f_P(R)} \frac{f_Q(-\phi^{-1}(R))}{f_Q(\phi^{-1}(P - R))}$$

Proof. By proposition 2, $div(f_Q) = div(f_{\phi(Q)} \circ \phi)$. Hence $f_{\phi(Q)} = \lambda f_Q \circ \phi^{-1}$ for some constant λ. If we combine this fact with the result of proposition 4, we can obtain this corollary.

Note that $P, Q \in E(\mathbb{F}_q)$, but $\phi(Q) \in E(\mathbb{F}_{q^k})$. If we apply the above corollary to compute the Weil pairing, we can reduce the full Miller part to the Miller lite part.

4.2   Computing $e_\ell(P, \phi(P))$

Lemma 1. *Given a rational function $f : E \to F_{q^k}$ with a pole of order ℓ at O. Define $g(X) = \frac{f(-X)}{f(\phi(X))}$ where $\phi(X)$ is a distortion map. Then*

$$g(O) = c_\phi{}^l$$

where c_ϕ is constant depending on the distortion map and l is the order of pairing.

Proof. This proof is similar to that of Lemma 1 of [11].
Consider the rational function $h(x) = \frac{x(X)}{y(X)}$ which has a zero of order 1 at $X = O$. Since f has a pole of order ℓ at O, the function $f_1 = \frac{f}{h^\ell}$ has neither a pole nor a zero at $X = O$, so $f_1(O)$ is finite and nonzero. By the same reason, $\psi_\phi(O)$ is finite and nonzero for the rational function $\psi_\phi(X) = \frac{h(-X)}{h(\phi(X))}$. Let $\psi_\phi(O)$ be c_ϕ. Hence $g(X) = \frac{f(-X)}{f(\phi(X))} = \frac{h(-X)^l f_1(-X)}{h(\phi(X))^l f_1(\phi(X))} = \psi_\phi(X)^l \frac{f_1(-X)}{f_1(\phi(X))}$, and $g(O) = c_\phi{}^l$.

In [21], it is claimed that $f_P(O)/f_Q(O) = 1$ if f_P and f_Q are normalized. While this normalization depends on the point P and Q, the constant c_ϕ only depends on the distortion map. So it can be precomputed. For distortion maps in the table 1, we compute the value of c_ϕ in the following lemma .

Lemma 2. $c_{\phi_1} = c_{\phi_5} = -1/\zeta$, $c_{\phi_2} = 1$, $c_{\phi_3} = c_{\phi_4} = c_{\phi_6} = i$

Proof. Since $-(x, y) = (x, -y)$ over the field of the characteristic $p \neq 2$ and $-(x, y) = (x, y + 1)$ over the field of the characteristic 2,

$$\psi_{\phi_1}(X) = \psi_{\phi_5}(X) = \frac{x}{-y} / \frac{\zeta x}{y} = -1/\zeta$$

$$\psi_{\phi_2}(X) = \frac{x}{y + 1} / \frac{x + s^2}{y + sx + t} = \frac{xy + sx^2 + tx}{xy + x + s^2 y + s^2}$$

$$\psi_{\phi_3}(X) = \psi_{\phi_4}(X) = \frac{x}{-y} / \frac{-x + r}{iy} = \frac{-ix}{-x + r}$$

$$\psi_{\phi_6}(X) = \frac{x}{-y} / \frac{-x}{iy} = i$$

Hence
$$c_{\phi_1} = c_{\phi_5} = -1/\zeta, \ c_{\phi_2} = 1, \ c_{\phi_3} = c_{\phi_4} = c_{\phi_6} = i.$$

Proposition 5. *Let* $Q = \phi(P)$. *Then for an injective separable distortion map* ϕ,
$$e_\ell(P, \phi(P)) = c_\phi{}^\ell \frac{f_Q(\phi(Q))}{f_Q(P)} = c_\phi{}^\ell \frac{f_P(Q)}{f_P(\phi^{-1}(P))}.$$

Proof. By proposition 2 and 4,
$$e_\ell(P, \phi(P)) = e_\ell(P, Q) = \frac{(f_Q \circ \phi)(Q + R)}{(f_Q \circ \phi)(R)} \frac{f_Q(-R)}{f_Q(P - R)}$$

We can consider $e_\ell(P, Q)$ as a rational function in the variable R. Then $e_\ell(P, Q)$ only has zeros or poles in the following cases.

$$\{\phi(Q + R) = Q \text{ or } O\}, \{\phi(R) = Q \text{ or } O\}, \{-R = Q \text{ or } O\}, \{P - R = Q \text{ or } O\}$$

Since ϕ is injective and $Q = \phi(P)$, we have
$$R = P - Q, P, -Q, \text{ or } O.$$

But the zeros and poles cancel each other out at each of these points. So the rational function $e_\ell(P, Q)$ has neither zeros nor poles and hence $e_\ell(P, Q)$ must be a constant function. If we choose $R = O$, then
$$\frac{f_Q(-R)}{f_Q(\phi(R))} = c_\phi{}^\ell$$

by Lemma 1. Hence
$$e_\ell(P, \phi(P)) = c_\phi{}^\ell \frac{f_Q(\phi(Q))}{f_Q(P)}.$$

If we apply the proposition 2 again,
$$c_\phi{}^\ell \frac{f_Q(\phi(Q))}{f_Q(P)} = c_\phi{}^\ell \frac{f_P(Q)}{f_P(\phi^{-1}(P))}$$

When computing $e_\ell(P, \phi(P))$, therefore, the Weil pairing is the same as the Tate pairing without the final powering. Hence we need only one Miller's algorithm to compute the Weil pairing. Moreover it is possible to make a deterministic Miller's algorithm according to the above result. In Miller's algorithm, $f_P(Q)$ is computed by multiplications of and divisions by $g(Q)$'s, where g's are lines passing through some multiples of P. Since $\{P, \phi(P)\}$ are linearly independent, these lines cannot pass through the point $\phi(P)$ and hence no $g(\phi(P))$'s are zero. Since the same holds when computing $f_Q(\phi(Q))$, no division by zero can occur during the computation of $e_\ell(P, \phi(P))$.

4.3   Analysis of Computational Savings

The main advantage of computing $f_Q(\phi^{-1}(R))$ instead of $f_{\phi(Q)}(R)$ is that we can replace the point multiplication in the extension field with the point multiplication in the base field. For computing the Weil pairing with order l, we need a point doubling or addition of P and $\phi(Q)$ in the Miller lite and the full Miller part, respectively, until we obtain lP and $l\phi(Q)$. After we double and add point Q, we apply the distortion map to doubling and addition of Q for doubling and addition of $\phi(Q)$. But we can't save multiplication in the extension field F_{q^k} for each step by computing the distortion map. Usually we must calculate one multiplication in the extension field. For distortion map $\phi(x, y) = (x + s^2, y + sx + t)$ which is used in supersingular curve over a field of characteristic 2, one squaring and one multiplication in the extension field are necessary. Hence we can save about $log(l)$ multiplications in the extension field by replacing the full Miller part with the Miller lite part. Another savings are obtained in computing the slope of the $g_{U,V}$. The slope λ of $g_{U,V}$ is $\frac{y(U)-y(V)}{x(U)-x(V)}$ and the tangent line slope is $\frac{3x(U)^2+a}{2y(U)}$ for the elliptic curves $y^2 = x^3 + ax + b$. So we need one inversion for $g_{U,V}$, one squaring and one inversion for $g_{U,U}$. If we compute $f_Q(\phi^{-1}(R))$ instead of $f_{\phi(Q)}(R)$, we can reduce $\frac{3\ell}{2}$ divisions and ℓ squarings in the extension field to the same number of divisions and squarings in the base field. Finally, the inversion of a distortion map in computing $f_Q(\phi^{-1}(R))$ does not influence the operation count. The computation of the inversion of distortion map is easy. For example, $\phi_1^{-1}(x, y) = (\zeta^2 x, y)$ and $\phi_2^{-1}(x, y) = (x + s^2, y + sx + t + 1)$. Moreover $\phi^{-1}(R)$ is evaluated just one time in the Miller's algorithm.

In particular, when computing $e_\ell(P, \phi(P))$, we don't need to evaluate the full Miller part. We reduce two Miller part to one Miller part. Hence we can save 50% of time.

5   Conclusions

In this paper, we proposed an improved implementation of the modified Weil pairings. When computing $e_\ell(P, \phi(Q))$, we can save some operations in the extension field by reduction the full Miller part to the Miller lite part. In [19], there is a comparison between the operation count of the full Miller's part and that of the exponentiation at the end of Tate pairing computation. We can choose the better one according to this comparison. But we must compare the operation counts of the Miller lite part with that of the exponentiation at the end of Tate pairing in case of supersingular curve with distortion map. This means we must reexamine the relative speed of the Tate and Weil pairing computations which is referred as the sixth open problems in [19]. When computing $e_\ell(P, \phi(P))$, the computation of the Weil pairing is the same as that of the Tate pairing without the final powering. So our algorithm saves about 50% of the computation cost compared to Miller's algorithm. Our method can be also applied to any Weil pairing method using a distortion map such as the parabola method[10] and the squared Weil pairing[11].

References

1. P. S. L. M. Barreto, H. Y. Kim, B. Lynn, M. Scott, "Efficient Algorithms for Pairing-Based Cryptosystems," Advances in Cryptology – Crypto 2002, Lecture Notes on Computer Science 2442, Springer-Verlag (2002), pp. 354–368.
2. P. S. L. M. Barreto, S. D. Galbraith, C. O'hEigeartaigh and M. Scott, "Efficient Pairing Computation on Supersingular Abelian Varieties," Cryptology ePrint Archive, Report 2004/375.
3. Available from http://planeta.terra.com.br/informatica/paulobarreto/pblounge.html
4. I. Blake, G. Seroussi, N. Smart, "Elliptic Curves in Cryptography," Cambridge University Press, 1999.
5. D. Boneh, M. Franklin, "Identity-based encryption from the Weil pairing," Advances in Cryptology – Crypto 2001, Lecture Notes on Computer Science 2139, Springer-Verlag (2001), pp. 213–229.
6. D. Boneh, B. Lynn, H. Shacham, "Short signatures from the Weil pairing," Advances in Cryptology – Asiacrypt 2001, Lecture Notes on Computer Science 2248, Springer-Verlag (2002), pp. 514–532.
7. L. S. Charlap, D. P. Robbins, "An elementary introduction to elliptic curves," CRD Expository Report No. 31, December 1988.
8. L. S. Charlap, R. Coley, "An elementary introduction to elliptic curves II," CCR Expository Report No. 34, July 1990.
9. J. C. Cha, J. H. Cheon, "An Identity-Based Signature from Gap Diffie-Hellman Groups," Practice and Theory in Public Key Cryptography – PKC 2003, Lecture Notes on Computer Science 2567, Springer-Verlag (2003), pp. 18–30.
10. K. Eisentrager, K. Lauter, P. L. Montgomery, "Fast Elliptic Curve Arithmetic and Improved Weil Pairing Evaluation," CT-RSA 2003, pp. 343-354.
11. K. Eisentrager, K. Lauter, P. L. Montgomery, "Improved Weil and Tate Pairings for Elliptic and Hyperelliptic Curves," ANTS 2004, pp.169-183.
12. G. Frey, M. Muller, H. Ruck, "The Tate Pairing and the Discrete Logarithm Applied to Elliptic Curve Cryptosystems," IEEE Transactions on Information Theory 45(5) (1999), pp. 1717–1719.
13. S. D. Galbraith, "Supersingular curves in cryptography," Advances in Cryptology – Asiacrypt 2001, Lecture Notes on Computer Science 2248, Springer-Verlag (2002), pp. 495–513.
14. S. D. Galbraith, K. Harrison, D. Soldera, "Implementing the Tate pairing," Algorithmic Number Theory Symposium – ANTS-V, Lecture Notes on Computer Science 2369, Springer-Verlag (2002), pp. 324–337.
15. F. He, "Efficient Identity Based Signature Schemes Based on Pairings," Selected Areas in Cryptography – SAC 2002, Lecture Notes on Computer Science 2595, Springer-Verlag (2003), pp. 310–324.
16. A. Joux, "A one-round protocol for tripartite Diffie-Hellman," Algorithm Number Theory Symposium – ANTS-IV, Lecture Notes on Computer Science 1838, Springer-Verlag (2000), pp. 385–394.
17. A. Joux, "The Weil and Tate Pairings as Building Blocks for Public Key Cryptosystems," Algorithm Number Theory Symposium – ANTS-V, Lecture Notes on Computer Science 2369, Springer-Verlag (2002), pp. 20–32.
18. M. Kim, H. Kim, K. Kim, "A New Identification Scheme based on the Gap Diffie-Hellman Problem," 2002 Symposium on Cryptography and Information Security (SCIS2002), Shirahama, Japan, Jan. 29 – Feb. 1, 2003, vol. 1/2, pp. 349–352.

19. N. Koblitz, A.J. Menezes, "Pairing-Based Cryptography at High Security Levels," Cryptology ePrint Archive, Report 2005/76.
20. A.J. Menezes, "Elliptic Curve Public Key Cryptosystems," Kluwer International Series in Engineering and Computer Science, 1993.
21. V. Miller, "The Weil Pairing, and Its Efficient Calculation," Journal of Cryptology, 17, 2004.
22. K. G. Paterson, "ID-based signatures from pairings on elliptic curves," Electronics Letters 38(18) (2002), pp. 1025–1026.
23. J.H. Silverman, "The Arithmetic of Elliptic Curves," Graduate Texts in Mathematics, vol. 106, Springer-Verlag, 1986.
24. J.Solinas,"ID-based digital signature algorithms," 2003, http://www.cacr.math. uwaterloo.ca/conferences/2003/ecc2003/solinas.pdf.
25. E. Verheul, "Evidence that XTR is more secure than supersingular elliptic curve cryptosystems," Advances in Cryptology - Eurocrypt 2001, Lecture Notes in Computer Science 2045 (2001), pp. 195-210.
26. F. Zhang, R. Safavi-Naini, W. Susilo, "ID-Based Chameleon Hashes from Bilinear Pairings," Cryptology ePrint Archive, Report 2003/208.
27. F. Zhang, R. Safavi-Naini, W. Susilo, "An Efficient Signature Scheme from Bilinear Pairings and Its Applications," Practice and Theory in Public Key Cryptography – PKC 2004, Singapore(SG), March 2004, Lecture Notes on Computer Science 2947, Springer-Verlag (2004), pp. 277–290.

Efficient Simultaneous Inversion in Parallel and Application to Point Multiplication in ECC

Pradeep Kumar Mishra

Centre for Information Security and Cryptography (CISaC)
University of Calgary, 2500 University Drive NW, Calgary, AB, Canada
pradeep@math.ucalgary.ca

Abstract. Inversion is the costliest of all finite field operations. Some algorithms require computation of several finite field elements simultaneously (elliptic curve factorization for example). Montgomery's trick is a well known technique for performing the same in a sequential set up with little scope for parallelization. In the current work we propose an algorithm which needs almost same computational resources as Montgomery's trick, but can be easily parallelized. Our algorithm uses binary tree structures for computation and using 2^{r-1} multipliers, it can simultaneously invert 2^r elements in $2r$ multiplication rounds and one inversion round. We also describe how the algorithm can be used when $2, 4, \ldots$ number of multipliers are available. To exhibit the utility of the method, we apply it to obtain a parallel algorithm for elliptic curve point multiplication. The proposed method is immune to side-channel attacks and compares favourably to many parallel algorithms existing in literature.

Keywords: Elliptic Curve Cryptosystems, Scalar Multiplication, parallel algorithm, Montgomery ladder, simultaneous inversion.

1 Introduction

Finite fields inversions are the bottleneck in implementation of many cryptographic and coding theoretic schemes. The efficiency of these schemes can be greatly enhanced if finite field inversions can be performed more efficiently. The cost of an inversion can be as high as thirty to fifty times the cost of a multiplication for a prime field [6], [16]. In many situations, the requirement is to compute inversions of several field elements (for example in SSL Handshake scheme [21], elliptic curve factorization [15] [19]). Montgomery's trick (see Section 2.2) is an elegant technique for *simultaneous* computation of the inverses of several field elements. Using this trick it is possible to compute the inverses of n elements using $3(n-1)$ multiplications and one inversion. However, Montgomery's trick is a strictly sequential algorithm with little scope for parallelization. In the current work, we introduce a new algorithm for simultaneous computation of the inverses of several field elements. It, like Montgomery's trick, requires only $3(n-1)$ multiplications. Using $n/2$ multipliers n field elements can be inverted by the proposed

D. Feng, D. Lin, and M. Yung (Eds.): CISC 2005, LNCS 3822, pp. 324–335, 2005.

algorithm in $2\log n$ parallel rounds. When n is moderately large, it may be difficult to employ $n/2$ multipliers for the purpose. In that case we show, how the the algorithm can be employed with lesser number of multipliers $(2, 4, 8, ...)$.

Elliptic curve cryptosystems (ECC), since their discovery in 1985 (independently by Koblitz'[12] and Miller [17]), are gradually phasing out other public key cryptosystems in many platforms. ECC derives its security from elliptic curve discrete logarithm problem (ECDLP). Except for some special cases there is no subexponential algorithm for solving ECDLP. This leads to a high level of security with smaller key sizes in comparison to other cryptosystems. This fact makes ECC suitable for small handheld devices. Elliptic curve point multiplication is the operation of computing mP, where m is a positive integer and P is a point on the curve. This is the basic operation on which elliptic curve cryptography is built. Consequently, there has been a tremendous amount of research on obtaining efficient algorithms for different situation. Interested readers can refer to [8] for an excellent discussion. One particularly important issue is resistance against side channel attacks([13, 14]). One important class of side-channel attacks are power attacks, which reconstruct the secret by measuring and analyzing the power consumption traces. Power attacks can be divided into two subclasses: simple power attacks (SPA) and differential power attacks (DPA). SPA uses data from one observation to reconstruct the secret key. DPA-like attacks use data from several computations and uses statistical tools for the same. An implementation is SCA resistant only if it is secure against both SPA and DPA-like attacks.

We use the parallel simultaneous inversion algorithm in elliptic curve point multiplication. In the current work we propose an algorithm which efficiently computes point multiplication and is secure against side-channel attacks. The point multiplication algorithm computes the point multiplication by repeatedly invoking a multiple simultaneous double and add algorithm. This multiple simultaneous double and add algorithm uses affine coordinates and invokes the simultaneous inversion algorithm for computing the inverses. The point multiplication method so obtained is resistant against SPA-like attacks and is applicable to the situation where the base point P is fixed. The algorithm can be made resistant against DPA-like attacks using Joye-Tymen countermeasure. The algorithm can be implemented using a fixed number $(2, 4, 8, \ldots)$ of multipliers. Our algorithm compares favourably against all existing SCA-resistant parallel algorithms.

2   Background

In this section we briefly outline the background required for the rest of the paper.

2.1   Elliptic Curve Preliminaries

Elliptic curve cryptography has a rich literature. Here we only describe (without proof) the essentials that we will require. Interested reader can refer [8] for details. In the current work we will concentrate on elliptic curves over fields of characteristic > 3 only. An elliptic curve E over such a field K is defined by an equation $y^2 = x^3 + ax + b$, where $a, b \in K$ and the curve is free from any singularity (i.e. $4a^3 + 27b^2 \neq 0$).

An elliptic curve point is represented using a pair of finite field elements. Two important algorithm in an implementation of ECC are ECADD and ECDBL. ECADD takes as input two points P and Q on the curve and returns their sum, $P + Q$. ECDBL takes as input a point P on the curve and returns $2P$. These algorithms in affine coordinates are shown in Table 1. Note that, in the addition algorithm we assume $P \neq \pm Q$.

Table 1. ECADD and ECDBL Algorithm

Algorithm ECADD	Algorithm ECDBL
Input : $P(x_1, y_1), Q(x_2, y_2)$	Input : $P(x_1, y_1)$
Output : $P + Q = (x_3, y_3)$.	Output : $2P = (x_4, y_4)$.
A1. $t_1 = (x_2 - x_1)^{-1}$	D1. $T_1 = (2y_1)^{-1}$
A2. $\lambda = t_1 * (y_2 - y_1)$	D2. $T_2 = 3x_1^2 + a$
A3. $x_3 = \lambda^2 - x_1 - x_2$	D3. $\Lambda = T_1 * T_2$
A4. $y_3 = \lambda * (x_1 - x_3) - y_1$	D4. $x_4 = \Lambda^2 - x_1 - x_2$
A5. return (x_3, y_3)	D5. $y_4 = \Lambda * (x_1 - x_3) - y_1$
	D6. return (x_4, y_4)

Let $[i], [m]$ and $[s]$ be the times required for one inversion, multiplication and squaring in the underlying fields respectively. Then, ECADD has complexity $1[i] + 2[m] + 1[s]$ and ECDBL has complexity $1[i] + 2[m] + 2[s]$. In the current work, we do not distinguish between a multiplication and a squaring. This may not be a realistic assumption when the underlying field is represented using a normal basis; in such a situation, squaring is virtually free. However, for standard (or polynomial) basis representation the cost of a squaring is nearly equal to that of a multiplication.

2.2 Montgomery's Trick

Montgomery's trick, as described below, is an elegant technique for computing inverses of several field elements. It computes inverse of n field elements with a total of $3(n - 1)$ multiplication and one inversion. However it is a strictly sequential algorithm with little scope for parallelization.

2.3 Side-Channel Attacks

Side-channel attacks (SCA), discovered by Paul Kocher et al.([13], [14]) are the most dangerous threat against ECC. SCA reveals the secret information by sampling and analyzing the side-channel information like timing, power consumption and EM radiation traces. An implementation of ECC must be side-channel resistant. SCA's which use data from only one computation are called SPA-like

Algorithm 1 (Montgomery's Trick)

Input: Field elements $x_1, x_2, \cdots, x_n$.
Output: $x_1^{-1}, x_2^{-1}, \cdots, x_n^{-1}$.
1: $a_1 = x_1$;
2: **for** $i = 2$ to n **do**
3:    $a_i = a_{i-1} x_i$;
4: Invert a_n;
5: $x_n^{-1} = a_{n-1} a_n^{-1}$;
6: **for** $i = n - 1$ to 2 **do**
7:    $a_i^{-1} = x_{i+1} a_{i+1}^{-1}$;
8:    $x_i^{-1} = a_{i-1} a_i^{-1}$;
9: $x_1^{-1} = x_2 a_2^{-1}$;

---

attack. Another class of attacks are called DPA-like attacks. DPA-like attacks use side-channel information from several computations and use statistical tools to analyze them.

Several countermeasures have been proposed in literature to guard ECC against side-channel attacks (see [3], [4], [9], [11], [20]). The algorithm proposed in this work uses a variant of Coron's dummy addition method [4] to resist SPA-like attacks. To thwart DPA-like attacks Joye-Tymen's curve randomization technique [11] can be easily integrated to it.

3   New Algorithm for Computing Simultaneous Inverses

In this section we describe our parallel algorithm for simultaneous inversion.

Let $x_1, x_2, \cdots, x_n$ be the field elements to be inverted. Let $A[1, \cdots, (2n - 1)]$ be an array of $(2n - 1)$ elements, each capable of storing one field element. The following algorithm computes the inverses simultaneously.

Algorithm 2 (Simultaneous Inversion (SINV))

Input: Field elements $x_1, x_2, \cdots, x_n$.
Output: $x_1^{-1}, x_2^{-1}, \cdots, x_n^{-1}$.
1: For $i = n$ to $(2n - 1)$, $A[i] \leftarrow x_{i-n+1}$;
2: For $i = (n - 1)$ down to 1, $A[i] \leftarrow A[2i] * A[2i + 1]$;
3: Invert $A[1]$, i.e. $A[1] \leftarrow A[1]^{-1}$;
4: **for** $i = 2$ to $2n - 1$ step 2 **do**
5:    $T \leftarrow A[i]$;
6:    $A[i] \leftarrow A[\lfloor i/2 \rfloor] * A[i \oplus 1]$;
7:    $A[i + 1] \leftarrow A[\lfloor i/2 \rfloor] * T$;
8: Output $A[i], (n \leq i \leq (2n - 1))$;

Proposition 1. *The cost of Algorithm 2 is $3(n - 1)$ multiplication and one inversion.*

Proof. It is obvious that Step 2 and 4 of the algorithm require $(n-1)$ and $2(n-1)$ multiplication respectively. There is one inversion in Step 3.

The algorithm requires $(2n-1)$ memory locations, each capable of holding one field element, $(2n-1)$ for the array $A[]$ and 1 memory location for T. The elements $A[n]$ to $A[2n-1]$ in the array store the input data and $A[1]$ to $A[n-1]$ are used for storing intermediate variables. Montgomery's trick also demands same amount of memory. Algorithm 2 was independently discovered by B. Möller [18] and was utilized by him in a sequential implementation of ECC. The beauty of Algorithm 2 is that it can be implemented in parallel.

3.1   Parallel Implementation

Let the elements to be inverted be $x_1, x_2, \cdots, x_n$ where $2^{r-1} \le n \le 2^r$. We assume that the algorithm is to be processed by 2^{r-1} multipliers and we have sufficient memory to store $2 \times n$ field elements. We name the multipliers as $P_1, P_2, \cdots, P_{2^{r-1}}$. In fact we do not need more than 2^{r-1} multipliers. The algorithm can also be run with less number of multipliers, but the number of rounds of parallel multiplication will go up.

Algorithm 3 (Simultaneous Parallel Inversion (PINV))

Input: Field elements $x_1, x_2, \cdots, x_n$.
Output: $x_1^{-1}, x_2^{-1}, \cdots, x_n^{-1}$.
1: **Initialisation:** For $i = n$ to $2n-1$, $A[i] \leftarrow x_i$;
2: **for** $k \leftarrow 1$ to r **do**
3:     **(kth Parallel Round:)**
4:     **for** $i = 2^{r=k}$ to $\min\{2^{r-(k-1)} - 1, n-1\}$; **do**
5:         $P_{i+1-2^{r-k}}$ computes $A[i] \leftarrow A[2i] * A[2i+1]$;
6: **r+1st parallel Round:**
7: Invert the element in $A[1]$ and store to $A[1]$;
8: **for** $k \leftarrow r+2$ to $2r+1$ **do**
9:     kth Parallel Round
10:     **for** $2^{k-(r+1)} \le i \le 2^{k-r} - 1$ **do**
11:         $P_{i-2^{k-(r+1)}+1}$ computes in parallel $A[i] \leftarrow A[\lfloor i/2 \rfloor] * A[i \oplus 1]$;
12: **for** $n \le i \le (2n-1)$ **do**
13:     output $A[i]$;

The proof of the following proposition is trivial and hence omitted.

Proposition 2. *Algorithm 3 correctly computes the inverses of 2^r elements in $2r$ rounds of parallel multiplication.*

3.2   Computing with Lesser Number of Multipliers

With 2^{r-1} multipliers Algorithm 3 can compute the inverses in $2r$ parallel rounds. Let the number of available multipliers be 2^p. Then the obvious way

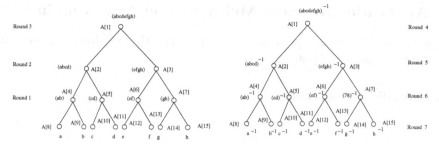

Fig. 1. Illustration for Algorithm 3 with $n = 8$ field elements

of carrying out the computations is to allow the available multipliers to compute one round of Algorithm 3 in as many parallel rounds as required.

To carry out the computations of round $k, (1 \leq k \leq r)$ of Algorithm 3, the 2^p multipliers will require $\lceil 2^{r-k}/2^p \rceil$ parallel rounds of computations. The $(r+1)$st round is an inversion round. Similarly, for round $k, r + 2 \leq k \leq 2r + 1$, the t multipliers will require $\lceil 2^{k-r-1}/2^p \rceil$ parallel rounds of computations. Hence we have,

Proposition 3. *With $t = 2^p$ multipliers Algorithm 3 can be computed in*

$$\sum_{k=1}^{r} \lceil \frac{2^{r-k}}{2^p} \rceil + \sum_{i=r+2}^{2r} \lceil \frac{2^{k-r-1}}{2^p} \rceil = 2 \sum_{k=1}^{r-1} \lceil \frac{2^k}{2^p} \rceil + 2^{r-p}$$

parallel rounds of computation besides one inversion round.

In the following we will denote by $\mathsf{COST}(r, p)$ the number of multiplication rounds required by Algorithm PINV to compute the inverses of 2^r elements using 2^p multipliers. Hence

$$\mathsf{COST}(r, p) = 2 \sum_{k=1}^{r-1} \lceil \frac{2^k}{2^p} \rceil + 2^{r-p}$$

In the Table 2 we show the number of parallel rounds required for inverting n number of elements by k number of multipliers using Algorithm 3.

Table 2. Number of parallel rounds required for inverting $n = 8, 16, 32$ elements with $k = 8, 4, 2$ multipliers by Algorithm 3

n/k	8	4	2
8	6	7	11
16	9	13	23
32	15	25	47

4   Application to Scalar Multiplication Algorithm in ECC

Before describing our new point multiplication algorithm we describe some auxiliary algorithms used by it.

4.1   Auxiliary Algorithms

First we describe a parallel algorithm for simultaneous add-and-double of several elliptic curve points. The steps (A1, D1, ... etc) in the algorithm t-ECADDBL refer to the steps in Table 1.

Algorithm 4 (t-ECADDBL)

Input: $P_1, Q_1; \cdots; P_t, Q_t$.
Output: $P_1 + Q_1, 2P_1; \cdots; P_t + Q_t, 2P_t$.
 1: Use PINV to perform the inversions in the
        steps A1(P_1, Q_1), D1(P_1); ...; A1(P_t, Q_t), D1(P_t);
 2: For $1 \le i \le t$, do in parallel A2(P_i, Q_i), D2(P_i);
 3: For $1 \le i \le t$, do in parallel A3(P_i, Q_i), D3(P_i);
 4: For $1 \le i \le t$, do in parallel A4(P_i, Q_i), D4(P_i);
 5: For $1 \le i \le t$, do in parallel D5(P_i);
 6: For $1 \le i \le t$, do in parallel A5(P_i, Q_i), D6(P_i);

It is easy to verify that, if $t = 2^r$ and $2t$ multipliers are available for computation then algorithm t-ECADDBL can be computed in $2r + 4$ multiplication rounds and one inversion round. If $k = 2^p$ multipliers are available, then each of Steps 2 through 4 will take $\lceil 2^{r+1}/2^p \rceil$ multiplication rounds and Step 5 will take $\lceil 2^r/2^p \rceil$ multiplication rounds. Step 1 requires $\mathsf{COST}(r+1, p)$ multiplication rounds. Hence we have,

Proposition 4. *With 2^p multipliers, Algorithm 2^r-ECADDBL can be computed in $3 \times \lceil 2^{r+1}/2^p \rceil + \lceil 2^r/2^p \rceil + \mathsf{COST}(2^{r+1}, p)$ multiplication rounds and one inversion round.*

Another algorithm we will frequently invoke is t-ECADD, which takes as input t pair of points $P_1, Q_1; \cdots; P_t, Q_t$ and computes the sums $P_1 + Q_1, \cdots, P_t + Q_t$. In fact, it is a straightforward modification of t-ECADDBL.

Also, we will invoke a similar algorithm t-ECDBL for simultaneous doubling of t input points. This algorithm is another straightforward modification of t-ECADDBL for t doublings and hence we do not describe it in details. The cost of 2^r-ECADD (resp. 2^r-ECDBL) using 2^p multipliers is $3 \times \lceil 2^r/2^p \rceil + \mathsf{COST}(r, p)$ (resp. $4 \times \lceil 2^r/2^p \rceil + \mathsf{COST}(r, p)$) multiplication rounds and one inversion round.

Algorithm t-ADD takes as input t points and computes their sum. Algorithm 2^r-ADD invokes 2^i-ECADD for $0 \le i \le r - 1$. Using the cost of 2^i-ECADD we obtain the cost for 2^r-ADD to be a total of $\sum_{i=0}^{r-1}(3\lceil 2^i/2^p \rceil + \mathsf{COST}(i, p))$ multiplication rounds and r inversion rounds.

Algorithm 5 (t-ECADD)

Input: $P_1, Q_1; \cdots; P_t, Q_t$.

Output: $P_1 + Q_1, \cdots, P_t + Q_t$.

1: Use PINV to perform the inversions in the steps $A1(P_1, Q_1), \ldots; A1(P_t, Q_t)$;
2: For $1 \leq i \leq t$, do in parallel $A2(P_i, Q_i)$;
3: For $1 \leq i \leq t$, do in parallel $A3(P_i, Q_i)$;
4: For $1 \leq i \leq t$, do in parallel $A4(P_i, Q_i)$;
5: For $1 \leq i \leq t$, do in parallel $A5(P_i, Q_i)$;

Algorithm 6 (t-ADD)

Input: $P_0, P_1, \cdots, P_{2^r - 1}$.

Output: $P_0 + P_1 + \cdots + P_{2^r - 1}$.

1: **for** $i = 1$ to r **do**
2: $\quad k = 2^{r-i}$;
3: $\quad (P_0, P_{2^i}, P_{2 \cdot 2^i}, P_{3 \cdot 2^i}, \ldots, P_{(k-1)2^i})$
$\quad = k\text{-ECADD}(P_0, P_{2^{i-1}}, P_{2 \cdot 2^{i-1}}, P_{3 \cdot 2^{i-1}}, \ldots, P_{(2k-1)2^{i-1}})$;
4: **return** P_0;

4.2   Parallel Algorithm for Point Multiplication

In this section, we present our new point multiplication algorithm. Our algorithm incorporates a countermeasure to resist SPA which is based on Coron's technique of dummy addition [4]. Our algorithm computes the point multiplication in parallel and is suitable for the situation when the base point is fixed. Applications for such an algorithm can be found in [8].

Let $w \geq 2$ be a positive integer. We express m in the base 2^w. Let $m = c_0 + c_1 2^w + \cdots + c_{t-1} 2^{w(t-1)}$, where each $c_j \in \{0, \ldots, 2^w - 1\}$ and $t = 2^r$ for some r. Then $mP = c_0 P + c_1 2^w P + \cdots + c_{t-1} 2^{w(t-1)} P$. For all j with $0 \leq j \leq t - 1$ we precompute $2^{jw} P$ and store it in a table $T[\,]$. Thus $T[j] = 2^{jw} P$ for $0 \leq j \leq t - 1$. This table is used to simultaneously compute $c_0 P, c_1 2^w P, \cdots, c_{t-1} 2^{w(t-1)} P$ using the right-to-left binary method. Finally we add them to obtain mP. Let the n-bit binary representation of m be $m_{n-1} \ldots m_0$. Note that $t = \lceil n/w \rceil$. We express c_j in binary, i.e., we write $c_j = c_j^0 + c_j^1 2 + \cdots + c_j^{w-1} 2^{w-1}$, where $c_j^i = m_{wj+i}$.

Note that the amount of computation is independent of the values of c_j^is. Hence the algorithm is SPA resistant. We now obtain the number of rounds required to compute algorithm PPMA.

Proposition 5. *Using 2^p multipliers, Algorithm PPMA requires $(r + w)$ inversion rounds and $(w+5)\lceil 2^r/2^p \rceil + 2\mathsf{COST}(r, p) + \sum_{i=0}^{r-1}(3\lceil 2^i/2^p \rceil + \mathsf{COST}(i, p)) + (w-2)(3\lceil 2^{r+1}/2^p \rceil + \mathsf{COST}(r+1, p))$ multiplication rounds to complete the point multiplication.*

Proof. Algorithm PPMA invokes 2^r-ECDBL, 2^r-ECADD and 2^r-ADD once each. Further, it invokes 2^r-ECADDBL a total of $(w - 2)$ times. Adding up all the costs gives us the required result.

Algorithm 7 (Parallel Point Multiplication Algorithm (PPMA))

Input: c_j^i for $0 \le i \le w - 1, 0 \le j \le t - 1$; table $T[\,]$.

Output: mP.

1: **for** $j = 0$ to $t - 1$ **do**

2:    $R_j = T[j]; Q_j^{(c_j^0)} = R_j; Q_j^{(1-c_j^0)} = 0;$

3: $(R_0, \ldots, R_{t-1}) = t\text{-ECDBL}(R_0, \ldots, R_{t-1});$

4: **for** $i = 1$ to $w - 2$ **do**

5:    $(Q_0^{(c_0^i)}, R_0, \ldots, Q_{t-1}^{(c_{t-1}^i)}, R_{t-1})$

$= t\text{-ECADDBL}(R_0, Q_0^{(1)}, \ldots, R_{t-1}, Q_{t-1}^{(1)});$

6: $(Q_0^{(c_0^{w-1})}, \ldots, Q_{t-1}^{(c_{t-1}^{w-1})}) = t\text{-ECADD}(R_0, Q_0^{(1)}, \ldots, R_{t-1}, Q_{t-1}^{(1)});$

7: res $\leftarrow t\text{-ADD}(Q_0^{(1)}, \cdots, Q_{t-1}^{(1)});$

8: return(res);

4.3 DPA Resistance

It is easy to see that the Joye-Tymen countermeasure can be easily integrated into the proposed scheme for resistance against DPA like attacks. If C is represented by the equation $y^2 = x^3 + ax + b$ then a random curve C' isomorphic to C can be found out by choosing a random element $\alpha \in K$ and taking the curve $y^2 = x^3 + a'x + b$, where $a' = \alpha^4 a$ and $b' = \alpha^6 b$. If the point P on C has coordinates (x, y) then $\sigma(P) = P'(x', y')$, where $x' = \alpha^2 x$ and $y' = \alpha^3 y$. Thus transforming the curve coefficients take $3[s] + 1[m]$ and transforming a point to the random curve takes $2[m]$ computations. The backward transformation is $\sigma^{-1}(x', y') = (x'/r^2, y'/r^3)$, which takes $1[i] + 1[s] + 3[m]$ computation. In the current scheme we have to transform all the t points in the table $T[\,]$ to the random curve. So we require $3[s] + 1[m]$ computation for transforming the curve coefficients and $2t[m]$ computation for transforming all the points in $T[\,]$ to the random curve and $1[i] + 1[s] + 3[m]$ computation to bring back the result to the original curve. Thus to implement the countermeasure we require $1[i] + 4[s] + (2t + 4)[m]$ computations. These steps can also be computed in parallel taking lesser number of parallel rounds of computation. For example if the window size w is 5, then the amount of computation required is $1[i] + 4[s] + 68[m]$ and with 2 multipliers it can be computed in 36 parallel multiplication and 1 inversion round.

4.4 Hardware Requirement

As the proposed algorithm is for parallel implementation, more hardware support is required for its implementation. However for an ECC implementation the finite field multiplication is the most dominant operation. That is because the additions are very cheap and the costlier inversions are very few. Although, the proposed algorithm uses affine coordinates, there are very few inversions than multiplications. So one inverter is sufficient. Also as additions are very cheaper operations, one can perform the additions sequentially by one finite field adder. Thus the parallel algorithm requires only more than one multiplier for its implementation. Also, it is flexible in the sense that one can use any number of multipliers in an implementation. In literature, there are proposals for elliptic and hyperelliptic curve coprocessors with more than one multiplier (see for example [1]). The proposed algorithm can be implemented in those devices.

The proposed algorithm uses a precomputed table and hence demands more memory for implementation. To store the table $T[]$, t points are to be stored. If the window size is 5, then 32 points are to be stored. For a medium term security, the ECC point size has been prescribed to be at least 320 bits or 40 bytes in length. In view of memory requirement the proposed algorithm is not suitable for memory constrained devices.

5   Results and Comparison

In this section, we present performance results of the proposed point multiplication algorithm for a typical 160 bit ECC.

In Table 3 we display the number of multiplication and inversion rounds required for computation of point multiplication when the scalar is a 160 bit integer. The first column stands for various window sizes. The second, third and fourth column display the amount of computation required if 8, 4 or 2 multipliers respectively are used. Each table element is a pair of two numbers, the former (resp later) specifying the number of multiplication (resp inversion) rounds required for the computation of the point multiplication. For example, using 2 multipliers and with window size equal to 5, a 160 bit point multiplication can be carried out with 907 multiplication rounds and 10 inversion rounds. If we assume that an inversion is equal to 30 multiplication, then for window size $w = 5$ and using two multipliers, we will require around 1207 multiplication rounds using PINV. Adding additional computation required to make the scheme DPA resistant, it will equivalent of 1273 multiplication rounds.

Table 3. Number of multiplication and inversion rounds required for PPMA for a 160-bit scalar multiplier for various window sizes. Note $2^r = 160/w$.

# multipliers →	8	4	2
Window size	#[m]-rnds, #[i]-rnds	#[m]-rnds, #[i]-rnds	#[m]-rnds, #[i]-rnds
5	251, 10	464, 10	907, 10
10	273, 14	492, 14	955, 14
20	298, 23	506, 23	965, 23

The parallel algorithm presented in [7] with two multipliers computes 160 point doublings and 40 point additions on average. Using Jacobian coordinates, the computation will take ($10[m]$ for a doubling and $11[m]$ for a mixed addition) more than 2000 multiplication rounds. The scheme proposed in [5], uses a parallelized encapsulated-add-and-double algorithm using Montgomery arithmetic.

This algorithm using two multipliers takes $10[m]$ computations per bit of the scalar ($1600[m]$ for a scalar of length 160 bits). Our algorithm does that in 1207 multiplication with 2 multipliers, which is a speed-up of around 25% over the algorithm in [5]. In [10], the authors have proposed several parallel schemes for computing point multiplication in ECC. Their best scheme (in Jacobian coordinates) computes a 160 bit point multiplication in 1593 multiplication rounds. Our methods can be seen to be much efficient than this method.

6   Conclusion

In the current article, we have proposed a new parallel algorithm for computing several finite field inversions simultaneously. The algorithm takes 1 inversion and $3(n-1)$ multiplication to compute inverse of n finite field elements. Although cost wise it is as efficient as Montgomery's trick, it is easily parallelizable. The algorithm can be utilized in many situations like SSL handshake scheme, elliptic curve factorization or elliptic curve encryption and digital signature schemes. We have also demonstrated how the scheme can be utilized to speed-up the elliptic curve point multiplication algorithm over prime fields. The proposed point multiplication algorithm uses affine coordinates, resistant against side-channel attacks and performs better than all previously known parallel algorithms.

Acknowledgment. Author is greatly indebted to Palash Sarkar and Rana Barua of Indian Statistical Institute, Kolkata, India for their valuable discussions and suggestions on the topic.

References

1. G. Bertoni, L. Breveglieri, T. J. Wollinger, C. Paar Finding Optimum Parallel Coprocessor Design for Genus 2 Hyperelliptic Curve Cryptosystems. ITCC (2) 2004: 538-546, IEEE Computere Society.
2. E. Brier, I. Dechene, and M. Joye Unified point addition formulae for elliptic curve cryptosystems In N. Nedjah and L. de Macedo, Eds, Embedded Cryptographic Hardware: Methodolgies & Architectures, Nova Science Publishers, 2004
3. E. Brier and M. Joye. Weierstrass Elliptic Curves and Side-Channel Attacks. In *PKC 2002*, LNCS 2274, pages 335-345, 2002.
4. J.-S. Coron. Resistance against Differential Power Analysis for Elliptic Curve Cryptosystems. In *CHES 1999*, LNCS 1717, pp 292-302, Springer-Verlag, 1999.
5. W. Fischer, C. Giraud, E. W. Knudsen, J. -P. Seifert. Parallel Scalar Multiplication on General Elliptic Curves over $\mathbf{F}_p$ hedged against Non-Differential Side-Channel Attacks, Available at IACR eprint Archive, Technical Report No 2002/007, http://www.eprint.iacr.org.
6. K. Fong, D. Hankerson, J. Lòpez, and A. Menezes. Field inversion and point halving revisited. *IEEE Transactions on Computers*, 53(8):1047–1059, Aug. 2004.
7. J. M. G. Garcia, R. M. Garcia. Parallel Algorithm for Multiplication on Elliptic Curves. Cryptology ePrint Archive, Report 2002/179, (2002), Available at http://eprint.iacr.org

8. D. Hankerson, A. Menezes and S. Vanstone *Guide to Elliptic Curve Cryptography*, Springer-Verlag, 2004.
9. T. Izu, B. Moller and T. Takagi. Improved Elliptic Curve Multiplication Methods Resistant Against Side Channel Attacks. Proceedings of Indocrypt 2002, LNCS 2551, pp 296-313, Springer-Verlag, 2002.
10. T. Izu and T. Takagi. A Fast Parallel Elliptic Curve Multiplication Resistant against Side-Channel Attacks In *PKC 2002*, LNCS, pp 280-296, Springer-Verlag 2002.
11. M. Joye and C. Tymen. Protection against Differential Sttacks for Elliptic Curve Cryptography. *CHES 2001*, LNCS 2162, pp 377-390, Springer-Verlag, 2001.
12. N. Koblitz. Elliptic curve cryptosystems. *Mathematics of Computation*, 48(177):203–209, January 1987.
13. P. Kocher. Timing Attacks on Implementations of Diffie-Hellman, RSA, DSS and Other Systems, *Crypto'96*, LNCS 1109, pp. 104-113, Springer-Verlag, 1996.
14. P. Kocher, J. Jaffe and B, Jun. Differential Power Analysis. In *CRYPTO'99*, LNCS 1666, pp. 388-397, Springer-Verlag, 1999.
15. H. W. Lenstra. Factoring Integers with Elliptic Curves. Ann. of Math., 126(1987), 649-673.
16. A. Menezes, P. C. Van Oorschot, and S. A. Vanstone. *Handbook of applied cryptography*. CRC Press, 1997.
17. V. S. Miller. Uses of elliptic curves in cryptography. In H. C. Williams, editor, *Advances in Cryptology – CRYPTO '85*, volume 218 of *LNCS*, pages 417–428. Springer-Verlag, 1986.
18. B. Möller. Personal Communication.
19. P. L. Montgomery. Speeding The Pollard and Elliptic Curve methods of Factorization. Math. Comp. 48(1987), 243-264.
20. E. Oswald. On Side-Channel Attacks and Application of Algorithmic Countermeasures. *Ph.D. Thesis*, Graz University of Technology, Austria, 2003.
21. H. Shacham and D. Boneh. Improving SSL Handshake Performance via Batching. In *CT-RSA*, LNCS 2020, Springer-Varlag, 2001.

Key Management for Secure Overlay Multicast

Jong-Hyuk Roh[1] and Kyoon-Ha Lee[2]

[1] Information Security Research Division, ETRI, Korea
[2] Dept. of Computer Science and Engineering, Inha University, Korea

Abstract. Recently, the research focus of multicast has been put on overlay multicast. In overlay multicast, while the multicast routing, data replication and group management have been extensively studied, an important but less studied problem is security. In particular, adding confidentiality to overlay multicast is needed. To achieve confidentiality, data encryption keys are shared among the multicast group members. There is a need for key distribution scheme to solve the rekeying overhead. We introduce the key management solution called KTOM (Key Tree in Overlay Multicast). We described the operations of KTOM and compare the performance with other schemes, namely, host-to-host encryption, whole group encryption and SOT scheme.

Keywords: Overlay Multicast, Secure Multicast, Key Management, Key hierarchy.

1 Introduction

As expectations for the Internet to support multimedia applications grow, new services need to be deployed. One of them is the group communication service. There is more than a decade of important research and development efforts. However, the deployment of multicast routing in the Internet is far behind expectations, because of technical and marketing reasons [5]. Therefore, overlay multicast schemes have been proposed as the alternative group communication solution. Here, routers only perform unicast forwarding, while end hosts perform all multicast functions.

Many of the group communication services require data confidentiality for information protection and for charging purpose. Providing confidentiality in IP multicast has been extensively studied. However, they cannot be directly applied in overlay multicast, mainly due to the fundamental difference in data forwarding.

To offer data confidentiality in overlay multicast, we may think of two straightforward basic methods. One is the host-to-host encryption. Each overlay connection on the data delivery tree shares a unique data encryption key. In forwarding packets, each host has to first decrypt the packet received from its parent, and then re-encrypt the packets before forwarding them to each of its children using the corresponding key of the connection. This leads to continuous decrypt/re-encryption processing overhead depending on packet arrival rate. The other is

D. Feng, D. Lin, and M. Yung (Eds.): CISC 2005, LNCS 3822, pp. 336–345, 2005.
© Springer-Verlag Berlin Heidelberg 2005

whole group encryption. All group members share a universal group key. Then, only one encryption in sender and one decryption in the receiver are needed. In this case, whenever there is a membership change, a new group key is generated which has to be communicated and made known to all the members. This leads to rekey processing overhead depending on how often group membership changes [2, 3].

Either host-to-host encryption or whole group encryption may not perform satisfactorily given a certain data rate and group dynamics. To solve these problems, SOT(Secure Overlay Tree) is proposed. Group member are divided into several clusters. Instead of sharing a group key among all members, members in a cluster share a *cluster key*. Whenever a member joins or leaves the group, it actually joins or leaves a cluster. Hence, rekey messages are only delivered within a cluster. However, multicast packets need to be re-encrypted when the cross the boundary of clusters. This method is similar to Iolus [7].

Although SOT solved the problems of two basic scheme, SOT reduces the advantages of two schemes. The advantage of host-to-host encryption is the fast rekey processing and the advantage of whole group encryption is the fast transmission of multicast data using a universal group key. In the rekey processing, SOT is slower than host-to-host encryption and in the data transmission, SOT is slower than whole group encryption.

The performance of overlay multicast is lower than that of native multicast routing protocols because data forwarding at the end host is necessarily less efficient than using multicast routers in the backbone[8, 9]. So, the delay of data forwarding is the critical issue in the security overlay multicast.

In this paper, we proposed the key management scheme called KTOM (Key Tree in Overlay Multicast) which uses the key tree mechanism to reduce the rekey overhead. In the data transmission, KTOM need one encryption and one decryption because of using a universal group key.

2   Related Works

In this section, we describe the two basic schemes and SOT.

2.1   Basic Schemes

Host-to-Host Encryption. Each pair of peers that are neighbors in the multicast distribution tree share a symmetric key. Upon receiving a packet from a parent node, a member decrypts the packet using the key shared with parent. Then it re-encrypts the packet using the key shared with child node and forwards to child node. By this scheme, when the membership changes, only its parent and children needed to be rekeyed. However, this scheme requires per-packet processing on every node re-encryption. Therefore, the nodal processing overhead is expected to be high for high-bandwidth applications [2, 3].

Whole Group Encryption. Sender encrypts the data using a universal group key k_g. When a member receives the data packet, it simply delays the packet to its child nodes and decrypts the packet using a k_g. Therefore, This scheme has good performance in the data transmission. However, whenever one of the group member joins or leaves, the group key has to be changed. This incurs $O(N)$ re-key messages to all the existing N members, who are required to process the rekey messages. Clearly, the overhead of rekey is expected to be high for dynamic group [2, 3].

2.2 SOT

Group members are divided into non-overlapping clusters of size m. Instead of sharing a group key among all members, members in a cluster share a cluster key. When the membership changes, rekey messages are only delivered within a cluster. Only $O(m)$ rekey messages are processed for each join/leave. SOT loosely maintains its cluster size by splitting and merging. Every cluster has a cluster leader, which manage the cluster for coordinating operations such as rekeying, merging and splitting. Packets are re-encrypted only when they cross the boundary of clusters, and only take place at the ingress and egress nodes of a cluster. In other words, SOT uses "whole cluster encryption" within clusters and "host-to-host encryption" between clusters [2]. Either host-to-host encryption or whole group encryption may not perform satisfactorily given a certain data rate and group dynamics. SOT reduces the disadvantages in the two basic schemes using a hybrid scheme where the group members are divided into clusters. However, SOT has worse performance than whole group encryption in the multicast message transmission, because messages are re-encrypted when they cross the boundary of clusters. And the rekey overhead of SOT is more than host-to-host encryption.

3 Key Tree in Overlay Multicast

In this section, we describe KTOM scheme in detail. To quickly transmit the multicast data, KTOM uses a single group key. And to reduce the rekeying overhead, the key tree mechanism is employed in KTOM.

3.1 Key Tree

Logical Key Hierarchy (LKH) is often used to offer data confidentiality in IP multicast [1, 6]. In LKH, one universal group key is used to transmit multicast data as whole group encryption. The main purpose of LKH is to reduce rekeying overhead. However, However, LKH cannot be directly applied in overlay multicast, because there is fundamental difference between IP multicast and overlay multicast in the data transmission [2, 4].

LKH is independent on the network topology. So, subgroup members in the key tree could not neighbor each other. When the membership changes, the rekey messages are generated per each subgroup. In this situation, the rekey message of one subgroup is duplicated several times and delivered to each different region. This problem becomes serious in the overlay multicast, because end hosts perform data forwarding and duplicating process. Our key management tree match

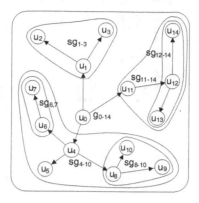

Fig. 1. Subgroup in overlay multicast

the network topology in such a way that the neighbors on the key tree are also physical neighbors on the network. By localizing the delivery of rekey messages to small regions of the network, our scheme lessens the amount of traffic crossing portions of the network that do not have users who need to be rekeyed.

Fig. 1 shows the subgroup in overlay multicast. Group members are divided into subgroups to build the key tree. Subgroups are composed hierarchically. The algorithm that generates subgroup is eshown in Fig. 2. This rule is that if the node has one or more child node, it makes the subgroup that includes all its children and itself. In Fig. 1, the sender u_0 that send multicast data has child nodes, u_1, u_4, and u_{11}. Then, group g_{0-14} that includes all group members is generated. Each u_1, u_4, and u_{11} has the child node, then sg_{1-3}, sg_{4-10}, and sg_{11-14} is generated. Also, each u_6, u_8, and u_{12} has the child node, subgroups $sg_{6,7}$, sg_{8-10}, and sg_{12-14} are generated in the subgroup.

KTOM has a trusted key server responsible for generating and securely distributing keys to users in the group. And the key server manages the key tree

```
subgroup (struct stnode CurrentNode)
{
    if (CurrentNode has one or more ChildNodes) {
        MakeSubgroup(CurrentNode, All ChildNodes);    /* Make a subgroup */
        Struct stnode TempNode = First ChildNode;
        while (TempNode != NULL) {
            subgroup(TempNode);
            TempNode = Next ChildNode;
        }
    } else
        return;
}
```

Fig. 2. Subgroup generation

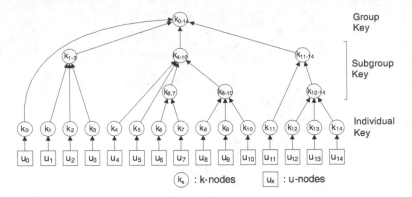

Fig. 3. Key tree

that changed whenever the user joins or leaves. Fig. 3 shows the key tree that includes subgroups and members in Fig. 1. The key tree is composed with two types of nodes: u-nodes representing users and k-nodes representing keys. There are three types of keys. The first type is a *group key*, used to encrypt/decrypt multicast data; the second type is a *subgroup key*, used to encrypt/decrypt other keys instead of the actual data; the last type is the *individual key*. Each member holds the keys along the path from u-node itself all the way to the root. Therefore, for the case of user u_6, u_6 holds k_6, $k_{6,7}$, k_{4-10}, and k_{0-14}. Each subtree in the entire key tree is a subgroup and each member is assigned to more than one subgroup. For example, member u_6 belongs to groups $sg_{6,7}$, sg_{4-10}, and g_{0-14}.

3.2   Member Joining

A new member u_x contacts the key server s to join the multicast group. For a join request from user u_x, server s performs the authentication and authorization process. If the join request is granted, the individual key k_x of u_x is generated and is shared by u_x and s.

A new member u_x finds a node that called the joining point in the overlay multicast tree. u_x first contacts the root of the tree, chooses the best node among the root's children, and repeat this top-down-process until it finds an appropriate parent. After finding the joining point, the key tree is modified. The modifying method of key tree is different according to the position of joining point.

The Joining Point Is Not the Leaf Node. If a new member u_x is attached to the root node or the interior node, u_x joins the existing subgroup that is composed with joining point and its children. According to this situation, server s modifies the key tree. Server s creates a new u-node for user u_x and a new k-node for its individual key k_x. The new k-node is attached to the k-node of joining subgroup. And, to guarantee backward secrecy, all keys along the path from joining point to the root node need to be changed.

For example, if a new member u_x is attached to u_1, k-node k_x is attached to k-node k_{1-3} in the key tree. To guarantee backward secrecy, the key of this k-node is changed to $k_{1-3,x}$. Moreover, the group at the root is changed from k_{0-14} to $k_{0-14,x}$. User $u_4, \ldots, u_{14}$ only need the new group key $k_{0-14,x}$. User u_1, u_2, u_3 and u_x need not only new group key but also the new subgroup key $k_{1-3,x}$. Server s creates and sends the following three rekey messages:

$$s \rightarrow u_4, ..., u_{14} : [k_{0-14,x}]_{k_{0-14}}$$
$$s \rightarrow u_1, u_2, u_3 : [k_{0-14,x}, k_{1-3,x}]_{k_{1-3}}$$
$$s \rightarrow u_x : [k_{0-14,x}, k_{1-3,x}]_{k_x}$$

Note the first message. There is no single key that is shared only by $u_4, \ldots, u_{14}$. However, old group key k_{0-14} can be used to encrypt the new group key because u_x does not know this key k_{0-14}. At the second message, subgroup key k_{1-3} that is shared only by u_1, u_2, and u_3 is used for encryption.

The Joining Point Is the Leaf Node. If a new member u_x is attached to leaf node, the new subgroup that includes u_x and joining point is generated. Server s creates not only a new u-node and a new k-node for u_x, but also new k-node for new subgroup. The k-node for u_x is attached to the k-node for new subgroup.

For example, a new member u_x is attached to u_3, server s creates the new subgroup $sg_{3,x}$ and the k-node $k_{3,x}$. The k-node $k_{3,x}$ is attached to k_{1-3} and k_x is attached to $k_{3,x}$. To guarantee backward secrecy, key k_{0-14} and k_{1-3} must be changed. Server s creates and sends the following four rekey messages:

$$s \rightarrow u_4, ..., u_{14} : [k_{0-14,x}]_{k_{0-14}}$$
$$s \rightarrow u_1, u_2 : [k_{0-14,x}, k_{1-3,x}]_{k_{1-3}}$$
$$s \rightarrow u_3 : [k_{0-14,x}, k_{1-3,x}, k_{3,x}]_{k_3}$$
$$s \rightarrow u_x : [k_{0-14,x}, k_{1-3,x}, k_{3,x}]_{k_x}$$

3.3   Member Leaving

After granting a leave request from user u_x, the data transmission tree and key tree are updated. The modifying method of key tree is different according to the position of u_x.

The Departing Node Is Not the Leaf Node. If the departing user u_x is the root node or the interior node in the data transmission tree, the existing user u_y among the child nodes of u_x replaces u_x to transmit multicast data. In the overlay multicast, to reduce the transmission overhead of each node, there is the maximum number of children node, called maximum degree d_{max}. When u_y replaces u_x, children of u_x become the children of u_y. If the sum of new children and existing children exceeds the maximum degree d_{max}, the user u_z among the existing children of u_y replaces the old position of u_y. This process can be repeated.

For example, the maximum degree d_{max} in the overlay multicast of Fig. 1 is 3. When the departing user is u_4, let's assume that the case u_8 replaces u_4 is the optimal choice to provide the maximal throughput. In this case, the sum of children of u_8 exceeds d_{max}. Therefore, u_9 replaces the old position of u_8. (See Fig. 4.)

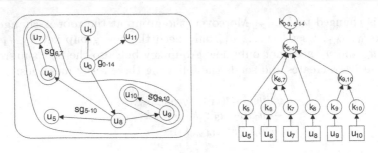

Fig. 4. Member leaving

Server s modifies the key tree according to the above situation. The subgroup sg_{5-10} takes the place of sg_{4-10} and the $sg_{9,10}$ takes the place of sg_{8-10}. To guarantee forward secrecy, the universal group key k_{0-14} must be changed to $k_{0-3,5-14}$. And, the old k-node k_{4-10} and k_{8-10} is changed to the new k-node k_{5-10} and $k_{9,10}$. Server s creates and sends the following five rekey messages:

$$s \rightarrow u_1, u_2, u_3 : [k_{0-3,5-14}]k_{1-3}$$
$$s \rightarrow u_{11}, ..., u_{14} : [k_{0-3,5-14}]k_{11-14}$$
$$s \rightarrow u_5 : [k_{0-3,5-14}, k_{5-10}]k_5$$
$$s \rightarrow u_6, u_7 : [k_{0-3,5-14}, k_{5-10}]k_{6,7}$$
$$s \rightarrow u_8, u_9, u_{10} : [k_{0-3,5-10}, k_{5-10}, [k_{9,10}]k_9, [k_{9,10}]k_{10}]k_{8-10}$$

When the rekey messages are encrypted, the key k_{0-14} and k_{4-10} must not be used. Because the departing node u_4 knows that keys.

The Departing Node Is the Leaf Node. In the case that the departing user u_x is the leaf node in the data transmission tree, the process is simple. The only user u_x is removed from the transmission tree. According to this situation, server s modifies the key tree. If u_x has sibling node, the u-node and k-node of u_x are only removed from the key tree. Unless, the subgroup includes u_x and its parent node is removed. In the key tree, u-node and k-node of u_x and k-node of subgroup is removed from the key tree. And, the k-node of u_x' parent is attached to the k-node of upper subgroup.

For example, if the departing user is u_2, only u-node and k-node of u_2 are removed. If the departing user is u_7, the subgroup $sg_{6,7}$ is removed. In the key tree, u-node and k-node of u_7 and k-node of $sg_{6,7}$ are removed. In the case that u_7 leaves the group, to guarantee forward secrecy, the group key k_{0-14} and subgroup key k_{4-10} must be changed. Server s creates and sends the following five rekey messages:

$$s \rightarrow u_1, u_2, u_3 : [k_{0-6,8-14}]k_{1-3}$$
$$s \rightarrow u_{11}, ..., u_{14} : [k_{0-6,8-14}]k_{11-14}$$
$$s \rightarrow u_5 : [k_{0-6,8-14}, k_{5-6,8-10}]k_5$$
$$s \rightarrow u_8, u_9, u_{10} : [k_{0-6,8-14}, k_{5-6,8-10}]k_{8-10}$$
$$s \rightarrow u_6 : [k_{0-6,8-14}, k_{5-6,8-10}]k_6$$

4   Performance Evaluation

In our simulation, we compare the performance of KTOM with the two basic schemes and SOT. The simulation parameters are listed in Table 1.

Fig. 5 shows the average time of multicast data transmission for different group sizes. This elapsed time is from the sender encrypts the message to all receivers decrypt the message. KTOM and whole group encryption show the better performance than SOT and host-to-host encryption, because the re-encryption is not needed in two schemes.

Table 1. Parameters used in simulation

Parameter	Value
Group size	100 ~ 10000
Degree of multicast tree	4
Link delay	5 ms
Data packet size	10000 bytes
Cluster size in SOT scheme	100
Process time of a symmetric crypto-op. for data	1 ms
Process time of a symmetric crypto-op. for key	0.1 ms

The average time of join processing for different group sizes is shown in Fig. 6. As the group size increases, the processing time of KTOM and whole group encryption increases. Because the universal group key is used, the entire group member need rekey process in the two schemes. However, the processing time of host-to-host encryption and SOT scheme does not increase, because the members need to be rekeyed are limited.

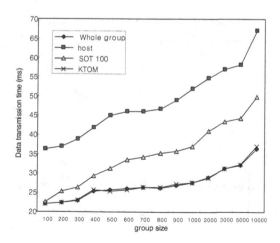

Fig. 5. Data transmission time

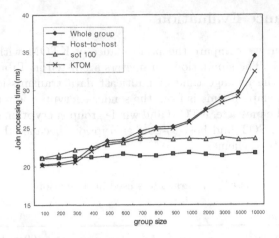

Fig. 6. Join processing time

Fig. 7 shows the leave processing time. The average leave time of KTOM is similar to the average join time. The average leave time of host-to-host encryption and SOT scheme has less good performance than the join processing time. In the host-to-host encryption, when member joining, the number of members need to be rekeyed is only two. However, when member leaving, if departing member is not leaf node, the number of members need to be rekeyed can be more than two.

In SOT, rekey messages are only delivered within a cluster. When member joining, the cluster leader generates the new cluster key k, encrypts k by the old cluster key and multicast it within the cluster. However, when member leaving, the cluster leader generates the new cluster key k, it multicast k within the cluster along the overlay tree using host-to-host encryption, i.e., members re-

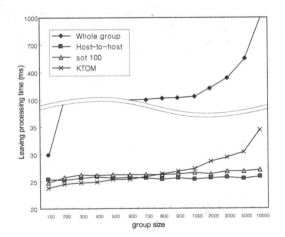

Fig. 7. Leave processing time

encrypt k using neighbor keys before forwarding it [2]. Therefore, when the group size is less than 700, KTOM has better performance than SOT and host-to-host encryption. In the whole group encryption, this incurs $O(N)$ rekey messages to all the group N members.

To summarize, in the data transmission, whole group encryption and KTOM scheme are significantly faster. In the join/leave processing, host-to-host encryption and SOT scheme is better. The choice of best key management scheme depends on the application needs: minimizing rekeying latency or minimizing data multicasting latency. However, the delay of data forwarding is the critical weakness of the overlay multicast. Therefore, we believe that minimizing data forwarding latency is better choice in the secure overlay multicast.

5   Conclusion

In this paper, we describe a protocol called KTOM to provide data security in overlay multicast. The weakness of overlay multicast is the delay of data forwarding. So, KTOM uses a whole group key not to make matters worse. To reduce the rekeying overhead, KTOM employs the key tree mechanism. Also, by matching the key management tree to the overlay multicast topology, KTOM could localize the delivery of rekeying messages.

We compare the performance of KTOM with the SOT scheme and two basic schemes. According to the simulation results, KTOM can achieve much better performance than other schemes in the data transmission. And, key tree mechanism reduces the rekeying overhead.

References

1. C. K. Wong, M. Gouda, and S. S. Lam, "Secure Group Communications Using Key Graphs," IEEE/ACM Transactions on Networking, vol. 8, pp. 16-29, Feb. 2000.
2. W.-P. K. Yiu and S.-H. G. Chan, "SOT: Secure Overlay Tree for Application Layer Multicast," IEEE International Conference on Communications, vol. 3, pp. 20-24, Jun. 2004.
3. C. Abad, I. Gupta, and W. Yurcik, "Adding Confidentiality to Application-Level Multicast by Leveraging the Multicast Overlay," IEEE International Conference on Distributed Computing Systems Workshops, pp. 5-11 Jun. 2005.
4. A. Ganjam and H. Zhang, "Internet multicast video delivery," in Proceedings of the IEEE, vol. 93, pp. 159-170, Jan. 2005.
5. A. El-Sayed, V. Roca, and L. Mathy, "A Survey of Proposals for an Alternative Group Communication Service," IEEE Network, vol. 17, pp. 46-51, Jan.-Feb. 2003.
6. K. Chan and S.-H. G. Chan, "Key Management Approaches to Offer Data Confidentiality for Secure Multicast," IEEE Network, vol. 17, pp. 30-39, Sep.-Oct. 2003.
7. S. Mittra, "Iolus: A Framework for Scalable Secure Multicasting," in Proceedings of ACM Sigcomm, pp. 277-288. 1997.
8. P. Francis, "Yoid: Extending the Internet Multicast Architecture," Technical Report, ACIRI, Apr. 2000.
9. B. Zhang, S. Jamin, and L. Zhang, "Host Multicast: A Framework for Delivering Multicast to End Users," INFOCOM, vol. 3, pp. 1366-1375, Jun. 2003.

Design and Implementation of IEEE 802.11i Architecture for Next Generation WLAN*

Duhyun Bae, Jiho Kim, Sehyun Park[**], and Ohyoung Song

School of Electrical and Electronic Engineering,
Chung-Ang University,
221, HukSuk-Dong, DongJak-Gu, Seoul, Korea
{duhyunbae, jihokim}@wm.cau.ac.kr,
{shpark, song}@cau.ac.kr

Abstract. The drive for high data rate and QoS support in wireless LANs has pushed the IEEE to develop IEEE 802.11n and IEEE 802.11e. For higher throughput, new MAC mechanisms such as Block Ack in IEEE 802.11e and frame aggregation in IEEE 802.11n are being currently discussed and these mechanisms needs short response time in each MPDU processing. In this paper, we propose a design of IEEE 802.11i hardware architecture to support these new MAC mechanisms. We reduce the response time in the crypto engine to short constant interval by using the dual S-Box scheme in WEP and TKIP processing and by adopting parallel structure in CCMP. In our method, the key management block is used to eliminate the computational burden for key and per packet counter management in 802.11i device driver. Our design features 195 Mbps in WEP, TKIP, and 562 Mbps in CCMP throughput respectively at 50 MHz frequency, which are targeted to Altera Stratix FPGA device.

1 Introduction

When the IEEE 802.11 standard was published, it included an optional security protocol called WEP. However, as the IEEE and Wi-Fi Alliance realized that WEP is not safe against attacks, IEEE 802.11 task group I presented the RSN (Robust Security Network) architecture that uses WEP (Wired Equivalent Privacy), TKIP (Temporal Key Integrity Protocol) and CCMP (Counter with CBC-MAC Protocol) to protect WLAN traffic in MAC (Medium Access Control) layer [1][2].

For higher data throughput, new MAC mechanisms such as Block Ack [9] in the IEEE 802.11e and frame aggregation [10] in the IEEE 802.11n are being discussed. Because these mechanisms have short interval among MPDUs, a response time in a crypto hardware engine should be short. In this paper, we define the response time as an interval between the first data input time and the first processed data output time. We may reduce the response time by increasing a clock frequency in the crypto en-

---

[*] This research was supported by the MIC(Ministry of Information and Communication), Korea, under the Chung-Ang University HNRC(Home Network Research Center)-ITRC support program supervised by the IITA(Institute of Information Technology Assessment).

[**] Corresponding author.

D. Feng, D. Lin, and M. Yung (Eds.): CISC 2005, LNCS 3822, pp. 346–357, 2005.

gine. But, power consumption is a critical factor especially to wireless communication device of a mobile terminal. As a clock frequency becomes faster, dynamic power consumption in circuit increases. Therefore, in order to support new mechanisms in IEEE 802.11e and 802.11n, new design methods of an IEEE 802.11i hardware is needed to reduce the response time.

In this paper, we reduce the processing overhead of RC4 key scheduling and the response time by using the dual S-Box scheme. On CCMP design process, the parallel structure is adopted so that we reduce the processing time and the response time.

In 802.11i, a pair-wise key [2] is used for MPDU encapsulation. Therefore, an AP (Access Point) should manage pair-wise keys for each a mobile terminal. In addition, because a per-packet counter [2] - such as IV (Initialization Vector) in WEP, TSC (TKIP Sequence Counter) in TKIP and PN (Packet Number) in CCMP - is used for generating a per-packet key, the AP should manage these counters for each a mobile terminal. In IBSS (Independent Basic Service Set), the management of pair-wise keys and per-packet counters should be needed since a mobile terminal acts as an AP. But, these managements through a 802.11i device driver may cause system overheads. Thus, we introduce key management block to reduce system overhead in the device driver. By means of key and counter management in hardware, our design can decrease the system overheads and the response time.

The presented design in this paper has the following features:

- Parallel operation in CCMP
- Dual-port ram is used, allowing for higher memory transfer efficiency
- The dual S-Box scheme for the key scheduling of RC4
- Supporting all protocols – WEP, TKIP and CCMP – in IEEE 802.11i
- Reduced response time to support Block Ack mechanism in IEEE 802.11e and frame aggregation mechanism in IEEE 802.11n
- 2 interface: PCI interface for device driver, MAC interface for 802.11 MAC hardware
- Key Management: Pair-wise key and per-packet counter management

2 Design Considerations

New versions of the IEEE 802.11 standard specify new MAC mechanisms to reduce the acknowledgement overhead. The Block Acknowledgement (Block Ack) mechanism is currently being discussed in the IEEE 802.11 task group E. The message sequence chart for Block Ack mechanism in 802.11e is illustrated in Fig. 1. The Block Ack mechanism allows a burst of frames to be transmitted before any acknowledgement. After sending the block of frames, the sender sends a block acknowledgement (BlockAck) frame, in which the correctly received frames' information is included. All the frames are separated by a short interframe space (SIFS) period.

In IEEE 802.11n task group, single and multiple destination frame aggregation is being discussed. Some proposal specifies a standardized frame aggregation for both single and multiple destinations to improve network efficiency and interoperability. For example, frame aggregation in TGnSync proposal is a MAC layer function that

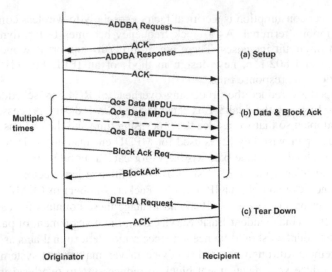

Fig. 1. The message sequence chart for block ack mechanism in IEEE 802.11e [9]

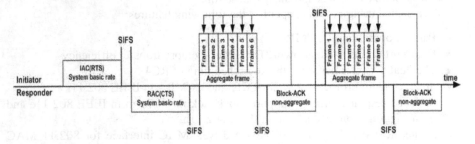

Fig. 2. The frame aggregation process in TGnSync proposal [10]

bundles several MAC frames into a single aggregate frame for transmission. The frame aggregation process in TGnSync proposal is illustrated in Fig. 2.

As mentioned above, new MAC mechanisms in IEEE 802.11e and 802.11n have a short interval among MPDUs. In the IEEE 802.11i, the encapsulation process is per formed per MPDU. Therefore, the response time in the crypto engine must be short. If the latency between the end time of a previous MPDU processing and the start time of the encapsulation or decapsulation of the following MPDU is not negligible, we can't support new MAC mechanisms.

We may reduce the response time by increasing a clock frequency in the crypto engine. But, in wireless device, which are usually resource-constrained, power consumption is a critical factor especially to a mobile terminal. In general, as a clock frequency becomes faster, the dynamic power consumption increases. But, if the data throughput is high but only the response time has long term in the crypto engine, we can adopt low clock frequency by reducing the response time and thereby we can decrease power consumption in the crypto engine.

As mentioned in Section 1, key and per-packet counter management through device driver can cause system overheads - such as matched key searching, per-packet counters management, the validity check of per-packet counter, data handshake for key, cipher suite, and per-packet counter between the device driver and the crypto engine. These system overheads increase the response time because appropriate data should be sent to the crypto engine before encapsulation or decapsulation. Therefore, key and per-packet counter management in hardware is necessary and it should not need additional processing time before encapsulation or decapsulation.

We may use SIFS as a factor to consider the maximum available response time. The total delay in MAC, PHY and the crypto engine must within the SIFS. Thus, the delay in the cipher core must be much smaller than the SIFS specified in other 802.11 standards. SIFS is $10\mu s$ in 802.11b and $16\mu s$ in 802.11a and 802.11n. In this paper, we assume the maximum available response time in the crypto engine is about $3\mu s$.

3   Review of Previous Designs and Our Motivation for RC4 and AES-CCM

RC4 is a stream cipher algorithm designed by Ron Rivest and was originally proprietary to RSA Data Security [5]. RC4 stream cipher algorithm which is used in WEP and TKIP has an overhead of the key scheduling which swaps S-Box memory 256 times before encryption or decryption. Consequently, it delays encryption, reduces throughput and increases the response time [7]. The procedure of RC4 algorithm is illustrated in Fig. 3.

The RC4 algorithm can be divided into 2 phases. The first phase is a key scheduling phase (KS-phase) and the second phase is a pseudorandom number generator (PRNG) phase. In WEP and TKIP, both the phases must be performed for every MPDU. In WEP and TKIP, the KS-phase initializes the S-Box with the WEP seed

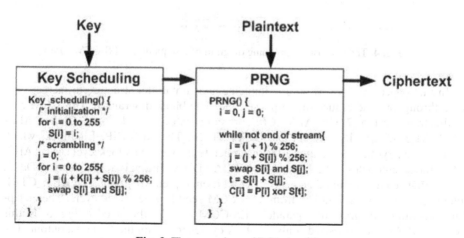

Fig. 3. The procedure of RC4 algorithm

key and the PRNG generates pseudorandom numbers and encrypts by XORing the plaintexts and the key streams [4].

AES (Advanced Encryption Standard) in CCM (Counter with CBC-MAC) mode [3] is used in CCMP. AES-CCM algorithm consists of two processes: one is MIC calculation with CBC-MAC (Cipher Block Chaining Message Authentication Code) mode and the other is data encryption with counter mode [2]. In AES-CCM, one AES core can be used to both MIC (Message Integrity Code) calculation and data encryption. In general, there are two methods in designing AES-CCM core in hardware: One is sequential structure that calculates MIC firstly and then performs encryption later by using one AES core. The other is the parallel structure design that computes the MIC in CBC mode and performs encryption in the counter mode simultaneously by using two AES core.

The sequential structure design can lead to a significant savings in code and hardware size because it uses only one AES core. However, because the first encrypted data are ready after MIC calculation, the response time increases. Moreover, as the payload size increases, this design increases the response time linearly. For example, if 1024 bytes is a payload size and it takes 11 clock cycles for MIC calculation of 128 bit data, the total MIC calculation of 1024 bytes will take 748 clock cycles as described in Fig. 4. At 100 MHz clock frequency, it will take 7.48 μs. If 2048 bytes is a payload size, the total time of MIC calculation will take 14.52 μs, which is more than SIFS in IEEE 802.11b.

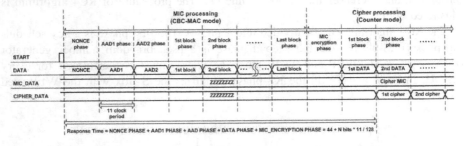

Fig. 4. The encapsulation timing diagram of a sequential AES-CCM core

In this paper, AES-CCM core is implemented in parallel structure to increase the data throughput and reduce the response time. The block diagram of AES-CCM core is illustrated in Fig. 7. Our AES-CCM core consists of 5 blocks: AES-Cipher, AES-MIC, KEY_CTRL, INPUT_IF, and OUTPUT_IF. The AES-CIPHER block, which performs encryption, generates 128 bit cipher text every 11 clock cycle. The AES-MIC block computes MIC about NONCE, AAD (Additional Authentication Data), and MPDU data field and then generates 64 bit encrypted MIC data. The KEY_CTRL block generates one round key from AES-CCM seed key per clock cycle. The encapsulation timing diagram of a parallel AES-CCM core is illustrated in Fig. 5. In this design, AES-CCM core needs only 44 clock cycles to obtain the first data output. The important result is that the response time doesn't depend on the payload size.

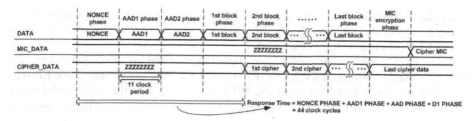

Fig. 5. The encapsulation timing diagram of a parallel AES-CCM core

4 The Design of Protocol Cores and the IEEE 802.11i Hardware

4.1 WEP and TKIP

In WEP and TKIP, RC4 algorithm is used. As mentioned in Section 3, RC4 algorithm has a significant response time due to key scheduling. In this paper, we introduce new method for the key scheduling, in which RC4 module has two S-Boxes and two key scheduling modules. When one pair of S-Box and key scheduling module is used to perform encryption or decryption, the other pair is used to perform key scheduling about other RC4 key. In other words, while the present MPDU is being encrypted in the PRNG which must access one of the two S-Box storing data for key stream, the other S-Box with a key scheduling module is used to prepare for key scheduling for the next MPDU. To encapsulate the next MPDU, we can skip key scheduling just by using the latter S-Box and go to the PRNG-phase immediately. Thus, if the data field size of a MPDU currently being processed is more than 256 bytes, which it takes 512 clock cycles to encrypt or decrypt, the key scheduling for the next MPDU is performed at the same clock cycles in the other S-Box and key scheduling module.

In WLAN, most of packets are control and management packets that have a small size between 64-127 bytes. But we don't need to encapsulate these packets. The data packet is typically about 1024 bytes, which it takes 2048 cycles to encapsulate [8]. The key scheduling requires 512 cycles. Therefore, the dual S-Box scheme can save 512 cycles every MPDU except the first one.

In encapsulation process, a sender can know a per-packet counter for the next MPDU whether its destination is the same as the destination of the MPDU currently begin encapsulated or not. Therefore, the key scheduling for the next MPDU can be immediately performed. In decapsulation process, a receiver receives successive MPDUs from one sender and can know the per-packet counter of the first MPDU after receiving the extended header. Because the extended header follows the MAC header, we can calculate the per-packet counter for the next MPDU by adding 1 to the current per-packet counter. So, just after receiving the extended header, we can start the key scheduling for the next MPDU. By this scheme, we can reduce the latency due to RC4 key scheduling, so that we can reduce the response time and increase the data throughput.

The block diagram of WEP module is illustrated in Fig. 6. The WEP module consists of RC4 module, CRC-32 module, INPUT_IF (Input Interface), and OUTPUT_IF (Output Interface) module. The RC4 module performs RC4 stream cipher processing and the CRC-32 module generates 32 bit CRC (Cyclic Redundancy Check) value.

After the WEP module is initialized, the RC4 module starts key scheduling phase. Then, 8 bit data are encrypted by the RC4 module and 32 bit CRC value is processed by the CRC-32 module per 2 clock cycles.

TKIP uses a per-packet key mixing function to combine a temporal key, the TA(Transmitter Address), and the TKIP Sequence Counter (TSC) into the WEP seed to defeat weak-key attacks against the WEP key. TKIP has the additional latency caused by key mixing before RC4 key scheduling. However, it is negligible since the key mixing algorithm is not complicate [2]. The block diagram of the TKIP module is illustrated in Fig. 6.

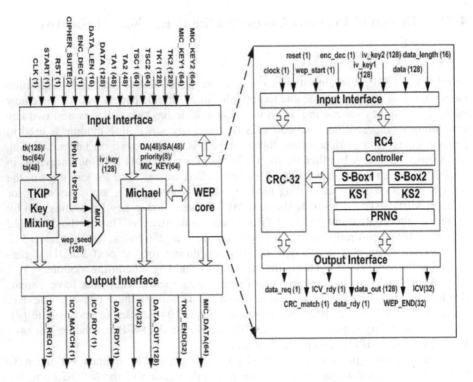

Fig. 6. The block diagram of WEP module and TKIP module

The TKIP module consists of 5 sub-modules: WEP module, MICHAEL module, TKIP Key Mixing module, Input Interface module, and Output Interface module. The TKIP Key Mixing module performs TKIP phase1 and phase 2 key mixing. The MICHAEL module generates MIC data. The TKIP module can be used in either WEP or TKIP operation mode depending on cipher_suite signal as shown in Fig. 6.

4.2   CCMP

CCMP is based on the CCM mode of operation of the AES encryption algorithm. The CCM mode consists of Counter Mode (CTR) for confidentiality and Cipher Block

Chaining-Message Authentication Code (CBC-MAC) for authentication and integrity [2][6].

The block diagram of CCMP module is illustrated in Fig. 7. The Construction Block generates NONCE and AAD. The KEY_CTRL module generates round keys from AES-CCM seed key.

4.3 IEEE 802.11i Hardware Architecture

The implemented IEEE 802.11i hardware has the following functions: (1) Encapsulation and decapsulation for WEP, TKIP, CCMP (2) Key Management (key searching, key addition, key deletion, per-packet counter management) (3) Reporting TKIP and CCMP countermeasure to device driver using PCI interface. The block diagram of the IEEE 802.11i hardware is illustrated in Fig. 8.

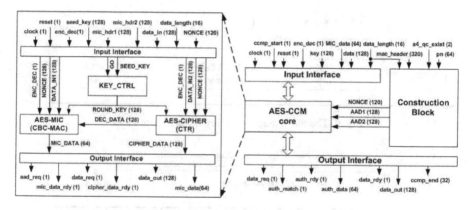

Fig. 7. The block diagram of CCMP module and AES-CCM module

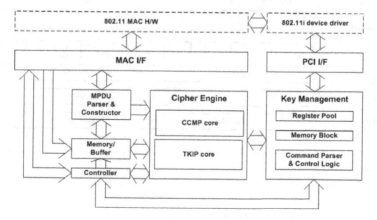

Fig. 8. The block diagram of the IEEE 802.11i hardware

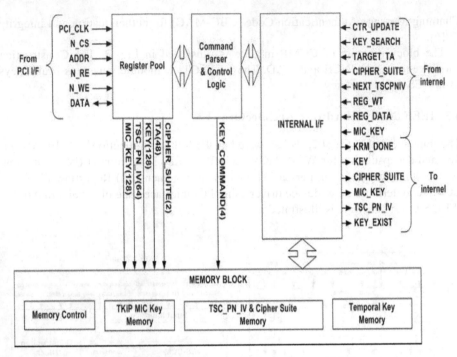

Fig. 9. The block diagram of key management block

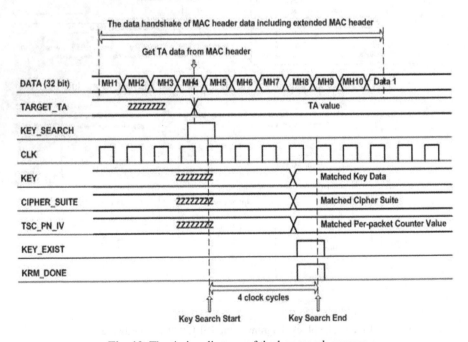

Fig. 10. The timing diagram of the key search process

The design has 2 interfaces: MAC and PCI interfaces. The MAC interface receives MPDU and control signals from the 802.11 MAC hardware and sends the encapsulated or decapsulated MPDU to the 802.11 MAC hardware. In order to support IEEE 802.11i key management function, the IEEE 802.11i hardware receives a command and data related to key management from the 802.11i device driver through the PCI interface.

The block diagram of the key management block is illustrated in Fig. 9. The key management block provides key management functions such as key addition/deletion from the device driver through the PCI interface and key search and per-packet counter update from the controller of the cipher engine shown in Fig. 8 through the Internal Interface. When a key addition command is assigned by the device driver, the key management block saves cipher suite, initial per-packet counter, and temporal key to memory. In case of TKIP, it saves a TKIP MIC key too.

We can reduce the overheads of key and per-packet counter management in the 802.11i device driver and the response time by using the key management block in the IEEE 802.11i hardware. In addition, no more clock cycle is needed for key and per-packet counter management. For example, we can obtain matched key, cipher suite, and per-packet counter during the handshake process of MAC header data including the extended MAC header in decapsulation process. The timing diagram of the key search process is illustrated in Fig. 10.

In addition, the IEEE 802.11i hardware can check the validity of the per-packet counter, which is used to prevent the replay attack by comparing the received per-packet counter in the extended header with the saved per-packet counter in the key management block.

5 Performance Measurement and Verification

The IEEE 802.11i hardware was synthesized and implemented using Quartus II compiler and targeted to Altera Stratix FPGA device.

Our design can support up to 195 Mbps in WEP, 195 Mbps in TKIP, and 562 Mbps in CCMP at 50 MHz clock frequency. This satisfies MAC data processing speed of all standards. The data speed of MAC layer is 11 Mbps in IEEE 802.11b and 54 Mbps in IEEE 802.11a and 802.11g. Our design can support all these standards [1].

Table 1 shows performance of WEP and TKIP for the 1024 bytes payload at a 50 MHz clock frequency. In this result, WEP and TKIP have similar performance since

Table 1. Performance of WEP and TKIP for the 1024 bytes payload at a 50 MHz clock frequency

Category	WEP	TKIP
Throughput without the dual S-Box	160 Mbps	157 Mbps
Throughput with the dual S-Box	195 Mbps	195 Mbps
Response Time without the dual S-box	11.08 μs	11.92 μs
Response Time with the dual S-box	0.8 μs	0.8 μs

both protocols use the same cipher algorithm of RC4. By using the dual S-box scheme, the data throughput and the response time have been improved. Specially, the response time has been 10 times improved.

Table 2 shows performances of CCMP for 1024 byte payload at 50 MHz clock frequency. In CCMP, we improve data throughput nearly 2 times than the sequential structure design's and reduce the response time significantly by adopting the parallel structure. In addition, the response times at WEP, TKIP and CCMP are not dependant on the payload size, but only dependant on the clock frequency.

Table 2. Performance of CCMP for 1024 bytes payload at 50 MHz clock frequency

Category	CCMP
Throughput in the sequential structure	285 Mbps
Throughput in the parallel structure	562 Mbps
Response Time in the sequential structure	14.96 μs
Response Time in the parallel structure	0.88 μs

Table 3 shows the design comparison between our design and a typical one with CCMP designed by a sequential structure and WEP by a single S-Box scheme. The number of logic gates used in our design is as about 2 times as in a typical design's. But, if the critical response time is 3 μs, the typical design should uses 200 MHz clock frequency in TKIP and more than 250 MHz in CCMP to reduce response time as the payload size becomes larger than 1024 bytes. But, our design can use the lower clock frequency considering the data throughput, the response time, and the performance constraints specified in 802.11e and 802.11n. We can use 25 MHz clock, which results in about 100 Mbps data throughput and 1.6μs response time in TKIP. The clock frequency is an important factor since the distribution of the clock signal over the circuit can consume a lot of energy even if the switching activity within the circuit is very low. So, it is important to make the clock as slow as possible while still staying within performance constraints. The minimum of the clock frequency achievable in a typical design is as 10 times as our design's Therefore, even if our design doubles the number of the logic gates, the total power consumption of our design is compatible with a typical design's.

Table 3. Design comparison

TKIP		CCMP	
Category	Logic Used	Category	Logic Used
Without pre-computing S-Box	4225	Sequential design	5565
With pre-computing S-Box	7718	Parallel design	9598

6   Conclusion

In this paper, we propose the IEEE 802.11i hardware architecture that supports WEP, TKIP and CCMP protocols and also supports new MAC mechanisms in other 802.11

standards. In WEP design, we reduce the response time and increase the data throughput by adopting the dual S-Box scheme. In AES-CCM module design, we obtain the constant response time and double the data throughput by adopting the parallel structured AES-CCM core. Besides, we can reduce the overheads of key and per-packet counter management in device driver by using key management block in 802.11i secure engine.

As a result, our design can support up to 195 Mbps in WEP, 195 Mbps in TKIP, and 562 Mbps in CCMP at 50 MHz clock frequency. This satisfies MAC data processing speed of all standards which is 11 Mbps in IEEE 802.11b and 54 Mbps in IEEE 802.11a and 802.11g. The response time at 50 MHz clock frequency is less than 1 μs in all protocols, which is enough to support new MAC mechanisms in 802.11e and 802.11n. We can conclude that our design can support new MAC mechanisms that include Block Ack in 802.11e and frame aggregation in 802.11n and reduce power consumption because our design has the shorter response time and the data throughput achievable at the lower clock frequency.

References

1. IEEE P802.11, The Working group for Wireless LANs, http://www.ieee802.org/11/
2. IEEE standard 802.11i, July 2004.
3. D.Whiting, Hifn, R.Housley, N.Ferguson, MacFergus, "Counter with CBC- MAC(CCM)" RFC 3610, September, 2003
4. K.H. Tsoi, K.H. Lee and P.H.W Leong, "A Massively Parallel RC4 Key Search Engine", IEEE Symposium on Field-Programmable Custom Computing Machines (FCCM'02) 1082-3409/02 2002.
5. Jon Edney, William A. Arbaugh, "Real 802.11 security: Wi-Fi Protected Access and 802.11i" Addison Wesley, 2003.
6. Ho Yung Jang, Joon Hyoung Shim, Jung Hee Suk, In Cheol Hwang and Jun Rim Choi, "COMPATIBLE DESIGN OF CCMP AND OCB AES CIPHER USING SEPERATED ENCRYPTOR AND DECRYPTOR FOR IEEE 802.11I", ISCAS 2004.
7. Wang Shunman, TaoRan, WangYue, ZhangJi, "WLAN and Its Security Problems", IEEE 2003.
8. P. Prasithsangaree and P. Krishnamurthy, "Analysis of Energy Consumption of RC4 and AES Algorithms in Wireless LANs", GLOBECOM 2003
9. IEEE standard 802.11e/D13.0 January 2005
10. Matthew S. Gast, "802.11 Wireless Networks – 2nd Edition" O'REILLY, 2005.

Automatic Alignment of Fingerprint Features
for Fuzzy Fingerprint Vault

Yongwha Chung[1], Daesung Moon[2], Sungju Lee[1], Seunghwan Jung[1],
Taehae Kim[1], and Dosung Ahn[2]

[1] Department of Computer and Information Science, Korea University, Korea
{ychungy, peacfeel, sksghksl, taegar}@korea.ac.kr
[2] Biometrics Technology Research Team, ETRI, Daejeon, Korea
{daesung, dosung}@etri.re.kr

Abstract. Biometrics-based user authentication has several advantages over traditional password-based systems for standalone authentication applications. This is also true for new authentication architectures known as *crypto-biometric* systems, where cryptography and biometrics are merged to achieve high security and user convenience at the same time. Recently, a cryptographic construct, called *fuzzy vault*, has been proposed for crypto-biometric systems. This construct aims to secure critical data(e.g., secret encryption key) with the fingerprint data in a way that only the authorized user can access the secret by providing the valid fingerprint, and some implementations results for fingerprint have been reported. However, all the previous results assumed that fingerprint features were pre-aligned, and automatic alignment in the fuzzy vault domain is a challenging issue. In this paper, we perform the automatic alignment of fingerprint features by using the geometric hashing technique which has been used for model-based object recognition applications. Based on the preliminary experimental results, we confirm that the proposed approach can align fingerprint features automatically in the domain of the fuzzy vault and can be integrated with any fuzzy fingerprint vault systems.

Keywords: Crypto-Biometric, Fuzzy Fingerprint Vault, Geometric Hashing.

1 Introduction

Current cryptographic algorithms have a very high proven security, but they suffer from the key management problem: all these algorithms fully depend on the assumption that the keys will be kept in absolute secrecy. If the secret key is compromised, the security provided by them immediately falls apart. Another limitation of these algorithms is that they require the keys to be very long and random for higher security, which makes it impossible for users to memorize the keys. As a result, the cryptographic keys are stored securely and released based on some alternative authentication mechanism. If this authentication succeeds, keys can be used in encryption/decryption procedures. The most popular authentication mechanism used for key release is based on passwords, which are again cryptographic key-like strings but simple enough for users to users to remember. Hence, the plain text protected by a cryptographic algorithm is only as secure as the password(weakest link) that releases

D. Feng, D. Lin, and M. Yung (Eds.): CISC 2005, LNCS 3822, pp. 358–369, 2005.

the correct decrypting keys. Simple passwords compromise security, but complex passwords are difficult to remember and expensive to maintain. Further, passwords are unable to provide non-repudiation: a subject may deny releasing the key using password authentication, claiming that her password was stolen[1].

Many of these limitations of password-based key release can be eliminated by incorporating biometric authentication. Biometric authentication refers to verifying individuals based on their physiological and behavioral traits. It is inherently more reliable than password-based authentication as biometric characteristics cannot be lost or forgotten. Further, biometric characteristics are difficult to copy, share, and distribute, and require the person being authenticated to be present at the time and point of authentication. Thus, biometrics-based authentication is a potential candidate to replace password-based authentication, either for providing complete authentication mechanism or for securing the traditional cryptographic keys. In this paper, the fingerprint has been chosen as the biometrics for user authentication. It is more mature in terms of the algorithm availability and feasibility[2].

A biometric system and a cryptographic system can be merged in one of the following two modes[2-16]: (i) In biometrics-based key release, the biometric matching is decoupled from the cryptographic part. Biometric matching operates on the traditional biometric templates: if they match, cryptographic key is released from its secure location, e.g., a smart card or a server. Here, biometrics effectively acts as a wrapper mechanism in cryptographic domain. (ii) In biometrics-based key generation, biometrics and cryptography are merged together at a much deeper level. Biometric matching can effectively take place within cryptographic domain, hence there is no separate matching operation that can be attacked; positive biometric matching "extracts" the secret key from the conglomerate(key/biometric template) data. An example of the biometric-based key generation, called *fuzzy vault*, was proposed by Juels and Sudan[11]. This cryptographic construct, as explained in later sections, has the characteristics that make it suitable for applications that combine biometric authentication and cryptography: the advantages of cryptography(e.g., proven security) and fingerprint-based authentication(e.g., user convenience, non-repudiation) can be utilized in such systems.

In this paper, we focus on the fuzzy vault, especially fuzzy fingerprint vault. Recently, some implementations results for the fuzzy fingerprint vault have been reported by assuming that fingerprint features were pre-aligned. However, an automatic approach to align fingerprint features in the fuzzy vault domain needs to be developed, and it is challenging because the alignment should be performed in a non-invertible transformed domain[14-16]. That is, an alignment should be performed between the enrollment template added by a lot of the "chaff" points and the input template without such chaff points. In this paper, we propose an approach of automatic fingerprint alignment by using the geometric hashing technique[17] which has been used for model-based object recognition applications. We first modify the original geometric hashing technique suitable for 1:N identification applications to 1:1 fingerprint verification applications. And then, a hash table for the fuzzy fingerprint vault has been designed as an alignment invariant representation. Based on the preliminary experimental results, our approach by using the hash table generated for the fuzzy fingerprint vault can align the fingerprint features accurately in real-time. We believe our approach can be integrated with any fuzzy fingerprint vault systems and provide both high security and user convenience as crypto-biometric systems.

The rest of the paper is structured as follows. Section 2 explains the overview of the fuzzy fingerprint vault and the geometric hashing, and Section 3 describes the proposed fingerprint alignment based on geometric hashing. The experimental results are given in Section 4, and conclusions are made in Section 5.

2 Background

2.1 Crypto-Biometric Systems

Davida, et al.[8] suggested on-line biometric authentication which moved biometric data from a central server into a signed form on a portable storage device, such as a smartcard. Their system was essentially a PKI-like environment that did local fingerprint matching. Its main flaw is that it required some local authentication authority to have a key capable of decrypting the template stored on the storage device. While they address the key management issues, the basic premise is still that of local fingerprint matching, and is therefore inherently insecure.

There were other innovative, yet similar methods that did not perform biometric matching. The first is the *fuzzy commitment* scheme[10]. Here, a secret(presumably a private key used for later authentication) is encoded using a standard error correcting code such as Hamming or Reed-Solomon, and then XOR-ed it with a biometric template. To retrieve the secret, a slightly different biometric template can again be XOR-ed, and the result put through an error correcting decoder. Some small number of bit errors introduced in the key can be corrected through the decoding process. The major flaw of this system is that biometric data is often subject to reordering and erasures, which cannot be handled using this simple scheme. A second paper[9] has a similar theoretical foundation to this work, but aims toward a completely different application. Here, Monrose, et al., attempt to add entropy to users' passwords on a computer system by incorporating data from the way in which they type their password. Since the biometric being used here so so radically different from fingerprints, their results are not applicable to this work.

Recently, Juels and Sudan[11] proposed the *fuzzy vault*, a new architecture with applications similar to Juels and Wattenberg's fuzzy commitment scheme, but is more compatible with partial and reordered data. In the fuzzy commitment, Alice can place a secret value k(e.g., private encryption key) in a vault and lock(secure) it using an unordered set A . Bob, using an unordered set B , can unlock the vault (access k) only if B overlaps with A to a great extent. The procedure for constructing the fuzzy vault is as follows: First, Alice selects a polynomial p of variable x that encodes k(e.g., by fixing the coefficients of p according to k). She computes the polynomial projections, $p(A)$, for the elements of A . She adds some randomly generated "chaff" points that do not lie on p , to arrive at the final point set R . When Bob tries to learn k (i.e., finding p), he uses his own unordered set B . If B overlaps with A substantially, he will be able to locate many points in R that lie on p . Using error-correction coding, it is assumed that he can reconstruct p(and hence k). The security of the scheme is based on the infeasibility of the polynomial reconstruction problem(i.e., if Bob does not know many points that lie on p, he can not feasibly find the parameters of p, hence he cannot access k). Note that since this fuzzy vault can work with unordered sets(common in biometric templates, including fingerprint minutiae data), it is a promising candidate for crypto-biometric systems.

Based on the fuzzy vault, some implementations results for fingerprint have been reported. For example, Clancy et al.[14] and Uludag, et al.[15,16] proposed a *fuzzy fingerprint vault*. Note that, their systems inherently assumes that fingerprints(the one that locks the vault and the one that tries to unlock it) are pre-aligned. This is not a realistic assumption for fingerprint-based authentication schemes, and limits the applicability of their schemes[16].

2.2 Geometric Hashing

In a model-based recognition system, a set of objects is given and the task is to find instances of these objects in a given scene. The objects are represented as sets of geometric features, such as points or lines, and their geometric relations are encoded using a minimal set of such features. The task becomes more complex if the objects overlap in the scene and/or other occluded unfamiliar objects exist in the scene.

Many model-based recognition systems are based on hypothesizing matches between scene features and model features, predicting new matches, and verifying or changing the hypotheses through a search process. Geometric Hashing[17] offers a different and more parallelizable paradigm. It can be used to recognize flat objects under weak perspective. Because of such robustness, geometric hashing has been used for many applications. In the following, for the sake of completeness, we briefly outline the geometric hashing technique. Additional details can be found in [17].

Fig. 1 illustrates the geometric hashing algorithm. The algorithm consists of two procedures, preprocessing(or enrollment) and recognition(or identification).

Preprocessing

The preprocessing procedure is executed off-line and only once. In this procedure, the model features are encoded and are stored in a hash table. The information is stored in a highly redundant multiple-viewpoint way. Assume each model in the database has n feature points. For each ordered pair of feature points in the model chosen as a basis, the coordinates of all other points in the model are computed in the orthogonal coordinate frame defined by the basis pair. Then, (model,basis) pairs are entered into the hash table bins by applying a given hash function f to the transformed coordinates.

Recognition

In the recognition procedure, a scene consisting of S feature points is given as input. An arbitrary ordered pair of feature points in the scene is chosen. Taking this pair as a basis, the coordinates of the remaining feature points are computed. Using the hash function on the transformed coordinates, a bin in the hash table (constructed in the preprocessing phase) is accessed. For every recorded (model,basis) pair in the bin, a vote is collected for that pair. The pair winning the maximum number of votes is taken as a matching candidate. The execution of the recognition phase corresponding to one basis pair is termed as a probe. If no (model,basis) pair scores high enough, another basis from the scene is chosen and a probe is performed.

Note that, the basis set can be chosen as a set of single points, point pairs, or triple points depending on the required functionality for occlusion, rotation, translation, and perspective. Also, the object features can also be represented by other geometric features such as lines.

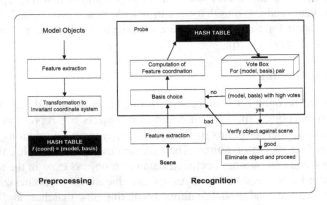

Fig. 1. Illustration of the Geometric Hashing

3 Fingerprint Alignment Based on Geometric Hashing

This section explains a proposed fingerprint alignment approach for the fuzzy vault based on the geometric hashing technique. To modify the original geometric hashing technique suitable for 1:N identification applications to 1:1 fingerprint verification applications, the model used for identifying an object from the database is excluded in the our approach.

To explain our approach, we describe the fuzzy vault in more detail. Alice can place a secret value m in a vault and lock it using an unordered locking set L. Bob, using an unordered unlocking set U, can unlock the vault only if U overlaps with L to a great extent. The procedure for constructing the fuzzy vault is as follows: Secret value m is first encoded as the coefficients of some degree k polynomial in x over a finite field $GF(q)$. This polynomial $f(x)$ is now the secret to protect. The locking set L is a set of t values $l_i \in GF(q)$ making up the fuzzy encryption key, where $t > k$. The locked vault contains all the pairs $(l_i; f(l_i))$ and some large number of chaff points (α_j, β_j), where $f(\alpha_j) \neq \beta_j$. After adding the chaff points, the total number of items in the vault is r. In order to crack this system, an attacker must be able to separate the chaff points from the legitimate points in the vault. The difficulty of this operation is a function of the number of chaff points, among other things. A legitimate user should be able to unlock the vault if they can narrow the search space. In general, to successfully interpolate the polynomial, they have an unlocking set U of t elements such that $L \cap U$ contains at least $k + 1$ elements. The details of the fuzzy vault can be found in [11,14-16].

In general fingerprint verification systems, a fingerprint feature, called as a *minutia*, can be specified by its coordinates, angle, and its type. Let $m_i = (x_i, y_i, \theta_i, t_i)$ represent a minutia. The coordinates show the position of the minutia. The angle shows the direction of the minutia. Finally, the type shows if the minutia is an ending point or a bifurcation point. However, the geometric characteristics of minutiae of a user vary over acquisition. That is, a fingerprint image can be translated, rotated, enlarged, or shrinked in each acquisition. Hence, a direct comparison between two fingerprint images is impossible, and alignment between them is needed.

In the same manner, to use the fingerprint feature as locking and unlocking sets, alignment is an essential step. As the locking set to lock the secret includes a number of chaff points, alignment between the two fingerprints used for locking and unlocking sets is more difficult than in the typical feature space. Hence, we modify the geometric hashing technique to be adapted for fuzzy fingerprint alignment.

Our approach consists of two processes: *enrollment* and *verification* processes. Enrollment process consists of minutiae information acquisition stage, enrollment hash table generation stage again. In minutiae information acquisition stage, minutiae information includes *genuine minutiae* of a user and *chaff minutiae* generated randomly. According to the geometric characteristics of the minutiae information, a table, called an *enrollment hash table*, is generated.

Let $m_i = (x_i, y_i, \theta_i, t_i)$ represent a minutia and $L = \{m_i \mid 1 \le i \le r\}$ be a locking set including the genuine and chaff minutiae. In L, the genuine and chaff minutiae can be represented by $G = \{m_i \mid 1 \le i \le n\}$ and $C = \{m_i \mid n+1 \le i \le r\}$, respectively. Note that, the enrollment hash table is generated from L.

In the *enrollment hash table generation stage*, an enrollment table is generated in such a way that no alignment is needed in the verification process for unlocking vault by using the geometric hashing technique. That is, alignment is pre-performed in the enrollment table generation stage. In verification process, direct comparisons without alignment are performed in 1:1 matching between the enrollment hash table and an input fingerprint in order to select the genuine minutiae(G) only. Each step in the enrollment hash table generation stage is explained in detail in the following.

1) Reference Point Selection Step
In reference point selection step, a minutia is selected as the first minutia from the set of enrollment minutiae(L). The first minutia is denoted by m_1 and the other remaining minutiae are denoted as $m_2, m_3, \ldots, m_r$. At this moment, the minutia, m_1, is called as *basis*.

2) Minutiae Transform Step
In minutiae transform step, minutiae $m_2, m_3, \ldots, m_r$ are aligned with the first minutia m_1, and then quantized. Let $m_j(1)$ denote the transformed minutiae, *i.e.*, the result of the transform of the jth minutia with respect to m_1. Also, let T_1 be the set of transformed minutiae $m_j(1)$, *i.e.*, $T_1 = \{m_j(1) = (x_j(1), j_j(1), \theta_j(1), t_j(1)) \mid 1 < j \le r\}$, and T_1 is called the m_1-transformed minutiae set. (Eq. 1) represents the translation and rotation such that features $(x_1, y_1, \theta_1, t_1)$ of m_1 is translated and rotated into $(1,1,1, t_1)$. Let $_{TR}m_j(1)$ denote the minutia translated and rotated from the jth minutia with respect to m_1.

$$_{TR}m_j(1) = \begin{pmatrix} _{TR}x_j(1) \\ _{TR}y_j(1) \\ _{TR}\theta_j(1) \\ _{TR}t_j(1) \end{pmatrix} = \begin{pmatrix} \cos(\theta_1) & \sin(\theta_1) & 0 & 0 \\ -\sin(\theta_1) & \cos(\theta_1) & 0 & 0 \\ 0 & 0 & 1 & 0 \\ 0 & 0 & 0 & 1 \end{pmatrix} \begin{pmatrix} x_j - x_1 \\ y_j - y_1 \\ \theta_j - \theta_1 \\ t_j \end{pmatrix}, where\ 1 < j \le r \qquad \text{(Eq. 1)}$$

$$m_j(1) = \begin{pmatrix} x_j(1) \\ y_j(1) \\ \theta_j(1) \\ t_j(1) \end{pmatrix} = \begin{pmatrix} \lfloor_{TR}x_j(1)/\alpha + 0.5 \rfloor \\ \lfloor_{TR}y_j(1)/\alpha + 0.5 \rfloor \\ \lfloor_{TR}\theta_j(1)/\beta \rfloor \\ _{TR}t_j(1) \end{pmatrix} \qquad \text{(Eq. 2)}$$

To reduce the amount of information, quantization is required both in coordinates and angles. This quantization is summarized in (Eq. 2), where α is the quantization parameter for coordinates and β is the quantization parameter for angles. α is determined by the range of coordinates in the extraction stage in the enrollment process, whereas β is determined by the required precision in the verification process.

3) Repeat Step

Step 1) and step 2) are repeated for all the remaining minutiae. When step 1) and step 2) are completed for all the minutiae of the enrollment user, the enrollment hash table is generated completely.

After enrollment process, verification process to separate the chaff minutiae(C) from the genuine minutiae(G) in the enrollment hash table should be performed. In verification process, minutiae information(unlocking set U) of a verification user is obtained and a table, called *verification table*, is generated according to the geometric characteristic of the minutiae. Then, the verification table is compared with the enrollment hash table, and the subset of genuine minutiae is finally selected. Note that, *minutiae information acquisition stage* and *table generation stage* are performed in the same way as in the enrollment process.

In comparing between the enrollment and verification hash tables, the transformed minutiae pairs with the same coordinates, the same angle, and the same type are determined. The minutiae pairs having the maximum number and the same basis are selected as the subset of genuine minutiae(G).

Note that, because of the noises and local deformation during acquisition, extracted minutiae from the same finger may have different coordinates and angles over each acquisition. To solve this problem, an adaptive elastic matching algorithm in which tolerance levels are determined according to the polar coordinates of the minutiae was proposed in [18]. In this paper, the coordinate plane is divided into several fields according to the distance from the origin. Each field has its own level of tolerance for x- and y-coordinates. The first field has tolerance level of [-3, 3] which means errors between -3 and 3 in x-or y-coordinate are tolerated. Two transformed minutiae in the first field are considered to have matching coordinates if their coordinates do not differ more than this error range. Tolerance level for angles is 22.5 degree for all transformed minutiae. Note that, this reduction of the search space required in a straightforward implementation of the geometric hashing can reduce the execution time significantly.

For the purpose of explanation, we illustrate our approach with a simple example as shown in Fig. 2. Fig. 2(a) shows the example of the input set for the enrollment hash table generation stage which includes both the genuine(represented as white circles) and the chaff(represented as black circles) minutiae, and Fig. 2(b) shows the input set for verification. Then, Fig. 3 shows the transformed minutiae plotted in the hash table once the first minutia(m_1) is used as the basis. To generate the enrollment

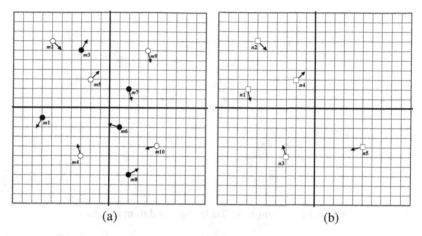

(a)   (b)

Fig. 2. Example of Minutiae: (a) enrollment minutiae(white circles: genuine minutiae, black circles : chaff minutiae), (b) verification minutiae

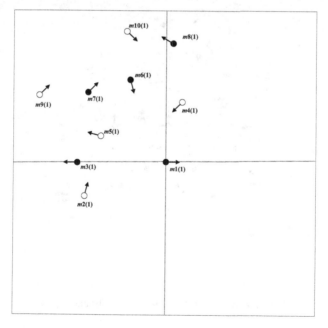

Fig. 3. Transformed Minutiae using Basis Minutia(m_1)

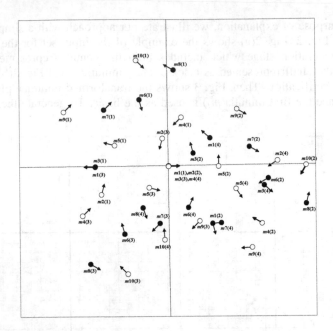

Fig. 4. Enrollment Hash Table generated from Fig. 2(a)

Fig. 5. Verification Result with Fig. 2(b) and Fig. 4

hash table, we repeat the same transformation with bases using all the remaining mi-nutiae. Fig. 4 shows the enrollment hash table generated from the minutiae shown in Fig. 2(a). For simplicity, Fig. 4 uses only four bases from 1 to 4. Finally, Fig. 5 shows the verification result with the input minutiae shown in Fig. 2(b) and the enrollment hash table generated from Fig. 2(a). Minutiae transformed by the second basis(n_2) are superposed on the enrollment hash table. The matched pairs are represented as dotted circle. As shown in Fig. 5, our approach can separate the chaff minutiae(C) from the genuine minutiae(G) in the enrollment hash table without any alignment information.

4 Implementation Details and Experimental Results

For the purpose of evaluating of the automatic fingerprint alignment, a data set of 4,272 fingerprint images composed of four fingerprint images per one finger was collected from 1,068 individuals by using the optical fingerprint sensor[19]. The reso-lution of the sensor was 500dpi, and the size of captured fingerprint images was 248×292.

As in [16], we selected the number of the chaff minutiae as 200. Thus, the size of the enrollment hash table is (the number of the genuine minutiae in the enrolled fin-gerprint + 200)×(the number of genuine minutiae in the enrolled fingerprint + 199). Also, for each enrolled fingerprint, we generated 200 chaff minutiae by using a ran-dom number generator.

Preliminary experimental results were encouraging. With the enrolled fingerprint and the input fingerprint, the proposed approach can align them accurately(shown in Fig. 6) and the results of the alignment, *i.e.*, pairs of the genuine minutiae, can be delivered to the fuzzy vault module to release the secret. We will report full experi-mental results in the final version of this manuscript.

To evaluate the execution performance of the proposed approach, we also meas-ured the execution times on a PC(Pentium4 CPU 2.8GHz, 512MB). The average execution times of the enrollment and the verification processes were 3.1 seconds and

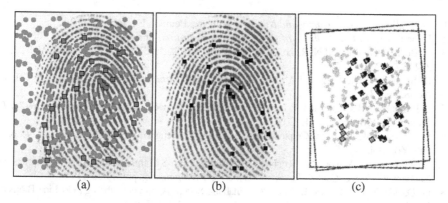

(a)	(b)	(c)

Fig. 6. Results of Automatic Alignment using Geometric Hashing: (a) an enrolled fingerprint image overlaid with the genuine minutiae(shown as gray boxes) and the chaff minutiae(shown as gray circles), (b) an input fingerprint image overlaid with the genuine minutiae(shown as black boxes), (c) result of alignment

1.3 seconds, respectively. Note that, the enrollment process is a one time process and can be carried out off-line, whereas the verification process is executed on-line repeatedly. The proposed approach can perform the verification process in real time.

5 Conclusions

In this paper, an approach to align fingerprint features automatically in the domain of the fuzzy fingerprint vault has been proposed. By employing the geometric hashing technique which has been used for model-based object recognition applications, we can achieve automatic alignment of fingerprint features in the domain of the fuzzy vault. We first modified the original geometric hashing technique suitable for 1:N identification applications to 1:1 fingerprint verification applications. And then, a hash table for the fuzzy fingerprint vault has been designed. To evaluate the effectiveness of our approach, we conducted preliminary experiments. Based on the experimental results, our approach by using the hash table generated for the fuzzy fingerprint vault can align the fingerprint features accurately in real-time and can be integrated with any fuzzy fingerprint vault systems. Currently, we are conducting more experiments to obtain optimal design parameters and to reduce the size of the hash table.

Acknowledgement

This research was supported by the MIC(Ministry of Information and Communication), Korea, under the Chung-Ang University HNRC-ITRC(Home Network Research Center) support program supervised by the IITA(Institute of Information Technology Assessment.

References

1. W. Stallings, *Cryptography and Network Security*, Pearson Ed. Inc., 2003.
2. D. Maltoni, *et al.*, *Handbook of Fingerprint Recognition*, Springer, 2003.
3. R. Bolle, J. Connell, and N. Ratha, "Biometric Perils and Patches," *Pattern Recognition*, Vol. 35, pp. 2727-2738, 2002.
4. B. Schneier, "The Uses and Abuses of Biometrics," *Communications of the ACM*, Vol. 42, No, 8, pp. 136, 1999.
5. S. Prabhakar, S. Pankanti, and A. Jain, "Biometric Recognition: Security and Privacy Concerns," *IEEE Security and Privacy*, pp. 33-42, 2003.
6. U. Uludag, *et al.*, "Biometric Cryptosystems: Issues and Challenges," *Proc. of IEEE*, Vol. 92, No. 6, pp. 948-960, 2004.
7. D. Maio and D. Maltoni, "A Secure Protocol for Electronic Commerce based on Fingerprints and Encryption," *Proc. of Conf. on Systems, Cybernetics, and Informatics*, pp. 519-525, 1999.
8. G. Davida, Y. Frankel, and B. Matt, "On Enabling Secure Applications through Off-Line Biometric Identification," *Proc. of Symp. on Privacy and Security*, pp. 148-157, 1998.
9. F. Monrose, M. Reiter, and S. Wetzel, "Password Hardening based on Keystroke Dynamics," *Proc. of ACM Conf. on Computer and Comm. Security*, pp. 73-82, 1999.
10. A. Juels and M. Wattenberg, "A Fuzzy Commitment Scheme," *Proc. of ACM Conf. on Computer and Comm. Security*, pp. 28-36, 1999.

11. A. Juels and M. Sudan, "A Fuzzy Vault Scheme," *Proc. of Symp. on Information Theory*, pp. 408, 2002.
12. J. Linnartz and P. Tuyls, "New Shielding Functions to Enhance Privacy and Prevent Misuse of Biometric Templates," *LNCS 2688 - Proc. of AVBPA*, pp. 393-402, 2003.
13. Y. Dodis, L. Reyzin, and A. Smith, "Fuzzy Extractors: How to Generate Strong Keys from Biometrics and Other Noisy Data," *LNCS 3027 - Proc. of EuroCrypt*, pp. 523-540, 2004.
14. T. Clancy, N. Kiyavash, and D. Lin, "Secure Smartcard-based Fingerprint Authentication," *Proc. of ACM SIGMM Multim., Biom. Met. & App.*, pp. 45-52, 2003.
15. U. Uludag, S. Pankanti, and A. Jain, "Fuzzy Fingerprint Vault," *Proc. of Workshop Biometrics: Challenges arising from Theory to Practice*, pp. 13-16, 2004.
16. U. Uludag, S. Pankanti, and A. Jain, "Fuzzy Vault for Fingerprints," *LNCS 3546 - Proc. of AVBPA*, pp. 310-319, 2005.
17. H. Wolfson and I. Rigoutsos, "Geometric Hashing: an Overview," *IEEE Computational Science and Engineering*, Vol. 4, pp. 10-21, Oct.-Dec. 1997.
18. N. Ratha and A. Jain, "A Real-Time Matching System for Large Fingerprint Database," *IEEE Trans on PAMI*, Vol. 18, pp. 799-813, 1996.
19. D. Ahn, et al., "Specification of ETRI Fingerprint Database(in Korean)," *Technical Report – ETRI*, 2002.

Classification of Universally Ideal Homomorphic Secret Sharing Schemes and Ideal Black-Box Secret Sharing Schemes

Zhanfei Zhou

State Key Laboratory of Information Security,
Graduate School of the Chinese Academy of Sciences,
Beijing, China
zhouzhanfei@is.ac.cn

Abstract. A secret sharing scheme (SSS) is homomorphic, if the products of shares of secrets are shares of the product of secrets. For a finite abelian group G, an access structure $\mathcal{A}$ is G-ideal homomorphic, if there exists an ideal homomorphic SSS realizing the access structure $\mathcal{A}$ over the secret domain G. An access structure $\mathcal{A}$ is universally ideal homomorphic, if for any non-trivial finite abelian group G, $\mathcal{A}$ is G-ideal homomorphic.

A black-box SSS is a special type of homomorphic SSS, which works over any non-trivial finite abelian group. In such a scheme, participants only have black-box access to the group operation and random group elements. A black-box SSS is ideal, if the size of the secret sharing matrix is the same as the number of participants. An access structure $\mathcal{A}$ is black-box ideal, if there exists an ideal black-box SSS realizing $\mathcal{A}$.

In this paper, we study universally ideal homomorphic and black-box ideal access structures, and prove that an access structure $\mathcal{A}$ is universally ideal homomorphic (black-box ideal) if and only if there is a regular matroid appropriate for $\mathcal{A}$.

Keywords: Universally ideal homomorphic secret sharing scheme, black-box secret sharing scheme, chain group, regular matroid.

1 Introduction

A secret sharing scheme (SSS) involves a dealer p_0, a finite group P of n participants and a collection $\mathcal{A}$ of subsets of P called the access structure. A SSS realizing an access structure $\mathcal{A}$ is a method by which the dealer distributes shares of a secret to the participants such that any qualified subset $A \in \mathcal{A}$ can reconstruct the secret from its shares, whereas any non-qualified subset $A \notin \mathcal{A}$ can't reveal any partial information about the secret in information theoretic sense. If an access structure $\mathcal{A}$ consists of all the subsets whose cardinality is at least a certain threshold t, then it's called a (t, n) threshold access structure. SSS's were first introduced for the threshold case by Blakley [4] and Shamir [18] in 1979. SSS's for general access structures were proposed by Ito et al. [13]. Given any access structure, they show how to construct a SSS realizing it.

D. Feng, D. Lin, and M. Yung (Eds.): CISC 2005, LNCS 3822, pp. 370–383, 2005.
© Springer-Verlag Berlin Heidelberg 2005

Karnin et al. [15] showed that in a SSS, the cardinality of every share domain is not less than that of the secret domain. Fortunately, for some access structures, there are SSS's realizing them without information expansion [5]. A SSS is ideal, if the cardinality of every share domain is the same as that of the secret domain. An access structure is ideal, if there exists an ideal SSS realizing it. Brickell [5] was the first to introduce the notion of ideal access structure. [1, 6] revealed the relation between ideal access structures and matroids.

A SSS is homomorphic, if the secret domain and every share domain are multiplicatively closed, and the products of shares of secrets are shares of the product of secrets. Benaloh [2] firstly found the property of homomorphism in some SSS's, and pointed out that this property will make SSS be widely used in application. Now, SSS's have become one of the most important components, from which distributed protocols such as shared signatures and multiparty computations et al. are builded [19, 3]. Hereafter, homomorphic SSS's were investigated by Frankel and Desmedt et al. [12, 11]. For a finite abelian group G, an access structure $\mathcal{A}$ is G-ideal homomorphic, if there is an ideal homomorphic SSS realizing $\mathcal{A}$ over the secret domain G. An access structure $\mathcal{A}$ is universally ideal homomorphic, if $\mathcal{A}$ is G-ideal homomorphic for any non-trivial finite abelian group G. Liu and Zhou [16] generalized the notion of representation of a matroid over a finite field to that over a ring, and proved that for a finite cyclic group G with order m, an access structure $\mathcal{A}$ is G-ideal homomorphic if and only if there is a matroid appropriate for $\mathcal{A}$, which is representable over $\mathbb{Z}_m$.

A black-box SSS is a special type of homomorphic SSS. The difference between a black-box SSS and other SSS's is that a black-box SSS is over arbitrary finite abelian groups, whereas an ordinary homomorphic SSS is over a specified finite abelian group. In addition, in a black-box SSS, only black-box access to the group operations and to random group elements is required. In some distributed protocols, the shared secret is from a group with a secret order. The proposition of black-box SSS's provides a solution to sharing secret from a group with a secret order. Black-box SSS's were firstly proposed by Desmedt and Frankel [8]. In [9], Desmedt and Frankel showed a black-box SSS. Recently, Cramer and Fehr [7] made a improvement by showing an optimal black-box SSS.

In this paper, classification of universally ideal homomorphic SSS's and ideal black-box SSS's will be investigated. As we known, all the results about black-box SSS's have been for threshold access structures. In this paper, ideal black-box SSS's realizing general access structures will be discussed. This paper is organized as follows. In Section 2, we will introduce some notions and related results. In Section 3 and 4, we will discuss the classification of universally ideal homomorphic SSS's and the property of the dual of a universally ideal homomorphic access structure. In Section 5, we will discuss ideal black-box SSS's. In Section 6, we will show the existence of a universally ideal homomorphic (black-box ideal) access structure by the terminology of matroid.

2 Notions and Related Results

2.1 Secret Sharing Schemes

Let $P = \{p_1, p_2, \cdots, p_n\}$ be a set of participants, a non-empty collection $\mathcal{A}$ of subsets of P is called an access structure, if $A \in \mathcal{A}$ and $A \subseteq B \subseteq P$ implies $B \in \mathcal{A}$. For an access structure $\mathcal{A}$ over P, let $\mathcal{A}_m = \{A \in \mathcal{A} : B \subset A \Rightarrow B \notin \mathcal{A}\}$. Obviously, $\mathcal{A}$ and $\mathcal{A}_m$ can be determined each other. On the other hand, for $\mathcal{E} = 2^P \backslash \mathcal{A}$, let $\mathcal{E}_M = \{A \in \mathcal{E} : B \supset A \Rightarrow B \notin \mathcal{E}\}$. An access structure $\mathcal{A}$ is degenerate, if $\bigcup_{A \in \mathcal{A}_m} A \subset P$. An access structure $\mathcal{A}$ is trivial, if $|A| = 1$ for any $A \in \mathcal{A}_m$. In this paper, we always assume that the access structure $\mathcal{A}$ is non-degenerate and non-trivial unless we specify it definitely elsewhere.

In what follows, we will give a formal definition of SSS's.

Definition 2.1. *Let* $P = \{p_1, p_2, \cdots, p_n\}$ *be a set of participants,* $\mathcal{A} \subseteq 2^P$ *be an access structure over* P, *and* $S_0, S_1, \cdots, S_n$ *be finite sets. For convenience, the random variable corresponding to the share of participant* p_j *is still denoted by* p_j *for* $j = 1, 2, \cdots, n$, *and the random variable corresponding to the secret is denoted by* p_0. *Let the subset* $\pi \subseteq S_0 \times S_1 \times \cdots \times S_n$ *be a probability space of random vector* $(p_0, p_1, \cdots, p_n)$ *such that for any distribution rule* $\alpha \in \pi$, *the probability* $P(\alpha)$ *of choosing* α *is greater than zero, where the distribution rule* $\alpha = (s_0, s_1, \cdots, s_n)$ *represents a probable method of distributing shares of the secret* $s_0 \in S_0$ *among the set of participants.* π *is a SSS realizing the access structure* $\mathcal{A}$, *if the following conditions are satisfied.*

(1) $\forall A \in \mathcal{A}, H(S_0|A) = 0,$
(2) $\forall A \notin \mathcal{A}, H(S_0|A) = H(S_0),$

where $H(\cdot)$ *is an entropy function.*

Let $P' = P \cup \{p_0\}$ and $A = \{p_{j_1}, p_{j_2}, \cdots, p_{j_k}\}$ be a subset of P', where $0 \leq j_1 \leq \cdots \leq j_k \leq n$. For $\alpha = (s_0, s_1, \cdots, s_n) \in \pi$, let $\alpha(A) = (s_{j_1}, s_{j_2}, \cdots, s_{j_k})$ be the restriction of α to A. The set $S_0' = \{\alpha(p_0) : \alpha \in \pi\}$ is the secret domain of π, and $S_j' = \{\alpha(p_j) : \alpha \in \pi\}$ is the share domain of participant p_j, where $1 \leq j \leq n$. For convenience, the secret domain is still denoted by S_0 and the share domain of p_j is denoted by S_j for $1 \leq j \leq n$.

Definition 2.2. *Let* G *be a non-trivial finite abelian group (i.e.* $|G| \geq 2$*), and* $\pi \subseteq G^{n+1}$ *be a SSS realizing access structure* $\mathcal{A}$ *over* P *such that the secret domain of* π *is* G. *For distribution rules* $\alpha = (a_0, a_1, \cdots, a_n)$ *and* $\beta = (b_0, b_1, \cdots, b_n)$ *in* π, *define a multiplication* $\alpha * \beta = (a_0 b_0, a_1 b_1, \cdots, a_n b_n)$ *of* α *and* β. *The SSS* π *is ideal homomorphic, if* $\alpha * \beta \in \pi$ *for any* $\alpha, \beta \in \pi$. *In this case, access structure* $\mathcal{A}$ *is called* G-ideal homomorphic.

It has been proved [11] that if $\mathcal{A}$ is G_i-ideal homomorphic, then $\mathcal{A}$ is G-ideal homomorphic, where $G = G_1 \times G_2$, $i = 1, 2$. An access structure $\mathcal{A}$ is universally ideal homomorphic, if $\mathcal{A}$ is G-ideal homomorphic for any non-trivial finite abelian group G.

In this paper, we always deal with an abelian group as an additive group and the multiplication between distribution rules as an addition between them.

2.2   Black-Box Secret Sharing Schemes

Let M be a $t \times m$ matrix over $\mathbb{Z}$, and the map $\psi : \{1, 2, \cdots, m\} \longrightarrow$ $\{p_1, p_2, \cdots, p_n\}$ be surjective, (M, ψ) is called a labelled matrix over $\mathbb{Z}$. For a labelled matrix (M, ψ), we say that the jth column $(j = 1, \cdots, n)$ of M is labelled by $\psi(j)$ or that "$\psi(j)$ owns the jth column". For a subset $A \subseteq \{p_1, p_2, \cdots, p_n\}$, $M(A)$ denotes the restriction of M to the columns jointly owned by A. Similarly, for $\alpha \in \mathbb{Z}^m$, $\alpha(A)$ denotes the restriction of α to the coordinates jointly owned by A.

Definition 2.3. *Let $\mathcal{A}$ be an access structure over P, and (M, ψ) be a labelled matrix over $\mathbb{Z}$ as described above. (M, ψ) is a black-box SSS realizing $\mathcal{A}$, if for any $A \in \mathcal{A}$, there is a $\lambda_A \in \mathbb{Z}^{|\psi^{-1}(A)|}$ such that for any non-trivial finite abelian group G, $\alpha = gM$ satisfies the following conditions.*

(1) $\forall A \in \mathcal{A}$, $s = \alpha(A)\lambda_A^T$,
(2) $\forall A \notin \mathcal{A}$, $\alpha(A)$ contains no information about s,

where $g = (g_1, g_2, \cdots, g_t)$ is uniformly distributed on G^t, subject to $g_1 = s$.

A black-box SSS (M, ψ) is ideal, if $m = n$. An access structure $\mathcal{A}$ is black-box ideal, if there is a ideal black-box SSS realizing $\mathcal{A}$.

2.3   Matroids and Ideal Homomorphic Secret Sharing Schemes

In this section, some basic concepts of matroid and related results will be introduced. For further details about matroid, please refer to [21].

Definition 2.4. *Let V be a finite set, $\mathcal{I}$ be a collection of subsets of V, and $\mathcal{M} = (V, \mathcal{I})$. $\mathcal{M}$ is a matroid over V, if $\mathcal{I}$ satisfies the following conditions.*

(1) Empty set $\emptyset \in \mathcal{I}$,
(2) $X \in \mathcal{I}$ and $X \supseteq Y$ imply $Y \in \mathcal{I}$,
(3) If X, $Y \in \mathcal{I}$ and $|Y| = |X| + 1$, then there exists $y \in Y \backslash X$ such that $X \cup \{y\} \in \mathcal{I}$.

For a matroid $\mathcal{M}$, a set $X \subseteq V$ is independent, if $X \in \mathcal{I}$; otherwise X is dependent. Furthermore, a maximal independent subset of V is called a base of $\mathcal{M}$, the collection of bases is denoted by $\mathcal{B}$. A minimal dependent subset of V is called a circuit of $\mathcal{M}$, the collection of circuits is denoted by $\mathcal{C}$. A matroid $\mathcal{M}$ is connected, if for any x, $y \in V$, there is a circuit containing x, y. The rank function $\rho : 2^V \longrightarrow \mathbb{Z}$ of the matroid $\mathcal{M}$ is defined by $\rho(A) = \max\{|X| : X \subseteq A \subseteq V, X \in \mathcal{I}\}$, and $\rho(V)$ is called the rank of $\mathcal{M}$. x is dependent on A, if $x \in A$ or there is a circuit C such that $C \backslash A = \{x\}$, and denoted by $x \sim A$. A is closed, if for any $x \in V \backslash A$, x is not dependent on A (denoted by $x \not\sim A$). $\sigma(A) = \{x \in V : x \sim A\}$ is a closure of A. Obviously, $\sigma(A)$ is the minimal closed set containing A. A hyperplane of a matroid $\mathcal{M}$ is a maximal closed proper subset of the matroid. Let $\mathcal{M}$ be a matroid over V, then there is a matroid $\mathcal{M}^*$ such that $\mathcal{B}^* = \{V \backslash B : B \in \mathcal{B}\}$ is the collection of bases of $\mathcal{M}^*$, which is called the dual matroid of $\mathcal{M}$. Obviously, $(\mathcal{M}^*)^* = \mathcal{M}$. Usually, a circuit, base of $\mathcal{M}^*$ is called a cocircuit, cobase of $\mathcal{M}$.

Theorem 2.1 (Circuit Axiom of Matroids). *Let V be a finite set and $\mathcal{C}$ be a collection of subsets of V, then $\mathcal{C}$ is a collection of circuits of a matroid over V if and only if $\mathcal{C}$ satisfies the following conditions.*

(1) If $C_1, C_2 \in \mathcal{C}$ and $C_1 \neq C_2$, then $C_1 \not\subset C_2$.
(2) If C_1, C_2 are two different elements of $\mathcal{C}$, and $x \in C_1 \cap C_2$, then there is $C \in \mathcal{C}$ such that $C \subseteq (C_1 \cup C_2) \backslash \{x\}$.

Usually, a matroid $\mathcal{M}$ can also be denoted by $\mathcal{M} = (V, \mathcal{C})$. Theorem 2.1(2) is called circuit elimination axiom. In fact, there is a strong circuit elimination axiom as follows.

Theorem 2.2. *Let C_1, C_2 be two different circuits of a matroid $\mathcal{M}$ and $x \in C_1 \cap C_2$, then for any $y \in C_1 \backslash C_2$, there is a circuit C such that $y \in C \subseteq (C_1 \cup C_2) \backslash \{x\}$.*

Theorem 2.3. *If B is a base of a matroid $\mathcal{M}$, then for any $x \in V \backslash B$, there is a unique circuit $C = C(B, x)$ such that $x \in C \subseteq B \cup \{x\}$, which is called a fundamental circuit of x with respect to B.*

Theorem 2.4. *Let $\mathcal{M} = (V, \mathcal{I})$ be a matroid, then $H \subseteq V$ is a hyperplane of $\mathcal{M}$ if and only if $V \backslash H$ is a cocircuit of $\mathcal{M}$.*

Let R be a commutative ring with an identity and K be an R-module. A finite set B of R-module K is perfect, if for any minimal linearly dependent subset $\{x_1, x_2, \cdots, x_t\} \subseteq B$, there are invertible elements $r_i \in R^*$ ($1 \leq i \leq t$) such that $\sum_{i=1}^{t} r_i x_i = 0$, where R^* is the set of invertible elements of ring R. Let $\mathcal{C} = \{X \subseteq B : X$ is a minimal linearly dependent subset$\}$, it can be proved that for a perfect set $B \subseteq K$, $(B, \mathcal{C})$ is a matroid, and called a modular matroid [16]. In fact, for the above modular matroid, the rank of a set in this matroid is the same as the maximum of cardinalities of linearly independent subsets. Furthermore, it can be easily proved that if B is perfect, then the module generated by B is free.

Definition 2.5. *Let $\mathcal{M}$ be a matroid over V and R be a commutative ring with an identity. A matroid $\mathcal{M}$ is representable over R, if there exist a free R-module K and a map $\varphi : V \longrightarrow K$ such that $\varphi(V)$ is perfect and φ preserves rank.*

Since a module generated by a perfect set is free, the notation of a free R-module in the above definition can be replaced by an R-module. Obviously, Definition 2.5 coincides with representability of a matroid over a field, which has been defined in [21].

Theorem 2.5. *If a matroid $\mathcal{M}$ is representable over a field $\mathbf{F}$, then the dual matroid $\mathcal{M}^*$ is also representable over the filed $\mathbf{F}$.*

In the following, we will introduce result about ideal homomorphic access structures [16].

Definition 2.6. *Let $\mathcal{A}$ is an access structure over P and $\mathcal{M} = (P', \mathcal{C})$ be a matroid over P'. If*

$$\mathcal{A}_m = \{C \backslash \{p_0\} : p_0 \in C \in \mathcal{C}\}$$

then the matroid $\mathcal{M}$ is said to be appropriate for the access structure $\mathcal{A}$.

Theorem 2.6. *For a cyclic group G with order m, an access structure $\mathcal{A}$ over P is G-ideal homomorphic if and only if there is a unique matroid $\mathcal{M} = (P', \mathcal{C})$ appropriate for $\mathcal{A}$, which is representable over $\mathbb{Z}_m$.*

3 Universally Ideal Homomorphic Secret Sharing Schemes

In this section, we will study classification of universally ideal homomorphic SSS's. Firstly, let's generalize the notion of chain group over an integral domain to that over a commutative ring with an identity. Readers can refer to [21] for details about chain groups over an integral domain.

Let R be a commutative ring with an identity, and V be a finite set. A chain on V over R is a map $f : V \longrightarrow R$. $\|f\| = \{v \in V : f(v) \neq 0\}$ is said to be a support of f. If $\|f\| = \emptyset$, f is said to a zero chain, and denoted by 0.

The sum of chains f and g on V over R is defined by:

$$(f + g)(v) = f(v) + g(v) \quad \forall\, v \in V$$

For $r \in R$ and a chain f on V over R, the product rf is defined by:

$$(rf)(v) = rf(v) \quad \forall\, v \in V$$

Let N be a collection of chains on V over R, if N is closed under the above operations, then N is an R-module, and called a chain group on V over R.

Let N be a chain group on V over R, a non-zero chain $f \in N$ is elementary, if for any chain $g \in N$, $\|g\| \subset \|f\|$ implies $g = 0$. An elementary chain $f \in N$ is normal, if $f(v)$ is invertible for any $v \in \|f\|$. A chain group N on V over R is normal, if for any elementary chain $f \in N$, there is a normal chain $g \in N$ such that $\|g\| = \|f\|$.

In what follows, we will introduce the relation between normal chain groups and matroids.

Theorem 3.1. *Let V be a finite set, R be a commutative ring with an identity, and N be a normal chain group on V over R, then for $\mathcal{C} = \{\|f\| : f \in N$ is elementary$\}$, there is a matroid over V such that $\mathcal{C}$ is a collection of circuits of this matroid, denote this matroid induced by N by $\mathcal{M}(N)$.*

Proof. Let C_1, $C_2 \in \mathcal{C}$ be different circuits and $v \in C_1 \cap C_2$. Since N is a normal chain group, there exist normal chains f_i such that $\|f_i\| = C_i$, where $i = 1$, 2. Let $f_i(v) = r_i$ $(i = 1, 2)$ and $g = r_2 f_1 - r_1 f_2$, then $g \in N$. Since $g(v) = 0$, $\|g\| \subseteq C_1 \cup C_2 \backslash \{v\}$. Choose an element $v' \in C_1 \backslash C_2$, $g(v') = r_2 f_1(v')$. Since f_1

is normal, $g(v') \neq 0$. Hence, there exists a elementary chain $g' \in N$ such that $\|g'\| \subseteq \|g\| \subseteq C_1 \cup C_2\backslash\{v\}$. From the above proof, it's obvious that C satisfies the Circuit Axiom of Matroids, then there is a matroid M over V such that C is a collection of circuits of the matroid M.   □

Theorem 3.2. *Let V be a finite set and $M = (V, C)$ be a matroid over V, where C is a collection of circuits of the matroid M. Then for a commutative ring R with an identity, the matroid M is representable over R if and only if there is a normal chain group N on V over R such that $M(N) = M$.*

Proof. Let $N(V, R)$ be the set of all chains on V over R, and K be an R-module. Suppose that the map $\varphi : V \longrightarrow K$ is a representation of the matroid M over R, and the map $\phi : N(V, R) \longrightarrow K$ is defined by $\phi(f) = \sum_{v \in V} f(v)\varphi(v)$. Let $N = \ker \phi = \{f \in N(V, R) : \phi(f) = 0\}$. Obviously, N is a chain group on V over R. It is easy to verify that for a chain $f \in N$, f is elementary if and only if $\{\varphi(v) : v \in \|f\|\}$ is a minimal linearly dependent set. By the definition of representation of a matroid, if $\{\varphi(v) : v \in \|f\|\}$ is a minimal linearly dependent set, then there exist invertible elements $r_v \in R^*$ $(v \in \|f\|)$ such that $\sum_{v \in \|f\|} r_v \varphi(v) = 0$. Let $f'(v) = \begin{cases} r_v & v \in \|f\| \\ 0 & v \notin \|f\| \end{cases}$, then $f' \in N$. Hence there is a normal chain $f' \in N$ such that $\|f\| = \|f'\|$, and N is a normal chain group.

Let C' be a collection of circuits of the matroid $M(N)$. From the above proof and the definition of representation of a matroid, it is obvious that $C = C'$. Hence $M(N) = M$.

On the other hand, let N be a normal chain group on V over R such that $M(N) = M$, and the map $\phi : N(V, R) \longrightarrow N(V, R)/N$ be a canonical homomorphism. Construct a mapping $\varphi : V \longrightarrow N(V, R)/N$ such that $\varphi(v) = \phi(f_v)$, where $f_v(v') = \begin{cases} 1 & v' = v \\ 0 & v' \neq v \end{cases}$. It is easy to verify that a chain $f \in N$ is elementary if and only if $\{\varphi(v) : v \in \|f\|\}$ is a minimal linearly dependent set. Since the chain group N is normal, for any minimal linearly dependent set $\{\varphi(v) : v \in C \subseteq V\}$, there is a normal chain f' such that $\|f'\| = C$. Let $f' = \sum_{v \in C} f'(v) f_v$, where $f'(v) \in R^*$ $(v \in C)$ are invertible, then $\sum_{v \in C} f'(v)\varphi(v) = \sum_{v \in C} f'(v)\phi(f_v) = \phi(f') = 0$. Hence $\{\varphi(v) : v \in V\}$ is perfect. Since $f \in N$ is elementary if and only if $\{\varphi(v) : v \in \|f\|\}$ is a minimal linearly dependent set, φ preserves rank.   □

Let N be a chain group over the ring $\mathbb{Z}$ of integers, a chain $f \in N$ is called an integral chain. An elementary chain $f \in N$ is primitive, if $f(v) = \begin{cases} \pm 1 & v \in \|f\| \\ 0 & v \notin \|f\| \end{cases}$. A chain group N over the ring $\mathbb{Z}$ of integers is regular, if for any elementary chain $f \in N$, there exist a primitive chain $g \in N$ and an element $r \in \mathbb{Z}$ such that $f = rg$. Since the only invertible elements of ring $\mathbb{Z}$ are ± 1, obviously, a normal chain group over $\mathbb{Z}$ is regular. A matroid M is regular, if there is a regular chain group N such that $M(N) = M$. As a special case of Theorem 3.2, A matroid M is representable over $\mathbb{Z}$ if and only if there is a regular chain group N such that $M = M(N)$.

Let f, $g \in N$ be integral chains on V, and $m \geq 2$ be a positive integer. g is an m-representative of f, if for any $v \in V$, $g(v) \equiv f(v) \pmod{m}$ and $|g(v)| < m$.

Theorem 3.3 ([21]). *Let N be a regular chain group on V, and $f \in N$. Then for any positive integer $m \geq 2$, there is a chain $g \in N$, which is an m-representative of f.*

Theorem 3.4. *If a matroid $\mathcal{M}$ is regular, then for any positive integer $m \geq 2$, $\mathcal{M}$ is representable over the ring $\mathbb{Z}_m$.*

Proof. Let the matroid $\mathcal{M}$ be regular, then there is a regualr chain group N such that $\mathcal{M} = \mathcal{M}(N)$. For any chain $f \in N$, let f' to be a chain over the ring $\mathbb{Z}_m$ such that $f'(v) = f(v) \pmod{m}$ for all $v \in V$. Obviously, $N' = \{ f' : f \in N \}$ is a chain group over the ring $\mathbb{Z}_m$. Let $\mathcal{C}$ be the collection of circuits of the matroid $\mathcal{M}$, and $\mathcal{C}' = \{\|f'\| : f' \in N'$ is elementary$\}$. For any circuit $C \in \mathcal{C}$, there exist a primitive chain $f \in N$ such that $\|f\| = C$. By the definition of a primitive chain, $\|f'\| = C$ is obtained, then there is a $C' \in \mathcal{C}'$ such that $C' \subseteq C$. On the other hand, for any $C' \in \mathcal{C}'$, there is a chain $f \in N$ such that $\|f'\| = C'$. By Theorem 3.3, there is an m-representative g of f such that $\|g\| = \|f'\| = C'$. Hence, there is a $C \in \mathcal{C}$ such that $C \subseteq C'$. Since the elements in $\mathcal{C}$ (and those in $\mathcal{C}'$) can not contain each other properly, then $\mathcal{C} = \mathcal{C}'$. For any elementary chain $f' \in N'$, there is a primitive chain $g \in N$ such that $\|g\| = \|f'\| \in \mathcal{C}$. Obviously, $g' \in N'$ is a normal chain and $\|g'\| = \|g\| = \|f'\| \in \mathcal{C}$. Then N' is a normal chain group over $\mathbb{Z}_m$. From the above proof, $\mathcal{M} = \mathcal{M}(N) = \mathcal{M}(N')$ is obtained. □

Theorem 3.5 ([21, 20]). *If $\mathcal{M}$ is a matroid, then the following statements are equivalent.*

(1) $\mathcal{M}$ is regular.
(2) $\mathcal{M}$ is representable over finite fields $GF(2)$ and $GF(3)$.

Now, we can obtain the main theorem of this paper.

Theorem 3.6. *An access structure $\mathcal{A}$ over P is universally ideal homomorphic if and only if there is a regular matroid $\mathcal{M} = (P', \mathcal{C})$ appropriate for $\mathcal{A}$.*

Proof. Let $\mathcal{A}$ be universally ideal homomorphic, then $\mathcal{A}$ is $\mathbb{Z}_2(+)$ and $\mathbb{Z}_3(+)$-ideal homomorphic. By Theorem 2.6, there is a unique matroid $\mathcal{M}$ appropriate for $\mathcal{A}$, which is representable over the fields $GF(2)$ and $GF(3)$. By Theorem 3.5, the matroid $\mathcal{M}$ is regular.

On the other hand, suppose that there is a regular matroid $\mathcal{M}$ appropriate for the access structure $\mathcal{A}$. Then for any positive integer $m \geq 2$, the matroid $\mathcal{M}$ is representable over the ring $\mathbb{Z}_m$, so $\mathcal{A}$ is $\mathbb{Z}_m(+)$-ideal homomorphic. So for any non-trivial finite abelian group G, the access structure $\mathcal{A}$ is G-ideal homomorphic. □

4 Dual Access Structures

In this section, we will discuss the property of dual access structures. Firstly, let's introduce the notion of dual access structures, which has been studied in [10, 14, 17].

Definition 4.1. *Let $\mathcal{A}$ be an access structure over P. It's easy to verify that $\mathcal{A}^* = \{A \subseteq P : P\backslash A \in \mathcal{E}\}$ is also an access structure over P, which is called the dual access structure of $\mathcal{A}$. Denote $2^P\backslash\mathcal{A}^*$ by $\mathcal{E}^*$.*

Lemma 4.1 ([10, 17]). *Let $\mathcal{A}$ be an access structure over P. Then*

(1) $\mathcal{A}_m^* = \{A \subseteq P : P\backslash A \in \mathcal{E}_M\}$
(2) $\mathcal{E}_M^* = \{A \subseteq P : P\backslash A \in \mathcal{A}_m\}$
(3) $\mathcal{A}^{**} = \mathcal{A}$

Lemma 4.2. *Let $\mathcal{A}$ be an access structure over P, and the matroid $\mathcal{M} = (P', \mathcal{I})$ be appropriate for $\mathcal{A}$. Let $\mathcal{H}_{p_0} = \{H \subseteq P : H$ is a hyperplane of the matroid $\mathcal{M}\}$, then $\mathcal{H}_{p_0} = \mathcal{E}_M$.*

Proof. Choose a hyperplane $H \in \mathcal{H}_{p_0}$ arbitrarily, then for any $A \in \mathcal{A}_m$, $A \nsubseteq H$. Otherwise, there is a set $A \in \mathcal{A}_m$ such that $p_0 \sim A \subseteq H$, contradiction. Furthermore, for any $p \in P\backslash H$, $p_0 \sim H \cup \{p\}$. Hence there is a circuit C such that $C\backslash(H \cup \{p\}) = \{p_0\}$, then $H \cup \{p\} \supseteq C \cap (H \cup \{p\}) = C\backslash\{p_0\} \in \mathcal{A}_m$. From the above proof, we can deduce that H is a maximal subset of P not containing $A \in \mathcal{A}_m$, namely, $H \in \mathcal{E}_M$.

On the other hand, choose $H \in \mathcal{E}_M$ arbitrarily. Assume that H is not closed, then there is $p \in (P \cup \{p_0\})\backslash H$ such that $p \sim H$. By the definition, there is a circuit C_1 such that $C_1\backslash H = \{p\}$. If $p \in P\backslash H$, then there is $A \in \mathcal{A}_m$ such that $p \in A \subseteq H \cup \{p\}$. Let $C_2 = A \cup \{p_0\}$, then $p \in C_1 \cap C_2$ and $p_0 \in C_2\backslash C_1$. By Theorem 2.2, there is a circuit C_3 such that $p_0 \in C_3 \subseteq C_1 \cup C_2\backslash\{p\}$, and $C_3\backslash H = \{p_0\}$, ie., $p_0 \sim H$. If $p = p_0$, then $p_0 \sim H$. From the above proof, there is $A \in \mathcal{A}_m$ such that $A \subseteq H$, contradicted with $H \in \mathcal{E}_M$. Since $H \in \mathcal{E}_M$, for any $p \in P\backslash H$, there is $A \in \mathcal{A}_m$ such that $p \in A \subseteq H \cup \{p\}$. Let $C = A \cup \{p_0\}$, then $p \sim C\backslash\{p\} \subseteq H \cup \{p\}$. Hence $\sigma(H \cup \{p_0\}) = P \cup \{p_0\}$. In addition, since $p_0 \sim A \subseteq H \cup \{p\}$, $\sigma(H \cup \{p\}) = \sigma(H \cup \{p_0\}) = P \cup \{p_0\}$. $\qquad\square$

Let $\mathcal{C}_{p_0}^* = \{C \subseteq P' : p_0 \in C \in \mathcal{C}^*\}$, by Theorem 2.4, Lemma 4.1 and Lemma 4.2, $\mathcal{C}_{p_0}^* = \{C \subseteq P' : P'\backslash C \in \mathcal{H}_{p_0}\} = \{C \subseteq P' : P'\backslash C \in \mathcal{E}_M\} = \{C \subseteq P' : C\backslash\{p_0\} \in \mathcal{A}_m^*, p_0 \in C\} = \{A \cup \{p_0\} : A \in \mathcal{A}_m^*\}$. Thus, we obtain the following result.

Lemma 4.3. *If a matroid $\mathcal{M}$ is appropriate for an access structure $\mathcal{A}$, then the dual matroid $\mathcal{M}^*$ is appropriate for the dual access structure $\mathcal{A}^*$.*

By Theorem 2.5 and Theorem 3.5, if a matroid $\mathcal{M}$ is regular, then the dual matroid $\mathcal{M}^*$ is also regular. By Theorem 3.6 and Lemma 4.3, we can obtain the following result.

Theorem 4.1. *If an access structure $\mathcal{A}$ is universally ideal homomorphic, then the dual access structure $\mathcal{A}^*$ is also universally ideal homomorphic.*

5   Ideal Black-Box Secret Sharing Schemes

In this section, we will discuss the classification of ideal black-box SSS's.

At first, let's introduce the property of representation of a regular matroid over the ring $\mathbb{Z}$.

Let $N(V, \mathbb{Z})$ be the set of all integral chains on V, where $V = \{v_1, v_2, \cdots, v_n\}$. Let f be a integral chain, and denoted by $f = (f(v_1), f(v_2), \cdots, f(v_n))$. Suppose that N is a regular chain group on V, denote the induced matroid by $\mathcal{M} = \mathcal{M}(N)$. Assume that the rank of the matroid $\mathcal{M}$ is t, without loss of generality, let $B = \{v_1, v_2, \cdots, v_t\}$ be a base of the matroid $\mathcal{M}$. By Theorem 2.3, for any v_i $(t+1 \leq i \leq n)$, there is a fundamental circuit $C(B, v_i)$ of v_i with respect to B such that $v_i \in C(B, v_i) \subseteq B \cup \{v_i\}$. Since N is regular, for any fundamental circuit $C(B, v_i)$ $(t+1 \leq i \leq n)$, there is a primitive chain f_i such that $\|f_i\| = C(B, v_i)$. Without loss of generality, let $f_i(v_i) = 1$, where $t+1 \leq i \leq n$. For any $f \in N$, let $g = f - \sum_{i=t+1}^{n} f(v_i)f_i$, then $g \in N$. Since $\|g\| \subseteq B$ and B is a base of the matroid $\mathcal{M}$, $g = 0$. It's easy to verify that $\{f_i : t+1 \leq i \leq n\}$ are linearly independent. Hence $\{f_i : t+1 \leq i \leq n\}$ is a base of the regular chain group N. By using $\{f_i : t+1 \leq i \leq n\}$ as row vectors, we can construct a matrix M_1 such that the ith row of M_1 is f_{t+i}. Since $\|f_i\| \cap (V \backslash B) = C(B, v_i) \cap (V \backslash B) = v_i$, M_1 is a matrix with the following form,

$$\begin{pmatrix} & \vline & 1 & & & \\ & \vline & & 1 & & \\ A & \vline & & & \ddots & \\ & \vline & & & & 1 \end{pmatrix}$$

where A is an $(n-t) \times t$ matrix over $\mathbb{Z}$.

For $f, g \in N(V, \mathbb{Z})$, let $\langle f, g \rangle = \sum_{v \in V} f(v)g(v)$, and $N^* = \{g \in N(V, \mathbb{Z}) : \langle f, g \rangle = 0, \forall f \in N\}$. Obviously, N^* is a chain group on V over $\mathbb{Z}$. Since $\{f_i : t+1 \leq i \leq n\}$ is a base of N, N^* can be generated by $\{f_i : 1 \leq i \leq t\}$, where $\|f_i\| \cap B = v_i$ and $f_i(v_i) = 1$ for $1 \leq i \leq t$. On the other hand, since $\{f_i : 1 \leq i \leq t\}$ are linearly independent, $\{f_i : 1 \leq i \leq t\}$ is a base of N^*. By using $\{f_i : 1 \leq i \leq t\}$ as row vectors, we can construct a matrix M_2 such that the ith row of M_2 is f_i and M_2 has the following form,

$$\begin{pmatrix} 1 & & & & \vline & \\ & 1 & & & \vline & \\ & & \ddots & & \vline & -A^T \\ & & & 1 & \vline & \end{pmatrix}$$

where A^T is the transpose of the matrix A.

Let $\gamma_i = (f_1(v_i), f_2(v_i), \cdots, f_t(v_i))^T$, where $1 \leq i \leq n$. Suppose that K is a module generated by $\{\gamma_i : 1 \leq i \leq n\}$, construct a map $\varphi : V \longrightarrow K$ such that

$\varphi(v_i) = \gamma_i$ $(1 \leq i \leq n)$. In what follows, we will prove that $\varphi : V \longrightarrow K$ is a representation of the matroid $\mathcal{M}$ over $\mathbb{Z}$.

Lemma 5.1. *Let $\mathcal{M} = (V, \mathcal{C})$ be a regular matroid, and φ be a map as described above, then φ is a representation of the matroid $\mathcal{M}$ over $\mathbb{Z}$.*

Proof. By the construction of φ, it's easy to verify that for any subset $C \subseteq V$, C is a circuit of the matroid $\mathcal{M}$ if and only if $\{\gamma_i : v_i \in C\}$ is a minimal linearly dependent set. Then for any minimal linearly dependent subset $\{\gamma_i : v_i \in C \subseteq V\}$, there is a primitive chain f such that $\|f\| = C$, i.e., there are invertible elements $f(v_i)$ $(v_i \in C)$ such that $\sum_{v_i \in C} f(v_i) \gamma_i = 0$. Hence $\{\gamma_i : 1 \leq i \leq n\}$ is perfect. Since a subset $C \subseteq V$ is a circuit of the matroid $\mathcal{M}$ if and only if $\{\gamma_i : v_i \in C\}$ is a minimal linearly dependent set, φ preserves rank. Now, we have proved that φ is a representation of the matroid $\mathcal{M}$ over $\mathbb{Z}$. $\qquad\square$

By the definition of representation of a matroid, for any base B of a regular matroid $\mathcal{M}$, $\{\gamma_i : v_i \in B\}$ is a base of the module K, then the restriction $M_2(B)$ of the matrix M_2 to B is invertible.

In the following, we will discuss the condition, under which an access structure is black-box ideal.

Theorem 5.1. *An access structure $\mathcal{A}$ over P is black-box ideal if and only if there is a regular matroid $\mathcal{M} = (P', \mathcal{C})$ appropriate for $\mathcal{A}$.*

Proof. Let the access structure $\mathcal{A}$ is black-box ideal, then by the definition of black-box SSS, $\mathcal{A}$ is G-ideal homomorphic for any non-trivial finite abelian group G, i.e., $\mathcal{A}$ is universally ideal homomorphic. Hence there is a unique regular matroid $\mathcal{M}(P', \mathcal{C})$ appropriate for $\mathcal{A}$.

On the other hand, let $\mathcal{M} = (P', \mathcal{C})$ be a regular matroid appropriate for $\mathcal{A}$. Suppose that the rank of the matroid $\mathcal{M}$ is t. Let φ be a representation of the matroid $\mathcal{M}$ over $\mathbb{Z}$ constructed as above. Construct a matrix M such that the ith column vector of M is $\varphi(p_i)$ $(1 \leq i \leq n)$, and let $\psi : \{1, 2, \cdots, n\} \longrightarrow \{p_1, p_2, \cdots, p_n\}$ be a map such that $\psi(i) = p_i$ for $1 \leq i \leq n$.

Now, let's prove that the labelled matrix (M, ψ) is a black-box SSS realizing the access structure $\mathcal{A}$. For any $A \in \mathcal{A}$, there is $A' \in \mathcal{A}_m$ such that $A' \subseteq A$. Since $A' \cup \{p_0\}$ is a circuit of the matroid $\mathcal{M}$, $\{\varphi(p_i) : p_i \in A'\} \cup \{\varphi(p_0)\}$ is a minimal linearly dependent set. On the other hand, $\{\varphi(p_i) : 0 \leq i \leq n\}$ is perfect, then $\varphi(p_0)$ is a linear combination of $\{\varphi(p_i) : p_i \in A'\}$. Hence $\varphi(p_0)$ is a linear combination of $\{\varphi(p_i) : p_i \in A\}$, i.e., there is $\lambda_A \in \mathbb{Z}^{|A|}$ such that $\varphi(p_0) = M(A)\lambda_A^T$. For any non-trivial finite abelian group G, let $g = (g_1, g_2, \cdots, g_t) \in G^t$ be distributed uniformly, subject to $g_1 = s$, and $\alpha = gM$.

For any $A \in \mathcal{A}$, from the above proof, there is $\lambda_A \in \mathbb{Z}^{|A|}$ such that $M(A)\lambda_A^T = \varphi(p_0) = (1, 0, \cdots, 0)^T$, then $s = g(1, 0, \cdots, 0)^T = gM(A)\lambda_A^T = \alpha(A)\lambda_A^T$.

For any $A \in \mathcal{E}_M$, by Lemma 4.2, A is a hyperplane of the matroid $\mathcal{M}$. Let A' be a maximal independent subset of A, then for any $p_i \in A \backslash A'$, $\varphi(p_i)$ is a linear combination of $\{\varphi(p_i) : p_i \in A'\}$. On the other hand, by the definition of hyperplane, $A' \cup \{p_0\}$ is a base of the matroid $\mathcal{M}$, then $M'(A' \cup \{p_0\})$ is an invertible matrix, where $M' = (\varphi(p_0)|M)$. Hence there is a solution satisfying the system of linear equations $(x_1, x_2, \cdots, x_t)M'(A' \cup \{p_0\}) = (1, 0, \cdots, 0)$. In addition, from the above proof, the system of linear equations $(x_1, x_2, \cdots, x_t)M'(A' \cup \{p_0\}) = (1, 0, \cdots, 0)$ has the same solutions as $(x_1, x_2, \cdots, x_t)M'(A \cup \{p_0\}) = (1, 0, \cdots, 0)$, so the system of linear equations $(x_1, x_2, \cdots, x_t)M'(A \cup \{p_0\}) = (1, 0, \cdots, 0)$ has at least a solution. Let $\zeta = (z_1, z_2, \cdots, z_t) \in \mathbb{Z}^t$ be a solution of the above system of linear equations, obviously, $z_1 = 1$. For any $s' \in G$, let $\beta = \alpha + (s' - s)\zeta M$, it's easy to verify that $\beta(A) = \alpha(A)$ and the secret determined by β is s'. Now, we have finished proving that the labelled matrix (M, ψ) is a black-box SSS. $\square$

6   A Class of Universally Ideal Homomorphic (Black-Box Ideal) Access Structures

In this section, we will give a class of universally ideal homomorphic access structures using the terminology of matroid. At first, let's discuss representability of graphic matroids.

Suppose that $T = (V, E)$ be a graph, where V is the set of vertices of the graph T, and E is the set of edges of the graph T. Let $\mathcal{I} = \{X \subset E : X$ does not contain cycles of graph $T\}$, it's easy to verify that $\mathcal{I}$ is a collection of independent sets of a matroid, which is called a cycle matroid of the graph T, and denoted by $\mathcal{M} = (E, \mathcal{I})$ [21]. The set of circuits of the matroid $\mathcal{M} = (E, \mathcal{I})$ is that of cycles of the graph T. A matroid $\mathcal{M}$ is graphic, if there exists a graph $T = (V, E)$ such that $\mathcal{M} \simeq (E, \mathcal{I})$.

Similar to representability of a graphic matroid over a field, we have the following theorem.

Theorem 6.1. *Let* $T = (V, E)$ *be a finite graph, then the graphic matroid* $\mathcal{M} = (E, \mathcal{I})$ *is representable over* $\mathbb{Z}_m$ *for any positive integer* $m \geq 2$.

Proof. Let K be a free module over the ring $\mathbb{Z}_m$ such that $\dim K = |V|$. Construct an injective map $\phi : V \longrightarrow K$ such that $\{\phi(v) : v \in V\}$ are linearly independent. For an edge e adjacent to vertices v_i, v_j $(j > i)$, let $\varphi(e) = \phi(v_j) - \phi(v_i)$. Since $\{\phi(v_i) : v_i \in V\}$ are linearly independent, φ is injective.

Now, let's prove that φ is a representation of the graphic matroid $\mathcal{M} = (E, \mathcal{I})$ over ring $\mathbb{Z}_m$.

Choose a minimal linearly dependent subset of $\{\varphi(e) : e \in E\}$ arbitrarily, without loss of generality, let it be $\{\varphi(e_i) : 1 \leq i \leq k\}$, then there are non-zero elements $r_i \in \mathbb{Z}_m$ such that $\sum_{i=1}^{k} r_i\varphi(e_i) = 0$, where $i = 1, 2, \cdots, k$. Let T_0 be a subgraph of T such that the set of edges $E(T_0) = \{e_i : 1 \leq i \leq k\}$, and the set of vertices $V(T_0)$ is that of the vertices which are adjacent to the edges of $E(T_0)$. Assume that $v \in V(T_0)$ is only adjacent to one edge of T_0. Since $\{\phi(v_i) : v_i \in V(T_0)\}$ are linearly independent, it will lead to a contradiction to linearly dependence of $\{\phi(e_i) : 1 \leq i \leq k\}$. So there is no vertex of the graph T_0 with degree 1, and there exists a cycle $C \subseteq E(T_0)$. If $C \subset E(T_0)$, without loss of generality, let $C = \{e_1, \cdots, e_l\}$, where $1 \leq l < k$, then there exist

$r_i \in \{-1, 1\} \subseteq \mathbb{Z}_m^*$ $(i = 1, \cdots, l)$ such that $\sum_{i=1}^{l} r_i \varphi(e_i) = 0$, contradicted to the minimal linearly dependence of $\{\varphi(e_i) : 1 \leq i \leq k\}$. So $\{e_i : 1 \leq i \leq k\}$ is a cycle and there exist $r_i \in \{-1, 1\} \subseteq \mathbb{Z}_m^*(1 \leq i \leq k)$ such that $\sum_{i=1}^{k} r_i \varphi(e_i) = 0$. Hence $\{\phi(e) : e \in E(T)\}$ is perfect.

Let X be an independent set of $\mathcal{M} = (E, \mathcal{I})$, if $\{\phi(x) : x \in X\}$ is a linearly dependent set, then there exists a minimal linearly dependent set $\{\varphi(x) : x \in Y \subseteq X\}$. From the above proof, $Y \subseteq X$ is a cycle, contradicted.

On the other hand, if $\{\varphi(x) : x \in X\}$ is a linearly independent set, then X is independent. Otherwise, there exists a cycle $C \subseteq X$, then $\{\varphi(x) : x \in C\}$ is a linearly dependent set. From the above proof, we conclude that φ preserves rank.

Hence φ is a representation of $\mathcal{M} = (E, \mathcal{I})$ over the ring $\mathbb{Z}_m$.   □

For an access structure $\mathcal{A}$, if there is a graphic matroid appropriate for $\mathcal{A}$, then by the above theorem and Theorem 2.6, $\mathcal{A}$ is G-ideal homomorphic for any cyclic group G with order m ($m \geq 2$). So $\mathcal{A}$ is G-ideal homomorphic for any non-trivial finite abelian group G ($|G| \geq 2$). Thus, we have

Theorem 6.2. *For an access structure $\mathcal{A}$, if there is a graphic matroid appropriate for $\mathcal{A}$, then $\mathcal{A}$ is universally ideal homomorphic.*

Acknowledgement

We thank Kewei Lü for discussions about this paper.

References

1. A. Beimel and B. Chor, Universally ideal secret sharing schemes, *IEEE Transaction on Information Theory*, vol.IT-40, no.3 pp.786-794, 1994.
2. J. C. Benaloh, Secret sharing homomophisms: keeping shares of a secret secret, *Advances in Cryptology-CRYPTO'86*, Lecture Notes in Computer Science, vol.263, pp.251-260, 1987.
3. M. Ben-Or, S. Goldwasser and A. Wigderson, Completeness theorems for non-Cryptographic fault tolerant distributed computation, *Proceedings of the 20th Annual ACM Symposium on Theory of Computing (STOC'88)*, pp.1-10, 1988.
4. G. R. Blakley, Safeguarding cryptographic keys, *Proc. AFIPS 1979 Nat. Computer Conf.*, vol.48, pp.313-317, 1979.
5. E. F. Brickell, Some ideal secret sharing schemes, *Journal of Combinatorial Mathematics and Combinatorial Computing*, vol.6, pp.105-113, 1989.
6. E. F. Brickell and D. M. Davenport, On the classification of ideal secret sharing schemes, *Journal of Cryptology*, vol.4, no.2, pp.123-134,1991.
7. R. Cramer and S. Fehr, Optimal black-box secret sharing over arbitrary abelian groups, *Advances in Cryptology - CRYPTO '02*, Lecture Notes in Computer Science, vol.2442, 1990.
8. Y. Desmedt and Y. Frankel, Threshold cryptosystem, *Advances in Cryptology - CRYPTO'89*, Lecture Notes in Computer Science, vol.435, pp.307-315, 1990.

9. Y. Desmedt and Y. Frankel, Homomorphic zero-knowledge threshold schemes over any finite abelian group, *SIAM Journal on Discrete Mathematics*, 7(4), pp.667-679, 1994.

10. M. van Dijk, A linear construction of perfect secret sharing schemes, *Advances in Cryptology-EUROCRYPT'94*, Lecture Notes in Computer Science, vol.950, pp.23-36, 1994.

11. Y. Frankel and Y. Desmedt, Classification of ideal homomorphic threshold schemes over finite abelian groups, *Advances in Cryptology-EUROCRYPT'92*, Lecture Notes in Computer Science, vol.658, pp.25-34, 1993.

12. Y. Frankel, Y. Desmedt and M. Burmester, Non-existence of homomorphic general sharing schemes for some key spaces, *Advances in Cryptology-CRYPTO'92*, Lecture Notes in Computer Science, vol.740, pp.549-556, 1993.

13. M. Ito, A. Saito and T. Nishizeki, Secret sharing schemes realizing general access structure, *Proc. IEEE Global Telecommunication Conf., Globecom 87*, pp.99-102, 1987.

14. W.-A. Jackson and K. Martin, Geometric secret sharing schemes and their duals, *Designs, Codes and Cryptography*, vol.4, no.1, pp.83-95, 1994.

15. E. D. Karnin, J. W. Greene and M. E. Hellman, On secret sharing systems, *IEEE Transaction on Information Theory*, vol.IT-29, no.1, pp.35-41, 1983.

16. Mulan Liu and Zhanfei Zhou, Ideal homomorphic secret sharing schemes over cyclic groups, *Science in China*, Ser. E, Vol.41, no.6, Dec, 1998.

17. G. S. Simmons, W.-A. Jackson and K. Martin, The geometry of shared secret schemes, *Bulletin of the Institute of Combinatorics and its Applications*, pp.71-88, 1991.

18. A. Shamir, How to share a secret, *Communication of the ACM*, vol.22, no.11, pp.612-613, 1979.

19. V. Shoup, Practical threshold signatures, *Advances in Cryptology-EUROCRYPT 2000*, Lecture Notes in Computer Science, vol.1807, pp.207-220, 2000.

20. K. Truemper, Matroid decomposition, Boston: Academic, 1992.

21. D. J. A. Welsh, Matroid theory, London: Academic, 1976.

New Methods to Construct Cheating Immune Multisecret Sharing Scheme*

Wen Ping Ma[1] and Fu Tai Zhang[2]

[1] Key Laboratory of Computer Network and Information Security,
Ministry of Education, Xidian University, Xi'an 710071, P.R. China
wp_ma@mail.xidian.edu.cn
[2] The School of Mathematics and Computer Science,
Nanjing Normal University, Nanjing 210097, P.R. China
zhangfutai@njnu.edu.cn

Abstract. In this paper, the constructions of cheating immune secret sharing and multisecret sharing are studied. Based on the theories of matrix and linear block codes over finite field, some new methods to construct cheating immune secret sharing, strictly cheating immune secret sharing and multisecret sharing immune against cheating are proposed. Some cryptographic properties of the constructed secret sharing are analyzed as well.

Keywords: Quadratic Function, Secret Sharing, Cheating Immune Function, Multisecret Secret Sharing.

1 Introduction

Secret sharing is an indispensable tool in key management, multiparty computation, group cryptography and distributed cryptography. Unfortunately, many existing secret sharing systems are easily subjected to cheat by dishonest participants in the process of reconstruction. In such secret sharing systems the dishonest participants may submit fake shares to the combiner so that the combiner cannot reconstruct the original shared secret, but the dishonest participants may find the original shared secret in some way. Tompa and Woll [1]discussed the problem of cheating prevention in secret sharing in 1988. Since then, a considerable effort has put into the investigation of cheating prevention in secret sharing systems. A notable work in this line of study is the research on cheating immune secret sharing systems initiated by Josef Pipprzyk and Xian Mo Zhang [4]. They studied the problem of cheating prevention and the construction of cheating immune secret sharing schemes in [4, 5, 6, 7].

Cheating immune secret sharing schemes are divided into two classes, i.e., the computational secure schemes and unconditional secure ones. In computational secure cheating immune secret sharing schemes, the combiner checks the

---

* This work was supported by the National Science Foundation of China under the grant No.60373104 and Key Project of Jiangsu education bureau, China, under grant number 03KJA520066.

D. Feng, D. Lin, and M. Yung (Eds.): CISC 2005, LNCS 3822, pp. 384–394, 2005.

validity of the shares submitted by the participants before he reconstructs the shared secret, so any false shares may probably be found out in this stage and the cheaters are likely to be detected. One solution for computational secure cheating immune secret sharing is publicly verifiable secret sharing. M.Stadler et. al considered this problem in [8, 9, 10]. Josef Pieprzyk and Xian-Mo Zhang [4] pointed out that cheating by dishonest participants can also be prevented without using the method of public key cryptography. The prevention here is meant that the dishonest participants cannot derive the original shared secret correctly from the invalid secret computed by the combiner, furthermore, the invalid secret reveals no information about the original shared secret.

Multisecret sharing was probably first discussed in [2]. The problem of cheating prevention in this type of secret sharing schemes was also first considered by Josef Pieprzyk and Xian Mo Zhang [5]. They gave the fundamental concepts of multisecret sharing immune against cheating and some ideas to construct multisecret sharing immune against cheating.

In this paper, we further study the problem of cheating prevention in secret sharing systems. Based on quadratic function over finite field, the cheating immune secret sharing, strictly cheating immune secret sharing and multisecret sharing immune against cheating are constructed. Some cryptographic properties of these secret sharing schemes are also analyzed.

2   Secret Sharing System Immune Against Cheating

2.1   Basic Model of Cheating Immune Secret Sharing Scheme [4]

Let $GF(p)$ denote a finite field with p elements, where p is a prime number or a power of a prime number. We use $GF(p)^n$ to denote the vector space of dimension n over $GF(p)$.

For vectors $x = (x_1, x_2, \cdots, x_n)$, $\delta = (\delta_1, \delta_2, \cdots, \delta_n)$ in $GF(p)^n$, define vectors $x_\delta^+ \in GF(p)^n$, $x_\delta^- \in GF(p)^n$ as follows :

$$(x_\delta^+)_j = \begin{cases} x_j, & \text{if } \delta_j \neq 0 \\ 0, & \text{if } \delta_j = 0 \end{cases}$$

$$(x_\delta^-)_j = \begin{cases} 0, & \text{if } \delta_j \neq 0 \\ x_j, & \text{if } \delta_j = 0 \end{cases}$$

where $j = 1, 2, \cdots, n$.

Let $\tau = (\tau_1, \tau_2, \cdots, \tau_n)$, $\delta = (\delta_1, \delta_2, \cdots, \delta_n)$ be two vectors in $GF(p)^n$. By the notation $\tau \leq \delta$ we mean that $\tau_i \neq 0$ implies $\delta_i \neq 0$, for all $i \in \{1, 2, ..., n\}$. We use $\tau < \delta$ to denote $\tau \leq \delta$ and the Hamming weight $HW(\tau)$ of τ (the number of nonzero coordinates of τ) is less than the Hamming weight $HW(\delta)$ of δ. If $\delta' \leq \delta$, and $HW(\delta') = HW(\delta)$, we write $\delta' \approx \delta$. For $\tau, \delta \in GF(p)^n, \delta \neq 0, \tau \leq \delta$, $u \in GF(p)$, and a mapping f from $GF(p)^n$ to $GF(p)$, define

$$R_f(\delta, \tau, u) = \{x_\delta^- | f(x_\delta^- + \tau) = u\}.$$

We also simply write $R(\delta, \tau, u)$ in place of $R_f(\delta, \tau, u)$ if no confusion occurs.

Now, we consider a secret sharing system. Suppose the secret to be shared is randomly chosen from $GF(p)$, namely the secret space is $GF(p)$. There are n participants(or share-holders) $P_1, P_2, \cdots, P_n$, a dealer D and a combiner in the system. Denote $P = \{P_1, P_2, \cdots, P_n\}$. Two phases are involved in a secret sharing scheme. One is share distribution, and the other is reconstruction. In the share distribution phase, the dealer D randomly splits a secret K into n shares in $GF(p)$, and distributes in secret each participant one share.In reconstruction phase, all participants submit their shares to the combiner who computes the shared secret using a function f from $GF(p)^n$ to $GF(p)$. The function f is called the defining function as it determines the secret sharing.

Let $\alpha = (s_1, s_2, \cdots, s_n) \in GF(p)^n$ be the share vector, i.e., s_j is the share distributed to participant P_j by the dealer, $K = f(\alpha)$ be the shared secret.

Let $\alpha + \delta$ be the vector whose coordinates are *shares* submitted to the combiner by the participants. We call $\delta = (\delta_1, \delta_2, \cdots, \delta_n) \in GF(p)^n$ a cheating vector, and P_i is a cheater if and only if $\delta_i \neq 0$. The collection of cheaters is determined by the vector $\delta = (\delta_1, \delta_2, \cdots, \delta_n)$ uniquely.

It is assumed that in pooling phase, dishonest participants always submit invalid shares, and honest participants always submit their valid shares. We also suppose the dishonest participants change their *shares* from time to time, and there is at least one cheater in the system, this implies $\delta \neq 0$.

Consider the vector $\alpha + \delta$. It is obvious that $\alpha + \delta = \alpha_\delta^- + \alpha_\delta^+ + \delta$, here α_δ^- is submitted by the honest participants (or we can say the nonzero coordinates of α_δ^- are shares submitted to the combiner by the honest participants), and $\alpha_\delta^+ + \delta$ by the dishonest ones (the nonzero coordinates of α_δ^+ are shares held by the dishonest participants). In this case, the combiner will output an invalid secret $K^* = f(\alpha + \delta)$.

For the defining function f, share vector α and cheating vector $\delta = (\delta_1, \delta_2, \cdots, \delta_n)$, the number

$$\rho_{\delta,\alpha} = \frac{\sharp(R(\delta, \alpha_\delta^+ + \delta, K^*) \cap R(\delta, \alpha_\delta^+, K))}{\sharp R(\delta, \alpha_\delta^+ + \delta, K^*)}$$

is the probability of successful cheating by dishonest participants with respect to δ, α, where $\sharp X$ denotes the number of elements in the set X.

It is obvious that $\rho_{\delta,\alpha} > 0$ since the share vector α is always in the set $(R(\delta, \alpha_\delta^+ + \delta, K^*) \cap R(\delta, \alpha_\delta^+, K))$ and the number of cheaters is equal to $HW(\delta)$. It was proved in [4] that $max\{\rho_{\delta,\alpha} | \alpha \in GF(p)^n\} \geq p^{-1}$ for arbitrary $\alpha \in (GF(p))^n$ and nonzero $\delta \in GF(p)^n$.

Definition 1. A secret sharing is said to be k-cheating immune if $\rho_{\delta,\alpha} = p^{-1}$ for every $\delta \in GF(p)^n$ with $1 \leq HW(\delta) \leq k < n$ and every $\alpha \in GF(p)^n$.

Let f be a quadratic function, if $f(x_\delta^- + \tau + \delta) - f(x_\delta^- + \tau)$ is a non-constant affine function for arbitrary $\delta, \tau \in GF(p)^n$ with $1 \leq HW(\delta) \leq k$ and $\tau \leq \delta$, we call f has property $B(k)$.

Let f be the defining function, $\delta = (\delta_1, \delta_2, \cdots, \delta_n)$ be a nonzero vector, α be an original vector, the nonzero vector $\tau, \tau \leq \delta$ be an active cheating vector, the number

$$\rho_{\delta,\tau,\alpha} = \frac{\sharp(R(\delta,\alpha_\delta^+ + \tau, K^*) \cap R(\delta,\alpha_\delta^+, K))}{\sharp R(\delta,\alpha_\delta^+ + \tau, K^*)}$$

expresses the probability of cheaters' success with respect to δ, τ and α.

Definition 2. A secret sharing is said to be strictly k-cheating immune if $\rho_{\delta,\tau,\alpha} = p^{-1}$ for every $\delta \in GF(p)^n$ with $1 \le HW(\delta) \le k < n$, every $\alpha \in GF(p)^n$ and any nonzero vector $\tau, \tau \le \delta$.

Next, we will study how to use quadratic functions over finite field to construct cheating immune secret sharing.

A function f from $GF(p)^n$ to $GF(p)$ is said balanced if

$$\sharp\{\alpha : \alpha \in GF(p)^n, f(\alpha) = b, \forall b \in GF(p)\} = p^{(n-1)}$$

For quadratic functions, the following theorem can be easily proved.

Theorem 1. *Let* $Q(x_1, x_2, \cdots, x_n) = \sum_{i,j=1,i\le j}^n a_{ij} x_i x_j + \sum_{i=1}^n a_i x_i$ *be a quadratic function over finite field $GF(q)$ with characteristic not equal to 2, then the function $Q(x_1, x_2, \cdots, x_n)$ is balanced if and only if there exists $\omega \in GF(q)^n$ such that $Q(x + \omega) - Q(x)$ equals to a constant, and $Q(\omega) \ne 0$.*

2.2   A New Construction of Cheating Immune Secret Sharing

Let $\alpha = (a_1, a_2, \cdots, a_m)$ be a nonzero vector over $GF(p)$ with characteristic not equal to 2, and $\sum_{i=1}^m a_i = 0$, $b_0, b_1, \cdots, b_{n-1} \in GF(p)$, and $\sum_{i=0}^{n-1} b_i \ne 0$. Define a function $\lambda_{n,m}$ on $GF(p)^n$ as:

$$\lambda_{n,m}(x_0, x_1, \cdots, x_{n-1})$$
$$= \Sigma_{i=0}^{n-1} b_i x_i + (x_0, x_1, \cdots, x_{n-1}) A(\alpha, n)(x_0, x_1, \cdots, x_{n-1})^T$$
$$= \Sigma_{i=0}^{n-1} b_i x_i + \Sigma_{j=0}^{n-1} x_j (a_1 x_{[j+1]_{(n)}} + a_2 x_{[j+2]_{(n)}} + \cdots + a_m x_{[j+m]_{(n)}})$$

where $j = i_{(n)}$ iff $j = i \bmod n$.

$A(\alpha, n)$ is an $n \times n$ matrix over $GF(p)$ determined by the vector $\alpha = (a_1, a_2, \cdots, a_m)$ as follows:

$$A(\alpha, n) = \begin{pmatrix} 0 & a_1 & a_2 & \cdots & a_m & 0 & \cdots & 0 \\ 0 & 0 & a_1 & \cdots & a_{m-1} & a_m & \cdots & 0 \\ \cdots & & & & & & & \\ 0 & 0 & 0 & 0 & 0 & 0 & 0 & 0 \\ a_m & 0 & 0 & \cdots & 0 & 0 & \cdots & a_{m-1} \\ a_{m-1} & a_m & 0 & \cdots & 0 & 0 & \cdots & a_{m-2} \\ \cdots & & & & & & & \\ a_2 & a_3 & a_4 & \cdots & & \cdots & & a_1 \\ a_1 & a_2 & a_3 & \cdots & 0 & 0 & \cdots & 0 \end{pmatrix}$$

Theorem 2.   *1. $\lambda_{n,m}(x_0, x_1, \cdots, x_{n-1})$ is balanced.*
2. If $n \ge km + k + 1$, then the function $\lambda_{n,m}(x_0, x_1, \cdots, x_{n-1})$ satisfies the property $B(k)$.

Proof. 1. Because $\lambda_{n,m}(1,1,\cdots,1) = \sum_{i=0}^{n-1} b_i \neq 0$, we have $\lambda_{n,m}(x_0 + 1, x_1 + 1, \cdots, x_{n-1} + 1) - \lambda_{n,m}(x_0, x_1, \cdots, x_{n-1}) = \sum_{i=0}^{n-1} b_i = $ constant. From theorem 1, $\lambda_{n,m}(x_0, x_1, \cdots, x_{n-1})$ is balanced.

2. Let $\delta \in GF(p)^n$, with $HW(\delta) \leq k$, and $\tau \leq \delta$. Suppose $HW(\delta) = k$, write $\delta = (0, \cdots, \delta_{i_1}, \cdots, \delta_{i_2}, \cdots, \delta_{i_k}, \cdots, 0)$ where $0 \leq i_1, i_2, \cdots, i_k \leq n - 1$, $\delta_{i_1} \neq 0, \delta_{i_2} \neq 0, \cdots, \delta_{i_k} \neq 0$. If $n \geq km + k + 1$, then there exists at least one element $k \in \{0, 1, 2, \cdots, n - 1\}$ such that k belongs to just one of the classes

$$\{\{(i_j - 1) \bmod n, (i_j - 2) \bmod n, \cdots,$$

$$(i_j - m) \bmod n, (i_j + 1) \bmod n, (i_j + 2) \bmod n, \cdots, (i_j + m) \bmod n\}, 1 \leq j \leq k\},$$

thus $f(x_{\bar{\delta}} + \delta + \tau) - f(x_{\bar{\delta}} + \tau)$ contains the term $a x_k, a \in GF(p), a \neq 0$. This implies that the function $\lambda_{n,m}(x_0, x_1, \cdots, x_{(n-1)})$ satisfies the property $B(k)$.

Theorem 3 ([4]). *Let k, s be two positive integers satisfying $s \geq (k + 1)$, h_i be a balanced quadratic function with property $B(k)$ on $GF(p)^{n_i}$ for each $i = 1, 2, \cdots, s$. Set $n = n_1 + n_2 + \cdots + n_s$. Defining the function f on $GF(p)^n$ as $f(x) = h_1(y_1) + h_2(y_2) + \cdots + h_s(y_s)$, where $x = (y_1, y_2, \cdots, y_s)$, h_i and h_j have disjoint variables if $i \neq j$. Then the secret sharing with defining function f is k-cheating immune.*

3   The Construction of Multisecret Sharing Immune Against Cheating

3.1   Basic Model of Multisecret Sharing Immune Against Cheating [2, 5]

The multisecret sharing system is defined by a mapping $F : GF(p)^n \to GF(p)^m$. The function F is equivalent to the following function group :

$$\begin{cases} f_1 : GF(p)^n \to GF(p) \\ f_2 : GF(p)^n \to GF(p) \\ \qquad \cdots \\ f_m : GF(p)^n \to GF(p) \end{cases}$$

We denote this function group by $[f_1, f_2, \cdots, f_m]$, and call it the defining function of the multisecret sharing.

Let δ be a nonzero vector in $GF(p)^n$, $\tau \leq \delta$, and $\mu \in GF(p)^m$, set

$$R_f(\delta, \tau, \mu) = \{x_{\bar{\delta}} : f(x_{\bar{\delta}} + \tau) = \mu\}.$$

We simply denote $R_f(\delta, \tau, \mu)$ as $R(\delta, \tau, \mu)$ if no confusion occurs.

Let $u^* = f(\alpha + \delta)$, the number

$$\rho_{\delta,\alpha} = \frac{\sharp(R(\delta, \alpha_{\bar{\delta}}^+ + \delta, u^*) \cap R(\delta, \alpha_{\bar{\delta}}^+, u))}{\sharp R(\delta, \alpha_{\bar{\delta}}^+ + \delta, u^*)}$$

expresses the probability of successful cheating with respect to δ and α.

A multisecret sharing is said to be k-cheating immune if $\rho_{\delta,\alpha} = p^{-m}$ hold for every $\delta \in GF(p)^n$, with $1 \le HW(\delta) \le k$, and every $\alpha \in GF(p)^n$.

We call the nonzero vector $\delta = (\delta_1, \delta_2, \cdots, \delta_n)$ a cheating vector, nonzero vector $\tau \le \delta$ an active cheating vector, α the original vector, then the value

$$\rho_{\delta,\tau,\alpha} = \frac{\sharp(R(\delta, \alpha_\delta^+ + \tau, u^*) \cap R(\delta, \alpha_\delta^+, u))}{\sharp R(\delta, \alpha_\delta^+ + \tau, u^*)}$$

expresses the probability of successful cheating with respect to δ, τ, α.

A multisecret sharing is said to be strictly k-cheating immune if the the probability of successful cheating satisfies $\rho_{\delta,\tau,\alpha} = p^{-m}$ for every nonzero $\delta \in GF(p)^n$ with $1 \le HW(\delta) \le k < n$, any $\alpha \in GF(p)^n$, and any nonzero vector $\tau \le \delta$.

Definition 3. Let $[f_1, f_2, \cdots, f_m]$ be the defining function of a multisecret sharing, k a positive integer, and $k < n$. $[f_1, f_2, \cdots, f_m]$ is said satisfying the property $B(k)$ if there exists $a_1, a_2, \cdots, a_m \in GF(p)$ such that $\Sigma_{i=1}^m a_i[f_i(x_\delta^- + \tau + \delta) - f_i(x_\delta^- + \tau)]$ is a non-constant affine function, where $(a_1, a_2, \cdots, a_m) \ne (0, 0, \cdots, 0)$, $1 \le HW(\delta) \le k, \tau \le \delta$.

Thus $[f_1, f_2, \cdots, f_m]$ satisfies the property $B(k)$ iff any nonzero linear combination of $f_1, f_2, \cdots, f_m$, i.e., $\Sigma_{i=1}^m a_i f_i$ satisfies the property $B(k)$, where a_1, $a_2, \cdots, a_m \in GF(p)$, and $(a_1, a_2, \cdots, a_m) \ne (0, 0, \cdots, 0)$.

3.2   The New Construction of Multisecret Sharing Immune Against Cheating

Let $GF(p)$ be a finite field whose characteristic is not equal to 2. Set

$$\Delta = \{(x_1, x_2, \cdots, x_m) : x_i \in GF(p), i = 1, 2, \cdots, m, \Sigma_{i=1}^m x_i = 0\},$$

then Δ is a linear subspace of dimension $m - 1$ of vector space $GF(p)^m$.

A set of base of linear subspace Δ is:

$\alpha_1 = (a_{11}, a_{12}, \cdots, a_{1m})$,
$\alpha_2 = (a_{21}, a_{22}, \cdots, a_{2m})$,
$\cdots$

$\alpha_{m-1} = (a_{(m-1)1}, a_{(m-1)2}, \cdots, a_{(m-1)m})$.

For each $i \in \{1, 2, \cdots, m - 1\}$, we construct an $n \times n$ matrix

$$A(\alpha_i, n) = \begin{pmatrix} 0 & a_{i1} & a_{i2} & \cdots & a_{im} & 0 & \cdots & 0 \\ 0 & 0 & a_{i1} & \cdots & a_{i(m-1)} & a_{im} & \cdots & 0 \\ \cdots & \cdots & \cdots & \cdots & \cdots & \cdots & \cdots & \cdots \\ 0 & 0 & 0 & \cdots & 0 & 0 & \cdots & a_{im} \\ a_{im} & 0 & 0 & \cdots & 0 & 0 & \cdots & a_{i(m-1)} \\ a_{i(m-1)} & a_{im} & 0 & \cdots & 0 & 0 & \cdots & a_{i(m-2)} \\ \cdots & \cdots & \cdots & \cdots & \cdots & \cdots & \cdots & \cdots \\ a_{i2} & a_{i3} & a_{i4} & \cdots & \cdots & \cdots & \cdots & a_{i1} \\ a_{i1} & a_{i2} & a_{i3} & \cdots & 0 & 0 & \cdots & 0 \end{pmatrix}$$

Let $\lambda(\alpha_i, n) = (x_1, x_2, \cdots, x_n)A(\alpha_i, n)(x_1, x_2, \cdots, x_n)^T$,

$f_{11}(x_1, x_2, \cdots, x_n) = x_1 + \lambda(\alpha_1, n)$,

$f_{21}(x_1, x_2, \cdots, x_n) = x_2 + \lambda(\alpha_2, n), f_{22}(x_1, x_2, \cdots, x_n) = 2x_2 + \lambda(\alpha_2, n)$

$\cdots$

$f_{(m-1)1}(x_1, x_2, \cdots .x_n) = x_{m-1} + \lambda(\alpha_{m-1}, n)$,

$f_{(m-1)2}(x_1, x_2, \cdots, x_n) = 2x_{m-1} + \lambda(\alpha_{m-1}, n)$.

From theorem 1, each function constructed above is balanced.
Let $(x_1, x_2, \cdots, x_{nm}) \in GF(p)^{nm}$, we can write

$(x_1, x_2, \cdots, x_{mn}) = (y_1, y_2, \cdots, y_m)$, $y_i \in GF(p)^n, i = 1, 2, \cdots, n$.

Now we construct the following functions:

$f_1(x_1, x_2, \cdots, x_{mn}) = f_{11}(y_1) + f_{11}(y_2) + \cdots + f_{11}(y_m)$,

$f_2(x_1, x_2, \cdots, x_{mn}) = f_{21}(y_1) + f_{22}(y_2) + f_{21}(y_3) + \cdots + f_{21}(y_m)$,

$\cdots$

$f_{m-1}(x_1, x_2, \cdots, x_{mn}) = f_{(m-1)1}(y_1) + f_{(m-1)1}(y_2) + \cdots + f_{(m-1)2}(y_{m-1}) + f_{(m-1)1}(y_m)$.

Namely, the $i'th$ term of $f_i(x_1, x_2, \cdots, x_{mn})$ is f_{i2}, and the other terms of $f_i(x_1, x_2, \cdots, x_{nm})$ are $f_{i1}, i = 2, \cdots, (m-1)$.

Theorem 4. *If $n \geq km + k + 1$, then the function group:*

$$\begin{cases} f_1(x_1, x_2, \cdots, x_{nm}) \\ f_2(x_1, x_2, \cdots, x_{nm}) \\ \quad \cdots \\ f_{m-1}(x_1, x_2, \cdots, x_{nm}) \end{cases}$$

is a balanced function from $GF(p)^{nm}$ to $GF(p)^{m-1}$, and satisfies the property $B(k)$.

Proof. We use the fact that a function group $[g_1, g_2, \cdots, g_{m-1}]$ is balanced iff for any nonzero linear combination of $g_1, g_2, \cdots, g_{m-1}$, i.e, $\Sigma_{i=1}^{m-1} a_i g_i$ is balanced, where $a_1, a_2, \cdots, a_{m-1} \in GF(p)$, and $(a_1, a_2, \cdots, a_{m-1}) \neq (0, 0, \cdots, 0)$. Now, for the function group $[f_1, f_2, \cdots, f_{(m-1)}]$, we have

$a_1 f_1 + a_2 f_2 + \cdots + a_{m-1} f_{m-1}$
$= [(a_1 x_1 + a_2 x_2 + \cdots + a_{m-1} x_{m-1}) + y_1 \Sigma_{i=1}^{m-1} a_i \lambda(\alpha_i, n) y_1^T]$
$+ [(a_1 x_{n+1} + 2a_2 x_{n+2} + \cdots + a_{m-1} x_{n+m-1}) + y_2 \Sigma_{i=1}^{m-1} a_i \lambda(\alpha_i, n) y_2^T] + \cdots +$
$[(a_1 x_{(m-2)n+1} + a_2 x_{(m-2)n+2} + \cdots + 2a_{m-1} x_{(m-2)n+m-1}) +$
$y_{m-1} \Sigma_{i=1}^{m-1} a_i \lambda(\alpha_i, n) y_{m-1}^T]$
$+ [(a_1 x_{(m-1)n+1} + a_2 x_{(m-1)n+2} + \cdots + a_{m-1} x_{(m-1)n+m-1}) +$
$y_m \Sigma_{i=1}^{m-1} a_i \lambda(\alpha_i, n) y_m^T]$.
$\Sigma_{i=1}^{m-1} a_i \lambda(\alpha_i, n) = \lambda(\Sigma_{i=1}^{m-1}(a_i \alpha_i), n)$

Since $a_1, a_2, \cdots, a_{m-1} \in GF(p)$ are not all zero, thus there exists at least a nonzero element in $a_1 + a_2 + \cdots + a_{m-1}, a_1 + 2a_2 + \cdots + a_{m-1}, \cdots, a_1 + a_2 + \cdots +$

$2a_{m-1}$, hence we know from theorem 1, the function $a_1f_1+a_2f_2+\cdots+a_{m-1}f_{m-1}$ is balanced. This proves the function group $[f_1, f_2, \cdots, f_{m-1}]$ is balanced.

For each $i \in \{1, 2, \cdots, m-1\}$, the function $\lambda(\alpha_i, n)$ satisfies the property $B(k)$, so we know from the theorem 2, $\lambda(\Sigma_{i=1}^{m-1}a_i\alpha_i, n)$ satisfies the property $B(k)$ when $n \geq mk + k + 1$ and $a_1, a_2, \cdots, a_{m-1} \in GF(p)$, with $(a_1, a_2, \cdots, a_{m-1}) \neq (0, 0, \cdots, 0)$. This implies the function group $\lambda(\alpha_i, n), i = 1, 2, \cdots, m-1$ satisfies the property $B(k)$, namely $[f_1, f_2, \cdots, f_{m-1}]$ satisfies the property $B(k)$.

The following theorem can be proved using the similar way as in [4].

Theorem 5. *Let k, s be two positive integers satisfying $s \geq q(k + 1)$, h_i be a balanced function with property $B(k)$ from $GF(p)^{n_i}$ to $GF(p)^m$ for each $i = 1, 2, \cdots, s$. Set $n = n_1 + n_2 + \cdots + n_s$. Defining the function f from $GF(p)^n$ to $GF(p)^m$ as $f(x) = h_1(y_1) + h_2(y_2) + \cdots + h_s(y_s)$, where $x = (y_1, y_2, \cdots, y_s)$, h_i and h_j have disjoint variables if $i \neq j$, then the multisecret sharing with defining function f is k-cheating immune.*

4 On the Construction of Strictly Cheating Immune Multisecret Sharing

Theorem 6. *Given a multisecret sharing defining function $f : GF(p)^n \longrightarrow GF(p)^m$, the following statements are equivalent:*

(1) the multisecret sharing is strictly $k-$cheating immune,
(2) For any integer l with $1 \leq l \leq k$, any $\delta \in GF(p)^n$ with $HW(\delta) = l$, any $\tau_1 \leq \delta, \tau_2 \leq \delta, 0 \leq HW(\tau_2)$, and any $\mu, \nu \in GF(p)^m$, we have

$$\sharp(R(\delta, \tau_1, \nu) \cap R(\delta, \tau_1 + \tau_2, \mu)) = p^{n-l-2m},$$

(3) The system of equations:

$$\begin{cases} f(x_\delta^- + \tau_1 + \tau_2) = \mu \\ f(x_\delta^- + \tau_1) = \upsilon \end{cases}$$

has precisely $p^{(n-l-2m)}$ solutions on x_δ^-, for any $\tau_1 \leq \delta, \tau_2 \leq \delta, 0 < HW(\tau_2)$, and any $\mu, \nu \in GF(p)^m$.

The proof is similar to the proof of theorem 3 in [5].

If $m = 1$, the multisecret sharing with its defining mapping $f : GF(p)^n \longrightarrow GF(p)^m$ is a secret sharing. Thus the theorem is also right for ordinary secret sharing.

Definition 4. The function f of degree two is said to have the strict property $B(k)$ if for any $\delta \in GF(p)^n, 1 \leq HW(\delta) \leq k$, any $\tau_1 \leq \delta$, any $\tau_2 \leq \delta$ and $0 < HW(\tau_2)$, $f(x_\delta^+ + \tau_1 + \tau_2) - f(x_\delta^+ + \tau_1)$ is a non-constant affine function.

Similar to theorem 4, the function f of degree two which satisfies the strictly property $B(k)$ can be used to construct the strictly cheating immune secret sharing.

In the following, a method to construct strictly cheating immune multisecret sharing will be given.

Theorem 7. *[5] Given a multisecret sharing with its defined mapping* f : $GF(p)^n \to GF(p)^m$, *then the multisecret sharing is strictly* $k-$*cheating immune iff for any integer* r *with* $0 \leq r \leq k-1$, *any subset* $\{j_1, j_2, \cdots, j_r\}$ *of* $\{1, 2, \cdots, n\}$ *and any* $a_1, a_2, \cdots, a_r \in GF(p)$, *the mapping*

$$f(x_1, x_2, \cdots, x_n)|_{x_{j_1}=a_{j_1}, x_{j_2}=a_{j_2}, \cdots, z_{j_r}=a_{j_r}}$$

is the defining mapping of a $(k-r)$ *cheating immune secret sharing.*

Let $GF(p)$ be a finite field whose characteristic is not equal to 2. Suppose $C^/$ is a $(n^/, k^/, d)$linear cyclic codes over $GF(p)$ such that for every codeword $\alpha = (a_1, a_2, \cdots, a_m) \in C^/$, such that $\Sigma_{i=1}^{m} a_i = 0$, and $k^/ \geq d, n^/ - k^/ \geq d$. Let C be $(n^/ - d, k^/ - d, \geq d)$ shortened cyclic codes, rewrite the parameter $(n^/ - d, k^/ - d, \geq d)$ as $(m, k, \geq d)$.

Let $\alpha = (a_1, a_2, \cdots, a_m) \in C$ be a nonzero code of the code C, b_0, b_1, $b_2, \cdots, b_{n-1} \in GF(p)$, such that $\Sigma_{i=0}^{n-1} b_i \neq 0$, $\lambda_{n,m}$ be a function on $GF(p)^n$ defined by :

$$\lambda_{n,m}(x_0, x_1, \cdots, x_{n-1}) = \Sigma_{i=0}^{n-1} b_i x_i + (x_0, x_1, \cdots, x_{n-1}) A(\alpha, n) (x_0, x_1, \cdots, x_{n-1})^T$$

Theorem 8. *1.* $\lambda_{n,m}(x_0, x_1, \cdots, x_{n-1})$ *is balanced.*
2. If $n \geq 2m^2 + m + 1$, *the function satisfies strict property* $B(d)$.

Proof. 1), From the theorem 1, it is easy to prove that $\lambda_{n,m}(x_0, x_1, \cdots, x_{n-1})$ is balanced.

2),Let $h(x_{i_1}, x_{i_2}, \cdots, x_{i_{n-r}}) = \lambda_{n,m}(x_0, x_1, \cdots, x_{n-1})|_{x_{j_1}=a_1, \cdots, x_{j_r}=a_r}, 0 \leq r < d, x_{i_1} = y_1, x_{i_2} = y_2, \cdots, x_{i_{n-r}} = y_{n-r}$.

Consider the function $h(y_1, y_2, \cdots, y_{n-r})$. Recall that for each j, $1 \leq j \leq n-r$, x_j appears precisely in $2m$ quadratic terms of

$$\lambda_{n,m}(x_0, x_2, \cdots, x_{n-1}) : x_j x_{[j+i]_{(n)}}, x_j x_{[j-i]_{(n)}}, i = 1, 2, \cdots, m.$$

Let $\delta \in GF(p)^{n-r}$ be an cheating vector with $HW(\delta) = l, 1 \leq l \leq m, \tau \leq \delta$ be an active cheating vector. Write $\delta = (\delta_1, \delta_2, \cdots, \delta_{n-r})$,
$J = \{j | \delta_j \neq 0, 1 \leq j \leq n-r\}$, $\sharp J = HW(\delta) = l \leq d - r$, if i, j do not belong to J, the term $y_i y_j$ does not appear in $h(y_\delta^- + \delta + \tau) - h(y_\delta^- + \tau)$.
Since $n - r > n - m > 2m^2 + 1$, $\lceil \frac{n-r}{m-r} \rceil \geq 2m + 1$, there exist $j_0 \in J$ and l_1 such that $l_1 \geq 2m + 1$, we have

$$[j_0 + l_1]_{(n-r)} \in J, \{[j_0 + 1]_{(n-r)}, [j_0 + 2]_{(n-r)}, \cdots, [j_0 + l_1 - 1]_{(n-r)}\} \cap J = \varnothing.$$

Let $[j_{l-1}]_{(n-r)}, [j_{l-2}]_{(n-r)}, \cdots, j_0$ be all elements of J, and $[j_0 + l_1 - 1]_{(n-r)} = [j_{(l-1)}]_{(n-r)}$.

Because every codeword in $C^/$ has minimum weight not smaller than d, there exists some element $[i_0]_{(n-r)} \in \{[j_0 + 1]_{(n-r)}, [j_0 + 2]_{(n-r)}, \cdots, [j_0 + m]_{(n-r)}\}$ such that $a x_{[i_0]_{(n-r)}}$ $(a \neq 0)$ appears in $\Sigma_{s=0}^{l-1} \delta_s (a_1 x_{(j_s+1)} + a_2 x_{(j_s+2)} + \cdots + a_m x_{(j_s+m)})$, thus $ax_{[i_0]_{(n-r)}}, (a \neq 0)$ appears in $h(y_\delta^+ + \tau + \delta) - h(y_\delta^+ + \tau)$. This proves that h has the property $B(d-r)$.

Suppose a set of base of the codes C is

$\alpha_1 = (a_{11}, a_{12}, \cdots, a_{1m})$,

$\alpha_2 = (a_{21}, a_{22}, \cdots, a_{2m})$,

$\cdots$

$\alpha_k = (a_{k1}, a_{k2}, \cdots, a_{km})$.

To construct matrix $A(\alpha_i, n), i = 1, 2, \cdots, k$.

let $\lambda(\alpha_i, n) = (x_1, x_2, \cdots, x_n) A(\alpha_i, n)(x_1, x_2, \cdots, x_n)^T$,

$f_{11}(x_1, x_2, \cdots, x_n) = x_1 + \lambda(\alpha_1, n)$,

$f_{21}(x_1, x_2, \cdots, x_n) = x_2 + \lambda(\alpha_2, n)$, $f_{22}(x_1, x_2, \cdots, x_n) = 2x_2 + \lambda(\alpha_2, n)$,

$\cdots$

$f_{k1}(x_1, x_2, \cdots .x_n) = x_k + \lambda(\alpha_k, n), f_{k2}(x_1, x_2, \cdots, x_n) = 2x_k + \lambda(\alpha_k, n)$.

From theorem 1, each function constructed above is balanced.

Let $(x_1, x_2, \cdots, x_{nk}) \in GF(p)^{nk}$. Write $(x_1, x_2, \cdots, x_{kn}) = (y_1, y_2, \cdots, y_k)$, $y_i \in GF(p)^n, i = 1, 2, \cdots, n$.

Now, we construct the following functions:

$f_1(x_1, x_2, \cdots, x_{kn}) = f_{11}(y_1) + f_{11}(y_2) + \cdots + f_{11}(y_k)$,

$f_2(x_1, x_2, \cdots, x_{kn}) = f_{21}(y_1) + f_{22}(y_2) + f_{21}(y_3) + \cdots + f_{21}(y_k)$,

$\cdots$

$f_k(x_1, x_2, \cdots, x_{kn}) = f_{k1}(y_1) + f_{k1}(y_2) + \cdots + f_{k2}(y_k)$.

The i'th term of $f_i(x_1, x_2, \cdots, x_{kn})$ is f_{i2}, and the other terms of $f_i(x_1, x_2, \cdots, x_{nk})$ are $f_{i1}, i = 2, \cdots, k$.

Theorem 9. If $n \geq 2m^2 + m + 1$, then the function group:

$$\begin{cases} f_1(x_1, x_2, \cdots, x_{nk}) \\ f_2(x_1, x_2, \cdots, x_{nk}) \\ \qquad \cdots \\ f_k(x_1, x_2, \cdots, x_{nk}) \end{cases}$$

is a balanced function form $GF(p)^{kn}$ to $GF(p)^k$, and satisfies the strict property $B(d)$.

The proof is similar to that of the theorem (4) and (8).

Similar to theorem 5, the construction of strictly cheating immune multisecret sharing can be given easily by the construction above.

5   Conclusions

In this paper, we have presented some methods to construct the cheating immune secret sharing functions, strictly cheating immune secret sharing and multisecret sharing immune against cheating, some cryptographic properties of related schemes are analyzed as well.

Acknowledgements

We would like to thank the anonymous referees for their helpful comments and suggestions.

References

1. M.Tompa and H.Woll. How to Share a Secret with cheaters. Journal of Cryptology, Vol.1, No.2, pp.133-138, 1988.
2. Wen-Ai Jackson, Keith M.Martin and Christine M.OKeefe. Multisecret Threshold Schemes. Advance in Cryptology-Crypto' 93, Lecture Notes in Computer Science, 773, pp. 126-135, Springer-verlag, 1994.
3. Kaisa Nyberg and Lars Ramkilde Knudsen. Provable Security against Differential Cryptanalysis. Advance in CryptologyCrypto' 92, Lecture Notes in Computer Science, 740, pp. 566-574, Springer-verlag, 1992.
4. Josef Pieprzyk and Xian-Mo Zhang. Cheating Prevention in Secret sharing over $GF(p)$. INDOCRYPT 2001, Lecture Notes in Computer Science, 2247, pp. 226-243, Springer-Verlag, 2001.
5. Josef Pieprzyk and Xian-Mo Zhang. Multisecret Sharing Immune against cheating. Informatica-An International Journal of Computing and Informatics, Volume 26, Number 3, 271-278, 2002.
6. Josef Pieprzyk, Xian-Mo Zhang. Construction of cheating immune secret sharing. ICISC2001, Lecture Note in Computer Science, 2288, 226-243, Springer-Verlag2002.
7. Hossein Ghodosi, Josef Piepreyk. Cheating prevention in secret sharing. ACISP2000, Lecture Notes in Computer Science, 1841, 328-341, Springer-Verlag, 2000.
8. M. Stadler. Publicly verifiable secret sharing[A]. In Advances in cryptology. EUROCRYPT' 96[C], LNCS 1070, 190-199, Springer-Verlag, Berlin, 1996.
9. Fujisaki E, T. Okamoto. A practical and provably secure scheme for publicly verifiable secret sharing and its applications[A]. Advances in Cryptology, EUCRYPTO' 98[C], 32-47, Springer-Verlag, Berlin, 1998.
10. B. Schoenmakers. A simple publicly verifiably secret sharing scheme and its application to electronic voting[A]. CRYPTO' 99[C], 148-164, Springer-Verlag, Berlin, 1999.
11. R, J. McEliece. Finite fields for computer scientists and engineers. Kluwer Academic, 1987.
12. Wen Ping Ma, Moon Ho Lee. New methods to construct cheating immune functions. Information Security and Cryptology -ICISC2003, LNCS 2971, 79-86, Springer-Verlag, Berlin, 2003.

Detection of Unknown DoS Attacks by Kolmogorov-Complexity Fluctuation

Takayuki Furuya, Takahiro Matsuzaki, and Kanta Matsuura

Institute of Industrial Science, The University of Tokyo,
4-6-1 Komaba, Meguro-ku, Tokyo 153-8505, Japan
{matu, kanta}@iis.u-tokyo.ac.jp

Abstract. Detection of unknown Denial-of-Service (DoS) attacks is a hard issue. What attackers do is simply to consume a large amount of target resources. This simple feature allows attackers to create a wide variety of attack flows, and hence we must find a sophisticated *general metric* for detection. A possible metric is Kolmogorov Complexity (KC), a measure of the size of the smallest program capable of representing the given piece of data flows because DoS attacks, known or unknown, are anyway launched by computer programs. However, there are no established DoS-detection methods which make use of this possibility. And to make matters worse, it is well known that KC cannot be rigorously computed. In this paper, we compare three different KC estimation methods including a new proposal of our own, and propose a new DoS-detection method by monitoring *fluctuation of KC differentials*.

1 Introduction

Denial-of-Service(DoS) attacks have recently become serious [1]–[5]. What DoS attackers do is simply to consume a large amount of resources of remote targets. This simple feature allows attackers to create a wide variety of attack flows, and hence we must find a sophisticated general metric to detect such flows.

Heuristic countermeasures against DoS include tracing the attacker after being attacked like IP traceback [6], an agent-based packet marking [7], and filtering packets on the spot by watching source IP addresses of packets [8] like ingress filtering [9]. However, these countermeasures suffer from a deployment problem; they need deployment by a lot of collaborating nodes, and the cost of the deployment keeps many nodes from the deployment. Although intrusion detection systems (IDSs) can be used independently by a host being attacked, traditional IDSs [10]–[12] suffer from large false negative rates when flows are constituted from combination of DoS attacks and legitimate packets. Escape from the false-negative problem often comes to anomaly-detection approaches which in turn suffer from large false positive rates and need a help of application-specific knowledge [13] or data fusion [14]. Therefore, it is important to find a sophisticated *general metric* for DoS detection that can be used by a victim alone.

D. Feng, D. Lin, and M. Yung (Eds.): CISC 2005, LNCS 3822, pp. 395–406, 2005.

A possible metric for this purpose is Kolmogorov Complexity (KC), a measure of *the size of the smallest program capable of representing the given piece of data flows* because DoS attacks, known or unknown, are anyway launched by computer programs. There is a literature [15] which suggests this possibility. However, there are no established DoS-detection methods which make use of that suggestion. And to make matters worse, it is well known that KC cannot be rigorously computed. In other words, we must estimate the KC of the sampled flows, and then design a DoS-detection procedure based on the estimation.

In this paper, we prepare three different KC estimation methods including a new proposal of our own in Section 2. Then, in Section 3, we firstly investigate the basic characteristics of KC when used for monitoring flows that may contain DoS attack flows. Based on the results of the basic investigation, we propose a new DoS-detection method by monitoring *fluctuation of KC differentials* in Section 4. Finally, Section 5 concludes the paper.

2   Background Knowledge

2.1   Kolmogorov Complexity

KC is regarded as the minimum size of programs which produce given data. The KC of a finite binary string x is defined as follows [16]:

$$\min_{p:\mathcal{U}(p)=x} l(p) \tag{1}$$

where $l(x)$ is the length of string x, $\mathcal{U}$ is a universal computer, and $\mathcal{U}(p)$ is the output of a program p by $\mathcal{U}$.

Let us suppose a completely random string. The length of a program which produces such a random string completely depends on the length of the string. In other words, programs to generate other strings should be smaller than the ones to generate completely random strings. This line of thought can be expressed in the following formula if we denote KC of a binary string X by $K(X)$.

$$K(X_1 \| X_2) \leq K(X_1) + K(X_2) + \log l(X_1 \| X_2) + c \tag{2}$$

where $X_1 \| X_2$ is the concatenated string of X_1 and X_2, and c is a constant.

For further details, [17] is to be referred, but we explain the reason why we are interested in the use of KC for DoS detection by showing an intuitive example. Consider two strings $X_1 = 10010110101110\ldots$ and $X_2 = 01101001010001\ldots$. Each of the two strings looks random but they are strongly associated with each other. The right-hand side of the formula (2) depends on the length of the string X_1 as well as that of X_2. On the other hand, the program description of X_1 can be used to produce X_2 in a program that produces the concatenated string $X_1 \| X_2$ in the left-hand side of (2). Therefore, the KC of the concatenated string becomes smaller than the right-hand side of (2).

This line of thought could be applied to detect DoS attacks as follows: if the value of the left-hand side of (2) becomes much smaller than that of the right-hand side, we might be able to judge the suspicious flow is generated by a small number of programs, possibly DoS-attack tools.

2.2 Estimation of Kolmogorov Complexity

In [16], it was proved that KC cannot be rigorously computed. Therefore, if we want to implement an application that uses KC, we must somehow estimate KC.

Probabilistic Method. In the related study [15], they suggest that one may be able to find the suspicious flow including DoS attacks when the value of the left-hand side of (2) becomes much smaller than the value of the right-hand side. When they tested this idea for DoS detection, they calculated the following differential at probes by sampling packets regularly:

$$\{K(X_1) + K(X_2) + ... + K(X_m)\} - K(X_1||X_2|| ... ||X_m). \tag{3}$$

If this value (we will refer to this as KC differential, in the following) is close to 0, the suspicious flow is thought to be legitimate. On the other hand, if packets have high correlation, data string $X_1 X_2 \ldots X_m$ can be expressed by a smaller program, so the value of (3) becomes larger. The KC estimation method proposed in [15] is as follows:

$$\hat{K}(X) \approx l(X) H \left(\frac{X\#1}{X\#1 + X\#0} \right) + \log_2 \{l(X)\} \tag{4}$$

where

$$H(p) = -p \log_2 p - (1 - p) \log_2 (1 - p) \tag{5}$$

$X\#1$ and $X\#0$ are the number of 1's and 0's in X, respectively.

However, by our observation, this estimation method raises a problem. For example, the estimated value of the KC of

- a data string in which the same number of 1's and 0's appear alternately (e.g. "1010101010101010")

is equal to that of

- a data string of the same length in which the same number of 1's and 0's appear not alternately but randomly (e.g. "1001101011101000"),

although a shorter program can be used for producing the former alternate string than that for the latter random string.

Estimation by Lempel Ziv. In our study, we also test "Lempel Ziv 78" KC estimation method (hereafter, we will refer to this method simply as *Lempel Zip*) [18]. Lempel Ziv partitions a given string into prefixes that has not appeared before. This algorithm makes codebook that will enable long strings to be encoded with small indexes. Suppose there is a binary string as follows:

10110100100110100100111010010011000010.

This string can be partitioned as follows:

$$1,0,11,01,00,10,011,010,0100,111,01001,001,100,010.$$

If there are fewer partitioned strings and longer ones, the string is thought to be highly correlated with partitioned strings that are previously appeared. Therefore, it is possible to refer to the program routine used to describe the former strings when we describe the script for the partitioned strings. So, the size of the program to describe whole the string becomes smaller and the value of KC becomes smaller, too. There have been proposed revised version of Lempel Ziv, so [18] may be referred to for further details. In our study, we implement Lempel Ziv by using the following formula:

$$\hat{K}(X) \approx L\{2 + \log_2(L - 2)\} \tag{6}$$

where L is the number of the partitioned strings. If there are smaller number of partitioned strings, the size of the program to describe whole the string becomes smaller, therefore the value of KC becomes smaller.

Our Proposal for KC Estimation. When we try to detect DoS attacks, it is necessary to sample packets in the same flow and to examine the correlation in the data string X itself in order to avoid the problem observed for the probabilistic KC estimation method. Hence, our KC estimation of X includes the examination of the correlation between the first half F_X and the second half S_X of the bitstring $X = F_X || S_X$. In particular, we take bitwise logical equivalence of F_X and S_X, and sum up all the outputs of the equivalence operations. Let us denote the sum by n (e.g. $n=2$ when $X = \underline{00}1 || \underline{01}1$ where the underlined bits contribute to the sum). Intuitively, n shows how similar the string S_X is to the string F_X or the string $\bar{F}_X$, in which each bit of the number of F_X is inverted. Finally, our KC estimation method is as follows:

$$\hat{K}(X) \approx l(X) P\left(\frac{n}{\frac{l(X)}{2}}\right) + \log_2 l(X) \tag{7}$$

where

$$P(y) = \begin{cases} 2y & \text{if } 0 \leq y < \dfrac{1}{2} \\ 2 - 2y & \text{if } \dfrac{1}{2} \leq y \leq 1. \end{cases}$$

3   Basic Experiments

The existing work [15] shows nothing but a brief suggestion about the use of KC for DoS detection. As mentioned in the introduction, in order to make use of this suggestion, we must somehow estimate the KC of the sampled flows, and then design a specific DoS-detection procedure. So we start from investigation about how each KC estimation works when DoS attacks come.

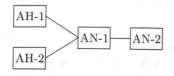

Fig. 1. Network topology used in the experiment

3.1   Detection by KC Differential Itself

First, we sample packets from a flow, and calculate KC of each packet($X_1, X_2, ...$) and of the concatenation of them all. Next, we use the resultant KC values to calculate KC differential written as (3).

The authors of [15] observed that the KC differential of packets X_1, X_2, ..., X_m generated by one attacking program was larger than that of a legitimate flow generated by many independent programs installed at different places. So they hoped that, if the KC differential is larger than a certain threshold, the suspicious flow could be thought to include DoS attacks. By contrast, if the KC differential is smaller than the threshold, the flow is thought to be legitimate. The threshold would be decided experimentally.

The existing study [15] suggested the idea explained in the previous paragraph. However, it doesn't include enough information to re-experiment. That is, the description of concrete procedure (including sampling) is not given there, and hence one could not be sure whether their implementation is tuned up well for DoS detection or not.

Therefore, in this section, we firstly compare the result which can be achieved by the KC estimation method used in the study [15], the result by Lempel Ziv, and the result by our KC estimation method. Thus we experimentally explore toward the best KC estimation method to detect DoS attacks.

3.2   Network Setup

In the same way as in [15], the network topology was set for this experiment as illustrated in Fig 1. We are going to examine the possibility of detecting DoS attacks against the node AN-2 at the node AN-1. Regarding OS, we used Windows XP Home Edition at the node AN-1, Windows Me at AH-1, and Vine Linux version 2.5 at AH-2.

The study [15] compares

- the KC differential which is computed by their KC estimation method when there is a flooding from AH-2 to AN-2 and nothing from AH-1

with

- the KC differential when there are a flooding from AH-2 to AN-2 and legitimate packets sent from AH-1 to AN-2.

The study [15] didn't examine a case in which all the packets coming to AN-2 are composed of legitimate ones. Therefore, as a comprehensive study, we examine the legitimate-flow-only case as well in the next section.

In summary, we examine the following three cases:

((**Flooding**)).   There is a flooding (either Syn Flood or ICMP echo flood) from
   AH-2 to AN-2 but nothing else.

((**Mixed flow**)).   There is a flooding (either Syn Flood or ICMP echo flood)
   from AH-2 to AN-2 as well as a legitimate flow from AH-1 to AN-2.

((**Legitimate**)).   There is a legitimate flow from AH-1 to AN-2 but nothing
   else.

3.3   Sampling Packets

By using popular simulation tools such as synk4, we generated Syn flood or
ICMP echo flood as a DoS attack flow from node AH-2 to AN-1. Also, we
adopted apache [19] to set up a web server at AN-2 and browsed the website by
a browser operated at AH-1 in order to generate a legitimate flow between AH-1
and AN-2. We used WinDump [20] for extraction of packets.

We sampled packets for 20 seconds for the previously mentioned three cases:
((Flooding)), ((Mixed flow)), and ((Legitimate)). We tried a lot of different sampling intervals between 0.1 and 1 second. Foe instance, we collected 200 packets
when the sampling interval was 0.1 (most-frequently sampled case), and collected 20 packets when the sampling interval was 1 (least-frequently sampled
cases).

3.4   Results

When we used Syn flood as an attack, the KC differentials for different sampling
intervals were computed as shown in Figs. 2 (a), 3 (a), and 4 (a). Figures 2 (a),
3 (a), and 4 (a) were obtained when we estimated KC by using the method in
[15], Lempel Ziv, and our method, respectively. In those figures, the horizontal

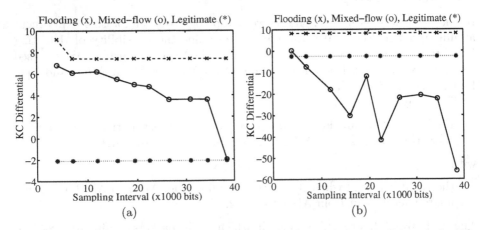

Fig. 2. KC differentials (vertical axis) for different sampling intervals (horizontal axis)
when we use KC estimation method by [15]. (a) is in the case of Syn Flood attack, and
(b) is in the case of ICMP echo flood.

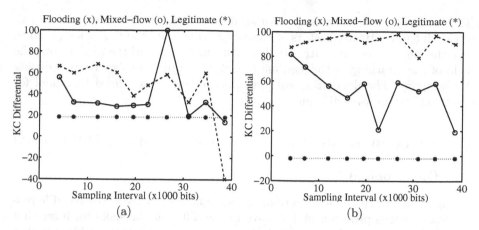

Fig. 3. KC differentials for different sampling intervals when we use KC estimation method by Lempel Ziv. (a) is in the case of Syn Flood attack, and (b) is in the case of ICMP echo flood.

axis shows sampling interval by bit($\times 10^3$) and the vertical axis shows KC differential. The solid lines correspond to the case of ((Mixed flow)), the dashed lines correspond to the case of ((Flooding)), and the dotted lines correspond to the case of ((Legitimate)). Likewise, when we used ICMP echo flood as an attack, the KC differentials for different sampling intervals were computed as shown in Figs. 2 (b), 3 (b), and 4 (b).

Figures 2–4 tell us that one will face a limitation of the DoS detection method suggested in [15]; since we have no normalization method regarding the KC differentials, we have no idea of finding a fixed threshold for detecting different attacks. To make matters worse, the solid lines (i.e. the KC differentials for the

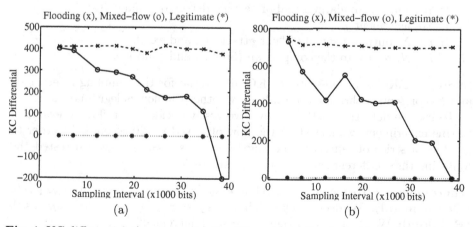

Fig. 4. KC differentials (vertical axis) for different sampling intervals (horizontal axis) when we use our KC estimation method. (a) is in the case of Syn Flood attack, and (b) is in the case of ICMP echo flood.

((Mixed flow)) case) show fluctuation for different sampled intervals. In the real-world, due to legitimate packets of lower-layer protocols, the flow is supposed to be either mixed flow or legitimate flow. And in the case of the mixed flow, the ratio of the attacking to the legitimate packets are most likely changing during the sampling. The fluctuation suggests that to find such a fixed threshold for detection is even more difficult.

4   Detection by Monitoring Fluctuation of KC-Differential

4.1   Our Proposal

As suggested in the previous section, the straightforward use of the KC differential has a serious problem: we will have to use different threshold for flows that have different ratios of attacks to legitimate packets. Another problem is that we must use different threshold to detect different DoS attacks, which suggests this naive method cannot be used for detection of unknown DoS attacks.

However, let us have a different, positive look at the KC differential fluctuation. In short, we can observe that changing sampling intervals would be helpful for DoS detection. We can expect that some amount of legitimate packets are anyway included in the flow even when attacked. Therefore, the KC differential under attack should be decreased when we increase the sampling interval. On the other hand, when no attack is contained in the flow, KC differential should remain almost the same value for different sampling intervals.

So we propose the following DoS-detection method.

1. Prepare a series of different sampling intervals s_1, s_2, $\cdots$, s_N according to a sampling-change strategy.
2. Initialize $j := 1$;
3. Check whether $|\Delta KC(s_j) - \Delta KC(s_{j+1})| > \delta$ or not.
4. If Yes, output an alarm signal of "attack detected", and exit.
5. If No, increment j.
6. If $j = N$, output a signal of "not attacked", and exit.
7. If $j < N$, return to the comparison (Step 3) and continue.

In Step 3, $\Delta KC(s_j)$ represents the KC differential for the sampling interval s_j, and δ represents a threshold to evaluate whether the flow is legitimate or not.

To use the detection method above, we firstly decide which flow to evaluate; in this experiment, we picked up the flow observed for 20 seconds. In order to produce a series of different sampling intervals s_1, s_2, $\cdots$, s_N, we tested the following three different sampling-change strategies:

(Incremental): We increment s_j. That is, $s_2 - s_1 = s_3 - s_2 = \cdots = s_N - s_{N-1} > 0$.
(Decremental): We decrement s_j. That is, $s_2 - s_1 = s_3 - s_2 = \cdots = s_N - s_{N-1} < 0$.
(Random): We randomly change s_j when we increment j.

4.2 Evaluation

Evaluation for DoS attack detection performance is done in the following way.

We heuristically optimized the threshold δ but used the same value for the same combination of KC estimation method and sampling-change strategy. That is, the threshold is fixed regardless of the simulated attacks. This means that we do not use prior knowledge about attacks to be detected.

The results obtained when we use the incremental strategy, the decremental strategy, and the random strategy, are shown in Tables 1, 2, and 3, respectively.

As clearly shown in those tables, our KC estimation method gives much smaller false positive rates (FPRs) and false negative rates (FNRs) than the other methods. The difference among the three sampling-change strategies are not evident. However, for any of the three strategies, we can see that our KC estimation method gives FPRs and FNRs that are small enough to motivate us to go further studies in this direction.

4.3 Discussion

This paper considers the following six methods to detect DoS attacks:

1. Evaluate the absolute values of KC differential by using [15]'s KC estimation method.
2. Evaluate the KC differential fluctuation by using the KC estimation method proposed in [15].
3. Evaluate the absolute values of KC differential by using the Lempel Ziv KC estimation method.
4. Evaluate the KC differential fluctuation by using the Lempel Ziv KC estimation method.
5. Evaluate the absolute values of KC differential by using our KC estimation method.
6. Evaluate the KC differential fluctuation by using our KC estimation method.

In addition, we test three different strategies (Incremental, Decremental, and Random) for changing sampling intervals when we use the three methods 2, 4, and 6. It should be noted that the only one existing paper that uses KC for DoS detection [15] suggests the method 1 only. The other five methods were tested by us in this paper for the first time.

Table 1. False positive rate (FPR) and false negative rate (FNR) obtained when we used the incremental strategy for changing the sampling intervals

Estimation (Attack)	FPR [%]	FNR [%]
Kulkarni's (Syn flood)	26.2	47.4
Kulkarni's (ICMP echo flood)	30.8	10.2
Ours (Syn flood)	7.4	18.6
Ours (ICMP echo flood)	0.5	0.6

Table 2. False positive rate (FPR) and false negative rate (FNR) obtained when we used the decremental strategy for changing the sampling intervals

Estimation (Attack)	FPR [%]	FNR [%]
Kulkarni's (Syn flood)	32.2	50.7
Kulkarni's (ICMP echo flood)	29.9	7.9
Ours (Syn flood)	3.9	18.1
Ours (ICMP echo flood)	0.6	8.9

Table 3. False positive rate (FPR) and false negative rate (FNR) obtained when we randomly changed sampling intervals

Estimation (Attack)	FPR [%]	FNR [%]
Kulkarni's (Syn flood)	29.2	49.0
Kulkarni's (ICMP echo flood)	30.3	17.0
Ours (Syn flood)	7.6	18.3
Ours (ICMP echo flood)	8.6	12.7

The methods 1, 3, and 5 have the problems mentioned at the beginning of subsection 4.1. The method 2, 4, and 6 are better than the methods 1, 3, and 5 in this respect. Among the method 2, 4, and 6, the method 6 is by far the best in terms of FNR and FPR.

One might wonder why our method based on KC works so well by asking about the idea that legitimate flows are typically random while malicious packages are strongly correlated (for example, by asking whether the idea is a generally accepted and realistic assumption or not). However, our results do not support that idea; even if we are allowed to say KC represents randomness, the randomness itself cannot be used for detection of unknown DoS attacks as shown in Section 3. Instead, our DoS detection method watches how significantly the randomness changes when the sampling interval is changed. This paper experimentally supports the effectiveness of that method although deeper theoretical discussion is left as a future work.

Other future works include implementation issues. Although one would be afraid that the proposed method might need too much computation to realize real-time detection, we do not have to be pessimistic. In the area of intrusion detection, there are a lot of experiences for reducing computational cost [21]. Since the proposed detection method uses basic logical and arithmetic operations, there is a good hope of having efficient implementation. When we look around existing works, even the analysis of large firewall logs was studied [22] where DoS detection is within their scope as well. And fortunately, Figs. 2–4 suggest that we can use the same detection method even when the sampling intervals are confined within a region of large intervals. So there is a possibility for us to find an efficient sampling-change strategies by using a limited region of sampling intervals. The similarities of the FNR and FPR performances among the three sampling-change strategies are good news for us as well; we may be able to integrate them in a dynamic way to seek for better efficiency. Although we have started the efficiency improvement according to the observation above, we do not report it in this paper due to the immaturity of the results and the lack of space. Finally, the feature of KC as a layer-independent general metric is worth noting; this feature suggests a possibility of integration with other methods [23]–[25] including detection methods in lower-layers [26] and OS [27]. If the situation allows us to regard the speed as an insignificant matter, then integration with a meta-level metric such as attacking spectrum [28] would be a possible direction as well.

5   Concluding Remarks

This paper firstly examined the detailed features of Kolmogorov Complexity (KC) when it is used for DoS detection without prior knowledge about specific attacks. After observing the features, we reached our proposal of a new DoS detection method: monitoring the fluctuation of KC differentials for different sampling intervals of the flow. The best implementation that uses our own KC estimation method gives remarkably better false negative rates and false positive rates than the other implementations.

We hope that information-theoretic insights would contribute to solutions for difficult network-security issues as the KC did in this study.

References

1. "Distributed   Denial   of   Service   (DDoS)   Attacks/tools".   `http://staff.washington.edu/dittrich/misc/ddos/`
2. Felix Lau, Stuart H. Rubin, Michael H. Smith, and Ljiljana Trajovic, "Distributed Denial of Service Attacks", In Proceedings of IEEE International Conference on Systems, Man, and Cybernetics, pp.2275–2280, October 2000.
3. Jussipekka Leiwo, Tuomas Aura, and Pekka Nikander, "Towards Network Denial of Service Resistant Protocols", In Proceedings of the 15th International Information Security Conference (IFIP/SEC 2000), Kluwer, pp.301–310, August 2000.
4. K. Matsuura and H. Imai, "Modified Aggressive Modes of Internet Key Exchange Resistant against Denial-of-Service Attacks", IEICE Transactions on Information and Systems, vol.E83-D, no.5, pp.972–979, May 2000.
5. J. Mirkovic and P. Reiher, "A Taxonomy of DDoS Attack and DDoS Defense Mechanisms", ACM SIGCOMM Computer Communication Review, vol.34, no.2, pp.39–54, April 2004.
6. H. Alifri, "IP Traceback: A New Denial-of-Service Deterrent?" IEEE Security & Privacy, Vol.1, No.3, MAY/JUNE 2003.
7. U. K. Tupakula and V. Varadharajan, "A Practical Method to Counteract Denial of Service Attacks", In Proceedings of the 26th Australasian Computer Science Conference (ACSC2003), Volume 16, Feb. 2003.
8. T. Peng, C. Leckie, and K. Ramamohanarao, "Detecting Distributed Denial of Service Attacks Using Source IP Address Monitoring", manuscript, ARC Special Research Center for Ultra-Broadband Information Networks.
9. P.Ferguson and D.Senie, "Network Ingress Filtering: Defeating Denial of Service Attacks Which Employ IP Source Address Spoofing", RFC 2827, May 2000.

10. D. Denning, "An Intrusion-Detection Model", IEEE Transactions on Software Engineering, vol.13, no.2, pp.222-232, 1987.
11. M. Thottan and C. Ji, "Proactive Anomaly Detection Using Distributed Intelligent Agents", IEEE Network, vol.12, no.5, pp.21-27, 1998.
12. R. A. Kemmerer and G. Vigna, "Intrusion Detection: A Brief History and Overview", Supplement to IEEE Computer, Security & Privacy, pp.27-30, 2002.
13. C. Krügel, T. Toth, and E. Kirda, "Service Specific Anomaly Detection for Network Intrusion Detection", In Proceedings of the 2002 ACM Symposium on Applied Computing, pp. 201–208, March 2002.
14. C. Siaterlis and B. Maglaris, "Towards Multisensor Data Fusion for DoS Detection", In Proceedings of the 2004 ACM Symposium on Applied Computing, pp.439–446, 2004.
15. A.B.Kulkarni, S.F.Bush, and S.C.Evans, "Detecting Distributed Denial-of-Service Attacks Using Kolmogorov Complexity Metrics", Tech. Report, GE Research & Development Center, 2001CRD176, December 2001 (Class 1)
16. T. Cover and J. Thomas, Elements of Information Theory. John Wiley & Sons, Inc., New York, pp.144-153, 1991.
17. Ming Li and Paul Vitanyi, "An Introduction to Kolmogorov Complexity and Its Applications". Springer, Berlin, 1993
18. S. C. Evans et al., "Kolmogorov Complexity Estimation and Analysis", Tech. Report, GE Research & Development Center, 2002GRC177, October 2002(Class 1)
19. http://www.apache.org/dyn/closer.cgi
20. http://netgroup-serv.polito.it/windump/install/Default.htm
21. H. Dreger, A. Feldmann, V. Paxson, and R. Sommer, "Operational Experiences with High-Volume Network Intrusion Detection", In Proceedings of the 11th ACM conference on Computer and Communications Security, pp. 2–11, October 2004.
22. H. Tongshen, Xiamin, C. Qingzhang, and Y. Kezhen, "Design and Implement of Firewall-Log-Based Online Attack Detection System", In Proceedings of the 3rd International Conference on Information Security (InfoSecu'04), pp. 146–149, November 2004.
23. Jelena Mirkovic et al., "A Taxonomy of DDoS Attacks and DDoS Defense Mechanisms", Tech. Report, UCLA CSD, CSD-TR-020018, 2002.
24. S. Cheung and K. N. Levitt, "Protecting Routing Infrastructures from Denial of Service Using Cooperative Intrusion Detection", In Proc. of New Security Paradigms Workshop '97, pp.94-106, September 1997.
25. J. Sun, H. Jin, H. Chen, Q. Zhang, and Z. Han, "A Compound Intrusion Detection Model". In Proc. of ICICS (5th International Conference on Information and Communication's Security), LNCS 2836, pp.370–381, October 2003.
26. W. Xu, T. Wood, W. Trappe, and Y. Zhang, "Wireless Monitoring and Denial of Service: Channel Surfing and Spatial Retreats: Defenses against Wireless Denial of Service", In Proceedings of the 2004 ACM Workshop on Wireless Security, pp. 80–89, October 2004.
27. F. Kargl, J. Maier, and M. Weber, "Protecting Web Servers from Distributed Denial of Service Attacks", In Proceedings of the 10th International Conference on World Wide Web, pp. 514–524, 2001.
28. A. Hussain, J. Heidemann, and C. Papadopoulos, "Denial-of-Service: A Framework for Classifying Denial of Service Attacks", In Proceedings of the 2003 Conference on Applications, Technologies, Architectures, and Protocols for Computer Communications, pp. 99–110, August 2003.

MIPv6 Binding Update Protocol
Secure Against Both Redirect and DoS Attacks[*]

Hyun-Sun Kang and Chang-Seop Park

Department of Computer Science,
Dankook University,
Chonan, Choongnam, Republic of Korea, 330-714
{sshskang, csp0}@dankook.ac.kr

Abstract. We propose a new binding update (BU) protocol between mobile node (MN) and correspondent node (CN) for the purpose of preventing redirect attacks and DoS attacks observed from the existing BU protocols and enhancing the efficiency of the BU protocol. Home agent plays a role of both authentication server validating BU message and session key distribution center for MN and CN. Also proposed is stateless Diffie-Hellman key agreement based on cryptographically generated address (CGA). Security of our proposed protocol is analyzed and compared with other protocols.

1 Introduction

Mobile IPv6 (MIPv6) [1] has been designed as a solution for enabling a wireless mobile node (MN) to move freely from one point of attachment to the IPv6 Internet to another, without disrupting ongoing transport connection. In MIPv6, two types of IPv6 addresses are defined for MN. The one of them is a fixed home address (HoA) on MN's home network, and the other is a care-of address (CoA) on the foreign network that is dynamically assigned to MN when it moves into the foreign network. In order for the MN to receive the packets destined to its home address, while it is away from home, it should perform a home registration notifying its home agent (HA) of a new CoA by sending a binding update (BU) message. HA updates the mobility binding for the MN, which is an association between the HoA and the CoA, as a result of successful binding update. So, all the subsequent packets for MN can be tunneled to MN through HA. When a stationary host (called correspondent node, CN) wants to send packets to MN, they will be first sent to the MN's HoA since it does not know the MN's current CoA. Then, HA on the MN's home network will relay the packets to the MN's CoA. However, MN can respond by sending directly to CN. The route optimization mechanism introduced in MIPv6 can be used to solve the above triangular routing problem. After receiving a BU message from MN, CN keeps MN's HoA and CoA in the binding cache entry and can send packets directly to MN. However, if BU messages are not authenticated at all, several redirect and denial-of service (DoS) attacks can be possible. Suppose CN is communicating with MN. The attacker sends

---

[*] This work was supported (in part) by the Ministry of Information & Communications, Korea, under the Information Technology Research Center (ITRC) Support Program.

D. Feng, D. Lin, and M. Yung (Eds.): CISC 2005, LNCS 3822, pp. 407–418, 2005.
© Springer-Verlag Berlin Heidelberg 2005

to CN a spoofed BU message conveying both MN's HoA and the attacker's address as MN's CoA, in order to redirect packets intended for MN to the attacker. Furthermore, the packets for MN can be redirected to any other host to do flooding attack against it or the subnet to which it belongs. Besides them, several potential attacks against the unauthenticated BU message have been observed [2, 3, 4]. Eventually, the BU messages to CN should be protected.

Most of authentication mechanisms proposed so far for protecting BU protocol between MN and CN do not depend on any security infrastructures such as public key infrastructure (PKI) or trusted key distribution center (KDC), so that how to establish a security association between MN and CN is the main point of the proposed authentication mechanisms. The return routability (RR) procedure included in MIPv6 [1] and the cryptographically generated address (CGA) [5, 6] are used to protect the BU messages exchanged between MN and CN. However, those schemes are insecure and inefficient.

In this paper, we propose a new BU protocol between MN and CN for the purpose of mitigating the security problems observed from the existing BU protocols and enhancing the efficiency of the BU protocol. In Section 2, previous works related with our proposal are introduced. A new secure and efficient binding update protocol is proposed and analyzed in Section 3 and 4, respectively. A comparative analysis with other BU protocols will be also given in Section 5. Finally, concluding remarks are given in Section 6.

2 Previous Works and Their Problems

The main part of secure BU protocols between MN and CN is a mechanism for CN to verify both HoA and CoA sent by MN, namely for CN to assure itself that MN is in fact addressable at its claimed CoA as well as at its HoA. Therefore, the mechanism should be properly designed in such a way to stand against various types of redirect and DoS attacks. In this section, we analyze the mechanisms proposed so far to protect the BU messages, and point out the observed vulnerabilities or weaknesses.

2.1 Return Routability Procedure

The RR procedure [1] cooperates in enhancing the security of the BU protocol of MIPv6. The main purpose of the RR procedure is to establish a kind of session key called "binding management key (Kbm)" between MN and CN, which will be used to protect the subsequent binding update (BU) / binding acknowledgement (BA) messages. For this purpose, CN generates and sends two keying materials, kh and kc, to MN through MN's HoA and CoA, respectively. The keying materials are computed based on HoA and CoA, respectively, together with CN's secret key. If MN really owns both HoA and CoA, MN can receive two keying materials based on which session key $Kbm = h(kh, kc)$ can be computed, where $h()$ is one-way hash function.

However, the RR procedure has a security weakness. The RR procedure does not provide a strong binding between HoA and CoA. Suppose kh_1 and kc_1 are exchanged between MN_1 and CN for HoA_1 and CoA_1, and kh_2 and kc_2 are exchanged between MN_2 and CN for HoA_2 and CoA_2. Since two messages conveying the keying materials are sent without encryption, the keying materials can be easily eavesdropped, so that the attacker can derive a valid session key $Kbm' = h(kh_1 \mid kc_2)$ to fabricate a false BU message for HoA_1 and CoA_2. Furthermore, the RR procedure is not efficient since it accompanies 8 distinct message flows to complete one BU protocol run.

2.2 BU Protocols Based on CGA

CGA is used to derive a 64-bit interface identifier of the IPv6 address for the purpose of binding the IPv6 address of MN to its public key. Given MN's public key PK_{MN} and private signing key SK_{MN}, the interface identifier (IID) of MN's HoA is derived from h(subnet prefix of HoA, PK_{MN}). A detailed process of generating a CGA is given in [7]. In CGA-based BU protocol in [5], the MN sends to CN a BU message (<u>CoA</u>, <u>CN</u>, HoA, ... , PK_{MN}, $Sig(SK_{MN})$), where two underlined fields represent the source/destination addresses and $Sig(SK_{MN})$ is a digital signature generated using MN's private signing key SK_{MN}. The CN verifies the signature using the public key, PK_{MN}, after checking if the IID of HoA can be derived from the public key. DoS attack against CN can be mounted by sending a storm of above BU messages to CN since CN should perform several signature verification operations which are computationally expensive.

In a basic SUCV protocol [6], a more refined CGA-based BU protocol is proposed using a concept of Client Puzzle [12] to cope with DoS attack against CN. However, the time required to solve the puzzle has an undesirable effect on the efficiency of BU protocol. The basic SUCV protocol also uses Diffie-Hellman (D-H) key agreement to share a common key between CN and MN. In sucvP2 message, the D-H public value g^y (mod p) is not protected at all so that the man-in-the-middle (MITM) attack can be mounted, where g is a generator of a group Z_p and p is a large prime. One solution to this problem is for CN to use CGA and sign the sucvP2 message. Unfortunately, the solution gives rise to another DoS attack against CN, namely if MN sends a storm of faked sucvP1 messages to CN, CN should perform a lot of public key operations to sign the corresponding sucvP2 messages. Basically, the BU protocol based on CGA [5, 6] gives a computational burden to the hardware-limited MN since each BU message requires MN to generate a digital signature.

2.3 BU Protocols Based on Security Proxy

In other proposals for securing BU protocols [6, 8, 9], MN's HA plays a role of a security proxy for the purpose of offloading a burden of performing public key operations from the hardware-limited MN. When MN sends a request message to HA, MN's HA starts an authenticated D-H key agreement protocol with CN, in order to create a session key between HA and CN. Using a response message, the session key is securely transported to MN. Then, the session key can be used to secure BU and BA messages between MN and CN. The BU protocol proposed in [8] is based on the existence of a global-wide PKI for authenticated D-H key agreement, so that it is limited for practical deployment. Instead of employing a global PKI, both an extended SUCV protocol in [6] and a variant of [8] proposed in [9] use a CGA-based digital signature for authenticated D-H key agreement between HA and CN.

Unfortunately, the BU protocol in [9] has a fatal security flaw. Namely, HA generates a CGA using a pair of its public and private signing key, and then constructs a self-signed public-key certificate using its private signing key. The certificate is used for authenticated D-H key agreement between HA and CN. However, since the certificate is self-signed, any node whose IPv6 address is CGA can construct its own self-signed certificate and then pretend to CN that it is HA serving a specific MN. In other word, an attacker can mount several attacks against both MN and CN.

3 A New Proposal

3.1 Design Principles

Our design starts with a fact that MN's HA has already maintained correct and fresh binding information supplied by MN through home registration. So, it is assumed that MN does not register incorrect CoA during home registration since misbehaving MN for redirect or DoS attacks can be traced through HA and consequently home agent service to MN can be terminated. This kind of assumption has also been mentioned in [10, pp. 158]. Consequently, it is not required for MN to prove an ownership of its CoA to HA during home registration.

A concept of CGA is also employed in our proposed protocol. However, contrary to the previous schemes [5, 6] using CGA for signing BU messages, CGA is used for the purpose of authenticated D-H key agreement between HA and CN. HA generates a HoA for MN as follows. Again, let g be a generator of a group Z_p, where p is a large prime. HA chooses a random y and computes $g^y \bmod p$. From now on, "mod p" is omitted for the simplicity of notations. The interface identifier of MN's HoA is computed as $h(\text{MN's subnet prefix}, g^y)$. At the initial service registration, the HoA is assigned to MN. It should be noted that the D-H value y is not known to MN. In the same manner, CN also generates and keeps a pair of x and g^x. CN's interface identifier is also computed as $h(\text{CN's subnet prefix}, g^x)$. Both g^x and g^y are a kind of long term key. Our CGA can be more refined to enhance the security like in [7]. With this approach, the public key operation such as signature generation or verification can be eliminated.

In our protocol, HA plays a role of both an authentication server and a key distribution center. First, when MN sends a BU message to CN, CN becomes an authenticator for the MN. Since CN does not have any information to authenticate MN, CN should ask MN's HA to authorize the message on behalf of itself, which means MN's HA becomes an authentication server (authorizer) for the CN. In other word, CN can check the validity of the BU message through HA. Second, MN's HA distributes a session key to be used between MN and CN based on both a static security association (SA) between MN and HA and a dynamically-generated SA between CN and HA. So, we assume that there is a pre-established SA between HA and MN, which is also used to secure home registration between HA and MN [11]. On the other hand, CN dynamically establishes a SA with HA using CGA-based D-H key agreement. Exploiting established security associations, the HA cooperates in sharing a new session key between MN and CN. In the following description, we will denote the concatenation operator by | and the XOR operator by $\oplus$. $H(\ )$ is the keyed hash function, and $MAC(K)$ is the MAC computed over all the preceding field values using the key K. We also use node's entity name to denote its IPv6 address.

3.2 Stateless Diffie-Hellman Key Agreement Based on CGA

In this subsection, a concept of stateless D-H key agreement is introduced, which is a main module of our proposed protocol in the following subsection. We consider a following scenario associated with D-H key agreement. Node A sends a query message to node B as in Fig.1-(a), where IPv6 addresses of node A and B are CGAs derived from D-H public values g^x and g^y, respectively. Then, the node B sends back to the node B a pair of query and response which is protected with $MAC(KS)$, where KS = $h(g^{xy})$. For the simplicity of explaining the main point, we assume here that the Query-Response protocol is performed only once between node A and node B, in order to disregard a possibility of replay attack.

Suppose node A maintains state information related with the query message it sends. Then, a stateful D-H key agreement is performed between two nodes. After sending a query message to the node B, the node A expects to receive the response message whose source address is B. Suppose an attacker wants to modify the Response and generate the corresponding $MAC(KS)$. The attacker C on the path between the node B and the node A cannot replace g^y in the response message by g^z which is the attacker's D-H public value without changing the source address B, since the one-way property of $h(\ )$ makes it infeasible for the attacker C to find g^z generating B.

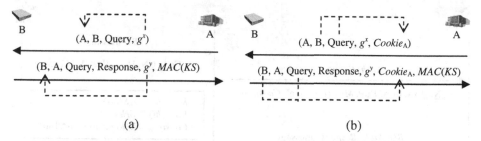

(a)   (b)

Fig. 1. Stateful and Stateless CGA-based D-H Key Agreement

On the other hand, suppose the node A does not maintain any state information related with the query message it sends. Then, a stateless D-H key agreement is performed. Since the node A does not know whom it has sent the query message to, the MITM attack can be successfully mounted as follows. As a result of substituting ($\underline{C}$, B, Query, g^z) for ($\underline{A}$, B, Query, g^x), the attacker C can share $KS_{BC} = h(g^{yz})$ with the node B. Subsequently, the attacker can modify the following response message sent from the node B.

($\underline{B}$, C, Query, Response, g^y, $MAC(KS_{BC})$)
Namely, after generating $KS_{CA} = h(g^{zx})$ to be shared with the node A, the following modified message is sent to the node A. However, the node A accepts the message as long as C can be derived from g^z and $MAC(KS_{CA})$ is valid.

(<u>C</u>, A, Query, Response', g^z, $MAC(KS_{CA})$)

In order to fix the problem in the stateless D-H key agreement, we introduce the $Cookie_A = H(K_A, B \mid Query)$ generated by the node A, as in Fig.1-(b), where K_A is node A's secret key. Since the cookie contains the information about both B and Query, the node A can check the source address of the response message, which means that the above MITM attack is not feasible. The main reason we introduce the stateless D-H key agreement is to protect the node A from DoS attacks, which will be evident in the next subsection.

3.3 Proposed Binding Update Protocol

It is assumed that HA keeps a binding cache entry for MN, which consists of MN's HoA, CoA, K_{HM}, (y, g^y), SN_{HA}, and lifetime (LT_{HA}). K_{HM} is a pre-shared symmetric key between MN and HA, and g^y, a kind of long term key, is a D-H public value used to derive a CGA for MN. SN_{HA} is a pre-shared sequence number between MN and HA through the home registration and is used to derive a session key for MN and CN. We treat MN and HA as a single entity from a security point of view. Fig.2 shows a series of messages exchanged among MN, CN, and HA for the purpose of securing binding update to CN.

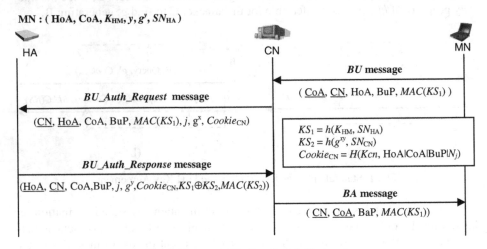

Fig. 2. Proposed Binding Update Protocol

BU message

First, MN sends to CN a *BU* message containing its HoA and new CoA together with BuP (binding update parameter). The BuP has a sequence number (SN_{CN}) field which is used to derive a session key for CN and HA and a lifetime (LT_{CN}) field. The entire *BU* message is authenticated with $MAC(KS_1)$, where $KS_1 = H(K_{HM}, SN_{HA})$. We assume that the SN_{CN} in BuP starts with a random number chosen by MN if the *BU* message is the first one to the CN.

BU_Auth_Request message

Since CN cannot process the *BU* message directly, CN constructs and sends a *BU_Auth_Request* message to HA for verification of the *BU* message on behalf of itself. However, CN does not maintain any state information about the messages it sent to HA or received from MN. A stateless D-H key agreement is performed between HA and CN. On the other hand, CN keeps an array of nonces, *ArrayN*, consisting of a pre-configured number, n, of entries. Each entry of the array consists of an index, a nonce value, a lifetime, and a flag bit called 'pending nonce'. When constructing the message, CN chooses an index j whose flag bit is set to zero, computes $Cookie_{CN} = H(Kcn, \text{HoA} \mid \text{CoA} \mid \text{BuP} \mid N_j)$ using the corresponding nonce value N_j from the array, and sets the flag to one. *Kcn* is a secret node key of CN. When a *BU_Auth_Response* message is received from HA, the flag bit corresponding to the index j in it is set to zero, and the corresponding nonce value should be updated. However, If CN does not receive the corresponding *BU_Auth_Response* message from HA within the lifetime, CN assumes packet losses to occur and the flag bit corresponding to the index j in it is set to zero, and the corresponding nonce value should be updated. Basically, CN configures a maximum number, n, of *BU* messages it can handle at the same time, each of which it is willing to assign a distinct nonce value to. So, if there is no entry whose flag bit is set to zero, additional *BU* messages should be dropped.

HA first check if both HoA and CoA contained in the message are matched with those in its binding cache. Then, HA computes KS_1 in the same way as MN did and checks if $MAC(KS_1)$ is valid. Also verified is if the interface identifier of CN can be derived from g^x. If any of three tests fails, HA drops the message silently. Otherwise, a D-H key agreement is performed based on g^x contained in the message and y contained in the binding cache for MN, and $KS_2 = H(g^{xy}, SN_{CN})$ is computed. When the *BU_Auth_Request* message is proven to be valid, HA constructs and sends to CN a *BU_Auth_Response* message authorizing the *BU* message requested by MN, which includes the information for the D-H key agreement and session key to be shared between CN and MN. The messages exchanged between HA and CN contains $Cookie_{CN}$ to make CN stateless for the purpose of defending CN against DoS attacks.

BU_Auth_Response message

After receiving the *BU_Auth_Response* message from HA, CN checks if CoA, HoA, and BuP contained in it are consistent with $Cookie_{CN}$. If they are not consistent, the message is silently dropped. Otherwise, CN performs a stateless D-H key agreement based on g^y to compute $KS_2 = H(g^{xy}, SN_{CN})$, after verifying if the interface identifier of MN can be derived from g^y and consequently KS_1 can be obtained from $KS_1 \oplus KS_2$. Now, a common session key, KS_1, is shared between MN and CN. Finally, the entire message is authenticated using $MAC(KS_2)$. If the authentication is successful, CN sets the flag bit to zero, corresponding to the index j in the message, and update the nonce value indexed by j. Otherwise, CN drops the message silently.

BA message

If the *BU_Auth_Response* message is valid, CN sends to MN a *BA* message after creating or updating the binding cache entry for MN. The message is authenticated based on $MAC(KS_1)$. BaP (binding acknowledgement parameter) contains the same values as BuP or different values modified by CN.

4 Security Analysis

In this section, we analyze the security of the proposed binding update protocol against the various threats and attacks [2, 4] observed during the process of designing several secure binding update protocols. We concentrate on both redirect attacks and resource exhaustion attacks against our BU protocol.

4.1 CGA-Based Diffie-Hellman Key Agreement

A plain D-H key agreement messages should be authenticated to prevent from the MITM attack. However, the stateless D-H key agreement based on CGA alone cannot prevent the MITM attack as explained in subsection 3.2. In our protocol, it is supplemented by both MAC and $Cookie_{CN}$. The main purpose of an attacker on the path between CN and HA is to modify a part of $BU\_Auth\_Response$ message so that CN stores a false HoA', CoA', and BuP' in its binding cache. First of all, the D-H value g^y is replaced by g^z chosen by the attacker, where HoA' is derived from g^z as one-way hash function output.

$BU\_Auth\_Response$ message = (<u>HoA</u>, <u>CN</u>, CoA, BuP, j, g^y, $Cookie_{CN}$, $KS_1 \oplus KS_2$, $MAC(KS_2)$), $KS_2 = H(g^{xy}, SN_{CN})$
$BU\_Auth\_Response$ message' = (<u>HoA'</u>, <u>CN</u>, CoA', BuP', j, g^z, $Cookie_{CN}'$, $R \oplus KS_2'$, $MAC(KS_2')$), $KS_2' = H(g^{xz}, SN_{CN})$

It should be mentioned that the attacker cannot expect a specific HoA' in advance since g^z determines HoA'. Then, the attacker should obtain the key KS_2' to compute a valid $MAC(KS_2')$ as a result of modifying a part of the message. However, there are two obstacles the attacker should jump to succeed. First, it is not possible to construct a valid $Cookie_{CN}' = H(Kcn, HoA' | CoA' | BuP' | N_j)$ since the attacker does not know the secret node key, Kcn, of CN. Furthermore, the attacker cannot split KS_1 from $KS_1 \oplus KS_2$, so that he can not construct $KS_1 \oplus KS_2'$, but $R \oplus KS_2'$, where R is a random number chosen by him. Eventually, CN obtains R instead of KS_1 so that the BA message cannot be accepted by MN, even though the attacker could compute $Cookie_{CN}'$.

4.2 Redirect and Flooding Attacks

There are two types of redirect attacks against a normal BU protocol. In the first type of redirect attack (Type 1 Redirect Attack), an attacker uses other MN's HoA fraudulently for the purpose of redirecting the message flow destined for the MN to another node. Suppose an attacker knows that MN possessing a specific HoA is communicating with CN. If the attacker can send to CN a successful BU message containing the attacker's CoA and MN's HoA, the attacker can hijack the connection between MN and CN. Using the same technique, any host in the network can be a victim of flooding attack with redirected messages. However, in our protocol, such redirect attacks are not feasible since the attacker does not have K_{HM} or KS_1 based on which the BU message can be authenticated through HA. Those keys are known only to the legitimate MN owning the specific HoA and the corresponding HA. Furthermore, since the attacker's CoA is not identical to that of binding cache for MN on the HA side, the faked BU message cannot be processed. Especially, the attacker does not know a valid pair of D-H public/secret values corresponding to the target MN's HoA.

The second type of redirect attack (Type 2 Redirect Attack) is committed by a malicious MN using his own HoA abnormally. Namely, after starting to download a big file from CN, the MN sends a false BU message to CN to redirect it to other host. Most of proposed BU protocols [1, 5, 6, 9] cannot defend against such an attack. However, such an attack can be prevented or mitigated in our protocol. HA maintains a fresh and correct pair of HoA and CoA for the malicious MN. When sending a false BU message containing HoA and a false CoA to CN, the $BU\_Auth\_Request$ message containing such information cannot be processed by HA since it does not match with the information stored in binding cache of HA. Subsequently, the malicious MN may try to forge the corresponding $BU\_Auth\_Response$ message approving its BU message as soon as sending the false BU message to CN. Because the MN does not have the D-H secret key y corresponding to his HoA, the MN cannot compute a valid $MAC(KS_2)$, so that it cannot forge the corresponding $BU\_Auth\_Response$ message. On the other hand, suppose the malicious MN registers HoA and a false CoA through home registration against our initial assumption that MN does not misbehave during its home registration. When sending a false BU message with such a false CoA to CN, the MN can successfully redirect the message flow to flood other host. However, two evidences remained at HA's and CN's binding cache can be exploited to point out the malicious MN.

4.3 Resource Exhaustion Attacks

DoS attacks exhausting the target node's memory and computing resources are major threats on the Internet. An attacker can flood a target node with a storm of messages, which causes it to perform computationally-expensive public-key operations or to create a lot of states in it during protocol executions. We show how our protocol can be protected against flooding MIPv6 nodes with a storm of false messages.

First, the attacker sends a storm of useless BU messages to CN. The CN performs a lightweight keyed hash operation to generate a cookie, but does not create any state in it for each received message. At this phase, CN does not have any efficient means to filter out such messages, so the corresponding useless $BU\_Auth\_Request$ messages are constructed and sent to HA. If there is no more nonce whose flag bit is set to zero, additional BU messages will be dropped by CN. Second, in order to defend against the attack sending a storm of $BU\_Auth\_Request$ messages, our original protocol can be slightly modified as follows. A small amount of memory called "request_identity" in addition to the binding cache entry for MN is allocated to store the sender's identity of the $BU\_Auth\_Request$ message, CN. After receiving the normal $BU\_Auth\_Request$ message from CN, HA performs a normal operation to check the validity of the message. If it is successful, HA store the identity of CN to the memory. Suppose an attacker records the $BU\_Auth\_Request$ message, and subsequently send a storm of identical $BU\_Auth\_Request$ messages to HA. HA checks if the identity of sender exists in the binding cache for MN whose home address is in the message. Since it has already existed in the binding cache, such messages are silently dropped without causing HA to perform CGA-based D-H operation. To save the memory space of request_identity, the identity stored can be deleted if we set a lifetime to it. Third, a storm of recorded identical $BU\_Auth\_Response$ messages sent to CN can be filtered out using the nonce index j. As mentioned before, CN maintains an array of nonces, $ArrayN$. In the normal operation, the flag bit corresponding to the index in the message is set to one if the processing of the message is successful. However, if several messages containing an identical index value are received, those are not processed and dropped since the flag bit has been set to zero or the corresponding index value has been changed.

4.4 Attacks Using Fictional HoAs

Even though it's not feasible to find a pair of D-H public/secret keys corresponding to a specific HoA due to a property of one-way hash function, an attacker can generate any D-H public/secret key pair, based on which he can fabricate an fictional HoA, and he can subsequently send a faked BU message to CN. Due to this weakness, CN's binding update cache might be filled with useless binding information if a storm of faked BU messages are received and processed by CN. This problem is applicable not only to our protocol, but also to other CGA-based BU protocol [5, 6, 7, 9]. However, we show here that such attack is not effective for our protocol.

Suppose an attacker generates a set of D-H parameters (z_1, g^{z_1}), (z_2, g^{z_2}), ..., (z_m, g^{z_m}), and then derives the corresponding fictional IPv6 HoAs (HoA$_1$, HoA$_2$, ..., HoA$_m$) together with arbitrary CoAs (CoA$_1$, CoA$_2$, ..., CoA$_m$). The attacker now constructs and sends to CN several faked BU messages (BU_1, BU_2, ..., BU_m) based on the fictional HoAs and CoAs. After receiving BU_i for $i = 1, 2, ..., m$, CN sends the corresponding $BU\_Auth\_Request_i$ message to HA which is associated with HoA$_i$ in the faked BU_i message. However the message is not processed by the HA since the HoA$_i$ is fictional. When sending each faked BU_i message, the attacker can also construct and send faked $BU\_Auth\_Response_i$ message to CN for the purpose of both making CN perform several D-H operations and CN's binding cache to be filled with useless information. In order for each faked $BU\_Auth\_Response_i$ message to be processed by CN, the message should contain the cookie generated by CN, which means that the attacker should overhear each $BU\_Auth\_Request_i$ message generated by CN, and the attacker should perform several D-H operations same as CN does. So, sending a storm of faked BU messages based on fictional HoAs is not effective for DoS attack against CN.

5 Comparative Analysis

A long latency associated with Mobile IPv6's BU protocol can significantly impact delay-sensitive applications. Therefore, it is desirable to minimize the number of message flows among MIPv6 entities during BU protocol. As shown in Table 1, our protocol and Basic SUCV protocol are most efficient in terms of the number of message flows. Also shown are the comparative amounts of both Diffie-Hellman and digital signature operations performed by MN, CN, and HA.

Except for the Return Routability procedure [1] which has fatal security vulnerabilities, our protocol is also more efficient than other protocols in terms of computational complexity of performing public key operations. For security comparisons, we selected three attacks mentioned in Section 4, two types of redirect attacks and resource exhaustion attack. Even though not shown at the above table, the proposed BU protocols including ours are secure against other attacks such as reflection and amplification attacks which are usually mentioned [2, 3, 4] in designing a secure BU protocol.

Table 1. Comparisons of our Protocol with other Protocols

[1] Return Routability [6-1] Basic SUCV   [6-2] Extended SUCV [8] PKI-based Proxy
[9] CGA-based Proxy
DH = the number of D-H operations
DS = the number of digital signature generations / verification operations

	[1]	[6-1]	[6-2]	[8]	[9]	Our Proposal
# of message flows	8	4	7	9	9	4
MN's computation	None	DH(1) DS(2)	None	None	None	None
CN's computation	None	DH(1) DS(2)	DH(1) DS(2)	DH(1) DS(1)	DH(1) DS(1)	DH(1) DS(0)
HA's computation	None	None	DH(1) DS(2)	DH(1) DS(1)	DH(1) DS(1)	DH(1) DS(0)
Security Infrastructure	None	None	None	PKI	None	None
Redirect Attack (Type 1)	Insecure	Secure	Secure	Secure	Insecure	Secure
Redirect Attack (Type 2)	Insecure	Insecure	Insecure	Mitigated	Insecure	Mitigated
Resource Exhaustion Attack	Secure	Insecure	Insecure	Secure	Insecure	Secure
Attack using fictional HoA	Insecure	Insecure	Insecure	Secure	Insecure	Secure

6   Concluding Remarks

We have proposed a new secure and efficient BU protocol between MN and CN for route optimization. Our approach has been to test the validity of new BU information through HA as a kind of security proxy, assuming that HA keeps fresh and correct BU information. HA also plays a role of session key distribution center for MN and CN. Also proposed has been a new feature called stateless Diffie-Hellman key agreement protocol based on CGA, which allows MN to do non-public-key operations and generates a couple of new security association among MN, CN, and HA. Our protocol is also shown to be more secure and efficient than other protocols.

References

1. Johnson, D., Perkins, C. and Arkko, J., Mobility Support in IPv6, RFC 3775, June 2004.
2. Aura, T., Roe, M. and Arkko, J., Security of Internet Location Management, In Proc. The 18th Annual Computer Security Applications Conference, Las Vegas, Dec. 2002.

3. Aura, T., Mobile IP Security, Security Protocols: The 10th Int'l Workshop, Cambridge, U.K., Apr. 17-19, 2002, LNCS 2845, Springer Verlag, 2003.
4. Nikander, P., Arkko, J. and Aura, T., Montenegro, G., Nordmark, E., Mobile IP version 6 Route Optimization Security Design Background, draft-ietf-mip6-ro-sec-02, Oct. 2004.
5. O'Shea, G. and Roe, M., Child-proof Authentication for MIPv6 (CAM), ACM Computer Communications Review, 31 (2), July 2001.
6. Montenegro, G., Castelluccia, C., Statistically Unique and Cryptographically Verifiable Identifiers and Addresses, In Proc. ISOC Symposium on Network and Distributed System Security (NDSS 2002), San Diego, Feb. 2002.
7. Aura, T., Cryptographically Generated Addresses, RFC 3972, March 2005.
8. Deng, R., Zhou, J., and Bao, F., Defending against Redirect Attacks in Mobile IP, In Proc. The 9th ACM conference on Computer and communications security, Washington D.C., Nov 18-22, 2002.
9. You, I. and Cho, K., A Security Proxy Based Protocol for Authenticating the Mobile IPv6 Binding Updates, Computational Science and Its Applications – ICCSA 2004: International Conference, Assisi, Italy, May 14-17, 2004, LNCS 3043, Springer Verlag, 2004.
10. Soliman, S., Mobile IPv6 : Mobility in a Wireless Internet, Addison-Wesley, 2004.
11. Arkko, J., Devarapalli, V. and F. Dupont, Using IPsec to Protect Mobile IPv6 Signaling between Mobile Nodes and Home Agents, RFC 3776, June 2004.
12. Aura, T., Nikander, P., and Leiwo, J., DoS-resistant Authentication with Clients Puzzles, Security Protocols: The 8th Int'l Workshop, Cambridge, U.K., Apr. 25-27 2000, LNCS 2133, Springer Verlag, 2001.

Author Index

Lecture Notes in Computer Science

For information about Vols. 1–3722

please contact your bookseller or Springer

Vol. 3775: J. Schönwälder, J. Serrat (Eds.), Ambient Networks. XIII, 281 pages. 2005.

Vol. 3773: A. Sanfeliu, M.L. Cortés (Eds.), Progress in Pattern Recognition, Image Analysis and Applications. XX, 1094 pages. 2005.

Vol. 3772: M. Consens, G. Navarro (Eds.), String Processing and Information Retrieval. XIV, 406 pages. 2005.

Vol. 3771: J.M.T. Romijn, G.P. Smith, J. van de Pol (Eds.), Integrated Formal Methods. XI, 407 pages. 2005.

Vol. 3770: J. Akoka, S.W. Liddle, I.-Y. Song, M. Bertolotto, I. Comyn-Wattiau, W.-J. van den Heuvel, M. Kolp, J. Trujillo, C. Kop, H.C. Mayr (Eds.), Perspectives in Conceptual Modeling. XXII, 476 pages. 2005.

Vol. 3768: Y.-S. Ho, H.J. Kim (Eds.), Advances in Multimedia Information Processing - PCM 2005, Part II. XXVIII, 1088 pages. 2005.

Vol. 3767: Y.-S. Ho, H.J. Kim (Eds.), Advances in Multimedia Information Processing - PCM 2005, Part I. XXVIII, 1022 pages. 2005.

Vol. 3766: N. Sebe, M.S. Lew, T.S. Huang (Eds.), Computer Vision in Human-Computer Interaction. X, 231 pages. 2005.

Vol. 3765: Y. Liu, T. Jiang, C. Zhang (Eds.), Computer Vision for Biomedical Image Applications. X, 563 pages. 2005.

Vol. 3764: S. Tixeuil, T. Herman (Eds.), Self-Stabilizing Systems. VIII, 229 pages. 2005.

Vol. 3762: R. Meersman, Z. Tari, P. Herrero (Eds.), On the Move to Meaningful Internet Systems 2005: OTM 2005 Workshops. XXXI, 1228 pages. 2005.

Vol. 3761: R. Meersman, Z. Tari (Eds.), On the Move to Meaningful Internet Systems 2005: CoopIS, DOA, and ODBASE, Part II. XXVII, 653 pages. 2005.

Vol. 3760: R. Meersman, Z. Tari (Eds.), On the Move to Meaningful Internet Systems 2005: CoopIS, DOA, and ODBASE, Part I. XXVII, 921 pages. 2005.

Vol. 3759: G. Chen, Y. Pan, M. Guo, J. Lu (Eds.), Parallel and Distributed Processing and Applications - ISPA 2005 Workshops. XIII, 669 pages. 2005.

Vol. 3758: Y. Pan, D.-x. Chen, M. Guo, J. Cao, J.J. Dongarra (Eds.), Parallel and Distributed Processing and Applications. XXIII, 1162 pages. 2005.

Vol. 3757: A. Rangarajan, B. Vemuri, A.L. Yuille (Eds.), Energy Minimization Methods in Computer Vision and Pattern Recognition. XII, 666 pages. 2005.

Vol. 3756: J. Cao, W. Nejdl, M. Xu (Eds.), Advanced Parallel Processing Technologies. XIV, 526 pages. 2005.

Vol. 3754: J. Dalmau Royo, G. Hasegawa (Eds.), Management of Multimedia Networks and Services. XII, 384 pages. 2005.

Vol. 3753: O.F. Olsen, L.M.J. Florack, A. Kuijper (Eds.), Deep Structure, Singularities, and Computer Vision. X, 259 pages. 2005.

Vol. 3752: N. Paragios, O. Faugeras, T. Chan, C. Schnörr (Eds.), Variational, Geometric, and Level Set Methods in Computer Vision. XI, 369 pages. 2005.

Vol. 3751: T. Magedanz, E.R. M. Madeira, P. Dini (Eds.), Operations and Management in IP-Based Networks. X, 213 pages. 2005.

Vol. 3750: J.S. Duncan, G. Gerig (Eds.), Medical Image Computing and Computer-Assisted Intervention – MICCAI 2005, Part II. XL, 1018 pages. 2005.

Vol. 3749: J.S. Duncan, G. Gerig (Eds.), Medical Image Computing and Computer-Assisted Intervention – MICCAI 2005, Part I. XXXIX, 942 pages. 2005.

Vol. 3748: A. Hartman, D. Kreische (Eds.), Model Driven Architecture – Foundations and Applications. IX, 349 pages. 2005.

Vol. 3747: C.A. Maziero, J.G. Silva, A.M.S. Andrade, F.M.d. Assis Silva (Eds.), Dependable Computing. XV, 267 pages. 2005.

Vol. 3746: P. Bozanis, E.N. Houstis (Eds.), Advances in Informatics. XIX, 879 pages. 2005.

Vol. 3745: J.L. Oliveira, V. Maojo, F. Martín-Sánchez, A.S. Pereira (Eds.), Biological and Medical Data Analysis. XII, 422 pages. 2005. (Subseries LNBI).

Vol. 3744: T. Magedanz, A. Karmouch, S. Pierre, I. Venieris (Eds.), Mobility Aware Technologies and Applications. XIV, 418 pages. 2005.

Vol. 3742: J. Akiyama, M. Kano, X. Tan (Eds.), Discrete and Computational Geometry. VIII, 213 pages. 2005.

Vol. 3740: T. Srikanthan, J. Xue, C.-H. Chang (Eds.), Advances in Computer Systems Architecture. XVII, 833 pages. 2005.

Vol. 3739: W. Fan, Z.-h. Wu, J. Yang (Eds.), Advances in Web-Age Information Management. XXIV, 930 pages. 2005.

Vol. 3738: V.R. Syrotiuk, E. Chávez (Eds.), Ad-Hoc, Mobile, and Wireless Networks. XI, 360 pages. 2005.

Vol. 3735: A. Hoffmann, H. Motoda, T. Scheffer (Eds.), Discovery Science. XVI, 400 pages. 2005. (Subseries LNAI).

Vol. 3734: S. Jain, H.U. Simon, E. Tomita (Eds.), Algorithmic Learning Theory. XII, 490 pages. 2005. (Subseries LNAI).

Vol. 3733: P. Yolum, T. Güngör, F. Gürgen, C. Özturan (Eds.), Computer and Information Sciences - ISCIS 2005. XXI, 973 pages. 2005.

Vol. 3731: F. Wang (Ed.), Formal Techniques for Networked and Distributed Systems - FORTE 2005. XII, 558 pages. 2005.

Vol. 3729: Y. Gil, E. Motta, V. R. Benjamins, M.A. Musen (Eds.), The Semantic Web – ISWC 2005. XXIII, 1073 pages. 2005.

Vol. 3728: V. Paliouras, J. Vounckx, D. Verkest (Eds.), Integrated Circuit and System Design. XV, 753 pages. 2005.

Vol. 3727: M. Barni, J. Herrera Joancomartí, S. Katzenbeisser, F. Pérez-González (Eds.), Information Hiding. XII, 414 pages. 2005.

Vol. 3726: L.T. Yang, O.F. Rana, B. Di Martino, J.J. Dongarra (Eds.), High Performance Computing and Communications. XXVI, 1116 pages. 2005.

Vol. 3725: D. Borrione, W. Paul (Eds.), Correct Hardware Design and Verification Methods. XII, 412 pages. 2005.

Vol. 3724: P. Fraigniaud (Ed.), Distributed Computing. XIV, 520 pages. 2005.

Vol. 3723: W. Zhao, S. Gong, X. Tang (Eds.), Analysis and Modelling of Faces and Gestures. XI, 4234 pages. 2005.